RESTORING THE FOUNDATIONS

An Integrated Approach to Healing Ministry

Second Edition

II Corinthians 7:1
Having therefore these promises, dearly beloved,
let us cleanse ourselves from all filthiness of the flesh and spirit,
perfecting holiness *in the fear of God.*

Chester and Betsy Kylstra

Restoring the Foundations
Second Edition
Copyright by Proclaiming His Word, Inc., 1994, 1996, 2001.
All Rights Reserved.

Published by   Proclaiming His Word Publications
2849 Laurel Park Highway
Hendersonville, NC 28739
828-696-9075, 877-214-8076
office@phw.org

First Printing: 2000, Second Printing: 2003, Third Printing: 2004
Fourth Printing: 2006, Fifth Printing: 2007.

Cover Concept: Chester Kylstra
Cover Graphic Artists: Phil Pink, Art Cox, James Cline and CCP Bayou Printing.

Bible quotes are from several Bible versions. The particular Bible version is indicated by the following abbreviations.

KJV
The *King James Version* of the Bible.

NIV
The Holy Bible, New International Version. Copyright 1973, 1978, 1984, by the International Bible Society. All Rights Reserved.

NAS
New American Standard Bible. Copyright THE LOCKMAN FOUNDATION, 1960, 1962, 1963, 1968, 1971, 1973, 1975, 1977. A corporation not for profit. La Habra, California. All Rights Reserved.

AMP
The Amplified Bible. Copyright by Zondervan Publishing House, 1965, Grand Rapids, Michigan. All Rights Reserved.

Wuest
The New Testament: An Expanded Translation by Kenneth S. Wuest. Copyright Wm. B. Eerdmans Publishing Co. 1961, Grand Rapids, Michigan. All Rights Reserved.

Preliminary Edition, Workbook: -7, March 1994.
First Edition, Workbook: -3, September 1996.
Second Edition, Workbook: -5, August, 2007. ISBN 0-9649398-1-9
Second Edition, Paperback: -5, August, 2007. ISBN 0-9649398-2-7

Summary
Table of Contents

Detailed
Table of Contents

Part 2 Foundational Ministry Areas   101

Table of Figures

Table of Tables

Appendices

Table of Testimonies

Acknowledgments
Second Edition

Very little that is worthwhile has ever been done totally solo. The people who have given love, inspiration, physical and financial help are usually not in front of the camera helping to collect the prize but off to the side cheering or praising the Lord in their hearts. We have had much support in producing this second edition of *Restoring the Foundations*.

Our friend and mentor, Bishop Bill Hamon, always preaches, "Its time to update and relate." Well, dear friend, at last we have updated!

Phil Pink, owner and manager of CCP Bayou Printing, Valpariso, Florida, has given his and his staff's time as a gift to create the new book cover for the second edition. Thanks immensely for helping us better communicate our message. We are so pleased and grateful.

One special group of people have been by our side as they shared the vision and worked full-time with Proclaiming His Word Ministries. They have served in the Healing House, trained RTF ministers, and led seminars. They are Steve and Cindi Bishop, Mike and Michele Green, Tommy and Pat James, Phil and Gloria Prather, and Crawford and Dorathy Railey. They have prayed with us, cried with us, and helped take the Restoring the Foundations ministry to many parts of the world. In addition, they have also been in our face to "get the book done." Thank you, guys, for all of the above.

We are also grateful to our office staff Jeannie Mack, Hugh and Arleen Stevenson, and Bonnie Kunkle, who do an excellent job of keeping things running, so we can focus on writing and ministry. We also want to thank and acknowledge former office staff, Lois Blanchard, and Mike and Wendy Caulley, for their contributions to the ministry and for helping us finish projects and travel.

We are greatly appreciative of those pastors, churches, and RTF ministers that have taken Restoring the Foundations ministry into their hearts and congregations. It is exciting to us to see more and more people having access to RTF ministry.

We want especially to acknowledge and thank David and Linda Roeder and Pastors Leon and Donna Walters (Indiana), and Joe and Debbie Senesi and Pastors Greg and Susie Williamson (New York). You have shown us what it's like when pastors get behind an anointed ministry team and we see a church RTF program flourish. You have inspired us to present better and clearer the RTF ministry resources and vision.

Our editors, Val Cindric, James and Frances Morrison, and Mike Green, have been a great blessing. Thank you for your time and creative contributions.

Finally, our friends, Jim and Polly Altman (Atlanta), have so graciously loaned us their wonderful cabin, which provided a quiet and beautiful place to write. We are so appreciative of your generosity.

As you can see, we have not flown solo but on the wings and prayers of our friends and helpers.

Foreword
Second Edition

Restoring The Foundations helps individuals return to their true foundations: the foundations of their soul, mind and spirit. As they go through the four Problem/Ministry Areas, they receive enlightenment, healing, deliverance, and restoration.

My wife and I were greatly blessed by going through the ministry of **Restoring The Foundations**. These truths and ministries were such a blessing and so restorational that I requested that all of my CI Board of Governors receive the ministry. We also challenged all 500 of our Ministers in the Christian International Ministries Network to go through the restoration process and then establish it in their Church as an on-going ministry.

The truths presented in this book are not theories but proven, divine biblical principles and practices that bring transformation and restoration. During the 46 years of my ministry, I have been exposed to almost every ministry available in the Body of Christ. I can truly say that *Restoring The Foundations* expresses the most balanced and workable ministry in this area that I have ever witnessed or experienced. This book and its application in the ministry the Kylstras have developed is being used by the Holy Spirit to take the spots and wrinkles out of Christ's Church.

I have worked with Chester and Betsy Kylstra for many years. Their "10 M's" are in proper order in their personal lives. The evidence of the fruit of their ministry can be seen in the hundreds of transformed Christian lives, the many rescued marriages, and restored ministers.

We thank you and bless you, Chester and Betsy, for your commitment to God to bring such truths of ministry to Christ's Corporate Church.

Dr. Bill Hamon
Founder and President of Christian International Ministries Network

Author of:

The Eternal Church
Prophets and Personal Prophecy
Prophets and the Prophetic Movement
Prophets Pitfalls and Principles
Apostles, Prophets and the Coming Moves of God
Prophetic Destiny and the Apostolic Reformation
Fulfilling Your Personal Prophecy

Acknowledgments
(First Edition)

As in all major efforts, many others have provided us much support and help producing this manuscript.

We would like to thank Pastors Buddy and Mary Crum and Life Center Church, Dunwoody, GA, for believing in us and our vision while it was still in the formative stages. They helped to birth and nurture it into reality. Our hearts will always be knitted with you. We are grateful for the RTF ministry team members who volunteered for the training process and then, with faithfulness and anointing, served the church and the Body of Christ. A special "thank you" to Charles and Jackie Clifton for continuing to share in the vision and for helping to bring it forth. Your love and support have been invaluable. Thank you all for letting us impart into your lives. You have been a fruitful testimony. You have demonstrated that this approach to healing does indeed bring lasting healing. We have all learned so much together.

Thank you, Christ Redeemer Church, San Antonio, Texas, and your RTF ministry teams for continuing to grow with us and helping to convince us that "the book must be written." You also gave us an opportunity to see that the Integrated Approach to Healing Ministry could bring healing not only to an individual but to an entire congregation as well.

We are grateful to Bishop Bill Hamon and Christian International Ministries for their loving reception of us and our ministry. We are also thankful for the many lives that have been enriched at CI, including our own. You have given much needed caring, support, prayers, facilities, and even release time to do this writing. Most of all, thank you for continuing to enlarge our vision.

In addition, some very special people have contributed directly to the preparation of this book. Our dear friend Jeannie Mack has made manifold copies of each chapter. Marge Wolfe has brought great encouragement as well as her tireless editorial skills to bear on the project. George Payne has generously provided needed publishing know-how and other encouragement. Jerome Lukas caught the concept for the cover and persevered to illustrate it. We also give a *big* thank you to those of you who have contributed to Proclaiming His Word, Inc. Your support provided the equipment necessary for the writing and production of this book and also covered the expense of printing.

Without your help, we could not have brought this effort to completion.

Preface
Second Edition

We are pleased and excited to release this Second Edition of ***Restoring the Foundations***. It represents the completion of a strong directive from the Lord to "spread the word" of the power and effectiveness of the Integrated Approach to Healing Ministry to as many in the Body of Christ as possible. The time is short, and He **is** coming back for a bride without spot or wrinkle.[1]

Putting out an updated edition of *Restoring the Foundations* has been a wonderful challenge. We have worked to incorporate the fresh understandings and revelation gained in the RTF ministry room and through our friends and co-workers.

In these past four years since the first edition was written, we have fine-tuned our initial understanding of each ministry area. We have also received increased revelation about the Soul/Spirit Hurt area and further developed our knowledge of specific strongholds. In addition to including these in the second edition, we have also added helpful preparation/submission prayers to the core ministry chapters, especially for those who use this book for personal ministry. We have added an index, which will help all of us as we look-up specific topics. We have also updated the Ministry Application Form in the Appendix.

The most significant change in appearance is that *Restoring the Foundations* (RTF) is now a paperback book with a new cover. (It will also continue to be available in the three-ring binder format.)

It has been evident for some time that we needed to change the "name" of what we are doing from "counseling" to "ministry" — for it is truly ministry. Through the Lord's power and goodness, what takes place goes far beyond our traditional understanding of counseling. Although we have used the words interchangeably, the secular world does not. We feel it is time to make the break with past terminology. As a result, we have changed the wording in this second edition from Counselor to Minister; from counseling to ministry; from counselee to ministry receiver. While this last term still seems awkward, we know we are moving in the right direction.

---

[1] Please see Eph 5:27.

Restoring the Foundations has been the basis for a training book, *Ministry Tools for Restoring the Foundations*[1] (Kylstras and Dorathy Ferguson Railey, 1995). It has served as the primary resource material for numerous seminars and been the basis for the *Issue-Focused Ministry* cell/small group publications. *Restoring the Foundations* has undergirded the Healing House ministry, in which almost 2000 individuals have received 15 hours of ministry based on its principles.

Our zeal to share the revelation in this book with the Body of Christ has increased rather than waned. It is with much excitement that we are seeing it translated into other languages.

Many people have shared how significant *Restoring the Foundations* has been to them and its impact on their lives.. Recently a man commented, "Next to the Bible, *Restoration the Foundations* is the most valuable book I own." Needless to say, it is tremendously satisfying to us to have this book so well received.

We pray that this second edition will further accomplish God's purpose, especially now that we are four years closer to the time when Jesus will come back for us, His Bride, called to be without spot or wrinkle. Our hope is that God's healing and freedom will come to each person who reads and applies the principles found here.

Chester and Betsy Kylstra
September, 2000

---

[1] Information about the *Ministry Tools* manual is included in the resource section on page 435.

Preface
(First Edition)

This book represents many years of our personal healing and training by the Holy Spirit. Even as He was healing us from our own hurts and bondages, He was training us to minister to and train others. **Restoring the Foundations** (RTF) ministry is a very effective approach to ministry.

God has given us a revelation of His intense desire to see His people healed, delivered, and set free. This desire is so great that He took a professional secular counselor/teacher (Betsy) and a professional aerospace, software engineer/teacher (Chester), and gradually developed a healing/deliverance ministry team responsive to His Holy Spirit. He has given us a desire to share this knowledge through **Restoring the Foundations** ministry by training, equipping, and activating others. This book is one of the vehicles to be used for sharing these basic understandings, with biblical support for the concepts and principles.

Cover
The soldier/warrior[1] on the book's cover stands contemplating/surveying the temple ruins[2] while he assesses how to restore the building according to God's plan (shown in his hands). His mission is to make it a suitable temple for the Holy Spirit.[3] The starting place is the **foundation**, which must be **restored** first so that the rest of the temple can be properly supported as it is reconstructed.

This book covers the basic, **foundational**, **restorational** tasks that need to be accomplished in every saint's life as God the Holy Spirit does His work of sanctification.[4] This **foundational ministry** provides a good base upon which other, more specific, kinds of ministry, discipleship, and equipping can be built.

We think of this process as **Restoring the Foundations** ministry. It is an Integrated Approach to Healing Ministry that deals with the four **foundational** Problem/Ministry Areas of: (1) Sins of the Fathers and Resulting Curses, (2) Ungodly Beliefs, (3) Soul/Spirit Hurts, (4) and Demonic Oppression. The key phrase, **Integrated Approach to Healing Ministry,** means ministry to all of these areas in concert under the direction and power of the Holy Spirit. The result yields more effective, lasting results than ministry to only one, two, or even three of these areas during the same time period.

This **restoration** process, which is going on in each saint's life, also coincides with the **restoration** of the Church. It fits in with, and is a part of, the **restoration** of the apostles and prophets.[5,6] **Restoring the Foundations** ministry (and other similar healing ministry approaches) has been brought forth by God at this time to

---

[1] Eph 6:10-18, 2 Tim 2:1-4.

[2] Isa 44:26, 58:12, 61:4; Acts 3:20-21; Gal 6:1.

[3] 1 Cor 3:16-17, 6:19-20.

[4] Rom 15:16; 1 Cor 6:11; 1 The 4:3.

[5] Hamon, Bill, *Prophets and the Prophetic Movement*, Destiny Image, Shippensburg, PA, 1990.

[6] Hamon, Bill, *Apostles, Prophets, and the Coming Moves of God*, Destiny Image, Shippensburg, PA, 1997.

bring **foundational** healing and freedom to the Church. He particularly wants His five-fold ministers[1] healed and free so that they can fulfill their part in preparing the Bride for the coming of the Lord and the **restoration** of all things.[2]

Three levels of **foundations** are being **restored** today. The **foundation** of each saint, the **foundation** of the local church, and the **foundation** of Christ's Church universal. As each individual saint is restored, all three of these **foundations** are being **restored**, healed, strengthened, enabled, and equipped. As a result, the entire temple is being **restored**, thus preparing the way for the return of the Lord.[3]

Putting It Into Practice

The Biblical understandings and concepts as expressed in ***Restoring the Foundations*** must be translated into practice in order to be effective. We have developed several teaching/training/apprenticeship programs for the local church and para-church ministries. These programs equip RTF lay ministers, cell/small group leaders, and other five-fold ministers. We are grateful for the anointing and the abundant fruit coming forth in all of these areas.

Testimonies: Caution Note

A caution note is in order before we launch into the main portion of the book. Although we received permission to use the personal testimonies of the people portrayed in the ministry illustrations, we have changed their names to protect their identity. If you think you recognize someone by the events of the story, please remember that we have ministered to hundreds of people with similar problems. As Paul writes in First Corinthians 10:13, "There hath no temptation taken you but such as is common to man: but God [is] faithful, . . . " (KJV)

Preliminary Edition

The preliminary edition of ***Restoring the Foundations*** was prepared for the March, 1994, Prophetic Counseling conference held at Christian International, Santa Rosa Beach, Florida. Due to the press of time, we were not able to complete several supportive chapters and other finishing details.

Final First Edition

We had not expected it to take another two years before we could set aside the time needed to complete and publish the final First Edition, but it has. Over the last two years, God has opened many ministry doors and expanded our ministry reach by bringing others to co-labor with us. While these have been positive changes, it has hindered the finishing of *Restoring the Foundations*. It is now completed. We hope that you like it.

May God Bless you and bring you to a new level of revelation of His healing Grace as you read and study this book.

Chester and Betsy Kylstra
September 1996

---

[1]   Please see Eph 4:8, 11-12.
[2]   Please see Acts 3:21.
[3]   Please see Isa 40:3 and Mal 3:1.

Prologue
Sandy's Story[1]

We will call her Sandy,[2] this lady at the center of the storm. Our first contact with Sandy and her husband occured at the church where we were meeting some of the church elders and prospective couples to be trained and equipped to conduct Restoring the Foundations (RTF) ministry.

Middle-aged, well-dressed, and distinguished, she and her husband appeared "normal" in every sense of the word. Over the years, they had served the congregation well with much honor and respect as elders. A strong teacher of the Word, Sandy had also been the head counselor at the church — until all of "this" had come out.

They were understandably cautious and reserved as we were introduced. Why shouldn't they be? We were to be their "restorers," the ones through whom God would bring their healing (at least the initial part of it). They questioned whether or not they could really trust us; whether or not we could really help them through and out of their devastation.

*Could Sandy really be helped? Had she gone **too** far?*

We learned later that Sandy wasn't at all sure she could be helped. She lived with the fear and the torment that maybe she had gone "too far." Had she committed the "unpardonable" sin? Could God really "be there" for her in spite of all she had done? Or even worse, maybe she was inherently "too defective, too evil" and beyond God's ability to restore.

We were also wondering, "Have we gotten ourselves in over our heads (again)? Could God really use us in this situation? Could we really discover the root(s) of the sin and expose the open doors through which the enemy had come. Could we clear out the 'legal' rights Satan had and get the doors closed? Could we help make a way for God's restoration and healing to come?"

We didn't know for sure, but we did know our God and His mercies that "are new every morning." Numerous times previously, He had "come through" when we were beyond our experience and skill level. We knew that His desire to heal His people was far greater than ours. We had strong reason to believe that Sandy could and would be restored.

As we visited, Sandy visibly began to relax. We felt that she had accepted us and would submit to the RTF ministry process.

---

[1] Sandy's Story, with her testimony about God's freedom, cleansing, and healing, is interwoven throughout Part 2 and 3 of *Restoring the Foundations*. It concludes with the Epilogue after Chapter XVI in Part 4.

[2] Sandy (not her real name) and her husband have given us full permission to use their story, with the sincere prayer and hope that it will help others gain freedom from Satan's bondages.

The First Ministry Session

When we met with Sandy that first morning, it was clear that this case was not going to fall into the normal pattern of Restoring the Foundations (RTF) ministry. As we had grown to expect (and desire), we would need to trust the Holy Spirit to weave the elements of the Integrated Approach to Healing Ministry together in a way that Sandy's healing would come. (Actually, we wouldn't have it any other way. The only worthwhile healing has to come from the Lord and under His direction.)

The initial Interview.

After the "startup" events,[1] we launched into gathering information about Sandy. We wanted to know about her current life, the "sin" that had prompted the church to bring us to minister to her (and others); her ancestors, her family, her growing-up years, her successes and failures. We wanted to know all about her, particularly those things that would give us understanding about how she had arrived at her current situation. We wanted to listen to her *and* to the Holy Spirit's comments and illumination about what she was saying.

In order to spare you the many hours of ministry during which we obtained information about Sandy, we are going to present several main threads that ran through the fabric of her life. In Part 2 and 3, where we present the four Problem/ Ministry Areas and the discussion on Demonic Strongholds, we will show how the Holy Spirit led us as we ministered to these "threads." It was fascinating and tremendously exciting to see how the Holy Spirit unraveled the complexity of her situation and then gave us the strategy that confounded and defeated the enemy, bringing the victory.

One Additional Note of Importance

Sandy's depth of wounding and bondage was much greater than what we usually find in the Body of Christ. She was not the "typical" church leader or member ministered to by RTF lay ministers. As you will see, the severity of the Demonic Strongholds and the intensity of the lies she believed, along with the Soul/Spirit Hurts, required much more ministry than the five sessions of the "Thorough" format.[2] So, dear reader, please don't read Sandy's story thinking that this is "normal" RTF ministry. It is the "Extended" format. Rather, read it to learn the lessons God wants you to learn, so you will be better equipped to minister to those God brings your way. Also, read it to rejoice with us at God's wonderful mercy, power, and grace that He would bring such freedom and healing to one of His children and allow us to participate in it. He truly is doing amazing things in the earth today!

---

[1] In the first session, after a little conversation, we like to start with an Opening Prayer. Then we go through the person's Application Form. (There is a sample Application Form in Appendix A.) We go over the Limited Liability and Limited Confidentiality in great detail, making sure that the person understands what we can and can't do and when we may bring designated Ministry Oversight into the picture. Then we are ready to move on into the interviewing process.

[2] Please see Chapter XV, "RTF Ministry Formats," for a discussion of the different formats or types of ministry conducted.

Her Sin

What had brought Sandy's life to a halt and stopped her ministry in its tracks as a much-loved church counselor and Bible teacher? It was a shocking adulterous affair. With paramount courage she had faced her friends in the congregation and confessed her eight-year adulterous relationship with their (and her) pastor. If a Richter scale could have measured personal devastation, her reading would have been an "8" and the church's "7.5." The revelation of her sin caused a "faith" quake that left almost nothing standing. It exposed the deception behind their pastor's resignation several months previously for reasons of "fatigue."

Filled with grief and self-hate, Sandy realized how her sin was shattering the very people she had helped to shepherd for eight years.

The Key Threads

Sandy had an intertwining of complex problem areas.

It was soon obvious that Sandy was coming out of years of **deception** and a life ruled by **fear**. We were dealing with an intertwining of complex problem areas, including strong evidence of much occult involvement in Sandy's family line.

In our years of RTF ministry, we have learned that when the symptoms of **control, deception, fear, sexual sin, and infirmities are present**, there is almost always occult background somewhere in the family line. Sandy had all five of these indicators, **big time**!

The foundational wound appeared to be **abandonment**. This was the primary door through which everything else had entered and become established. It was the "basis" for many other strongholds and oppressions.

Abandonment was given opportunity right from the start. Sandy was an unwanted child. Her young parents were struggling financially and had two children already. These stresses generated much strife in the family. While still in the womb, Sandy was essentially **abandoned** by both parents. Her mother did want a girl and eventually came to idolize her daughter. The damage to Sandy, however, had already been done.

In her early years, Sandy's father was often away from home. He essentially became an **absentee father**.

Fear also got an early grip on the young child. The **occult** immediately begin to use both fear and **terror** to bring her into submission. As a little girl, she would often experience a "presence" at the door of her bedroom in the late night hours. "I'll kill you if you move," the evil voice threatened. The sound of eerie music that seemed to come from the church across the street added to the fear. Lying in her bed and paralyzed with **fear**, Sandy wondered if she would survive the night.

Sandy's sense of **abandonment**, along with the whispered lies of the demons, caused her to conclude early in life that she must be a "**bad**" girl. It was "obvious" since nobody wanted to be with her, and all those **terrorizing** things kept happening to her. Believing herself to be "bad" helped Sandy move into a "**deceptive, secret life.**" By age six, she felt **isolated and all alone** with nobody to help her.

Often **left alone** at night, Sandy would lie for hours on the floor in the center of the house. She picked a spot where no one could see her if they looked through any of the windows. Feeling **too abandoned** and **afraid** to tell her parents, she blamed herself and often thought, "I'm **stupid** to be **afraid.**" As a result, she led a **double life** that made her appear good and happy on the outside but **fearful**, **abandoned**, **isolated**, **and bad** on the inside.

Between six and ten years of age, the **fears** became even more paralyzing.

Like many little girls, Sandy worked hard to get her father's attention when he was home. This proved successful in her early years, and she enjoyed being known as "daddy's little girl." Between the ages of eight and twelve, she performed with him on the stage numerous times. He was so proud of her. Things changed, however, as she approached the teen years, and Sandy became clumsy and awkward. On one occasion, when she even forgot her lines in their play, sheer **terror** and **panic** overtook her. After this traumatic turning point, she **lost her special place** as daddy's little girl.

Many of these early events dramatically reinforced her feelings that she was "just a **bad** person."

At age twelve, at a camp meeting, Sandy's mother **abandoned** her (she didn't protect her, but put her "at risk.") with an evangelist (spiritual authority). At their first contact, he asked her to **look into his eyes**. Overtaken by his hypnotic power, which, in this case, was a form of occult control, Sandy became helpless to resist. When it was over, she was his and would do whatever he suggested. At first her mother would visit to the evangelist alone but later he told her to bring Sandy also. He would engage them in "prayers" and other activities that left Sandy feeling tremendous **shame**, **embarrassment**, and **humiliation**. Once again, the belief that she was **"bad"** was reinforced. After all, if she were normal, these things wouldn't be happening to her. Adding to her confusion was the fact that, in spite of all of her negative feeling, she also liked the attention. Being needed by this man made her feel special.

After two summers of being captivated by the evangelist, Sandy was **abandoned** by him when he told her mother not to bring the child anymore. While relieved to be free from his control, she felt **abandoned** and rejected once again.

This became the first of three rejections she experienced from a spiritual authority, after being used by each one.

In the sixth grade, Sandy had a special relationship with a boy who liked her. After her jealous girlfriends persuaded Sandy to reject him, they began to pursue him. This experience further enforced Sandy's feelings of abandonment and betrayal. The young man later became a brilliant doctor with a balanced personality.

For years, Sandy carried regrets and "what ifs" concerning this traumatic episode. Once again she concluded that she was to blame. If her girlfriends could **betray** her so easily, she must just be "bad." Perhaps she deserved to miss the opportunity for a good marriage.

In her late teens, Sandy felt **abandoned** once again when her two older brothers went away to college. With one brother, she had experienced a special protective relationship. His departure left her feeling vulnerable and **unprotected**.

By the time Sandy arrived at college, she had an interesting dichotomy with respect to the issue of control. On the one hand, she was easily dominated by authority figures, boyfriends, or an important friend. She would be or do almost anything to receive acceptance and approval. If occult power was being used, she was completely **passive** while being **controlled**.

When *she* was in **control**, however, Sandy became strong-willed and assertive. With the presence of many controlling figures in her life and family line, it was natural for Sandy to be controlling. She was a "survivor." She was determined to protect herself from exposure of her "bad" self and the resultant hurt and pain.

Sandy did smoke and do the usual "college" sins, but, interestingly, she was not sexually promiscuous. This points to the fact that sexual sin was not the main stronghold, but that it was "used" by the other strongholds.

In high school and college, others saw her as popular, fun, outgoing, and a good friend. Sandy, however, saw herself as not close to anyone. She had to **hide** her "true" self (which she saw as "**bad**") from them. As she put it, "I have defilement on the inside, so I have to look good on the outside."

One year after college, Sandy married. Her husband, however, **emotionally abandoned** her and caused further separation as he "picked at" and verbally abused their oldest daughter.

Sandy felt a great **fear** of other people's **anger** and **rage**. Her father had almost hit her one time when he was in a rage, and he did hit her brother. This **fear of anger** being directed at her, carried into Sandy's marriage, causing further separation with her husband.

Moving into her adult years, Sandy continued her **double life**, hiding the deep hurts and disappointments and acting, on the outside, as if everything was fine.

During the eight years of adultery with the spiritual leader (her pastor), her **double life** continued. This pattern of behavior was normal for her now.

She actually **believed** that God wanted her to participate in the adultery in order to help this man's self-esteem and bring about his eventual healing. Like her previous seducers, this pastor had hypnotic eyes, which she felt powerless to resist. Interestingly, Sandy reported, "Every time I was with him, I fully believed that it would be the last time."

Two years before the end of their affair, God gave Sandy a revelation, including specific questions and scriptures, which directed her to "come out." She wrote out the revelation and even showed it to her pastor. He merely laughed. The grip of her strongholds were so intense that she was unable to break free. As a result, she continued in her sin.

In the end, this pastor also **abandoned** her for another woman, leaving Sandy **feeling discarded**, **betrayed**, and used.

Much more could be revealed about Sandy's history, but this synopsis provides a good overview of some key themes and the "stealing, killing, and destroying"[1] work of Satan in her life.

In Parts 2 and 3 of *Restoring the Foundations*, we will continue Sandy's story as we present the four Problem/Ministry Areas and Demonic Strongholds. Different pieces of her story will illustrate how God used the Integrated Approach to Healing Ministry to bring forth her freedom and healing in each of these areas. If you can't wait to read the rest of her story, you can "skip ahead" by looking in the Table of Testimonies for the page number of each section of "Sandy's Story."

---

[1] Please see John 10:10.

I

INTRODUCTION

*And [they that shall be] of thee shall **build** the old waste places:*
*thou shalt **raise up** the **foundations** of many generations; and thou shalt be called,*
*The **repairer** of the breach, The **restorer** of paths to dwell in.*
Isaiah 58:12

They will be called oaks of righteousness, . . .
*They will **rebuild** the ancient ruins and **restore** the places long devastated;*
*they will **renew** the ruined cities that have been devastated for generations. . .*
you will be called priests of the LORD, you will be named ministers of our God.
Isaiah 61:3-4

Many people in the world, including Christians, are trapped, wounded, and "feeling" helpless, much as Sandy[1] was. Like many others, we were once among that group. By the Grace of God we were given the keys of the Kingdom[2] that enabled us and now others to receive God's restorative healing, deliverance, and freedom. This book reveals the keys needed to unlock the chains that bind our lives and block and hinder our Christian growth. These keys allow us to be among the people whom Isaiah prophesied would "raise up the foundations of many generations." May we seek to be among those involved in "Restoring the Foundations."

A. Christian Prophetic Prayer Ministry

There are four components to **Restoring the Foundations** ministry. These are the "bedrock," or foundation, of what we do. These components are **Christian Prophetic Prayer Ministry**.

Christian

It is Christ-Centered.

Everything we do is Christ-Centered. Jesus the Christ, the Anointed One of God, through His sacrifice on the Cross and His resurrection from the dead, made a way for every promise of God to be "Yea and Amen."[3] It is His Holy Spirit in the ministry sessions that accomplishes the significant and eternal work. Without the Holy Spirit's presence, NOTHING of eternal value would be accomplished. We help others appropriate His finished work into their lives, so they can be made whole.

It is the Holy Spirit who accomplishes the eternal work.

---

[1] Please see the first part of Sandy's testimony in the Prologue, page xix.
[2] Please see Isa 22:22, Mat 16:19, Lk 11:52, Rev 1:18.
[3] Please see 2 Cor 1:20.

Prophetic

Why it is "prophetic."

"Prophetic" simply means that we listen to and hear the Voice of the Lord. As appropriate, we speak out His word(s) as His Holy Spirit speaks to us.[1] This form of ministry is prophetic for two reasons.

"Prophetic" means the sum total accumulation of God's revelation over the generations.

- One, the basis for RTF ministry is the Holy Bible as it is illuminated by the accumulation of all of the revelations that God has released to the church, particularly since the time of the Reformation. This revelation comes through the Rhema Word of God as He breathes Life into the Scriptures. As we minister and train, we teach **present truth**[2] understanding of the revelations of God applicable to the four Problem/Ministry Areas.[3] We also show how to apply these truths using the Integrated Approach to Healing Ministry so that God's healing can come with great depth and permanency.

"Prophetic" means hearing God's Rhema Word for the individual.

- Two, we depend heavily on the voice of the Holy Spirit to lead and guide us as we minister. We don't want to minister by the dead letter of the law[4] but by the Living Word. Much of what we minister to is unseen and would remain unknown if the Holy Spirit did not reveal it.

  Before the ministry begins, we listen to verify that God wants us to minister to a particular individual. If the answer is "Yes," we then listen to seek revelation knowledge about the individual in order to minister as effectively as possible. During the ministry session, we depend on the gifts of the Holy Spirit[5] to bring forth life-changing healing as God's Rhema[6] Word reveals Knowledge, Understanding, Wisdom, Discernment, Anointing, and Healing.

Prayer

*God wants **two-way** communication.*

Everything we do is bathed in prayer. Prayer is direct communication and communion with God. We speak to God and **expect** Him to speak to us. We depend on a two-way conversation to bring Him into the ministry situation. God is given total access to direct us according to His Will, so that His freedom and healing can come into the person's life.

We start and end each ministry session with prayer. These are not ritualistic prayers, but a deliberate action from the heart to ensure that God is in charge of each session and that the effects of Satan are minimized.

---

[1] Please see Jn 10:4, and Chapter IV, "Hearing God's Voice."

[2] Please see 2 Pet 1:12.

[3] We define and discuss the four Problem/Ministry Areas on page 7, as well as the Integrated Approach to Healing Ministry.

[4] Please see 2 Cor 3:6.

[5] Please see 1 Cor 12:7-11.

[6] A "*rhema*" word is a specific word from God, for a specific individual, at a specific time, for a specific situation. In contrast, "*logos*" is a general word, addressed to a general audience, applicable to all time and situations. The most frequently used word for "word" in the Greek New Testament is "*rhema,*" not "*logos.*" For one example, please see Rom 10:17.

Ministry

The word "minister" means "one who serves." Ministry, of course, is "doing" the serving. We minister the healing touch of the Lord Jesus Christ and His finished work on the Cross. In the ministry room, we are there to serve the individual (or group), to help him (them) do what needs to be done to appropriate what God has already provided.

B. Restoring the Foundations Ministry

Since the initial release of *Restoring the Foundations*, many people and churches have made use of this ministry approach. They have used the Integrated Approach to Healing Ministry and the principles and revelation expressed within this book. Many of them refer to this approach to ministry as "Restoring the Foundations (RTF) ministry." We have decided to go with this trend and use the terminology "Restoring the Foundations ministry," or "RTF ministry," throughout this book.

C. What's in a Name? Counselor or Minister?

Jesus the Christ is: "Wonderful Counselor."

As we explained in the Preface to this Second Edition, we previously used the word "counseling" and "counselor" interchangeably with "ministry" and "minister." After all, Wonderful Counselor is one of the Names of the Christ.[1] However, the modern use of the words "counseling" and "counselor" have specialized meaning. For example, one meaning is to give advice (counsel) as a doctor or lawyer might. Further, there is a legal meaning, as in a "licensed mental health 'counselor'." So we have decided to stop using the words "counseling," "counselor," and "counselee."

Since our purpose is to minister the wisdom, grace, and restoration power of the Wonderful Counselor[2] and not man's wisdom and knowledge, we want to avoid any misrepresentation or confusion. We have settled on the words "ministering," "minister," and "ministry receiver," to indicate the process (serving others), the one doing the process (the server), and the one receiving the process (receiving the ministry). These words will be used throughout this book. We also are in the process of changing all of our books, publications, and documents, to this updated terminology.

---

[1]　Please see Isa 9:6 and 11:2-4a.
[2]　Please see Acts 3:21.

D. God's Purpose

Before we proceed any further, let us make our purpose clear. We don't want to be ministering just for the sake of ministering. Our goal is to accomplish God's will and purpose in the ministry receiver's life and help him establish a more meaningful relationship with God.

The primary purpose for RTF ministry is not to make the receiver feel or function better because he has received physical or emotional healing or been set free from demons. We, of course, rejoice when a person is healed or delivered, but this is not God's main objective for personal ministry.

What is God's primary purpose for us as individuals? **Scripture makes it clear that He wants us to be transformed and conformed into the image of Christ.**[1] He wants godly offspring who exhibit His nature and character, who think like He thinks, talk like He talks, and view themselves and others as He views them. In other words, our heavenly Father wants children who are like their "daddy."[2]

God wants sons and daughters who are like Him.

> 2 Cor 3:18
> And we, who with unveiled faces all reflect the Lord's glory, **are being transformed into his likeness** with ever-increasing glory, which comes from the Lord, who is the Spirit. (NIV)

> Rom 8:29
> For those God foreknew he also **predestined to be conformed to the likeness of his Son**, that he might be the firstborn among many brothers. (NIV)

As this is accomplished, we are increasingly able to love Him (and others) with an unconditional love — an *agape* love. This **is** His image since "God is Love."[3]

If this is God's purpose, what part do we have in making it happen?

Being "Born Again"

Step One: Ye must be born again! (Jn 3:7)

The first step in the process of being conformed into the image of Christ is to be "born again,"[4] to be "converted," to be born "from above." When God's incorruptible seed is placed inside of us by the Holy Spirit, we become a son of God.

> 1 Pet 1:23
> Being born again, not of corruptible seed, but of **incorruptible (seed)**, by the word of God, which liveth and abideth for ever. (KJV)

---

[1] Besides 2 Cor 3:18 and Rom 8:29, please see Gal 4:19; Eph 4:13, 15, 23; 2 Pet 1:4; and 1 Jn 2:6.
[2] Please see Rom 8:15.
[3] Please see 1 Jn 4:8.
[4] Please see Jn 3:3, 5.

Being "Holy"

At the moment of being born again, we "legally" become "holy" because God sees us in accordance with the results of the Cross. Interestingly enough, at the same time, we begin the *process* of becoming "holy." God wants us all to be "holy."

Step Two: You must be sanctified: be separated, be purified.

To be "holy" means to be "separated, set apart." We are instantly holy because we are translated out of the kingdom of darkness into Christ's kingdom.[1] Our ownership likewise is transferred from Satan to Jesus Christ. We are separated and set apart for God, just as He is separate from the world. We are "consecrated" to God. All of these phrases are merely different ways of saying, "We are holy."

Of course, "holy" also means "purity." This is where "sanctification" comes into the picture. None of us are "pure" when we are born again. The job of the incorruptible seed, the nature of God, that has been planted within us must sprout up and take over, bringing forth purity in the process. All kinds of things can help or hinder this growth, but the process of becoming holy, of becoming pure, is "sanctification."

Peter exhorts us to choose to be like God:

> 1 Pet 1:15-16
> [15]But just as he who called you is holy, so be holy in all you do; [16]for it is written: "Be holy, because I am holy." (NIV)

Cooperating with the Holy Spirit

The basic responsibility of the Holy Spirit is to promote, activate, and energize the sanctification process in each of our lives. We can cooperate with the Holy Spirit and help the process along (which, by the way, is the best approach), or we can resist the Holy Spirit and hinder or even stop the process. Resisting the Holy Spirit is never a good idea. He is determined to have a fit temple[2] for both Himself and us, and we are wise to let go of the things that displease God and that are harmful to us. He has many, much better "things" for us anyway.

Salvation is an ongoing decision.

Just as our initial salvation is a choice we must make, the continuation of our salvation is likewise an ongoing choice. Paul admonishes us to actively choose to work with the Holy Spirit, striving to be cleansed of "all filthiness of flesh and spirit." There is a purpose in this. It is to "perfect" (complete) ourselves and to work toward holiness.

> 2 Cor 7:1
> Having therefore these promises, dearly beloved, **let us cleanse ourselves from all filthiness of the flesh and spirit, perfecting holiness** in the fear of God. (KJV)

Can we really "cleanse ourselves" from filthiness of our flesh and our spirit? If we can, how do we do this?

---

[1] Please see Col 1:13.
[2] Please see 1 Cor 3:16-17, 6:19; 2 Cor 6:16; and Eph 2:21.

Being Cleansed

Many ways and/or disciplines of holiness lead to sanctification: Reading and/or meditating on the Word of God, the Bible; praying in one's natural tongue or in the Spirit; listening to the Holy Spirit; praise and worship, etc. Each of these different ways is a part of the process **if** we will embrace them.

It is the Holy Spirit who really does the cleansing. But we have to cooperate.

As the Holy Spirit shows us areas of unholiness in our lives, we must respond in obedience and do the necessary forgiving, releasing, repenting, and praying for healing and restoration. With the help of the Holy Spirit, we can break curses and perform self-deliverance, thereby doing spiritual warfare for ourselves. We can also allow other Christians, trained by the Holy Spirit, to help us with areas we don't know how to, or **don't even know exist**. This is what we call "ministry."

Being Stuck

No matter how well we pursue the spiritual disciplines, it seems that each of us, sooner or later, runs into walls, barriers, and obstacles of some sort that we, seemingly, can't break through.

Some of us have this happen right after we are born again. Certain obvious obstacles that are already "in place" have us "stuck." We don't know how to get "unstuck." We need help from others, and, "We need it **now**!"

Pride, independence, rebellion: the Holy Spirit knows how to work with us no matter what.

Some of us would like to "just do it" on our own without help from others. This attitude possibly reflects an element of pride. This is why God deliberately puts us in families and makes us dependent on each other. In fact, James clearly states that we are to call on the elders in the church and to pray for each other when we have need. It doesn't matter whether we would prefer to do it on our own or not. Stuck or not, like it or not, we are dependent on each other.

> Jam 5:14-16
> [14]Is any one of you sick? He should **call the elders of the church** to pray over him and anoint him with oil in the name of the Lord. [15]And the prayer offered in faith will make the sick person well; the Lord will raise him up. If he has sinned, he will be forgiven. [16]Therefore **confess** your sins **to each other and pray for each other** so that you may be healed. The prayer of a righteous man is powerful and effective. (NIV)

The Need for Formal Ministry

There have always been those in the church who are the "elders." These mature believers have grown in the Lord and gained God's wisdom and peace. Because their lives are guided by the Holy Spirit rather than by their carnal nature, we naturally recognize them as the ones to go to for help.

Formalizing the ministry should promote safer, more effective ministry, leading to faster maturing, healed saints.

By training people to be RTF "ministers," we are formalizing this natural occurrence and equipping mature Christians to be more effective at their "job" than they might be otherwise. Setting up a Restoring the Foundations church "program" provides a safe system to more effectively help needy church members to receive healing. This way, the entire church, including that "stuck" or independent person, can grow and mature in the Lord.

This formalized ministry approach to the four foundational Problem/Ministry Areas makes it possible for every Christian to understand more fully God's revelation in these areas. At the same time, it provides a structure that for training others to be effective RTF ministers.

E. Overview of the Four Problem/Ministry Areas

As Christians we all struggle in the same four problem areas. As a result, we all need help in getting free. Thus, the four problem areas are also the four areas needing ministry. Hence the phrase, the four "Problem/Ministry Areas."

Restoring the Foundations ministry is built around the need for an Integrated Approach to Healing Ministry, which includes all four of the identified problem areas. This is necessary to achieve deep and lasting freedom and healing in the life of the person to whom we are ministering. Let's take a brief overview of these four areas.

- **Sins of the Fathers and the Resulting Curses (SOFCs)**
  This problem is rooted in the second commandment (Ex 20:3-6) where God visits "the iniquities of the fathers upon the children unto the third and fourth generations." In order to get free of this curse, God requires us to confess our ancestors' sin, as well as our own sin (Lev 26:40). We help the person focus on the confession of sin (I Jn 1:9) and challenge him to appropriate Christ's finished work on the Cross to break curses (Gal 3:13) and recover the "legal ground" from the enemy (Col 2:14).

- **Ungodly Beliefs (UGBs)**
  Some UGBs are inherited from our ancestors (i.e., parents, grandparents). Others are formed from hurtful circumstances or experiences in our own lives. These Ungodly Beliefs need to be changed into Godly Beliefs (GBs). This is accomplished through a carefully structured procedure of repentance, renouncing, and receiving God's Truth to renew our minds (Rom 12:2). This procedure also removes "legal ground" as we break our agreements with demons.

- **Soul/Spirit Hurts (SSHs)**
  Jesus came to heal the brokenhearted (Lk 4:18). As we "wait upon the Lord" with "listening prayer," He heals the hurts of our soul and spirit. He does this by showing us what He wants to heal, as we acknowledge our areas of pain. Then, after we take care of necessary forgiveness, releasing, and renouncing, He heals what He has revealed. All "legal ground" given to the enemy from our sinful responses to the hurts is recaptured as well.

- **Demonic Oppression (DO)**
  It is now relatively easy to disassemble and destroy the Demonic Oppression structures (Mk 16:17), since they have lost their "legal ground." We have "co-labored with Christ"[1] to bring freedom and healing to the first three ministry areas. It is a delight to help others gain this freedom.

The Integrated Ministry brings the Integrated Healing.

Completing the Integrated Approach to Healing Ministry to the four problem areas brings the "integrated healing" into our lives. This can be a major life-changing occurrence. Not only are we transformed, but God's purpose is accomplished as we are conformed into the image of His Dear Son, Jesus the Christ. This further opens the door for intimate fellowship with God and His empowerment, making it possible for us to live the "overcoming"[2] Christian life.

In Part 2, we present the four Problem/Ministry Areas more completely and discuss how to minister to them. After all, this is the primary purpose for writing this book. First, we need to consider some reasons why people resist ministry of any kind, even when they are clearly suffering heavy blows in their lives and appear to be "losing the battle."

F. Why Some Don't Seek Help

Several unfortunate misconceptions block people from getting ministry when they need it. We want to expose these misconceptions and help you think through them. Please don't let any of these misconceptions keep you, or others to whom you minister, from God's further healing and freedom. These misconceptions are:

Deadly misconceptions!

- I was perfected at the time of my salvation.
- My past no longer affects me once I am saved.
- Once saved, I will *automatically* grow up into the image of Christ.

These "vicious" misconceptions bring passivity into our Christian walk and cause us to put up with hassles and oppression from demons. They create guilt, discouragement and hinder our maturing into godliness. In extreme cases, these misconceptions can cause us to reject our Christianity and walk away from Christ. Over all, they are very deadly. Let's look at them one by one.

I was Perfected at the Time of my Salvation.

This misconception acts as a smokescreen to keep Christians from receiving much needed help. If we suppose ourselves to be "perfected," then we don't see the need for help and have no reason to seek it. We are supposed to "have it all together."

If I'm already perfected, why am I acting the way that I am, and feeling the way that I feel?

If we have problems, this really puts us in a bind. Where can we go for help? How can we testify about the "overcoming" life if we are not "overcoming?" This misconception can be a major cause of confusion. It can even result in "giving up" on Christianity.

---

[1]   Please see 1 Cor 3:9.
[2]   Please see Lk 10:19, Jn 16:32, Rom 12:21, 1 Jn 2:13-14, 4:4, 5:4-5, and Rev 2:7, 11, 17, 26, 3:5, 12, 21, 21:7 for wonderful scriptures about "overcoming."

The concept, "I was perfected at the time of my salvation" comes from a misinterpretation of a very wonderful verse of scripture, Second Corinthians 5:17. Let's read it.

> 2 Cor 5:17
> Therefore if any man [be] in Christ, [he is] a new creature: old things are passed away; behold, all things are become new. (KJV)

This verse tends to be interpreted as, "Old things are passed away, so they don't have any effect on me. Since I am a new creature, I have no problems. Neither are there any 'open doors' from the past through which the enemy can get to me."

An Example

Suppose you have a terrible problem with rejection, and you get "saved." You will likely still suffer from feelings of rejection. It is the exception rather than the rule that you will be delivered from rejection and its effects on and in your life at the time of your salvation. This issue is so deeply rooted, has so many interconnections, and has so much "legal ground" that it is not easily eliminated. Before you will be completely free, God will have you work through most of the different aspects of rejection. It's not that God **can't** heal you, but He does follow His Word. Usually, certain "legal" transactions have to occur, such as forgiving someone or confessing sin. You have a part to play in your healing. For example, you may need to **make some decisions** that nullify previous decisions made by yourself and/or your ancestors.

If you say to yourself, "I'm a new creation, I don't have any right to still feel rejection," and yet you do feel rejection, what will happen? Most likely, self-condemnation, frustration, and a sense of failure will develop in your life.

Spiritual Realm

Once our spirit comes alive with the rebirth, we are new creatures. The spirit is instantly regenerated. That is a fact. The body and the mind/soul, however, are not instantly regenerated. They must go through the process of "becoming new" through the sanctification process. Other scriptures wouldn't make any sense if this weren't true. Actually, all we have to do is look around at other people — or look in the mirror — to know that this is truth.

When we read 2 Cor 5:17 in context, we realize that Paul is talking about the spiritual realm. He is writing about *not* knowing Christ any longer after the flesh but knowing Him after the spirit.

Greek Verb Tense

Further, when we look up the Greek verb in the phrase "all things are become new," we find the word *"ginomai"* translated "are become." *Ginomai* is a "perfective" verb tense, which has to do with a past event that has **ongoing** consequences, **not completed** consequences. A "long-winded" translation might be: "All things are become, and are continuing to become, new." Our past salvation was an "event," and it continues to have ongoing consequences. We can rejoice that God's salvation continues to work in our lives. No Christian wants to be "stuck" in his or her past (or current) condition.

Neighboring Scriptures

Do other scriptures support the "already perfected" concept? No, they don't. In fact, we don't have to "travel far" at all to gain further understanding. All we have to do is to move ahead two chapters and back up two chapters. We can stay in the same book written by the same author to find more clarity.

In Second Corinthians, we read in context that:

> 2 Cor 3:18
> We . . . are being **transformed** into the same image from glory to glory. (KJV)

If we have already "arrived," we would not need to be transformed into Christ's image from glory to glory. This verse strongly implies a sense of time, a progress, a sequence of events leading us through the transformation process; i.e., the sanctification process.

Now, looking ahead two chapters at the other passage,

> 2 Cor 7:1
> **Let us cleanse ourselves** from all defilement of flesh and spirit, perfecting (completing) holiness in the fear of God. (KJV)

Again, this verse implies a time process for cleansing and perfecting holiness. Even more, it squarely lays a responsibility upon us to do, or to be involved in, the cleansing. In other words, it is our responsibility to make ourselves available to the Holy Spirit and to be obedient to His directions. When we cooperate, He can do the actual cleansing.

Neither of these two verses gives us any room to be "perfected" **at** salvation. They both suggest a time aspect, a process, a series of "ongoing consequences."

Numerous other scriptures contain the same time aspect, implying an ongoing process and action. Some of these scriptures are:

> Rom 12:2
> Be ye **transformed** by the renewing of your mind. (KJV)

> 2 Tim 2:21
> Therefore if a **man cleanse himself** of these things, he will be a vessel of honor. (KJV)

> Jam 1:27
> Pure religion and undefiled before God and the Father is this, . . . **to keep oneself unspotted (polluted)** from the world. (KJV)

> 1 Jn 3:3
> And every man that hath this hope in him **purifieth himself**, even as he is pure. (KJV)

If we are already perfected, all these scripture verses about what we need to do in order to grow and be clean and sanctified would be unnecessary. Let us not be deceived by the misconception that we are supposed to be perfected already. If you have accepted this lie, let us encourage you to let go of it.

My Past no Longer Affects Me once I am Saved

The good news is that our past is truly forgiven. The price for our sins has been paid through the Cross of Christ. The bad news, however, is that the past *does* still affect us.

Our body and mind/soul are still "in process." Past habits of sin and ongoing weaknesses of the flesh need correcting. The beliefs of the mind, the continued action of ancestral curses, the hurts to our soul and spirit, and the influence of demonic spirits — all these still need attended to. We don't get rid of **all** the demonic oppression just because we get saved.

Sometimes, God sovereignly moves in our lives and sets us free. You may have experienced a glorious deliverance in some area of your life, for example, from addiction to alcohol or lust or cigarette smoking. Generally, however, this wonderful freedom does not come instantaneously to every area of our lives. The good new is that more freedom and healing is always available.

God wants us to come to Him, grab hold of Him, and receive His healing for the other areas in our lives; **all** of the other areas. It is wise to go back into the past and bring the various issues before God and do what is necessary to cleanse them. Then, we can move into the future without dwelling on the past or having it jeopardizing our future.

Once Saved, I will Automatically Grow Up into the Image of Christ

It would be nice if this third misconception were true. After all, puppies grow up into dogs and kittens into cats, so surely we will automatically grow up into the image of Christ. Right? No, unfortunately, we don't.

We have to take an **active** stance. All the way through, the Bible addresses the issue of being active in our Christian life. We can't get away from this very prevalent concept. Particularly in the Epistles, Paul admonishes us to be active. He exhorts us to "put off the old man" and "put on the new man," etc. That takes action on our part. We are to engage in warfare, overcome evil with good, overcome Satan, repent, turn away from, etc. Each of these commands tell us to do something. We are to be active and engage ourselves with the Truth as we work with the Holy Spirit. As we become actively involved, we will grow spiritually and mature into the things of God.

What will happen if we simply stand still and become passive? The answer is, we will go backwards. When we let the flesh go its own way without fighting against it, it will take us back into sin. When we don't know how to stand against demonic forces, they will push us toward sin. Demons encourage the flesh. That's why we must be actively engaged in the process of our cleansing and standing against the enemy. Otherwise, we will not only **not** automatically "grow up," but we will slide back into immaturity and catering to the flesh.

Betsy didn't like warfare and balked at being active. She remembers how mad she got at a pastor who said, "Everybody has to get into God's army and be prepared to fight!"

She thought, "Glory to God, I'm a pacifist! I don't want to be in anybody's army!" The more she read the Word, however, the more she had to acknowledge, "I am in an army. I might as well accept it because I am here whether I like it or not. There are spiritual attacks, and there is a battle going on over my life. I am being shot at. I need to learn how to defend myself and 'shoot back'!"

Once we realize that we have powerful spiritual weapons that enable us to fight victoriously, our concept of being in God's army changes.[1]

In order to receive God's healing and freedom, you need to know two more verses, that you can put in your arsenal of weapons (besides the ones presented two pages earlier). These verses further confirm why your active participation is absolutely necessary.

> Rom 8:13
> For if you live according to the sinful nature, you will die; but if by the Spirit **you put to death** the misdeeds of the body, you will live, . . . (NIV)

> Col 3:1-2
> [1]Since, then, you have been raised with Christ, **set your hearts on things above**, where Christ is seated at the right hand of God. [2]**Set your minds on things above**, not on earthly things. (NIV)

Lastly, it is hard to be an overcomer if you are passive. We listed all of the overcomer scriptures in the footnote on page 10 Let these encourage you.

It is time to let go of all misconceptions concerning our need for further healing after we have been born again. It is also time to get rid of any other misconceptions we have about God and His kingdom. Now is the time to receive all that He has for us, whether it comes directly from the Holy Spirit or indirectly through one of God's human instruments.

---

[1]   Please see Chapter V, "God's Weapons for Spiritual Warfare."

G. What's Ahead

The remainder of this book is divided into four parts.

Part 1 (Foundational Understandings) covers five topics that we consider fundamental to being a Restoring the Foundations minister. We trust you will enjoy reading these basics even if it is a review for you. These truths are also fundamental to the Christian Life, so you may receive a personal benefit as well as an "equipping" benefit as you read.

Part 2 (Foundational Problem/Ministry Areas) has the "meat" of the Restoring the Foundations Integrated Approach to Healing Ministry. The four Problem/Ministry Areas briefly discussed in the Overview Section of this chapter are covered in depth in this part.

Part 3 (Foundational Applications) contains four chapters. The first, "Soul Ties, the Ties that Bind," is an important concept, and a wide-spread problem. We almost always have to help a ministry receiver break and remove Soul Ties. The "Demonic Strongholds" chapter presents how the four Problem/Ministry Areas can sometimes occur within one demonic structure, requiring the application of the Integrated Approach to Healing Ministry to that one situation. The final two chapters expose "super-strongholds" that hinder and trap many people. Be sure to read about the "Control-Rebellion-Rejection Stronghold" and the "Shame-Fear- Control Stronghold."

Part 4 (Foundational Implementations) wraps up the main part of the book. The RTF Ministry Formats Chapter comes first. It pulls the information and understandings of Parts 1 and 2 together and presents the possible RTF ministry formats. In addition, we outline the required preparation for RTF ministers that correspond to the different formats and describe suitable ministry receivers for each format.

The last chapter, "Final Thoughts for RTF Ministers," offers a distillation of many years of hard won wisdom for Christian ministers. Please read it. It may save you some, or much trouble.

Don't miss the "Epilogue," where the testimony of Sandy is brought up to date. It describes how she doing today and what has happened in the intervening years since her ministry.

We have included four Appendices. The first contains an example RTF ministry Application Form, as well as several supportive forms, that you can use as starting points for your church ministry program. The other three appendices go into more detail about topics important to Restoring the Foundations but unsuitable for inclusion in the main portion of the book.

At the very back, you will find several pages describing the RTF training steps for the Thorough RTF Ministry Format, along with information about available resources from Proclaiming His Word Ministries.

We hope you enjoy *Restoring the Foundations*. We want it to be a blessing to you. Our prayer is that you will learn much more about God's provisions and how to receive them for yourself and for others. We also pray that the Holy Spirit will minister to you as you read and study it.

Part 1

Foundational Understandings

Restoring the Foundations ministry builds upon the fundamentals of the Christian faith. Our goal is to present several fundamental areas that we consider essential, yes, even crucial, for the RTF minister not only to understand but to "live in" on a daily basis. Furthermore, we want you to be able to explain and minister these understandings to each individual (or group of people) to whom you minister. Before anyone can completely enter into the ministry process and maximize his receiving from God, the recipient needs to understand the reasons behind the difficulties in his life. We want him to carry away from the ministry process the tools he will need, not only to retain his freedom and healing but also to continue to grow and mature in his Christian walk.

After we complete the Foundational Understandings part of *Restoring the Foundations*, we will have the basics needed to go on into Part 2, where we present the Integrated Approach to Healing Ministry as expressed through the four Problem/Ministry Areas.

II

THE POWER OF THE CROSS IN THE CHRISTIAN LIFE

. . . to us who are being saved it (the Cross) is the power of God.
1 Corinthians 1:18

At the heart of Christianity is the Cross of Jesus Christ. At the heart of our faith is the Cross. At the heart of all effective Christian Ministry stands the Cross.

The Cross is the source of God's greatest provision for us. The Cross represents the exchanged life, in which we give Jesus all that we are and have in exchange for Himself and all that He has done for us. Through the Cross, He gives us the provisions for a victorious life: forgiveness of sin, victory over the power of sin, victory over Satan and his demons, power over sickness and disease, and triumph over death itself. The Cross provides the basis for reconciliation with Him and with our Abba Father. Because of the Cross, we can live an abundant, joyful life on earth as well as experience the glorious knowledge of eternal life.

The Cross gives power and potency to every area of Christian Ministry. It is the avenue to newness of life. At the Cross we can come and lay down the sin in our lives and receive forgiveness and the release from our guilt. Because of the Cross, curses are broken. Against the truths of the Cross, we can measure and expose the Ungodly Beliefs that have infiltrated our minds and crippled our lives. The love shown through the Cross assures us that Jesus cares about healing our broken hearts and lives. Because Satan was defeated at the Cross, Jesus gives us the authority to cast out demons. The Cross is the power and provides the legal basis for the RTF ministry.

In this chapter, we are going to look at the Cross from three different, but related, directions. First, let's look at some **essential background truths** of the Cross: God's provision for our forgiveness, God's substitutionary atonement, and the love of the Father and Son as manifested in the Cross.

Secondly, let's look at the ways in which the Cross applies directly or indirectly to each of the four Problem/Ministry Areas: **Sins of the Fathers and Resulting Curses, Ungodly Beliefs, Soul/Spirit Hurts,** and **Demonic Oppression.**

Thirdly, let's look at the importance of the person himself, the ministry receiver, **appropriating the Cross in his own life.**

17

The Cross Doesn't Make Sense

Before we begin talking about the Cross itself or its application to Christian Ministry, take a moment to reflect on the past. Imagine that you, along with Jesus' disciples, are standing at the foot of the Cross. You, like they, are appalled that this Jesus you have followed is being killed in the same torturous way as a common criminal. Overwhelmed by the horrible events happening so quickly, you are outraged by the brutality. You want to run away and pretend the shocking scene is only a nightmare. You want to wake up and find that the sun is shining and it is just another day to follow your Master as He walks about teaching and doing wonderful miracles. But you cannot pretend. In the past hour, darkness has heavily spread over Jerusalem. What is happening? This doesn't make sense. Nothing makes sense any more, especially the Cross. You don't want to watch. Some of the words that Jesus spoke not long ago come back to you — words about going to Jerusalem to die, but you never quite believed Him. Now it is happening. What does it all mean?

In a very real way, we modern disciples of Jesus do not understand the Cross any better than the early disciples did. We have the facts but struggle with the meaning.

Those of us raised in the western world are trained to think in terms of the logical consequences of cause and effect. We understand well the formulas where one term equates another. We try to apply our best logic to the Cross, but our logic fails us. We have to make the paradigm shift that comes from seeing the Cross through the eyes of faith. Only then does the Cross "make sense." It takes God's revelation. It takes a willingness to lay down our logic and say,

> God, You are the one who determined the meaning of the Cross. In order to understand it, I have to get out of my system of thinking and into Your system.

Contrasting the way an unsaved man sees the Cross with one who is born again, the Apostle Paul said,

> 1 Cor 1:18
> For the story and message of the Cross is sheer absurdity and folly to those who are perishing and on their way to perdition, but to us who are being saved, it is the [manifestation of] the power of God. (AMP)

If we rephrased this scripture to further encompass our age of rationality, it might read like this.

> For the story and message of the Cross is sheer absurdity and folly to those who approach it from the point of view of their own reason and logic, but to us who see it through the eyes of faith, who see God's meaning, it is the manifestation of the power of God.

"Lord, we ask You today, to help us make that crucial paradigm shift!"

A. Background Truths of the Cross

Before we touch on the essential background truths of the Cross, let's listen in on a conversation that might have happened a long time ago, as measured in earth time.

1. An Imagined Conversation

As you think about the Cross, have you ever thought about the conversation that might have taken place between the Son and the Father before the world was established? Think of the magnified anticipation they must have experienced as the finalized design for man became clear. While waiting for man to be brought forth, the Father and Son are talking and considering the consequences of this dangerous venture.

The Son says, "I feel good about most aspects of this plan. The only uneasiness I feel has to do with giving man free will. Do We have to do it this way? Do You think there is any possibility that they would turn their backs on Us?"

The Father ponders awhile and then replies, "You know, Son, that bothers Me more than anything else, too, but unless We let them choose to love Us, it won't truly be love."

Another long silence transpires. Then the Son speaks. "You know, if they turn away, if they reject Us, I think I would do anything to bring them back."

"Anything, Son, anything?" the Father queries. Then He asks, "Would You be willing to go to earth and die for them?"

An even longer pause. Slowly and thoughtfully, the Son replies. "It would be hard, but I would do it. It could make all of the difference."

The Father adds, "It would be hard for Me, too."

Perhaps it was at a point in time like this that the Lamb was slain before the foundation of the world.[1] Man had not yet been created; Jesus had not yet come to earth; and Jerusalem had not yet been built; but in many ways at that moment, Jesus set his face like a flint to go to Jerusalem and die for us.

2. The Cross' Message: Forgiveness

In the ministry setting, the rich truths of the Cross stand as a backdrop. It is as if a curtain of truth were wrapped around the participants. The truths are there to be brought in as needed, to personalize the depth of God's love, to know and to feel the on-going power of His redemption, and to realize the basis of His forgiveness in our lives.

---

[1] Please see Rev 13:8.

Through the Cross the principle of God's forgiveness, as well as His legal right to forgive us, is established. How does Jesus' dying on a Cross enable God to forgive us? It was God who decided that Jesus' substitutionary death would satisfy all of His wrath about our sin and become sufficient payment for the required judgment. Only then would His justice be met.

After the Cross, God would and could stand ready to forgive if we personally meet His conditions of repentance and forgiving others.

> 1 Jn 1:9
> If we confess our sins, He is faithful and just to forgive us our sins, and to cleanse us from all unrighteousness. (KJV)

God is eager to see us released from our guilt. He is ready to toss our sin into His sea of forgetfulness. He desires to wash away our crimson stains and clothe us in the whiteness of His righteousness. He wants to forgive us and to give us a "new beginning."

Forgiveness is central to everything that takes place in ministry. The person to whom we are ministering needs to receive God's forgiveness, forgive others, and often to forgive himself as well. Because of the Cross, he can receive God's forgiveness, coming back into fellowship with Him. He can have a fresh beginning. It is the power of God's forgiveness that provides a "basis" for a person to forgive himself. Otherwise, self-forgiveness would be an empty ritual.

Although God's desire to forgive sin is centered at the Cross, He requires an additional condition besides repentance. This area lies at the heart of most Christian ministry: God requires us to forgive others.

If we cannot forgive others, we have no legal right to expect our Father, God, to forgive us. Frequently, the ministry receiver is hurt, bitter, or disappointed with other people. It is clear; he needs to forgive. This, however, can be an agonizingly painful process. Often, looking at the Cross will help bring him strength and resolve to forgive. At the Cross, he is confronted with how much he has been forgiven. At the Cross, he can reflect on the unfolding compassion and grace Jesus demonstrated toward those who crucified Him. At the Cross, he may cry out for Jesus to give him the grace and power to forgive those who have sinned against him.

3. The Cross's Message: Substitution

A second concept essential to understanding the Cross is that of "substitution."[1] God Himself decided what could be substituted for what. He declared that Jesus' sinless blood could be substituted for our sin-filled blood. He declared that Jesus' sinless blood could be shed in place of our blood since the Law requires that everything be cleansed with blood.[2]

---

[1] For a further discussion of substitution, please see *Cross of Christ* by John Stott, InterVarsity Press, Downers Grove, IL 60515, pages 133-163.
[2] Please see Heb 9:22.

His people, the Israelites, had been well-prepared by God to understand the concept of substitution. For almost a thousand years, He laid a foundation for understanding His system. This system provided that the blood of one life could be substituted for the blood of another life to pay for sin. Before anyone could come back into right relationship with God, the price of sin had to be paid.

Early in Israel's history, at the time of the Passover, God experientially showed the Israelites that the blood of a pure lamb could be **substituted** for the death of their first-born son.

Then, through the Law given to Moses, God instituted a sacrifice system in which various animals had to be killed and the animal's blood offered as a **substitute** for man's blood to pay for his sin.

God, through Aaron the high priest, demonstrated that "one" (animal) could take upon himself the sins of many and carry them away. On the Day of Atonement,[1] Aaron called together the entire congregation. As he laid hands on the head of the chosen goat, he named the sins of each family, transferring their sin to it. The ceremony might have sounded something like this:

> And I now lay on this goat the Shallums' sin of stealing and lying and murmuring. And now I lay on this goat the Shimeahs' family sin of . . .

After all the sins were laid upon the head of the goat, then the Law prescribes,

> Lev 16:22
> . . . the goat shall bear on itself all their iniquities to a solitary land; and he shall release the goat in the wilderness. (NAS)

Such sacrifices had to be made over and over again. The Day of Atonement occurred on a yearly basis.

Although the sacrifice system and the Day of Atonement both cleared the way for the re-establishment of right relationship with God, neither of them had the power to redeem men's hearts. These methods were at best a maintenance system.

God, Himself, was paving the way for His people, then and NOW, to understand that Jesus' blood could be substituted for ours and our sins could be laid upon Jesus and He would carry them away on our behalf.

At the Cross, Jesus' life blood was **substituted for ours. His sacrifice was made "once for all," for all the sins that would ever be committed. This sacrifice was, and is, good forever.**

> Heb 7:27
> Unlike the other high priests, He [Jesus] does not need to offer sacrifices day after day, first for His own sins, and then for the sins of the people. He sacrificed for their sins **once for all** when He offered Himself. (NIV)

---

[1] Please see Lev 17.

4. The Cross's Message: Love

In a world of violence and broken relationships — a world in which our entire nation has a sense of emotional abandonment — God's unconditional covenant love seems radical by contrast. He gave His most precious gift, His only Son, to us. His greatest desire is a relationship with us. Jesus willingly laid down His own life for us. Such unfathomable love, all for the sake of relationship!

Speaking of the new covenant relationship that would be established through the Cross, God said through Jeremiah,

> Jer 31:33
> . . . I will put My law within them, and on their heart will I write it; and I will be their God and they shall be my people. . . . (AMP)

This is Relationship!

Demonstrating His love, Jesus

> Phil 2:7- 8
> [7] . . . stripped Himself [of all privileges and rightful dignity] so as to assume the guise of a servant (slave), in that He became like men and was born of a human being.
> [8] And after He had appeared in human form, He abased and humbled Himself [still further] and carried His obedience to the extreme of death, even the death of [the] Cross! (AMP)

In John's gospel, Jesus shows a sense of relentless divine mission, a divine "must." His eye seems focused on the Cross as He sets His face like a flint to go to Jerusalem and die. He manifests a paramount sense of being in charge, of holding the reins, of knowing He is the one to make the ultimate decision.

> Jn 10:17-18
> 17 Therefore doth my Father love me, because I lay down my life that I might take it again.
> 18 No man taketh it from Me but I lay it down of Myself. I have power to lay it down, and I have power to take it again. . . . (KJV)

He made the choice for us. Jesus made the choice on behalf of us. Loving us, He poured out His blood.

Just before the crucifixion, Jesus tried to help His disciples understand what His Cross was going to mean in terms of the potential for a new relationship with Him and with the Father. He took the familiar cup of wine saying,

> 1 Cor 11:25
> . . . This cup is the new covenant in My blood. . . . (NAS)

A literal translation of this passage from the Greek reads,

> 1 Cor 11:25
> . . . This cup is the covenant **new in its nature,** a covenant which is **within the sphere of my blood.** . . . (Wuest)

"Why? Why? Why?" we ask, almost incredulously. Why was He willing to go through the shame and the pain of the excruciating Cross? For the restoration of our intimate, lasting, covenant, love relationship with Him and with the Father! Powerful! Can we hear it? The possibility of new relationship was the "joy set before Him."[1] That was what He wanted: a relationship, our love in return.

> 2 Cor 5:14-15
> For the love which Christ has [for me] presses on me from all sides, holding me to one end and prohibiting me from considering any other, wrapping itself around me in tenderness, giving me an impelling motive, having brought me to this conclusion, namely, that One died on behalf of all, therefore all died, and that He also died on behalf of all **in order that those who are living no longer are living for themselves but for the One who died on their behalf and instead of them,** . . . (Wuest)

God's justice was satisfied. The sin gap was breached. A whole new relationship between God and man was made possible. It is as if Jesus were saying, "I died for you that you might live for Me and in close relationship with Me."

The meaning of the Cross is so lovingly personal. As Christian ministers, we have a precious opportunity. We are ministering to those who have chosen to live for Him. As we apply the Cross to each ministry area, with the leading of God's Holy Spirit, we can help make the unfathomable love of the Father and of the Son real and personal to them.

B. Relationship to Each Ministry Area

The Cross undergirds and relates to each ministry area. It relates very directly to Sins of the Fathers and the Resulting Curses and to deliverance from Demonic Oppression. The Cross relates in significant ways, though more indirectly, to Ungodly Beliefs and to Soul/Spirit Hurts.

1. The Cross Applies to Sins of the Fathers and Resulting Curses

First Peter has a powerful description relating the Cross to the Sins of the Fathers. In it, Peter exhorts the believers:

> 1 Pet 1:17-19
> [17]. . . conduct yourselves in fear during the time of your stay upon earth;
> [18]knowing that you were not redeemed with perishable things like silver and gold from **your futile way of life inherited from your forefathers,**
> [19]but with **precious blood,** as of a lamb unblemished and spotless, **the blood of Christ**. (NAS)

---

[1]   Please see Heb 12:2.

Peter cautions his readers to remember that Jesus paid a price for them to be set free from the sinful ways handed down generation after generation from their ancestors. They are to be different. They are to live holy lives.

As we appropriate that same precious blood, in the authority of Jesus' Name, we too can separate ourselves from the sinful patterns existing in our generational lines.

At the same time we break free from areas that have dominated our family's past, we must covenant ourselves together with the Lord once again as the One who gives us the power to walk in holiness.

It is through the Cross that curses can be broken. **Curses are consequences, or penalties, of sin, which are put into action when we break God's laws. Curses frequently continue from one generation to the next, especially when the original sin involved the occult or when there has been no repentance for the initial sin.** The judgments that curses represent, however, can be stopped when we appropriate the Cross. Jesus has already paid for the sin.

> Gal 3:13
> Christ delivered us by payment of ransom from the curse of the law by becoming a curse in behalf of us, because it stands written, Accursed is everyone who is suspended upon a tree, . . . (Wuest)

In Deuteronomy, God's Law states that everyone who hangs on a tree is cursed.[1] According to God's system, when Jesus hung on the Cross, He was cursed. As He hung there, He became our substitute. He took upon Himself all the curses that should have come upon us because neither we, nor our forefathers, have been able to keep the Law.[2]

The rest of the Galatians passage goes on to give Jesus' ultimate purpose in becoming a curse for us.

> Gal 3:14
> . . . in order that to the Gentiles the blessings of Abraham might come in Jesus Christ, to the end that the promise of the Spirit we [Jew and Gentile] might receive through faith. (Wuest)

Jesus took the curse for us so we could have all of God's covenant blessings, including the presence of the Holy Spirit in our lives!

The fact that Jesus took our curses on the Cross is the essential basis for our being able to break the power of any curses that are operating in our lives or in the lives of the people to whom we minister.

---

[1] Please see Deu 21:23. The Hebrew word for "tree" meant any kind of upright wooden object, living or dead. The cross qualified as a "tree."

[2] Please see Deu 28.

2. The Cross Applies to Ungodly Beliefs

The Cross brings salvation and redemption. It is only the redeemed man who has a desire for God's truth, who wants his mind transformed, who wants Godly Beliefs. The redeemed man wants to weed out the ungodly lies he has believed and to transform his once worldly mind. The redeemed man, however, needs a standard.

Jesus is our standard of truth. He put it this way:

> Jn 14:6
> . . . I am the way, and the truth, and the life. . . . (NAS)

He wants us to know Him personally. He wants us to know His life, His character, His teachings. When we know these truths, only then will the lies be exposed — the lies that we have believed about ourselves, about others, and even about God.

To know Him as our truth, we need to abide in Him. John's gospel says,

> Jn 15:4,7
> [4]maintain a living communion with Me, and I with you.
> [7]. . . (If) my words are at home in you, . . . (Wuest)

When we are in Christ and His words are at home in us, we will know the truth. His truth will be in our midst. Over time, His truth will begin to set us free from the lies that plague us.

There is a second sense in which the Cross is related to our minds being renewed, to having Godly Beliefs replace our Ungodly Beliefs. The Cross, in itself, is truth laden and truth compacted. Intrinsic to the Cross are the truths of redemption and victory over sin, sickness, Satan, and death. Implicit in the Cross is the truth of Jesus' love for us. These truths give us value and significance, purpose and destiny, life and hope.

From these truths, we can extract Godly Beliefs. For example, one obvious Godly Belief inherent in the Cross is, "I am valuable enough for Jesus to die for me." That revelation alone can strike a death blow to all of the lies about unworthiness. They are clearly and eternally refuted.

In another example, through the crucifixion and resurrection, Jesus shows us that God's plan wins, no matter what the circumstances.

Many other significant truths are wrapped up in the Cross. Once we embrace them, they give us the basis for replacing our Ungodly Beliefs with Godly Beliefs.

3. The Cross Applies to Soul/Spirit Hurts

As we look at how the Cross applies to the Soul/Spirit Hurt area, we encounter a new fact about ourselves: We are "broken hearted" any time we are alienated or separated from God the Father and from Jesus. Until we know Him and walk with Him, our hearts, the core of our being, are fragmented and incomplete. Through the Cross, Jesus provided a way of reconciliation, a way for our relationship with God to find wholeness and restoration.

In a more specific application of the Cross to Soul/Spirit Hurts, God's Word tells us that Jesus "bore our griefs and carried our sorrows."[1] Legally, positionally, He took them upon Himself. Our job now is to release them to Him, to give them to Him to carry, so we can receive our healing from Him.

Because of the events that Jesus went through surrounding His experience of the Cross, we can trust Him to understand our worst hurts. He experienced rejection by religious leaders, abandonment by His closest friends, betrayal by one of His own, slander and false reports, and undeserved mockery and beating. Isaiah says He was:

> Isa 53:3
> . . . despised and forsaken of men, a man of sorrows and acquainted with grief. (NAS)

Jesus can understand our heartbreaks! He wants to heal our hearts today.

4. The Cross Applies to Demonic Oppression

Jesus came to defeat Satan. John puts it this way.

> 1 Jn 3:8
> . . . For this purpose the Son of God was manifested, that He might destroy the works of the devil. (KJV)

On the Cross, Jesus defeated Satan and all of the demonic powers. In Colossians, Paul describes Jesus as leading the procession of defeated demonic hosts.

> Col 2:15
> [Jesus] stripped off and away from himself the principalities and authorities. He boldly made an example of them, leading them in a triumphal procession. . . . (Wuest)

As Satan is legally defeated, so are all of his underlings, which comprise the various levels of demonic forces. Having won victory over Satan and his forces, Jesus has authority over him. He shared that authority with us as believers when He told us to cast out demons in His Name.[2]

---

[1] Please see Isa 53:4.
[2] Please see Mk 16:17.

C. Appropriating the Cross

Let us turn our attention now to the concept of appropriation. Appropriation has to do with "receiving." Webster's dictionary defines "to appropriate" as "to take exclusive possession of, to own." God wants us to receive, apply, and own the provisions, the realities, and the victories of the Cross.

At the time of the Last Supper, Jesus gave a wonderful demonstration of appropriation. When He broke the bread and poured the wine, it was important to Him to give it to **each** individual. Each disciple needed to receive individually. He didn't just say, "I'm going to eat this bread, and it's going to represent all of us." It was important to Him that each individual partake; that each person reach out and say, "Yes, I receive this."

> 1 Cor 11:24
> . . . Take, eat: this is my body, which is broken for you: . . . (KJV)

He wanted the disciples not merely to "look" at the bread representing His Body but to take it and to eat it — to receive it into themselves (symbolically to receive Him into themselves). Eating and drinking provides a tremendous symbol of receiving because what we eat and drink goes into every cell. It nourishes; it changes; it brings life. Jesus was saying, "Take Me in; let Me be your life." He was saying, "Receive, receive, receive!"

Jesus undoubtedly shocked and offended the Jews when He said to them:

> Jn 6:53
> Unless you eat the flesh of the Son of Man and drink His blood, you have no life in yourselves. He who eats My flesh and drinks My blood has eternal life. (NAS)

What did Jesus mean by this statement? Jesus was saying that believers must take Him within themselves. It is not enough for Him just to be on the outside. He wants us to receive Him completely.

How then do we receive, appropriate, begin to "own" what He has provided for us?

Any time that we appropriate what God has provided, we appropriate (receive) **by faith**. We received salvation **by faith**.[1] We receive physical healing **by faith**. We receive all of the provisions God has for our lives by faith. Our faith is not based on hype or emotion but on His faithfulness. **Our faith is in the fact that He keeps His promises as we meet His conditions**.

The great joy of the ministry process finds its essence in the appropriation of God's freeing, healing, and deliverance provisions into the life of our ministry receiver. Jesus wants each of us to receive and personally own all that He did for us on the Cross. When we break curses, it is because Jesus became a curse for us.

---

[1] Please see Jn 1:12.

We apply the truth that curses have no legal right to operate in our lives. As we deal with Ungodly Beliefs, we look to Him and to the truths established in His Cross. As we pray for hurts to be healed, we can take the hurts to Jesus, who (already) has carried our griefs and sorrows. As we cast out demons, we are only reinforcing the victory that He won at the Cross. As we receive the gift of the Cross that Jesus has given and apply it to our lives, we can receive these great victories ourselves.

III

GOD'S LAW AND THE CHRISTIAN LIFE

Great peace have they who love your law, and nothing can make them stumble.
Psalms 119:165

We can well imagine you wondering:

"Why a chapter about the Law in a book on healing, deliverance, and freedom? What does that have to do with Restoring the Foundations Ministry? After all, we are New Testament Christians. We don't have to worry about the Law. Didn't Paul write in Romans, 'Ye are not under the law, but under grace'"?[1]

If this is you, we invite you to come along with us. We will help you gain an appreciation for God's Law and how to be in harmony with it. Let's look at several truths we want you to receive from this chapter:

1. God's Law definitely applies to us as Christians and to everyone else.
2. There are consequences, sometimes severe consequences, even for Christians, who violate or break God's Law.
3. It is far wiser to conform with and align with God's Law than try to fight or buck it. Why try to swim upstream when you can swim downstream? God says, "Get with the flow!"
4. God has provided a way to get free of past mistakes, failures, sin, etc. We are not necessarily trapped. But, once free, let us walk in obedience from now on.

We want you, as ministers, to know how to help the people to whom you are ministering get free from entanglements, oppression, and misconceptions about what it means to be free.

If you already have an appreciation and understanding of God's Law, come along with us anyway. It is exciting to study and learn how God intends for us to relate to the Law on this side of the Cross.

It is true that we are living "under" grace, but it's not true that we can ignore the Law, which is the implied conclusion when we take the above quoted scripture out of context.

---

[1] Please see Rom 6:14.

A. Things to Know

Let's start by defining what type(s) of law we, as Christians, need to take into consideration.

1. Types of Law

Natural Law

God established natural, physical laws on "day one" of Creation.[1] Light was released, and with it all of the laws of physics, chemistry, metallurgy, meteorology, etc., came into action. By the end of the second day, material had been created out of raw energy; the land and sky were in place.

Starting on day three, God began to bring forth living creatures. He established the biological and physiological laws, such as the biochemical laws, laws of reproduction, etc. The most important law, the one that He really wanted us to understand, was stated at least twice for each group of living creatures. That is, that **each one produced (reproduced) after his own kind**.[2] It is here that the universal **law of sowing and reaping** was put into action. God then crowned His creation by creating man in His image. He gave man not only the ability to reproduce his physiological nature but also to reproduce God's spiritual abilities and characteristics.

We will continue to talk about some of these laws because God uses the natural to teach us about the spiritual. That is, the realm in which He exists.

First Law Requiring Obedience

God gave a commandment to Adam,

> Gen 2:17
> . . . but you must not eat from the tree of the knowledge of good and evil,
> for when you eat of it you will surely die. (NIV)

God gave a commandment that included the consequence if the commandment was disobeyed. Although Adam (and Eve) had been clearly informed of the consequence, they disobeyed anyway and experienced the result: *death! Spiritual death came first as they lost fellowship with God. Physical death came later.*

God had given a law, a commandment, and they violated it. They experienced the consequences. To this day, we as their children, continue to experience the consequence. We now know about good and evil. Sadly, we could have been spared all that this knowledge represents.

---

[1] Please see Gen 1:3-5.
[2] Please see Gen 1:11-25.

Law of Moses

Many years later, God instructed Moses to write down and codify His Law into the first five books of the Bible: the "Torah" or "Pentateuch." This Law had different parts dealing with moral, ceremonial, and civil aspects of His covenant with Israel.

This Law, however, did not originate with Moses. We have many scriptural examples of men who lived long before Moses who knew how to relate to God and obey His Law. For example, Cain and Abel both brought a sacrifice to God.[1] Enoch[2] and Noah[3] both knew God and had fellowship with Him. Abraham gave a tithe to Melchizedek,[4] and was known for the many altars[5] to God that he built. All of these show us that God's Law was in place and "in operation" before His formal covenant with Israel through Moses.

Much of the Law is applicable to all of mankind. We see proof of this in the Prophets, as they bring Oracles or Burdens[6] against the various nations of the earth that were violating God's Law. These nations experienced the consequences of their disobedience.

When the Bible refers to the "Law," it is usually the Law of Moses. Sometimes the Psalms and the Prophets are included.

God's Law

In one sense, all "Law" is a representation of God. Since God cannot lie and because everything He says "happens," the Law "shows" us God. Romans states this explicitly as:

> Rom 1:20
> For since the creation of the world God's invisible qualities — his eternal power and divine nature — have been clearly seen, being understood from what has been made, so that men are without excuse. (NIV)

We feel that God's nature, character, heart, desires, plans, etc. are seen through His Law. That is why the Psalmist could express his love of the Law in such a powerful way.

When we separate out the ceremonial and cultural aspects of the Law, leaving the natural, moral, and relational aspects, what do we have left? A picture of God and His dealings with mankind.

God's Law for the New Testament Christian

In the New Testament, Jesus makes it clear that we are still subject to the moral Law of God. Jesus not only repeats the Ten Commandments, but He extends them. The sin is not "just" in breaking of the commandment by "doing" something, but in breaking the commandment by what seems to be a lesser action: by merely "thinking" about doing something. For example, He extends the penalty

---

[1] Please see Gen 4:3-5.
[2] Please see Gen 5:22, 24.
[3] Please see Gen 5:29-9:29.
[4] Please see Gen 14:17-20.
[5] Please see Gen 12:8, 13:4, 18, 22:9.
[6] Please see as examples Isa 13:1, 19:1, 23:1, Nah 1:1.

for murder to being angry at one's brother,[1] and He equates lusting after a woman in one's heart to actually committing adultery.[2]

An essential difference exists between us at this time in history and the Israelites who lived (and still do) under the Law of Moses. We are free of the ceremonial and of many civil (cultural) along with all physical actions that the Israelites had to observe for righteousness' sake. God was using these requirements in the natural to teach them (and us) about the spiritual. For example, Paul makes it very clear in Galatians that we do not have to be circumcised (a physical act) in order to be in covenant with God.

> Gal 5:6
> For in Jesus Christ neither circumcision availeth any thing, nor uncircumcision; but faith which worketh by love. (KJV)

In Colossians, He takes away all need to follow dietary restrictions or special days observances in order to achieve righteousness (i.e., salvation). These external things were only a "shadow of things to come."[3]

The New Testament makes it clear that the Law we are to observe now involves God's moral commandments and the conditions within His conditional promises. In order to gain His promises of salvation, forgiveness, healing, freedom from demonic torment, etc., certain conditions must be met. We do it by faith, through the provisions that Jesus has made available to us. We will refer to this part of the Law as "the Moral/Promises Law."

Abuses of the Law

In our introduction to this chapter, we quoted a person who believes that the Law does not apply to him because of the statement: "Ye are not under the law, but under grace."[4] This belief puts him in danger of abusing the Moral/Promises Law and failing to mature in his Christian life. He could go to either of several extremes, which we describe as the "Libertarian," "Cheap Grace," and "Indifferent."

The "**Libertarian**" feels totally free of any restraint. He is free to indulge himself in anyway and at anytime that he wants. There are no consequences because he is "under grace!" "Christ bought my freedom." Carnal pleasures of the mind and body occupy his time and energy. He doesn't know what the Christian life is really all about. He doesn't know Jesus as Lord. He is deceived.

The "**Cheap Grace**" person is similar to the Libertarian but with some differences. He **knows** that he continually sins, that his decisions are controlled by his flesh, and that he is not advancing in maturity. He always has another excuse/justification, however, as to why he is not able to take control of his life and become a serious disciple of Christ. His "ace in the hole" is his total trust in God's faithfulness to His Word. He knows that God is "faithful and just" to **always** forgive us when we confess our sin and ask forgiveness. So, every time he sins, he just asks for forgiveness. It's that simple. Or is it?

---

[1]   Please see Mat 5:21-22.
[2]   Please see Mat 5:27-28.
[3]   Please see Col 2:16-23.
[4]   Please see Rom 6:14.

32

The most likely extreme for a person to adopt is to be "Indifferent." He really doesn't understand the Law or know its purpose. He just knows that God was always angry with the Israelites. He is very glad that Jesus came and died on the Cross so God won't be upset with him. He doesn't have to be concerned about the Law. He's glad he can live under the New Testament, where all he has to do is "love everybody."

We will have more to say about these subjects as we go along, but now let's dig deeper into God's Moral/Promises Law. Stay alert and be on the lookout for "Mr. Libertarian," "Mr. Cheap Grace," and "Mr. Indifference."

2. God's Law "Is"

In Pat Robertson's book, *The Secret Kingdom,*[1] he laid out a number of the laws in the Kingdom of God, including: the law of reciprocity, the law of use, the law of perseverance, the law of responsibility, the law of greatness, the law of unity, the law of fidelity, the law of change, the law of miracles, the law of dominion, plus a number of others. Pat observed that these laws in the invisible kingdom of God operate just as reliably as the natural laws that scientists have discovered. God, of course, designed the natural laws, like gravity, into the universe where they operate perpetually.

If you jump off a building, at any time of the day or night, the earth will pull on you. Actually, the earth is always pulling on us. Usually, though, we are standing or lying on something that keeps us from moving toward the earth. But the force of gravity is **always** in operation.

The laws of the invisible kingdom function in the same way. They are **always** in operation. God's Law "**is**."

The laws of God operate whether someone is saved or unsaved. He "sendeth rain on the just and on the unjust."[2] They operate all of the time, day or night, summer or winter.

We can't "break" God's Law. All we can do is violate it. The Law remains unbroken. *We* are the ones broken on His Law.[3]

When we violate a law, whether natural or spiritual or moral, God doesn't have to sit around watching us and waiting for it to happen. He is not "up there" with a big fly swatter, just waiting for a chance to use it.

"Ah hah, there is another one. Take that!" Swat!

No, God is smarter than that, and much more merciful. The consequence of violating any part of His Moral/Promises Law is built into the universe. The law contains its own result just as a seed knows how to grow itself into the correct plant or animal. God doesn't "push a button" to set the consequence into action. It simply starts happening. God doesn't have to pay any attention to it at all!

---

[1] Robertson, Pat, *The Secret Kingdom*, World Publishing, Dallas, TX, 1992.
[2] Please see Mat 5:45.
[3] Please see Mat 21:44.

As children, if we touched a hot stove, we experienced the natural consequence. Our parents did not have to run over and suddenly make the stove hot or cause our finger to have pain; it just happened.

If we get angry at someone and deal with it in a sinful way, certain consequences are put into motion. The results will become apparent, sooner or later.

One last thing. God has not had a legislative meeting in heaven and repealed any part of His Moral/Promises Law, nor has He added any parts. God's Law/Word stands.[1] Even though we are living in the New Testament period, we cannot ignore the Law. The Old Testament shows us the Law, the New Testament clarifies it and extracts the Moral/Promises portions for us as Christians. We remain subject to it, and He expects us to obey it. Being a Christian does not automatically separate us from the consequences of God's Moral/Promises Law. Why not? Because His Law "**is**."

B. How did Jesus Relate to the Law?

What was Jesus' attitude toward the Law? What did He think about it? Was He subject to the Law or not?

Jesus speaks in Matthew,

> Mat 5:17-18
> 17 Think not that I am come to destroy the law, or the prophets: **I am** not **come** to destroy, but **to fulfill**.
> 18 For verily I say unto you, Till heaven and earth pass, one jot or one tittle shall in no wise pass from the law, **till all be fulfilled**. (KJV)

Likewise in Luke, Jesus says,

> Lk 24:44
> . . . These [are] the words which I spake unto you, while I was yet with you, that **all things must be fulfilled**, which were written in the law of Moses, and [in] the prophets, and [in] the psalms, **concerning me**. (KJV)

The Law pointed to Jesus, and He came to fulfill it. He made it clear that the wrap-up of the ages would not occur until **all** of the Law is fulfilled.

> Lk 16:17
> It is easier for heaven and earth to disappear than for the least stroke of a pen to drop out of the Law. (NIV)

Jesus' did not come to break God's commands or to be above nor ignore the Law, but to **fulfill** the Law. In fact, He lived His life according to the Law. His was a sin-free life, in which He was obedient in every way to the Father.

---

[1]   Please see Mat 24:35. Parallel passages in Mk 13:31, Lk 21:33.

As the sinless, spotless Lamb who met all of the requirements of the Law, He was the perfect sacrifice. Jesus was willing to die a painful death in order to fulfill the prophetic word written in the scriptures.

> Mat 26:53-54
> 53 Thinkest thou that I cannot now pray to my Father, and he shall presently give me more than twelve legions of angels?
> 54 **But how then shall the scriptures be fulfilled**, that thus it must be? (KJV)

Jesus honored and respected the Law. It was His absolute standard. As His first coming was a part of fulfilling the Law, His second coming will be part of fulfilling the Law.

C. How does God Expect Us to Relate to the Law?

God expects us to obey and fulfill the Moral/Promises Law. The Sermon on the Mount, the Beatitude, and all of His commandments to us, demonstrate this.

1. Direct Commandments

Jesus says in Matthew,

> Mat 5:19
> Whosoever therefore shall break one of these least commandments, and shall teach men so, he shall be called the least in the kingdom of heaven: but whosoever shall do and teach [them], the same shall be called great in the kingdom of heaven. (KJV)

Jesus clearly admonishes us not to break the commandments nor to teach others to do so. We are to obey the laws of God, to do the laws of God, so that we are in alignment with God and Christ in fulfilling all that He wants us to do.

In the story of the woman caught in adultery,

> Jn 8:10-11
> 10 When Jesus had lifted up himself, and saw none but the woman, he said unto her, Woman, where are those thine accusers? hath no man condemned thee?
> 11 She said, No man, Lord. And Jesus said unto her, Neither do I condemn thee: **go, and sin no more**. (KJV)

Jesus released her through forgiveness and then makes it clear that she is not to continue the practice of sin. "Go and obey the Law," He is commanding her.

Later we have the story about the man who laid beside the pool for 38 years. Jesus said to him,

> Jn 5:14
> . . . Behold, thou art made whole: **sin no more, lest a worse thing come unto thee**. (KJV)

Going back into sin can bring a larger consequence. Jesus warned them against the effects of the Law of Sowing and Reaping, as well as the Law of Multiplication. He wanted them to have "the good life" and not to be continually subjected to the judgments that come from violating God's Law.

2. The "Good News" of the Law in Romans

In Galatians and in Romans, Paul writes more about the Law of God than anywhere else. It is a tough assignment because, on the one hand, he is trying to help Christians, particularly Jewish Christians, get free of the observances of the Law that have no righteousness value, such as circumcision, observances of particular days and seasons, etc. Yet, on the other hand, he did not want them to move into "Cheap Grace," with its false sense of freedom and license to sin willfully.

A continual tension exists between Grace and Law (meaning Legal Observances) and between Freedom and License (to sin). Every time Paul finishes expounding on grace, he immediately counters with words such as, "But don't sin!"[1]

Not only does Paul give us God's commandment to keep the Law, but the Bible makes it clear that Paul himself did his best to keep the Law. We read in Acts,

> Acts 24:14-16
> [14] . . . I believe everything that agrees with the Law and that is written in the Prophets, [15]and I have the same hope in God as these men, that there will be a resurrection of both the righteous and the wicked. [16]So I strive always to keep my conscience clear before God and man. (NIV)

Passages on the Moral/Promises Law

Several scripture verses found predominately in the book of Romans show a reasoned progression of thought.[2] They move from the purpose of the Law to being lead by the Spirit in order to fulfill the Law without the believer becoming bound by the Law.

> Rom 3:20
> Therefore **no one** will be declared righteous in his sight by observing the law; rather, **through the law we become conscious of sin**. (NIV)

> Rom 7:6
> But now, by dying to what once bound us (the law), **we have been released from the law so that we serve in the new way of the Spirit**, and not in the old way of the written code (law). (NIV)

---

[1] Please see for example, Rom 6:1-2, 6:15.

[2] Please remember that Paul "wrote" Romans (and his other epistles) as a letter by dictating it to a scribe, as the Holy Spirit gave him inspiration. He was not writing a theological treatise, logically presented and organized. We have rearranged his presentation to show the logical progression.

Rom 6:1-2
[1]What shall we say, then? **Shall we go on sinning so that grace may increase?** [2]**By no means!** We died to sin; **how can we live in it** any longer? (NIV)

Rom 6:15
. . . **Shall we sin because we are not under law but under grace? By no means!** (NIV)

Gal 2:21
I do not set aside the grace of God, for **if righteousness could be gained through the law, Christ died for nothing!** (NIV)

Rom 2:13
For it is **not those who hear the law** who are righteous in God's sight, **it is those who obey the law who will be declared righteous**. (NIV)

Rom 3:31
Do we, then, **nullify the law by this faith?** Not at all! Rather, **we uphold the law.** (NIV)

Rom 8:4
In order that the righteous requirements of the law might be <u>fully</u> met in us, who do not **live** according to the sinful nature but **according to the Spirit.** (NIV)

Gal 5:18
But **if you are led by the Spirit, you are not under law**. (NIV)

We are not "under the Law." In other words, we are not to be pressed down and crushed by it but, rather we are to "uphold the Law." We are to meet the "righteous requirements of the Law," not in our own strength nor by our own will power but by living "according to the Spirit," by being "led by the Spirit," and by God's Grace that empowers us to live as testimonies of His Mercy and Grace. Yes, it is safe to say that the Law is "very" important.

3. How to Fulfill the Moral/Promises Law

If we are expected to uphold and fulfill the Law as Jesus did, how do we do it? Jesus points us in the right direction. Consider the following scriptures.

Do it by Love

Mat 22:37-40
[37]Jesus replied: "'**Love the Lord your God with all your heart and with all your soul and with all your mind.**' [38]This is the first and greatest commandment. [39]And the second is like it: '**Love your neighbor as yourself.**' [40]**All the Law and the Prophets** hang on these two commandments." (NIV)

In other words, if we do as He has directed, we will be able to fulfill all moral and righteousness commandments contained in the Pentateuch and the Prophets. Becoming free and healed is a part of being able to walk in this scripture.

> Rom 13:10
> Love does no harm to its neighbor. Therefore **love is the fulfillment of the law**. (NIV)

Other passages that direct us to love our neighbor are in Galatians 5:14 and James 2:8. As we express our love in this way, we become aligned with God's nature and character. We become Christlike.

Until we are healed, however, most of us can hardly love ourselves, much less love our neighbors. We are usually so hurt that we can't believe God really loves us, so we have a hard time loving Him and fulfilling His commandments. We need to be healed and experience God's love in our lives, then we can turn from being "self" focused to being "other" focused.

Do it by the Fruit of the Spirit

> Gal 5:22-23
> [22]But **the fruit of the Spirit is** love, joy, peace, patience, kindness, goodness, faithfulness, [23]gentleness and self control. **Against such things there is no law.** (NIV)

Paul describes nine types of Christian behavior that are not against the Law of Moses. Exhibiting love, joy, peace, patience, kindness, goodness, faithfulness, gentleness, and self-control will not bring the Pharisees' wrath. These fruits only become evident, however, as we live in grace and are led by the Spirit.

Do it by Being in Christ

> Rom 10:4
> For **Christ is the end of the law**—the limit at which it ceases to be, for the Law leads up to **Him Who is the fulfillment of its types**, and in Him the purpose for which it was designed to accomplish is fulfilled.—That is, the **purpose of the Law is fulfilled in Him**—as the means of righteousness (right relationship to God) **for everyone who trusts in *and* adheres to *and* relies on Him**. (AMP)

> Jer 31:33
> "This is the covenant I will make with the house of Israel after that time," declares the LORD. "**I will put my law in their minds and write it on their hearts**. I will be their God, and they will be my people." (NIV)

As we are born again, as we allow the sanctifying work of the Holy Spirit to proceed in our lives, God's Law will be in our minds and hearts. We will want to fulfill it. It will be "natural" for us.

D. Results of Violating God's Law

If we (and our ancestors) had not violated the Law of God, it is a possibility that we might not experience any problems in our lives. Isn't that an amazing thought? We woudn't need others to pray with us! Unfortunately, we, and our ancestors, did violate and *are* violating the Law of God. That is why we need help.

What would life be like if we no longer violated God's Law. What if we had received complete ministry for all four Problem/Ministry Areas? We would have taken care of the Sins of the Fathers and Resulting Curses? Our lives would be rid of all ungodly attitudes and thinking. Our minds and hearts would be completely renewed and aligned with God's nature, character, and Word. Our hearts would be totally healed and all internal Demonic Oppression would be gone.

There would still be external forces trying to tempt us. Demons, however, would likely avoid our sphere of authority for fear of what might happen to them! As a result, we wouldn't need much, if any, continuing ministry!

Does such a scenario appear to be "Mission Impossible?" Unfortunately, yes. Sin has so saturated this world system that getting totally free of it and its consequences this side of heaven seems highly unlikely. This is why an understanding of the Law and how it relates to ministry cannot be overlooked. When people come for ministry, the question to ask is, "How are they living contrary to the Law of God?"

Consequences

When we violate God's Law, several things begin to happen.

Natural Consequence Activated

An "effect" goes out from us and triggers, or sets in motion, the natural consequence. We discussed this process earlier in the section, God's Law "Is," when we stated that the consequences are "built into" the Law. The consequence might be minor or major, a nuisance or a calamity. The result depends on whether we are activating blessings by our obedience or cursings by our disobedience.

Pain

One consequence almost always occurs: **pain**. In fact, most people come for ministry because they are in pain. Turmoil, confusion, torment, guilt, shame, anger; the list goes on and on. Pain drives us to God. Jesus promises peace. Peace that is not understood.[1] Receiving God's peace is conditional upon doing things God's way.

---

[1] Please see Jn 14:27 and Phil 4:7.

Spiritual Separation

Another consequence of breaking God's Law is a spiritual separation from God.

> Isa 59:2
> But your iniquities have separated you from your God; your sins have hidden his face from you, so that he will not hear. (NIV)

Even when we, as Christians, sin, a degree of separation occurs. How much and for how long depends on many factors. But as we presented earlier in the chapter about the Cross, God's Father heart has provided a way for the separation to be rectified, reconciled, and ended.

Give "Place"

Unfortunately, when we sin, we give legal opportunity for Demonic Oppression. In Ephesians, Paul expresses this clearly when he writes,

> Eph 4:26-27
> 26 Be ye angry, and sin not: let not the sun go down upon your wrath:
> 27 Neither **give place** to the devil. (KJV)

A "place" is like legal ground. It is an "inhabited" space, a snare.[1]

In Proverbs we have an "interesting" little verse.

> Prov 26:2
> Like a fluttering sparrow or a darting swallow, an undeserved curse does not come to rest. (NIV)

This verse shows that an "undeserved" (KJV has "causeless") curse cannot find a place to "rest," or land. It has "no place." On the other hand, when we or our ancestors sin, we give a "place." Satan uses these opportunities to do his work of stealing, killing, and destroying.[2]

In the ministry setting, we want to explore and find those places that have given opportunity for curses and Demonic Oppression and then bring about God's healing and freedom.

How can we fulfill the law so that we won't have these horrible consequences come upon us? Please refer back to the section on "How to Fulfill the Moral/Promises Law." We must live by the Spirit and love God, love ourselves, and love our neighbor. But when we do sin, we have a solution.

---

[1]　Other scriptures expressing this concept are 2 Cor 2:11 and 2 Tim 2:26.
[2]　Please see Jn 10:10.

E. Solution for Violating God's Moral/Promises Law

Christians have two advantages over the rest of the world regarding violating God's Law: (1) We have a remedy when we violate God's Law, and (2) we have the opportunity to ask the Holy Spirit for grace and empowerment to avoid breaking God's Law in the future.

When a non-Christian breaks the Law and experiences the consequences, he becomes more and more burdened and oppressed. He has no way to get free of the load. Christians do not necessarily escape the consequences (depending on the type of consequences and how rapidly they respond), but we do have a solution for the penalty that comes from breaking the Law.

The place to receive help is at the Cross. We have already discussed the awesome provision of the Cross. One additional fact is that the Cross is the place of judgment, where the consequences of **all** of the violations of God's Law were poured out on one man, Jesus Christ.

One of the main reasons Jesus came was to save us from the judgments of the Law, such as "an eye for an eye, a tooth for a tooth," etc.[1] When we receive Jesus, the Anointed One, as our Savior, we are in a position to receive His substitutional carrying of the judgments due us.

Being saved from the judgments of God does not usually happen automatically. We have to know God's remedy and receive it by faith. We must meet God's conditions.

Remarkably, the Law contains within itself the provisions for obtaining freedom from the Law! Isn't that fascinating? The very principle that draws the line and states, "On this side of the line is sin, and on this side is obedience," also contains the promises pointing the way out of the trap (curse) of violating the Law.

The promises showing us how to be saved and have our citizenship legally transferred to the Kingdom of God are the promises that result in our healing.

These promises, however, do not come with a blanket guarantee. In fact, **all** come with conditions that must be met — what we call the **"If Then"** clauses. In these promises, God says, **"If** you will do 'that,' **then** I will do 'this.'"

As we proceed through the Forgiveness chapter and into Part 2, we will repeatedly appropriate Christ's redeeming work on the Cross. Why? Because the Cross made it possible for us to "enter into" God's promises. However, the key point in every case will be, "Am I willing to meet God's condition?"

For example, let's look at God's conditional promise in First John. John writes,

> 1 Jn 1:9
> If we confess our sins, he is faithful and just to forgive us [our] sins, and
> to cleanse us from all unrighteousness. (KJV)

When and if we do our part (confess our sins), God will do His part (forgive us and cleanse us from the resulting unrighteousness) because He is faithful and just.

---

[1] Please see Ex 21:23-25.

F. Specific Laws Relevant to RTF Ministry

As we minister, a number of God's laws are relevant. They can affect us spiritually, both negatively and positively. The Holy Spirit is calling us to "go with the flow." In other words, we need to go with God's laws and be in harmony with God's laws so they work to our benefit rather than our detriment.

In this discussion, we will focus on four of God's laws:

- Sowing and Reaping
- Multiplication
- Time to Harvest
- Believing in your Heart

All these laws are intimately interrelated and operate at the same time. Although they have a combined impact, we will look at them one at a time.

1. Sowing and Reaping

In Genesis Chapter one, God declared that everything was to reproduce after its own kind.

The basic principle sets forth the fact that living "things" will produce seed that has all of the information needed to bring forth a harvest of like "things."

When seed is planted, it normally sprouts and grows into a mature plant, producing a harvest. If the soil is bad, fertilizer is lacking, and water is unavailable, a stunted crop or even crop failure may result. In God's kingdom, however, a harvest normally results. If the seed is planted in good soil, a harvest of 30-, 60-, or even a 100-fold is possible.[1]

Since this is a general principle not restricted to the physical realm, it is valid at all levels: at the spiritual and soulish levels, as well as at the physical level.

In Galatians, Paul declares this for us.

> Gal 6:7-8
> [7]Do not be deceived: God cannot be mocked. **A man reaps what he sows**.
> [8]The one who sows to please his sinful nature, from that nature will reap destruction; the one who sows to please the Spirit, from the Spirit will reap eternal life. (NIV)

Paul says, "Do not be deceived." Don't be confused about this, don't be mistaken. This is a reality that cannot be altered. The law of God's kingdom states that wherever we plant our seed, that's where we will reap the harvest. Whatever type of seed is planted, in general, that is what we will get in return.

---

[1]   Please see Mk 4:20.

The Law of Retribution found in Exodus follows the principle that "like" results in "like."

> Ex 21:23-25
> [23]. . . you are to take life for life, [24]eye for eye, tooth for tooth, hand for hand, foot for foot, [25]burn for burn, wound for wound, bruise for bruise. (NIV)

Other scriptures setting forth this same principle include Mat 7:1: "Judge not, that you be not judged," Romans 2:1-3, and a passage in Isaiah.

> Isa 3:10-11
> [10]Tell the righteous it will be well with them, for they will enjoy the fruit of their deeds. [11]Woe to the wicked! Disaster is upon them! They will be paid back for what their hands have done. (NIV)

If we sow wicked seed, we will receive a wicked harvest.

The Laws of Sowing and Reaping, of Retribution, of Judging are still in operation today.

If we get angry and blast someone, we plant seeds of anger in the soulish realm *and* the spiritual realm. We are setting ourselves up to receive a harvest of anger coming back at us.

If a son says, "My dad was a terrible father who beat me all the time. He is no good," that child has judged his father and set the stage to enter into the same sins and to receive that same kind of judgment when he becomes a father himself.

In families of alcoholics, the children are likely to say, "I will never be like my dad (or mom)." In reality, they usually become alcoholics themselves as a result of planting "judging seeds" and then reaping the consequences.

It is important to recognize that the Law of Sowing and Reaping will produce either positive or negative results. It all depends on the type of seed. When godly seeds are planted, godly/positive results will occur. This powerful law is so universal in function that it will work for or against anyone — even Christians — in every possible realm.

Be sensitive to this law in your own life and in the lives of the people to whom you minister. It can be the source of much trouble. The good news is that all consequences of violating God's Law of Sowing and Reaping can be taken to the Cross. Frequently, the negative harvesting can be brought to a stop, depending on the type of seed that was planted.

2. The Law of Multiplication

God has designed a seed to reproduce after its own kind. He also designed a seed to produce a plant or animal to multiply by producing many more seeds. God seems to always want increase, whether it is more fruit or more sons, etc.[1] God is the God of multiplication.

As the cycle of planting and harvesting, planting again and harvesting again continues, a surplus of seed should result each time. This seems to be true for **every** type of seed, whether soulish or spiritual, positive (i.e., godly) or negative (i.e., ungodly).

With a natural crop, the actual yield depends on many factors such as rainfall, soil quality, sunshine, etc. The yield from soulish and spiritual seeds can also vary greatly, depending on the conditions.

Unfortunately, we often have more faith for negative seeds than we do for positive seeds. We like to dwell on our fears and worries; our "what ifs." It's easier to have fear and the expectation of bad things happening than it is to expect good-things to happen. As a result, our harvest of negative seeds is frequently greater than from our positive seed planting.

Do you see why having our minds renewed is so important? This is why we go into such depth studying how these laws relate to Ungodly Beliefs. We want to help you personally while also giving you the tools to help others.

First, we must stop the planting of negative seeds. Then we must accelerate the planting and multiplication of positive, godly seeds. We want a yield of "good fruit" as described in the parable of the sower.

> Mk 4:20
> Others, like seed sown on good soil, hear the word, accept it, and produce a crop—thirty, sixty or even a hundred times what was sown. (NIV)

3. The Time to Harvest

We need to realize that a certain period of time is required from the planting of the seed until the harvest. During this transition time is when we need our faith to carry us through. We need hope to substain us. We must keep in mind that there is a transition time, the time to harvest, because we will have the old, negative seed still coming to harvest even as the new crop is developing. We have to be aware that both will be happening simultaneously.

Every type of seed has a "time to harvest." For example, think about giving birth. While a human pregnancy (only) lasts about nine months, it takes two years for an elephant to have a baby. In Genesis we read,

> Gen 8:22
> As long as the earth endures, seedtime and harvest, cold and heat, summer and winter, day and night will never cease. (NIV)

---

[1] Please see Jn 15:8 for one example.

God ordained a rhythm, a cycle, an elapse of time between seedtime and harvest.

> Ecc 11:1
> Cast thy bread upon the waters: for **thou shalt find it after <u>many days</u>**. (KJV)

> Gal 6:9
> And let us not be weary in well doing: **for in <u>due season</u> we shall reap**, if we faint not. (KJV)

> Heb 6:12
> That ye be not slothful, but followers of them **who through faith and <u>patience</u> inherit the promises**. (KJV)

Each of these verses emphasizes the time requirement.

The Hebrews passage is particularly difficult for those of us who are "Now Faith" people. We don't like the word "patience." We want what we are "believing for" **NOW** and not later nor after a season of "patience."

Although faith is "now," it takes time before the harvest comes to pass. Abraham never saw the fulfillment of many of the promises God gave him, but his descendants did. Even so we, as Abraham's spiritual descendants, benefit from God's promises to him.[1]

As we change our Ungodly Beliefs into Godly Beliefs, we need to expect a passage of time before we see evidence of the new harvest. If we continue to work with the Godly Beliefs, good seeds will be planted and things in our life — and things in the life of those to whom we minister — will begin to change.

4. Believing in Your Heart

This law comprises the first three laws already mentioned and wraps them into one. To illustrate this law of believing, we will go to Mark, where God has given us a key verse. When we receive the revelation(s) contained in this verse and how it relates to all realms of life, we will have received a tremendous advantage in living the overcoming life.

> Mk 11:23-24
> [23]I tell you the truth, if anyone says to this mountain, "Go, throw yourself into the sea," and does not doubt in his heart but believes that what he says will happen, it will be done for him. [24]Therefore I tell you, whatever you ask for in prayer, believe that you have received it, and it will be yours. (NIV)

In Mark 11:23, Jesus states a general spiritual principle. How do we know that? Because verse 11:24 starts with "therefore," indicating that a conclusion is about to be made from the general principle just stated.

---

[1]   Please see Gal 3:14.

Jesus says that "anyone" (or in the KJV, "whosoever") who can "say," "not doubt," and "believe," will thereby receive what he said. "Anyone," includes saved or unsaved, worthy or unworthy, righteous or unrighteous. It doesn't matter. Anyone means "whosoever!"

If this seems too broad and all encompassing, we would have to agree. It seems too good to be true. And yet, at times, a gift of faith comes, and God's miracle appears. For the unsaved, they hope for better, but don't expect it.

Many Christians do better at applying this law in negative, ungodly ways than in the positive, godly realm. Suppose you believe in your heart that you are "no good," that you will be rejected, that everyone hates you, that you will be abandoned, and that no one is ever going to relate to you in a positive way. If you believe these lies 100 percent and have great faith (fear) for these negative statements, "it will be done 'for you'" In other words, we will receive the negative things that we are "believing for," even if we really don't want them!

Those things that we "believe in our heart" *do* come out of our mouths! As Jesus said in Matthew,

> Mat 15:18
> But those things which proceed out of the mouth come forth from the heart; and they defile the man. (KJV)

This fact provides another motivation to have our Soul/Spirit Hurts (i.e., our hearts) healed. When that happens, we can speak out of a healthy heart rather than a sick one. We don't want to defile ourselves any more than we already have; we don't want to plant any more of the wrong kind of seeds.

Let's look once more at the phrase, "what we say." We don't actually need to speak aloud what is in our heart for it to impact our lives. When we think a thought repeatedly, such as "I'm a rejected person," the circulating thought can plant seeds and build an expectancy as powerful as if we had actually said the words out loud. This expectancy will eventually bring forth a harvest.

As ministers, we want to help the person to whom we are ministering identify and understand the negative things (i.e., Ungodly Beliefs) that are in his or her heart. Then God's solution for violating His Law can be brought to bear on the problem. Our goal is to help the person bring to a stop the negative things he doesn't want in his life.

In verse 24, Jesus draws the conclusion that we should apply the general spiritual principle for godly, positive results. He indicates that we need to apply the law to the things God puts on our hearts to pray for. He encourages us to be wise and apply God's laws in a way that furthers the kingdom, furthers the blessings, and furthers the promises He has made available to us. Be wise, don't do it the old, worldly way — the "before we got saved" way when we operated out of Soul/Spirit Hurts and Ungodly Beliefs. By applying the keys He has given us, we can get free!

G. Final Remarks

Well, what do you think? Do you have any new thoughts about God's Law? A new appreciation for what God has done for us? Did you find "Mr. Libertarian," or "Mr. Cheap Grace," or maybe "Mr. Indifference" loitering around in your mind or heart? We hope this chapter stirred some new "pondering" about God's Law and that you will join us in celebrating with the Psalmist:

> Psa 119:97
> Oh, how I love your law! I meditate on it all day long.

IV

HEARING GOD'S VOICE

. . . your ears will hear a voice behind you, saying, "This is the way; walk in it."

Isaiah 30:21

Some people equate the idea of "hearing" God's voice with "spooky" images of ghosts and goblin and things that "go bump in the night." "I'm not sure I want to hear God's voice," they may say.

At Mt. Sinai, the Israelites made a similar complaint. Their fear of death[1] overcame their desire to be close to God and hear His voice.[2] They preferred to have Moses go up and talk to God while they stayed home and played with idols.[3]

If you are not able, or are fearful, of hearing God's voice, let us challenge you with a question. How can we, as the Body of Christ, function if we can't or won't listen to our "head?"[4] We don't want to be a body separated from its head, yet that is the condition of much of the church today. Let us encourage you to use this chapter as a launching pad to begin hearing the voice of God. May you then go on to more in-depth lessons on learning to hear His voice.[5,6]

For other Christians, particularly those attending prophetic churches, it is considered a "normal experience" to hear God's voice. They accept the fact that God wants to have an ongoing verbal relationship with them. They have daily conversations with God and also bring God's Rhema Word[7] to others. They are a "prophetic" people. We believe that God wants, and is raising up, a prophetic people today.

For RTF ministers and other Holy Spirit led ministers, hearing God's voice is absolutely essential to their walk with the Lord. If we are to be instruments[8] in the Master's hands, we must be able to be guided by Him. What a huge advantage this gives us! It takes the responsibility for healing and deliverance out of our hands and leaves it where it should be — where it really is — in God's hands.

---

[1] Please see Ex 20:18-19.

[2] Please see Ex 19:9, 17, 20:22.

[3] Please see Ex 32:1.

[4] Please see Eph 1:22.

[5] An excellent student book is *Communion with God*, by Mark Virkler, Communion with God Ministries, Inc., Elma, NY 14059, 716-652-6990, 1987.

[6] The resource for the prophetic is *Prophets and Personal Prophecy*, by Dr. Bill Hamon, Destiny Image, Shippenburg, PA 17257, 717-532-3040, 1987.

[7] We defined God's *"rhema"* word in a footnote on page 2.

[8] Please see 2 Tim 2:21.

A. We Must Learn to Hear

Hearing the voice of God does not come automatically. There is a tendency for Christians to assume that once they are born again, they will automatically be in communication with God. This may be true to an extent. However, most Christians, if they have heard God at all, can remember hearing from God only one or two times in their lives. This is usually at a time of danger or during a critical juncture point. They hold on to these special Rhema words from God as precious experiences, as they rightly should. On the other hand, they don't seem to have an awareness that God would like to speak to them on an ongoing, daily basis.

We suspect that all of us have been hearing God's voice, but we did not identify "it" as God's voice. We need to learn how God talks to us, whether in the "still small voice," or by visions, or with dreams, or . . . in any way He chooses. God speaks in many different ways as we will discuss in a moment.

"Other" voices may also be speaking to us, confusing the issue of "Who is speaking?" Some people to whom we have ministered had so many demonic voices telling them what to do that their lives stayed in confusion and torment. They were absolutely unable to pick God's voice out of the clamor.

Biblical Examples

Several Biblical examples encourage us that we must learn to hear God's voice. The one we like the best concerns Samuel.

> 1 Sam 3:2-10
>
> [2]One night Eli, whose eyes were becoming so weak that he could barely see, was lying down in his usual place. [3]The lamp of God had not yet gone out, and Samuel was lying down in the temple of the LORD, where the ark of God was. [4]Then **the LORD called Samuel.**
>
> **Samuel answered, "Here I am**." [5]And he ran to Eli and said, "Here I am; you called me."
>
> But Eli said, "I did not call; go back and lie down." So he went and lay down.
>
> [6]**Again the LORD called, "Samuel!"** And Samuel got up and went to Eli and said, "Here I am; you called me."
>
> "My son," Eli said, "I did not call; go back and lie down."
>
> [7]Now **Samuel did not yet know the LORD: The word of the LORD had not yet been revealed to him**.
>
> [8]The **LORD called Samuel a <u>third</u> time**, and Samuel got up and went to Eli and said, "Here I am; you called me."
>
> **Then Eli realized that the LORD was calling the boy**. [9]**So Eli told Samuel, "Go and lie down, and if he calls you, say, `<u>Speak, LORD, for your servant is listening</u>**.'" So Samuel went and lay down in his place.
>
> [10]**The LORD came and stood there, calling as at the other times, "Samuel! Samuel!"**
>
> **Then Samuel said, "Speak, for your servant is listening."** (NIV)

We can learn much from this passage. But, for now, notice that Samuel heard the Lord three times and did not recognize Him. He thought Eli was calling him. Did God sound like Samuel's spiritual authority? After Eli told Samuel how to respond to the Lord, the boy answered on the third call. The word of the Lord had at last "been revealed to him." Samuel had learned how to hear God and recognize His voice.

Another encouraging example for those of us who do not always feel confident that we are hearing God, comes from Jeremiah, one of the great prophets. In the latter part of his book, when he is already a well-trained and seasoned prophet near the end of his life, we find an intriguing story. It concerns his buying some land from a cousin. God had Jeremiah do it as a prophetic "act," to illustrate that even though the nation of Israel was going into captivity, someday land would again be bought and sold by Israelites. They would be coming back! The story is in Chapter 32. Hear the relief in the master prophet's voice when he said,

> Jer 32:8
> So Hanameel mine uncle's son came to me in the court of the prison **according to the word of the LORD**, and said unto me, Buy my field, I pray thee, that [is] in Anathoth, which [is] in the country of Benjamin: for the right of inheritance [is] thine, and the redemption [is] thine; buy [it] for thyself. <u>**Then**</u> **I knew that this [was] the word of the LORD.** (KJV)

When his cousin Hanameel showed up and spoke the very words that God had said he would, Jeremiah could declare with certainty, "Then I knew that this [was] the word of the LORD."

Jeremiah, like the rest of us, was prophesying by faith. When we do anything by faith, it is not yet a certainty. If it were, it wouldn't be "faith." It is always a relief when something we have done by faith is confirmed.

God's Promises and Directives to Listen

God promises us that we will know His voice. As in every relationship, however, we learn to recognize someone's voice by hearing it over and over again. This is true even for the Lord's voice.

> Jn 10:4-5, 16
> [4]When he has brought out all his own, he goes on ahead of them, and **his sheep follow him because they know his voice.** [5]But they will never follow a stranger; in fact, they will run away from him because **they do not recognize a stranger's voice.**
>
> [16]. . . **They too will listen to my voice,** . . . (NIV)

Prophetic people practice[1] hearing God's voice in a safe environment, such as in a school for prophetic training.[2] There they can learn to recognize it and be among His sheep who know His voice.

---

[1] Please see Heb 5:14.

[2] For example, Christian International Ministries has prophetic conferences, as well as the Ministry Training College where people come for one or more years resident training in the prophetic.

This final scripture comes with a powerful command. On the Mount of Transfiguration, God Himself speaks out of the cloud, saying,

> Mat 17:5
> . . . This is my Son, whom I love; with him I am well pleased. **Listen to him!** (NIV)

"Yes, Lord. We will learn how hear so we can listen to You!"

B. How God Speaks

The one thing that often stops us from hearing God is a preconceived notion about how God speaks and how we should listen. If He doesn't speak the way we expect, we usually don't hear Him. The key is to focus on "communication" and not merely on "speaking/hearing."

As an example of God "speaking" more than one way, let's go back to Samuel and read the first verse of Chapter 3, the chapter we were studying a moment ago.

> 1 Sam 3:1
> The boy Samuel ministered before the LORD under Eli. **In those days the <u>word of the LORD</u> was rare; there were not many <u>visions</u>.** (NIV)

Notice how this verse equates "the word of the LORD" with "visions." What we normally think of as "speaking and hearing" is placed on the same level with "seeing" visions.

Through our experiences in ministry, we have learned to define the "word of the Lord" very broadly. In reality, it encompasses every possible method of communicating, including God using other people and situations to pass His message to us.

We need to learn how to hear from the Lord for ourselves. To be more precise, we need to learn how to "perceive" God when He speaks.

Hearing/Seeing/Feeling

Our spiritual "hearing" senses can be placed into three broad categories: hearing, seeing, and feeling. We may "hear" God's voice as Samuel did. We may "see" God's voice as in visions. We may also "feel" God's voice through our senses.

Table A[1] lists thirteen different ways that God speaks. (Yes, He uses these ways, even today.) These thirteen ways do not operate totally independent of each other. Much overlapping occurs as one way blends into another way. For purposes of this study, though, we have divided them into these separate categories. As you read through these descriptions, think about whether each particular "way" is "hearing," "seeing," or "feeling."

---

[1] These "ways" are condensed and organized from many different sources.

Table A
Ways God Speaks

1.	Hearing His Voice Audibly	1 Sam 3:10 , Acts 9:3-7
2.	Hearing His Voice in Our Spirit. (the still small voice)	1 Kin 19:12, Jn 14:26
3.	Dreams	Gen 15:1, 20:3, 28:12, 31:10, 31:24, 37:5-10, etc. Dan 2, Mat 1 & 2 (plus many more)
4.	Inward Vision. (Word of Knowledge or Wisdom)	Jn 5:19-20, 8:38, 40.
5.	Praying in the Spirit with Interpretation	1 Cor 14:5-6, 13-15, 26
6.	Word of Knowledge, Wisdom, Discernment	1 Cor 12:7-11, Heb 5:14
7.	Illumination of Scripture	
8.	Seeing His Words in Our Spirit (A form of Inward Vision)	
9.	Experiencing Another's Emotions (Word of Knowledge)	1 Cor 12:7-11
10.	Experiencing Another's Physical Feelings (Word of Knowledge)	1 Cor 12:7-11
11.	Personal Prophecy	1 Cor 12:7-11
12.	Song of the Lord (singing personal prophecy)	1 Chr 25:1-2, 5, 7
13.	Outward or External Vision	Ex 3:2-17, Josh 5:13-15, Acts 9:3-7

---

1. Audible Voice

We have come to understand that God rarely speaks audibly. However, there are two scriptural examples in Table A. Also, a number of people have shared with us their experiences of hearing God speak to them out loud. Such audible messages seem to be reserved for times when God really wants to get someone's attention. The person may not be listening or may be unaware that God wants to communicate. An audible message from God may come at times of great danger. Do not, however, expect God to speak to you this way. You don't want to be knocked to the ground as happened with Paul![1] This won't be necessary if you are listening for God's voice in one of the other, less dramatic, ways.

---

[1] Please see Acts 9:3-7, 22:6-11, 26:12-18.

53

2. Still Small Voice

The most common way God speaks to us comes as a whisper from deep inside, as a still small voice. Before we learn that God is attempting to communicate, we may have ignored this voice, or thought it was our conscience speaking. We may have labeled it a "hunch" or "intuition."

This manner of communication can take a number of forms and overlap several of the other ways. In its "pure" form, we literally hear this "still small voice" on the inside of ourselves, coming up out of our spirit-man region, i.e., from our "belly."[1] It is our responsibility *not* to ignore it nor discount it as unimportant. If we respond appropriately, this voice will often warn us about potential problems or disasters, as well as provide encouragement and guidance.

On many occasions, we have been protected from possible accidents or awkward situations by heeding this still small voice. Other times we have ignored it and ended up with a mess on our hands. We have learned to pay attention to the still small voice no matter when it occurs or what we are doing at the time.

As we present a procedure for hearing the voice of God later in this chapter, we will be listening for the "still small voice."

3. Dreams

The Bible records many incidents in which men (and women) adjusted their actions based on a dream from God. This is a fascinating way for God to communicate. As with other spiritual communications, we have to sort out what is from God and what isn't. We don't want to confuse dreams birthed in our minds or counterfeit dreams from demons with dreams from God.

Certain characteristics usually accompany a dream is from God. If the dream occurs just as you are waking up or if it is intense and vivid (frequently in full-blown color), it is very likely from God. Other dreams may also be from God, but it is more difficult to be sure. When we are uncertain, we can ask Him for wisdom and discernment.

Some people hear from God most frequently via dreams, even when they are able to hear Him speak other ways. For some other people, however, this is the only way God can get through to them. Since they don't slow down long enough during their waking hours to let God get a word in edgewise, He communicates when they are "unconscious" and not distracted.

A number of good Christian books[2] explain how to identify and understand godly dreams. If you desire to dig in deeper, you may want to study these books. We

---

[1] Please see Jn 7:38.

[2] One that is especially suited for prophetic people is *Dreams and Visions* by Jane Hamon, Regal Books, a division of Gospel Light, Ventura, CA, 2000. You may call the Christian International bookstore to order at 888-419-2432.

have found, however, that if we pray and ask the Holy Spirit for the dream's interpretation, He will reveal it to us. This principle does not work well, however, when we don't want to know the truth. This usually happens because we assume the interpretation will be negative or because we may not want to do what God asks of us!

Interpretation Guidelines

A couple of guidelines for dream interpretation might be helpful. For instance, be sensitive to the emotional content of the dream. In other words, "How did you feel?" The main message might be contained in the emotional response to the dream and its events more than in the literal symbols and action within the dream.

Another guideline is to be aware that the "other" people in the dream rarely represent themselves literally. Rather, these "people" may be symbols representing different parts of ourselves, possibly to express a current conflict or unresolved problem/decision. They also may be symbols to represent a concept. For example, in your dream, your pastor may represent a spiritual authority figure and not necessarily or literally himself.

RTF Ministers

For RTF ministers, dreams are another way that God speaks to us about the people to whom we are going to minister. He may reveal needed information we need to help them remove hindrances to receiving His healing. We can also learn through their dreams. We may encourage them to keep a "dream journal" and to share it with us as we go through the ministry progress.

One way to record your dreams is to keep a pad of paper and a small flashlight by the side of your bed. Before you go to sleep, ask the Holy Spirit to speak to you in the night on behalf of the person to whom you are ministering. Don't be surprised if God awakens you at 3:00 A.M. with a dream He has just given you fresh in your mind. Write it down, starting with the last remembered segment of the dream. Then use that segment as a "hook" to the previous segment. Frequently, it is possible to work all the way back to the beginning of the dream by writing it down in reverse order. Then go back to sleep. You can sort out your notes in the morning and ask the Holy Spirit to interpret them for you.

4. Inward Vision

The still small voice can also express itself as a "picture" in our spirit. While similar to using our imagination (notice the root word "image"), in this case, God creates the image rather than us.

Dr. David Yonggi Cho wrote many years ago that visual symbols are literally the "language" of the spirit. In other words, images and visual symbols are the means for communication to take place in the spirit realm. Dreams are an obvious example of this, but images and visions while awake are also common. So it should be expected that "visions" are frequently used by the Holy Spirit to communicate with us.

Let us add one word of caution when "watching" for God's voice. It is important to let the image come up out of your spirit and develop on its own without your help in "thinking it up."

You may want to meditate on scriptures in the Gospel of John where Jesus says that He only does what He **sees** the Father doing, and He only says what He **hears** the Father saying.[1] Would that we all live with that kind of communication with God.

As you pray for your ministry receiver, it is not unusual to have an Inward Vision. The Word of Knowledge or Wisdom often comes in this form. If you don't understand the Inward Vision, ask the Holy Spirit to clarify the meaning and then wait to "hear" the still small voice.

Frequently, our ministry receiver will "hear" God with an image or vision in his own spirit, particularly during the "Waiting Upon the Lord" Listening Prayer. Over and over again, God brings awesome healings via the action within an ongoing, inner vision. It is better than any box-office hit at your local theater!

5. Praying in the Spirit with Interpretation

Interpretation of "tongues" is one of the nine gifts of the Spirit listed in First Corinthians chapter 12. To shed some light on this topic, let's look at Romans chapter 8, where Paul writes two verses for us to consider. They are:

> Rom 8:26-27
> [26]In the same way, **the Spirit helps us in our weakness**. We **do not know what we ought to pray** for, but **the Spirit himself intercedes for us with groans that words cannot express**. [27]And he who searches our hearts knows the mind of the Spirit, because **the Spirit intercedes for the saints in accordance with God's will**. (NIV)

We get further clarity about the Spirit's "groans" from Jude as he urges us to build ourselves up as we "pray in the Holy Spirit."

> Jude 1:20
> But you, dear friends, build yourselves up in your most holy faith and **pray in the Holy Spirit**. (NIV)

As we pray in the Holy Spirit, speaking in an unknown tongue, we have the promise of Romans 8:27 that the Holy Spirit is praying for us (the saints) according to God's will. Whether we understand it or not doesn't matter.

Our experience with speaking in tongues is that it "charges" our spirits in a way similar to "charging" a battery. As we do it, the other forms of communication are often activated. Sometimes an interpretation of what we have been praying "in the Spirit" comes to our awareness as an impression of words in English. Speaking these words brings the communication from God. We have heard from God, either for our personal benefit or for the benefit of our ministry receiver.

---

[1] Examples are Jn 5:19-20, 30; 6:38; 8:28-29, 38; 10:32. 38; 14:31; 15:15.

6. Word of Knowledge, Wisdom, Discernment

These methods of communication are three of the nine gifts of the Holy Spirit listed in First Corinthians, chapter 12. They are "gifts," in that we don't have to "earn" them. Paul writes that the Holy Spirit manifests these gifts for the "common good."[1] We appreciate the Holy Spirit bringing forth these gifts during the ministry since they always benefit the person(s).

The information we receive might be a fact (Word of Knowledge) or how to deal with something in the form of a plan or strategy (Word of Wisdom). It could also be a discernment of spiritual information (Discernment of Spirits), revealing what demons are present, as well as their functions and their legal ground.

We can receive, or perceive, this information from the Lord in a variety of ways. Frequently it is a "knowing." We "know" that we know that we know. Something "clicks" in our "knower" like a deposit in the bank, and we know. Other times we may have a vision, a still small voice, emotions, or a sensation of pain. As we learn to trust our accuracy in receiving the voice of the Lord and to act on the information, much healing and freedom will come through our ministry.

7. Illumination of Scripture

Have you ever talked to someone who exclaimed, "This Bible verse 'leaped' off of the page and into my spirit!"? Maybe you have had this experience yourself. This is God communicating by making the Logos become a Rhema word. Even people who haven't learned to hear God's voice in other ways can easily receive from His written Word. God uses this method to reveal either a specific application of the word for a specific situation or a deeper understanding of the meaning of the scripture. Those called to be teachers frequently experience hearing God's voice in this way.

8. Seeing His Words in our Spirit

Sometimes people literally see letters and words in their spirit — like words on a billboard. Similar to Inward Vision, this form of communication does not appear as "pictures" of objects and scenery but as a "picture" of writing.

The words may be anything. They can be someone's name, an address, a phone number, or an entire sentence. Since the purpose of the vision and what we are to do with the information is usually quite clear, the interpretation generally is not a problem.

---

[1] The phrase "common good" is from the NIV translation.

9. Experiencing Another's Emotions

This way of communicating, which is a form of the Word of Knowledge, allows our own emotions "to echo" those of another person. Before we become familiar with this particular style of God's communication, it can feel quite strange. One moment we are feeling fine, the next moment we begin to "emphasize" with the person, feeling depressed, sad, confused, or any multitude of human emotions. It doesn't have to be a negative emotion, but it usually is. The Holy Spirit allows us to experience the same feelings our ministry receiver is experiencing. This knowledge aids us in unraveling the person's tangled problems.

10. Experiencing Another's Physical Feelings

This communication can be just as or even more strange than experiencing someone else's emotions. To suddenly have a pain or discomfort or an unfamiliar sensation somewhere in our body can be quite disconcerting. If we know this is one of the ways the Holy Spirit brings the Word of Knowledge, then we are more able to "flow" with it. We are to use it to guide our prayers for healing and for commanding demons of sickness, disease, and pain to leave. Sometimes this type of communication tells us how the person is reacting physiologically to fear or worry or panic. Again, the message is for the benefit of the one to whom we are ministering.

11. Personal Prophecy

In one sense, everything involved with communication from God is prophecy. This is true as long as we define "prophecy" as God speaking forth His mind, heart, and counsel. The phrase "personal prophecy" narrows us down to speaking forth a word personally to an individual. This is not a significant communication method during the ministry process. The Holy Spirit normally uses other forms of communication to direct the ministry. Sometimes, however, as part of the Opening or Closing Prayer, the Holy Spirit will have one of the RTF ministers speak a personal word of encouragement, understanding, insight, and/or comfort.[1]

12. Song of the Lord

There is something about singing a personal prophecy from the Lord that goes right to the heart. This intensely powerful communication can cut away years of childhood hurt or neglect, replacing it with healing acceptance, love, security, and a feeling of worth. At that point, major healing can occur for the ministry receiver. Our advice is: Do not allow yourself to become casual with this way of communication. (That is, do not automatically sing to every person to whom you minister.) Rather, treat this method with respect, and sing only when the Holy Spirit makes it clear that He has a song for the ministry receiver.

---

[1]   Please see 1 Cor 14:3.

13. Outward or External Vision

Every now and then, we hear of a person who experienced a vision that seemed "outside" of himself. He felt as if he were in a different place with different surroundings, experiencing what was happening there. In one sense, this is merely an extension of the Inward Vision, even if rather amazing.

We personally have not experienced this in the RTF ministry setting, but some people have, particularly during the Soul/Spirit Hurts ministry. As we conducted the "Waiting Upon The Lord" Listening Prayer, Jesus would so involve them in His healing process that the person would "go somewhere else," losing all awareness of us and the room. When the Lord was finished, the person would "come back" and again become aware of his actual surroundings. A deep, personal, and lasting healing always results from this intimate and intense encounter with the Lord.[1]

C. Procedure for Listening/Seeing

Many different procedures for listening to/watching the voice of the Lord have been suggested by others. In case you don't have a procedure you use, we would like to present the following one for you to try. We have found it very helpful. It is similar to the one given by Mark and Patti Virkler in their student workbook.[2]

This procedure is for your private time with the Lord. It allows the Holy Spirit to train you to hear and recognize God's voice, and to sharpen your ability to hear in many different situations. If you persist with this practice, soon you will hear reliably in the middle of a RTF ministry session or while teaching or preaching.

We like to record what we are asking and what God is saying about the various topics we cover. Let us encourage you to have a prayer journal at hand so you can write down and "run" with what He says to you.

> Hab 2:1
> And the LORD answered me, and said, **Write the vision, and make [it] plain upon tables, that he may run that readeth it**. (KJV)

1. Preparation

Keep in mind that everything in the kingdom of God is done by faith,[3] including hearing God's voice. During this time of listening, you will not always know for certain that you have truly heard from God. We suggest that you withhold judgment until the prayer time is finished, so the "flow" will not be interrupted.

---

[1] Please see Chapter IX, "Soul/Spirit Hurts," for an in-depth presentation of how to help a person have this type of encounter with the Lord.

[2] Please see footnote on first page of this chapter.

[3] Please see Heb 11:6.

As you prepare your heart, think about the extensiveness of God's kingdom and the multitudes of people and creatures of all kinds with whom He constantly communicates. Contemplate the vastness and reliability of His communication network. Surely He can handle one more small link (you) of those seeking to tap into His vast wisdom.

Actually, God has been waiting for us to join in. He is more eager to talk to us than we are to give the time for listening.

Since God speaks to us in many different ways, we must decide to be sensitive to whatever way(s) He uses at any one time.

2. Prayer

We like to always start with prayer. We pray an "Opening Prayer" similar to the one given in the *Ministry Tools for Restoring the Foundations* training manual.[1] We suggest that you pray as you start, including the following items as necessary.

Also, if you need to speak forgiveness to anyone or ask forgiveness from God for any sin, this is a good time to do it. If you are not sure whether or not this is necessary, ask the Holy Spirit. He is "always" faithful to reveal this to us.

If the Devil has been successful in bringing up the "unworthiness" or "fear" issues again, this is also a good time to lay these to rest "again." Go through the Ministry Steps of forgiveness and repentance for these sins. Then, agree with the Devil that, in ourselves, we are unworthy. But, we are claiming by faith the righteousness and worthiness that Jesus has purchased for us. Our personal worthiness is not even an issue.

Then renounce your fear(s)! Remind yourself of what God has to say about fear.[2]

Bind all demons, including unworthiness and fear. Forbid any demonic interference during this time of listening to the Lord. Expressly bind any voices that would like to masquerade as the voice of the Lord.

Ask God to open up a clear communication link between yourself and Him. Be ready to "reach" out with your faith "antenna" and tune into His continuous flow of words coming from His throne room.

3. Express Thankfulness

As we move toward the listening time, we like to transition with "Thanksgiving." It is easy to be thankful to God when we consider all that He has done for us. This is a good time to "count our blessings." Also, thanksgiving will tune our spirits into the voice of the Lord. As the Psalmist said,

---

[1] Information about *Ministry Tools* is included on page 435.
[2] Please see 2 Tim 1:7, 1 Jn 4:18.

Psa 100:4
Enter his gates with **thanksgiving** and his courts with praise; **give thanks to him** and praise his name. (NIV)

In previous verses, the Psalmist uses the phrase "come before Him with joyful songs." It is good to worship and praise Him with song. He is Worthy! This time of thanksgiving, worship, and praise not only helps us prepare to hear God's voice, but it is fun, heart-lifting, inspiring, and faith-building. We write our thanksgivings in our prayer journal, as our spirit becomes attuned to God's Holy Spirit.

4. Listen and Record

Writing down those things for which we are thankful provides a natural transition to hearing God as either the still small voice or seeing images or any of the other ways listed. You will want to continue recording what is flowing through your spirit.

If you see an image, record the essential features about it. If you don't understand what it means, ask the Holy Spirit to clarify. As you hear Him explain the vision, record the words.

You may find yourself alternating between listening, writing, asking, expressing thanksgiving, repenting, and receiving healing. During this time, you may receive God's guidance and direction about decisions you need to make, areas where you need to be cautious, or ways you have given Satan opportunities to attack and hassle you.

Chester still remembers the day that God showed him an image of a rough, crudely shaped statue, and said to him, "I've gotten you to the point where I'm not going to have to use the hammer and chisel so much anymore. From now on, I will mostly be using the coarse file and grinding tools." While Chester felt he was supposed to be grateful for this progress, he wasn't sure about having the coarse file and grinding tools applied either.

5. Judge the Word

After the Holy Spirit has brought the prayer time to a close, and you have "tuned" back to the physical world, read back over what you have written. The question, "Was this really God?" needs to be settled.

First, pray over the various words you have written, and consider how you and the Holy Spirit respond to them. Verify that they don't contradict the truths and principles of the Bible. If you have received any directive words, or important decisions, etc., continue to ask the Lord about these topics for several days during your prayer time. Go to the person providing you with spiritual oversight/covering/authority, and ask him or her to pray with you to discern whether or not this message is from God.

Here, as everywhere, God has provided safeguards. In His Logos Word He says,

> Deu 19:15
> . . . A matter must be established by the testimony of two or three witnesses. (NIV)[1]

If you are cautious and insist on the confirmation of several witnesses, your heavenly Father understands. He knows that the deceiver is at work. Don't rush into anything that seems to be from God if there is any question in your mind and/or spirit. Let it "season" for a while, as you continue to seek confirmation from several sources. Only when you have the peace of God that passes all understanding[2] should you proceed to act, particularly on important, major issues.

D. Hindrances to Hearing/Seeing God's Voice

We have already mentioned two of the hindrances to hearing God: the Ungodly Beliefs of **unworthiness** and **fear**. These two lies probably do more than anything else to keep us from hearing God. Yet, both are definitely of the kingdom of darkness. Do not give them any opportunity to oppress you. God can free us from these beliefs and heal the wounds that give them place.

The third hindrance is plain, old-fashioned **sin**. This will definitely hinder your hearing God. Any ongoing, besetting sin can keep you bound in guilt and shame, in failure and defeat, in hopelessness and helplessness. You will probably not even attempt to approach God, much less expect Him to receive you if sin has a foothold in you life. As always, God's Law has the solution[3] as well as healing of the separation[4] that sin brings.

The fourth hindrance to hearing God's voice comes from **demons** that block our spiritual eyes and ears. Certain demons specialize in trying to prevent our receiving *anything* from God, whether it involves reading our Bible, hearing God in our spirit, or functioning in the gifts of the Holy Spirit. These demons operate during our Bible time, prayer and/or listening time, or while in church, particularly when the preacher is about to deliver his main point.

The proper solution, of course, is to get rid of these demons. In most cases, however, these demons don't leave easily because they are usually occult empowered demons. You will most likely need help to get free. Go to your spiritual oversight for help, read through this book and apply the Ministry Steps, receive ministry from a trained RTF church team, come to the CI/PHW Healing House, etc. Do something! Don't let these demons succeed in their determination to keep you out of your God ordained destiny!

In the meantime, you can bind[5] and stop the action of every demon whose mission is to block your receiving from God. Don't let them do their dirty work. Stand on your authority as a child of God and forbid their operation!

---

[1]   Also please see Deu 17:6; Mat 18:16, 20; 2 Cor 13:1; 1 Tim 5:19; Heb 10:28.
[2]   Please see Col 3:15 and Phil 4:7.
[3]   Please see 1 Jn 1:9.
[4]   Please see Isa 59:2.
[5]   Please see Mat 16:19, 18:18.

E. God's Purpose for Speaking in the Ministry Setting

The desire of God's heart is to heal us and set us free. As we realize that He desires this for us even more than we do, it becomes easier to open our hearts and believe that He really wants to speak to us. When God speaks, He brings His **promises** to focus on **our** situation, **our** entrapment, and **our** fears.

As we listen on behalf of our ministry receiver, before and during the ministry sessions, God has at least three purposes He wants to accomplish when He communicates with us.

1. To Reveal Roots

Do you want to be free of pain?

When a person comes for ministry, he or she has one agenda: To be free from pain.

As he begins to tell us about his life, he shares stories of successes and failures. He will describe his "growing up" years, his parents, and relationships with their siblings and friends. Experiences that wounded their hearts and shaped their outlook on life come to the surface. While sharing these personal facts, they may exhibit some emotions and relate their "symptoms."

Although the symptoms provide clues to underlying problems, the "roots," we do not want to focus on them. God uses the symptoms to help lead us to the roots. Freedom and healing come from dealing with the roots and not the symptoms. This is what distinguishes Christian ministry led by the Holy Spirit from the world's form of "counseling." God wants to eliminate the roots and, thereby, eliminate the entire "tree" of symptoms that does not reflect the image of Jesus the Christ in the person's life.

> Mat 3:10
> And now also the ax is laid unto the root of the trees: therefore **every tree** which **bringeth not forth good fruit** is hewn down, and cast into the fire. (KJV)

In RTF ministry, we work with the Holy Spirit, using "dual listening." That is, we listen to the person to whom we are ministering with "one ear," and to the Holy Spirit with the "other ear." We listen for God to reveal the root causes behind the stories that we are hearing. We listen for what Sins of the Fathers and Resulting Curses might be active. We ask the Holy Spirit when the sins were committed and the curses initiated. We desire to discern the Ungodly Beliefs that are in the person's heart as we listen to his words. We ask, "Holy Spirit, what lies or Ungodly Beliefs (UGBs) underlie his statements of bitterness, hurt, and anger? How did they get their foothold?" We also want to know, "What Soul/Spirit Hurts are producing trees of anger, hate, bitterness, depression, etc." In addition, we seek to know what Demonic Strongholds have become entrenched so we can pull them out by their roots.

We want to know "what's there" that has hindered or prevented God's healing and freedom from coming to the person. What conditional promises haven't had their conditions met yet? Then the next question is, "What needs to be done so God *can* bring freedom and healing."

2. To Reveal How to Minister

We appreciate very much the revelations and understandings that the Holy Spirit has given to us over the years. Many of them came during actual ministry sessions as He showed us what to do next and "why." These understandings make up this book. They have led to what we call the Integrated Approach to Healing Ministry as we bring together the Ministry Steps for the four Problem/Ministry Areas.

The real issue, however, is what do we do when "Mr. Christian" is expectantly sitting in front of us. Do we follow by rote the filled-out application forms and various other aids we have scattered throughout this book?

Positive results will come from this approach since we would be meeting God's conditions for some of the problems in Mr. Christian's life. To "customize" the Integrated Approach to Healing Ministry for each individual, however, works much better. This is what the Holy Spirit does while we continue listening to Him. As we prayerfully ponder the ministry notes and filled-out forms, and listen to the person, God reveals the roots that need attention. He also gives us the strategy, i.e., the order of events and the "when to do what," as the different revelations come to us. This strategy includes showing us when, if at all, we are to share the information with the ministry receiver.

The flow of the ministry process is such that each part builds upon what has gone before. The Integrated Approach to Healing Ministry is a "framework," upon which we "hang" the Holy Spirit's revelations as we move through the various parts. The strategy develops as He shows where the "roots" fit on the framework and how to minister to each one.

As we encounter each part of the framework, we simply do what the Holy Spirit has already told us or what He is telling us to do at that moment. When He says to let the person talk, we remain quiet. When it's time to ask a question, direct him, or to minister, we speak up. The Holy Spirit lets us know when to be sympathetic and bring comfort, and when to be confrontative and ask the person to face reality. He *is* the Wonderful Counselor.[1]

---

[1] Please see Isa 9:6 and 11:2-4a.

3. To Reveal His Plan and Purpose for the Person

When God begins to reveal more of His plan and purpose for our ministry receiver, this can take different forms.

Sometimes the Holy Spirit cautions us not to "rescue" the person from his discomfort or pain. He lets us know that the person has not yet reached a place of surrender and submission. If we "rush in" to "rescue" the person, God's plan can be thwarted. This knowledge has made us more sensitive in all areas of life. After all, we desire to work in concert with God and not in opposition to Him.

We want to determine the character traits God is seeking to develop in the person. How do we focus the ministry thrust to bring out these areas? What questions do we ask, and where do we dig down deep? God will give us this type of information because He loves the person too much to leave him in the place where he is.

Is God calling the person to new faith levels? Does He want him to begin to take authority over a larger arena?[1] Does he need to begin to walk in godly headship over his household? Is God calling him to deal with specific areas of hurt and pain? Knowing these things helps guide the ministry as we wait for healing of the soul and spirit and the removing of blocks to reach the desired progress.

Does God want a new, deeper level of fellowship and relationship with the person? Is He wooing him to come into a more intimate relationship? How do we minister to him to help him build trust toward God and to soften his heart.

We want the Holy Spirit to guide us so that God's plans and purposes are accomplished.

Lastly, when we can hear God's voice and flow in His gifts, we are much more ready to confront the enemy of our soul. In the next chapter, we will learn what we need to know to successfully confront and deal with Satan and his works.

---

[1] Please see Section, "What are Our Spheres of Warfare?" in next chapter.

V

GOD'S WEAPONS FOR SPIRITUAL WARFARE

Thou [art] my battle ax [and] weapons of war:
for with thee will I break in pieces the nations,
and with thee will I destroy kingdoms;
Jeremiah 51:20

For the weapons of our warfare [are] not carnal,
but mighty through God to the pulling down of strong holds;
Casting down imaginations, and every high thing
that exalteth itself against the knowledge of God,
and bringing into captivity every thought to the obedience of Christ;
2 Corinthians 10:4-5

It is fair to ask, "Is there really a war going on?"

The short answer is, "Yes." The long answer is contained in the rest of this chapter, as well as in many books lining the shelves of bookstores. Our basic book, the Bible, is a book about war and warfare from beginning to end.

Restoring the Foundations ministry is based on the Bible. There would be no need to write this book if we were not at war. It is a battle manual for extracting captives from the enemy's hands and turning them into healed, free, active, and able soldiers.

This chapter is for you and for the people to whom you will minister. Please use it first of all for yourself and then on behalf of your ministry receiver, the person for whom you are warring. Finally, teach him how to conduct warfare for himself before completing the RTF ministry session(s).

A. What is the War All About?

The short answer is, "You." The long answer is, "You."

An enemy is fighting for our soul, and he is determined to take us to hell with him. He hates God and all who side with Him. He doesn't want us to find out about God and His way of salvation. But, if we do, he works overtime to keep us from maturing spiritually. If this happens, despite his best efforts, he tries to keep us from becoming effective in our God-given destiny and in our warfare against him.

The Holy Spirit's job is to sanctify us regardless of the enemy and his efforts. Whether He succeeds or not largely depends on our decisions to cooperate by meeting the requirements of God's conditional promises.

1. The War is About Us

When Adam and Eve disobeyed, the serpent (Satan) acquired authority over the world system. He tempted them, and they fell. From the moment he was removed from his high position with God,[1] Satan hated mankind. Why? Because he knew man was going to take his place as the one in close fellowship with God. Satan was, and is, in a rage.

As we discussed in the chapter on the Cross, God had already allowed for the possibility of man exercising his free will in disobedience. He had prepared the Lamb slain from the foundation of the earth,[2] since, by His own Law, a man's life had to be paid for, or redeemed, with blood. God "bought" us back from the authority of Satan.

> 1 Cor 6:20, 23
> 20 **For ye are bought with a price**: therefore glorify God in your body, and in your spirit, which are God's.
> 23 **Ye are bought with a price**; be not ye the servants of men. (KJV)

> 1 Pet 1:18-19
> [18]For you know that it was not with perishable things such as silver or gold that **you were redeemed** from the empty way of life handed down to you from your forefathers,
> [19]but **with the precious blood of Christ, a lamb** without blemish or defect. (KJV)

The way was prepared for us to be redeemed, to ensure that we could be in the kingdom of God and that His purchase of us was effective. This redemption, however, comes with one stipulation: We must *choose* whether or not we get free of the enemy's captivity. We can decide to accept or reject God's redemption; it is available for "whosoever."[3]

---

[1] Please see Isa 14:12-24, Eze 28:12-19.
[2] Please see Rev 13:8
[3] Please see Jn 3:16.

2. The War is About Our Mind

Where does the battle rage? In the realms of the soul and spirit. It goes on in our thoughts. The places of infiltration are buried in our belief systems, distorted by our ancestral inheritance (of curses and ungodly traditions), and latent within the wounds to our soul and spirit. The army of the father of lies[1] directs a continuous stream of propaganda to our minds, coming not only directly into our thoughts but also through our eye and ear gates.[2]

Unsaved people have no awareness that this barrage of thoughts may not be their own. If they did, they would try to defend against it. Once we are saved, however, defending against the temptations and lies becomes possible if we are willing to enter the battle.

Helmet of Salvation

First of all, God has given us the Helmet of Salvation. Since we will be discussing this article of defense in the "What are Our Weapons" Section, we will not do it here. At this point, we need to know that there is protection for our minds and that the onslaught of thoughts can be reduced and filtered by having the Truth of the Lord Jesus Christ protecting our minds.

Taking Captive Every Thought

Secondly, we can take control over the thought "stream" going through our minds. We are **not** helpless victims. God tells us to be in charge, to be overcomers. In one of the theme verses of this chapter, Paul writes:

> 2 Cor 10:5
> **Casting down imaginations**, and **every high thing that exalteth itself against the knowledge of God**, and **bringing into captivity every thought to the obedience of Christ**; (KJV)

The language of this verse is "to take charge!" "Do it!" Expose the lies! Be careful what we let circulate through our minds. Examine every thought carefully. Be active. Ask the question, "How does this thought stack up against the measuring stick of Christ, i.e., Holiness?"

God's Measuring Stick

We like to use John 10:10 as a good, have-it-at-the-ready, measuring stick. Read this verse again, thinking of it as a gauge against which to measure every thought.

> Jn 10:10
> The thief cometh not, but for to steal, and to kill, and to destroy: I (Jesus) am come that they might have life, and that they might have [it] more abundantly. (KJV)

---

[1]   Please see Jn 8:44.
[2]   Please see Mk 4:24.

Measure every thought. Ask yourself: Is it involved with bringing life and life more abundantly, or is it involved with death: with stealing, killing and destroying within our lives and areas of responsibility?

Not every thought can be analyzed so easily. For some thoughts, we have to consider the possible fruit or let it "sit" on the back burner for a while until its true "colors" can be determined. For the vast majority of thoughts, ideas, decisions, etc., John 10:10 stands as a God-given standard for our use as we become serious about the warfare over our minds.

3. The War is About Our Body

Besides the main arena of warfare over our minds, Satan attacks our bodies in an attempt to stop our progress — and because he hates us. These attacks can take many forms. He brings addictions of all types, i.e., food, drink, drugs, medicines, TV, pornography, sex, etc. He brings worldly diseases in various forms — from "normal" types of sickness to unusual and "rare" plagues. He initiates accidents, injuries, and premature death to the body, over and over again.

> 1 Pet 5:8
> Be self controlled and alert. Your enemy the devil prowls around like a roaring lion **looking for someone to devour**. (NIV)

Remember, the unsaved person has no defense. He is helpless.

The saved person must work to renew his mind and recognize that he is in a war with an enemy who has targeted him and his loved ones. He needs to learn of the deceptions in the world concerning proper care and maintenance of his "earth" suit. He has to know that he is on the winning side and that weapons are available to enforce the victory. Then, he has to decide to use these weapons. It is better, however, if he first learns his position in the battle and is trained to use his weapons.

B. What is Our Position?

Our position is determined more by knowing and believing, i.e., faith, than by an actual location. While our bodies may be here in the earth realm, our strength, authority, and victory come from the spiritual realm. The real action takes place in our natural spiritual home. Once the battle is settled "over there," the result is manifested "over here."

Heavenly Places
As believers we operate from a "high" location where we are "seated in heavenly places." If we are a part of Christ's body, everything that can be named is "already" under our feet.[1] Paul beautifully clarifies this understanding in Ephesians.

---

[1] Please see Josh 10:24-26.

Eph 1:19-23, 2:6
[19]And his incomparably great power for us who believe. That power is like the working of his mighty strength, [20]which he exerted in **Christ when he raised him from the dead and seated him at his right hand in the heavenly realms**, [21]far above all rule and authority, power and dominion, and every title that can be given, not only in the present age but also in the one to come. [22]And **God placed all things under his feet** and appointed him to be head over everything for the church, [23]which is his body, the fullness of him who fills everything in every way.

[6]And **God raised us up with Christ and seated us with him in the heavenly realms** in Christ Jesus, (NIV)

When we are seated at the right hand of God, we are in the place of supreme authority. Many other passages affirm that Christ delegated His authority to us, the Church. Two of them are:

Mat 28:18-19
[18]Then Jesus came to them and said, "**All authority in heaven and on earth has been given** to me. [19]**Therefore go** and make disciples . . ." (NIV)

Lk 10:19
I have given you authority to trample on snakes and scorpions and **to overcome** all the power of the enemy; nothing will harm you. (NIV)

Because of Christ's finished work[1] on the Cross, He has the authority and victory over **all** the powers of darkness. He has passed this authority on to us. We need to know and believe that we are operating from a "high" place.

In "Him"
It is a mystery how we can be "in Christ" at the same time that He is "in us." But it is so. Believe it and live out of it. This truth will make all the difference.

Many wonderful scripture passages are based on this concept. Reading John 14 and 15, and Ephesians 1,[2] brings this understanding alive. One verse is particularly applicable for this chapter:

Jn 15:5
I am the vine; you are the branches. If a man remains in me and I in him, he will bear much fruit; apart from me you can do nothing. (NIV)

We want to produce much fruit. We want to help the kingdom of God advance. We want to be good soldiers. But unless He is "in us" and we are "in Him," we can do nothing.

---

[1]   Please see Jn 19:30.
[2]   Other passages include Jn 6:56, Acts 17:28, Rom 8:1, 12:5, 1 Cor 1:30.

Partnership with God

One of the wonderful joys of being a Christian is that we are on God's side. Many times, He does the fighting.[1] Other times, He lets us do it. Whatever the "battle" plan, we already know that we are on the winning side.

> Eph 6:10
> Finally, my brethren, **be strong in the Lord, and in the power of his might**. (KJV)

God provides us with the armor we need to protect ourselves and He provides the weapons[2] to attack and defeat the enemy. All we have to do is to show up for duty!

Satan's Status

It is important to have it firmly settled in our hearts that Satan is totally defeated, and that he has no "legal" power or authority on his own. All he has is the authority and rights that men give to him by subjecting their will, authority, and rights as members of the human race to his demonic control. If all of us stopped cooperating with him and listening to him, he would be totally ineffective. That isn't likely to happen before the battle at the end of the age,[3] so we each need to do our part to render him ineffective in "our sphere" (i.e., our area of authority and responsibility) of the world.[4] After all, we operate from heavenly places because we are "in Him." God has provided everything we need, and Satan is totally and absolutely defeated. What more could we want?

Consider these three powerful scriptures about Jesus and Satan.

> 1 Jn 3:8
> . . . For this purpose the Son of God was manifested, that he might destroy the works of the devil. (KJV)

> Acts 10:38
> How God anointed Jesus of Nazareth with the Holy Ghost and with power: who went about doing good, and healing all that were oppressed of the devil; for God was with him. (KJV)

> Col 2:15
> And having disarmed the powers and authorities, he made a public spectacle of them, triumphing over them by the cross. (KJV)

Sounds to us like the war is all over! Jesus says that we will do greater works than He did.[5] Why not apply these truths in the area of spiritual warfare?

---

[1]   Please see 2 Chr 20:15-17.
[2]   We will discuss these in the next section of this chapter.
[3]   Please see Rev 19 and 20, 20:10.
[4]   Please see Gen 1:26, 28.
[5]   Please see Jn 14:12.

C. What are Our Weapons?

We have defensive weapons and offensive weapons.

We have two classes of weapons: defensive weapons and offensive weapons. We want to use both effectively.

Nature of our Weapons
Going back to the theme verse once again, the nature of our weapons are described.

> 2 Cor 10:4
> For the weapons of our warfare are not of the flesh, but divinely powerful for the destruction of fortresses. (NAS)

Anytime we battle out of our own fleshly strength and reasoning of the mind, we become much less effective than we could be. We want to use God's divine weapons.

1. Defensive Weapons

The key passage concerning our spiritual armor is found in Ephesians 6:10-18. Paul lists six items of armor and warfare: five defensive/protective items, and one defensive/offensive weapon. As the armament of a well-equipped Roman soldier, these weapons were the latest technology, the most up-to-date, the most effective. They were the "bullet-proof vests" of today, the "smart" bombs, the "Stealth fighters." Compared to the far superior battlegear God has provided for us, such manmade weapons are totally inadequate. Our weapons are of a different nature and operate in the spiritual dimension.

In Ephesians, Paul is amplifying on an Old Testament passage found in Isaiah.

> Isa 59:17
> He put on **righteousness as his breastplate**, and the **helmet of salvation** on his head; he put on the **garments** of vengeance and wrapped himself in zeal as in a cloak. (NIV)

God's armor has been available to His people for thousands of years. He wants **us** to make good use of these defensive items. Let us encourage you to read and meditate about them. The five defensive pieces are:

- the Girdle of Truth
- the Breastplate of Righteousness
- the Boots of the Preparation of the Gospel of Peace
- the Shield of Faith
- the Helmet of Salvation

These articles of defense cover us from every angle, except from the rear. But God takes care of this as well. In Isaiah we read:

> Isa 52:12
> . . . for the LORD will go before you, the God of Israel will be your **rear guard**. (NIV)

One last thing. We can ask God to send His ministering spirits[1] with us for protection wherever we go. At times, we may need some of His BIG ones.

2. Offensive Weapons

The military teaches its leaders that "the best defense is an offense." The same is true for spiritual warfare. We want to take our "divinely powerful" offensive weapons and use them on the enemy before he launches an attack at us. Two principles apply to these offensive weapons.

First, as mentioned earlier in the section on "Satan's Status," we must apply our authority to keep the Devil's army shut down and bound up. Our strategy should be to keep an attack from even starting.

Second, it is a Biblical principle that after every victory (or advancement), the enemy launches a counterattack. In our spiritual warfare, we would be wise to plan on this and counterattack (or neutralize) the counterattack before it gets started.

We expect to have many victories in the ministry sessions. We expect to see lives changed in significant ways so that the captives will be set free. Our mission is to defuse, confuse, and scatter the enemy's counterattack attempt as part of the mop-up action, which usually takes place during the Closing Prayer.

Prayer

As we pray for the person to whom we are going to minister, we are interceding for him. In many ways, we are "standing in the gap"[2] for him, as Jesus did for us. Our intercession, however, would be totally ineffective if Jesus the Christ had not already accomplished His substitution for us.

Prayer is our communication link with our commander-in-chief. In the broadest term, however, prayer includes "commanding," "declaring," "decreeing," "breaking," "interceding," and "releasing." **In a very real sense, all of the weapons, both defensive and offensive, are put into action through prayer.**

a. The Word of God

The sixth item Paul includes in the Ephesians passage on the armor of God is an attack weapon, the Sword of the Spirit. The apostle clearly defines this as the Word of God.[3]

---

[1] Please see Heb 1:14.
[2] Please see Eze 22:30.
[3] Please see Eph 6:17.

So much could be said about the Word of God. First of all, the Bible is the Word of God. Within the Bible, numerous passages define and explain the Word of God. Many books have been written about the Word of God.

We strongly desire that all we do in ministry, not to mention in our "normal Christian life," be based on the Word of God, the Logos Word. God has provided a written standard for us to use to judge truth versus error, authority versus usurped authority, our rights versus deception.

In the ministry room, we also depend extensively on the Rhema Word of God. As defined earlier, it comes in the form of the Gifts of the Spirit (word of knowledge, word of wisdom, prophecy, discernment of spirits, gifts of healing, miracles, faith.)[1] for a specific individual at a specific time for a specific situation. This is what makes what we do "Prophetic Ministry."

The "Word of God" as a phrase is used throughout the Bible. One scripture stands out from the others:

> Heb 4:12
> For the word of God [is] quick, and powerful, and sharper than any two-edged sword, piercing even to the dividing asunder of soul and spirit, and of the joints and marrow, and [is] a discerner of the thoughts and intents of the heart. (KJV)

As we minister, we observe the Word of God doing exactly these things. It is an awesome experience.

b. Name of Jesus

Jesus gave us the right to use His Name.[2] In effect, He said, "Go represent Me. Be my ambassador. Here is My Name to use whenever you need credibility, whenever you sign a legal document, whenever you have to pay for something."

His Name is His authority. We established earlier that He has all authority and that He has passed it on to us, His church.

We use His Name to bind and to loose. This is a very basic, very important, activity for us to do — both in our own lives and in the ministry room. In Matthew, Jesus states:

> Mat 18:18-20
> 18 Verily I say unto you, Whatsoever ye shall bind on earth shall be bound in heaven: and whatsoever ye shall loose on earth shall be loosed in heaven.
> 19 Again I say unto you, That if two of you shall agree on earth as touching any thing that they shall ask, it shall be done for them of my Father which is in heaven.
> 20 For where two or three are gathered together in **my name**, there am I in the midst of them. (KJV)

---

[1] Please see 1 Cor 12:7-11.
[2] Please see Jn 14:13-14, 15:16, 16:23-27.

We should note one more thing about the importance of His name. In Old Testament times, a name had meaning. A person's name said something about them. Jesus' Hebrew name is *"Yeshua"*, meaning "God saves." Every time someone said His name, they were saying, "God saves." Jesus was constantly reminded of His mission. Of course, the angel[1] told Mary what to name Jesus. God wanted all of Israel and the surrounding countries to know that "God saves."

God still wants us to know that "God saves." As we use the Name (i.e., the authority) of Jesus in every situation, we are declaring that God is present and here with us to save. Even more, the nature, the character, and, in a sense, even the person of Jesus is brought into the situation when we use His Name.

c. Cross of Christ

In an earlier chapter, we discussed the Cross at length. It is one of our primary spiritual weapons.

What does the cross represent? Death. Death is separation. The Cross is used to put the old nature to death. It is used to bring to death anything that is evil, against God, or against His promises.

Everything ungodly that we have inherited from our ancestors must be brought to the Cross. This is the place to stop curses.[2] When we bring our old, bad seeds of Ungodly Beliefs to the Cross, new life springs up out of their death. Our sinful ways of coping with Soul/Spirit Hurts need to be left at the Cross. Demons were defeated at the Cross. It blocks them from the new life in our bodies, minds, and spirits. Demons hate the Cross, the place of defeat. As we repent and bring our sin to the cross, it separates us from the old way of life and propels us on to the new.

d. Blood of Jesus

"The life is in the blood." God established this truth with Noah and formalized it with Moses.[3] Combined with the Law of Judgment,[4] it takes the shedding of blood to cover sin, to make atonement, to bear the judgment.

As we read the scriptures, the sacrifice of the perfect, unblemished Lamb and the shedding of His Blood has great significance. We have discussed this at length in the chapter on the Cross.

There are many very significant New Testament scriptures to study about the Blood.[5] Also, the scriptures in the Pentateuch about the blood from sacrificed animals point toward and give us a picture of God's use of the Blood of Christ.

---

[1] Please see Lk 1:31.
[2] Please see Gal 3:13.
[3] Please see Gen 9:4-6 and Lev 17:11, 14.
[4] Please see Ex 21:23.
[5] Please see Mat 26:28 (parallel Mk 14:24), Jn 6:53-56, Rom 3:25, 5:9, Eph 1:7, Col 1:20, Heb 9:12, 14, 22, 10:19, 13:12, 20, I Pet 1:18-20, I Jn 1:7, Rev 1:5, 12:11.

Nothing compares to the power of the blood of Jesus. As ministers we can "apply" the Blood by faith on behalf of our ministry receiver (just as the Priests did on behalf of Israel in the Old Testament.) As we apply the Blood, it cleanses, sanctifies, brings life, and sets him apart from his sin and from the world.

We have personally experienced how much the demons hate the Blood of Jesus. To them, it is like a burning poison. It is life, whereas they are death. Applying the Blood to the legal ground occupied by demons drives them off. They can't stand it, nor can they stand being reminded of their defeat at the Cross.

Apply the Blood liberally, as much, and as often as needed. We will never run out of the Blood. The old hymn says it so well,

There is a Fountain

There is a fountain filled with blood, drawn from Immanuel's veins;
And sinners, plunged beneath that flood, lose all their guilty stains:
Lose all their guilty stains, lose all their guilty stains;
And sinners, plunged beneath that flood, lose all their guilty stains.

And it never will run dry, no, it never will run dry;
There is a fountain filled with blood, and it never will run dry.[1]

3. Other Offensive Actions

Several other actions can be used to make the weapons of our warfare more effective. We will also mention these actions later when we need to apply them at different points in the ministry process.

Praise
While ministering to an individual, we frequently praise God as we do as a group in corporate worship. It is easy to praise when God has come forth and demonstrated His healing, His freedom, His Love, His compassion, etc. Praise can also be used during spiritual warfare. Praise drives the demons wild and "clears the air" when oppression begins to build. Singing and worship brings an awareness of the presence of God[2] and allows His anointing to break the yoke of bondages.

Laying on of Hands
We often ask the permission of our ministry receiver to (appropriately) lay our hands on him. This allows for an impartation of love and comfort, particularly during a time when old hurts are surfacing. During deliverance, laying on of hands provides an increased sensitivity to the presence of demons. This helps in our discernment of the spirits. Besides, demons dislike hands with the anointing of God placed on what they consider to be "their house." It "stirs" them "up."

---

[1]   "There is a Fountain," by William Cowper, 1771.
[2]   Please see Psa 22:3.

Dispatching Angels

While we don't directly dispatch angels ourselves, we have no hesitation in asking God to dispatch them.[1] They are here for our benefit, so, why not use them? We don't want any unemployed angels! Keep in mind, however, that this is not a frivolous request. Using proper respect, we can ask our Father to send His angels to accomplish a certain mission. We want to ensure, however, that what we are asking God to do with His angels agrees with His Logos, or Rhema Word!

D. What are Our Spheres of Warfare?

As Christians, we want to be kingdom minded with a worldwide vision for the advancement of the kingdom of God. At the same time, we need to be self or "individual" minded as we focus our attention and prayer onto one person. As we "war" on behalf of ourselves or on behalf of one person, we also want to be aware that we are affecting an ever-expanding area of influence. One way to list these spheres of warfare and influence is:

- Ourselves (or the person to whom we are ministering)
- Our family (or the family of the person)
- Our Church and/or Place of Business (or the same for the person)
- Our Region
- Our Nation
- Our World

In order to actually advance the kingdom of God into the larger arenas, it is important to enter into agreement with others who have authority and responsibility within the same spheres. As we apply the understanding about the four Problem/ Ministry areas that we have for the individual to the larger arenas, these larger regions will come under the dominion of the kingdom of God.

What does God desire most? To see His redemption brought to entire groups or regions of people. Do we expect the Church to reclaim the "entire" world for God this way? No, we do not. Our Bible indicates that the Man on the white horse[2] will have to come with His army before the "entire" world comes under His authority. In the meantime, He wants us to repossess as much enemy territory as possible — and certainly the territory that is included within our responsibility.

---

[1] Please see Heb 1:14.
[2] Please see Rev 19:11-21, 20:7-10.

E. How Do We Fight?

Restoring the Foundations was written to teach us how to fight, first for ourselves and then for the people to whom we minister. This book is designed to help you become a first-rate Restoring the Foundations (RTF) minister. You could accomplish this on your own with the Holy Spirit leading you through it; or, you could be trained through Proclaiming His Word Ministries and benefit from direct contact with the training methods, approaches, and anointing that He has given to us. However you do it, you will repeatedly perform the ministry steps presented in Part 2. Briefly, they are:

- Submission to God
- Confession and Taking Responsibility
- Forgiveness and Repentance
- Assuming Legitimate Authority
- Praying and Receiving
- Pouring Out and Releasing
- Declaring and Breaking
- Binding and Loosening
- Casting Out
- Being Filled with the Holy Spirit

We hope you enjoy the journey!

F. God's Promise

We want to conclude this chapter with a portion of Psalm 18,[1] a Psalm of David. Take this Psalm as your own, as if God was speaking these promises directly to you.

> Psa 18:30-50
>
> 30 [As for] God, his way [is] perfect: the word of the LORD is tried: he [is] a buckler to all those that trust in him.
>
> 31 For who [is] God save the LORD? or who [is] a rock save our God?
>
> 32 [It is] God that girdeth me with strength, and maketh my way perfect.
>
> 33 He maketh my feet like hinds' [feet], and setteth me upon my high places.
>
> 34 **He teacheth my hands to war**, so that a bow of steel is broken by mine arms.
>
> 35 Thou hast also given me the **shield of thy salvation**: and **thy right hand hath holden me up**, and thy gentleness hath made me great.
>
> 36 Thou hast enlarged my steps under me, that my feet did not slip.
>
> 37 I have pursued mine enemies, and overtaken them: neither did I turn again till they were consumed.
>
> 38 I have wounded them that they were not able to rise: they are fallen under my feet.
>
> 39 For **thou hast girded me with strength unto the battle**: thou hast subdued under me those that rose up against me.
>
> 40 Thou hast also given me the necks of mine enemies; that I might destroy them that hate me.
>
> 41 They cried, but [there was] none to save [them: even] unto the LORD, but he answered them not.
>
> 42 Then did I beat them small as the dust before the wind: I did cast them out as the dirt in the streets.
>
> 44 As soon as they hear of me, **they shall obey me**: the strangers (demons) shall submit themselves unto me.
>
> 45 The strangers (demons) shall fade away, and be afraid out of their close places.
>
> 46 The LORD liveth; and blessed [be] my rock; and let the God of my salvation be exalted.
>
> 47 [It is] God that avengeth me, and subdueth the people under me.
>
> 48 **He delivereth me from mine enemies**: yea, thou liftest me up above those that rise up against me: thou hast delivered me from the violent (strong) man.
>
> 49 Therefore will I give thanks unto thee, O LORD, among the heathen, and sing praises unto thy name.
>
> 50 **Great deliverance** giveth he to his king; and showeth mercy to his anointed, to David, and **to his seed for evermore**.

---

[1]   Originally recorded in 2 Sam 22:31-51.

VI

FORGIVENESS
THE KEY TO FREEDOM

Forgive, and ye shall be forgiven:
Lk 6:37

Recently, Betsy heard a story about two old-maid sisters, Mary and Mabel, who lived together. Because of their extreme differences, they had irritated each other for years. Now in their eighties, each one had developed a bundle of resentments toward the other. One January, Mabel became seriously ill and was hospitalized. The sisters' well-meaning Christian friends, knowing well the bitterness between them, encouraged Mary to ask Mabel's forgiveness while there was still time to set things right. Obligingly, Mary made her way to the hospital and said to her frail sister, "Mabel, you've been so hard to live with all these years, but I just want you to know that I forgive you for all the horrible things you've done, and you need to forgive me too." Then, after a pause, she added, "But Mabel, if you should happen to get well, just forget everything I just said."

In this chapter, that is **not** the kind of forgiveness that we are going to be writing about! In God's economy, **forgiveness is the principal activity and heart attitude needed to pave the way for freedom.** It is the **key to freedom**. As long as unforgiveness is present, God's hand of protection, mercy, and restoration is hindered at best and stopped at worst. Although often the hardest part of the ministry process for the ministry receiver, forgiveness is the prerequisite for lasting healing.

Directions of Forgiveness

Forgiveness flows:
- *Toward others*
- *From God*
- *To self*

We want to discuss forgiveness from the three essential directions: the ministry receiver forgiving **others**, the receiver asking **God's** forgiveness, then the receiver forgiving **self**, which allows the fullness of God's forgiveness to be received. The scriptures underlying these different directions of forgiveness are given in Table B on page 87.

A. Forgiving Others

Forgiving others. The words are easy to say, aren't they? Forgiving others may be the greatest challenge the ministry receiver faces. In this section, we want to look at what is involved in forgiving others, the scriptural principles, some common misconceptions and hindrances to forgiveness. We will also study ways the minister, working with much grace, can help the receiver to overcome the hindrances. Table B on page 87 contains some relevant scriptures.

Forgivenss sets the stage for freedom and healing.

In the ministry process, forgiveness sets the stage for unhindered healing in the four major ministry areas: Sins of the Fathers and Resulting Curses, Ungodly Beliefs, Soul/Spirit Hurts, and Demonic Oppression. As soon as the initial interview is completed, we want to begin the process of forgiveness, unless we hear the Holy Spirit say otherwise.

1. Illustrations

*Forgiveness releases **both** parties.*

Most Christians know the power of forgiveness to change lives and to bring healing to bodies. Forgiveness breaks the powerful spiritual bond that locks people into a negative way of relating to each other. To our amazement, we have even seen the person who has been forgiven begin to act differently, even when he does not know that forgiveness has taken place.

Several years ago we worked with a young Bible college student whose father was a pastor. It was one of those situations where the ministry had come first. As a result, her father had not been present at those meaningful moments and events. The daughter's bitterness had created a deep estrangement between them. As we worked through the process of forgiveness with her, she was able to forgive her father. Then we said to her, "You can expect your relationship with your father to change." We said that in faith because we had seen it work so many times.

Forgiveness bears the fruit of reconciliation.

A month later, over Thanksgiving, she attended the traditional service at her father's church. After giving a Thanksgiving message, her father became uncharacteristically personal and began to share his heart with the people. He said, "You know, there are a lot of ways that I've have failed, and one of them is in my relationship with my daughter. And yet I am thankful that we have a God of new beginnings, and I am very thankful for my daughter." With that, he walked out of the pulpit and into the congregation. He put his arms around her, asked for her forgiveness, and expressed his love for her. Shocked but also thrilled, she immediately realized why this had happened. By forgiving her father, she had helped set in motion the restoration of their relationship. The families in the congregation, touched by this reconciliation, began to follow suit by sharing their love for each other and giving thanks for that which is most precious in life. When we forgive, we break a negative bond or bondage that exists with those people we are holding something against. This young woman's forgiveness set her father free to express the love in his heart.

*Abused people **need** God's grace in order to forgive.*

Several years ago, Betsy was ministering with a young woman who had been an incest victim. Abused by her brother over a period of four or five years, she had allowed hatred to dominate her life. Over the months, as she expressed her anger and pain, Betsy often mentioned, "God wants to bring you to a place where you can begin to forgive your brother." At the time, the young woman was so hurt that she didn't want to hear anything about forgiveness. At this point, Betsy prayed and interceded for God to somehow break through and touch her life.

Bitterness leads to ulcers and colitis.

One day she called Betsy saying, "I'm home from work. I have ulcers that are bleeding; I'm in such incredible pain that I cannot go to work. The doctor says that I may need surgery. I don't see how I can come to my ministry session this afternoon." Encouraging her to try to come anyway, Betsy began asking the Lord how to minister to her. What the Lord revealed really shook Betsy. He said, "Her bitterness has already caused the stomach ulcers. If it goes on, it will destroy her colon, and eventually affect a third area of her body. It will then progress into a life-threatening condition."

After conferring with the pastor who had referred the young woman to her, they both felt Betsy should share what God had shown her. Betsy was not thrilled at the prospect.

She was instantly healed from bitterness and pain!

As they met that afternoon, Betsy said, "I have to tell you something. I just have to. I don't feel as if I have a choice. God loves you too much to want you to go on like this." While sharing with the young woman, Betsy began to weep. She was feeling the grief of God over the destruction taking place in the woman's life: The destruction from the sexual sin and now the consequence of this woman's own bitterness.

In answer to prayer, the message found its way into the young woman's heart, and God's amazing grace helped these tentative words come out of her mouth. "God, please bring me to a place where I can forgive my brother." It was a horrendous thing. Betsy could see the physical and emotional struggle taking place as the woman gave up her bitterness. Afterward, she looked wilted.

Suddenly, she stood up, looked at Betsy, and cried out, "The pain is gone, the pain is gone, the pain is gone!" They danced around the living room glorying in God's instant healing miracle. The pain never returned. As she forgave and released that bitterness, her body was healed right there and right then.

A story once told by a Methodist pastor and retold to us by Rodney Unruh sums up the importance of forgiveness.

Once upon a time two men went into the forest to cut wood. As they labored together, one of the men was bitten on the ankle by a poisonous snake. As his foot and leg began to swell to threatening proportions, the man became frightened and angry. Grabbing an ax, he started beating the brush into which the snake had disappeared. His friend attempted to dissuade him from his search, telling him how important it was that they get immediately to the hospital He knew time was limited to stop certain death from creeping into his friend's blood stream. But the wounded man refused to listen. He flailed angrily at the tall grass and bushes as he shouted, "I'm not leaving here until I've killed that snake."

In all of life's attacks upon us, Jesus is our Doctor, and Jesus is our Healer. We must make the choice to rush ever so quickly into His loving mercy and provision of Grace, or . . . . We can choose to kill snakes, until the venom of unforgiveness and bitterness claims our spiritual lives.

2. Definition of Forgiveness

*Forgiveness is setting the other person **free**, so you can be **free**.*

Forgiveness is the setting of one's will, the making of a decision (a decree, a decision at the spiritual level) **that a release is granted to the offending person or situation** (sometimes it's an organization or a body of people more than just an individual). When we forgive, we choose to set them free. We don't hold the resentment; we don't hold the bitterness; we let go of our plans for retaliation. We let go of the feeling, "They owe me something." We set them free. It's important for the receiver to forgive all who have contributed to his hurts and bondages.

Webster's definition of "forgive" is helpful, particularly the definition for "pardon," which really comes closest to the biblical meaning of "forgiveness."

Definition: Forgive "to give before or ahead of"

1) To cease to feel resentment against (an offender)
2) To grant relief from payment

Definition: Pardon "to grant freely"

1) The excusing of an offense without exacting a penalty
2) Divine forgiveness

---

3. Scriptural Principles

Have you, like us, ever wanted God to make a special exception in your "case?" As painful as forgiveness can be, it ultimately brings about our healing in God's providential plan. His principles are very clear. As we discuss them, please refer to Table B on page 87.

a. God Requires Us to Forgive Each Other

*Forgiveness is **non-negotiable**.*

__Issues of:__
- *Fairness*
- *Feelings*
- *Right or Wrong*

__are not relevant!__

God's Word clearly spells out His requirement for Christians: We are to relate to one another without bitterness, grudges, or anything that puts up a barrier between us and our brother or sister. When it comes to forgiveness, the scriptural principles are uncompromising and non-negotiable. Forgiveness does not depend on fairness, on whether a person feels like it or not, or who was in the wrong. God simply tells us repeatedly that we **MUST** forgive.

God, our loving heavenly Father, not only cares about how we relate to Him, but HE also cares about how we relate to our brothers and sisters in Christ. How we relate to everyone in His creation. He doesn't want us to have coldness to each other, or to mentally "X" people out. Chester used to think it was all right to avoid people. God made it clear that His way was different. He said, "Your avoidance of people is unacceptable. It is not My nature." God wants us to forgive one another, so that we have "cleaned-out," right relationships. That's His expectation. He permits no "ifs," "ands," "buts," or "special situations." No matter what the offense, He simply says, "**Forgive**."

b. God Covers All of the Angles

We must forgive if we have anything against anyone, or if we know that someone is having a problem with us.

The Gospel of Mark describes how we should respond when someone has offended us:

If you have been offended, you must . . .

> Mk 11:25-26
> ²⁵. . . if you have anything against anyone, forgive him and let it drop—leave it, let it go—in order that your Father Who is in heaven may also forgive you your own failings and shortcomings and let them drop.
> ²⁶But if you do not forgive, neither will your Father in heaven forgive your failings and shortcomings. (AMP)

How could anything so plain take so much grace?

Matthew covers it from the other direction when we know someone is offended with us:

If you have been offended, you must . . .

> Mat 5:23-24
> ²³If therefore you are presenting your offering at the altar, and there remember that your brother has something against you,
> ²⁴leave your offering there before the altar and go your way; first be reconciled to your brother, and then come and present your offering. (NAS)

God asks us not only to forgive, but to be willing to take the initiative for reconciliation when needed.

Scripture offers no loopholes. God covers forgiveness from both directions. In the first case He says, "If you have aught against anyone, then you must forgive." Then He comes at it from the other direction and says, "If you think anyone is holding something against you, then go and get it worked out." In each case, we are to initiate the forgiveness.

c. God wants Forgiveness from the Heart

God wants us to forgive from the heart. Matthew says:

> Mat 18:35
> So shall my Heavenly Father also do to you (talking about sending tormentors) if each of you does not forgive his brother from your heart.
> (NAS)

That takes God's grace. We can't always start by forgiving from our heart, but we can begin by making the decision to forgive. Then we can enter into a healing process that if we persevere can bring us to the place of wholehearted forgiveness.

d. God's Consequences of Unforgiveness are Sure

The consequences of unforgiveness are:

- *Not forgiven*
- *Out from under God's protection*
- *Tormentors*

If we do not forgive others, God will not forgive us.[1] God may also remove his protection from us, causing us to be turned over to the tormentors.[2] We believe that the tormentors can come in many forms: from bodily illness to tormenting demons.

> That is enough for me, knowing that if I don't forgive, He's not going to forgive me. I'm not willing to pay the price of having Him not forgive me, of being out from under His protection, or of being turned over to the tormentors. I'm willing to do whatever it takes.

e. God Wants as Much Forgiveness as Necessary

*It is easier to forgive **before** the offense.*

How much forgiveness is enough? Forgiveness needs to take place as long as there is remaining hate, bitterness, resentment, blame, or a desire for vengeance or punishment toward another person. In Matthew 18:21-22, Jesus tells the disciples that we need to forgive in an unlimited way. We need to live in an attitude of forgiveness. Larry Lea, in his teaching on "The Lord's Prayer," said that he would begin the day by setting his will to forgive whatever happened to him that day. He prepared himself to hold no offense.

4. Two Common Misconceptions Around Forgiveness

Two common misconceptions frequently hinder a person's ability to forgive. It is important for the minister to be sensitive to the Holy Spirit and to the ministry receiver to discern if these misconceptions are in operation.

a. Forgiveness Equals Healing?

Forgiveness plus healing from the hurts is a two-step process.

A common misunderstanding is that once the offender is released, all the pain will automatically leave one's heart. No! That is not true. Frequently, because a person still feels pain, he thinks, "Well, there must be something wrong with my forgiver," so he "cranks up" and forgives again. When the offense is forgiven, the healing has only just begun. The person then **needs God to come and heal his heart and take away the pain**.[3] That is the way the pain will leave.

*Healing involves **all** of the ministry areas.*

If the person experienced the kind of hurt/offence that follows a generational pattern, he also needs **generational sins and curses** broken in his life. If these are not broken, the same type of hurt may be repeated. It is likely that he needs his **mind renewed** from any lies he has come to believe about himself, others, and God. If not, he will continue to attract the same types of hurtful situations to himself. Also, please note that he still frequently needs **deliverance** from the demons that otherwise will keep reminding him of the painful incidents.

---

[1] Please see Mat 6:14-15, and Mk 11:26.
[2] Please see Mat 18:35.
[3] Please see Chapter IX, "Soul/Spirit Hurts."

Table B
Scriptures Concerning Forgiveness

God's Minimum Requirement is that We Forgive

Lk 17:3-10   We are unworthy servants; we have only done our duty (when we forgive).

Forgive Those Offending You

Mk 11:25-26   Forgive if you have aught against any, else God won't forgive you.

Mat 6:14-15   If you forgive men when they sin against you, God will also forgive you.

Mat 18:15-17   Procedure for reconciliation with an offending brother.

If You have Offended Someone

Mat 5:23-24   For God to accept your gift, you are required to go and be reconciled to your brother.

God wants Forgiveness from the Heart

Mat 18:35   You will be turned over to the tormentors if you do not forgive from your heart.

God wants as much Forgiveness as Necessary

Mat 18:21-22   Forgive up to seventy times seven.

After We have Given and Received Forgiveness, God's Heart is to Forgive

Isa 43:25   "I blot out your transgressions **for my own sake** and remember your sins no more."

Isa 1:18   "Come, let us reason together, so that your scarlet sins shall be white as snow, . . ."

Jer 31:31ff   "Put My Law within them . . . for they shall know me . . . for I will forgive their iniquity and remember their sin no more." (KJV)

God's Forgiveness and Cleansing

1 Jn 1:7-2:2   "If we confess our sins, he is faithful and just to forgive us our sins, and to cleanse us from all unrighteousness." (KJV)

b. Forgiveness is <u>only</u> a Decision?

*Forgiveness is just the **beginning** as it opens the door to the healing process*

Another misconception is that forgiveness is limited to being a **decision only** — over and done with, period. Although forgiveness is a decision, it is more than **the simple act of deciding. In most situations (and this is certainly true for the more seriously wounded person) forgiveness is a process** that takes time. The wounded person must also do his part by acknowledging unforgiveness, looking at the full impact of his hurt, working through painful memories, and then reaching a place of forgiveness. There are no short cuts. Pretending would only sabotage true healing.

Forgiveness can be both a gut-wrenching matter and the initial start for the healing process. Much patience, prayer, and leading of God's Spirit are needed for both receiver and minister during this time. The minister should be true to what the scripture says about forgiveness while at the same time not threatening, shaming, or pressuring the receiver into a form of meaningless forgiveness that is only lip service. At the same time, he must be willing to confront a ministry receiver's endless excuses for not forgiving, if that should be the case.

5. Blocks to Forgiving Others

In this section, we want to address some of the major issues or blocks with which people wrestle during the forgiveness process.

a. Some are Ignorant of the Scriptures

*You may have to **teach** them about forgiveness.*

Some people are simply ignorant of what scripture says. They may be new believers or simply come from churches that don't teach much on forgiveness or emphasize reading the Bible. We need to explain the scripture so that they can understand what the Bible says. Once they hear the Word, they will have to decide whether to be obedient or not concerning forgiveness.

b. Misconception: I Have to <u>Feel</u> Forgiving

*You may have to teach them that how they **feel** is not relevant.*

Do we have to **feel forgiving** in order to forgive? No! Forgiveness starts with a decision. First it is an act of the will. We have discovered that if a person will ask God to bring him to a place where he can choose to forgive, God will honor that. When forgiveness has been chosen and acted upon, eventually the feelings of forgiveness will follow.

c. It's Too Big to Forgive

*The epitome of **Pride** is thinking our sin is **too big** for God.*

Sometimes an offense has been so overwhelming and devastating in the receiver's life that he feels, "I know that I should forgive, but I just can't." The wrong done seems insurmountable. Forgiveness takes time and it takes God's grace.

d. Some Fear Forgiveness

Forgiving is not the same as denying the offense.

The ministry receiver may **fear** forgiving. This often happens if he **mistakenly** equates forgiveness with **excusing or ignoring** the offense. He must realize that it is possible to release the offender from blame while, at the same time, acknowledging the full impact of the hurt and/or abuse in his life. He needs to be reassured that by forgiving, he is **not** saying the offense is "okay." It is **not** tacit acceptance that he should accept of more hurt or abuse of the same kind.

The ministry receiver may **fear** that if the offender is released from blame, he gets off "scot-free." Forgiving, however, does not negate holding the offender responsible for his actions.

Fear of failure will try to hinder the process.

Some receivers **fear** that if they forgive, then the minister will expect them to be healed, and they know that they won't be. As a result, they do not want to risk having expectations put on them that they know they can't fulfill.

*What if they are **more** vulnerable after they forgive?*

Some receivers **fear** that if they forgive, they will be in a more vulnerable position to the one who has offended them. "Maybe I was unable to protect myself from hurt, but at least I don't have to forgive." A ministry receiver sometimes **fears** that if he forgives, the situation will get worse. He feels a kind of protective power in not forgiving. Since thoughts of vengeance generate power, some people may resist forgiving because it means laying down a cherished defense at a time when he is still feeling helpless.

e. We may Think We have Already Forgiven

*The Holy Spirit will bring **all** things to our remembrance.*

Occasionally, we think we have forgiven everything when we haven't. That happened to Betsy once in a prayer group setting. She asked the leader to pray about a concern she had. He replied, "I would be glad to, but the Lord is saying that you are holding unforgiveness. We need to deal with that first." Surprised, she responded, "No, I don't think so. I know I've forgiven everybody." Betsy thought that she was squeaky clean. "Well," he gently added, "Would you be willing to ask the Holy Spirit one more time if there is any unforgiveness in any part of your life?" Feeling foolish, but wanting her concern prayed for, she agreed. Led by the Holy Spirit, Betsy spent the next 45 minutes forgiving many people in her past that the Holy Spirit revealed to her while the prayer group interceded. We don't always remember what needs to be forgiven.

f. Power Over Other Person

This one is interesting. Somehow, the ministry receiver feels that as long as he holds unforgiveness (and probably anger as well), he has power over the other person. It appears that this is a way to counter being a victim. Unfortunately, this strategy for survival is not in agreement with God's Word. God says to be empowered by His Holy Spirit, not by carrying unforgiveness.

g. Recognize a Spirit of Unforgiveness and a Spirit of Control

The kingdom of darkness will do its best to hold its captives.

The demonic **spirit of unforgiveness**, which tends to be passed down family lines, will do everything it can to prevent forgiveness. An entire family can be bitter and unforgiving. It's like the Hatfields and McCoys without the shoot out. Instead, they "shoot it out" in hostile words or with cold, undermining behaviors accompanied by unforgiveness. It is wise for the minister to do deliverance if he discerns this spirit in operation. Then the receiver is much more able to forgive.

Do whatever deliverance is necessary.

Demons of control also promote confusion and strife within a family through continual defensive reactions. They hinder the forgiveness process by promoting the above mentioned fears and feelings of inadequacy and shame. Frequently the control spirits are actually religious spirits, manifesting as control. Again, do whatever deliverance is necessary in order to free the ministry receiver enough so that forgiveness can be accomplished.

6. There are Aids to Forgiving Others

The minister can be the key in helping the receiver forgive.

The minister can be a significant resource in helping the ministry receiver to forgive. His intercession, his love and patience, and his ability to confront or encourage as the Spirit leads him, make a big difference. The following are ways we have encouraged and confronted during the forgiveness process.

a. The Enabling Power of the Holy Spirit.

Here is the place for powerful intercession.

When a person is wrestling with forgiveness, don't merely pray a simple prayer. Call on the enabling power of the Holy Spirit to help that person do what he couldn't do on his own. He also needs to seek the Holy Spirit's help. We remind the receiver that he has full access to the same Holy Spirit who enabled Jesus to say, "Father, forgive them, for they know not what they do."[1]

b. The Cross is the Model of God's Forgiveness

*All of our sin and pain **pales** in the light of the Cross.*

Although we always pray for wisdom to present the great realities of our faith with anointing, the Holy Spirit will never lead us to manipulate or force people. In this regard, breakthroughs have come by asking the receiver to ponder the price Jesus paid for him personally to receive forgiveness. When led, we ask him to focus on his specific sins. This helps him gain a more personal appreciation of the Cross.   Then a thought provoking question may be posed: "Is forgiving others truly asking you to do more than Jesus has done for you?" Forgiving others acquires a different perspective when we see ourselves in the light of the Cross.

c. Consider the Offender

"Hurt people hurt people" helps bring compassion.

"Hurt people hurt people," Sandra Wilson[2] is fond of saying. That simple statement spells out a tremendous truth. It can **soften the receiver's heart** toward his offender to consider the pain in the other person's life. Did he get the love he needed? What hurts and traumas did he experience? Was he emotionally abandoned, abused, or caught in some web of deception? Again, the purpose is not to coerce through pity, but to help look at the facts and provide the Holy Spirit an opportunity to work compassion through this information.

Severely abused people need time for healing before they are ready to forgive others.

A note of caution is due here. In ministering with people who are survivors of physical, sexual, or severe verbal abuse, forgiveness is usually a long process. It takes time for the receiver to go through numerous painful events and let go of his blame, hate, and desire for vengeance. It takes time for God's healing to come into his heart. No deeply hurt person is ready to begin the forgiveness process by looking at the hurts of his offender. This compassion usually comes later as the forgiveness and healing process works deeper into the ministry receiver's life.

d. Knowing Satan's Schemes

In Second Corinthians, Paul makes a direct connection between not forgiving others and Satan's ability to outwit us. He writes:

---

[1] Please see Lk 23:34.

[2] Sandra D. Wilson, *Hurt People Hurt People*, Thomas Nelson Publishers, Nashville, TN, 1993.

2 Cor 2:10-11

[10]If you forgive anyone, I also forgive him. And what I have forgiven—if there was anything to forgive—**I have forgiven** in the sight of Christ for your sake, [11]**in order that Satan might not outwit us**. **For we are not unaware of his schemes.** (NIV)

When we hold unforgiveness, we have allowed Satan to outwit us.

Sometimes it helps us to decide to forgive others when we realize that, by holding unforgiveness, we have fallen into one of Satan's traps and allowed him to outwit us. As a result we have left wide open doors for Demonic Oppression.

> **Prayer:** Father, You have made it clear that You require me to forgive. You desire the healing and freedom for me that forgiveness brings. So today, I choose to forgive all who have set me up to enter into sin and all who have hurt me. I choose to release them, each and every one. I let go of all judgments against them, and I let go of all punishments for them I have harbored in my heart. I turn all of this, and all of them, over to You.
>
> Holy Spirit, I thank You for working forgiveness into my life, for giving me the grace I need to forgive, and for continuing to enable me to forgive. In Jesus' Name. Amen!

B. Asking God's Forgiveness: Repentance

*Forgiving others establishes the **basis** for receiving God's forgiveness.*

Once we have completed the process of forgiving others, then we can come before God's throne and, with faith, ask for and receive the forgiveness He promises us **if** we meet His conditions.

Let's look at this part of forgiveness called repentance. After we have forgiven others, we are in a position to confess our sins to God and to ask for His forgiveness. If we ask God's forgiveness with a repentant heart — a heart that is sorry and ready to change direction, God promises that He will grant forgiveness and cleansing to us. We read in Psalm 51:

Psa 51:17
A broken and a contrite heart, oh God, Thou will not despise. (KJV)

1. An Illustration

An Englishman had lived a racy life filled with gambling, women, and drugs. As a result, he became powerfully addicted. God drew him out of his gutter life, miraculously saved him, and set him free. The man became an evangelist. Some years later, as he was preaching in one of London's famous old cathedrals, he faced an unexpected challenge. As he mounted the pulpit of the packed-out service, he noticed a letter lying open on top of the Bible. Immediately, he saw that it was from one of his former gambling buddies, one who knew the most sordid details of his life. The letter said, "How dare you bring God's message! I know what you're really like. I am here in the audience, and if you dare to preach, I'm going to get up and expose you. I'm going to tell everything what you have done." The letter went on to list a number of the evangelist's specific sins. It ended by saying, "If you've got any sense in this world, you will walk away from that pulpit right now and never try to do this again."

Wherefore I say unto thee, Her sins, which are many, are forgiven; for she loved much: but to whom little is forgiven, [the same] loveth little. (Lk 7:47, KJV)

By the time the evangelist finished reading the letter, he had already made his decision. In hushed tones, he began to read this letter to the audience. Concluding, he said, "I want you to know that everything this man has said about me is true, and there's a whole lot more that he didn't even list. But more important than that, I want you to know that I have taken all of this to the Lord. I have repented, and I have received so costly a forgiveness, paid for me at the Cross. Tonight I want to talk to you about the power of true repentance and God's great forgiveness."

As he was speaking the people began silently to weep. In their faces, there was no judgment, and there was no condemnation. They saw in front of them a repentant, healed man who clearly knew the grace of God. It was as if the light of God shone out of him that night. Some of the people made their way to the altar while others stood and began to publicly confess their sins and desire to repent. As God's Spirit of repentance filled the people, revival broke out in the meeting and spread to neighboring villages until it had touched much of England. It all started with the simple sharing of what God can do when we come in a true spirit of repentance.[1]

2. The Meaning of Repentance

*True repentance is marked by a **radical** change in the direction of a life.*

The act of repentance is simple. It is coming to God to confess our sin with a heart of regret about what we have done and a heart commitment to turn and go God's way. Repentance means **to turn around and go in a different direction**, purposed intentionally to change. It translates into, "God, I am sorry and I am willing to take action. I am willing to work, to change, and to let You help me stand against temptation. I set my face against sin. I am willingly pay the price to remove myself from all 'setups' that could draw me back into it." The consequences of true repentance are radical. They can include changing patterns, confronting, getting rid of things, and letting go of "friends" and avoiding places where we like to hang out. We become careful about what we let come into our ear gates and our eye gates, what we let come out of our mouths, and what we let dominate our minds. Repentance is radical. The arrow that represents one's life points in a new direction.

3. Scriptural Basis: God's Heart Concerning Our Repentance

In First John, John lovingly assures us that:

1 Jn 1:9
If we confess our sins, He is faithful and just to forgive us our sins and to cleanse us from all unrighteousness. (KJV)

---

[1] Story recounted by Jim Darnel, Liberty Church Westside, Pensacola, FL, 1985.

*We **need both** forgiveness **and** cleansing.*

God promises two things, forgiveness and cleansing. His response to our confession is restoration: restoration of our lives and our relationship with Him as we are freed from guilt, shame, and defilement. He not only pours Holy Ghost "Clorox" on us, He also reaches out and takes us by the hand.

Speaking God's forgiveness is awesome and powerful.

It is important for the ministry receiver to be assured, to have it settled in his heart that he is truly forgiven. Often, we speak God's promise directly to him, affirming that he is now forgiven. Two wonderful scriptures allow us, as elders in the Body of Christ, to be God's representative when this confirmation is needed.

> Jn 20:23
> **If you forgive anyone his sins, they are forgiven**; if you do not forgive them, they are not forgiven. (NIV)

> Jam 5:14-16
> [14]Is any one of you sick? He should call the **elders of the church to pray over him** and anoint him with oil in the name of the Lord. [15]And the prayer offered in faith will make the sick person well; the Lord will raise him up. **If he has sinned, he will be forgiven**. [16]Therefore confess your sins to each other and pray for each other so that you may be healed. The prayer of a righteous man is powerful and effective. (NIV)

4. Hindrances to Repentance

In some instances, ministry receivers have trouble asking for God's forgiveness. Others have no difficulty in asking but have trouble receiving. We need to discuss these possible trouble spots.

*We are **never** beyond God's **patience** to forgive.*

Besetting Sin
Failure, shame and hopelessness encompass the person who has a **besetting sin**.[1] He has known the joy of temporary victory only to fall again to the hated thoughts or behavior. He feels guilty and hypocritical, for "asking again." The **unqualified nature of God's promise** needs to be emphasized. Just as God has required of us unconditional forgiveness of others, so too, He has required Himself to forgive us unconditionally if we confess our sins with a right heart.[2]

*We are **never** beyond God's **ability** to forgive.*

Sin too Great
A similar problem occurs when the receiver believes that **his sin is too great.** He considers his sin "humongous" because it is so heinous and of such long duration. He continually "whips" himself, because he knew better but chose sin anyway. In all cases, he feels totally unworthy to ask God to forgive him. As RTF ministers, we try to help him realize that God's Word is true and valid for him regardless of his feelings. A person struggling with unworthiness needs a **revelation of God's heart toward him** before he can face God, asking for forgiveness.

---

[1]   Please see Heb 12:1.
[2]   Note that the only condition is not blaspheming the Holy Spirit (Mat 12:31-32).

No Realization of Sin

True repentance requires a revelation of true sin.

An opposite problem occurs when a person has **no realization that he has sinned** and, thus, no awareness that repentance is needed. People have to come to a place of repentance by being first brought to a knowledge of the truth.

.. I came not to call the righteous, but sinners to repentance. (Mk 2:17, KJV)

This was the case in our own lives regarding some experimental activities we later came to realize were in the occult arena. Conviction and repentance came as our eyes were opened to the passages of scripture defining how abhorrent these things are to God. Actually, many people are blind to the need to repent from "dabbling in the occult," especially when it was entered into with innocence or as a game.

Disappointment with God

Satan wants us to blame and mistrust God.

Trauma, tragedy, difficult life circumstances, and "unanswered prayer" all can **cause our faces and hearts to be turned away from God**. Trust is broken and alienation takes over. Searching seems to produce no satisfactory answers. When there is **disappointment with God**, it is hard for a person to deal with God at all, but particularly to repent, because he is in the habit of blaming God for the pain in his life.

Chapter IX contains additional discussion on this issue.

Our approach is to acknowledge the distress and not gloss over the pain of unanswered questions, while at the same time helping the person to see that it was never God's desire for him to be hurt. So many times we are putting the blame in the wrong place. We're shaking our fist at God when we need to be shaking our fist at the enemy or acknowledging the weakness of our own flesh. Sin is operating in the world, and Satan is also out to destroy whom he may.[1] Sometimes there are no satisfactory answers, and we have to reach a place of choosing to trust God's goodness even when we do not understand. In Chapter IX, "Soul/Spirit Hurts," we discuss in depth various aspects of ministering to this hindrance in the "Anger/ Disappointment Toward God" Section.

5. Receiving God's Forgiveness

What about the person who is repentant and can eat plenty of "humble pie" but can't accept that God truly forgives him? His "forgiven" receiver isn't working. Have you known anyone like that? Betsy had a dear friend who spent hours on her face repenting only to come away saying, "God hates me, God hates me." She had trouble receiving His forgiveness.

Do you have a "broken" receiver?

Wouldn't it be great if there were a shop for broken "forgiven" receivers? You, dear friend, may be that shop! Broken "forgiven" receivers are repaired as people come to have an understanding, **a revelation**, if you please, **of the Father's heart**.

---

[1]　Please see 1 Pet 5:8-9.

How well Betsy remembers the day that she came upon this verse in Isaiah:

> Isa 43:25
> I, even I, am He who blots out your transgressions **for My own sake** and remember your sins no more. (NIV)

For "Your own sake," God? Yes, that is Your heart. That's the Gospel message. For Your own sake because, above all, You want to be in fellowship and in loving relationship with us. The light began to break in on Betsy's heart. The God of the universe wanted to forgive **her sin** for **His own sake**.

"Come now, let us reason together," says the LORD. "Though your sins are like scarlet, they shall be as white as snow; though they are red as crimson, they shall be like wool." (Isa 1:18, NIV)

Yes, forgiveness was always His plan. Yes, the Lamb was slain from the foundation of the world.[1] God has always made a way for restored relationship; from institution of the sacrificial system to the Cross, where He forgave Sin and it became a settled issue. Relationship is the gospel message. Why? Because God wants a relationship with us.

God forgave Moses the murderer and David the adulterer. Jesus forgave the woman taken in adultery and the thief on the Cross next to Him. To illustrate God's heart toward the repentant sinner, Jesus told the story of the watching, waiting Father opening His arms to his repentant son. That is the Father's heart. It was while we were yet sinners, while we were still in the pig pen, that Jesus died for us. Our heavenly Father provides forgiveness for the sake of relationship because **He** wants it. God says in Jeremiah:

> Jer 31:33-34
> [33]. . . I will put My law within them, and on their heart . . .
> [34]**for they shall all know Me** from the least of them to the greatest of them, declares the Lord, for I will forgive their iniquity, and their sin I will remember no more. (NAS)

> **Prayer:** Father, now that I have forgiven all others, I thank You that I can now come to receive Your forgiveness. So I come to You, through the shed blood of Jesus and the power of His Cross, asking You to forgive me of all of my sins. I acknowledge and take responsibility for each and every time I have violated Your commandments, as well as for the iniquity that is in my heart.
>
> Holy Spirit, thank You for working forgiveness into my life, for healing me, and for cleansing me from all unrighteous. Thank You, Father, for restoring me to fellowship with You. In the Name of Jesus Christ, I pray. Amen!

---

[1]   Please see Rev 13:8.

C. Forgiving Self

When the ministry receiver has received God's forgiveness, then, because he has been forgiven, he is in a position to forgive himself if needed. Whether self-forgiveness is needed or not depends on the receiver and how he feels about himself. Has he been holding guilt, self-condemnation, self-hate, etc., because of some foolish or very painful sin of the past? Forgiving himself may be needed before God can flush away the guilt, self-condemnation, and self-hate. At times, he must forgive himself to keep God's available gift of forgiveness from being blocked. Our goal is to help him **thoroughly and completely receive God's forgiveness,** which sometimes includes forgiving himself.

1. Scriptural Basis for Self-Forgiveness

There is no Bible verse that directly instructs us to forgive ourselves. Therefore, if someone wants to avoid this step, he can justify it as "non-scriptural." We submit, however, that certain principles are expressed in the Bible that strongly encourage self-forgiveness. Also, we frequently see great freedom and release come when a person forgives himself. Why avoid a step that might bring more healing, deliverance, and freedom?

We start out with the second commandment, as Jesus declared in Matthew.

> Mat 22:39
> And the second [is] like unto it, Thou shalt love thy neighbour as thyself.
> (KJV)

When a person is holding self-hate, etc., he is not loving himself and usually not loving his neighbor either. Self-forgiveness can lead to self-acceptance, peace, and "loving" one's self. Then the "neighbor" can benefit as well.

Now, let's go back to the verses that direct us to forgive others. For example, in Mark Jesus said:

> Mk 11:25
> . . . forgive, **if ye have ought against any**: that your Father also which
> is in heaven may forgive you your trespasses. (KJV)

The "any" that a person may have "ought against" could be himself! Let's clear out all "ought!"

2. Blocks to Forgiving Self

In actual fact, sometimes the hardest part of forgiveness is to forgive oneself. Pride says, **"Your sin is too big to forgive,"** and Unworthiness says, **"You don't deserve forgiveness, you deserve to keep feeling miserable."** Both try to block self-forgiveness.

In addition, the demonic spirit of Unforgiveness, which works to prevent a person from forgiving others, will also work to keep him from self-forgiveness. This spirit will also team up with the demon of self-hate to stop the ministry. Deliverance may be needed, as well as helping the person choose to love himself as God loves him.

3. Procedure

How to speak self-forgiveness.

We have found it effective to have the receiver say his own name and declare his forgiveness. For example, Susie would say, "Susie, because God's forgiven you, I choose to forgive you also." It is also okay to say, "I choose to forgive myself for . . . ."

It is so important to speak this release to ourselves when needed. The Holy Spirit will show you when the ministry receiver needs to do this.

Prayer: Father, because you have forgiven me, I choose to forgive myself and to release myself from all accusations, judgments, hatred, slander, mistakes, stupidity, and falling short of the mark. I choose to accept myself just as I am because You accept me. I choose to love myself because You love me. I even expect to begin to like myself.

Holy Spirit, I ask You, I give You permission, I expect You, to work Your work of sanctification in me. I fully embrace this truth and look forward to working with You so I can be changed into the image of Christ. In the Name of Jesus Christ I pray. Amen!

D. Procedure Used to Minister Forgiveness

At the end of each chapter on the four Problem/Ministry Areas, we have listed the Ministry Steps for that ministry area. The first steps **always** involve **confession** and **forgiveness**. This is truly the **key to freedom**. In this chapter, we provide an overview of the procedure for ministering forgiveness since it is used throughout the entire ministry process.

We follow the Biblical prescription for forgiveness, which is to first forgive others and then ask for God's forgiveness. If self-forgiveness is needed, it should come last, since it is based on God's forgiveness of us.

While we present an order of forgiveness in the following paragraphs, the order may be varied as circumstances and the Holy Spirit directs.

1. Forgiveness Cross

Use of the Forgiveness Cross.

We use a memory aid that we call "The Forgiveness Cross," as shown here. First, we consider the horizontal bar of the Cross. It reminds us that we are to speak out forgiveness toward other people who have hurt us or injured us in any way. The vertical part of the Cross reminds us to look upward, saying, "God, forgive me, a sinner," and we receive His forgiveness coming down. The circle reminds us to forgive ourselves, completing the forgiveness process.

We have the person receiving ministry follow the forgiveness procedure by starting with the horizontal arm of the cross **(himself to others)**, then proceed to the vertical arm **(God to him)**, and then, if needed, finish with the halo/circle **(himself to himself)**.

Figure 1: Forgiveness Cross

2. Forgiving Others: Phase One

Phase One of Forgiving Others involves ancestors.

In forgiving others, we follow an order. While it has no spiritual value in itself, it does help us keep our place in the process. We work from the past to the present. We start on the father's side of the family. If there has been a father and a stepfather, we start with the father since he is the actual blood line. We go back to the grandfather or great grandfather if sinful patterns are known that far back.

Special considerations apply if the ancestors are deceased.

If the people are deceased, we follow Biblical pattern and have the ministry receiver **confess** the sin to God. It is **not** appropriate, however, to speak forgiveness to dead relatives because what they have done is settled and sealed. We no longer have the authority to release **them** from their sin. However, as part of confessing their sin, it is very appropriate, and essential, that we appropriate the power of the Cross to **release ourselves** from the effect or consequences of their sin.

If the ancestors are living, we have the receiver both **confess** and **forgive**, i.e., **release** and **pardon**.[1]

Once the father's side is taken care of, we repeat the process with the mother's side. We again start from the past and work toward the present.

Parents require special attention.

We take care to be thorough in the area of parents. Most of our hurts come from family. Most people have extreme loyalty to their parents — even those who were hurtful. For this reason, they tend to deny negative experiences. Some describe their parents as they wish they had been. In this case, the person ministering needs to ask the Holy Spirit for revelation. We need to know how hard to press the receiver to remember and forgive, and when the receiver is ready to remember and forgive. Sometimes this comes after several sessions have occurred. At other times, God says, "Save it for the future." In other words, the person is not yet ready for ministry to the deeper memories and hurts.

Break Generational Sins and Curses at this point in the ministry.

Once sins have been confessed and forgiveness spoken, we ask the receiver to **repent** of any ways he has entered into his ancestors' sin. (He may need to forgive himself as well.) We are now ready to break generational sins and curses. This Problem/Ministry Area is discussed in depth in the next chapter.

3. Forgiving Others: Phase Two

Phase Two of Forgiving Others involves the growing-up years and adulthood.

Phase two of forgiving others involves the rest of the ministry receiver's family. We continue moving from the past to the present, so his siblings and others, such as step-parents, who impacted his early years come next.

We continue with the growing-up years, covering possible **significant relationships** such as teachers, scout leaders, coaches, past romantic relationships, pastors, church leaders, and friends. Just mentioning each category usually causes the ministry receiver to be aware of those people needing forgiveness.

---

[1]   Please see Lev 26:40. We have more to say about this in the next chapter.

Next, we bring up people involved with the ministry receiver's adult life. We usually start with bosses and other authority figures. Then his spouse, if he is married, and/or ex-spouse if he is divorced. Then we come to his children, when applicable.

We always give the Holy Spirit an opportunity to remind us of needed forgiveness.

Before leaving the "Forgiving Others" area of forgiveness, we ask the ministry receiver to seek the Lord asking Him to reveal any further forgiveness that may be needed.

More forgiveness will be needed in other parts of the ministry process. As Ungodly Beliefs are revealed, as hurts are exposed, and during deliverance, we remain alert to the possibility that more forgiveness may be necessary. We take care of these issues as they surface in each ministry area.

4. Repentance: Asking God's Forgiveness

Frequently, as the receiver is forgiving others, he will see his part or involvement in a situation and naturally, without being prompted, ask God's forgiveness. For example, a wife who is forgiving her husband for foolish spending, might pray, "And God forgive me for not being financially accountable, either, and not helping to establish a budget." If repentance has not naturally occurred, then it is appropriate for the minister to suggest areas where it is needed.

5. Forgiving Self

It is always wise to provide an opportunity for the receiver to forgive himself. You can facilitate this by saying, "Just take a moment and see if you have really received God's forgiveness. If you have, do you now need to forgive yourself?" Don't be in a hurry. Sometimes very significant healing occurs during this time as the receiver releases for the first time guilt, self-condemnation, self-hate, worthlessness, etc.

Part 2

Foundational Problem/Ministry Areas

As we finish the Foundational Understandings part of *Restoring the Foundations*, please take a moment and ponder the various topics we have presented. All of them are fundamental to the Christian life whether or not you become an RTF minister. Our prayer is that you will use these basic building blocks to establish a firm foundation under your Christian walk. We also pray that you will build on this foundation by adding the four Foundational Problem/Ministry Areas to your understanding.

The order in which the four Problem/Ministry Areas are presented is also their usual order in the ministry process. The ministry builds to a climax as we recover the legal ground given over to the enemy in each of the Problem/Ministry Areas.

First, we reclaim the ground given due to the iniquity of our ancestors being "visited" down the family line. We call this Problem/Ministry Area "Sins of the Fathers and the Resulting Curses." (SOFCs "for short.")

Then we proceed to root up any ungodly thinking that agrees with the enemy. We want to replace this thinking with God's view of things, by exchanging Ungodly Beliefs (UGBs) for Godly Beliefs (GBs).

The third area restores "broken hearts," as we use "Waiting Upon the Lord" Listening Prayer for God to heal Soul/Spirit Hurts (SSHs). God wants to heal every wound and wipe away every tear, allowing us to get rid of the various negative emotions (i.e., resentments, anger, frustrations, rage) attached to them. Exposing and redeeming the associated sin further recovers legal ground from the Devil.

We are then ready for the fourth Problem/Ministry Area which involves casting out the demons that have used all of the above mentioned types of "legal ground" as the basis for their Demonic Oppression (DO). This is usually easy to do after we have completed the first three Problem/Ministry Areas. In most cases, the Devil's demons don't "have a leg to stand on" any longer since we have removed all their legal ground.

Each of these chapters on the four Problem/Ministry Areas has a detailed list of Ministry Steps at the end of each chapter. You can use these as you work with the Holy Spirit to bring more healing into your life.

VII

SINS OF THE FATHERS
AND
RESULTING CURSES

Thou shalt not bow down thyself to them (idols), nor serve them:
for I the LORD thy God [am] a jealous God,
visiting the iniquity of the fathers upon the children
unto the third and fourth [generation] of them that hate me;
Exodus 20:5

. . . knowing that you were . . . redeemed . . . from your futile way of life
inherited from your forefathers, . . . with . . . the blood of Christ.
1 Pet 1:17-19

The Sins of the Fathers (and Mothers) and the resulting Curses (SOFCs) are a major source of oppression for all mankind. Why? Because we, our father's descendants, "take on," or "enter into," these same sins. This controversial and misunderstood Problem/Ministry Area has unfortunately been neglected and seldom addressed even among Christians. When the sins and curses coming down a family line are alcoholism, drugs, or sexual abuse, the problem is easily identified. The root cause and how to eradicate it from the family line, however, remain a mystery. With "less serious" sins the source of the problem is usually not even identified as generational. People simply explain the behavior by concluding, "Oh, he's just like his father, and you know what he was like!"

This chapter presents scriptures and relevant information showing how we are "set up" for problems because of the Sins of the Fathers. This leads into a discussion of the curses that result from these sins. Then both areas are illustrated in some detail. The Sins of the Fathers (and mothers) intertwine so tightly with the resultant Curses and the self-sins of the children, that these subjects are treated in this chapter as a unit. Then we discuss "good" side of this topic; the scriptures revealing God's solution to the Sins and to the Curses. Finally, we will explain how to minister to these areas.

Before we fully begin, however, let's look at some background issues related to the Sins of the Fathers.

A. Definition of Sins of the Fathers (SOFCs)

One purpose of this chapter is to clearly explain the meaning of "Sins of the Fathers" and the "Resulting Curses" (SOFCs). Let's begin by considering this simple definition for Sins of the Fathers. Curses are defined later in this chapter.

> **"Sins of the Fathers"** represents the accumulation of all sins committed by our ancestors. It is the heart tendency (iniquity) that we inherit from our forefathers to rebel (i.e., be disobedient) against God's laws and commandments. It is the propensity to sin, particularly in ways that represent perversion and twisted character. The accumulation continues until God's conditions for repentance are met.

B. God's Point of View

As we get ready to explore this topic in detail, let's start by considering God's point of view. How does He evaluate our fathers and mothers, our grandparents and great grandparents, etc., in terms of their actions and thoughts?

1. God Sees Us as Families

The twentieth century western mind sees man very individualistically, as if we can look at one man at a time. "It's my life, and I'm responsible for it. Period. No one else is affected," is a typical attitude. This is *not* how God thinks. God sees man in terms of families. He thinks in terms of generations. How often do we find in Scripture, "I am the God of Abraham, Isaac and Jacob?" He sees us not just as individuals but as integral parts of families that have existed over the generations.

At times, He speaks of several hundred years as if it were an extremely short time. Consider His promise to give Abraham the land of Canaan.[1] Over 400 years passed between the time of the promise and the realization of the promise.

From the foundation of the world, God planned every individual. In His mind, we already existed (a very real existence from His point of view) before we were born. Hebrews portrays Levi as having already tithed because he existed in Abraham's loins when Abraham tithed. This verse is representative of God's view:

> Heb 7:9-10
> 9 And as I may so say, Levi also, who receiveth tithes, paid tithes in Abraham.
> 10 For **he was yet in the loins of his father**, when Melchisedec met him. (KJV)

---

[1]   Please see Gen 15:7-8, 16, Ex 12:40-41, Act 7:5-6, 13:20, Gal 3:16-17.

We must look at families as God does.

Levi was part of Abraham. In this case, Levi received the blessings of Abraham's actions. They were credited to him as well as to Abraham.

God also sees us this way. We are a part of, and credited with, both the blessings and the iniquity of our fathers. We can "shed" the iniquity part by following a wonderful pattern God provides for our freedom. This includes sharing His viewpoint. Are we willing to receive His view and lay down our own way of thinking?

2. The God of Mercy is also a God of Justice

When first considering the effects of the Sins of the Fathers, it is natural, to cry out, "But God, this is unfair. I shouldn't be affected by what others have done. I don't even know most of them." We begin to complain from our point of view, without considering the nature or character of God. Let's attempt to shift our perspectives, and see what God says about Himself.

> Ex 34:6-7
> [6]. . . The Lord, the Lord God, **compassionate**, and **gracious**, **slow to anger**, and **abounding in lovingkindness and truth**;
> [7]who **keeps lovingkindness**, who **forgives iniquity**, **transgression**, and **sin**; yet He will by no means leave the **guilty unpunished**, **visiting the iniquity** of fathers on the children and on the grandchildren to the third and fourth generations.[1] (NAS)

The NIV translates this last phrase, "He **punishes** the children and their children for the sin of the fathers to the third and fourth generation." This passage is similar to the one in Exodus 20:5, the foundational scripture for Sins of the Fathers and Resulting Curses.

God is good, merciful, **and just**. He stands ready to forgive, and will forgive, as soon as His conditions are met. Otherwise, His justice, so basic to His nature, prevails, and the iniquities of the Fathers are passed down upon their children. He must **punish the guilty**.

We need to choose our parents carefully!

God's justice results in the children being affected by the pressure of inherited iniquity (perverseness) as well as the pressure of possible curses because of their father's (and mother's) sin. Someone has said, "The moral is we need to choose our parents carefully!"

*There is **bad news** and **good news**.*

The bad news is that we are affected by our parents' sins. The good news is that God has provided the way for our freedom from all the effects of their iniquity.

---

[1]   Please see Num 14:18, Isa 14:21, Lam 5:7, Dan 9:4-19.

3. What God Requires, God Provides

The Lamb was slain from the foundation of the world.

Ever since God instituted with the Israelites His requirement of the sacrificial system He has provided a way, His way, for man's sins to be forgiven and his guilt to be cleansed. God's plan culminated in Jesus, the "Lamb slain from the foundation of the world."[1] What is man's part in this plan? It is to confess his sin and turn from it.

In Leviticus 26:40-42,[2] God gives us a pattern and a promise for freedom. If we confess our sins and the sins of our fathers, and we humble ourselves, He will remember His covenant. That is, He "remembers" that we are part of His family. This is called "Identification Repentance" because we identify with our ancestors and repent on their behalf as well as our own. This breaks the power of the pressure of Sins of the Fathers and the Resulting Curses. Excellent examples of this principle are found in Daniel 9, Ezra 9, and Nehemiah 2 and 9.

Confession and repentance are God's provision for us:

> 1 Jn 1:9
> If we **confess** our sins, he is faithful and just to forgive us [our] sins, and to cleanse us from all unrighteousness. (KJV)

When the father (or mother) has sinned, that sin stands in need of being confessed. If it is not confessed by him, then it passes on to his children. Like an "outstanding" debt, the father's sin hangs out "there" impacting the man's descendants (and most likely also others) until it is addressed through confession and cleared out. God's grace will eventually enable a descendant, or perhaps a spiritual leader, to confess the sin. This person is effectively "standing in the gap" identifying with the family, and confessing on the families behalf. This is why this procedure is called "Identification Rependance."

4. God is the Same, He does not Change

Some people contend that God's conditions applied only to the Israelites since He entered into the covenant with them through the Ten Commandments and the Law. Scriptural evidence clearly opposes this position and indicates that God "weighs" all nations of the earth with the same scales. If you are unsure about this, remember that the books of the Prophets contain many "oracles" against the nations surrounding Israel as well as oracles directed toward Israel. God spoke forth judgment when sin exceeded His mercy "limit" and there was no indication of repentance.

Jesus declared the fate of the "sheep" and the "goat" nations.[3] This shows that there are many different groups of people, some godly and some ungodly, who would be judged by His standards.

---

[1]   Please see Rev 13:8.

[2]   This scripture is discussed a little later in the section, "Scriptural Basis for Freedom from Sins of the Fathers and Resulting Curses" in this chapter.

[3]   Please see Mat 25:32-33.

*God's character
and nature
are shown
in His Word.*

We believe that God's Word, both Old and New Testament, clearly shows forth His character and nature, as well as His mercy and justice. Since we are made in His image,[1] He expects us to have the same character and nature, regardless of our nationality. In Old or New Testament, God is the same. We read in Hebrews and in James:

> Heb 13:8
> **Jesus Christ the same** yesterday, and today, and for ever. (KJV)

> Jam 1:17
> . . . **the Father** of lights, **with whom** is **no variableness**, neither **shadow of turning**. (KJV)

We must conclude that all of us are subject to God's laws: the blessings and the cursings. All we have to do is to look around and we see them in operation.

5. The Importance of Appropriation

But wait, someone will say, "Why do we have to go and dredge up all this stuff from the past? Didn't Jesus pay the price for the required justice?"

*Have we
appropriated
what Jesus has
done for us?*

Praise be to God! Yes, Jesus did take the judgment and wrath of God that is due us.[2] We submit that the correct question to ask is, "Have we **appropriated**, **personally received**, **and applied** what He has done for us?" We need to receive the freedom Jesus bought for us by using God's provision. How do we do that? By confessing the Sins of our Fathers and our own sin and then appropriating what Jesus has done at the Cross to break the power of the sin to continue to affect us.

*Everything that we
receive from God
is by faith, i.e., by
appropriation.*

Salvation through Jesus Christ has been available for nearly 2000 years, yet none of us is automatically "born again" at our birth. We must by faith "receive" (i.e. appropriate)[3] salvation for ourselves. The same is true for physical healing, deliverance, finances, direction, gifts of the Spirit, love, etc. **All** are received by faith. Faith is believing that a promise of God applies to us and receiving that promise as realized. Until we know about these promises and provisions, we cannot, by faith, **receive**[4] what Christ has provided for us. This is true for everything that we receive from God. We must receive and apply the wonderful freedoms gained for us at the Cross. We receive by faith. Sometimes we receive by somebody else's faith and sometimes its by our own, but you must always appropriate God's provision by faith.[5] We break the effects of generational sins by faith that the promises in God's Word are true and that Jesus has indeed:

> Col 2:14
> **Canceled out** the **certificate of debt**, consisting of decrees against us . . .
> And He has taken it out of the way, **having nailed it to the cross**. (NAS)

This is the good news. We receive it and by faith apply it, breaking the power of the Sins of the Fathers on the basis of the truth of the Word.

---

[1] Please see Gen 1:26-27.
[2] Please see Rom 5:9-10, Eph 2:5, 1 Thes 5:9.
[3] Please see the "Appropriation" Section in Chapter II, "The Power of the Cross in the Christian Life."
[4] Please see story of the Sower, Mk 4:3-20. The good soil **received** the Word.
[5] Please see Heb 11:6.

6. The Fairness Issue

As we mentioned earlier, some people want to say, "It's not fair; the world is not fair." For those who think life should be fair, all we can say is, "Sorry." Things haven't been "fair" since the Garden of Eden when sin entered into the world. Jesus has made a way for victory to be enforced in our own individual lives and those of our families, but life and the world still aren't "fair." The only "fairness" comes from God who has provided the "payment" for the penalty of sin if we choose to accept it. We can use the Cross to break the effects of the Sins of the Fathers coming down our family line and start a new family line. As a result, the consequences of sin do not continue on to our descendants. This is **the** greatest inheritance that we can pass on to our children and their children, etc.

7. An Important Distinction

Understand that the passing down of iniquity is just that: **the passing down of iniquity**. The iniquity does cause a "pressure" to be applied to us (and our descendants), but it does not **force** us to sin. Iniquity does not mean automatic condemnation or death.

> Deu 24:16
> The fathers shall not be put to death for the children, neither shall the children be put to death for the fathers: every man shall be put to death for his own sin.[1] (KJV)

General Rule:

Each man dies for his own sin.

Inheriting iniquity is very different from being condemned to death. God makes it clear throughout His word that each person is going to die for his own sin. For example, in Second Chronicles we see this law applied by the king.[2] In Jeremiah, we see it reinforced again.[3] The entire 18th Chapter of Ezekiel clearly spells out how each man will die for his own sin and not for his father's, even if his father were a terrible sinner.

Exception to the Rule:

Children dying for their fathers sin.

While the above statements express the general rule, it must be pointed out that the Bible gives us some exceptions to this rule. There are situations when the children *do* die because of their parents' sin. When we offend God past His limit of Righteousness, then entire family lines may be sentenced to death. These cases are discussed in the "Scriptural Basis for Sins of the Fathers" section.

Without God's intervention into His own laws of justice, without God Himself paying the penalty for our sin, there would be no hope for us.

> Rom 3:23
> For **all have sinned**, and come short of the glory of God: (KJV)

> Rom 6:23a
> For the **wages of sin [is] death**; (KJV)

---

[1]   This statute is acted upon in 2 Chr 25:3-4 and re-affirmed in Jer 31:29-30.
[2]   Please see 2 Chr 25:3-4.
[3]   Please see Jer 31:29-30.

Because God did intervene, however, we have the blessed hope:

> Rom. 6:23b
> . . . but the **gift of God [is] eternal life through Jesus Christ** our Lord.
> (KJV)

This very important topic is discussed further in the Scriptural Basis section.

8. Personal Responsibility

Are you "Entering into" the Sins of your Fathers.

We cannot "blame shift." We are responsible for our sin.

Another frequently asked question is, "Why do we have to suffer for what our fathers did?" The answer is, "We don't," if we deal with the sin God's way. We will suffer only if we "enter into" the same sins and make "their" sins "our" sins and then do not appropriate God's provision for freedom. The phrase, "We enter into their sins," describes the process of taking their sins as our own. Although our ancestors set us up, we are now held accountable by God for these sins. As a result, we will die for our own sin if we don't receive God's provision. Why not take advantage of the godly principle of Identification Repentance?[1] You can apply the power of the Cross to nullify all the pressure of generational sins and to break the power of the associated curses from your life.

The issue is too important to ignore. God always requires us to be responsible and accountable for our own lives! Our **response** to the pressures, curses, environment, and demonic forces that we inherit determines our personal standing with God.

C. Understanding the Interrelationship of the Ministry Areas

The Integrated Ministry leads to lasting healing and freedom.

God has revealed to us an Integrated Approach to Healing Ministry. This means that the four major Problem/Ministry Areas negatively affecting a person's life must *all* receive ministry in the same general time frame in order to bear lasting healing and freedom. These four areas are the "Sins of the Fathers and Resulting Curses," "Ungodly Beliefs," "Soul/Spirit Hurts," and "Demonic Oppression." The ancestral sins and curses must be worked through and cleared out, the mind must be renewed with God's truth, the invisible hurts of the inner person must be healed, and demonic forces must be removed. Each of these problem areas is unique and yet they are very interrelated. If one or more of these areas is not ministered to, the already healed areas may be undermined and the healing gained might be lost.

We refer to these four problem areas needing ministry the four "Problem/Ministry Areas." In each of the four core chapters of this book we present one of these four Problem/Ministry Areas. In each core chapter we have included a section showing how that particular area is integrally related to the other three Problem/Ministry Areas. We hope you will come to appreciate the value of this Integrated Approach to Healing Ministry as it is expressed in Restoring the Foundations ministry.

---

[1] The phrase "Identification Repentance" is a modern term used by various intercessory organizations, i.e., Generals of Intercession, to represent "standing in the gap" and "making up the hedge" as we identify with, and repent for, other people and their sin.

1. How Sins of the Fathers and Curses are Related to Ungodly Beliefs

Parents often repeat the Sins of their Fathers (and mothers). They may replicate sinful attitudes, prejudices, and/or values, which their children assimilate from their parents. In addition, the parents' sin usually has hurtful consequences in the lives of the offspring, causing them to form wrong or Ungodly Beliefs based on their hurts.

Recently, we ministered to a woman who came from a family line that for at least two generations (as far as we knew) had physically abandoned their children and left them for others to raise. As this woman experienced the wounding of sudden abandonment she formed many Ungodly Beliefs about herself and her value, about what life is like, and about her parents. Later, she had a very difficult time loving or trusting God. Her beliefs were very divergent from God's truth. Now in her fifties, she is weeding out these Ungodly Beliefs and replacing them with God's Truth, i.e., Godly Beliefs.

2. How Sins of the Fathers and Curses are Related to Soul/Spirit Hurts

Sins of the Fathers put pressure on the next generation to enter into those same sins. Sometimes a person, through godly teaching and/or commitment, is able to withstand those pressures. Most commonly, however, the sins are continued with the usual consequence of the hurts being inflicted on others as well as on the person who is sinning. Think of the number of hurts caused by an alcoholic, especially if he is married and has children. Usually, the immediate family, extended family, friends, and business associates are all affected. The resulting curses usually involve some form of alienation, destruction, or death that causes major hurts to all involved.

3. How Sins of the Fathers and Curses are Related to Demonic Oppression

Sins of the Fathers and Curses work hand in hand with demons to create an ugly, vicious cycle. The initial sin gives an opening through which demons can oppress. Then, once established, the demons endeavor to continue down the family line, where they exert pressure on the descendants to sin in the same way as their fathers. The sin provides license for the demons to continue their oppression, causing the cycle to continue generation after generation.

In many cases, demons are the agents (or mechanisms) that carry out the curses coming from the Sins of the Fathers.

D. Preparing for SOFCs Ministry

As we prepare to minister to an individual, we like to pray beforehand and ready ourselves to hear God on behalf of our ministry receiver. The Application Form helps us in this preparation. A copy of this form is included in Appendix A.

As we prayerfully consider the information on this form, the Holy Spirit highlights and pinpoints the major issues in the person's life. In addition, He usually identifies the root causes underneath the symptoms. This information helps reduce the ministry interview time by making us aware of the most important information and the Lord's direction for ministry.

Are you ready now to open your mind and heart to further explore the scriptures concerning the Sins of the Fathers?

Exercise: As we progress through the remainder of this chapter, we want to encourage you to complete a copy of the Generational Patterns portion of the Application Form (in Appendix A). Then when we discuss the Ministry Steps at the end of the chapter you can work through the steps using your personal information. The form will also be helpful as we cover the other Problem/Ministry Areas.

Prayer: Lord, I desire to be fully cleansed and restored, so I can be an effective warrior in Your army and also come to know You more intimately. I ask that Your Holy Spirit reveal to me those areas where I need freedom from the Sins of my Fathers and the Resulting Curses. As I read this book, show me what applies to me along with the underlying roots. Thank You, Lord, for Your death on the Cross that provides the basis for my freedom. In the mighty Name of Jesus Christ, Amen!

E. Scriptural Basis for Sins of the Fathers

The need for ministry to Sins of the Fathers and Resulting Curses is rooted in the Second Commandment. In the following pages, we want to share with you what God has to say in His written Word about this Problem/Ministry Area. We will be referring to Table C on page 121, which contains the references to a number of relevant scriptures.

1. Foundational Scripture for Sins of the Fathers

Two foundational scriptures express the Problem/Ministry Area of Sins of the Fathers and Resulting Curses. These scriptures are Exodus 20:5-6,[1] the second commandment, and Exodus 34:6-7, a scripture expressing the same concept. We have already examined Exodus 34:6-7 (see page 105). In the second commandment, God expresses His hatred for idols and idolatry. He gets angry with jealousy, releasing a curse that causes the iniquities of the fathers to come onto the children to the third and fourth generation.

General curse of iniquity is passed unto the children.

> Ex 20:4-6
> 4 Thou shalt not **make** unto thee any graven image, or any likeness [of any thing] that [is] in heaven above, or that [is] in the earth beneath, or that [is] in the water under the earth:
> 5 Thou shalt **not bow down thyself** to them, nor **serve** them: for I the LORD thy God [am] a jealous God, **visiting the iniquity of the fathers upon the children unto the third and fourth [generation] of them that hate me**;
> 6 And showing mercy unto thousands of them that love me, and keep my commandments. (KJV)

This is the general curse placed on the children because of the sin (iniquity) of the fathers. Let's analyze this passage in some detail, looking at "idolatry," "iniquity," and "fathers."

a. Idolatry

God hates idolatry. He hates what it does to us. He hates the problems we get into and the openings we give Satan to oppress us. He says not to "make," "bow down to," nor "serve" idols. In the NAS, "not bow down" is translated "not worship them."

As usual, ignorance of the law is no excuse.

Most Americans, as well as other "civilized" people, will say, "I don't worship idols. I don't even know what an idol is." Knowing the definition of the word "idolatry" is not necessary to participate in it. Ignorance about what constitutes an idol or what idolatry is does not hinder the making of idols nor the practicing of idolatry. In actuality, idolatry is rampant in America as it was with all of our ancestors, regardless of the country from which they came.

---

[1] This passage is repeated in Deu 5:9-10.

Idolatry occurs whenever we put our trust in the "thing" or "situation" more than we put our trust in God. Jesus said, "For where your treasure is, there will your heart be also."[1] We can infer from this statement that our hearts and our treasure will be "at the same place." If that place is not "in" God, worshipping God, serving God, trusting God, and acknowledging Jesus as Lord, then it must be some other place. To the degree that we are "other" focused more than God focused, we are involved in idolatry.

Is your trust primarily in God, or elsewhere?

Idolatry occurs whenever we put our **trust** in the "thing" or "situation" more than we put our trust in God. It occurs as we look for information, power, fulfillment, and satisfaction in things apart from God. It creeps in when we put our life energies into things God hates. When we ask the question, "What is the focus and basis of my life?" the answer is either God or idolatry.

Do you think that we live in an idolatrous nation?

Idolatry includes all of the obvious forbidden areas, such as spiritualist churches, occultism, cults, all false religions (any that do not acknowledge the Lord Christ Jesus and His blood sacrifice for their atonement). This list includes psychics, witchcraft, satanism, secret societies based on occult (or "hidden") powers and bloody oaths. This includes groups such as the Masons, Shriners, and Rosicrucians who use their lower level members as a deceived "front."

Idolatry also includes the less obvious things: any excessive love, passion, or veneration of something such as money, possessions, beauty (the body), power, fame, rock stars, ungodly causes (homosexual rights beyond normal human rights, abortion, the environment), etc. Do you agree that we live in an idolatrous nation?

God says that we shall not bow down to other things, which means we shall not worship, focus on them, admire, or acknowledge them **as superior** or as a **replacement** to God. God says He is a jealous God. He is jealous for our attention, our affection, and our undivided heart.

The word for **jealous** in Hebrew is "*qanna.*" It is associated with the word "**red**." God is red in the face with anger when we ignore Him and give to other created things[2] the adoration, honor, and glory due Him. Many times in the Old Testament,[3] God states His zeal, His "redness," toward the children of Israel. Deuteronomy 6:15 explicitly ties together His jealousy and His anger. He was serious then, and He is serious now. **Don't let yourself get involved with other things that either block your heart from God or draw your heart away from God.**

Do you "hate" God?

The last phrase of Exodus 20:5 is also relevant. God concludes that we "hate" Him when we are involved in idolatry. This is a strong statement. If we concede that the results of hate in the one who "hates" is being separated or estranged from the one "hated," then idolatry separates us from God. He considers us to be in alliance "with the other side" when we "bow down to" or "serve" idols, and He becomes jealous and angry. He wants a relationship with us, not separation.

---

[1] Please see Mat 6:21, KJV.
[2] The entire passage in Rom 1:18-32 is significant. Please note specifically 1:25.
[3] Besides the above mentioned scriptures, please see Ex 34:14, Deu 4:24, 6:15, Josh 24:19, Eze 39:25, Neh 1:2, Zech 1:14, 8:2.

*Idolatry causes
the curse of
iniquity to be
passed down the
generations.*

As our ancestors worshipped and/or served other gods, the sin of idolatry resulted in the curse, which clearly states that the iniquity in their hearts would be passed down to the next three or four generations. As these generations then "**enter into**" the Sins of their Fathers, they continued the curse unto an additional three or four generations. This cycle continues with each generation, until and unless it is broken by the power of the Cross. We see this cycle in operation as God spoke to Israel through Jeremiah:

> Jer 16:11-12
> [11]Then say to them, "It is **because your fathers forsook me**," declares the LORD, "and followed other gods and served and worshipped them. They forsook me and did not keep my law. [12]But **you have behaved more wickedly than your fathers**. See how **each of you is following the stubbornness of his evil heart instead of obeying me**." (NIV)

As we look at the intensity with which God dislikes idolatry and the obvious destructive effect it has on humans, we can't help wondering: Does **all** sin have its basis in idolatry in one way or another? Having other gods before the true, living God steals from His place in our lives. Since Satan is behind **everything** that stirs the iniquity (rebellion) in our hearts (flesh), idolatry in one way or another leads to worshipping Satan rather than God.

b. Iniquity

The word "iniquity" is interesting. While not part of our normal, everyday English vocabulary, merely saying it creates a sense of "wrongness" or sly deceptiveness. Yuck! Who would want to be involved in "iniquity?"

*All of us have
iniquity in our
hearts.*

The truth is: We all are! Why? Because none of us had perfect parents or ancestors. All of us have received the "visiting" of our ancestors' iniquity. Just what have we inherited, anyhow?

*Iniquity is the
heart tendency
to rebel.*

Iniquity is a heart condition, an inner tendency of man to **break God's heart**. God created mankind for love, companionship, and fellowship. He wanted and still desires a love relation with us. But it has to be on His terms, His conditions. After all, He is God. He gave us the privilege of free will so we can freely choose, under His conditions, to love Him and acknowledge Him as Father. Having free will, we can choose to move away from God and **do our own thing**. When Adam and Eve chose to make their own decision about God's requirement regarding eating of the tree of the knowledge of good and evil,[1] they moved into disobedience, i.e., rebellion.[2] This tendency of the heart to rebel has been with us ever since.

> Jer 17:9-10
> 9 The **heart [is] deceitful above all [things]**, and **desperately wicked**: who can know it?
> 10 **I the LORD search the heart**, [I] try the reins, even to give every man according to his ways, [and] according to the fruit of his doings. (KJV)

---

[1] Please see Gen 2:16-17.
[2] Please read this sad story in Gen 3:1-7.

Iniquity is sin. Sin is also the outworking of iniquity.

Sin has its roots in the heart condition of iniquity/rebellion. Sin is the outworking of this heart tendency. We will wait until the section on Self-Sins to discuss sin and its various meanings in detail.

Iniquity is "lawlessness, wickedness, depravity, unrighteousness, transgression, perversion." The following chart helps us further define these words.

Iniquity involves:	
lawlessness	without, or "outside of," the law; not regulated by or based on law; not restrained or controlled by law; unruly
wickedness	morally bad, evil, fierce, vicious; causing or likely to cause harm or trouble
unrighteousness	contrary to the right way or thing; unjust; lacks right standing with God
transgression	crossing the line; going beyond the limits set or prescribed; violating a command or law, i.e., moving outside the law of God
perversion	turning away from what is right or good; corrupt; contrary to the evidence or the direction of the judge on a point of law; obstinate in opposing what is right, reasonable, or accepted, i.e., perverting the normal godly way

All of these words are included in "iniquity." When God says that we have iniquity in our hearts, He is painting a ugly picture. He is challenging us to be serious to work with Him to remove iniquity from our hearts.

c. Fathers

When the scriptures use "fathers," as in Exodus 20:5, the meaning not only includes the actual father of a person but also the mother, the grandparents, and the entire family line. All of these people have contributed to the iniquity and sin passed on to the children. We see this scripturally, and we see it experientially as the curse has its "outworking" in this world.

Ahab and Jezebel

One scripture explicitly names both the father and the mother as the source of their son's sin. In First Kings we read how Ahab marries "outside of the family" with disastrous consequences for Israel.

> 1 Kin 16:30-31
> 30 And **Ahab** the son of Omri **did evil** in the sight of the LORD **above all that [were] before him**.
> 31 And it came to pass, as if it had been a light thing **for him to walk in the sins of Jeroboam** the son of Nebat, that **he took to wife Jezebel** the **daughter** of **Ethbaal king of the Zidonians**, and **went and served Baal**, and **worshipped him**. (KJV)

115

Ahab is credited with doing even more evil than the "fathers" before him. Then, as if that was not enough, he marries Jezebel whose father is the king of Zidon (Sidon). Sidon was known for its worship of the goddess Ashtoreth. This city is named after "Sidon," the firstborn of Canaan,[1] whom Noah cursed.[2] Thus, by marrying into an idolatrous family line, Ahab added to the problems that Israel was already experiencing. This king further added to the resulting curses that would affect his descendants for generations to come as they struggled with the accumulated iniquity of their fathers (and mothers).

We see the fruit of this marriage further on in First Kings:

> 1 Kin 22:51-53
> 51 **Ahaziah the son of Ahab** began to reign over Israel in Samaria the seventeenth year of Jehoshaphat king of Judah, and reigned two years over Israel.
> 52 And **he did evil in the sight of the LORD**, and **walked in the way of his father**, and **in the way of his mother**, and **in the way of Jeroboam** the son of Nebat, **who made Israel to sin**:
> 53 For **he served Baal**, and **worshipped him**, and provoked to anger the LORD God of Israel, **according to all that his father had done**. (KJV)

Jezebel has the "honor" of being so bad and causing so much evil in Israel that she is mentioned in the above passage along with Ahaziah's father (Ahab) and Jeroboam, one of Ahaziah's forefathers. Truly, Ahaziah was an example of the Sins of the Fathers and mothers at work in a family line.

Mary the Mother of Jesus

Do only fathers contribute to our iniquity?

We want to comment on one "theory" used to "prove" that only the fathers and **not** the mothers contribute to the iniquity passed on to their children. This theory states that since Jesus had a human mother and "yet was without sin," that Mary's iniquity and/or sin was not passed on to Him. All that He inherited was from His Father, who, of course, being God, had no sin. Yet, if this were the case, then Jesus would not have experienced any temptation. Remember, iniquity is the tendency and the pressure to rebel and enter into sin. As we stated earlier, this doesn't automatically mean that we **have to** sin, but that we are likely to.

The scriptures tell us that Jesus was "tempted in every way, yet was without sin:"

> Heb 4:15
> For we do not have a high priest who is unable to sympathize with our weaknesses, but we have one **who has been tempted in every way**, just as we are—**yet was without sin**. (NIV)

---

[1]　Please see Gen 10:15.
[2]　Please see Gen 9:25-27.

Having God as His Father did not make it easier for Jesus. Hebrews also states:

> Heb 2:14, 17-18
> [14]Since the children have flesh and blood, **he too shared in their humanity**
>
> [17]. . . **he had to be made like his brothers in every way**, in order that he might become a merciful and faithful high priest in service to God, and that he might make atonement for the sins of the people. [18]Because **he himself suffered when he was tempted**, he is able to help those who are being tempted. (NIV)

*Jesus **was able** to experience temptation **because** He had a human mother.*

We believe that these passages, as well as the ones in the Gospels describing Jesus' temptation by the Devil,[1] actually support the opposite theory: that Jesus **was able** to be tempted precisely because He did have a human mother and did receive the iniquity of the Israelite family line through Mary. It was because He entered "the sheep pen by the gate,"[2] i.e., by being born through the womb of a woman, that He "legally" entered the domain of Adam and so could be the second Adam.[3] This made it possible for Him to be "made like his brothers in every way," including having the ability to be tempted, to suffer in temptation, to be pressured by the iniquity of His mother. Yet He did not sin. He chose not to sin, in spite of the iniquity inherited from Mary.

d. Law of Judgment

Now let's look at the last passage in the first group of verses in Table C (page 121), which is from Exodus:

> Ex 21:23-25
> [23]But if there is serious injury, you are to take **life for life**, [24]**eye for eye, tooth for tooth, hand for hand, foot for foot**, [25]**burn for burn, wound for wound, bruise for bruise**. (NIV)

*We are all **subject** to the Law of Judgment.*

*We must **appropriate** the truth that Jesus has **already** fulfilled the law for us.*

Here we see the law of Sowing and Reaping used to establish restitution for injury. This is the terrible Law of Judgment that expresses the "just" side of God's nature. This is God's expression of "fairness." He has arranged the universe so that every "evil" results in more evil, just as every "good" results in more good. Since He knew that we would all be helpless[4] and unable to get free of this law, His "mercy" side sent Christ to provide a way to get free of this law. Jesus fulfilled this law on our behalf. Again, the key to freedom from this law is to **appropriate** by faith the truth that Jesus has already suffered (paid) the judgment for our sin.

---

[1]   Please see Mat 4:1, Mk 1:13, and Lk 4:2, 13.
[2]   Please see Jn 10:1.
[3]   Please see 1 Cor 15:45-47.
[4]   Please see Rom 5:6, Eph 2:12.

2. Sins of the Fathers at Work

The second group of scriptures in Table C (page 121) allows us to observe the effects of the Sins of the Fathers upon the children. First, we have a summary statement from God as He lays out the consequences of Israel's potential disobedience:

> Lev 26:39
> And **they that are left** of you **shall pine away in their iniquity** in your enemies' lands; **and also in the iniquities of their fathers** shall they pine away with them. (KJV)

The children will suffer and "pine away" because of **both** their iniquity and their fathers' iniquity. While God is warning them not to be disobedient, He is also stating that they are *going to be* disobedient.

Second, we can read about the various kings and how they "entered into" and, in many cases, magnified their father's sins. Several brief phrases out of the following scriptures illustrate this point. You may want to look them up and study them in detail. Many additional scriptures could be used to show how the kings of both Judah and Israel entered into and added to the Sins of their Fathers. Of course, other people in Judah and Israel were also in this same fix, but their names are not recorded for us.

Israel's Kings

> 1 Kin 14:9, 16
> 9 But (**Jeroboam) hast done evil above all that were before thee**:
>
> 16 . . . And he (God) shall give Israel up because of the sins of Jeroboam, who did sin, and who made Israel to sin. (KJV)

> 1 Kin 15:25-26
> 25 And Nadab the son of Jeroboam
> 26 . . . **did evil in the sight of the LORD**, and **walked in the way of his father**, and in his sin wherewith he made Israel to sin. (KJV)

> 1 Kin 15:33-34
> 33 . . . Baasha the son of Ahijah (began) to reign . . .
> 34 And **he did evil in the sight of the LORD**, and **walked in the way of Jeroboam**, and in his sin wherewith he made Israel to sin. (KJV)

> 1 Kin 16:25-26
> 25 But Omri **wrought evil in the eyes of the LORD**, and **did worse than all that [were] before him**.
> 26 For **he walked in all the way of Jeroboam** the son of Nebat, and in his sin wherewith he made Israel to sin, to provoke the LORD God of Israel to anger with their vanities. (KJV)

> 1 Kin 16:30
> And Ahab the son of Omri **did evil in the sight of the LORD above all that [were] before him**. (KJV)

> 1 Kin 22:51-53
> 51 Ahaziah the son of Ahab . . .
> 52 . . . **did evil in the sight of the LORD**, and **walked in the way of his father** (Ahab), and **in the way of his mother** (Jezebel), and **in the way of Jeroboam** the son of Nebat, who made Israel to sin:
> 53 . . . **according to all that his father had done**. (KJV)

Finally, the evil became so horrendous that God could not withhold judgment any longer. God brought the Assyrian army against Israel (the northern kingdom) several different times, until every part of the nation was defeated, carried away, and dispersed among the nations.[1]

Judah's Kings

In studying Judah's kings, it is clear that although there was an occasional righteous king, the majority were very wicked just as Israel's kings were. Even in Judah the idolatry became so prevalent that God reached the limit of His mercy. Speaking through the prophet Jeremiah, God forewarns Judah that they have entered into the Sins of their Fathers and are committing even worse atrocities. They had become so insensitive that they did not even realize they had offended God by their deeds. They could not understand why God was punishing them.

> Jer 16:10-12
> 10 . . . and they shall say unto thee, **Wherefore hath the LORD pronounced all this great evil against us?** or **what [is] our iniquity?** or **what [is] our sin** that we have committed against the LORD our God?
> 11 Then shalt thou say unto them, **Because your fathers have forsaken me**, saith the LORD, and have **walked after other gods**, and have **served them**, and have **worshipped them**, and have **forsaken me**, and **have not kept my law**;
> 12 And **ye have done worse than your fathers**; for, behold, **ye walk** every one **after the imagination of his evil heart**, that they **may not hearken unto me**: (KJV)

Since their sin continued, God reached the point where even their repentance, if they had chosen to repent, would not, nor could not, stop the course of events. God was "weary."

> Jer 15:1, 6
> [1]Then the LORD said to me: "**Even if Moses and Samuel were to stand before me, my heart would not go out to this people**. Send them away from my presence! Let them go!" (NIV)
>
> 6 Thou hast forsaken me, saith the LORD, thou art gone backward: therefore will I stretch out my hand against thee, and destroy thee; **I am weary with repenting**. (KJV)

---

[1] Please see 2 Kin 17:6-23.

In Lamentations, the exile has come to pass. The destruction that Jeremiah prophesied has taken place. The people have collectively borne their Fathers' iniquities and are in a strange land as captives. The entire passage is very sad. Verse 7 sums it all up:

> Lam 5:7
> Our fathers have sinned, [and] are not; and we have borne their iniquities. (KJV)

Israel's Descendants

In Matthew, Jesus confronts the scribes and Pharisees and uses their own words to convict them that they are the descendants of murderers!

> Mat 23:30-32
> [30]And you say, "If we had lived in the days of our forefathers, we would not have taken part with them in shedding the blood of the prophets." [31]So you testify against yourselves that **you are** the **descendants of** those who **murdered** the prophets. [32]Fill up, then, the **measure of the sin of your forefathers**! (NIV)

Many more scriptures illustrate the Sins of the Fathers at work and coming down the generational lines. Just as God became weary with the sin of the Israelites, we become weary reading about it! It is grievous to our spirits. To prevent overdoing it, let us move on and look at God's justice concerning our own sin.

3. Each Dies for His Own Sin

The third group of scriptures in Table C on page 121 clearly confirms God's general law that each person dies for his own sin. Even though we are set up by our ancestors, we are all responsible for our deeds. This verse from Deuteronomy declares God's original statement of this principle. We encourage you to look up and study the other scriptures.

> Deu 24:16
> Fathers shall not be put to death for their children, nor children put to death for their fathers; **each is to die for his own sin**. (NIV)

4. We are All Under Iniquity

The three verses in the fourth group in Table C on page 121 contain an unpleasant description of the fallen state of mankind and the "wages" that we have earned because of our sin. God leaves no room for escape. It is pointless to try and impress God with our gracious conduct and good works that make us deserving of His approval. He is not impressed.

> Isa 64:6
> But **we are all as an unclean [thing]**, and **all our righteousnesses [are]** as **filthy rags**; and we all do fade as a leaf; and **our iniquities**, like the wind, **have taken us away**. (KJV)

We **all** need a savior. Praise God that He provided One for us.

Table C
Scriptures Concerning Sins of the Fathers

Sins of the Fathers

Ex 20:1-17, Deu 5:6-21	(Ten Commandments) The iniquity of the fathers visited upon the children unto the third and fourth generation.
Ex 34:6-7, Num 14:18	(God's description of Himself, of His Goodness) **Merciful** and **Just**
Ex 21:23-25	(Law of Judgment) "eye for an eye"

Sins of the Fathers at Work

Lev 26:39	Warning to Israel that they and their children will waste away in a foreign land.
1 Kin 15:26, 34, 16:25-26, 22:52-53	Descendants of Solomon corrupted by iniquity, leading nation into idolatry and corruption. In general, each one worse than the previous.
Jer 16:10-12	Descendants of Solomon and of Israel just before the Exile.
Lam 5:1-15	Children of Israel in Babylon during the Exile.
Mat 23:30-32	Scribes and Pharisees identifying with their ancestors who killed the prophets (particularly clear in the NIV).

Each Dies for His Own Sin

Deu 24:16	Original declaration: each dies for own sin.
2 Chr 25:3-4	King Amaziah of Judah applies Deu 24:16.
Jer 31:29-30	End of a proverb about sour grapes.
Eze 18:1-32	Clear outline of God's judgment and repentance principles.

We are All Under Iniquity

Rom 3:23	"For all have sinned and come short of the glory of God." (KJV).
Rom 3:10-18	Horrible description of the true nature of Man.
Rom 6:23	"For the wages of sin is death;" (KJV).

Special Exceptions where Children Die for their Father's Sin

Num 16:27-34	Rebellion of Korah, Dathan and Abiram results in the earth swallowing them and their men, their wives, children, and all of their possessions.
Josh 7:1, 18-26, 22:18-22	Sin of Achan results in his entire family and all possessions being stoned, burned, and buried.
2 Sam 12:14-18	David and Bathsheba's firstborn son dies at the age of seven days.
Jer 11:21-23, 13:14, 16:3-4	Death of the children as well as the fathers: of Anathoth and of Judah.
Lam 5:1-16 (:7)	"Our fathers sinned and are no more, and we bear their punishment."
Isa 14:20-23	Death of the children of the wicked of Babylon, no possession of their land, and destruction of their cities.

5. Special Exception Where Children Die for their Father's Sin

The last group of passages in Table C on page 121 shows some exceptions to the general rule of each person dying for his own sin. These exceptions occur when one's fathers and mothers have exceeded God's limit and brought upon themselves and their children complete destruction. While these examples of "Corporate Sin" and its effects on the people involved are not pleasant to read, they **are** part of God's Word to us. He is not a "respecter of persons," but He is a respecter of those who are obedient and those who are not.

> Rom 2:9-11
> [9]There will be **trouble and distress for every human being who does evil**: first for the Jew, then for the Gentile; [10]but **glory, honor and peace for everyone who does good**: first for the Jew, then for the Gentile. [11]**For God does not show favoritism**. (NIV)

The first passage describes Korah's rebellion, where he, his friends, and all of their family and possessions were swallowed by the earth.[1]

Then we have Achan's entire family being stoned, burned, and buried because Achan stole some of the "devoted things" that God had decreed were His during the victory at Jericho.[2]

Also, the first child of David and Bathsheba died for *their* sin, not his own. He died seven days after his birth, which was one day before he would have been presented before the Lord and dedicated to Him. It would appear that God prevented the dedication.[3]

Jeremiah prophesied against the men of Anathoth and their children because they sought to kill him and stop his prophesying. God stopped them instead and decreed that not even be a remnant of them would remain. Jeremiah also spoke God's Word against the people of Judah and Jerusalem, committing them all, including the sons (and daughters), to exile and destruction.[4] The book of Lamentations expresses the heartbreak of their descendants.

Isaiah prophesied against the wicked king of Babylon and his offspring. He decreed a complete end to the family line and complete destruction to the city, pronouncing it would become an uninhabited wasteland.[5]

These examples show that God does make exceptions to His general principle that "each one will die for his own sin." As we discussed in the introduction, God looks at families, and He looks over generations. If the Sins of the Fathers become excessive, there is the possibility that He will remove the entire family line.

---

[1] Please see Num 16:27-34.
[2] Please see Josh 7:1, 18-26, 22:20.
[3] Please see 2 Sam 12:14-18.
[4] Please see Jer 11:21-23, 13:14, 16:3-4.
[5] Please see Isa 14:18-22. Note that Babylon has remained uninhabited since its destruction by the Medes and Persians (Dan 5:30-31). It is reported that Sadam Hussein is attempting to reconstruct the city.

6. Mercy Triumps Over Justice

Let's end this section with the last three verses in Ezekiel 18, where God shares His heart. He desires mercy rather than justice.

> Eze 18:30-32
> 30 **Therefore I will judge you**, O house of Israel, **every one according to his ways**, saith the Lord GOD. **Repent, and turn [yourselves] from all your transgressions; so iniquity shall not be your ruin.**
> 31 Cast away from you all your transgressions, whereby ye have transgressed; and **make you a new heart and a new spirit: for why will ye die**, O house of Israel?
> 32 **For I have no pleasure in the death of him that dieth**, saith the Lord GOD: **wherefore turn [yourselves], and live** ye. (KJV)

Let's be sure we are operating in God's mercy for ourselves, and then help as many as possible also find God's mercy.

F. Thoughts Relevant to Sins of the Fathers

Here are a number of related and relevant topics that will help increase our understanding of Sins of the Fathers and how they operate.

1. Number of People Involved in Four Generations

One of the staggering aspects of "visiting the iniquity of the fathers upon the children unto the third and fourth generations" is the number of people involved. Adding up two parents, four grandparents, eight great-grandparents, and 16 great-great-grandparents, gives a total of 30 people! Thirty human beings, with their mixture of fleshy and godly desires, actions, beliefs, stumbling, falls, and besetting sins pass their iniquity on to each of us.

If there has been divorce and remarriage or adoption of children, even more people within four generations are involved. The greater tragedy, however, is that our parents also each had 30 people whose sin affected them, and the four grand-parents each had 30 people, etc. In other words, if we really trace it back, we inherit the iniquity of all past generations back to Noah and sons, and they

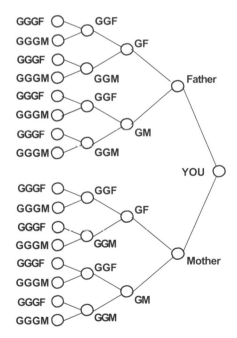

Figure 2: Thirty People in Four Generations

inherited from all of their generations back to Adam and Eve. This is the source of the innate, sinful nature of man. There would clearly be no escape from the consequences of many generations of sin if God had not planned from the beginning[1] for our release, healing, and freedom. Only when confession and rependence are "entered" into does the "visiting" come to a stop.

Our inheritance of physical characteristics may be by far the least of what we receive from our ancestors. Soul and spirit sins, iniquities, hurts, and oppressions probably have a far greater impact on our lives.

2. Inconsistencies

Some inconsistencies do exist in the way that generational sins operate and affect people. Sometimes certain sins may skip a generation or two. Other times, there seems to be a concentration or amplification of curses manifesting in a particular individual. **When one descendant seems to be a focus of the iniquity, past ancestral occultic involvement is often the reason.**

We have seen occult focuses on one or more individuals in the family line, resulting in unbearable oppression. Other family members, however, will seem not to be particularly affected. The occult iniquity keeps bouncing from here to there, wreaking its havoc on individual lives. Within three or four generations, some descendant will always be affected. This person will receive the iniquity, take it for his own, and pass it on down three or four more generations. This will continue until someone fulfills God's requirements for healing and freedom.

3. Mechanisms Transmitting the Sins of Fathers

Are you curious about how the "Sins of the Fathers" are passed down?

For those who have an inquisitive nature, like us engineers who like to know "how things work," the obvious question is, "What are the dynamics; how does it happen; what mechanism is at work that causes the Sins of the Fathers to come down the family line?"

The truth is, "We don't know, at least, not for sure." The following, however, are in the realm of speculative likelihood and/or strong possibility.

Genes

Are the "genes" involved?

Sins of the Fathers may be passed down through the genes. They could even affect the genes themselves, causing alterations to the gene structure and order. Who knows what physical and/or mental disorders might result from this?

Growing-Up Environment

Do we "absorb" them from our environment?

Sins of the Fathers could be partly propagated through the emotional and spiritual environment of our home. This could happen while we are being formed in the womb and also in our early, growing-up years. This is when we form our core beliefs and values in terms of how we are treated, resulting from the patterns of our parents' lives.

Sowing and Reaping

Is the law of Sowing and Reaping at work?

Also, as the Sins of the Fathers are passed down, they bring into action the Law of Sowing and Reaping or, more accurately, the Law of Judgment, with everything reproducing after its own kind.[2] Seeds of family violence, co-dependence, occult involvement, etc., clearly produce fruit of like nature generation after generation.

---

[1]   . . . the Lamb slain from the foundation of the world. (Rev 13:8).

[2]   Please see Gen 1 which contains many similar phrases.

Demons

Do demons carry out the Curses, pressuring us into the Sins of our Fathers?

Finally, we suspect that demons themselves help propagate the sin and iniquity. The most obvious are demons of anger, rejection, and abandonment, who run rampant throughout society. In addition, many children and grandchildren have testified to receiving demons from their parents or grandparents. We have heard on numerous occasions of a granddaughter experiencing the entrance of her grandmother's occult or "disease" demons at the time of the grandmother's death.[1] In some cases, this transference occurs during a formal, ritualistic ceremony.

The most likely situation is that a combination of the above factors are working in concert with each other. They probably occur in different proportions and frequencies within different people.

Summary

The likely main factors that transmit the Sins of the Fathers from one generation to the next and help the outworking of the curses are:

- genes
- growing-up environment
- Law of Sowing and Reaping
- Demonic Oppression

4. Frequently Occurring Sins of the Fathers

The following list of sins are frequently found within family lines. A minister ministering to Sins of the Fathers and the Resulting Curses should be particularly attuned to these possibilities.

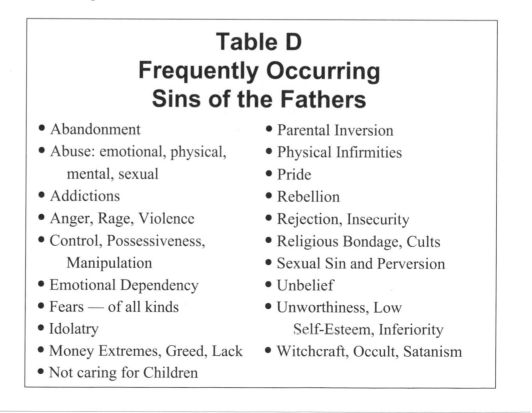

Table D
Frequently Occurring
Sins of the Fathers

- Abandonment
- Abuse: emotional, physical, mental, sexual
- Addictions
- Anger, Rage, Violence
- Control, Possessiveness, Manipulation
- Emotional Dependency
- Fears — of all kinds
- Idolatry
- Money Extremes, Greed, Lack
- Not caring for Children

- Parental Inversion
- Physical Infirmities
- Pride
- Rebellion
- Rejection, Insecurity
- Religious Bondage, Cults
- Sexual Sin and Perversion
- Unbelief
- Unworthiness, Low Self-Esteem, Inferiority
- Witchcraft, Occult, Satanism

---

[1] Mat 12:44 indicates how this may occur, as the demon returns to his "home."

Some of these are both sins and curses. The sins cause man to be disobedient, breaking God's law. Curses are the result of the sin, pressuring our descendants to enter into the same sin as their ancestors.

Fear is a good example of this "dual" role. Giving place to fears beyond normal human caution and prudence is sin because God has not given us a spirit of fear.[1] Fear is also a curse that frequently operates as a result of occult involvement. Regarding these sins, we minister to them as sins to be freed from and curses to be broken.

5. Some Short Illustrations

To help you see the relationship between God's commandment concerning idols and the outworking of the father's iniquity, let's look at some real life examples.

a. Sexual Sin and Divorce

Let's briefly trace the effects of sexual sin in one family.

Delores, a woman who loves and serves God, came from a family in which sexual sin was one of the Sins of the Fathers. It affected her life as well as her children's lives and her grandchildren. Sexual sin frequently links itself with marriage failure (as well as with shame). As we look at her family tree of descendants, note the amount of sexual sin and marriage failure.

1. Delores's first child, Samuel, was born out of wedlock and later given to a distant uncle and aunt to raise. He grew up, married, divorced, and remarried. He was faithful in marriage, but both of his daughters are sexually permissive. One had been molested.
2. Her second child, Barbara, is living with her boyfriend and doesn't intend to marry.
3. Her third child, Beverly, has been married several times. She has three children. The oldest is married and divorced and now sexually permissive.
4. Her fourth child, Paul, is separated from his former wife and sleeps with many women. He has never had any children.
5. Her fifth child, Steven, is having serious marriage problems and temporarily separated from his wife. Their children are still young.

Some of Delores' children are Christians, but they still have not escaped the pressures of sexual sin. Not a single one is happily married to his or her original mate.

b. Illustration: a Granddaughter of a Mason

One evening after everyone else had left the church offices, Betsy was still there ministering to Anna, a woman struggling to stay emotionally afloat. During the gathering of her generational history, it came out that Anna was the granddaughter of a 33rd degree Mason. As Betsy was having Anna confess the sins of her fathers, she came to the Masonic grandfather. "Now Anna, just confess the sin of Masonry in your family line, and . . . ."

---

[1] Please see 2 Tim 1:7.

126

That was as far as Betsy got. Anna rose up out of her chair a foot into the air. The demons associated with Masonry were manifesting. They were not happy that their "legal" ground was being taken away. Betsy decided that she would not go any further until Chester could join her. She and Anna bound the demons, prayed protection over Anna, and brought the session to a close. A few days later, we all gathered and proceeded through the rest of the SOFCs quite easily, including deliverance as necessary.

Anna herself was facing numerous problems in her marriage. She also had a very debilitating disease. Some months later, her precious, talented son died of a medical drug-related overdose. Anna's oldest daughter married a man after becoming pregnant. He later served a prison term for using and selling drugs. Her youngest daughter also has symptoms of a serious disease.

Could these problems relate back to the sin of masonry and its resulting curses? We also have to ask, "What occult Sins of the Fathers and the Resulting Curses were in operation in the first place that deceived and drew her grandfather into the clutches of this occult organization?"

Much that has been said about the Sins of the Fathers also applies to the subject of curses since the major source of curses comes from breaking God's laws (or commandments). After looking at another portion of Sandy's Story, we will shift the focus of our attention to Curses. Then we will discuss the scripture basis for freedom and ministering to Sins of the Fathers and the Resulting Curses.

c. Sandy's Story: Ancestral Deception

The ancestral sin and resulting curses were so intertwined with everything else in Sandy's life that we did not minister to SOFCs in the normal way.[1] It was necessary to continue to ministry to ancestral sins as a part of attacking the UGBs, SSHs and DO as new problems were uncovered.

Deception

God showed us several different ways that deception had created a powerful stronghold in Sandy's family line. During one of our sessions, we suggested to Sandy that "deception could be a major part of her immoral behavior." Shocked at the possibility, Sandy was sure that deception had never been an issue. (This was deception about the deception!)

During the next session, however, she came back to this topic and admitted that God had been speaking to her. She concluded, "Maybe deception had a small role in the total scheme of things, after all."

---

[1] When we minister, we like to move in a logical and orderly way from SOFCs to UGBs to SSHs to DO, progressively reclaiming the lost ground or "place." Because the problem areas were so interconnected, the procedure we used in ministering to Sandy was atypical and, consequently, not a good training model. We did what was necessary, however, to gain her freedom and healing as the Holy Spirit led us. In actuality, it is not uncommon for the "stereotype" training model to be "customized" by the Holy Spirit for each ministry receiver.

Sandy's eyes were being opened. By the following session, she realized that deception had indeed created a major veil over her mind. She began to acknowledge that she had led a double-life, a deceptive life, for essentially her entire life.

We continued to "cut away" at the area of deception, but it wasn't until we dealt with the Five Tower Stronghold[1] that she truly saw the magnitude of the deception in her life.

Sandy Writes

In one of Sandy's recent letters to us, she writes:

> This new life isn't just "the old life, cleaned up and made better." Even before my birth, Satan had begun his work in my ancestors that would limit and even control me. After I became a Christian, I was a "new creature in Christ," but I was still **me**. Generational sins, sins committed against me, and my own sin had already begun their deadly work. The salvation Christ brought to me now enabled me to overcome all of the works of the enemy — past, present, and future. However, I had been assaulted so early in life by his hateful plan that I can't even remember a time in my life that didn't have his fingerprints all over it. My cooperation with Satan through sin increased his power over me. For that, I take full responsibility and have repented. The new life of freedom into which I have entered has always been in God's heart for me and now I am unhindered in walking into it.

G. Curses

Since we have already discussed curses extensively in the first part of this chapter, it is almost anti-climactic to bring them up as a specific topic. Yet, much important information still needs to be presented. We will be using Table F on page 137 as our reference for scriptures relevant to Curses.

1. Just what is a Curse? Definitions

A curse protects the terms of a covenant.

The concept of a "curse" is found throughout the Old Testament and frequently in the New Testament. Generally, it involves a wish that "evil may befall another."[2] God's use of the word "curse" had the same meaning as Israel's contemporary world. All peoples understood what the word meant. The purpose of a "curse" was to protect the terms of a covenant by expressing the penalties that would be exacted if and when the covenant was violated.[3]

---

[1] We discuss this part of Sandy's Story in Chapter XII, "Demonic Strongholds."

[2] *The Interpreter's Dictionary of the Bible* (Nashville: Abingdon Press, 1985).

[3] Fee, Gordon D., and Douglas Stuart, *How to Read the Bible for All it's Worth* Grand Rapids: Zondervan Publishing House, 1982, page 136. Fee and Stuart provide a powerful correlation between God's covenant and "suzerain" covenants, common in Old Testament times, given by "an all-powerful overlord to a weaker, dependent vassal (servant)."

> A **Curse is the penalty** to be paid for the **breaking of a law**. Thus the biblical meaning regarding God's Law is "the consequence that will occur because of disobedience and rebellion against God's law."

In concept, it is completely analogous to our government specifying penalties for breaking the law. The fine of $95 for speeding, i.e., for breaking the law limiting our car speed to 55 mph, would be similar to a curse. The government would continue to search for us until we had paid the fine in full. Likewise, a curse will continue to search out the family line until the penalty is paid in full. Without the Cross, however, the penalty can never be paid in full.

God's curse must be paid in blood.

Unlike the world's governments, which accept money for their penalties, God's penalties can only be paid by the shedding of blood. God has always required the shedding of blood as payment, even in the garden with Adam and Eve.[1] The blood that He requires now is the blood of the perfect Lamb, Jesus Christ. Through His sacrifice on the Cross, we can by faith apply His blood to cover our sins, to pay the penalty, to stop the curse.

> Heb 9:22
> In fact, the law requires that nearly everything be cleansed with blood, and **without the shedding of blood there is no forgiveness**. (NIV)

Ken Copeland

A curse is being empowered to fail.

Another good definition of a curse comes from Ken Copeland. His definitions of both curses and blessings are:[2]

> A curse is being "empowered to fail."
> A blessing is being "empowered to succeed."

While this is a simplistic definition, it does get the point across.

Derek Prince

Derek Prince has a more elaborate definition of a curse.[3] As a Greek scholar, he has studied the scriptures in detail concerning curses and helped many people become free from the effect of curses. We consider him to be a respected authority well-versed in this subject.

> Curses are words spoken, with some form of spiritual authority (either good or evil), that set in motion something that will go on generation after generation. Behind the words is a spiritual power: God or Satan.

---

[1] The first blood was shed by God Himself on behalf of Adam and Eve: Gen 3:21.

[2] Ken Copeland of Kenneth Copeland Ministries, Fort Worth, TX, public communication at a conference, 1986.

[3] Derek Prince, *Curses: Cause and Cure*, Tape series No. 6011, Derek Prince Ministries, Fort Lauderdale, FL, 1983. Also see his book on *Blessings and Cursings*.

The Israelites did indeed experience being "empowered to fail," as they repeatedly broke their agreement with God. They have also experienced "something" set in motion that has gone on generation after generation. As a result of these curses, their history shows that they have gone through two complete exiles and scatterings. They are now being regathered for the third time, which is the final time according to Bible prophecy.[1]

2. Curses Operating in Several People's Lives

Our experience in ministry has uncovered certain "mysteries" in people's lives. These are mysteries in terms of the "unexplained." Consider these examples of unexplained events: frequent car accidents, business losses, bones that don't heal or that continue to be broken, infirmities that don't seem to respond to the usual treatments, people who suffer insanity, and multitudes of other problems. In one family, the first pregnancy for each woman in four generations was miscarried. Some families have a history of premature death.

In ministry, when we see the "unexplained," we become suspicious that a curse may be in operation. Why would one person who is a good driver have four rear-end collisions in a ten-year period? Why would a family's middle child be handicapped for two successive generations? Why would a businessman who had prospered begin to experience great losses? Why would a leg continue to ache and throb and defy medical help?

The frequent answer is that curses are operating in the lives of these people. In some cases, the reason behind the operation of curses was evident; in other cases, the reason was revealed by the Holy Spirit, either to us or to the ministry receiver, or to intercessors. Frequently, we had to "piece" together the information God had given to all of us to see the entire picture.

- The man who had so many car accidents had been living with a woman who was heavily involved in the occult and was angry with him for refusing to participate. She had been placing curses on him, setting the stage for accidents.
- The Holy Spirit revealed that the family whose middle child was handicapped had two ancestors who had witnessed the murder of a little boy. They had been "party to the crime" by remaining silent. Being involved in this crime had opened the door for physical curses to come on their descendants.
- The businessman who began to experience losses had ancestors who had owned slaves. Apparently the slaves had cursed the family.
- The woman with the terrible leg pain saw a picture in her spirit of her ancestors involved in slaughtering the French Huguenot Christians. This woman had experienced a remarkable number of near-death experiences. The spirit of death and pain were part of the curse that had come through the family line since the murdering of those Christians.

We will have to wait for another generation to see whether the ministry was effective in breaking the curse causing birth defects. In the other cases, freedom and healing either has come or is in the process of coming.

---

[1]   The Bible contains prophecy declaring that there shall be only two exiles! Then the root of Jesse will come and the animals will be at peace. See Isaiah 11, particularly verse 11.

3. Where do Curses Come From?

Generally, the most severe curses affecting a person's life are those that result from the Sins of the Fathers. Curses, as penalties for sin, come from only one source: God. Curses, as a desire to bring distress and failure into a person's life, can come from other sources. Unfortunately, we can also curse ourselves. In all cases, eliminating the effect of the curse from our lives is a wise thing to do!

- From God
- From Others/Word Curses
- From Self/Self-Curses

a. From God

The main source of curses is God. Shocking, isn't it? God, our heavenly Father, source of all good and perfect gifts,[1] is also the source of curses. God issued the first curses against the serpent and against the land in chapter three of Genesis. While the word "curse" is not used by God in His pronouncement against Adam and Eve, His words clearly convey a curse upon them. Other divine curses are seen in the flood[2] and in Moses' pronouncements against Egypt.[3]

Moses formalizes God's curses in the Pentateuch. Statements expressing the curses are "scattered" throughout the text, but the majority are in Leviticus 26 and Deuteronomy 27 through 32. God lays out the curses (or penalties) that will come upon the Israelites if they do not, ". . . keep the commandments, and the statutes, and the judgments, which I command thee this day, to do them."[4] God makes it very clear in Deuteronomy 11:

> Deu 11:26-28
> 26 Behold, **I set before you this day a blessing and a curse**;
> 27 A blessing, if ye obey the commandments of the LORD your God, which I command you this day:
> 28 And **a curse**, **if ye will not obey** the commandments of the LORD your God, but turn aside out of the way which I command you this day, to go after other gods, which ye have not known. (KJV)

Table E shows the main categories of curses (and also of blessings, for which we are grateful). These categories are from the book, *How to Read the Bible for All it's Worth*, by Fee and Stuart.[5] They show that the entire range of life is affected by curses as a result of breaking God's law.

While these curses were specifically directed to the Israelites, as part of God's covenant with them, it is clear that all peoples are cursed for rebellion against God, as we discussed earlier. The general condition for blessings or cursing from God for all of mankind is summed up in Proverbs:

---

[1] Please see Jam 1:17.
[2] Please see Gen 6:7, 13.
[3] Please see Ex 7 through 12.
[4] Deu 7:11. Similar statements are repeated many times throughout Leviticus and Deuteronomy.
[5] Fee and Stuart, *How to Read the Bible for All it's Worth*, op. cit.

> Prov 3:33
> The curse of the LORD [is] in the house of the wicked: but he blesseth the habitation of the just. (KJV)

Since any curse set into motion from God certainly has spiritual authority behind it, Derek Prince's criteria for a curse is met.

You may be wondering: Is God just waiting for us to make a mistake so He can activate a curse against us? No, revenge is not God's nature. Instead, it is likely that the "mechanism" for curses is in place as part of the fabric of the universe.

Judgment is brought forth as His laws are broken or violated. It is an expression of the Law of Sowing and Reaping. "Plant" a seed of disobedience, "reap" a harvest of judgment. This mechanism was probably put in place at the time of the Fall.[1] Since there is no way for us to escape by our own efforts from this continual cycle of sin and judgment, it was necessary for Christ to come to set us free.[2]

b. From Others: Word Curses

This is perhaps the more familiar source of a curse. We have all experienced someone "cursing" us or someone else. This type of curse usually doesn't have much power behind it, unless it comes from someone with spiritual and/or relational authority. If these people put forceful energy into cursing us and/or our ancestors, it may cause serious damage.

People, whom we or our ancestors have wronged by stealing, cheating, lying, deceiving, holding them in slavery, etc., may have cursed us (or them). These people may have released spiritual "pressures" and/or demonic power against us or our ancestors. This is particularly true if the people doing the cursing were witches, and/or if they were involved in any occult organizations, and/or if they were very emotional.

A number of times, we have encountered one particularly dangerous practice. Those in satanic or occult organizations often dedicate their descendants to the god of the "organization," or to Satan. This has happened several times with ministry receivers who had grandfathers active in the higher ranks of the Masons. Great Demonic Oppression can result from this curse placed on the family line until the "dedication" is broken.

Closer to home, we find our loving parents, who "curse" us with such warnings as "If you go out in the rain, you'll catch a cold," or "Don't play in the street, you'll get run over." Even worse are the curses that come from anger or "put-downs." For example, statements such as "You'll never amount to anything," and "You are a lousy daughter," are curses. The more subtle curses result from negative comparisons between siblings. A mother may say, "Linda is so pretty." Sister Judy, however, gets the message that she must be ugly. Dad may remark that "John is the smart one in the family." If you are John's brother, you begin to realize that you will never measure up to Dad's expectations.

---

[1]   Please see Gen 3.
[2]   Please see Gal 3:13.

It is clearly by God's grace that most of us survive the growing-up process and are able to function and be productive in society. Yet, the number of scars and unhealed wounds of the soul and spirit, along with the spiritual pressures and Demonic Oppression, can be astounding. This is why the Integrated Approach to Healing Ministry healing is so essential.

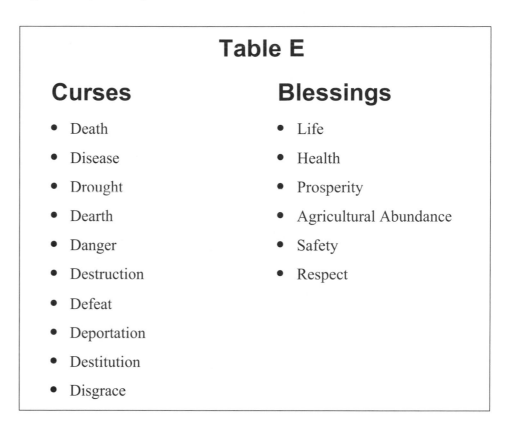

Table E

Curses	Blessings
• Death	• Life
• Disease	• Health
• Drought	• Prosperity
• Dearth	• Agricultural Abundance
• Danger	• Safety
• Destruction	• Respect
• Defeat	
• Deportation	
• Destitution	
• Disgrace	

To make matters worse, we have the media filling our minds with worry and fear. The ever-present TV brings the nation's worries and fears into our homes. Negative information can act as a curse if the viewer personally "receives" the statements as coming from an authority.

For example, as we were writing the first edition of this book, we heard on the TV news, "Over 50 percent of the population will die of cancer," and "AIDS patients will overflow the nation's hospital beds in the **1990s**." A person listening to this newscast could conclude (and believe) that he will contract and die of cancer, and that there will be no help for him from the medical system. Whether this actually becomes a "curse" or not depends on many factors, but the danger is real. Knowing the "truth" of God regarding this scare information is essential.

One biblical example of a person cursing those who had wronged him (and his family) is Gideon's son Jotham. Judges, chapter 9, relates this sad story as Abimelech, Gideon's son by a concubine who lived in Shechem,[1] is responsible for killing all 70 of Gideon's sons except Jotham. Jotham speaks a parable and a word curse[2] to Abimelech and the citizens of Shechem and Beth Milo. The sowing done by Abimelech yields a harvest of like nature. The remainder of chapter nine details

---

[1]   Please see Jud 8:30-31.
[2]   Please see Jud 9:20.

the sorry sequence of events eventually leading to the death of Abimelech and the men of Shechem, "And upon them came the (word) curse of Jotham the son of Jerubbaal (Gideon)."[1]

Another, even more chilling example is the Jews shouting,

> Mat 27:25
> Let his blood be on us and on our children. (NIV)

This is a self-curse for the shouting Jews, and a major ancestral curse for all of their descendants. Not a pleasant thought.

James writes a profound statement about cursing and wrong use of the tongue. He admonishes us to be careful what we say and not to bless God and curse men out of the same mouth.

> James 3:9-10
> 9 Therewith bless we God, even the Father; and therewith curse we men, which are made after the similitude of God.
> 10 **Out of the same mouth proceedeth blessing and cursing.** My brethren, these things ought not so to be. (KJV)

The guiding directive for all of us comes from Jesus, who gave us this command:

> Matthew 5:44
> But I say unto you, Love your enemies, bless them that curse you, do good to them that hate you, and pray for them which despitefully use you, and persecute you; (KJV)

c. From Self/Self-Curses

Even more sad than having our parents curse us is our cursing of ourselves. Unfortunately, we learned to do this from our parents, from our peer group, and from society, i.e., the media.

Familiar examples are:

- I can't start the day without my first cup of coffee.
- I will probably "blow" this job. (Expected failure)
- I can't remember names.
- I can't speak in front of people.
- Our family will always be poor.
- My children will always be left out.

Even the secular world realizes the power of repeated suggestions that programs the "subconscious" to carry out what we instruct it to do. Again, with sufficient emotion, repetition, and believing,[2] spiritual pressures and demonic forces can be loosened to help carry out the curse.

---

[1]   Please see Jud 9:56.
[2]   Please see Mk 11:23.

Paul, writing in First Corinthians,[1] shows us that we are not to be under bondage to anything (other than to the Lord Jesus Christ). He teaches us in Philippians[2] to be content in every situation, not to be dependent on our coffee, etc. Paul certainly doesn't even include, "I can't," in his vocabulary:

> Phil 4:13
> I can do all things through Christ which strengtheneth me. (KJV)

Paul believes in "self-blessing," not in "self-cursing."

4. How Curses are Carried Out

Are you curious about how curses are carried out?

The Bible is silent about how curses are carried out, as far as the actual mechanism is concerned. In some portions of Scripture, it appears that God Himself is orchestrating the penalty, as when He brings (or allows) one nation to be victorious over another, i.e., Babylon taking Israel into captivity. The books of Isaiah and Jeremiah strongly gives this impression. The Bible indicates that God killed all of the first-born males in Egypt in the last plague.[3] Sometimes He allows an evil spirit to carry out His purpose, as with Saul[4] and with Ahab.[5]

Is it a natural consequence?

Based on our earlier discussion of the laws of God, it seems that the judgment coming from breaking the laws is "built in" as a natural consequence. If we accept this view, we would conclude that the mechanism for carrying out a curse is automatically activated when the disobedience occurs. This is the essence of the Law of Sowing and Reaping.[6]

Are demons carrying out curses?

Then, of course, there is always Satan. While most of us never encounter him directly, his hierarchy of powers, principalities, dominions,[7] etc., apparently are eager to carry out every curse launched against us. His army seems to know our weaknesses and those areas where we have not yet appropriated God's healing and freedom into our lives. They also know when we sin and willingly take advantage of any openings we give them to come against us.

Also, the mechanisms carrying the Sins of the Fathers down the family line may also be carrying the Curses. These seems particularly likely for so-call hereditary diseases, where "defect" genes are blamed as the source. So we can summarize that curses are likely carried out by:

- genes
- growing-up environment
- natural consequence, i.e., "built in." (Law of Sowing and Reaping)
- demonic opportunity, i.e., "demons looking for open doors."[8]

---

[1] Please see 1 Cor 6:12 and 10:23.
[2] Please see Phil 4:11-12.
[3] Please see Ex 11-12.
[4] Please see 1 Sam 16:14.
[5] Please see 1 Kin 22:23.
[6] Please see Gal 6:7-8.
[7] Please see Eph 6:12.
[8] Please see Gen 4:7

5. Summary

There is the potential for a vast array of possible curses to come against us. Some come from God because of our ancestors' sins and our own sins. Others result from people cursing our ancestors and/or us. It is also possible to curse ourselves by speaking ungodly words from our hearts. Negative speech, of course, by itself does not produce a curse. However, when someone with spiritual and/or relational authority speaks evil against us, a resulting curse is a definite possibility.

There is some comfort in Proverbs 26:2:

> Prov 26:2
> As the bird by wandering, as the swallow by flying, so the **curse causeless shall not come**.

If we can stay pure before the Lord and appropriate what Christ did for us on the Cross,[1] then there is no cause for a curse to come upon us.

H. Scriptural Basis for Curses

Table F on the next page contains a number of scriptures relevant to Curses. We will not study these passages in depth as we did earlier with the Sins of the Father's scriptures. We have already discussed most of them anyhow. Their importance lies in assisting the minister both to encourage repentance and to instill faith in the ministry receiver. Also, it may be necessary to defend the application of the Gospel to this ministry area of Sins of the Fathers and Resulting Curses, i.e., apologetics.

In the fifth group of scriptures in Table F, Jesus commands us to "bless those that curse us."[2] Paul puts this very succinctly, "Bless and curse not."[3] In other words, we are directed to stop planting "curse seeds" and plant "blessing seeds." We are to stop the cycle of sinning, cursing, sinning, cursing, etc. We are commanded to bless and not curse because when we curse another, the Law of Judgment is put into motion, resulting in the fruit of the curse coming back on us.[4]

The last statement in the Bible about "the curse" is in Revelation 22:3. This beautiful promise makes it clear that one day, "No longer will there be any curse." We can say with John, "Even so, come, Lord Jesus."[5]

---

[1] Please see Gal 3:13.
[2] Please see Mat 5:43-44.
[3] Please see Rom 12:14.
[4] Please see Mat 7:1.
[5] Please see Rev 22:20.

Table F
Scriptures Concerning Curses

Reason for Curses from God

Dan 9:11	Transgression and disobedience of God's Law leads to curses and sworn judgments.
Deu 11:26-28	God sets before us a choice. We decide whether we obey or disobey His commandments.
Deu 28	Many curses listed for disobedience.

First Curses in Bible

Gen 3:14	To the serpent: cursed above all animals, crawl on belly, eat dust, head crushed.
Gen 3:16	To the woman: greatly increased pains in childbearing, . . . desire husband, be ruled over.
Gen 3:17-18	To the ground: cursed because of Adam, hard to produce good food, easy to produce thorns.
Gen 3:17-19	To the man: painful toil, sweating work, to produce food.

First Curse Spoken by a Man

Gen 9:25	"And (Noah) said, Cursed be Canaan; a servant of servants shall he be unto his brethren." (KJV)

Jews Cursing Themselves and Their Children

Mat 27:25	"Let his (Jesus') blood be on us and on our children." (NIV)

General Statements about Curses

Prov 3:33	"The LORD'S Curse is on the house of the wicked," (NIV)
James 3:9-10	[With the tongue] curse we men, ... Out of the same mouth proceedeth blessing and cursing. (KJV)
Prov 26:2	"Like a fluttering sparrow or a darting swallow, an undeserved curse does not come to rest." (NIV)

Jesus has the Last Word about Curses

Mat 5:43-44 Lk 6:27-28	". . . But I say unto you, Love your enemies, bless them that curse you, do good to them that hate you, and pray for them which despitefully use you, and persecute you;" (KJV)

Jesus Provides Freedom from the Curse

Gal 3:13	"Christ redeemed us from the curse of the law by becoming a curse for us." (NIV)

Last Statement about Curses in the Bible

Rev 22:3	"No longer will there be any curse." (NIV)

I. Self-Sins

Having discussed the Sins of the Fathers (and mothers) and the Resulting Curses, it is time to turn to the very important topic of Self-Sins. As the minister, you should be well versed in this information as you help lead your ministry receiver in repentance.

1. Response to the Set Up of Sins of the Fathers and Curses

We respond to the various pressures and temptations coming against us — self-curses, sinful acts, ungodly beliefs, the hurts we carry inside, demonic influence, etc. — in one of two ways. We can respond in a godly way, or an ungodly way. How we respond determines whether or not we are sinning, i.e., whether or not we are creating more ancestral sins and curses.

What is Sin?

This is probably one of the "top ten" age-old questions. Where do we draw the line between sin and non-sin? Let's take a brief look at what Scripture defines as sin and then consider what the theologians define as sin.

a. Scripture Defining Sin

Here are several passages from the Bible defining sin.

> Rom 14:22-23
> 22 Hast thou faith? have [it] to thyself before God. Happy [is] he that **condemneth not himself** in that thing which he alloweth.
> 23 And he that doubteth is damned if he eat, because [he eateth] not of faith: for **whatsoever [is] not of faith is sin**. (KJV)

This passage defines sin very broadly, "For whatever is not of faith is sin." The problem is knowing when we are operating out of the Logos and Rhema Word of God, i.e., "faith," and when we are operating out of a seared conscience.[1] That is, we might think that we are in faith when we are actually in presumption.

We see sin from another angle in 1 John:

> 1 Jn 3:4
> Whosoever committeth sin transgresseth also the law: for **sin is the transgression of the law**. (i.e., lawlessness) (KJV)

This view is still very general, but it clearly equates breaking God's law with sin. Further on in this book, John gives us another general statement:

> 1 Jn 5:17
> **All unrighteousness is sin**: (all wrongdoing) . . . (KJV)

---

[1] Please see 1 Tim 4:2.

Now, we have to ask, "What is unrighteousness?" If we come at this from the opposite direction, we know that "righteousness" is doing it God's way, doing it the "right" way. It also means "right standing" with God when we "do it" God's way, i.e., when we fulfill His requirements, which are His commandments.

James defines a very particular sin for us:

> Jam 2:9
> But if ye have respect to persons, ye commit sin, and are convinced of the law as transgressors. (KJV)

If we show favoritism, we sin. This certainly takes in all areas of prejudice and status.

b. Theologians Defining Sin

Let's turn to the theologians and briefly summarize their gleanings from the scriptures.

Theologians feel that the essence of sin is contained within First John.

> 1 Jn 2:16
> For all that [is] in the world, the **lust of the flesh**, and the **lust of the eyes**, and the **pride of life**, **is not of the Father**, but is of the world. (KJV)

This wonderful little verse shows three major categories of sin:

- Lust of the Flesh
- Lust of the Eyes
- The Pride of Life

If we go back and look at the temptation of Eve, we see that she was influenced by all three of these areas.

> Gen 3:6
> And when the woman saw that the tree [was] **good for food**, and that it [was] **pleasant to the eyes**, and a tree to be desired to **make [one] wise**, she took of the fruit thereof, and did eat, and gave also unto her husband with her; and he did eat. (KJV)

The serpent tempted Eve with the lust of the flesh (the fruit is "good for food"), with the lust of the eyes ("pleasant to the eyes"), and the pride of life ("make one wise;" in other words, "you shall be as gods"). She was touched and trapped in all three areas.

When Jesus was tempted in the wilderness, Satan attacked Him in all three areas.[1] He tried to get Him to turn the stones into bread after 40 days of fasting (lust of the flesh), to receive all of the kingdoms of the earth (lust of the eyes and pride of life), and to throw himself off of a pinnacle of the temple to demonstrate that He was the Son of God (pride of life). Jesus countered each time with the Word of God, and would have nothing to do with Satan's temptations.

---

[1]   Please see Mat 4:1-11 and Lk 4:1-13.

When Satan attacks us, he still attacks in these same three areas of sin. Like Jesus, we need to resist with our weapon the Word of God and tell Satan (or his henchmen) to "Get thee behind me."

Lust of the Flesh

The sins that are committed through the "Lust of the Flesh" are generally "doing" sins. They are desires and appetites of the body that gain control. Physical addictions such as food or drugs belong to this group.

Lust of the Eyes

The "Lust of the Eyes" generally produces sins of the soul, or "thinking" sins. Here the sin occurs in our thoughts, fantasies, the intent of our (soulish) will. Soulish addictions such as pornography belong to this group.

Pride of Life

The "Pride of Life" sins come out of the human spirit, or the "heart" of man according to Jesus.[1] This is the seat of the "iniquity" that we discussed earlier. The heart condition of man promotes this sin.[2] These sins can include trying to be holy by keeping rules (i.e., legalism) and hoping to earn our salvation by good works. Spiritual addictions such as pride of ownership or elitism belong to this group.

c. Summary

These three phrases comprise the main categories and motivations of sin. We have the **pride of life** inherited from our father, Adam. It has come all the way down the family line to us. This is the basic iniquity of the human heart: a tendency to rebel, to go our own way. Every person is born with this natural tendency. We have to receive God's salvation before we have an opportunity to stop being rebellious.

The other two areas, **lust of the eyes** and **lust of the flesh**, are inherited from our ancestors, from our environment, and from our peer groups. We "absorb" the standards of those around us. We are told that life is not complete and that we won't be happy unless we have a _____. So, until we get one, we are not happy.

Remember, you and I are each responsible for our own sin. Even though we enter this world "set up" and have all these influences working against us, we enter into the Sins of our Fathers and the Resulting Curses in only one way: By our own choice. God holds us accountable for the exercise of our free will. However, He also gives us the opportunity to choose His mercy and grace and enter into His family through the sacrifice of Jesus Christ on the Cross.

---

[1] Please see Mat 15:18-19.
[2] Please see Jer 17:9-10.

J.   Biblical Example of Sins of the Fathers and Curses

A number of biblical examples portray the Sins of the Fathers and Resulting Curses in action. One example, however, stands out above all the rest. The nation of Israel provides information about more generations than any other example. Technically speaking, this nation started with Abraham and continues until this day. For our illustration, however, we will use King David as the starting point.

1.   King David and His Descendants

David entered into adultery, deception, conspiracy, and murder.

King David sits as a premier example of king, priest, and prophet. He is the foreshadowing of the One who was yet to come, the Lord Jesus. As we read about his life in First and Second Samuel and in First Kings, David's many accomplishments are described, including his numerous victories in battle, conquests, favor with the people, and favor with God. He has everything going for him.

Then comes his encounter with Bathsheba — an encounter that both causes and marks the pinnacle of his career. From that point on, events in his life begin to deteriorate.

Now, you are possibly thinking, "Wait a minute, wasn't David forgiven?" The answer is, "Yes, he was forgiven," but the Sins of the Fathers and the Resulting Curses operating on his family line did not stop simply because he was forgiven. Forgiveness does not normally stop the "outworking" of curses. The Cross stops curses when we **appropriate** its freedom into our lives. If we don't appropriate the Cross, if we don't know we need to do so, the consequences/curses continue.

Forgiveness doesn't stop curses.

Some consequences continue no matter what. Why? Because a seed was planted that produced a harvest. The child conceived and born out of wedlock provides a simple example. The child is still with us even after the parents have repented and received God's forgiveness. At the other extreme, a person murdered does not come back to life after the murderer repents. Forgiveness is a wonderful gift from God, but it is only part of what needs to be done in order to stop curses.

David entered into the sins of **adultery**,[1] **deception**,[2] **conspiracy**,[3] and **murder**.[4] After David's (and Bathsheba's) sin, he is confronted by Nathan the prophet. Besides the humiliation of being exposed by Nathan, David receives a multi-part curse[5] from God. The curses are penalties of like nature to the sins he has committed. David and his descendants are going to reap what he has sown. As we discussed earlier, this curse includes the death of the child from the affair,[6] but this is only the beginning.

---

[1]   Please see 2 Sam 11:4.
[2]   Please see 2 Sam 11:8, 12-13.
[3]   Please see 2 Sam 11:14-15.
[4]   Please see 2 Sam 11:16-17.
[5]   Please see 2 Sam 12:10-14.
[6]   Please see 2 Sam 12:15-19. God spares David, but the penalty for adultery (death by stoning) falls onto the son. Is this fair, or consistent, with the previously mentioned scriptures about each one dying for his own sin?

David repents. We can read his confessional prayer in Psalm 51. This is a wonderful Psalm, one with which we all can identify. However, this doesn't stop the curses.

Later, one of David's sons, Amnon, **rapes** Tamar,[1] which leads to Amnon being **murdered** by Absalom.[2] **Deception**, **lying**, and **conspiracy** are all involved. Then Absalom himself **rebels** against his father, the King, and **conspires** to take over the kingdom.[3] The story ends with Absalom's **death**[4] and with much **destruction** in Israel, just as the prophet had spoken.

If we continue to follow the history of Israel and the line of David, we find the same Sins of the Fathers and the outworking of the Resulting Curses occurring time after time after time.

Solomon, the second son of David and Bathsheba, became king. While he was one of the wisest men to ever live, he was not wise in his later years. He married many foreign women and fell into the **traps of women, gold, horses, and idolatry**.[5]

While David's descendants (in Judah) included both good and bad kings, the overall pattern reveals definite flaws. God finally stops the royal succession coming through Solomon. He does this even though He had promised David:

> 2 Sam 7:16
> And thine house and **thy kingdom shall be established for ever** before thee: thy throne shall be established for ever. (KJV)

God cuts off Solomon's line with Jehoiachin,[6] the son of Jehoiakim,[7] and lets Israel go into captivity.

> Jer 22:30
> Thus saith the LORD, Write ye this man childless, a man [that] shall not prosper in his days: for no man of his seed shall prosper, sitting upon the throne of David, and ruling any more in Judah. (KJV)

Since we have the benefit of knowing the historical accounts, we can see that God did fulfill his promise to David through David's son Nathan (the third son born to David and Bathsheba).[8] This family line eventually lead to the birth of Jesus, the "supposed" son of Joseph.[9] Jesus **is now sitting** upon the throne of David **forever**.

Thus we have the fascinating situation of God keeping "all" of his promises to King David and Israel/Judah, both the cursing and the blessings. Yet the outworking of the Curses caused an ever-deepening spiral of wickedness and destruction. David's sin put in motion much trouble and heartache for his descendants.

---

[1] Please see 2 Sam 13:1-18.
[2] Please see 2 Sam 13:28-29.
[3] Please see 2 Sam 15.
[4] Please see 2 Sam 18:14.
[5] Please see Kin 11:4, 6.
[6] The names Coniah and Jeconiah are also used for Jehoiachin.
[7] Please see Jer 22:24-30.
[8] Please see 1 Chr 3:5, Lk 3:31.
[9] Please see Lk 3:23.

2. King David and His Ancestors

It seems fair to ask the questions, "What about David's ancestors? Did David fall into sin just 'out of the blue,' or did family pressures 'set him up?' Where did all of this sin begin?"

We know that David's grandmother was Ruth, a Moabite,[1] and that his great-grandmother was Rahab,[2] a Canaanite, the "keeper of the inn" in Jericho. So we have two heathen nations, known for their **idolatry** and **sexual sins**, grafted into the Israelite line preceding David **within four generations**.

Going back further, we do not know much about David's ancestors until we get back to Judah, a distance of ten generations.

In Genesis 38, we read about Judah, who has sexual relations with his daughter-in-law, Tamar, thinking she is a temple prostitute. We do not know Tamar's nationality, but Jewish tradition indicates that she is an Israelite. **Deception**, **fornication**, and **lying** are all involved in this sin, and perhaps **occult/idol worship**.

Judah's father, Jacob (Israel), reveals his tendency for **deceit**, **lying**, **cursing**, **cheating**, etc. All these sins are evident in his life, at least before his encounter with the angel of the Lord at the brook Jabbok.[3] His mother, Rebekah, entered into **deception** with Jacob, even **calling for the resulting curse** to be upon herself.[4] His wife, Rachel, **stole** her father's **household gods** and **lied** about them. This resulted in Jacob's **unintentional cursing** of her[5] and her early death.[6]

Both Abraham and Isaac were guilty of **lying**,[7] saying that their wives were their sisters. This, of course, was a half-truth, since they were half-sisters.

While the blessings of the fathers far outweighed the cursing, it is clear that David did not have a "pure" family line. Even though we don't know about his 10 nearest ancestors (except for Boaz, who was a righteous man following the Mosaic law), we know enough about David's family line to state with confidence that David was "set up" by his ancestors. Although he did indeed had a heart after God, David chose to enter into the Sins of his Fathers in his sin with Bathsheba.

David is a reminder to us all to be on guard. We must be careful not to assume that we cannot fall. God's favor may be on us, He may be using us mightily to further His Kingdom, but that is no guarantee that we can not be tempted and fall. Satan lies in wait like a roaring lion ready to pounce and bring us down in that one weak or unguarded moment. It is wise to be on the alert for the enemy's attack, particularly at the time of a great victory. Scripture shows that a counterattack often follows such a time. Our best defense is to be on guard and to stop the counterattack before it begins.

---

[1] Please see Ruth 1:22 and Mat 1:5.
[2] Please see Mat 1:5.
[3] Please see Gen 32:22-31.
[4] Please see Gen 27:12-13.
[5] Please see Gen 31:30-35, NIV.
[6] Please see Gen 35:16-20.
[7] Please see Gen 20:2, 26:7.

K. Scriptural Basis for Freedom

Once Christians discover that Sins of the Fathers and the Resulting Curses may be providing an opening for failure and oppression, most of them want to appropriate freedom. The scriptures in Table G provide us the basis for freedom.

1. Confession of Fathers' and Own Sins

God first states His condition(s) for restoration in Leviticus, surrounded by His warnings and dire consequences of Israel's anticipated rebellion.

> Lev 26:40-42
> 40 **If they** shall **confess their iniquity**, **and the iniquity of their fathers**, with their **trespass** which they **trespassed** against me, and that also they have walked contrary unto me;
> 41 . . . **if** then **their uncircumcised hearts be humbled**, and **they** then **accept of the punishment of their iniquity**:
> 42 **Then** will I remember my covenant with Jacob, and also my covenant with Isaac, and also my covenant with Abraham will I remember; and I will remember the land. (KJV)

As we prepare to apply the principles of this scripture to ourselves and our families, it would be helpful for you to reread the Section, "What God Requires, God Provides" (page 106). In this scripture, God has provided us a tremendous "pattern" to follow. One significant aspect of this pattern is that we are **not required to take responsibility** for our fathers' iniquity. It simply asks us to **acknowledge and confess** their iniquity. It asks us to accept responsibility for our own iniquity and to repent and be humbled. If we do what is asked, God states that He will remember His covenant(s). In other words, He will fulfill his promises of forgiveness and cleansing — of us and of the land. Of course, the "land" represents us also since we are God's promised land.

This scripture is the basis for "Identification Repentance," a modern term meaning that we "stand-in for" and represent our ancestors in confessing their sin.[1] This concept, when applied at the larger level, allows spiritual and civic leaders to "stand-in for" the former leaders and inhabitants of the land, confessing their sin. Applying this principle to an organization or a geographical area — a church or business, or a city or region — can yield great results in clearing out demonic principalities and paving the way for awakening and spiritual revival.

Scripture provides several very important examples of "Identification Repentance." Daniel, Nehemiah, and Ezra,[2] all prayed and confessed the Sins of their Fathers. Again, note that they do not ask forgiveness for their forefathers but only for themselves and their people. They **confessed** their forefather's sin.

---

[1] In Eze 13:5 and 22:30, God is looking for a man to "stand-in for" another.
[2] Please see Dan 9, Neh 1 and 9, Ezr 9.

Table G
Scriptures Concerning Freedom

Confession of Father's (and Own) Sins

Lev 26:40-42   **<u>If</u> they** shall **confess their iniquity**, <u>**and** the iniquity of their fathers</u>, with their **trespass** which they **trespassed** against me, and that also they have walked contrary unto me; . . . **if** then **their uncircumcised hearts be humbled**, and **they** then **accept of the punishment of their iniquity**: <u>**Then**</u> **will I remember my covenant** with Jacob, and also my covenant with Isaac, and also my covenant with Abraham will I remember; and I will remember the land. (KJV)

Dan 9:4-20   And I **prayed** unto the LORD my God, and **made my confession**, . . . **We have sinned**, and have **committed iniquity**, and have **done wickedly**, and have **rebelled**, even **by departing from thy precepts** and **from thy judgments**: . . . **all Israel have transgressed thy law**, even by **departing**, that they might **not obey thy voice**; <u>**therefore the curse is poured upon us**</u>, and <u>**the oath that [is] written in the law**</u> . . . And while **I [was] speaking, and praying, and <u>confessing</u> my sin and the sin of my people Israel**, and <u>**presenting**</u> my supplication before the LORD my God for the holy mountain of my God; . . . (KJV)

Appropriating the Cross

Gal 3:10-14   **All who rely on observing the law are under a curse**, for it is written: **"Cursed is everyone who does not continue to do everything written in the Book of the Law."** Clearly no one is justified before God by the law, because, "The righteous will live by faith." The law is not based on faith; on the contrary, "The man who does these things will live by them." **Christ redeemed us from the curse of the law by becoming a curse for us**, for it is written: "Cursed is everyone who is hung on a tree." **He redeemed us in order that the blessing** given to Abraham **might come** to the Gentiles through Christ Jesus, **so that by faith we might receive the promise of the Spirit**. (NIV)

Col 2:13-14   And when **you were dead** in your transgressions and the uncircumcision of your flesh, **He made you alive** together with Him, having **forgiven us** all our transgressions, having **canceled out** the **certificate of debt** consisting of decrees against us . . . and He has taken it out of the way, **having nailed it to the cross**. (NAS)

1 Pet 1:18-19   knowing that **you were** not **redeemed** with perishable things like silver and gold **from your futile way of life inherited from your forefathers**, but **with precious blood**, as of a lamb unblemished and spotless, **the blood of Christ**. (NAS)

Daniel prayed a tremendous confessional prayer of identification repentance during his and Israel's exile in Babylon. While reading in the book of Jeremiah, Daniel realized that the 70 years of captivity prophesied by the prophet was nearly completed.[1]

As you read this prayer, note how Daniel identifies with and confesses the sins of his forefathers. Then he confesses his own sin. At the very end, he asks the Lord to "hear, forgive, hearken, and do."

Dan 9:4-20

4 And I **prayed** unto the LORD my God, and **made my confession**, and said, O Lord, the great and dreadful God, keeping the covenant and mercy to them that love him, and to them that keep his commandments;

5 **We have sinned**, and have **committed iniquity**, and have **done wickedly**, and have **rebelled**, even **by departing from thy precepts** and **from thy judgments**:

6 Neither have we **hearkened** unto thy servants the prophets, which spake in thy name to our kings, our princes, and our fathers, and to all the people of the land.

7 O Lord, righteousness [belongeth] unto thee, but unto us confusion of faces, as at this day; to the men of Judah, and to the inhabitants of Jerusalem, and unto all Israel, [that are] near, and [that are] far off, through all the countries whither thou hast driven them, because of **their trespass** that they have trespassed against thee.

8 O Lord, to us [belongeth] confusion of face, to our kings, to our princes, and to our fathers, because **we have sinned against thee**.

9 To the Lord our God [belong] mercies and forgiveness, though **we have rebelled** against him;

10 Neither have we **obeyed the voice** of the LORD our God, to walk in his laws, which he set before us by his servants the prophets.

11 Yea, **all Israel have transgressed thy law**, even by **departing**, that they might **not obey thy voice**; <u>**therefore the curse is poured upon us**</u>, and <u>**the oath that [is] written in the law**</u> of Moses the servant of God, **because we have sinned against him**.

12 And **he hath confirmed his words**, which he spake against us, and against our judges that judged us, **by bringing upon us a great evil**: for under the whole heaven hath not been done as hath been done upon Jerusalem.

13 As [it is] written in the law of Moses, **all this evil is come upon us**: yet made we not our prayer before the LORD our God, that we might turn from **our iniquities**, and understand thy truth.

14 Therefore hath <u>**the LORD watched upon the evil, and brought it upon us**</u>: for the LORD our God [is] righteous in all his works which he doeth: for **we obeyed not his voice**.

15 And now, O Lord our God, that hast brought thy people forth out of the land of Egypt with a mighty hand, and hast gotten thee renown, as at this day; **we have sinned**, we **have done wickedly**.

---

[1] Please see Jer 25:11-12, 29:10.

> 16 O Lord, **according to all thy righteousness, I beseech thee**, let thine anger and thy fury be turned away from thy city Jerusalem, thy holy mountain: **because for our sins, and for the iniquities of our fathers**, Jerusalem and thy people [are become] a reproach to all [that are] about us.
>
> 17 Now therefore, O our God, hear the prayer of thy servant, and his supplications, and cause thy face to shine upon thy sanctuary that is desolate, for the Lord's sake.
>
> 18 O my God, incline thine ear, and hear; open thine eyes, and behold our desolations, and the city which is called by thy name: for **we do not present our supplications before thee for our righteousness, but for thy great mercies**.
>
> 19 O Lord, **hear**; O Lord, **forgive**; O Lord, **hearken** and **do**; **defer not**, for thine own sake, O my God: for thy city and thy people are called by thy name.
>
> 20 And while **I [was] speaking, and praying, and confessing my sin and the sin of my people Israel**, and **presenting** my supplication before the LORD my God for the holy mountain of my God; (KJV)

In this awesome prayer, Daniel identifies himself and the nation of Israel with their forefathers. He **confesses** his and their sins. He **agrees** with God that they were wrong and that God was right. He agrees with God that He had every right to bring the curses upon them "because we have sinned against him (God)." Then he calls on God's righteousness, mercy, and "for thine own sake," to restore the situation. This prayer is a great model for us.

In Nehemiah, we find two similar prayers.[1] These prayers have essentially the same ingredients as Daniel's prayer and serve as additional example prayers for us. Nehemiah 9:3 shows the Israelites following the Leviticus 26:40 pattern as they confess their sins and the iniquities of their fathers before beginning their corporate prayer. Ezra 9 follows a similar pattern.

As we choose to follow this Biblical pattern to humble ourselves and repent of the Sins of our Fathers, we and others are experiencing newfound freedom.

Tremendous testimonies are also being reported from around the world that Identification Repentance is breaking the power of demonic strongholds over geographic areas, and revival is coming forth.[2]

2. Appropriating the Cross

On this side of the Cross, Jesus has completely satisfied the requirements of God's judgment. He has provided freedom for us from the curses originating from the Sins of the Fathers and Resulting Curses, as well as from our own sin. Even better, whereas God also required the Israelites to accept the appropriate punishment for their sin (see Lev 26:40-42 on page 144), Jesus has already taken the punishment for us. All we have to do is to appropriate His Work on the Cross by faith!

---

[1] Neh 1:5-11, 9:5-37.
[2] Otis, George, Jr., "Transformations," a video produced by Sentinel Group, Inc., WA, 1999.

In Galatians, Paul writes:

> Gal 3:10-14
> [10]**All who rely on observing the law are under a curse**, for it is written: **"Cursed is everyone who does not continue to do everything written in the Book of the Law."** [11]Clearly no one is justified before God by the law, because, "The righteous will live by faith." The law is not based on faith; on the contrary, "The man who does these things will live by them." [12]**Christ redeemed us from the curse of the law by becoming a curse for us**, for it is written: "Cursed is everyone who is hung on a tree." [14]**He redeemed us in order that the blessing** given to Abraham **might come** to the Gentiles through Christ Jesus, **so that by faith we might receive the promise of the Spirit**. (NIV)

This promise is further amplified in Colossians:

> Col 2:13-14
> [13]And when **you were dead** in your transgressions and the uncircumcision of your flesh, **He made you alive** together with Him, having **forgiven us** all our transgressions,
> [14]having **canceled out** the **certificate of debt** consisting of decrees against us . . . and He has taken it out of the way, **having nailed it to the cross**. (NAS)

Peter also shows us the way out and explicitly ties redemption through the blood of Christ to the "futile" lifestyle inherited from our fathers.

> 1 Pet 1:18-19
> [18]knowing that **you were** not **redeemed** with perishable things like silver and gold **from your futile way of life inherited from your forefathers**,
> [19]but **with precious blood**, as of a lamb unblemished and spotless, **the blood of Christ**. (NAS)

We cannot keep God's law, and the Israelites could not and cannot today keep God's law. Our disobedience in breaking the law results in curses coming upon us. God Himself, in the likeness of man, "redeemed us from the curse of the law." Jesus is our substitution if we will receive Him as such by faith. He provides a legal answer to the outworking of God's judgments and to the curses that Satan wants to impose upon us. Jesus "canceled out the certificate of debt, consisting of decrees against us and which was hostile to us." Jesus is the answer to God's requirements and our inability to meet them. He alone sets us free.

3. What About Our Children?

We have been asked many times, "What effect will my ministry have on my children?" And/or, "What can I do to also help my children get free?"

One of the awesome things about breaking Sins of the Fathers and the Resulting Curses is that the person receiving this ministry brings the "passing down" to a halt at his generation. His descendants have a fresh start.

Babies born after the time of ministry are the first generation of a new family line, one rooted in the family of God. This is a tremendous blessing that one can give his descendants — perhaps, the most significant inheritance possible, next to helping them know the Lord Jesus.

For children who are already born, the effect of the parent's SOFCs ministry on them depends on their age, particularly their age relative to the age of accountability. The older they are, the less likely it is that they will receive significant freedom. We usually suggest that they be prayed for directly if they are over 4-5 years old.

Young Children
Young children, from infants to 4-5, can be ministered to while they are asleep. Anoint their beds with oil if you desire. Then, through prayer, move into a position of authority as both parent and intercessor. Using the same strategy you used to obtain your own freedom, continually apply the SOFCs Ministry Steps, moving from grouping to grouping. At the same time, you may want to cast out related demons.

Older Children
For older children, approximately nine to twelve-year olds, explain the basics of SOFCs to them and enlist their cooperation. Lead them through the Ministry Steps, again following the "family" strategy as you go through the groups. If they have not already been born again, this ministry may give them the freedom needed to make a godly choice. It would also be wise to continue to bind all demons oppressing them.

Adult Children
For mature children, the suggested approach is really the same as for "older" children. Help them become informed so they desire to receive the ministry for themselves. Perhaps, you might share your testimony with them. Consider asking their forgiveness for the ways your sins and hurts have caused them to be hurt. Let them know your heart; how much you desire their freedom. Depending on the age and personality of the child, you might share a copy of this book and encourage them to read it.

Obviously, wisdom is needed if the children are unsaved. How you actually approach them will depend on a number of factors. As always, seek the Holy Spirit for God's wisdom in all things, including whether or not to pray with them in this area — and if so, when, where, and how.

L. Ministering to the Sins of the Fathers and Curses

Ministering to the area of Sins of the Fathers and the Resulting Curses is very important. This is analogous to clearing away the faulty foundation upon which the ministry receiver's life has been built. At times this ministry to an individual may seem very straight-forward and "cut and dried," while at other times it can be extremely dynamic and powerful.

Regardless of the appearance, let us assure you that significant things are happening in the spiritual realm. Powerful forces are being released like rubber bands flying across the room. Demons are losing their place and heading for the unemployment line. The unseen universe is shaking as the profound reverberations of broken curses echo out from the Cross. A great cheer goes up in heaven. Another saint is getting free!

1. Strategy for the Ministry

We have found that the most effective ministry to the Sins of the Fathers and Resulting Curses ministry area takes place when we have a strategy. Our strategy involves grouping the core areas of sins that have most affected our ministry receiver's life and beginning with these. We start with the most significant and end with the least significant. Most often, these significant sin areas are closely related as with abandonment and sexual sin. (People who miss out on being loved look for love through sexual relationships.) Next, we include other closely related areas, such as the shame, fear, and control areas, associated both with abandonment and with sexual sin. Frequently there seems to be a cluster of about six to eight interrelated, core sin areas. After ministering to these, we move to the groups of lesser impact. We use the lists of groups in Generational Patterns portion of the Application Form (in Appendix A) as a worksheet to plan and organize the SOFCs ministry.

2. Receiving God's Blessings

In the Ministry Steps used for Sins of the Fathers and Resulting Curses, the last step can have deep personal significance for our receiver. This is a time when God can bring the blessings that He has always wanted for him. The Cross has been applied. The pressure of the sins and the power of curses has been broken. The slate of his life has been wiped clean. Now he is in a fresh position to receive from the Lord.

We ask the person to listen to the Lord in the last step. We either tape record or write the personal, life-giving blessings he receives as the Lord speaks.

If our receiver is unable to hear the Lord, then we share what the Lord is speaking to us or showing us. Don't let your ministry receiver miss the joy of this blessing!

3. Final Thoughts before Ministry

The minister needs to be particularly sensitive to the Holy Spirit during this ministry. He needs to be able to identify Sins of the Fathers and Resulting Curses operating in his receiver's life, including those known by the person himself and those unknown. The unknown ones, particularly those from more distant ancestors, may be discernible only by the gifts of the Holy Spirit.

> **Exercise:** As you pray the following Submission Prayer (or in your own words one similar to it), and work through the following Ministry Steps, you can use your completed Generational Patterns Form to help you and the Holy Spirit minister to those sins and curses that He has selected for this time.

4. Submission Prayer

The prayer on the next page can be used as a model as you help your receiver prepare to appropriate the freedom God desires for him. Please, however, avoid becoming "religious" and using this prayer by rote. We want our prayers to be of the Spirit and not of the letter.[1]

5. Steps to Freedom in Ministering to Sins of the Fathers and Curses

The progression of ministry is outlined in the following list of detailed steps. Generally, the minister will pray/declare ministry steps 8 and 9. Sometimes, however, the ministry receiver will include these as he is moving through the other steps. If so, that is great. It means that he is "grabbing hold" of the Gospel and applying it. Obviously, there is no need for the minister to repeat the same steps.

---

[1]   Please see 2 Cor 3:6.

SOFCs Submission Prayer: As a child of God, purchased by the blood of the Lord Jesus Christ, I choose to confess and acknowledge the sins of my ancestors. While I don't like the results of their sins on my life, I choose to forgive and release them and not to hold them accountable for each and every way that their sins have affected me.

I now renounce all of the sins of my ancestors and release myself from their effects, based on the finished work of Christ on the Cross.

Lord, I am sorry for all of the ways that I have entered into these same sins and allowed the curses to affect me. I ask You to forgive me for this and to wash me clean. I choose to receive Your forgiveness.

I affirm that I have been crucified with Jesus Christ and raised to walk in newness of life. On this basis, I announce to Satan and all his forces that Christ took upon Himself the curses and judgments due me. Thus I break every curse that has come upon me because of my ancestors. I also break all curses that have been released onto me by others. I also break all curses that I have spoken or thought about myself. I receive my freedom from every one of these curses.

Because of the above and because I have been delivered from the power of darkness and translated into the kingdom of God's dear Son, I cancel the legal rights of every demon sent to oppress me.

Because I have been raised up with Christ and now sit with Him in heavenly places, where I have a place as a member of God's family, I renounce and cancel each and every way that Satan and his demons may claim ownership of me. I cancel all dedications made by my ancestors of their descendants, including me and my descendants, in the name of Jesus. I declare myself to be completely and eternally signed over to, owned by, and committed to, the Lord Jesus Christ.

All this I do on the basis of the Truth revealed in the Word of God, and in the Name and with the Authority of my Lord and Savior, Jesus Christ. Amen!

Ministry Steps[1]

1. **Confess:** Have ministry receiver confess the Sins of his Fathers and his own sins.

2. **Forgive:** Have receiver forgive his ancestors and parents who are still alive for any and all sins that they have committed which have affected his life. Have him forgive them for specific sins as appropriate.

3. **Forgive:** Have receiver forgive every living person who has spoken word curses against him and/or his ancestors.

4. **Repent:** Have receiver ask God's forgiveness for entering into the Sins of his Fathers and for yielding to the Curses affecting him. Have him choose to turn away from any and all Sins of the Fathers, as well as his own personal sins.

5. **Forgive:** Have receiver forgive himself for his own personal sins, for self-curses, and for carrying guilt, shame, and self-hatred.

6. **Receive:** Speak forgiveness[2] and pray for cleansing.[3]

7. **Renounce:** Have receiver renounce any more involvement or "putting up with" the sins and curses.

8. **Appropriate:** Appropriate and apply the power of the Cross and the shed Blood of Christ to stop all judgments and curses.

9. **Break:** Break the power of any and all curses in the authority of the Name of Jesus and in His finished work on the Cross.[4] Refuse Satan any right to carry out any curses.

10. **Affirm:** Have receiver affirm that he has a new Father. Not only is he in a new kingdom,[5] but he is in a new family, where there are no Sins of the Fathers.[6]

11. **Receive:** Have receiver listen to the Holy Spirit, to reveal the blessing that God has for him in place of the sins and curses.

---

[1] A copy of a Ministry Card with a summary of these steps is in Appendix A.
[2] Please see Jn 20:23.
[3] Please see 1 Jn 1:9.
[4] Please see Gal 3:13.
[5] Please see Col 1:13.
[6] Please see 1 Jn 3:1-2.

VIII

UNGODLY BELIEFS

Let the wicked forsake his way, and the unrighteous man his thoughts:
and let him return unto the LORD, and he will have mercy upon him;
and to our God, for he will abundantly pardon.
Isaiah 55:7

. . . be ye transformed by the renewing of your mind,
that ye may prove what [is] that good, and acceptable, and perfect, will of God.
Romans 12:2

Everyone, to some extent, lives his life, out of wrong beliefs. We call these "lies" about ourselves, about others, and about God Ungodly Beliefs (UGBs). Why are they so dangerous? Because they affect our perceptions, our decisions, and our actions. You can see why God wants our minds renewed.

As we start this chapter we will share Tim's testimony and how the discovery of his Ungodly Beliefs resulted in the renewal of his mind. In other words, his Ungodly Beliefs were changed into Godly Beliefs.

Also in this chapter you will learn the difference between Ungodly Beliefs and Godly Beliefs, how they relate to the other three Problem/Ministry Areas, and why they must be ministered to in concert with these areas. As we discuss how and why Ungodly Beliefs are formed, you will learn to identify the most common ones. Since we Christians are also "infected" with Ungodly Beliefs (sorry!), we will explain the damaging results of living our lives based on them. We will then explore the scriptures that provide a basis and a methodology for identifying and changing Ungodly Beliefs into Godly Beliefs. You will learn how to "reprogram" your mind, so it is filled with Godly Beliefs. Lastly, we present Ministry Steps that allow you to break the power that Ungodly Beliefs have over your mind and appropriate God's power through Godly Beliefs.

Tim's Exposure to Ungodly Beliefs

Our hearts trembled as our new friend and recent ministry receiver, Tim, approached the podium to give his testimony. Waves of compassion mixed with tension swept over the congregation. A few short months before, Tim's pain-wracked existence had wavered between life and death when he overdosed twice in one week on cocaine and alcohol.

As Tim began to speak, a clarity and a steadiness came forth, confirming that God had truly done a deep, personal work in our friend's life. Tim shared about the recommitment to Christ that had taken place in his first ministry session, how his old belief system had been leading him to destruction, and how his new Godly Beliefs were bringing him into stability and new life.

"I want to touch on one core Ungodly Belief," he said. "This one came right out of my experience and combined with others for my destruction. I believed that I had to fend for myself because God could not be trusted. During my childhood, my father neglected me and failed to provide for my needs. As a result, I wandered through life feeling scared, insecure, and wondering how I was going to make it. I did all kinds of crazy things to provide for myself. The worst was allowing my body to be bought sexually. My looks and my body were the only things that I had any confidence in."

"The Kylstras helped me to see that I was believing a lie about God. We did some deliverance, prayed, and asked God to help me to begin believing the truth about Him. Then they told me to begin to pray/meditate every day on the Godly Belief that God loves me, and He is my provider. Over time, I began to change on the inside. At first I doubted that anything in my life would change since I was in deep financial debt at that time with no obvious way out. Although it was hard to keep believing, I started repeating these new phrases every day. After all, I didn't have anything to lose. As a result of this new belief about God, I started acting differently. I began by obeying God about tithing and learned how to manage my money better. Little by little, I began to believe that God **did** care and that He would provide."

"Before long, the miracles started happening. My salary increased by four times in four months, and I've taken home over half of it. At times I still fret a little bit. This past week I needed nearly $200 to fix my car. To make matters worse, I lost a few hours from work because I was sick. While I was sitting at home, I asked myself, 'Why aren't you worried? Why aren't you upset?' To my amazement, I began to see that my belief system really *was* changing. I was saying, 'Well, I know in my heart God is going to provide,' and I really believed it. That was a major turning point for me."

"Changing my beliefs about God's provision has had other implications. I no longer have to do those old, awful, sinful things to get someone else to take care of me."

As Tim finished, the congregation rose to their feet with a cheer. They clapped and shouted as they gave thanks to the Lord and rejoiced for the obvious changes God had worked in this young man they all had known.

A. Definition/Description of Ungodly Beliefs (UGBs)

Godly Beliefs agree with God (His Word, His nature, His character).

What is a belief system? It includes our **beliefs**, **decisions**, **attitudes**, **agreements**, **judgments**, **expectations**, **vows**, and **oaths**. Any beliefs that agree with God (His Word, His nature, His character) constitute our Godly Beliefs (GBs). Any beliefs that do not agree with God (His Word, His nature, His character), contribute to our Ungodly Beliefs (UGBs).

> **Ungodly Beliefs:** All **beliefs**, **decisions**, **attitudes**, **agreements**, **judgments**, **expectations**, **vows**, and **oaths** that **do not** agree with God (His Word, His nature, His character).
>
> **Godly Beliefs:** All **beliefs**, **decisions**, **attitudes**, **agreements**, **judgments**, **expectations**, **vows**, and **oaths** that **do** agree with God (His Word, His nature, His character).

Unfortunately, the major areas of our belief system are usually made up of UGBs. For example, what we believe about our right to exist, our purpose, our value, and the very source of our security — as well as what we believe about our relationships with other people and with God — is generally ungodly. As the Holy Spirit sanctifies our mind,[1] our belief system begins to change from a mixture of mostly UGBs to more and more GBs.

We can make some statements about real Godly Beliefs. That is, beliefs that do indeed agree with God rather then beliefs that we think agree with God.

> A real Godly Belief is reflected in our actions.
> A real Godly Belief is rooted in our heart.
> A real Godly Belief stands firm in the face of challenge.

The goal is to be transformed into the image of Christ,[2] having only GBs. While this goal may seem impossible to attain, we can decide to work with the Holy Spirit so that He can change us as rapidly as we can handle.[3] Perhaps the day will come when we can say with David:

> Psa 139:17
> How precious to me are your thoughts, O God! How vast is the sum of them! (NIV)

When we are tuned into His mind, we realize that God has a lot to say to us. Paul writes of this possibility in First Corinthians, as he is discussing Christians who are spiritual:

> 1 Cor 2:16
> . . . But we have the mind of Christ. (KJV)

If God has promised us His mind, let us not draw back but pursue a renewed mind with faith.

---

[1] Please see 2 Thes 2:13.
[2] Please see Rom 8:29.
[3] Please see 2 Cor 7:1.

The "Perfect" Ungodly Belief

How would you define a "perfect" Ungodly Belief (UGB).

> The "perfect" Ungodly Belief is one that appears to be absolutely **true** based on the **facts** of our experience and yet is absolutely **false** based on **God's Word**.

- No one loves me.
- I am all alone.
- I am defective.
- God doesn't love me.

Although these statements are completely false, most people who think this way do not even realize it. Why? Because UGBs are typically completely hidden from us. Until a UGB is pointed out to us, we continue on day after day, living our life based on a lie. When we finally recognize an UGB, we realize how completely at odds it is with God's Word. Most UGBs, however, are not "absolute" but rather a mixture of truth and error.

B. Understanding the Interrelationship of the Ministry Areas

Ungodly Beliefs are interrelated to the other three Problem/Ministry Areas. This is why they must be ministered to in concert with each of the other ministry areas if the ministry is to be permanently effective.

Although some measure of healing would come by ministering solely to UGBs, it will become apparent to you how **interrelated** UGBs are with each of the other ministry areas.

1. How Ungodly Beliefs are Related to Sins of the Fathers and Resulting Curses

After finishing a ministry session in which much generational sin had been exposed, Betsy commented to Chester, "Tell me the Sins of the Fathers affecting a person's life, and I will tell you most of his Ungodly Beliefs."

Think about it. The two are integrally related. The same sins that have plagued families for generations cause deception, clouded minds, rationalization, and unbelief in these same sin areas. For example, sexual sin causes many wrong, twisted beliefs about sex. Violence results in rationalization and "normalizing" of violence and wrong beliefs about it, as well as affecting the victim's beliefs about self-worth. The specific Sin of the Fathers is like the hub of a wheel and the UGBs are like the spokes going out from it. They become an extension of the sin. To deal with the spokes but not the hub would produce incomplete results as the roots would be left in place.

2. How Ungodly Beliefs are Related to Soul/Spirit Hurts

When a child becomes the victim of his father's drunken rage, his young heart is broken. Think for a moment about some of the UGBs that might develop. Eventually ideas might develop such as, "I must not be a lovable person," or "It is my fault that Dad is so angry."

Many of the negative beliefs that we have about ourselves, others, and God result from the ungodly, hurtful ways we have been treated. Hurts and wrong beliefs are like two hands that are placed together with the fingers intertwined and locked. The hurts must be healed as well as the mind renewed. If not, the hurts will cry out messages of denial to override the attempted process of renewing the mind. Hurts are like an infected wound, and the UGBs are like the pus coming from it. We can wipe away the pus, but more will develop unless the wound is healed. The wound affects the heart, the pus affects the mind. Both need to be healed.

Because sins are generational and sin causes hurts, the same types of hurts tend to be repeated generation after generation. As a result, the same kinds of UGBs continue to be generated and passed down. Sins of the Fathers, Soul/Spirit Hurts, and the resulting Ungodly Beliefs form a three-fold, negative cord that is only broken by our understanding, our faith, and the appropriation of God's freedom.

3. How Ungodly Beliefs are Related to Demonic Oppression

Our understanding of the importance of the Integrated Approach to Healing Ministry was greatly strengthened the day we supervised a ministry team that was trying to deliver a man named Clyde from a spirit of lust. The demon would not budge. The Holy Spirit revealed to the team that the demon's legal ground involved two UGBs based on this man's childhood experiences. Clyde's father had kept Playboy magazines under his bed and the boy often sneaked to look at them. Without realizing it, Clyde formed the beliefs that, "It is normal and manly for a man to have pornography in his house," and that, "Pornography is a normal part of the husband/wife relationship." When the ministry team identified and exposed these two beliefs as revealed by the Holy Spirit, Clyde repented and renounced them. The demon of lust was then easily and immediately cast out.

*God commands: "**No covenant with the enemy**." (Ex 23:31-33)*

Ungodly Beliefs provide legal permission for demons to stay. Why? Because we are in agreement with the Devil — rather than God — when we have an UGB. This connection between UGBs and the demonic has been validated in deliverance sessions many times over. It is best to minister to UGBs **before** doing deliverance since this removes "legal" ground for the demonic. Sometimes, however, the deliverance must be done first before we can begin to minister effectively. When this is the case, we still come back later — after finishing the ministry to Sins of the Fathers and Resulting Curses, Ungodly Beliefs, and Soul/Spirit Hurts — to do some "cleanup" deliverance. We want to insure that any demons that were able to enter in the interim are removed.

4. Summary

Thus we see how UGBs are clearly tied to the other three Problem/Ministry Areas. To minister only to UGBs — or to deal with the other Problem/Ministry Areas without including this one — would leave the ministry process incomplete and the ministry receiver vulnerable to losing his healing. We hope that you see the connections between the different areas and that you will not return to dealing with only one or two ministry areas such as deliverance or praying for hurts.

C. How Ungodly Beliefs are Formed

Ungodly Beliefs originate primarily from two sources: experiences of hurt and the natural or unredeemed mind of mankind. Let's look at these. We also want to explain how beliefs, once formed, are strengthened through a process we call the Belief-Expectation Cycle.

1. Ungodly Beliefs from Experiences of Hurt

The possibility of being hurt exists at every stage of life. These hurtful experiences add to the strength and intensity of our negative beliefs about ourselves and others.

a. Childhood Years

Most of our UGBs result from childhood hurts, traumas, and negative experiences. These make a very strong impression on us. For example, the child whose father misses all of his ball games, all of his birthday parties, and is never there when he needs guidance, may form such beliefs as the following:

- I am not important because my dad does not have time for me.
- Significant people in my life will not be there for me when I need them.

These UGBs will become incorporated into the very core of the hurt from which this child begins to live his life. These lies of abandonment embedded within his hurt will powerfully affect his life **until he learns how to get his hurt healed.** Even if he comes to recognize the lies, mental awareness is not enough. These UGBs will not be totally rooted out without heart-level, Jesus-level healing. This is also true for most of the UGBs we all have.

Even more serious UGBs are formed by the child who tries to intervene as his parents are fighting and is told, "Shut up, you pip-squeak. We didn't have all these problems before you came along." From this devastating experience, the child concludes:

- Things would be better if I had not been born. My life is a mistake.
- It is better to keep my mouth shut and my feelings to myself. If I express them, I will just get in trouble. I will just "stuff" my feelings.

Misshapen beliefs lead to misshapen lives.

In the same way a potter molds and shapes the clay, our hurtful experiences mold and shape our beliefs. If the foundation of our belief system laid during childhood is misshapen and distorted, the life that we built upon that foundation will also be misshapen and distorted.

b. Repetition of Hurts Reinforce the Ungodly Beliefs

The best way to learn something is through repetition!

We are particularly influenced by our families' often repeated statements, especially ones about ourselves. Some families continually reinforce with such statements as, "You will never amount to anything," or, "You are no good." In a friend's family it was, "Don't be a weenie," meaning, "Don't be a coward."

Our peers and school teachers also can play an important role repeating and reinforcing lies about ourselves. Have you ever heard your friends jeer, "Joey is a sissy, Joey is a sissy," or "Teacher's pet, teacher's pet?"

Such statements are often part of the child's daily diet. As a result, they become the bone and marrow of his UGBs system, a belief system that undermines his self-worth and ability to succeed.

c. Adult Years

In addition, negative experiences occurring during our adult years can cause further UGBs to be formed. The impact of problems in business, marriage, and church, or the experience of accidents, natural disasters, or tragedies can cause us to believe lies about ourselves, others, and God.

2. Ungodly Beliefs from the Natural Mind of Mankind

Worldly standards produce worldly beliefs.

The other large, tainted, source of UGBs comes from the **natural,** unredeemed mind of mankind. While these beliefs often seem logical and appealing, they reek with the worldly standards of man. In today's world they permeate and infuse our society. Concepts of worldly success, popularity, and the **self-made** man are held up as the ultimate goal. These Ungodly Beliefs encourage us to "be in charge," "to do our own thing," or in the words of various cult organizations, "to create our own reality." If God is mentioned, He is limited to the "God within" and considered more a "tool" than Lord. These beliefs are like poison gas — unseen but lethal. Surrounded by the beliefs that pervade our culture, we as Christians fail to detect how tightly they are woven into the fabric of our own partly sanctified minds.

It is the natural, unsanctified mind, attempting to handle and make sense out of life's hurts and traumas, that is chiefly responsible for the negative belief system that we have. As we attempt to protect ourselves from hurt, our mind wrests with the "what if?" As we allow our imagination to run wild, we worry about terrible things happening to us and convince ourselves that we are no good and shameful.

Because of our unredeemed belief system, God "insists" that our minds be renewed.[1]

---

[1] Please see Rom 12:2.

a. Family Heritage

Inherited family beliefs reflect Sins of the Fathers and Curses.

As our families pass on to us a special fishing rod, a set of old china, or the corner cupboard, our families also pass on their beliefs for better or for worse. Without realizing it, we "inherit" their beliefs about almost everything: life, politics, religion, education, and relationships. We receive their prejudices about other people, other races, other cultures, and even their pet peeve about the neighbor's dog. Our inheritance is very complete. Think of those times you've said, "I sound just like my mother (or father)." As one relay runner smoothly passes the baton to another, so parents pass on to their children their beliefs. Families are belief shapers without even realizing this truth!

b. Unintentional Teaching by Our Parents

Ungodly Beliefs can also be formed even when a parent has good motives like comforting and protecting his child. Jackie Clifton, a friend and co-laborer in ministry, shares the example of what a mother might say when her "precious" child comes home crying because the neighbor's "awful" child hit him.

The comfort sounds something like this. "There, there, don't cry. It doesn't hurt. You are just fine." Sound familiar? What UGBs might the child form if this kind of comfort were repeated? Perhaps the following:

- It must not be "okay" for something to really hurt.
- People who love me don't accept my real feelings.
- It is not all right to cry.

Most parents would not want their children to adopt such beliefs.

3. The Belief-Expectation Cycle

The dynamics of how Ungodly Beliefs are formed and continue to gain strength can be diagrammed as the Belief-Expectation Cycle as shown in the figure on the next page. In this cycle, we see the following process at work:

1. Our Ungodly Beliefs are formed out of hurtful Experiences, leading to . . .
2. Expectations arising from these Beliefs. These Expectations affect our . . .
3. Behavior, causing us also to influence the Behavior of others, leading to . . .
4. Experiences in line with these Behaviors, that confirm the Ungodly Beliefs.

This traps a person into a steadily worsening spiral of death.

The only way to stop this cycle is to intervene between the Experience and the Belief stages of this cycle. **We must choose to make God's truth our new belief.** As we receive the truth and let it begin to change our belief, we begin to expect positive events in our lives. This leads to constructive behavior and good experiences. The same cycle that was "killing" us now begins to reinforce the new GB, further strengthening it. The Law of Sowing and Reaping is now working for us rather than against us. Our trust in God's faithfulness builds, as the truth of His Word[1] works in our lives.

---

[1] Please see Jer 1:12.

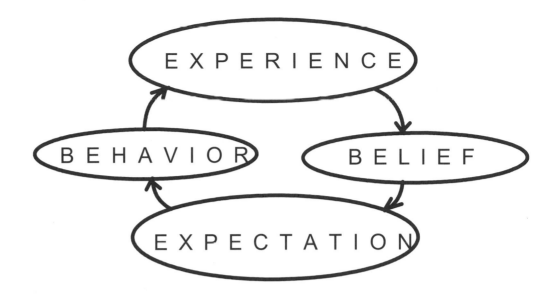

Figure 3: The Belief-Expectation Cycle

D. Typical Ungodly Beliefs

As we minister we encounter a large number of similar UGBs from person to person as we minister. We expect that this is due to the culture wide disintegration of the American family over the last fifty years and thus the common hurts we all have experienced. Reviewing our ministry notes, we have extracted those UGBs shared by the majority of people. These are tabulated on the following pages in two groups: those about ourselves and those about others.

What are your Ungodly Belief themes?

We have divided the table of "Ungodly Beliefs about Ourselves" into a number of "theme" categories. While this is not necessary, it indicates that different areas of our belief system may be either godly or ungodly (or a mixture). It is likely that you will have other themes that are significant for you (or for your ministry receiver).

The table of "Ungodly Beliefs about Others" is a distillation of many possible inclusions. There are a large number of other possible themes, and a huge number of possible UGBs. But the listed ones are a beginning as you develop an increased sensitivity to Ungodly thinking!

Men and women share complementary/ reinforcing Ungodly Beliefs.

We have also extracted some common complementary/reinforcing UGBs that men and women have about each other. These are presented in Table J on page 167. It seems that part of God's plan to conform us into the image of Christ usually includes a "helpmeet" who is "ideally" suited to draw out and expose our UGBs, as well as the other deficiencies of our flesh. This process can be particularly vicious when we have UGBs that "feed" into and confirm our spouse's UGBs. Once exposed, we have to choose whether to take these UGBs and our flesh to the Cross or defend our weaknesses and UGBs by resisting and fighting with our spouse and God. God wants us to choose to humble ourselves, and work with the Holy Spirit for further sanctification.

> **Exercise** We suggest that you use the Typical UGBs tables as a springboard for you and the Holy Spirit to identify some of your UGBs. Prayerfully consider the listed UGBs, marking those that you relate to, that seem to apply to you. If you realize other UGBs that you have, write them in the space provided or on an additional sheet of paper. Later on, we will give you an opportunity to write GBs to replace the ungodly ones. When we present the Ministry Steps, you can go through each UGB to remove it and plant the new belief.

E. Results of Ungodly Beliefs: Unnecessary Limitations

Our beliefs affect our identity, how we perceive ourselves, and how we relate to others, to the world around us, and to God. They determine how Christ-like we become and even the quality of our Christian lives. Ungodly Beliefs are like a vise-grip putting tight constraints on our lives, chokeing out the abundant life that Jesus promises.[1]

Ungodly Beliefs are like spiritual termites that quietly work behind the scenes, undermining and eating away at the faith established within us. They constantly "gobble, gobble, gobble," reducing our foundations.

*Ungodly Beliefs are **unbelief**.*

Ungodly Beliefs are, by definition, "unbelief." They hinder or block our faith in God and the truth of His promises. We hinder or shut off God's ability to bless us, since:

> Hebrews 11:6
> . . . without faith it is impossible to please God, because anyone who comes to him must believe that he exists and that he rewards those who earnestly seek him. (NIV)

God doesn't "reward" unbelief or lack of faith.[2]

By saying, "We are what we believe," we are not overstating the issue as the writer of Proverbs confirms:

Are you what you believe?

> Prov 23:7
> For as he thinketh in his heart, so [is] he . . . (KJV)

UNHAPPY RELATIONSHIPS   WANT TO HURT & DEFILE OTHERS
MOUNTAINS OF MOLEHILLS   FAITH ERODES
TAKE THINGS PERSONAL
PRISONER TO PUT-DOWNS

---

[1] Please see Jn 10:10.

[2] Please see Heb 3:15-4:11, particularly noting 3:19, 4:2, and 4:11.

Table H
Ungodly Beliefs about Ourselves

Theme: Rejection, Not Belonging

____ 1. I don't belong. I will always be on the outside (left out).

____ 2. My feelings don't count. No one cares what I feel.

____ 3. No one will love me or care about me just for myself.

____ 4. I will always be lonely. The special man (woman) in my life will not be there for me.

____ 5. The best way to avoid more hurt, rejection, etc., is to isolate myself.

____ 6. _____

Theme: Unworthiness, Guilt, Shame

____ 1. I am not worthy to receive anything from God.

____ 2. I am the problem. When something is wrong, it is my fault.

____ 3. I am a bad person. If you knew the real me, you would reject me.

____ 4. If I wear a mask, people won't find out how horrible I am and reject me.

____ 5. I have messed up so badly that I have missed God's best for me.

____ 6. _____

Theme: Doing to achieve Self-worth, Value, Recognition

____ 1. I will never get credit for what I do.

____ 2. My value is in what I do. I am valuable because I do good for others, because I am "successful."

____ 3. Even when I do or give my best, it is not good enough. I can never meet the standard.

____ 4. I can avoid conflict that would risk losing others' approval by being passive and not do anything.

____ 5. God doesn't care if I have a "secret life" as long as I appear to be good.

____ 6. _____

Theme: Control (to avoid hurt)

____ 1. I have to plan every day of my life. I have to continually plan/strategize. I can't relax.

____ 2. The perfect life is one in which no conflict is allowed, and so there is peace.

____ 3. _____

Theme: Physical

____ 1. I am unattractive. God shortchanged me.

____ 2. I am doomed to have certain physical disabilities. They are just part of what I have inherited.

____ 3. It is impossible to lose weight (or gain weight). I am just stuck.

____ 4. I am not competent/complete as a man (woman).

____ 5. _____

Theme: Personality Traits

____ 1. I will always be _____ (angry, shy, jealous, insecure, fearful, etc.).

____ 2. _____

Theme: Identity

____ 1. I should have been a boy (girl). Then my parents would have valued/loved me more, . . . etc.

____ 2. Men (women) have it better.

____ 3. I will never be known or appreciated for my real self.

____ 4. I will never really change and be as God wants me to be.

____ 5. _____

Theme: Miscellaneous

____ 1. I have wasted a lot of time and energy, some of my best years.

____ 2. Turmoil is normal for me.

____ 3. I will always have financial problems.

____ 4. _____

Table I
Ungodly Beliefs about Others

Theme: Safety/Protection

____ 1. I must be very guarded about what I say, since anything I say may be used against me.

____ 2. I have to guard and hide my emotions and feelings. I cannot give anyone the satisfaction of knowing that they have wounded or hurt me. I'll not be vulnerable, humiliated, or shamed.

____ 3. _____

____ 4. _____

Theme: Retaliation

____ 1. The correct way to respond if someone offends me is to punish them by withdrawing and/or cutting them off.

____ 2. I will make sure that _____ hurts as much as I do!

____ 3. _____

____ 4. _____

Theme: Victim

____ 1. Authority figures will humiliate me and violate me.

____ 2. Authority figures will just use and abuse me.

____ 3. My value is based totally on others' judgment/perception about me.

____ 4. I am completely under other people's authority. I have no will or choice of my own.

____ 5. I will not be known, understood, loved, or appreciated for who I am by those close to me.

____ 6. _____

____ 7. _____

Theme: Hopelessness/Helplessness

____ 1. I am out there all alone. If I get into trouble or need help, there is no one to rescue me.

____ 2. _____

____ 3. _____

Theme: Defective in Relationships

____ 1. I will never be able to fully give or receive love. I don't know what love is.

____ 2. If I let anyone get close to me, I may get my heart broken again. I can't let myself risk it.

____ 3. If I fail to please you, I won't receive your pleasure and acceptance of me. Therefore, I must strive even more (perfectionism). I must do whatever is necessary to try to please you.

____ 4. _____

____ 5. _____

Theme: God

____ 1. God loves other people more than He loves me.

____ 2. God only values me for what I do. My life is just a means to an end.

____ 3. No matter how much I try, I'll never be able to do enough or do it well enough to please God.

____ 4. God is judging me when I relax. I have to stay busy about His work or He will punish me.

____ 5. God has let me down before. He may do it again. I can't trust Him or feel secure with Him.

____ 6. _____

____ 7. _____

Table J
Husband/Wife Complementary/Reinforcing Ungodly Beliefs

Men Believe:	Women Believe:
Women control the household; men control at work.	Men don't know what to do around the house. It is easier to just do things myself.
Women are domineering and controlling.	Men are passive.
Women make too big a deal about special occasions.	Special occasions are not important to men.
Women are loose spenders. They can't be trusted with money. They don't have any restraint. They are always buying clothes and other things.	Men are tight with their money. They don't appreciate how hard it is to keep the house supplied with food, clothes, etc.
Women just want to talk about their feelings all of the time.	Men don't want an intimate, close relationship, in which a woman can share her innermost self.
Women just aren't interested in making love.	The only thing men are interested in is sex.
Women make having children too important. They get consumed with the children's lives.	Men see children as a bother. They would rather not have them.
My wife and children have ganged up against me. I can't even talk to my children.	My husband ignores me and our children. He just doesn't want to be close to us.
Women are just naturally more spiritual than men.	Men are not concerned about the spiritual life of their family.
My wife is lazy and doesn't keep the house in order.	My husband just finds fault with my housekeeping and doesn't see all that I do.

We use our UGBs to justify our fleshly (old man) behavior (sin), rather than allowing the Holy Spirit to sanctify us.

Are you justifying your flesh with Ungodly Beliefs?

Romans 6:6-7, 12
[6]For we know that our old self was crucified with him so that the body of sin might be done away with, that we should no longer be slaves to sin—[7]because anyone who has died has been freed from sin.

[12]Therefore do not let sin reign in your mortal body so that you obey its evil desires. (NIV)

Are your Ungodly Beliefs undermining your relationship with God?

Even our beliefs about God Himself have the power to make our Christian life a fulfilling, growing experience or one that is stagnant, frustrating, and unfulfilling. How could we have joy if we believed the following:

- No matter how hard I try, it will not be enough to please God.
- God is waiting for me to make a mistake.
- God cares for others more than He cares for me.

These beliefs undermine the very basis of any meaningful relationship with God.

Do you have portions of your identity based on Ungodly Beliefs?

In extreme cases, UGBs can result in a person having false or counterfeit identity. This occurs when he believes so many lies about himself that his God-given identity is obscured or covered over. Demonic entities work to reinforce the lies that keep the true identity covered.[1]

Ungodly Beliefs are blind spots.

Crippling Ungodly Beliefs, whether based on the natural mind or on experiences of hurt, are the enemy of our faith. Most of us are blind to them because they are buried deep within (blocked out) hurts. Also, they seem so natural since we have lived with them for so long. This is an area where we can seldom help ourselves, but we can greatly benefit by receiving ministry from others, particularly if they are trained to recognize and discern UGBs.

Examples of the Effects of Ungodly Beliefs

Two examples in the areas of "Significance and Security" and "Negative Expectation" will show how destructive UGBs can be.

a.　Significance and Security

Our real significance and security is in God. If we only verbally agree with this, and do not believe it in our heart, we have an UGB. Concerning this, the scripture says:

> Eph 1:6
> . . . wherein he hath made us accepted in the beloved. (KJV)

> Heb 13:5
> . . . for he hath said, I will never leave thee, nor forsake thee. (KJV)

Rather than believing God, we believe that we will be disliked, rejected, or abused. Therefore, we must strive to find acceptance.

We search for significance in many places other than God: in money, fame, sexual exploits, etc. Although His Word tells us that we are created in His image[2] for fellowship[3] and that He has a plan and a purpose[4] that will give us fulfillment, we don't believe it.

Striving and perfectionism are clear indicators.

As ministers, when we see striving and little rest in a person's life, we have an important clue that UGBs are in operation in the area of significance and security.

b.　Negative Expectations

If we are full of negative expectations and fear about what is going to happen to us, we are not believing nor trusting what God is saying in His Word:

---

[1]　Demonic identity personalities are not the same as multiple or fragmented personalities that have their origin from within the God-given identity.

[2]　Please see Gen 1:26, Rom 8:29, and 2 Cor 3:18.

[3]　Please see Gen 3:8 and 1 Jn 1:3.

[4]　Please see Eph 1:11, 2:10, and 2 Tim 1:9.

1 Jn 4:4

. . . and have overcome them (spirits of antichrist): because greater is he that is in you, than he that is in the world. (KJV)

Rom 8:37

Nay, in all these things we are more than conquerors through him that loved us. (KJV)

Jn 10:10

. . . I am come that they might have life, and that they might have [it] more abundantly. (KJV)

2 Pet 1:3-4

3 According as his divine power hath given unto us all things that [pertain] unto life and godliness, through the knowledge of him that hath called us to glory and virtue:
4 Whereby are given unto us exceeding great and precious promises: that by these ye might be partakers of the divine nature, having escaped the corruption that is in the world through lust. (KJV)

Mistrust and fears show us the Ungodly Beliefs.

Christians who expect lack, failure, and mistreatment by others or who worry about and fear every new experience are not walking in God's provision or promises. Second Peter 1:3 clearly states that:

2 Pet 1:3

His divine power has granted to us everything pertaining to life and godliness (when we meet the condition) through the true knowledge of Him . . . (NAS)

When we as ministers see a person living out of negative expectations, ministry for UGBs of fear is clearly indicated.

F. Sandy's Story: Sandy's "Evil Core" Stronghold

We want to share with you the events that took place as the Holy Spirit exposed the "Evil Core" stronghold (see Figure 4 next page). Two terribly vicious Ungodly Beliefs were key foundations holding this stronghold in place. Sandy's initial expression of these UGBs was:

No matter how much ministry I receive, no matter how much prayer goes up for me, no matter how many people pray, I am "evil" beyond God's ability to restore me. I am so bad that even God can't help me.

Can you recognize the two lies? Number one is, "I am inherently evil to the core." Number two is, "God can't help me." In her deception, Sandy was nullifying the power of the Cross![1]

Even with her desire and expectation of healing, Sandy was again leading the double life. On the one hand, she was "hoping" for freedom and healing. On the other hand, way down deep inside where she really lived, she believed her "case" was "hopeless." She thought that we were wasting our time.

---

[1]   Please see 1 Cor 1:17-18.

Once we recognized the "Evil Core" stronghold, we realized that it must be rooted out before we could make significant progress in Sandy's healing. (Of course, we did not yet know about the Five Tower Stronghold,[1] but the Holy Spirit was preparing the way.)

The series of ministry steps we went through is not necessarily the only sequence that would have brought freedom. It is, however, the sequence that we used as the Holy Spirit guided us. Because it is atypical, it is not a model for others to use. The Holy Spirit will likely have an entirely different approach for each ministry receiver oppressed by an "Evil Core" stronghold. The ministry pattern we used, however, is a good example of the need for an Integrated Approach to Healing Ministry.

SOFCs

We started by leading Sandy through confession and forgiveness of her ancestors for their involvement in the occult, witchcraft, deception, sexual sin, hopelessness, and gossip. We covered everything that might give "legal ground" to the "Evil Core." Then we had Sandy declare:

> I choose to be separated from the sins and curses of my ancestors. Your Word, Lord, says I have been brought out of darkness into Your kingdom of light. I receive that fully today. For every part of me not yet in the kingdom of light, I ask Your forgiveness, and I receive Your forgiveness.

Sandy then forgave, individually, several people who had spoken curses over her. She said, "I forgive each one who contributed to my believing that I am basically evil."

She then prayed for freedom.

> Father, I ask you to free me from deception. Let your truth flood every aspect of my being. Free me from the power these lies have had over my life and over my very identity. Free me from falling victim to another's control. Lord, set me free from my double life and all it involves: confusion, fear, and false responsibility. I renounce all demons promoting these sins and deception.

UGBs

Next came the UGBs related to the "Evil Core." Sandy confessed the sins of her ancestors and her own sins. These had set into motion the curses (coming down the family line) that promoted her UGBs. Gathering courage and determination, Sandy asked forgiveness and then spoke boldly through her tears, "I renounce the lies that:

1. I am basically evil, rotten at the core.
2. God, You can't save me out of this mess. I am so evil that Your Cross can't save me. This is too big for You and I will never be free."

Head still bowed, she forgave herself for the pride and arrogance associated with her former lies.

---

[1] We discuss this part of Sandy's Story in Chapter XII, "Demonic Strongholds."

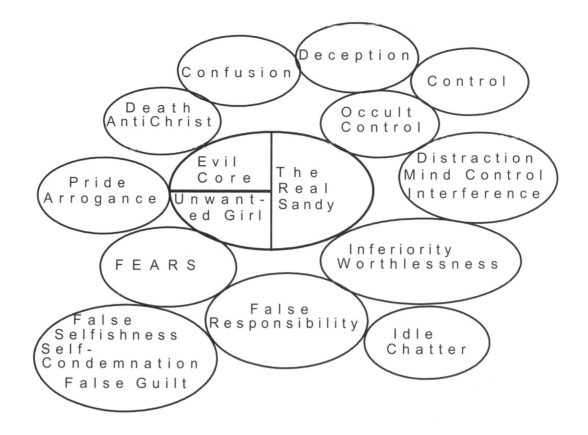

Figure 4: Sandy's "Evil Core" Stronghold

We continued to remove legal ground she had given to the stronghold. We had her break all "word curses" and "self-curses." These were negative words others had spoken to her or about her. She had agreed with them and taken the negative words and internalized them, repeating them to herself. We could see the life beginning to come back into her. The horrible oppression was beginning to lift. For the first time, she spoke as a person who truly had hope.

> I break all agreements with anyone who ever told me that I am bad. I break my agreement with myself that I am bad and will never get free.

DO

We had Sandy begin to renounce the demons promoting the lies in the "Evil Core." She renounced Deception, Unbelief, Hopelessness, Confusion, and others as well. We then began to cast out different demonic groupings that made up Sandy's entire "Evil Core" stronghold. The above diagram shows how we visualized this stronghold as the Holy Spirit revealed it to us and how the various groups "held on" to and reinforced each other.

The Holy Spirit had us start with the group Occult Control, which included Control. After casting them out, we moved on to Deception.

"I've not known who I was," Sandy said, looking up sadly. "I've been too busy being what I thought others wanted me to be!"

After that, Sandy reported that a thought went through her awareness. "Time to wrap this up. This is enough ministry!" We all chuckled, knowing the source of the thought, and continued on.

Next, we proceeded to cast out demons of Distraction, Mind Control, and Interference.

At that point the Holy Spirit gave Sandy an Inner Vision.[1] "I see a column of blackness that is shooting out of me!" she exclaimed. We realized that she was seeing the demons leaving. Rejoicing over the confirmation of our progress, we kept up the attack.

We commanded Fear to leave, especially the fear of "never being free of evil" and the fear of "always being bad." Then, we commanded a whole legion of fears to go. Sandy continued to see the demons leave. "I knew they were real," she said, almost awed, "but I had no idea I had so many."

Energized, she was "on a roll." All together, we came against many of the accusing spirits; Self-Condemnation, False Guilt, and even a spirit that accused her of being Selfish, when in actuality, she wasn't.

We knew that we were working our way in toward the center and getting closer to the "big guns." Death and Antichrist were sent to the same place as the previous demons.

As we were proceeding to the next grouping, Sandy suddenly saw the strategy of the Mental Tormenting demons. She saw that they would distract her and then condemn her for being distracted.[2] "I see it," she said jubilantly. "I see their strategy, and I'm not going to let them do that to me anymore!"

As the Holy Spirit led, we asked Sandy to forgive the three spiritual authority figures (the evangelist and the two pastors) who had hypnotically controlled her, abused her, promoted error, and then abandoned her. For the first time, drops of sweat lined her forehead. Slowly, painfully, she forgave each one. Then she broke all soul ties[3] with each of them.

Suddenly, she saw another Inner Vision. She saw three crowns fall off the three men and onto the ground. She knew what each crown represented. With no further prompting, she broke the power of all sins and curses of Idolatry of Authority, of Servitude, and of Temple Prostitution. She saw a symbolic representation of the dethroning of powers that had ruled her life.

A voice said to her, "You don't have to do that!"

"Oh, yes I do!" she spoke back. Then we cast out the demons behind the crowns.

Pride, Arrogance, Perfection (be perfect) were next. She gave and asked forgiveness and then broke the curse of "having to be perfect."

She heard the Holy Spirit say, "How much better it is to be free than 'good!'"

---

[1]   This is one of the ways God "speaks" (Chapter IV, "Hearing God's Voice").

[2]   We call this type of demonic tactic a "lose lose" or "double binding" strategy. They do their best to always keep us on the losing, failing, guilty side.

[3]   We discuss Soul Ties in Chapter XI.

We moved on to Inferiority and Worthlessness (I have to try harder to overcome my inadequacies.)

We could tell that the inner-most groupings of demons were getting worried. It was clear that they had thought they were more than adequately surrounded and protected by outer layers of demons plus Sandy's agreements with their lies. They had been confident that we would never get anywhere close to them. But we were burrowing our way in, continually having Sandy cycle through forgiveness, renouncing, casting out, etc., as needed. We would do what the Holy Spirit directed us to do to remove the next layer of obstacles and then press in further.

The intensity was building. Finally, we were closing in on the roots of this stronghold. We got rid of Idle Chatter and Words and then attacked the center.

"Out, 'Core of Evil,' and all remaining demons! Out in the Name of Jesus!" The manifestations rose to a peak. Now all that was left was Bad Girl: Unacceptable, Unwanted, Bad Girl.

"No mercy, you foul thing, that has tormented the real Sandy all of her life. Get out now, Unwanted, Unacceptable, Bad Girl." Things quieted down. Peace filled the room. Unwanted Bad Girl, the demon that had lied to Sandy since she was five or six years old, was gone. "Thank You Lord!"

It's Over
The "Evil Core" stronghold had been made up of many demonic forces that intertwined with, and lived next to, the real, God-given, personality of Sandy. Once the "Evil Core" was exposed and cast out, the real Sandy was left.

After the demolishing of the "Evil Core" stronghold, Sandy was amazed that her basic, core feeling about herself changed almost immediately. She stopped "feeling bad" about herself and began to feel "clean" on the inside and "loved by God." Even more amazing, the good feelings continued day after day. They did not go away!

If she herself had not experienced the change from one day to the next, she would not have believed that "just" casting out a "few" demons could make such a difference. Of course, it was not "just" casting out the demons that brought the freedom. Healing came from applying the Integrated Approach to Healing Ministry to her life: breaking the Sins of her Fathers and Resulting Curses; breaking soul ties; renewing her mind regarding her value and identity; healing her hurts, and then casting out the demonic forces. Major freedom was gained by the eviction of the demons that had deceived her into believing the lie that, "I am uniquely bad!"

Aftermath
Several weeks later, Sandy reported to us,

> The further I get away from it (the "Evil Core" stronghold) and the more I see how totally deceived and defiled I was, the more evil it looks. The "Evil Core" seems real close to the truth; therefore, it's hard to separate out the real evil from the flesh (evil).

Sandy's victory was not without its counterattacks. Demons were still able to affect her dreams. She would wake up from an occult dream feeling defiled and ugly. "This is who you really are!" Evil Core type demons were shouting lies at her. "It is just a matter of time. You will fall and we will get in." Their intent was to make Sandy feel violated, ashamed, and angry so she would give up and admit defeat. They wanted to convince her that it was hopeless and they had been right all along: she was "evil, evil to the core."

"I rejected Deception," she said. "I don't want to go back. I won't go back!"

She struggled from day to day. She knew how to identify with "Evil" or "Bad," but who was she really? What was "normal?" One day, God said to her in her quiet time, "I am teaching you what 'normal' is."

Sandy's "walking it out" took time. The bouts with occult dreams full of lies and terrors continued. We continued, too! We continued to pray for God to show us the remaining open doors. Renewed, we would work through the SOFCs, the UGBs, and pray for SSHs associated with each area of wounding. Then we would do the deliverance with the relevant demons. Slowly the intensity and frequency of the attacks decreased.

As you might expect, Sandy had several periods of grieving. She still felt stupid and deceived about having been drawn into the adulterous affair with her pastor. "The loss, the number of prime years wasted! I can never get them back." The extent of the feeling of loss was often overwhelming.

We cautioned her. "Don't let your guard down even during legitimate grieving periods. This, too, shall pass."

"Evil Core" was defeated. Although it tried, it has never regained a toehold. True victory was hers.

G. Higher Level of Truth than the Facts

In order for us to be transformed into the image of God, our thinking has to be changed so it lines up with God's **Truth** and not the **facts** of our experience. Here we are truly challenged.

First, there are the facts. Facts are what actually happened. For example:

- The accident happened.
- The person had a disease.
- The business closed.
- The person confessed sin.

Facts are true, based on our experience in the here and now.

But:

> There is a higher level of truth than the facts. And that is God's Truth. The real Truth is what He says about the situation.

Are you looking with natural eyes or with spiritual eyes?

God's truth is not seen by the natural man, who is looking at the facts, but by the spiritual man, who knows God's transforming power. It is seen and embraced through faith.

1 Cor 2:14-15
[14]But a natural man does not accept the things of the Spirit of God, for they are foolishness to him and he cannot understand them, because they are spiritually appraised.
[15]But he who is spiritual appraises all things, yet he himself is appraised by no man. (NAS)

But we are not just natural men. We are men and women whose spirits are alive and who have been born again. As a result, we can discern (appraise) the spiritual truth concerning what God says about a fact or situation. By the power of His Spirit working within us, we can embrace His Truth.

The following examples illustrate the difference between believing factual truth and believing God's truth.

1. Apparent Fact:	I am just a **nobody**, going nowhere.
God's Truth:	**God chose me** before the foundation of the world. His plans for me are good.
2. Apparent Fact:	The leadership of this church **can't be trusted**.
God's Truth:	God says **I am building** my Church.
3. Apparent Fact:	So much is changing; **I can't count on** anything.
God's Truth:	God says **I am the same** yesterday, today and forever. Put your trust in Me.
4. Apparent Fact:	I am going through **many trials** and difficulties.
God's Truth:	God will bring me through the trials and **mature me** in the process.

Can you hear the difference between believing the "reality" of our circumstances or believing and confessing God's **eternal Truth**? We don't negate the level of fact, but we can say, "God, there's something more, more than just the facts that my natural eyes are seeing and my natural circumstances are causing to happen. There's something more, and that's **Your Truth**."

Prayer: Lord, help me to be that spiritual man/woman who can discern and embrace Your **Truth**.

H. Scriptural Basis: Beliefs and Their Dynamics

As you may have noticed, we like to have a scriptural basis for everything we teach. Yet, since the Bible was not written to cover every detail of life, sometimes we have to infer from scriptural principles what the Logos has to say about a particular topic. We also depend on the Holy Spirit to teach us, as He "brings all things to our remembrance"[1] (KJV).

In the following pages, we have four tables of scripture relevant to Ungodly Beliefs. Take a moment and look at Table K, L, M, N on pages 177, 181, 185, and 187the main themes in each table. By focusing on these scriptures in some detail, we can understand beliefs and their dynamics and the resulting consequences in our lives.

1. Importance of What We Believe for Salvation

The first group of verses in Table K (Acts 16:31 and Rom 10:9-10) apply the Law of Sowing and Reaping[2] to believing, i.e., beliefs.

We include these verses to remind us of the importance of our belief system and how our beliefs can make the difference between heaven and hell. In Acts 16:31 we are promised, "**Believe** on the Lord Jesus Christ, and thou shalt be saved." Romans 10:9-10 contains the admonitions, "Confess with your mouth," and, "**Believe** in your heart." This passage lets us know **where** we have to believe. We have to believe down in the deep, central, core portion of ourselves — down in our heart. This is why we as Christians are called "**Believers.**" Our belief system was touched by the Holy Spirit, and we modified our beliefs to include the truth that God wanted to save us and that He had provided a **way** to save us.

If we plant **belief** seeds **contrary** to God's Word in our heart,[3] we sooner or later reap a harvest of like **contrary** nature.[4] As just discussed with the Belief-Expectation Cycle, this experience of "reaping" what we were already **expecting** further reinforces the UGBs, leading us into greater distress and frustration.

2. Importance of What We Believe in Shaping Situation

*Do we **create** our own reality?*

The next group of verses in Table K relate the importance of what we believe to the shaping of situations and events surrounding us. This concept is frequently taught by various occult, psychic, and secret societies. It is summed up in the phrase, "Creating your own reality." These people work hard at shaping/creating

---

[1] Please see Jn 14:26. Also, please refer back to Chapter IV, "Hearing God's Voice." We discern and verify that which comes from the spirit realm to ensure that we are indeed listening to the Holy Spirit and not to another spirit. Please see First Jn 4:1-6 for John's testing of the spirits. Paul writes about "another" spirit in Gal 1:8 and 2 Cor 11:13-15. Also, what we hear **must** agree with the Logos.

[2] Please see Chapter III, "God's Law and the Christian Life."

[3] Please see Mat 13:19.

[4] Please see Mat 15:18-20.

Table K
Scriptures Concerning Ungodly Beliefs (Set 1)

Importance of What We Believe for Salvation

Acts 16:31	**Believe** on the Lord Jesus Christ, and **thou shalt be saved**, and thy house. (KJV)
Rom 10:9-10	...if you **confess** with your mouth, "Jesus is Lord," and **believe in your heart** that God raised him from the dead, you will be saved. For **it is with your heart that you believe** and are justified, and it is with your mouth that you confess and are saved. (NIV)

Importance of What We Believe in Shaping Situations

Mk 11:22-24	And Jesus replied saying to them, Have faith in God (constantly). Truly, I tell you, whoever **says** to this mountain, Be lifted up and thrown into the sea! and **does not doubt at all in his heart**, but **believes that what he says will take place**, **it will be done for him**. For this reason I am telling you, whatever **you ask** for in prayer, **believe—trust** and **be confident**—that **it is granted to you,** and **you will [get it]**. (AMP)
Prov 23:7	For as he **thinks in his heart**, so is he. (AMP)
Gal 6:7-9	Do not be deceived: God cannot be mocked. **A man reaps what he sows**. The one who **sows** to please his sinful nature, from that nature will **reap** destruction; the one who **sows** to please the Spirit, from the Spirit will **reap** eternal life. Let us not become weary in doing good, for **at the proper time** we will **reap a harvest if** we do not give up. (NIV)
Heb 12:14-15	Make every effort to live in peace with all men and to be holy; without holiness no one will see the Lord. See to it that no one misses the grace of God and that no **bitter root** grows up to cause trouble and **defile many**. (NIV)
Mat 7:1-2	Do not judge, or you too will be judged. For in the same way you judge others, you will be judged, and with the measure you use, it will be measured to you. (NIV)
Luke 6:37-38	Judge not, and ye shall not be judged: condemn not, and ye shall not be condemned: forgive, and ye shall be forgiven: Give, and it shall be given unto you; good measure, pressed down, and shaken together, and running over, shall men give into your bosom. For with the same measure that ye mete withal it shall be measured to you again. (KJV)

their own reality, usually for selfish reasons. Some people involved probably think their motivations are not selfish, but they deceive themselves. Unless a person is born again, their motives are almost always self-centered. Believers, on the other hand, should be shaping situations and their responses to them under the direction of the Holy Spirit. That is the only way to plant godly seed and reap godly harvests.

Sowing and Reaping

When discussing the Laws of God, we often refer to Mark 11:22-24. Please read it as expressed in the Amplified version of the Bible in Table K on page 177. This important passage reveals the universality of the principle of sowing and reaping. As we plant "thought" seeds (in our heart), they do (eventually) affect our reality.

The principle of sowing and reaping is universal.

Verse 23 contains the general principle that if we **believe** in our heart — down in the soil of our heart where (thought) seeds are planted — and if we **don't doubt**, we shall **have** what we **say**. We usually read this verse from the prayer point of view since that is how Jesus applies the general principle of sowing and reaping. The power behind the Law of Sowing and Reaping, however, is at work all of the time and not just when we are praying. Whatever we plant with faith, expectancy, and absolute confidence that we shall have it, **we will have it**. Good or bad, **we will have it**.

When to Plant

Planting can go on continually.

It is a fact that we can plant a seed at any time of the year. In certain seasons there is a greater chance that the seed will sprout and come to harvest, but we **can** plant all year round: winter, spring, etc. Depending on where we live in the world, the seed may come up at any time of year or it may not come up at all. Likewise, we can plant thought seeds, good or bad, at any time.

Will there be a Harvest?

Whether or not we receive a harvest, and its magnitude, depends on many factors. One important factor is whether we "think" the thought repeatedly. Continued sowing is more likely to produce a harvest.

Another factor is faith. When prayer thoughts (whether out of faith or fear) go down into our heart and are received as the **truth**, the planted seed has a greater likelihood of sooner or later producing a harvest.

Childhood beliefs shape our reality.

Core Beliefs

The most "absolute" type of beliefs are those we grew up with, received, and made our own without even thinking about them. Since they were planted in the very core of our being, we don't even question whether they are true. We know that we know them without knowing that we know them. They are as **sure** as the truth that "The sun is going to come up in the morning" and "The sky is blue." These deeply planted belief/thought seeds produce a continuous harvest as the same thoughts go through our mind and into our hearts again and again. Usually we don't even notice them because they are such "givens." Planted again and again, they produce harvest after harvest, confirming and verifying the core belief(s).

Of course, the core beliefs that are lies produce a harvest that is ungodly. These can trap us into devastating Belief-Expectation Cycles.

Shaping Our Reality

As each harvest comes to maturity, the seeds are replanted in our heart. The expectations associated with the harvest also come to pass, further validating the belief. **We have shaped our reality**. God's universe has responded to our seed planting and produced a harvest according to our expectations, good or bad.

Since we all have a mixture of Godly and Ungodly Beliefs, we experience a mixture of good and bad happenings.

Demonic influences may also be at work with ungodly expectations by amplifying, accelerating, or stirring up the response. They attempt to make the situations appear worse than they might otherwise.

Believe, say, expect, receive!

To summarize: What we **believe** (in our heart), **say** (think), **expect** (to have), we will **receive**. God's Word promises this. As a result, our beliefs get reinforced by our experience, what we experience reinforces our beliefs, and around we go. "See the facts, here they are. I was rejected again. It proves that my belief, my expectation that I will be rejected, is valid." Our beliefs cause our expectations, the expectations shape our reality, and our reality influences our beliefs. Eventually, we find ourselves on a downward spiral that seems out of control.

Breaking Free of the "Bad" Harvest

It takes time to change a direction.

To break out of the downward spiral takes some effort. God has provided a way if we will appropriate it and allow the Law of the Time to Harvest[1] to work. It takes time to change the momentum of our experiences.

Becoming What We Believe

Continuing with the scriptures in Table K on page 177, Proverbs 23:7 is essentially another way to state the Law of Sowing and Reaping. We become what we believe we are. **If we don't like who we are, we need to change what we believe about ourselves.**

In Galatians 6:7-9, God states that whatever we sow — whether we sow to the flesh or we sow to the spirit — the Law of Sowing and Reaping will bring forth a harvest. Universal in nature, this law applies in all realms and to all people. This law operates no matter who plants the seed — a saved or an unsaved person. Sowing "thought" seeds (beliefs) produces a harvest in the soulish realm and/or possibly in the spiritual realm. Then, as others respond to the spiritual pressure of our expectations, they tend to "do" in the physical realm what it takes to conform to our expectations.

While we are on the subject of sowing and reaping, please note that the beatitudes reflect this same principle, particularly Matthew 5:7. "Blessed [are] the merciful: for they shall obtain mercy" (KJV).

Planting "Bitterness" Seeds

The God of peace will soon crush Satan under your feet. Rom16:20 (NIV)

Hebrews 12:14-15 refers to a root of bitterness. The context of the passage is "living at peace with all men." If we are not living at peace, then we are likely to be planting seeds of unforgiveness, anger, resentment, envy, and bitterness. Bitterness is a particularly "hardy" plant that usually underlies criticism, gossip, murmuring, complaining, etc. God is strongly admonishing us not to plant seeds of bitterness because the root will follow and the harvest will affect (defile) many others. The Law of Sowing and Reaping is at work again. God says to follow peace and not bitterness.

---

[1]   Please see more about this Law in Chapter III, "God's Law and the Christian Life."

Size of the Harvest

We reap in proportion to our planting.

Look next at Matthew 7:1-2. This passage belongs in the section on "Hazard of Believing Lies," but it is also an expression of the Law of Sowing and Reaping. It confirms that the amount of seed reaped relative to the number planted will be in proportion. If we plant with teaspoons, we will reap in proportion to teaspoons. If we plant with bushel baskets, our harvest will be relative to bushels. So it is with planting expectations, i.e., UGBs. The stronger, more intense our belief and the more we "think" it and plant it in our hearts, the larger the harvest.

Judging and Condemning

Luke 6:37, a companion verse to Matthew 7:1-2, says, "Judge not and you shall not be judged." The verse continues, "Condemn not and you shall not be condemned." Can you recognize the sowing and reaping process in these verses? If we don't plant seeds of condemnation, then we won't reap a harvest of condemnation. Next the verse reads, "Forgive and you shall be forgiven." This is the type of harvest we want to receive. This truth provides a powerful impetus for us to forgive other people — so that we will be forgiven.

Giving and Multiplying

Everyone who wants to be rich likes Luke 6:38, "Give and it shall be given unto you." This is God's Word. It says if we plant seeds by giving, "it" shall be given unto us. We can't avoid it. When applied in a godly way, this principle has very positive results. If, however, we apply it negatively, giving to others seeds of bitterness or hatred or anger or violence or rage or abuse, watch out! If we give away these types of "seed," then that's what we can expect in return. The amount will be "full measure, pressed down, shaken together, running over." But we don't want to reap this kind of harvest, do we?

3. Balancing Word: For the Spiritual Man

Judge righteous judgments.

If we only studied the verses in Table K, we probably would try to "stop thinking" altogether out of fear of "wrong thinking." The verses in Table L on the next page provide a balance to the previous group, particularly to Matthew 7:1 (judge not). It is possible to become so "non-judging" that other problems arise. God wants us to judge with "righteous" judgment[1] particularly when we are in a place of responsibility and authority. He wants us to be spiritually sensitive and discerning, aware of what's going on. As ministers, it is essential that we learn to judge by the Holy Spirit, so that we can discern both the good and evil in the people to whom we are ministering.[2]

Spiritual Discerning

Make spiritual judgments.

Look at First Corinthians 2:14-15. We see apostle Paul clearly stating, "The spiritual man makes judgments (discernments) about all things." God does want us to know what's going on around us. We are not, however, to take that understanding and comprehension and become judge and jury by handing out "guilty" verdicts, separating ourselves from other people, and being critical.

---

[1] Please see Jn 7:24.
[2] Please see Mal 3:18, Heb 5:14.

Table L
Scriptures Concerning Ungodly Beliefs (Set 2)

Balancing Word: For the Spiritual Man

1 Cor 2:14-15	The man without the Spirit does not accept the things that come from the Spirit of God, for they are foolishness to him, and he cannot understand them, because they are **spiritually discerned**. The **spiritual man** makes **judgments (appraises, discerns) about all things**, but he himself is not subject to any man's judgment: (NIV)
Jn 7:24	Stop judging by mere appearances, and make a right judgment. (NIV)
Jn 8:15-16	(reinforces Jn 7:24)
Heb 5:14	But solid food is for full-grown men (i.e., the mature Christian), for those whose **senses and mental faculties** (i.e., spiritual gifts) **are trained by practice to discriminate** and **distinguish** between **what is** morally **good** and **noble** and **what is evil** and **contrary** either to divine or human law (i.e., UGBs, things that are contrary to God's way). (AMP)
1 Thes 5:21	**Test everything. Hold on to the good.** (NIV)

God's Plan and Purpose for Our Beliefs

Rom 12:2	Do not be conformed to this world—this age, fashioned after and adapted to its external, superficial customs. But be transformed (changed) by the [entire] **renewal of your mind**—by its **new ideals** and its **new attitude**—so that you may **prove [for yourselves]** what is the good and acceptable and perfect will of God, even the thing which is good and acceptable and perfect [in His sight for you]. (AMP)
Eph 4:22-23	that, in reference to your former manner of life, you **lay aside the old self**, which is being corrupted in accordance with the lusts of deceit, and that you be **renewed in the spirit of your minds,** (NAS)
1 Pet 4:1	... **arm yourselves** likewise with the **same mind: (attitude)** ... (KJV)
Col 3:9-10	... seeing that ye have **put off the old man** with his deeds; And have **put on the new [man]**, which is **renewed in knowledge after the image** of him that created him: (KJV)
2 Cor 10:3-5	For though we walk in the flesh, we do not war after the flesh: (For the weapons of our warfare [are] not carnal, but mighty through God to the **pulling down of strongholds**;) **Casting down imaginations**, and **every high thing** that **exalteth itself against the knowledge of God**, and **bringing into captivity every thought** to the obedience of Christ; (KJV)

Righteous Judgment

John 7:24 instructs us how to judge, not by appearance but by righteous judgment. We do this by the Spirit. We should not go on appearance since Christ did not (and still doesn't).

> Isa 11:3 "And he will delight in the fear of the LORD. He will not judge by what he sees with his eyes, or decide by what he hears with his ears;" (NIV)

Appearance has to do with facts, with the situation, and how things seem to be. God wants us not to depend on the facts, the situation, or appearance, but to go by the truth, the Word of God. When we see somebody in sin, we are to know and understand what is going on, but not judge (condemn) the person. Rather, we are to help them get free.[1]

Practice

Hebrews 5:14 is a great verse. This passage not only encourages us to mature but offers a tremendous truth about maturing. The author of Hebrews is writing to people who are basically still babies. The *Amplified Version of the Bible* makes this very clear.

Develop spiritual gifts by training and practice.

Note the phrase, "**trained by practice**." The NIV has "**by constant use have trained** themselves." The KJV reads "**by reason of use have their senses exercised** to discern both good and evil." This verse contradicts the common attitude regarding spiritual gifts that we either have them or we don't, that we either use them or we don't.

We believe a better attitude is that we need to practice our spiritual gifts. The Word makes this clear, and experience verifies it. We need to exercise, we need to learn how to use the gifts that God has deposited within us. As we practice, as we mature, we become better able to discern between good and evil. This enables us to "judge" righteous judgments as a part of "discerning."

Prove (Test) All Things

The final verse in this group from Table L states, "Prove all things; hold fast that which is good" (KJV). If we don't discern, we can't prove, we can't judge, we can't hold on to the "good." We need to understand the balance to "judge not."

4. God's Plan and Purpose for Our Beliefs

The fourth group of verses in Table L on page 181 shows God's plan and heart for our beliefs. While our spirits were redeemed when we were born again, the redemption of our soul is "in process."[2] Renewing of the mind is a key element of the sanctification process. Our responsibility is to give ourselves to the process, cooperating with God rather than resisting Him.

---

[1] Please see Gal 6:1.

[2] The redemption of our body is yet to occur. Please see Rom 8:23.

Renewing the Mind

You can know the good and acceptable and perfect will of God.

Romans 12:2 is a key verse illuminating the sanctification process. In verse 12:1, Paul has just finished writing about presenting our bodies as a "living sacrifice" and that it's only reasonable for us to do so. Then he pens, "Do not be conformed to this world, . . . But be transformed (changed) by the [entire] renewal of your mind." Then the translators for the *Amplified Bible* qualify what this phrase means by adding "by its new ideals and new attitudes." Then comes the purpose statement, the reason for the renewing of our minds "so that you may prove [for yourselves] what is the good and acceptable and perfect will of God, even the thing which is good and acceptable and perfect [in His sight for you]."

Knowing God's Perfect Will

How many of us would like to know the perfect will of God in our lives? Of course, we all want this. In every situation, we would like to know God's good, acceptable and perfect will in our lives. How do we obtain this? The answer is this: We must have our minds renewed. As our minds become renewed, we think more like God, we become aware of how He looks at things, and we begin to look at things as He does instead of out of our own selfish, self-centered ways. We learn to know what is on His heart, how He wants us to pray, where He wants us to go, what He wants us to do. And so, we can begin to move in His good, acceptable, and perfect Will.

Healing brings trust and confidence.

As we receive His healing, we are not so fearful about what He might be wanting us to do. We grow in trust and confidence, working toward complete and absolute confidence in God. This enables us to hear His voice and to know His Will better and better and better. Thus, there is a one to one correspondence between having our minds renewed (which means getting rid of our UGBs and replacing them with GBs) and being able to know the good and acceptable and perfect Will of God.

We expect that most of us want our minds renewed so we can know God's good and acceptable and perfect Will. Then we can choose His perfect Will.

Renewing the Spirit of Your Minds

Paul, in Ephesians 4:23, again stresses the same theme. Here the phrase is, "Be renewed in the **spirit** of your **minds**." Isn't this an interesting phrase? "The spirit of your minds." We have been taught to think of the mind as being in the soul region, but here the spirit of our mind is to be transformed, to be renewed.[1]

In First Peter 4:1, Peter writes, "Arm yourselves likewise with the same **mind**," or we could say "with the attitude of Christ." As our mind is renewed, it should function more and more like the mind of Christ.

Colossians 3:10 is another wonderful verse expressing being "renewed in **knowledge** after the **image of Him**." Knowledge has to do with the mind (and spirit). This passage could be paraphrased: "Be renewed in (your) mind with knowing Him as He is."

---

[1] We say more about this topic in Appendix B, "Why Named Soul/Spirit Hurts."

Contrasts New Age with Christianity

This Colossians passage shows us the difference between humanism or New Age philosophy and Christianity. New Agers promote self-improvement, better self-image, etc., all of which is **self-centered**. Christianity, on the other hand, offers a "**Christ-centered**" life. It offers a "new Self" that is being conformed to the image of Christ, taking on **His** nature, character, attitudes, beliefs, likeness, and mind. It doesn't try to "improve" the "old Self."

Taking Thoughts Captive

*When the battle is won in the mind, **the battle is won.***

The well-known passage in Second Corinthians 10:3-5 instructs us to pull down strongholds, cast down **imaginations**, and use our spiritual weapons to come against "Every high thing that exalteth itself against the **knowledge** of God, and (to) bring into captivity every **thought** . . ." The battleground is in the mind. We need to apply God's weapons against everything that would try to keep our thought patterns and habits in the old way. Strongholds of fear, worry, bitterness, anger, shame, control, etc., need to come down and be replaced by Christ's thoughts.

Ungodly Beliefs are wide open doors inviting Satan to come into our mind.

All of these points are extremely important. We can only believe the truth by having our minds renewed. Otherwise, we are in danger because Satan has access to our minds through our UGBs.

5. Hazard of Believing Lies

The group of scriptures in Table M on page 185 shows the extreme danger of holding on to UGBs, particularly after realizing that they are lies we have believed. We would rather not include this section, but we must if we are to have a balanced and complete teaching on beliefs. We also strongly desire to encourage you to have your mind renewed so you will not be among those who deliberately choose to reject the truth. This places us in grave danger.

A Sinful Heart: Unbelief

An unbelieving heart is a sinful heart.

The author of Hebrews clearly understood the connection between unbelief, lack of faith, and disobedience. He makes it clear in Hebrews 3:12 that an unbelieving heart is a sinful heart. It seems clear that an unbelieving heart **cannot be** obedient because it is controlled by the old nature. The nation of Israel, who wandered for 38 years because of their unbelief, is our example. The adult males delivered out of Egypt died in the wilderness. On the other hand, a believing, faith-filled heart leads to obedience and entrance into God's Sabbath-rest.[1]

Unbelief is the Mother of all Sins!

David Wilkerson wrote on **unbelief** in one of his newsletters,[2] calling it, "**The Mother of All Sins**! This sin is . . . the one that gives birth to all others," he declares. Among his many valid points, he notes that, "**Our unbelief makes God a liar**!" We are afraid to take God at His Word and to **really believe** Him. We effectively say to God, "Your promises sound really good, but my problems are too big for you," or "Your promises are for others because I am too unworthy to receive anything." Declaring that God is a liar can be hazardous to one's health!

---

[1] Please see Heb 4:11.
[2] David Wilkerson, Times Square Church Pulpit Series, *The Mother of All Sins!*, World Challenge, PO Box 260, Lindale, TX 75771, 12-6-93.

Table M
Scriptures Concerning Ungodly Beliefs (Set 3)

Hazard of Believing Lies

Heb 3:12-4:9	"See to it, brothers, that none of you has a **sinful, unbelieving heart** that turns away from the living God. But encourage one another daily . . . so that none of you may be hardened by **sin's deceitfulness**. . . . "Today, if you hear his voice, do not harden your hearts as you did in the rebellion." . . . Was it not with those who sinned . . . to whom did God swear that they would never enter his rest if not to those who disobeyed? So we see that they were not able to enter, because of their **unbelief**. . . . Now **we who have believed** enter that rest . . . a **Sabbath-rest** for the people of God;" (NIV)
Rom 1:18-2:11	"The **wrath of God** is being revealed from heaven against all the godlessness and wickedness of men who **suppress the truth** by their wickedness, . . . For **although they knew God**, they neither glorified him as God nor gave thanks to him, . . . Therefore God gave them over in the sinful desires of their hearts to sexual impurity for the degrading of their bodies with one another. They **exchanged the truth** of God **for a lie**, . . . Furthermore, since they did not think it worthwhile to **retain the knowledge** of God, he gave them over to a **depraved mind**, . . . Although **they know** God's righteous decree . . . , they not only continue to do these very things but also approve of those who practice them. . . . God "will give to each person according to what he has done." . . . But for those who are self-seeking and **who reject the truth** and follow evil, there will be wrath and anger." (NIV)
2 Cor 4:3-4	"but if our gospel be hid, it is hid to them that are lost: in whom the **god of this world** hath **blinded the minds** of them which **believe not** (they're believing a lie), lest the light of the glorious gospel of Christ, who is the image of God, should shine unto them." (KJV)
2 Pet 1:9-10	"But if anyone does not have them (godly qualities), he is nearsighted and blind, and has **forgotten** that he has been cleansed from his past sins. Therefore, my brothers, be all the more eager to **make your calling and election sure**. For if you do these things, you will never fall," (NIV)
1 Tim 4:1-3	"The Spirit clearly says that in later times some will **abandon the faith** and **follow deceiving spirits** and **things taught by demons**. Such teachings come through **hypocritical liars**, whose consciences have been seared as with a hot iron. They **forbid** people to marry and **order** them to abstain from certain foods, which God created to be received with thanksgiving by those **who believe** and **who know the truth**." (NIV)
2 Thes 2:10-12	"And in every sort of **evil** that **deceives** those who are perishing. They perish because they **refused to love the truth** and **so be saved**. For this reason God sends them a **powerful delusion** so that **they will believe the lie** and so that **all will be condemned** who have **not believed the truth** but have **delighted in wickedness**." (NIV)

Exchanging the Truth for a Lie

*Choosing a
lie leads to a
downward spiral.*

The second passage in Table M focuses on the part of the Gospel we would rather not hear. In Romans, we read about the hazards of **exchanging the truth of God for a lie** (verse 25). If a person continues this downward trend, he may eventually be given over to a **depraved** (reprobate) **mind** (verse 28). A reprobate mind is one that can not be changed (again). A reprobate mind has turned away from God and the will has become set against His purpose and practice such that there is no way for it to be turned back. This is a deadly serious situation.[1]

Blinded?

In Second Corinthians 4:3-4, we see that those who are perishing (because they ignore the truth and believed a lie) have given the god of this world the ability to blind their minds. It is likely that this is true even if a portion of our mind is "believing not." The unbelieving part is an UGBs area.

*We must give
ourselves to
the process of
sanctification
and not hold
back!*

In Second Peter 1:9-10, we have the opposite view of this truth. If we do not grow in godly qualities, as Peter has enumerated in the earlier verses, then we open ourselves for the god of this world to blind us (2 Cor 4:4). We have become "nearsighted and blind." We are warned not to become casual but to press in, to "make your calling and election sure. For if you do these things, you will never fall." We grow in godly qualities as our minds are renewed and the truth is more and more firmly established.

Seduced?

In First Timothy 4:1-3 Paul writes, "Now, the Spirit speaks expressly, that in the latter times some shall depart from the faith giving heed to seducing spirits and doctrines of devils" (KJV). A doctrine is a teaching: a principle we believe. Doctrines of devils, obviously, would be contrary to the Word of God. If we are susceptible to being seduced by "hypocritical liars," then we may receive and believe lies, leading to a real danger of departing or abandoning the faith.

Deceived?

Second Thessalonians 2:10-12 warns us about Satan and deception. In verse 10, Paul warns Christians about the one coming "with all deceivableness of unrighteousness in them that perish; **because they received not the love of the truth, that they might be saved**" (KJV). Men have to be **willing** to receive the truth to be saved. "And for this cause (reason), God shall send them strong delusion, that they should believe a lie:" (KJV).

It is difficult to read these passages because we know Him as a loving, gracious Father God. He is also a judging God. If people reject Him and His truth, preferring to believe a lie, this scripture indicates that a strong delusion comes that confines them to the lie (the UGB). They become trapped. We do not want to be among this group, and we don't want anyone else to be in this group of people.

---

[1]   Please note that just a portion of one's belief system may be depraved causing a partial rather than a total reprobation.

Table N
Scriptures Concerning Ungodly Beliefs (Set 4)

How We are Progressively Saved

2 Thes 2:13	. . . because from the beginning God chose you to be saved through the **sanctifying work of the Spirit** and through **belief in the truth**. (NIV)
Jn 17:17	**Sanctify them by the truth**; **your word is truth**. (NIV)
Rom 1:17	For therein is the righteousness of God revealed from **faith to faith**: as it is written, The just shall live by faith. (KJV)
2 Cor 3:18	But **we all ... are changed into the same image from glory to glory**, [even] as by the Spirit of the Lord. (KJV)
Isa 26:3-4	Thou wilt keep [him] in perfect peace, [whose] **mind [is] stayed [on thee]**: because he **trusteth in thee**. **Trust ye** in the LORD for ever: for in the LORD JEHOVAH [is] everlasting strength: (KJV)
Col 3:1-2	Since, then, you have been raised with Christ, **set your hearts on (keep seeking) things above**, where Christ is seated at the right hand of God. **Set your minds (affection) on things above**, not on earthly things. (NIV)
Phil 4:8	Finally, brothers, whatever is **true**, whatever is **noble**, whatever is **right**, whatever is **pure**, whatever is **lovely**, whatever is **admirable**—if anything is **excellent** or **praiseworthy**—**think about such things**. (NIV)

6. How We are Progressively Saved

We are extremely grateful that our goal and destiny are different than those delighting in lies. Rather, we are on the path of progressively being saved. The verses in Table N illustrate this process. Second Thessalonians 2:13 states we are "saved through the **sanctifying** work of the Spirit and **through belief in the truth**." Sanctification is progressive conversion and holiness. Think back to the Introduction Chapter and our discussion on God's Purpose. Having our minds renewed is an important part of the process as we progressively think more and more like God. We were saved; we are being saved; and one day, we will be totally and completely and finally saved at the resurrection/translation.[1]

Sanctified?
John 17:17 further clarifies this progressive sanctification as we see that the Holy Spirit **sanctifies us by the truth**, the Word of God. This reminds us of Ephesians, where Paul writes,

> Eph 5:26
> To make her (the Church) holy, cleansing her by the washing with water through the word. (NIV)

Washing involves time — the time for sanctification.

---

[1] Please see Phil 2:12 and Rom 8:23.

Time to be Sanctified

Romans 1:17 and Second Corinthians 3:18 reveal the time process of sanctification. While we **are** righteous because of our legal standing with God, in another sense we are **becoming** more righteous — from **faith to faith** — as we grow in our faith walk. Likewise, we continue to reflect the glory of the image of the Lord in a stronger and stronger way as we progress from **glory to glory**.

"Stayed" Mind?

We are to become like Christ.

The real key to becoming like Jesus is revealed to us in Isaiah 26:3-4 and Colossians 3:1-2, the New Testament statement of the Old Testament truth. When our hearts/minds are "**stayed**" on God and not on earthly things, then we are not distracted away from whose we are and who we serve.[1] We become the image we are looking at and reflecting, as discussed in the previous paragraph.

"Think about Such Things"

Finally, in Philippians 4:8 Paul lays out for us the things that a renewed mind should be thinking. When the old belief system is largely replaced by godly thoughts coming from Godly Beliefs, we will be focused on the things of God.

I. Replacing Ungodly Beliefs With Godly Beliefs

Now that we have studied the dynamics of beliefs, let's learn how to replace UGBs with GBs.

A very important part of this process is to legally break our agreement with the Ungodly Belief and to legally join in agreement with God. Doing this step makes all of the difference in the ease of acquiring a belief system in alignment with God's Word, nature, and character.

As ministers, using this procedure with your ministry receivers will help them gain considerable freedom from the tyranny of their UGBs. As they talk, listen to them and to the Holy Spirit to hear the UGBs underlying their conversation.

Why Write UGBs and GBs?

We want a written statement in our own words that clearly declares God's truth to replace any lie(s) we have believed. Then we want to align our beliefs with God's. Written GBs help the process of removing the wrong beliefs (UGBs) that do not agree with God's Word. They help in releasing ourselves — and us releasing others — from the beliefs, judgments (labels), and expectations that keep us locked into **less** than God's best for us. We want to line ourselves up with His plans and purposes without putting limits on His abilities or His Grace.

> **Exercise:** Now you can continue the earlier Exercise on page 164, by writing the GBs to go with your UGBs.

---

[1]   Please see Acts 27:23.

1. Procedure for Replacing Ungodly Beliefs with Godly Beliefs

You may follow this procedure to help a ministry receiver change an Ungodly Belief into a Godly Belief.

1. Identify the Ungodly Belief

Identify a thought, belief, expectation, etc.; a "given," that the ministry receiver has that is not in agreement with God's Word, nature, or character.

One source of UGBs is the person's Application Form. Also, the Holy Spirit will expose the lies underneath the person's **fears**, **worries**, **anger**, **resentments, hurts**, **unbelief, doubts**, **bitterness**, **blaming, etc.**, as you listen.

The presence of these negative emotions can be brought out by helping him think about recent occurrences of hurt. If you will "dig" down under the emotions, you can determine the underlying beliefs. We encourage you to go for the root UGBs that support and undergird the obvious hurts and emotions. Every time you identify an UGB, see if you can dig deeper. Ask the Holy Spirit if there is a "more core" UGB under the identified one, until you feel you have arrived at the deepest level.

Remember that you will also identify additional core UGBs during the Soul/Spirit Hurts session as the lies embedded with the hurts are identified.

2. Write the Ungodly Belief

Write the UGB as a declarative statement, making it stark, blunt, and clear. The bluntness helps to emphasize the reality of the unbelief. Usually a belief can be stated in one or two sentences. If the ministry receiver can be honest with himself, he may be shocked at how much **fear**, **resentment**, and/or **unbelief** the statement contains.

Make a list of the UGBs that you feel cover the core issues in the ministry receiver's life. Limit your list to about 15 (maximum 20) statements so he isn't overwhelmed.

Number the UGBs and write them on a sheet of paper. Leave four or five blank lines between each one so you can later add the GBs and the ministry receiver can add supporting scriptures.

3. Write the Godly Belief

A **good** GB is a statement that agrees with the **truth** of God's Word. It expresses what God says about the ministry receiver or the situation. As we did with the UGB, we like to express the GB as a declarative statement.

Sometimes we write the GB for the ministry receiver. At other times, when he is mature in the Word, we work with him to write the GB during the session. We discuss his thoughts and give input, working until we have a solid GB that really fits. We either finish writing the GBs in the session or we let him complete the writing of his GBs as "homework" to bring back the next session. Make sure he has a list of UGBs and GBs at the end of the session to take with him even if there are some still to be completed.

Hints for Writing Effective Godly Beliefs

Use these hints to help construct an effective Godly Belief.

- Generally a GB is the opposite of the UGB. It expresses God's way of looking at the same concept/belief/principle that is revealed by the UGB. It must agree with the principles of Scripture.

- When the GB seems "too big a step" from the UGB, choose an intermediate GB that your receiver can believe — one that will help him move in the right direction.

- It may help to write a "progressive" GB that reduces the pressure to change immediately. A suggestion is, "As I am healed, I will be able to . . ."

- When needed you may include a phrase such as: "By God's grace, . . ." or "With His help . . ."

- Make sure the GB addresses the main issue of the UGB. It should counteract the essence of the UGB.

- Write the GB using the ministry receiver's words when possible. We are not looking for a nice religious statement but one that speaks to his heart.

- When writing GBs that include other people, be careful to not impose your, or the receiver's, will on them. Write a faith statement about what is possible with God's grace and with the cooperation of the people involved.

- Of course, the new GB must agree with Scripture. Make sure you are satisfied that the GB truly is godly before giving it your "stamp of approval."

4. **Use Scripture to support and verify that the new belief is godly**

   Assign the ministry receiver the homework task of finding scriptures that support the GB. Pray that the Holy Spirit lead him during his prayer time to the right scriptures. Instruct him to add the scriptures to the GB and to incorporate the GB and accompanying scriptures as a part of his prayer time. We want his faith to be solidly attached to the Word and not onto our opinion.

5. **Minister to the Belief System**

   Use the Ministry Steps at the end of this chapter (or the summary steps on the Ministry Card) to remove and break the power of the UGBs and to set the stage for the GBs to be established. Go through the steps of forgiveness, repentance, and renouncing. Declare and receive the new GBs.

6. **Fine Tune what has been written**

   Instruct the ministry receiver to improve the GBs using words that truly express what he knows God wants him to believe. Have him fine tune and adjust the statement until it "fits" him. Have him give you a copy of the final list so you can check it and verify that the Godly Beliefs truly are "godly."

7. Most Essential for Freedom

Stress to the ministry receiver that, if he desires to gain real freedom, it is important to pray, meditate, and think about his new Godly Beliefs for at least thirty days. This is the typical time that it takes to change any habit. We want the newly "planted" beliefs to be well rooted and to begin to manifest in his life. Have him continue to pray that the Holy Spirit will plant the new beliefs deep into his heart. Have him continue to meditate on their truth and meaning. The point is not merely positive confession but rather to have his heart changed so he can begin to think, make decisions, and have expectations corresponding to a GBs system.

2. Examples of Ungodly and Godly Beliefs

We will look at several examples, starting with UGBs/GBs about ourselves, then others, and then God.

a. Ungodly/Godly Beliefs Concerning Self

The following example illustrates that there are several different ways to express a Godly Belief. We want the one that best "fits" the ministry receiver.

Example: This is an UGB in the area of **"not belonging"** and "abandonment." The person for whom it was written had been left and ignored by his father. He had never bonded with either parent.

Ungodly Belief

I am alone in the world and have no one who cares.

Possible Godly Beliefs (We would choose one.)

- I am not alone in the world because God has given me Himself, my wife, and my family of God, i.e., the Church. I choose to reach out to them.

- God cares, my wife cares, and my brothers and sisters in Christ care for me and about me. I choose to be in relationship with them.

- I belong completely to God, my Father, Jesus, my brother, and the Holy Spirit, my comforter. I belong to my wife, as God has and is causing us to become one. I belong to the Body of Christ and they belong to me. I choose to let them be part of my life.

Is it a lie?

Observe how we have included statements such as "with God's help," or "by His grace He will enable me to . . . ," so that we don't have to face the entire transition from old to new in one step. Otherwise, our new GB could sound like a **lie** to us. For example, if we try to help someone change from "I can never remember names," to "I always remember names," it would be difficult to have faith for such a dramatic transition.

Example 1

Ungodly Belief

> I will always be lonely.

Godly Belief

> With God's help, I will begin to reach out to others and also to receive from them. He has designed me to fit into His Body, the Church.

Sometimes, in beliefs concerning Self, a GB amounts to a declaration (what I will decide to do), regardless of other people or situations.

Example 2

Ungodly Belief

> I always drift from job to job. I will never find my real direction.

Godly Belief

> I choose to submit myself to God and to go the way He leads me. He will direct me in the plan and purpose He has for me.

---

b. Ungodly/Godly Beliefs Concerning Others

What is possible for the other person?

In a situation in which the UGB involves another person, we need to look at what God says is **possible for that person** and not how he is behaving now.

Example 1

Ungodly Belief

> My husband always gets angry at me.

Godly Belief

> God can enable my husband not only to control the anger but to become completely free of this bondage.

Key: Separate the person from the problem.

Note that we no longer identify the problem with the person, but we separate him from the problem (i.e, the "anger," not "his anger"). We focus on what God says and on what God can do. The GB is a **statement of faith**.

c. **Ungodly/Godly Beliefs Concerning God Himself or His Word**

Ungodly Beliefs about God and/or His Word are very common. We must choose to believe what He says about Himself rather than our fears or resentments toward Him. It helps to remember that our beliefs about God are strongly influenced by our experiences and relationship with our earthly father.

Example 1

Ungodly Belief

God heals others, but He doesn't desire to heal me.

Godly Belief

God loves His children equally and desires His best for each one. He desires to heal me. I choose to receive His healing.

---

3. Practice

We have included Table O on page 195 as a practice page to help you become more acquainted with writing Ungodly and Godly Beliefs. This is your opportunity to put to work the teachings in this section. The first four pairs of UGBs/GBs are completed to give you additional examples. You can use the remaining space to practice on UGBs important to you.

If you are not sure where or how to start, refer back to the lists of examples of Ungodly Beliefs on pages 165 and 166. Also, re-read the instructions in this section on the Procedure for Replacing Ungodly and Godly Beliefs. Then take a deep breath and make the plunge!

Prayer: May the Holy Spirit illuminate your mind with revelation in hearing, discerning, writing, and ministering to UGBs. May this practice bring understanding and clarity in all aspects of working with the Holy Spirit to renew our minds. Amen!

J. Ministering to Ungodly Beliefs

As we have stated throughout this chapter, ministry to UGBs is among the most important of the four Problem/Ministry Areas. It is also a very rewarding ministry in which we see God transform lives as their minds are renewed.

1. Final Preparation before Ministry

Our preparation for ministry to Ungodly Beliefs.

The majority of the work in preparing to minister to UGBs takes place outside of the ministry session when we go back over the notes taken during the Interview and ministry to the Sins of the Fathers and Curses sessions. At that time, we note the obvious UGBs spoken directly by the ministry receiver as well as listen to the Holy Spirit as He shows us the UGBs "underneath" what the ministry receiver was saying. Prayerfully re-reading the notes and the noted UGBs usually leads to a "synthesis" of the material, allowing us to see patterns of thought and expectations that "group" into themes and threads of unbelief in the ministry receiver's life. Then we apply the steps in the earlier section on Procedure for Replacing Ungodly and Godly Beliefs to finish preparing for the ministry.

We try to not overwhelm the receiver!

Usually, we will try to have 10 to 15, with a maximum of 20, pairs of UGBs and GBs for the ministry receiver. Giving more than this at one time tends to be overwhelming. The ministry receiver may give up and not even try, particularly if one of his UGBs is that he fails at everything he tries!

Is it possible not to have any UGBs?

The other extreme is typified by a friend who attended one of our classes. After the session on Ungodly Beliefs, he said to his wife, "I just can't relate to any of these people in here. They all seem so excited as they realize what Ungodly Beliefs their ancestors have passed down to them, but I don't identify with a single one of them. I just don't have any Ungodly Beliefs!" His wife looked at him and said, "Well, I know at least one Ungodly Belief that you have." With some surprise, he said, "You do?" "Yes," she said, laughing. "Your Ungodly Belief is that you don't have any Ungodly Beliefs!" She proved to be correct when they later went through the RTF ministry.

Exercise: You should now be ready with your written Ungodly and Godly Beliefs pairs to move through the following Ministry Steps, allowing the Holy Spirit to help you free yourself from the UGBs and plant the GBs. Our prayers are with you as you set your will (2 Cor 7:1) to change the way your mind "works" so that you can be more like Jesus every day.

Table O
Practice Writing Ungodly and Godly Beliefs

UGB: Those important to me will abandon me at critical times and in critical events.

GB: God has promised to be with me always. He has also given me others in the Body of Christ who will be faithful friends.

Script: Mat 18:20, Prov 18:24

UGB: My spouse will never treat me the way I want to be treated.

GB: As I forgive and repent of my judgments about my spouse and the way that I have treated her/him, God is free to work in her/his life to bring about loving change.

Script: Eph 5:21-33

UGB: I will never fully be able to give or receive love, to have intimate, satisfying relationships with people.

GB: God, who is love, can and will teach me how to enter into 1 Cor 13 love. I choose to let down my defenses and to enter into His kind of love.

Script: 1 Cor 13:1-8, 1 Jn 4:8

UGB: God will not be pleased with me if I take time for myself to rest and play.

GB: God is holding the universe together. It will not fall apart if I rest or play. He desires for me to have a balanced life, to enjoy Him and His creation, as well as to do satisfying and fulfilling work.

Script: Eph 2:11, Heb 4:1-11

UGB: _____

GB: _____

Script: _____

UGB: _____

GB: _____

Script: _____

2. Submission Prayer

We again have a "model prayer" that you can use as you help your receiver prepare to renew his mind.

> **UGBs Submission Prayer:** Lord, according to Your Word in Romans 12:1-2, I choose to submit to the process of being transformed by the renewing of my mind. I ask You to search my heart today, invade my thought life, and make me aware of any wrong thinking or blind spots. I thank You that You have created me in Your image and that You desire to set me free from all negative ways that I view myself, others, and You, God. I commit my way to You, Lord, knowing that You will establish my thoughts.
>
> As You continue to renew my mind, I ask You to give me grace to cooperate with You fully in the process of changing my Ungodly Beliefs to Godly Beliefs. I receive Your mind, Lord Jesus.
>
> I declare that I have been redeemed, forgiven, and sanctified. I belong to Christ, my body is the temple of the Holy Spirit, and I shall have victory today as I submit myself to this renewing and transforming process on the authority of, and in the Name of, Jesus Christ. Amen!

3. Steps in Ministering to Ungodly Beliefs

Some of the following steps take place before the actual time of ministry to UGBs. Steps 1 and 2 are accomplished by the minister during the early sessions and as he prepares to minister. Then steps 4 through 12 are accomplished by the ministry receiver for each UGB. The minister has the privilege of praying for the power of the Cross to intervene into the ministry receiver's life in step 13.

Ministry Steps[1]

1. **Listen:** Identify possible UGBs by listening to the ministry receiver and to the Holy Spirit during the Interview and SOFCs sessions.
2. **Write:** Accumulate a written list of the possible UGBs. You may also write a list of new GBs to use as initial suggestions. [Either write new GBs before coming to the UGBs session, or write them during the ministry time (Procedure Step #3 on page 189) as the ministry receiver declares what he will believe to replace the UGBs (Ministry Step #12).]
3. **Offer:** Present one UGB at a time to the receiver during the UGBs session. Help him agree that he does indeed have this UGB and needs to take responsibility for it affecting his life. "Fine-tune" the UGB until it "fits" him. [The receiver may state that he does not relate to the presented UGB. If he doesn't relate to the UGB at all, you can either withdraw the UGB or suggest that you and the receiver pray and ask the Holy Spirit to show if and how the UGB applies to the receiver.]

---

[1]   A copy of a Ministry Card with a summary of these steps is in Appendix A.

4. **Confess:** Have receiver confess the sin of believing the UGB (lie) rather than the truth and living his life according to this lie. [If applicable, the ministry receiver should confess the Sins of his Fathers (and mothers) in believing and acting on the same lies.[1]]

5. **Forgive:** Have receiver forgive his ancestors (fathers and mothers) that have passed down to him the UGB. [If appropriate.]

6. **Forgive:** Have receiver forgive all others that may have influenced him to form the UGB.

7. **Repent:** Have receiver ask God's forgiveness for living his life based on this UGB.

8. **Forgive:** Have receiver forgive himself.

9. **Renounce:** Have receiver renounce the UGB and break its power from his life based on the finished work of Christ on the Cross. [Encourage him to be strong in setting his will and to make a spiritual "decree" to refuse the UGB any more importance in his life.]

10. **Construct:** Present the new GB or work with receiver to construct a new GB. [Fine-tune the GB until you and the receiver have a good "first draft."]

11. **Receive/Affirm:** Have receiver declare the GB and receive it into his belief system as the replacement for the previously removed UGB.

[Repeat the above steps until you have gone through all of the UGBs list.]

12. **Restore:** Pray for the receiver's new set of GBs.
    - Pray that God bring to an end the effects of the UGBs in his life.
    - Pray for the GBs to be planted into his heart.
    - Pray that the Word already in his heart will be brought to the surface of his mind and be available for use as a weapon against future, ungodly thoughts.
    - Pray for the discipline needed for him to meditate on his new GBs for at least 30 days.
    - Pray that the Holy Spirit will make him very sensitive to falling back into old thought patterns and that he will be able to take captive any such thoughts.[2]
    - Pray for new habit patterns of thought to be established.[3]

---

[1] Please see Lev 26:40-42.
[2] Please see 2 Cor 10:5.
[3] Please see Rom 12:2.

Post-Ministry: "Walking it Out"

The post-ministry phase of ministering to UGBs is extremely important to the success of establishing the new GBs in the heart and mind of your ministry receiver. Cover the following areas to prepare him for the "walking it out" phase of healing. If at all possible, the help of a mature saint should be enlisted for prayer support, accountability, and encouragement.

1. Inform receiver that the **legal power of the UGBs is broken**, but that he has to keep the doors shut to the old ways.

2. Charge him to **take control of his thoughts,** "bringing them into captivity to the obedience of Christ" (2 Cor 10:5), rather than allowing them to follow their natural course.   Take charge of any stray thought that "comes in."

3. Inform him that once the demonic deliverance is accomplished, any demonic temptation to continue in the old UGBs will be from the "outside," which will be much weaker than previous temptations. This **oppression will likely continue until the demons assigned to the ministry receiver become convinced that he will indeed stand firm in his new GBs. Demons will soon see his resolve in** allowing the Holy Spirit to help him develop a new belief system and that he is not going to believe demonic lies, either the old ones or any new ones that they might throw at him.

4. Have him **take responsibility to pray** that the Holy Spirit will continue to show him other UGBs and to do self-ministry so that additional healing and freedom may come.

5. Encourage him to **continue to "fine-tune" the GBs** so that they really speak to his heart. Have him search the scriptures and find verses that support the new GBs.

6. Have him **pray and meditate on his new GBs for at least one month** as part of his daily devotions. He should daily thank the Holy Spirit for planting the GBs deep into his heart.

7. Help him realize the tendency of the mind is to continue in the old habit patterns. Help him commit to **persevere for at least a month** with his new GBs to insure that the new habit patterns of thought are established. When a new GB is replacing a major, core UGB, he may need to periodically return to the GB and focus on it again while continuing to eradicate all traces of the original UGB.

IX

SOUL/SPIRIT HURTS

The Spirit of the Lord [is] upon me, . . .
he hath sent me to heal the brokenhearted, . . .
Luke 4:18-20

The pain of past hurt rules many lives. It simmers, it stifles, and sometimes it shuts a person completely down. Understanding scriptural principles brings comfort and hope, but it does not necessarily bring healing. Forgiveness releases a person from bitterness and from the bondage of negative ties to others, but it does not necessarily heal hurts. Demonic deliverance brings great freedom, but it does not heal hurts.

God heals hurts. He is waiting and ready to touch our deepest pain if we will let Him. In a sense, His healing is another divine exchange, in which we offer to Him our hurt and He offers to us His healing. Most of us do not know how to go about **receiving** this wonderful gift He has to offer.

In this chapter, we present a definition of Soul/Spirit Hurts and take an in-depth look at the consequences of hurts, as they affect our lives and personalities. Next, we look at hindrances to our receiving God's healing that come from these consequences. We then prepare to receive God's healing using a powerful approach we have named, "Waiting Upon the Lord" Listening Prayer. We can receive healing for ourselves and then lead others into the full healing God has provided.

In the first edition of *Restoring the Foundations* written in 1994, we did not include details about the "Waiting Upon the Lord" Listening Prayer approach process. At that time, we felt a caution not to expose too many details, but rather to reserve these for the training process. We wanted to first know that we had a mature, responsible RTF ministry team.

Well, a lot has changed in the Body of Christ in six years. Pastors and churches are much more welcoming of healing ministries such as Proclaiming His Word. Other ministries have published the details of the revelations God has shown them. And so we are excited that we now have the liberty to share with a more responsible and receptive church the details of how to bring effective ministry to the hurting. God wants you to know that an encounter with the living Christ Jesus in the midst of a painful memory brings a tremendous depth of healing. He wants you to know how to receive this healing.

199

A. Definition of Soul/Spirit Hurts (SSHs)

> Soul/Spirit Hurts are hurts on the "inside" of a person. They are wounds to the soul or the spirit of man that are carried and experienced within the person himself. They are not physical and they cannot be seen. Their presence is revealed by their symptoms, by the manifested evidence of unhealed emotions, behaviors, and thoughts.

Soul/Spirit Hurts (SSHs) surface when a person appears or a situation occurs that is similar to the person or situation involved with the original hurt. A common example is the stage fright people experience at the thought of being in front of a large group. Often this is related to an earlier painful experience in which the person was embarrassed or humiliated in front of others.

B. Background Information

Over the years, the topic of "inner healing" has generated much "discussion." Before proceeding further, let's address a couple of these issues and questions.

1. Why Named "Soul/Spirit Hurts?"

We have chosen to name this Problem/Ministry Area, "Soul/Spirit Hurts," instead of using one of the more familiar terms such as "inner healing" or "healing of emotions" or "healing of the memories."

First, our goal is to minister the necessary healing regardless of where it is needed — in the person's soul or spirit or both. Although we appreciate the teachings of Dennis and Rita Bennet[1] and others who have challenged us to consider the triune nature of man, that approach usually places the memories and emotions in the soul realm only. As a result, they believe healing is needed only in the soul realm.

A clear-cut distinction, however, between those functions occurring in man's soul and those taking place in his spirit is not easily accomplished. Scripture indicates that *both* the soul and the spirit have attributes of mind, memory, will, and emotion, as well as many other common characteristics. How, then, can we attempt to divide the functions of the innermost parts of man when Scripture provides no clear guidelines? Since our goal is healing, wherever it is needed, and not theological distinctions, an easy way to avoid this uncertainty is to minister to the soul and spirit as a unit, i.e., as "Soul/Spirit Healing," and let the Holy Spirit determine where the healing is actually needed.

---

[1] Dennis and Rita Bennet, *Trinity of Man*, Plainfield, IL, Logos International, 1979.

The second reason for using the term, "Soul/Spirit Healing," is simply that the terms "soul" and "spirit" are scriptural terms that are commonly accepted as parts of mankind. We prefer to use scriptural words and phrases.

Third, the definitions of the terms "soul" and "spirit" are broader than the terms "emotions" or "memories." We want to minister to the entire soul and/or spirit, wherever the wounding exists.

Please refer to Appendix B for an in-depth discussion of the issue of soul and spirit and what attributes belong to which part. We take an in-depth look at the Hebrew and Greek word meanings to help our understanding.

2. Controversies Concerning Soul/Spirit Healing

Is there a need for healing?

Are the methods valid?

The controversy surrounding the ministry of healing of the inner person usually centers around two points: (1) Whether inner healing is necessary; and (2) the "methods" used to minister to inner hurts. Both issues have stirred up a hornet's nest in the Body of Christ. We, of course, believe that inner healing is a vitally needed ministry, far more then most of us realize.

A number of books have been written in favor of ministering to the inner person. Other authors, however, are against it. If you read them all, you will have quite an education and perhaps even some clarity. The diversity of concepts and methods put forth by the different authors, however, makes it difficult to "define" the various terms. Even the term, "inner healing," has a diversity of meanings. As for the books written by authors against inner healing, their concerns generally fall into two basic categories.

Concern #1:

The use of secular, psychological terms.

Concern #2:

The leading of the counselee/ receiver in visualization.

Non-Scriptural Terms
Some practitioners of inner healing use secular, psychological terms and concepts that are not clearly defined or explained in the Bible. In other words, they are "non-scriptural." In addition, they incorporate visualization, imagination, and/or suggestions made by the counselor/minister to the counselee/ministry receiver. Of particular concern are suggestive, directive, or "leading" tactics. For example, the counselor may say, "Now, I want you to imagine that you're seeing Jesus and that He is coming into the situation with you, and He is there with you in this time of hurt," and so forth in this fashion.

Our approach, however, relies completely on the Holy Spirit, who has given us a safe and effective "method" that sets the stage for Him to bring His healing to the people of God. We are very excited about the "Waiting Upon the Lord" Listening Prayer approach, which will be discussed later in this chapter.

If you would like to study the controversies in more detail, please refer to the discussion in Appendix C, which contains a reference list of some of the many authors who have written about inner healing.

C. Our Personal Experiences of Healing

Long before either one of us (Chester or Betsy) had received the revelation through the Scriptures of Jesus healing the inner person, we experienced it! For each of us it was very unexpected.

The Father Heart of God was revealed to Chester.

Chester's experience occurred one hot summer day while we were driving our van from our home in Gainesville, Florida to the beach. He was lying in the back praying. When Chester was only two years old, his father died. Partly as a result of growing up without a father, he became introverted and a loner. For much of his life, he had hidden behind work and achievement.

On that life-changing day, God chose to reveal Himself to Chester as the Father that he had never had — as a personal Father-God who wanted a close relationship with him. As that revelation became real to Chester, tears flowed. His heart, which had been closed for so long, began to open. He says even now, "There are no words to describe the depth and profoundness of this experience as I realized that God, the very God of the universe, wanted a Father-son relationship with me. I still cannot talk about this in public without being filled with the awesomeness of His love." The healing that took place that day gave him a sense of belonging that has continued to increase.

Betsy's first experience of God healing her Soul/Spirit Hurts occurred about two years later on a wintry Sunday night. Jackie Canapa, a faith-filled friend who was visiting that evening, said that there was something Jesus wanted to touch in Betsy's life. Neither of them knew what it might be, but Jackie suggested that Betsy bow her head and ask Jesus to come and minister to her.

As Betsy followed Jackie's suggestion, she began to see a picture in her spirit of a tiny baby girl being born. Betsy describes her experience: "After a while, I saw Jesus come and pick up the baby girl. He looked at her with great delight in His face, and said, 'I am so glad that you are here. I planned your life a long time ago and I have such a wonderful plan for it.' Then I realized that the baby girl was me! As I saw Jesus welcoming me with tenderness and enthusiasm, I knew that He had a special purpose for my life. I had never experienced anything like that before. It had a profound and lasting effect on me."

*God adopts all **orphans**, and gives them purpose*

"For thirty-seven years, I had carried a painful doubt that maybe my life was a mistake. As a baby, I had been given up for adoption by a young, unmarried mother. She had wanted the best for me. Although in God's providence I was raised in a wonderful, godly family, I had never been able to put to rest the nagging feeling that I was the result of a sinful act and that I was lacking in some way. The Lord Jesus knew that I needed this healing. As the reality broke over me that I truly was planned and purposed by Him, my heart, so full of cracks and uncertainties, began to be healed."

D. Understanding the Interrelationship of the Ministry Areas

The Problem/Ministry Area of Soul/Spirit Hurts seems so personal, so intimate. How can it be related to the other Problem/Ministry Areas? As we shall see, it is exceeding closely related. Inner wounds are caused by Sins of the Fathers, Ungodly Beliefs, and Demonic Oppression. Then, these same three Problem/Ministry Areas are propagated by Soul/Spirit Hurts. It is important to realize and understand how these areas intertwine and impact each other in order to acknowledge the need for an Integrated Approach to Healing Ministry.

1. How Soul/Spirit Hurts are Related to Sins of the Fathers

Because the same types of sins are passed down in a family from generation to generation, the same curses continue to operate. As a result, many members of a family tend to repeat the same kinds of behaviors, hurting each other in similiar ways as their ancestors. These sinful, generational patterns and the resulting curses need to be broken in order to stop propagating the same hurts, sins, and curses. In breaking them, we set the stage for healing from the hurts.

The alcoholic family provides the classic example. The co-dependent family, where the children "can't leave home," offers another common example. We could continue, citing examples of the same Soul/Spirit Hurts continuing generation after generation.

2. How Soul/Spirit Hurts are Related to Ungodly Beliefs

Most Ungodly Beliefs are actually formed in hurtful situations. They result from hurtful family patterns. The Hurts underlying the Ungodly Beliefs must be healed before the belief system can be rebuilt founded on the Truth of God's Word, His nature, and His character. Otherwise, the hurt and the Ungodly Belief will serve to negatively reinforce each other.

If the heart says, "I'm hurting", and the mind that is being renewed says, "I'm healed," which one will win out? That's right, the heart! The unhealed hurt causes the heart to cry out, "This 'Godly Belief' is a lie! I can't receive it!" Why? Because the pain is still present. The hurt **must** be healed before God's truth can fully settle into the heart.

3. How Soul/Spirit Hurts are Related to Deliverance

Demons do not play fair. When hurt or trauma is experienced by someone, certain demons frequently invade: fear, failure, isolation, loneliness, shame, control, rejection, rebellion, depression, trauma, and death. Their work does not stop with the invasion. They continue to agitate and stir up the same hurts by "picking off the scabs," so to speak, and arranging events to cause more hurt.

Hurts also provide a launching place for demonic lies. Demons will amplify the hurt by the messages they send to the mind, such as, "No point in trying to make friends, nobody will like me." When we receive healing for our hurts, the demons are no longer able to amplify those hurtful memories.

If demons are blocking or distorting God's healing revelation, we sometimes do deliverance before praying for healing of hurts. Otherwise, we prefer to do the deliverance afterwards — when the "legal ground" of the sins associated with the hurts has been dealt with and the demons have no justification for remaining.

4. God's Overall Purpose

Deuteronomy 6:23 reads:

> Deu 6:23
> But He brought us out from there to bring us in and give us the land that he promised on oath to our forefathers. (NIV)

God wants to **bring us out** *in order* *to take us in.*

God wants to bring us out of the situation of hurt into the healing we need. He wants to set us free. His ministry is to bring us out of the Sins of the Fathers into His family line, where He is our Father and where no hurts nor sinful heritage exists. He wants to bring us out of the Ungodly Beliefs and have our minds renewed. Why? So we can think and act like Him and agree with His Word. He wants to bring us out of the snare of the Devil into the safety of His protection. He wants to bring us out of the world and into His Godly Kingdom. Our job is to make ourselves available to the Holy Spirit so our heavenly Father can accomplish His work in us.

E. Scriptural Basis for Soul/Spirit Healing

God is our *Jehovah Rapha*

God is our healer. No Spirit-filled Christian would question that **GOD** heals, particularly physical healing. Jehovah Rapha, the name for God used in Exodus 15:26, is used in the context of His bringing the Israelites out of Egypt. It also relates to His promise that if they obeyed His commandments and followed His statutes, then He would not put on them any of the diseases of the Egyptians. We could paraphrase this scripture as:

> Ex 15:26
> . . . None of the diseases of the world will be able to be on you because I am the God that healeth thee; I am Jehovah Rapha. (paraphrased)

Rapha: *to stitch or mend,* *to cure or heal,* *to position,* *to repair,* *to make whole.*

The basic meaning of the Hebrew word, "*rapha,*" is "to mend," as in stitching up or mending a torn cloth. Rapha also means "to cure or cause to be cured, to heal, to position, to repair, to make whole." When we say "Jehovah Rapha," we are saying, "God, the Mender, the One who makes us whole." Isn't that good? This is one of God's redemptive names. He wants each one of us to be whole.

Many Christians would agree that God wants to heal us physically but what about emotionally or mentally? Does He heal the inner person as well as the physical body? We have listed a number of relevant scriptures in Table P on page 207 that we feel show His heart for healing us wherever we need it.

> Is God interested in healing the "inner" person as well as the "outer"?

1. God Healing the Inner Person

Let's begin by looking in Table P at David's petition to God and see if we can identify with it. In Psalm 41:4, David petitions God to be merciful and to heal his soul. First, he acknowledges his sin before God because he knows that taking responsibility is an important requirement in obtaining God's mercy. David is asking God to heal his soul — a soul made sick from sin. David believed that his soul, his inner self, **could** be healed by God.

In Psalm 147:3, the writer pens, "He heals the **brokenhearted**, And binds up their **wounds** (or **sorrows**)." "Brokenhearted" refers to the wounds in the innermost portion of ourselves.

In Jeremiah 31:25, God speaks to Jeremiah that He "will [fully] satisfy the **weary soul**, and . . . replenish every **languishing** and **sorrowful** person" (AMP). In the Hebrew, both "weariness" and "sorrow" can refer to the mental or emotional condition of the inner person. God says He will **satisfy** and He will **replenish** the deepest part of man's being.

At another time (Jer 17:14), Jeremiah cries out, "Heal me, O LORD, and I will be healed; Save me and I will be saved, for Thou art my praise." The prophet is talking about much more than his physical condition. He is referring to his soul.

You are probably already familiar with the verse in the third epistle of John, in which the beloved apostle prays, "Beloved, I pray that in all respects you may prosper and be in good health, just as your soul prospers." (NAS) In addition to being a prayer for the prosperity and health of our soul, it is also a prayer for teaching prosperity in all areas of life, including financial prosperity.

2. Jesus Healing the Broken Hearted

Isaiah 53 presents a powerful prophecy concerning Jesus and His coming ministry to reveal the Father's heart to the people.[1] The Father desires to heal us. In the following verses, note the words we have printed in "bold" that have to do with emotions, or inner hurts.

---

[1] The 14th Chapter of John provides us with many examples of Jesus showing us the Father.

Isa 53:3-5

3 He was **despised** and **forsaken** of man, A man of **sorrows**, and acquainted with **grief**; And like one from whom men hid their face, He was **despised**, and we did **not esteem** Him.

4 Surely our **griefs** (**sickness**) He Himself bore, And our **sorrows**, He carried; Yet, we ourselves esteemed him **stricken**, **Smitten** of God, and **afflicted**.

5 But He was **pierced** (**wounded**) through for our transgressions, He was **crushed** for our iniquities; The **chastising** for our well-being fell upon Him, And by His **scourging** (**stripes**) we are healed. (NAS)

These verses offer a powerful listing of pain-related words that mostly refer to inner pain. For example, the Hebrew word for **sorrows** is used throughout the Old Testament to refer to mental or emotional pain. "*Choli*," translated **griefs**, means afflictions, casualties, weakness, and pain, as well as sickness and disease. It seems clear that more than the physical body is included in the healing and deliverance ministry of Jesus.

Isaiah also prophesied about the anointing, wisdom, and tenderness of Jesus' ministry in Isaiah 11:2-4. He declared that Christ would not rely merely on the five senses but He would be able to judge with righteousness and fairness.

In Isaiah 42:3, Isaiah expresses the divine care and tenderness with which Jesus would treat the souls of men. This is great comfort to hurting people.

The record of the gospels shows these prophetic words repeatedly fulfilled. Right from the beginning of His ministry, Jesus defined and declared His ministry to the inner man. Luke 4:18-19 records Jesus reading from Isaiah 61. He stated:

Lk 4:18-19

18 He hath sent me to heal the **brokenhearted**, to preach deliverance to the **captives**, and recovering of sight to the **blind**, to set at liberty them that are **bruised**,

19 to preach the acceptable year of the Lord. (KJV)

These powerful words were fulfilled as the anointing on Jesus Christ brought forth healing and freedom.

Portrait after portrait is recorded of God, through Jesus, meeting people at their point of pain. Ordinary people, trapped, rejected, outcast, or desolate, were touched by his heart of compassion, His words of life, His transforming power. Many encounters reveal His tremendous compassion. Consider the lepers whom He reached out and physically touched, defying all Jewish law.[1] What about the woman at the well,[2] whom He accepted and gave life-changing truth? Who can forget the woman caught in adultery whose death sentence He revoked and whose shame He remitted, saying, "Go and sin no more."[3] Then there were the scared, frustrated parents of demonized children, who had their precious ones healed and their own hearts mended when Jesus heeded their cries for help.[4]

---

[1]   Please see Mat 8:2-4, Mk 1:40-44, Lk 17:12-17.
[2]   Please see Jn 4:17-29.
[3]   Please see Jn 8:11.
[4]   Please see Mk 7:24-30 and 9:17-29.

Table P
Scriptures Concerning Soul/Spirit Hurts

The Ministry of Jesus Christ

Lk 4:18-19
(Isa 61:1-3)
"The Spirit of the Lord is upon me, because he hath anointed me to preach the gospel to the poor; He hath sent me to **heal** the brokenhearted, to preach **deliverance** to the captives, and recovering of sight to the blind, to set at **liberty** them that are bruised, To preach the acceptable year of the Lord. " (KJV)

Jn 21:15-19
" . . . 'do you truly love me more than these?' 'Yes, Lord,' he said, 'you know that I love you.' Jesus said, 'Feed my lambs.' . . ." (NIV)

Isa 11:2-4
"And the Spirit of the LORD will rest upon Him, the spirit of wisdom and understanding, the spirit of counsel and strength, . . . And He will not judge by what His eyes see, Nor make a decision by what His ears hear; But with righteousness He will judge the poor, And decide with fairness for the afflicted of the earth; . . ." (NAS)

Isa 42:3
"A bruised reed He will not break, and a dimly burning wick He will not extinguish; . . ." (NAS)

Isa 53:4
"Surely he took up our **infirmities** and carried our **sorrows**, yet we considered him **stricken** by God, **smitten** by him, and **afflicted**." (NIV)

God's Heart for Soul/Spirit Healing

Ex 15:26
". . . I will not bring on you any of the diseases I brought on the Egyptians, for I am the LORD, **who heals (rapha) you**." (NIV)

Psa 147:3
"He **heals** the brokenhearted, and **binds up** their wounds." (NAS)

Jer 31:25
"For I have **satiated** the weary soul, and I have **replenished** every sorrowful soul." (KJV)

David's Prayer

Psa 41:4
". . . Lord, be merciful unto me; **heal my soul**, for I have sinned against Thee." (KJV)

Psa 23:2-3
". . . he leadeth me beside the still waters. He **restoreth my soul:** . . ." (KJV)

John's Prayer

3 Jn 1:2
"Beloved, I pray that in all respects you may prosper and be in good health, just as your soul **prospers**." (NAS)

Jeremiah's Prayer

Jer 17:14
"Heal me, O LORD, and I will be healed; Save me and I will be saved, for Thou art my praise." (NAS)

Jesus ministers to Peter.

In John 21, we see Jesus dealing with the heart-broken Peter. Jesus knows what to do as He ministers to Peter's deep grief and remorse. Three times, Jesus asks, "Do you love me?" allowing Peter three opportunities to express his love and to receive Jesus' forgiveness and acceptance. As Jesus tells Peter to "feed My sheep" and "take care of My lambs," He reaffirms His trust in Peter to minister effectively. What healing that must have brought to Peter as he was still dealing with his act of betrayal. What could be more powerful than to be "reinstated" by the very One he had betrayed?[1]

Consider the question put so well by Max Lucado in his book *He Still Moves Stones.*[2]

*Max Lucado wrote, **He Still Moves Stones.***

> Why did God leave us one tale after another of wounded lives being restored? So we could be grateful for the past? So we could look back with amazement at what Jesus did?
>
> No. No. No. A thousand times no. The purpose of these stories is not to tell us what Jesus *did*. Their purpose is to tell us what Jesus *does*.
>
> "Everything that was written in the past was written to teach us," Paul penned. "The Scriptures give us patience and encouragement so that we can have hope" (Rom 15:4).
>
> These are not just Sunday school stories. Not romantic fables. Not somewhere-over-the-rainbow illusions. They are historic moments in which a real God met real pain so we could answer the question, "Where is God when I hurt?"
>
> He's not doing it just for them. He is doing it for me. He's doing it for you.

Lucado helps us see that when our hearts are broken, God wants to heal. If any of us are in emotional bondage or oppression, God wants to set us at liberty. This is Jesus' proclamation.

F. Information about Soul/Spirit Hurts

As we prepare to pray for Soul/Spirit Hurts, it helps to have an overall understanding about hurt. This section reviews some basics about Soul/Spirit Hurts.

1. Situations that Cause Hurt

The broken-hearted are near at hand.

We do not need to look far to find the broken-hearted. Daily, the media bombards us with reports of gang murders, rapes, and robberies. Violence and terror is apparent on all sides. More and more families are homeless. Witchcraft and occult practices have a stranglehold on many young people. Those who are ritually, sexually abused are being programmed in such a way that their personalities become fragmented, unable to function in normal society. Divorce rates continue to

---

[1] Peter's betrayal is recorded in all four gospels: Mat 26:31-35, 69-75; Mk 14:27-31, 66-72; Lk 22:31-34, 54-62; and Jn 13:37-38, 18:15-18, 25-27.

[2] Lucado, Max, *He Still Moves Stones*, Word Publishing, Dallas, TX, 1993, page 200.

escalate, leaving behind the untold stories of the adults and children whose lives are devastated. We read about the ongoing slaughter houses of abortion. The *Christian Herald* stated that 95 percent of the women who have had abortions regretted it (1994). The November 1993 National Aids Day yielded statistics that over 14 million people worldwide have AIDS. All of society is affected by situations and hurts such as those listed in Table Q.

Consider the hurts experienced by each person in your family. Now think about your friends. How about yourself? No doubt you could list a great variety of hurts which have different degrees of intensity. These hurts may have resulted from generational sin, they can be caused by others, or even self-imposed.

Hurts come from omission as well as commission.

Sometimes our hurts come not from what was done to us but from what was **not** done. What about the toddler who was never cuddled or hugged? How about the child who was never made to feel special? Consider the teenager whose parents missed his graduations, did not attend his birthday parties and failed to say, "God has a plan and purpose for your life."

Other hurts result from deep disappointments beyond our control: children who failed to meet our expectations, a promotion that never came, or a wanted pregnancy that never happened. Some of you reading this have experienced hurts that only God knows. Isn't it good to know that He cares, and that He wants to heal.

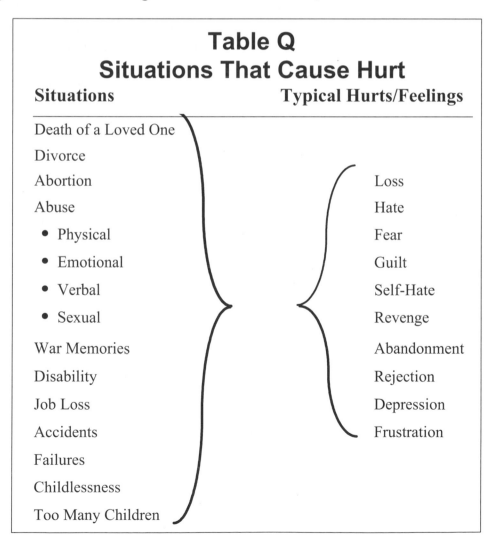

Table Q
Situations That Cause Hurt

Situations	Typical Hurts/Feelings
Death of a Loved One	
Divorce	
Abortion	Loss
Abuse	Hate
• Physical	Fear
• Emotional	Guilt
• Verbal	Self-Hate
• Sexual	Revenge
War Memories	Abandonment
Disability	Rejection
Job Loss	Depression
Accidents	Frustration
Failures	
Childlessness	
Too Many Children	

2. Levels of Hurt

What if it were possible to measure a person's mental, emotional, and spiritual "temperature" the same way we measure a physical temperature? Hurts, as we know, are hard to gauge. We can't take a traumatic experience in another person's life and calculate the depth of pain he suffered or how it affected his spirit and soul. We can't measure hurt from the outside.

There are degrees of hurt.

The degree and the intensity of hurts cover a tremendous range from the small pain, such as being left out of a ball game to the "gut-wrenching" trauma of losing a child-custody battle.

What about the long-lasting and ongoing hurt? Sometimes physical, sexual, or emotional abuse goes on for years, or the spouse is still unfaithful; the alcoholic still drinks every evening and weekend; the ridicule still continues.

Close friends of ours have a handicapped child. They say every time their son enters a new phase of development, they cry all over again, seeing what other children his age can do. **Ongoing hurt needs ongoing healing.**

At the extreme level of hurt are those deliberately and ritualistically traumatized to force disassociation. Examples of this are Satanic Ritual Abuse (SRA) and Political Programming. In the case of Political Programming the victimizers are after a totally controlled slave that will do their every wish yet remain undetectable.

G. Some Consequences of Hurt

It is not an exaggeration to say that the results of hurt are just as crippling to our soul and spirit as a debilitating disease is to our bodies. While the myriad of horrible consequences of hurt are far too many to discuss, we can list some of the major consequences.

1. Hurts begin in the family and affect the entire family.
2. Hurts affect the entire person.
3. Hurts cause others hurt.
4. Hurts cause lies (Ungodly Beliefs) to be established.
5. Hurts cause ongoing vulnerability and hopelessness.
6. Hurts cause shame.
7. Hurts cause defense mechanisms.
8. Hurts cause us to wear "masks."
9. Hurts cause restricted growth.
10. Hurts cause anger/disappointment toward God.
11. Hurts cause blocked emotions.
12. Hurts cause fragmented personality.
13. Hurts lead to Demonic Oppression.

We will elaborate briefly on most of these consequences. We will explore in more detail the "anger/ disappointment toward God" and "blocked emotions" consequences, since it is usually necessary to help a ministry receiver specifically deal with these areas before he can receive God's healing. Other consequences of hurt are discussed in the last two sections of Chapter XIII, "Control-Rebellion- Rejection Stronghold".

1. Hurts Begin in the Family and Affect the Entire Family

*It is not safe to be **real** in wounded families.*

Books galore have been written over the past 10 years about the devastation of dysfunctional behavior patterns affecting whole families. In their attempt to cope with already existing pain and hurt, families develop unspoken rules that lead to the denial of feelings, problems, and reality. At the center of these rules is the lie that "it is not safe to be real." The unspoken agreement within these dysfunctional families is:

- **Be Blind:** To your own perceptions of reality.
- **Be Quiet:** Do not discuss family problems with anybody.
- **Be Numb:** To your feelings and personal boundaries.
- **Be Careful:** No one can be trusted.
- **Be Good/Perfect:** It pays.

Such lies only create more pain. Why? For one reason: **Hurts that cannot be acknowledged cannot be healed.** Since most people grow up with some family dysfunction, nearly everyone carries unhealed hurts. These hurts contain lies (Ungodly Beliefs) that keep us trapped in our pain and dysfunction.

2. Hurts Affect the Entire Person

Hurts are like a poisonous gas seeping into every area of a person's life. Although quiet and unseen, they sap the life out of those exposed and can affect any of the following areas:

- **Physical Body:** A variety of ailments and diseases.
- **Behaviors:** Self-defeating; growth restricting of self and others; shut down of emotions.
- **Mind:** Painful flashbacks; Ungodly Beliefs; mistrust, distorted perceptions and goals.
- **Emotions:** Turbulent, negative emotions such as fear, hate, self-hate, anger, grief, defeat, mistrust, shame, rejection, abandonment.
- **Spirit:** Dullness, oppression; flickering life-flow; turning away from God.

*Hurt people are **easily** offended.*

All dimensions of a wounded person's life can be affected. He sees life through "gray tinted" glasses.

3. Hurts Cause Others Hurt

Considering others' situations brings compassion.

It would be easier if the hurting person wore a badge saying, "I am a hurting person, and I hurt other people. Contact at your own risk." Hurting people relate in ways that propagate hurt. Reflect on the hurts in the lives of those who have hurt you the most, and observe how their hurts drive them to inflict the very same hurts onto others.

4. Hurts Cause Lies (Ungodly Beliefs) to be Established

Embedded in every hurt are one or more lies. These core lies are usually "I AM" statements that affect our God-given identity. A common example might be, "I AM unlovable." These lies (Ungodly Beliefs) dictate our behaviors hour by hour. They breed other lies and work together with these other lies to keep us trapped. We have identified as many as five major Ungodly Beliefs in one deep hurt.

5. Hurts Cause Ongoing Vulnerability and Hopelessness

Hurts draw us to the very thing that causes more hurt.

UGBs empowered by our hurts propel us into the very life style we hate.

In her book, *Released From Shame,*[1] Sandra D. Wilson compares the operation of hurt/shame to Velcro with hoops and loops, looking for something to attach to. In our observation, hurt causes us to become enmeshed with the very thing that compounds the hurt. A fatherless girl, vulnerable because she is so needful of love and protection, is drawn to and becomes entangled with an older man who uses her sexually. We seem to seek out and expect to have happen to us the very thing that has caused us so much pain. The operation of our Ungodly Beliefs which are lodged in our hurts, set us up to perpetuate the very lifestyle that we hate.

6. Hurts Cause Shame

Shame is everywhere.

Writers, such as Sandra Wilson in her books *Released From Shame* and *Hurt People Hurt People,*[2] have done an excellent job in helping us to go deeper in understanding the correlation between hurt and shame. These books are strongly recommended for ministers, not only because of their quality but because a large percentage of the people that they minister to will be struggling with shame.

Through our own ministry, God has revealed an understanding of a unique way that shame collaborates with fear and control to yield an almost impenetrable stronghold of self-protection. We call it the Shame-Fear-Control Stronghold. When you are ready to learn more about this stronghold and how to identify and destroy it, please go to Chapter XIV.

---

[1] Sandra D. Wilson, *Released From Shame*, Intervarsity Press, Downers Grove, IL 60515, 1990.

[2] Sandra D. Wilson, *Hurt People Hurt People*, Thomas Nelson Publishers, Nashville, TN, 1993.

7. Hurts Cause Defense Mechanisms

Our psychology books are full of descriptions of the various defense, or coping, mechanisms that people put in place to survive. Even though these defenses may help a person make it from day to day, they also keep him trapped at a much narrower expression of life than the "life more abundant" that Jesus promises.[1] When true healing comes, defense mechanisms become a thing of the past!

8. Hurts Cause Us to Wear "Masks"

Who are we, really?

__Masks__ disguise our Hurt.

Deep hurt causes upheavals and distortions of our God-given identity. We may carry a false guilt about our very existence, a constant need to prove our worth, and a ruptured sense of belonging. Our real identity becomes unrecognizable because it is camouflaged by various defense mechanisms that we use either to express our hurt or to protect ourselves from further hurt. These behaviors are disguises, like masks, covering the real identity. Do we recognize the **hurt underneath these cover-ups, these disguises?**

The Shame-Fear-Control Stronghold is a major example of a (multiple) false identity and the "covering over" of the God-created personality. Please see Chapter XIV for more on this devastating stronghold.

Perfectionism and Performance Orientation can Mask Hurt

Can we earn our right to exist, for love and respect?

We work ourselves into exhaustion, ignoring family and compromising other values in order to win respect or love. Why? Because we carry the deep hurt of never feeling accepted and of having to **earn** love and respect. We struggle to be perfect and avoid criticism while knowing deep down inside that we can never be perfect enough. We are doomed to failure.

Anger, Blame, Criticalness, Sarcasm, and Bitterness can Mask Hurt

Anger is a symptom of feeling trapped, of being violated.

All of these behavior patterns can issue from hurt and frequently do. The anger comes from believing that we are trapped with no way out. There is also legitimate anger when our personhood has been violated. As a result, we find fault with others, blaming, criticizing, and being sarcastic, hoping that by putting others down, maybe we won't feel so bad about ourselves. If allowed to fester and grow, the anger develops into bitterness. We have seen the reality of Hebrews 12:16:

> Hebrews 12:15
> Looking diligently lest any man fail of the grace of God; lest any root of **bitterness springing up trouble [you], and thereby many be defiled**; (KJV)

---

[1]   Please see Jn 10:10.

Depression and Withdrawal can Mask Hurt

Depression is a sign of an ebbing life.

How long does it take us to recognize the broken heart underneath depression and withdrawal? When there is no safe place to vent our anger, when there is no hope of getting free from the trap around us, when we have no chance of success, when we have made a mistake so great that it is impossible to correct it, even for God, it is natural to lose the spark of life, become depressed, withdraw, and give up.

Passivity can Mask Hurt

Sometimes it is easier to give up.

One way to cope is to do nothing. We feel safe if we do nothing. At least we can't be blamed for failing at some attempt. Also, when we are trapped, we can't do anything anyway!

As we look at the patterns in our own lives, and as we prepare to minister to others, we must not be deceived by the disguises of hurt but be alert to the various masks that we all wear in order to survive.

9. Hurts Cause Restricted Growth

Hurts: the birthing place of fears!

Hurts restrict our vision of who we are and who we can become. We believe lies (Ungodly Beliefs) about ourselves. They blind us to our God-given identity and potential. Hurts also block intimacy in relationships, affecting who we relate to and what we let ourselves do. They are like invisible walls, holding us in and others out. They also act as invisible chains that will not let us move too far away from our hurt-distorted concept of ourselves. Hurts, the birthing place of fears, cripple our potential and keep us from becoming all that God has ordained for us.

Exercise: Stop a moment and ponder the following questions:

1. Think of some of the hurts in your own life and how they have held you back from opportunities you might have had, but you were scared to take the risk.
2. Think of the dreams that you have let go.
3. Think of people you would like to have talked to, but you couldn't because you didn't feel comfortable.
4. Think of the intimacy you wanted to have in a relationship, but it never happened.

Prayer: If considering any of these questions causes pain in your heart, pause a moment, pray, and ask the Holy Spirit to touch and heal the specific losses in your life. Then wait for Him to do so.

---

10. Hurts Cause Anger/Disappointment Toward God

Issues:

Does God really care?

Is He really there?

Can He really be trusted?

A natural result of hurt is to question God's "care," or to believe that if He does care, He cares more about other people than about us. Someone who feels God has hurt, betrayed, or abandoned him has a difficult time expecting to receive anything good, particularly healing, from God. The bottom line of the disappointment-with-God issue is a **trust** issue — a lack of trust in God.

Why would the one who "hurt" you want to heal you? People carrying hurt and/or disappointment often believe, "God doesn't care." This belief can form a barrier that blocks God's voice and puts a stranglehold on the relationship. Since the ability to hear God's voice greatly increases the effectiveness of receiving healing of Soul/Spirit Hurts, and since the major goal of RTF healing ministry is an improved relationship with God, we must address the issue of anger/ disappointment with God.

*Struggling with the **trust issue** is common.*

This is one of the most sensitive areas in which to minister. This delicate area is not unique to those who are severely wounded. Many devout, serious, searching Christians have struggled with these same questions, especially when they feel that God has not met their expectations or answered their prayers. They feel "He has not 'been there' for me." The serious believer has to come to terms with such unanswered questions as:

- God, where were You?
- God, if You love me so much, why didn't You intervene?
- God, why didn't You warn me not to get involved?
- God, why have I had to go through this?
- God, why don't You answer my prayers?
- Why do You seem so far away, so hidden, so silent?

Added to these questions are the "bigger" issues:

- Why is there so much suffering in the world?
- Why do people hurt and kill each other?

The gnawing belief that a caring God has abandoned us in our time of need **must** be addressed.

Obstacles to Acknowledging this Problem

*Religious attitudes make it difficult to be **real** with God.*

The problem of anger/disappointment toward God is greatly compounded in some Christian circles. Questioning God is considered sacrilegious, ungodly, and yes, even dangerous. As a result, attempting to work through real, negative feelings is seen as lack of faith, weakness, or rebellion. This makes it difficult for a person to admit these feelings to himself since he feels them to be too abhorrent, to scary to look at, and too shameful to acknowledge. He may fear disapproval from his pastor or other church friends. He may fear that God will be angry with him and punish him for having and expressing his real feelings. His relationship with God, however, will be greatly stifled until these feelings are exposed and resolved. Until they are, he will feel he is merely going through Christian "motions."

215

11. Hurts Cause Blocked Emotions

As the hurts begin to "pile up" in the life of a young child, the pain may reach a level where the child silently cries within himself, "Enough. I can't take any more. I have to get rid of this unbearable pain!"   And so he does.

He begins to separate himself from the pain. It is as if he puts it in a special "bottle" that encapsulates the pain and places it on the shelf. He has blocked the painful emotion from his conscience awareness. He feels ever so much better!

As this process is repeated, again and again, the line of "bottles" begins to get quite long. More and more of his emotional "being" has become encapsulated. Unfortunately, many of his positive feelings are bottled up along with the negative ones. His range of emotional expression and response becomes narrower and narrower. Eventually, he becomes emotionally neutral. Nothing bothers him anymore. He becomes that "steady" friend, the one you can count on in a crisis. He keeps his "cool" when others around him are all excited. He seldom feels pain, but then, he doesn't feel pleasure either.

This may seem like a desirable state, particularly if you have experienced a lot of pain in your life. It is merely a partial life, however. Jesus came that you might "have life and life more abundant."[1]   Bottled emotions, encapsulated emotions, blocked emotions, greatly diminish, even steal from your promised "life more abundant."

12. Hurts Cause Fragmented Personality

In extreme cases, hurts can be so severe that a person will go beyond "blocked emotions" and unconsciously create alternate personality fragments in his soul. These fragments, called "alters," isolate and protect the personality from the pain of the trauma. In most cases, the painful event may not even be remembered. This dissociation can result in separate and distinct personalities.[2]

The most common reasons for disassociation are physical or sexual abuse/trauma. In satanic ritual abuse (SRA),[3] the most extreme case, electric shock, drugs, and/or brain washing techniques are often deliberately used to fragment the personality. When memories of such abuse surface, the person needs care from someone experienced in ministering to these areas.

---

[1] Please see Jn 10:10.

[2] This phenomena was labeled Multiple Personality Disorder (MPD). The current term is Dissociative Identity Disorder (DID).

[3] The book by James G. Friesen, *Uncovering the Mystery of MPD*, Here's Life Publishers, Inc., San Bernardino, CA, 1991, presents an enlightened Christian approach to ministering to MPD or DID.

13. Hurts Can Lead To Demonic Oppression

Demons gain access when our natural spirit defenses are down due to trauma of any sort. So they work hard to "engineer" hurtful situations to cause hurt, as well as to gain "legal ground." This occurs because of our response to the hurt.   We respond with sinful behavior out of our pain. We shout and hurt back. We allow thoughts of revenge to circulate in our mind. We figure out how to shame and defeat our tormentor. Repeated sins become open doors for Demonic Oppression. If we could **always** respond in a godly way, we would not open any doors for oppression. Unfortunately, few, if any of us, are able to do this.

H. Possible Hindrances to Healing and Possible Solutions

As ministers, we come with great enthusiasm and anticipation to the time of healing. In about seventy percent of the people to whom we minister, the healing comes easily and without interference. It is absolutely thrilling how easily God's healing is received. In the other thirty percent, however, there are major, frustrating hindrances operating within the individual receiving healing. These hindrances can prevent him from receiving his healing. As ministers, we need to be "wise as serpents, and harmless as doves."[1] As we approach the healing session, we need to be prepared. We need to be on the offensive, knowing who the Healer is, ready to discern and cooperate with Him, and prepared to overcome any hindrances that may arise. Now let's look at what we may need to confront.

The most common hindrances that block the receiving of God's healing are:

1. unfamiliarity with the process
2. unconfessed sin
3. unforgiveness
4. major fears
5. analytical thinking
6. medication
7. anger/disappointment with God
8. blocked emotions
9. demonic blockage

Let's examine each of these in more detail, and look at some possible solutions to help the ministry receiver "break through" or "break free" of the hindrance.

1. Hindrance: Unfamiliarity with the Process

We take time to fully explain the healing process and answer the ministry receiver's questions. Happily, by this point in the ministry process, we have a gauge of how well he is hearing the Lord, and what way or ways he most often hears. Earlier, during the Sins of the Fathers and Resulting Curses ministry, we asked

---

[1] Please see Mat 10:16.

him to actively listen and to receive what God had for him once the curses were broken. This powerful listening experience provided excellent listening practice for our receiver and allowed us to assess his hearing ability. Still, however, if hearing the Lord is new to him, he may feel very tense and uncertain.

We assure each individual receiver that the Lord will speak to him in the ways with which he is most familiar. (We discuss this in more detail in the Preparing the Ministry Receiver section, page 198.) After the first time of receiving God's healing, most people relax and improve in their hearing. We often reassure our receiver that he cannot fail since there is no wrong way to do this process. We build faith that God wants to intervene in his life and bring healing even more than he wants to receive.

2. Hindrance: Unconfessed Sin

Unconfessed sin can block the entire Soul/Spirit Hurts session. New believers, particularly, haven't yet recognized that repentance for sin is one of God's most important requirements. We have never experienced a person being unwilling to confess sin and ask God's forgiveness once he understood the scriptures about forgiveness[1] and realized that unconfessed and unrepented sin can block the healing process. We usually lead the ministry receiver in a general "Submission Prayer"[2] as part of starting the healing time, and then we stay alert to help him repent any time this is necessary during the process.

3. Hindrance: Unforgiveness

Another powerful roadblock to receiving healing is unforgiveness of other people, organizations, or situations. It is important, as we deal with this area, to use discernment and avoid rigidity and legalism. We have seen the Lord deal very differently with different individuals. With some, He has not been willing to enter their memory in a visible way until forgiveness was completed. With other individuals, we have seen Jesus heal the ministry receiver first and then ask him to forgive. Often Jesus has helped the receiver to see his offender in a whole new way. The point here is to guide each individual as the Holy Spirit guides us rather than having a preconceived idea of how the forgiveness has to happen.

Often unforgiveness has been in our ministry receiver's life as a demonically empowered generational sin and curse. We may need to do deliverance before effective Soul/Spirit Healing can occur. Since we cleared the "legal ground" when we ministered to the SOFCs Problem/Ministry Area, we can move directly into deliverance as needed. Once free of the demon of unforgiveness and its related cousins of resentment, retaliation, bitterness, etc., our receiver is much more able to forgive or, at least, "be willing to be made willing."

---

[1]   Please see, for example, 1 Jn 1:9-10.
[2]   Soul/Spirit Hurts Submission Prayer is on page 256.

4. Hindrance: Major Fears

Natural fears, as well as demonically generated fears, can swarm to the surface and immobilize our ministry receiver as we attempt Soul/Spirit Healing. In each area of fear that we discuss in the following paragraphs, we need to discern whether binding/deliverance of demons and/or reassurance is needed.

Being out of Control

As we begin the healing session, the receiver will have just prayed a Submission Prayer, yielding the control of the session to the Lord. Near panic may ensue. The more wounded our receiver, the greater the challenge to give up his control. He may have lived for years with a fear of the unknown, and now he is being placed again in a situation of the **UNKNOWN**. He does not know what memory the Holy Spirit will bring to him, how much pain he will have to experience, or whether the healing will actually happen. He may feel very much out of control. He wants the healing, yet nothing in him wants to give up control!

Reliving Pain

Nothing in the ministry receiver wants to face the old pain. He is in an internal battle. As ministers, we need to reassure him that this time, facing the pain has a purpose and will have a conclusion. Entering into the pain again, in order to let the Lord heal it, will be entirely different from his past experiences of just being miserably overwhelmed with unending pain. It will be more than worth the temporary pain he has to endure.

Shame

Another strong, common fear is the fear of having a shameful, once-secret area exposed. Although our receiver has already confessed sin and repented in these areas, there is a greater level of intensity and feeling of shame and exposure as he re-enters the specific shameful memories. One man, who was on a pastoral staff, had kept secret a homosexual encounter for years. In our sessions he had confessed it and received God's forgiveness, yet he was still in bondage to the shamefulness of it. He just "didn't want to go there." As we reminded him that God's healing would bring him peace and restore his sense of cleanness and worthiness, he chose to receive healing. Wonderfully restored, he is now bringing healing ministry to many others. We need to encourage each individual — even though he may feel shamed momentarily — that both shame and the enemy's torment will be brought to an end.

Failure

The fear of failure is also common. In this case, the fear that he will not "do it right." A person with a strong history of failure will fear failing in this ministry situation. As with the other fears, both reassurance and deliverance may be necessary. Again, we reassure him that he cannot fail because there is no way to do this process wrong.

5. Hindrance: Analytical Thinking

Some very dear people have gone through life as analyzing machines. They analyze everything, particularly themselves, and any process in which they are engaged. It is a deeply ingrained habit and lifestyle. It can also be a primary way of staying in control. In addition, a demon may be empowering the analytical thinking as illustrated later in Cathy's healing testimony. A very analytical ministry receiver will be analyzing his own thoughts, particularly trying to figure out if he is hearing himself or, "Is this really God speaking?"

Unfortunately, analyzing will prevent him from fully entering into the memory. It will keep him in "head realm." We need to encourage/insist that our "analytical" receiver let go of evaluating his own thoughts and simply be present with the impression or memory that the Lord brings. We assure him that when the Lord speaks he will know it, because he will change. The healing will be real. Sometimes, we have to give several reminders to "Stop thinking."

6. Hindrance: Medications

Medications, particularly the anti-depressant or anti-anxiety drugs, are designed to limit the intensity of emotions as well as the range of emotions. We never tell a ministry receiver to discontinue his medication during his ministry (or any other time).[1] When the roots of depression are emotional and/or spiritual, however, his need for medication will end as the Lord's healing takes place.

As ministers, we do need to recognize that any receiver on anti-depressant drugs will have a much narrower range of emotions. He will have a narrow range of "feeling them" and a narrow range of "expressing them." He may report, "I just feel numb." Be encouraged that the Lord can still work with root causes and bring healing even when the drugs are blocking the ministry receiver's feelings. In some cases, however, it appears that, because of the medications, he receives less healing than he could have received. From person to person, the results can be quite variable.

7. Hindrance: Anger/Disappointment with God

A person who is angry at God cannot, at the same time, attempt to trust Him for healing. This can be a major block. Often, as we begin to minister, we encourage the ministry receiver to follow David's example and pour out his real feelings, as we discuss in the next section. We frequently need to remind him that God already knows how he feels. Sometimes we have to help him "unplug" his blocked negative emotions, which we also discuss in the next section.

---

[1] Note: Not all depression is rooted in hurts, nor does all depression have a spiritual basis. Some depression has physical roots, such as a chemical/hormonal imbalance. If this is the case, the ministry receiver will need medication until his physical condition is adequately treated.

a. Aids to Acknowledging Anger/Disappointment with God

We can help our ministry receiver deal with Anger/Disappointment toward God several different ways. However, one very important thing that we can do is intercession.

Intercession is important.

We have done more heartfelt, intercessory prayer, crying out to the Lord in this area than any other. We sometimes enlist the help of intercessors, asking them to pray and seek God on behalf of our receiver. We believe that intercession is many times the major key to getting the breakthrough.

Encourage Being Real

Gently lead.

Encourage the ministry receiver to acknowledge his true feelings toward God. It helps to be understanding rather than confrontive. If he is having trouble admitting his feelings, use softer words and a permissive tone unless the Holy Spirit leads you otherwise. This avoids defensiveness on his part.

> **Example:** It seems like you are upset, frustrated, or perhaps a little disappointed with God.

This suggestion is usually easier for him to admit than "anger." It doesn't seem so "awful."

Use Scriptural Examples

Show the person through scriptures that he is not alone or unique in his feelings. Moses, for example, was terribly upset with God:

Thank you, Lord, for examples like Moses and David.

Numbers 11:10-15
10 Moses heard the people of every family wailing, each at the entrance to his tent. The LORD became exceedingly angry, and Moses was troubled.
11 He asked the LORD, "Why have you brought this trouble on your servant? What have I done to displease you that you put the burden of all these people on me?
12 Did I conceive all these people? Did I give them birth? Why do you tell me to carry them in my arms, as a nurse carries an infant, to the land you promised on oath to their forefathers?
13 Where can I get meat for all these people? They keep wailing to me, 'Give us meat to eat!'
14 I cannot carry all these people by myself; the burden is too heavy for me.
15 If this is how you are going to treat me, put me to death right now—if I have found favor in your eyes— and do not let me face my own ruin."
(KJV)

David expresses his frustration with God as he cries:

Psa 10:1
Why dost Thou stand afar off, O LORD? Why does Thou hide thyself in times of trouble? (NAS)

Psa 13:1
How long, O LORD? Wilt Thou forget me forever? (NAS)

Psa 43:2
. . . Why hast Thou rejected me? . . . (NAS)

It is better to express than to stay stuck.

David asks, "Lord, where are You and what's happening in our relationship?" Isn't it good to know that someone who loved God as much as David could still deal with these questions? Yet God continued to love David. It's reassuring to know we can come and say, "God, why?"

The point is that it is **okay** to have these feelings and it is **okay** to express them. It is **not,** however, **okay** to stay stuck with these feelings.

Show Real Sources of Hurt

Expose the real enemies: Sin and Satan.

A turning point occurs when the ministry receiver realizes that the root cause of his hurt is sin in operation in the lives of other people and/or in his own life. Satan is always there, too, seeking whom he may devour,[1] encouraging sin to continue. A ministry receiver can often see that sin is the cause of hurt as a general principle, but he has trouble applying this truth in his own case. Sometimes we ask the ministry receiver to think about the person or people who have hurt him the most and identify the hurts operating in their lives. We pray for God's revelation of this important truth: Sin is the underlying cause. When this fact becomes clear, the ministry receiver can **stop blaming God** and begin to put the blame where it belongs. It takes the Holy Spirit to help the person see that God did not want those things to happen to him and that it wasn't His plan for him to be hurt.

*God doesn't **remove** us, but He goes **through** it with us.*

With some people, it may help to emphasize that God promises to be with us through the pain, the hurt, the disappointment, the things that we don't understand, and the grief process — not only in the past but also in the present as we face the pain. He wants to bring comfort and to raise up beauty from ashes. Isaiah 43:2 speaks powerfully about the fact that we will experience hard, trying, and hurtful times. That's a given. After all, we live in a fallen world. The good news is that we do not have to face these alone. The passage reads:

Isa 43:2
When thou passest through the waters, I will be with thee; and through the rivers, they shall not overflow thee: when thou walkest through the fire, thou shalt not be burned; neither shall the flame kindle upon thee. (KJV)

---

[1] Please see 1 Pet 5:8.

b. Verbalizing the Anger/Disappointment

When the ministry receiver, following David's example, pours out the deep pain of his resentment, abandonment, disappointment, and anger, etc., to the Lord, the relief can be immediate and healing can begin. We encourage him to do two things: to be very specific about his feelings and, secondly, to let himself **really** feel his feelings as he expresses his heart to God. In the majority of cases, just expressing his true feelings will lead him into a place of repentance.

Another phenomenon may occur first, however. Sometimes the ministry receiver, as he is verbalizing his upset with God, will immediately see or sense the hurtful memory where his anger/disappointment is rooted. He is already "there." In that event, it is natural to lead him right into the steps that allow further healing to take place. For some individuals, it is only **after** the healing of this specific memory when they realize that the Lord has not failed them and they can truly trust Him.

c. Repentance

The sin of misplaced blame.

*Learning to **trust God again** is key.*

Quite frequently, as the ministry receiver is engaged in the "Pouring Out My Complaint" to God process, he recognizes that he has been putting the blame in the wrong place. Then, on his own accord, he begins to ask God's forgiveness for blaming Him, instead of seeing the real source of his hurt. With some individuals, however, you may need to lead them in a brief prayer of repentance. Many tears have been shed as people sought God's forgiveness for misplaced blame. Repeatedly, this experience has been the turning-point in being able to receive from God and beginning to trust Him again.

d. God Redeems Hurt

*Our response to hurt can **determine** our destiny.*

God can bring **good** out of our hurts.[1] God can use hurt to develop us and to mature us if we don't let ourselves get stuck in it. Think about Joseph, for example. Many were the plans and purposes of God, but, oh, what he had to go through — and the hurts that he had to endure — before he got there! God can use hurt to chisel, to make, to strengthen, and to mold if we will give the hurt to Him. If we don't, the enemy uses it to keep us bound and wrapped in grave clothes, so that we can't move forward into all the Lord would have us to do and to be.

8. Hindrance: Blocked Emotions

Blocked emotions are somewhat like fear and rejection. Everybody has at least a few. When the ministry receiver comes for RTF ministry, it is our desire to help him release his "stuffed" emotions to God rather than keeping them suppressed and simmering down deep inside. We want to help him find, remove, and release the emotions bottled up for years. These emotions frequently include feelings of grief, bitterness, resentment, and frustration. Usually, our receiver is holding them in because it has not been safe to express them. Or he has been taught that it is a sign of weakness or a lack of faith to express them. Unfortunately, some religious teachings imply that Christians should "always be strong, joyful overcomers." This can cause people to hide their true, negative emotions even from themselves.

---

[1] Please see Rom 8:28.

Our goal is to help the individual receiver realize he has permission to be real with himself, with us, and with God, and that there is a safe, godly way to release and be free from blocked emotions. Let's look briefly at some steps we can use to accomplish this.

a. Explain the Biblical Precedent/Command

Colossians 3:8-10 basically commands us to get rid of negative emotions. Paul writes:

> Col 3:8-10
> [8]But now you must **rid yourselves** of all such things as these: anger, rage, malice, slander, and filthy language from your lips. [9]Do not lie to each other, since you have **taken off** your old self with its practices [10]and **have put** on the new self, which is being renewed in knowledge in the image of its Creator. (NIV)

Rid ourselves of both negative emotions and actions.

The King James Version has, "Now you must also **put off** all these things . . . ." The NIV has, "now you must **rid yourselves** of all such things as this . . . ." So, we are commanded to **get rid** of both negative emotions and negative behaviors.

In Ephesians 4:31, Paul echoes the same truth and then adds:

> Eph 4:32
> **Be kind** to one another, tenderhearted, forgiving each other, just as God in Christ also has forgiven you. (NAS)

*How to both "**get rid of**" and "**be kind**" in a godly way.*

As we look at these two commands — "**get rid of**," and "**be kind**" — it becomes clear that we are not to hurt other people in our process of "getting rid of." It is **not** permissible to spew our venom onto another person. What then do we do? David, the great psalmist, becomes our guide. He gives us numerous examples that act as signposts pointing in the same direction: Take the innermost issues of your heart to God. His message is unmistakable: **Be real with God.** Pour out your heart to Him. Hold nothing back before our heavenly Father who already knows everything that is hidden in our hearts. In modern terminology, "let it all hang out." David pours out everything that is troubling him to the Lord.[1]

Pouring Out My Complaint

Steve Cobb, a missionary friend, pointed out to us that Psalm 142 provides an excellent example of how David poured out his "complaint" to God and cried out for God to "bring his soul out of prison." It is another passage that gives us scriptural permission to be real with God.

David is our "model."

> Psa 142
> I cried unto the Lord with my voice; with my voice unto the Lord did I make my supplication. I poured out my complaint before Him. I showed before Him all my trouble. When my spirit was overwhelmed within me, then You knew my path and the way which I had walked. They have laid a snare for me. I looked on my right hand and beheld that there was no man there who would know me. Refuge failed me. No man cared for my soul. I cried unto Thee, oh Lord, I said, "Thou art my refuge and my

---

[1]   Please see Psalms 22:1-8, 35:15-17, 62:8, 64:1, 102:1-11, 19-20, 142.

portion in the land of the living." Attend unto my cry. For I am brought very low. Deliver me from my persecutors for they are stronger than I. Bring my soul out of prison that I may praise Thy name. The righteous shall compass me about, for Thou shall deal bountifully with me. (KJV)

Isn't this a beautiful pattern of openness to follow?

If other examples are needed to further illustrate this point, consider Moses[1] or Jesus in the garden of Gethsemane.[2] Jesus says, "My soul is exceedingly sorrowful, even unto death." And then He says to the Father, "If it be possible, let this cup pass from Me, nevertheless, not as I will, but as Thy will."

*Want a close relationship with God? **Be real**!*

We see in Scripture that those who are most **real** with God are those with the **closest** relationships to Him.

b. Helping the Ministry Receiver Give Himself Permission

In addition to seeing the biblical precedent for being real with God, it helps to remind our receiver that God already knows how he feels. Often, this comes as a surprise to him until he stops to think about it. Then, we remind him that he has had years of stuffing his emotions and telling himself, "You can't let that out; you can't say that. Don't let anyone know." What a shock to be told that he needs to let out his real feelings. This new idea represents a paradigm shift in his thinking and a threat to what has always been safe. He cannot just flip a switch and go from one mode of operating to another.

*There may be a need to **command** the release of stuffed emotions.*

Minister, be patient but firm here. Help the receiver give himself permission to do this. In extreme cases (this is more true with men than with women), we've had the receiver command his "inner self" to release the stored feelings. Now, that's really powerful, when you say to your inner self, **"I command you, in the name of the Lord Jesus Christ, to release those emotions you've stuffed for all these years."** Usually they begin to come out, sometimes as a dribble at first and sometimes like a flood. But they **will** eventually come out.

*Special considerations must be taken when dealing with **anger**.*

A note about anger: If anger is the primary emotion that has been held in, the ministry receiver may have many fears about releasing it. He may be afraid that he will go into a rage, lose control, or even go crazy. If this is verbalized, reassure him that you will not let him hurt himself or you or anything in the room. He may need to see scripturally that he does **not** have God's permission to hold on to anger. In Ephesians we read:

> Eph 4:26-27
> Be angry and sin not. Let not the sun go down on your wrath. (KJV)

God is not only telling us to keep our relationships straight but **also** not to hold on to anger. We are to take it to Him. That is **the** wonderful way He has provided.

---

[1] Please see Num 11:11-15.
[2] Please see Mat 26:38.

Please note that we do not have permission to "pour out" our anger onto others. Again in Ephesians:

> Eph 4:29-32
> [29]**Do not let any unwholesome talk** come out of your mouths, but only what is helpful for building others up according to their needs, that it may benefit those who listen. [30]And do not grieve the Holy Spirit of God, with whom you were sealed for the day of redemption. [31]Get rid of all bitterness, rage and anger, brawling and slander, along with every form of malice. [32]Be kind and compassionate to one another, forgiving each other, just as in Christ God forgave you. (NIV)

Paul clearly instructs us that our conversation with others should be a blessing to them, not cause more hurt. Our anger must be taken to God. This is the safe and godly way to deal with it.

God designed our emotions, including anger, for a reason.

We share about anger from the perspective that anger is a valid emotion included in our makeup by God. Sometimes it gets stirred up for unrighteous reasons or because our "flesh" does not like something. On the other hand, when we've been violated, when our personhood has been hurt or our core values disregarded, anger is a normal, natural emotion — an indicator that we should heed. We need to share with God the hurt underneath the anger as well as the anger itself.

c. Priming the Pump

*Use lines containing **feeling** words to help the receiver get started.*

After the ministry receiver agrees to try to be real with God in the area of his emotions, we ask him to begin to tell God about his hurt and pain. Some people immediately are able to do this. Others need some help getting started. If this is the case, we "prime the pump" by giving him some "lines" that begin to describe the hurt. We might suggest to him to say, for example, "Lord, I am just so hurt and angry about how my mother treated me. I still have nightmares about it." Or we might suggest, "Just tell the Lord what it was like for you to be locked in your bedroom all those afternoons when your mother was punishing you." After the priming, he may naturally continue, or more "feeling" lines may be needed.

The Holy Spirit will guide you in knowing how to lead your receiver. Do not get discouraged here. Remember, you are working to reverse the pattern of many years. If the receiver says a few things and then stops, give him more lines. Also, do not give up if he reports feeling "weird" by doing this. Be understanding, but be firm.

Releasing blocked emotions is a process.

Sometimes the ministry receiver may say feeling words but not be feeling them. He may still not be in touch with his emotions. Even so, this "pouring out" usually gets him one step closer to letting himself fully release them and be free of them and their effects in his life.

Releasing blocked emotions also releases forgiveness.

Once they have shared their pent-up emotions with God, a person will often spontaneously move into forgiving others who have hurt them. They are also able to **feel much closer to God.**

We encourage the receiver to continue the "pouring out" process at home and to use it whenever hurts occur or he becomes aware of other past hurts.

d. What if This Doesn't Work?

Sometimes the ministry receiver stays blocked even when we have implemented all of these suggestions. He may believe a hidden UGB, such as, "I will be punished if I say or feel anything negative." Other times the lie may be even more basic, such as, "I will just die if I let myself feel the pain."

Ask the receiver to let the Holy Spirit direct him to a time in his life when he shut down his feelings. Then work with the memory that the Holy Spirit reveals. Expose the lie that is embedded in the painful memory and have him repent of it and open himself to God's healing truth. He may just begin to "know" the truth, or he may see or sense Jesus, or Father God, telling him the truth. The truth will free him to begin to feel and express his emotions again.

Dissociation is a second reason a ministry receiver may stay blocked and be unable to get in touch with his pain even when trying. During a previous time of trauma, he may have disconnected from his emotional pain. Dissociation is a common unconscious defense mechanism that allows people to cope with their intense pain. If you discern dissociation in the ministry receiver, pray safety and protection over his life. Allow the Holy Spirit to lead your prayers for his healing. Don't try to push him. It is better to get specific training in dealing with dissociation before trying to minister in depth to a person with a severely fragmented personality.

9. Hindrance: Demonic Blockage

The last hindrance we want to be prepared to confront is demonic blockage. Did you know that demons take absolute delight in blocking the healing of hurts? They will interfere using every ingenious way possible. Unbelief, Doubt, and Skepticism demons will whisper, "This isn't going to work. Those ministers don't know what they are doing." The Unworthiness demon interrupts with, "God doesn't want to heal you anyway. Who do you think you are?" The Shame demon joins in the act with, "Now they are going to find out how bad you really are." Passivity says, "Why don't you just sit there and do nothing?" Stoicism demons cry out, "You know you've had it a lot better than most people. What are you whining about? You don't need healing, just 'suck it up.'" Meanwhile, the Mocking demons are laughing and ridiculing us, the ministers, as well as mocking God. The clamor can be so loud that it is a wonder that anyone breaks through and believes God more than the internal voices.

The strongest demons are the Occult blocking demons. They empower, strengthen, and magnify the forcefulness of all of the other demons. They cause deception and confusion. Often their presence is exposed as the receiver says, "I have a headache," or "I feel as if there is a tight band around my head." When there is strong occult bondage, at times we have been directed by the Holy Spirit to do all of the deliverance planned for the Demonic Oppression session before the Soul/Spirit Hurts ministry.

We must come to the SSHs session prepared to move aggressive against everything that could block the ministry receiver from receiving all the healing and freedom God has for him.

What is the message? **Come prepared!** Let's look at what is involved in our full preparation.

I. Preparation of the RTF Minister

The cry of our hearts, "Lord, would You come and heal this person?" represents the beginning of healing because of God's faithfulness as Jehovah Rapha. While we are trusting Him to do His healing work, we also need to prepare ourselves as well as our ministry receiver. This will help us better cooperate with Him throughout the healing process.

1. Releasing the Burden

For years, I, Betsy, carried the burden of trying to be the healer. That's right, me. I was declaring with my mouth that God **is** the healer but at the same time carrying the pressure of it as "my responsibility" to make something happen. Going into a Soul/Spirit Hurts session, I was tense and anxious. I ministered for several years in this miserable condition. At last the light broke through! What He wanted was simply for me to learn to cooperate with Him while He did the healing. It is an understatement to say, as I gave up my perceived responsibility (control), a multitudinous burden lifted. What about you? No matter what you may be confessing with your mouth, do you need to release yourself from false responsibility and put your total trust in God as the Healer? If so, do it today!

2. Understanding the "Insides" of a Memory

We must understand the "insides" of a memory before we can safely assist the Lord as He brings the healing to the memory. So before going further we want to explore the "insides of a memory."

We also want to be very sensitive to the fact that we are providing an opportunity for people to go deep within themselves and face painful, often distressing experiences that have been stored within their memories. We are entering a private, intensely personal realm that deserves our upmost respect. We have no more business charging into this vulnerable area of someone's life unprepared and untrained than a medical student has performing brain surgery his first year of medical school. We need to know what to look for in the memory and, more importantly, what to do with it. Memories needing healing contain the following ingredients:

- Hurtful Situations
- Negative Painful Feelings
- Ungodly Beliefs
- Demons (often)

Hurtful Situation

What are we trying to do? Our goal in working with a memory is to have our receiver re-experience his memory of a **hurtful situation** in such a way that Jesus, Father God, or the Holy Spirit is allowed to intervene and bring healing to all of his **negative, painful feelings.** (See examples later in this chapter.) Often, the Holy Spirit brings revelation to the hurting person or shows him pictures that bring relief, fresh understanding, and healing.[1] In other cases, people experience the active presence of Jesus, making it possible for them to interact with Him as He directs and heals. His action and His revelation bring healing of the negative emotions and pain. With God's fresh revelation, the ministry receiver begins to see himself as well as others from the Lord's perspective. He now has the healing **TRUTH** and not just the **FACTS**! This usually results in the automatic replacement of the Ungodly Belief (lies) associated with the memory with Godly Beliefs.

Negative Painful Feelings

Because **negative emotions** are such a strong component of hurtful memories, we often have our ministry receiver "pour out" his **hurtful emotions** to the Lord. (See "Pouring Out My Complaint" section on page 224.) This can be an important part of getting "unburdened" of the "trapped" aspect of a painful memory. As he pours out his complaint, he begins to feel less trapped and less alone.

Ungodly Beliefs

Ungodly Beliefs, incorporated into the pain of the memory, need to be exposed and healed. Often, a core **Ungodly Belief** becomes very evident as the healing takes place. Jesus or the Holy Spirit may address the lie directly. For example, as Jesus tells a person, "It wasn't your fault," the lie he has carried that, "Everything bad is always my fault," is exposed and replaced by the truth.

We add this **UGB** to our receiver's list of **Ungodly Beliefs** so he can later incorporate the truth that Jesus spoke to him into a Godly Belief. Doing this is a "backup." Why? Because when Jesus brings the truth into a hurtful memory the lie (**Ungodly Belief**), in most cases, is instantly replaced with the truth (Godly Belief). Sometimes, however, it necessary to continue to meditate on the Godly Belief to permanently plant God's truth into the receiver's heart and spirit. We firmly believe that these Ungodly Beliefs (lies) and Godly Beliefs (truth) need to be recorded in our notes and given to the person after the session. We have been amazed at how quickly we all forget the awesome things God has done!

More of a challenge to the RTF minister are the hidden, or less obvious, **Ungodly Beliefs** that spring from the core lie(s). A person believing, "Everything bad is always my fault," may also believe, "I am no good," and/or "I will never amount to anything."   Although these associated UGBs may never have been spoken each onc needs to be exposed and healed as well.

Another group of subtle **Ungodly Beliefs** are those that can powerfully serve to block a ministry receiver in several ways. These beliefs may hinder him from being able to hear from the Lord, receive a memory, or invite Jesus into his memory. A very evident example is, "I am too unworthy to receive anything from the Lord." When we suspect the presence of such a lie, we present it as a possibility to the ministry receiver. If he is willing, we take him through the Ungodly Belief steps on the Ministry Card to renounces the lie and come out of agreement with it.

We will likely find several Ungodly Beliefs in every painful memory.

---

[1] Please see Rob's story, page 245.

Demons (often present)

Demons constitute the fourth component of the memory. They are often attached to both the **Negative Painful Feelings** and the **Ungodly Beliefs** contained in the memory. These **demons** always try to block the healing. Count on it. Be prepared either to bind them or cast them out depending on their strength and degree of interference. As usual, let the Holy Spirit direct you. (See page 227, Hindrances: Demonic Blockage).

A vital part of ministry preparation is anticipating what we expect to find within a hurtful memory. Prepared and alert, we can be on the offense as we prayerfully help guide our ministry receiver.

J. Preparing the Ministry Receiver

Once you are prepared, the next crucial task is the thorough preparation of your ministry receiver. This preparation will determine, at least in part, how well he will be able to enter into the Soul/Spirit Healing experience. We discuss the following information with him to help him know what is expected: Both what he is to do, and what he is not to do.

1. Hearing the Lord

If needed, we review with our receiver how he usually hears the Lord. We have already shared with him from Chapter IV the different ways God speaks. If necessary, we remind him that he may have a thought, or a "knowing," or that he may see an image of a situation where he was wounded. We assure him that God will probably communicate with him in the way that is most familiar. A couple of cautions are usually needed.

a. Not "Thinking it Up"

First, we want ministry receiver to be still and wait to see/hear/sense God's voice. We emphasize that we are not asking him **to "remember" anything,** or **to "think it up,"** or **to select one of his (known) hurts. He is to receive, to be sensitive, and see what the Holy Spirit brings.** We also share that the hurtful memory can be connected to an event that occurred during any time period of his life, from conception until the present time.

b. Sharing without Censuring

Second, we tell the ministry receiver to share with us whatever the Holy Spirit may bring into his awareness. He is not to censure the memory in any way. Even if what he sees/hears/feels seems very insignificant or "fleeting" — or he doesn't understand what it means — his job is to share it. Why do we do want him to do this? Because as he shares, God usually causes his understanding to "open up" and become significant. In fact, we can point to numerous times when an initially "foggy" memory became clarified and meaningful ministry took place. We let the ministry receiver know that whatever comes into his awareness is what we are looking for. Nothing is too small, silly, or embarrassing if the Holy Spirit brings it to remembrance.

Also, remind him not to censure memories for which he has previously received ministry. The Holy Spirit may want to go deeper and provide a more complete healing.

2. Review the Ministry Steps

We review the steps on the ministry process.[1] This can be helpful in surfacing any remaining questions he may have. We make it clear, however that we will be leading him so that his focus can be on the Lord.

3. Maintaining God Focus

At this point, we prepare our receiver in terms of his focus which is to be on the Holy Spirit and what He reveals and/or on Jesus as He comes into the memory. We remind him that unlike the other sessions where the primary interaction has been with us, this will no longer be the case. We ask him to keep his eyes closed and to stay focused on Jesus and the memory even during times when we are talking to him.

4. "Pouring Out My Complaint"

Next, we instruct our ministry receiver how to do the "Pouring Out My Complaint" procedure[2] as David did in Psalm 142. We have him read this psalm out loud and share the ways he identifies with what David has written. We let him know that we will be asking him to enter into this same level of honesty as he shares his own painful feelings with the Lord.

5. Removing Possible Hindrances

It is important to alert our receiver that he may possibly experience some hindrances,[3] particularly demonic opposition. We reassure him that we are accustomed to interference and are prepared to work together to overcome all obstacles.

6. Giving Reassurance

The importance of giving reassurance cannot be overly emphasized. We must assure our ministry receiver that even though he may have intensely painful feelings when the memory returns, the pain won't last long. This time a redemptive purpose is at work: God's complete healing and eradication of his hurt. We assure him of the strong likelihood that in the midst of the hurt he will have an awareness of the presence of Jesus. Remind him the Lord has been present during every part of his life and that He promises never to leave us nor forsake us.[4] The Lord will be with him in this special time of healing.

---

[1] We do this either using the steps at the end of this chapter or from the Ministry Card. There is an image of this Card in Appendix A.

[2] Please refer back to the "Pouring Out My Complaint" process on page 224.

[3] You may refer back to the "Hindrances" section which starts on page 217.

[4] Please see Deu 31:6, Mat 28:20, and Heb 13:5.

7. Praying Submission Prayer

We let our ministry receiver know that as we start the healing ministry we want him to pray a Submission Prayer, both submitting to the healing process and turning over his control to the Lord. (Later, we will show him the prayer on page 256, and ask him to read it and see if he can agree with it. We will ask him if he would pray this prayer, adjusting it and/or putting it into his own words if he prefers.)

K. "Waiting Upon the Lord" Listening Prayer

This powerful ministry approach to bring healing for Soul/Spirit Hurts is very safe for the ministry receiver in terms of possible demonic interference or deception. It gives the Holy Spirit great latitude to control the ministry in "exactly the right way." As ministers, we merely follow along, being faithful stagehands.

In this section we want to present an overview of this approach. Then we will describe the basic ministry ingredients in detail. We will conclude by sharing several case histories of how these ingredients were used in actual ministry sessions.

1. Overview of the Ministry Ingredients[1]

Note that we are using the term "ingredients" rather than "steps." We usually do not need to do all of the following items with each person. We work with the Holy Spirit to move through only the **needed** ingredients. The ingredients are:

1. **Thoroughly prepare the ministry receiver.**
2. **Have the ministry receiver pray the Submission Prayer.**

Three Key Steps

3. **Determine the scope and starting point: General versus specific**

Key Step A =>

4. **Ask the Holy Spirit to reveal a memory or impression.**
   - Clarify the memory.*
   - Deal with any hindrances to receiving a memory.*

Key Step B =>

5. **Guide the process of "Pouring Out My Complaint" to the Lord.**
   - Work within the memory to "specify" and "feel" the feelings.

Key Step C =>

6. **When ready, invite Jesus into the memory.**
   - Deal with any hindrances blocking the awareness of Jesus.*
   - Keep the focus on what Jesus says and does.
   - Broaden what is acceptable.*
   - Three-way conversation (direct guidance from the Holy Spirit).*
   - Have ministry receiver give any remaining pain to Jesus.*

7. **Take notes (1) on what Jesus says and does and (2) on any revealed UGBs.** (These will be shared later with the ministry receiver.)

8. **Do "Clean Up/Follow Up" of remaining healing issues.**

(Ingredients continued next page.)

---

[1]   Please note that these ingredients are more complete and detailed than the Ministry Steps on the Ministry Card.

9. **Test healing by "Checking the Results."**
   - Deal with every negative feeling
   - Follow a Theme

   * The items marked with "bullets" are ingredients to be used as needed.

We want to emphasize again that hindrances can occur during any part of the SSHs healing ministry. Even though the above list has two references to hindrances don't be limited to only dealing with hindrances at these points in the process. We want you to be particularly alert to the two most important and very common hindrances: Disappointment with God and Blocked Emotions. Again, let us refer you back to these topics in the "Hindrances" section[1] so you can be well able to help the ministry receiver break through to healing.

2. Ministry Ingredients

Having presented the overview, let us now examine the ingredients in detail.

1. Thoroughly Prepare the Ministry Receiver
We prepare the ministry receiver by following the instructions given on pages 230-232.

2. Have the Ministry Receiver Pray the Submission Prayer
As we prepare to start the actual Soul/Spirit Hurts ministry, we have the ministry receiver read/pray the Submission Prayer (on page 256). We ask him to read it first to himself to see if he is in agreement with the prayer. We give him permission to change the wording into his own words if he prefers.

3. Determine the Scope and Starting Point: General versus Specific
Where do we start? Once we have prepare the ministry receiver we start very broad and general or we can start narrow and focused. When a life has been so dominated by one destructive issue or theme, we often feel led to begin with that focus rather than beginning in a broad and general way. Always ask the Lord where to start. It is a matter of revelation and discernment.

We explain to the ministry receiver our plan so he knows what to expect. If we want to start "broad," we ask the Holy Spirit to reveal **any hurt** He wants to heal. "Holy Spirit, please take Sam back to the memory You want to heal." Note that there is no focus, no limitation. If we choose to start "narrow," then we focus on one area that has been a key problem/issue in the ministry receiver's life. For example, we might say, "Holy Spirit, please take Sam back to a memory that contains the roots of his lust problem." Or, "Holy Spirit, please reveal to Laura a memory of when her fear first began."

4. Ask the Holy Spirit to reveal a Memory or Impression
We pray quietly and allow plenty of time for the ministry receiver to listen for a memory. Once he lets us know he has received a memory, we ask him to describe it in detail.

Clarify the Memory*
If the ministry receiver is not clear about the memory or doesn't understand it, we have him ask the Holy Spirit to clarify the memory and make it plain.

---

[1] Please see pages 220 and 223.

Deal with any Hindrances to Receiving a Memory*

If he still can not receive the memory clearly, we ask the Holy Spirit to show us what is hindering or blocking. We then take care of this obstacle. At this point in the ministry, the obstacle is usually blocking demons, needed forgiveness, or unfamiliarity with the process.

5. Guide the Process of "Pouring Out My Complaint" to the Lord

We want to help the minister receiver enter into the memory as much as possible, re-experiencing the event as well as his feelings. This will enable him to embrace a deeper level of healing. We do this by having him "Pouring Out My Complaint" (POC).

Once the minister receiver is in touch with his pain, we ask him to begin to share his pain and feelings with the Lord. Some ministry receivers are immediately able to do this. Others may need some help getting started. If so, we help him as discussed on pages 224-227.

Work within memory to "specify" and "feel" the feelings

Many times specific questions help the ministry receiver re-enter the memory. As he begins to report the memory, we ask him questions such as:

- "How old are you?"
- "Where are you?"
- "Is anyone else there?"
- "Describe what is happening and how you are feeling."
- "What is your fear like?"
- "Why are you afraid to tell anyone?"

These questions will not only help the ministry receiver become more focused, but will also assist him to specify and re-experience his feelings.

Once he has shared his pain with the Lord, we are ready to have him ask Jesus to come into the memory.

6. When ready, Invite Jesus into the Memory

In some cases the ministry receiver will already be experiencing Jesus being with him as he pours out his complaint. More often, however, at this point we ask the receiver to invite Jesus into the memory with him. We say, for example, "Ask Jesus to show you where He is." We ask him to report what Jesus is saying or doing.

Deal with any Hindrances blocking awareness of Jesus*

At this point, the main hindrances that prevent a ministry receiver from being aware of Jesus are unconfessed sin, unforgiveness, demonic interference and/or shame. If there is a problem, we ask the Holy Spirit which of these areas needs to be addressed.

Keep the Focus on what Jesus Says and Does

We encourage the ministry receiver to continue to keep his focus on Jesus. It is what Jesus says or does that brings the healing. All our efforts are directed toward helping this happen.

In our role, we **never tell** the ministry receiver what Jesus is doing or saying. For example, we **DO NOT** say, "Now Jesus is coming over to hug you." NO. NO. NO. Also, we **never command** or direct Jesus to do something. We never say, "Jesus, go take the baby out of his crib and hold him." This is another NO, NO.

We may **ask Jesus** if He will do something. For example, "Jesus, would You show this hurting child Your love?" **Asking is totally different from directing or demanding!** Sometimes Jesus responds to what we ask Him to do, and sometimes He doesn't! Our task is to stay tuned to the Holy Spirit, so that we are asking Jesus to do what He, through the Holy Spirit, is already telling us He wants to do. This is essentially the same as intercessory prayer, where the Holy Spirit has the intercessor praying God's will into a situation so God is released to do here on this earth what He wants to do.

Attempting to direct Jesus, or the Holy Spirit, and telling Him what to do or say is manipulation, control, and occultic. It will not result in true healing. It opens the door to illegitimate control by the minister and possible entry of spirit guides and other familiar spirits that would like to get involved.

We leave the Lord in control. He can appear to the ministry receiver however He wishes. We **ALWAYS** let Him **take the initiative!**

Broaden what is Acceptable*

Most often people are able to see Jesus with them in their hurtful memory. In other instances, they sense Him. Others do not see or sense Jesus, but rather have an overpowering sense of the Father's love and His presence. They report feeling bathed in the Father's love. Still others hear God speaking through the Holy Spirit. They hear words in their spirit such as, "I was always there for you." Others primarily hear scripture. Most amazingly, a few people to whom we have ministered did not see or sense anything specific, yet had a profound experience of God's peace replacing their feelings of hurt.

While we want to be totally open to whatever way God chooses to reveal Himself we must confess to having a preference. We have experienced particularly significant fruitfulness when the ministry receiver directly encounters Jesus within the memory. For that reason, we always begin by having the receiver invite Jesus to be there with him. If Jesus doesn't come into the memory, we must discern whether or not there is a blockage or whether God is choosing to heal in one of His other ways.

Three-Way Conversation (Direct Guidance from the Holy Spirit)*

For years we have used a three-way conversation as we worked with the ministry receiver within his memory. We have talked to the ministry receiver. (I.e., "Now, pour out your heart to the Lord.") We have talked to the Lord. ("Lord, would you come and heal John?") We have asked the receiver to report what the Lord was saying or doing. (I.e., "What is the Lord showing you?" "He is showing me that He wants me to forgive my mother.") God has brought tremendous fruit using this approach. Recently, Dr. Ed Smith has written about using this "three way conversation."[1] He says:

> I also talk to the Lord out loud during the process and carry on three-way conversations with Him. I ask the questions and allow the client to give response. I do not guide the moment but rather ask questions as to what the client senses Jesus is wanting him to do. I avoid leading questions that might be a subtle way of directing. I ask the Lord Jesus honest questions about my inadequacies. Such as, "Lord Jesus, I don't know what it is You are wanting to do, know, see, etc. Would you give us more understanding, direction, light, etc." I then trust that Jesus will speak to the person.

---

[1]   Smith, Dr. Ed M., *Beyond Tolerable Recovery, Basic Training Seminar,* Family Care Publishing, Campbellsville, Kentucky, 1999, pg. 140.

Notice the way it works. The minister asks the questions of the Lord, but is given the answer as the Lord speaks or brings revelation to the ministry receiver, who reports back to the minister. This roundabout way can be very helpful. It is another communication link to complement our direct listening to the Holy Spirit.

Have the Ministry Receiver Release Any Remaining Pain*

As we approach the end of bringing healing to a memory, we ask the ministry receiver to check whether or not he has any remaining pain. If some still remains, we direct him to give the pain to the Lord.

7. Take Notes (1) on what Jesus Says and Does and (2) on any Revealed UGBs.

Even though the ministry receiver may be tremendously affected by what Jesus says and does within the memory, we have noticed that he may quickly forget. We keep careful notes of what occurs so we can give him a record of these profoundly important events.

Jesus frequently speaks Truth into the lies associated with the SSH as part of bringing the healing. This usually completely destroys the power of the UGBs that were holding the hurt in place. However, it is important to record the truth and add what Jesus says to the Godly Beliefs list so that the ministry receiver can continue to meditate on it. If necessary, we lead the receiver in repentance for believing the lie or lies.

8. Do "Clean Up/Follow Up" of Remaining Healing Issues

In the Soul/Spirit Hurt area, we have often been reminded of Jesus raising Lazarus from the dead[1] and then His turning to His disciples and telling them to remove the grave clothes. Jesus has done the hard part. He has done the life-giving part. However, He directs His helpers to "loose him and let him go."[2]

It is the same in Soul/Spirit Hurts. Jesus, the Father, or the Holy Spirit have brought life and healing. Now we as ministers need to take care of the legalities. We need to be sure our "Lazarus" is completely unbound with no grave clothes in sight! This process involves ministering to any new areas that have been exposed.

Typical Clean Up/Follow Up jobs include making sure forgiveness is complete — especially self-forgiveness — that Soul Ties are broken, that newly identified Ungodly Beliefs are addressed, and that SOFCs are broken. If the presence of additional demons becomes evident, we need to either cast them out then or add them to our list for the upcoming deliverance.

9. Test Healing by "Checking the Results"

Dr. Ed Smith has contributed to the world of Christian inner healing ministry by sharing his godly revelation through Theophostic Counseling. We are appreciate his insight of "confirming the healing"[3] or "checking the results," once Jesus has brought the healing.[4] Checking the results allows us to determine if all of the negative emotion within the menory has been completely healed, or if there are some hurtful emotions still present.

---

[1] Please see Jn 11:1-45.

[2] Please see Jn 11:44.

[3] ibid, pg. 148.

[4] Note: Here we utilize the same principle of confirming but use the *Restoring the Foundations* Integrated Approach to Healing Ministry approach. It is not intended to represent the methodology of Theophostic Counseling.

The principle is to focus on whatever negative emotion the Lord has just healed, such as anger. We then ask the ministry receiver to search and see if he can find any remaining anger. In our experience, the receiver usually says, "No, Jesus has taken it all away," or something similar. There are times, however, when anger (or some other negative emotion) remains. In these cases, more healing is needed. The remaining anger is most often stored in one or more additional hurtful memories. We are thus alerted to follow the anger theme into other hurtful memories until the anger is completely healed in all of the memories.

Deal with every Negative Feeling

In addition, this process of "checking the results" helps the ministry receiver locate other negative feelings that are contained in the same memory. For example, he may say, "No, there is no more anger, but I do feel a lot of bitterness." What a wonderful entrée for the next area for healing. Now bitterness becomes the focus in the same memory. Once bitterness is dealt with we recycle and again "check the results." The approach is to continue until all negative emotions are healed.

Illustration

We were about to pray and wrap up the session with a ministry receiver when he spoke in a very irritated voice saying, "I'm feeling really angry." Although surprised, we asked the Holy Spirit to show him the root of his anger. The Holy Spirit took him back to the original memory of molestation, which we thought had been dealt with. This time Jesus healed him of his anger of being victimized. Again we thought we were finished. Then he began to weep because Jesus was dealing with his lifelong feeling of helplessness. As the Lord flashed memory after memory before this man, He showed him how He had been his source of strength in the many "helpless" situations of his life. Helplessness, that we had not even realized was there, was healed. We suddenly had a radiant, empowered man because Jesus had healed all of his negative emotions.

Follow a Theme

A number of years ago, the Lord taught us a tremendous lesson as we ministered to a man struggling with lust. The Holy Spirit revealed to him an early experience of molestation by a neighbor. Although Jesus healed him of this, none of us felt his healing was quite complete. As soon as we said, "Holy Spirit, show us what else needs to be healed to complete the process," the man immediately had two more memories of sexual defilement come to him. We then worked through each of these memories individually. It wasn't until Jesus had brought healing in all three of the memories that this man felt free. From that experience, we learned the importance of following a theme through several memories until we are assured that complete freedom has come.

We also have discovered that God is efficient. So often, when He heals a memory of a particular type, for example, rejection, He heals other memories of the same type/theme simultaneously. Sometimes, however, He wants to deal with several memories individually, especially if there is significant trauma involved in each one. We, as ministers, simply need to ask Him if there are related memories He wants to heal. Somctimes we will see a picture, like a map, showing several related memories connected by a time line. We share this information with the ministry receiver and have him ask the Holy Spirit to bring the next related memory.

3. Case Histories

The following are transcripts taken from actual ministry sessions and used with permission. Enjoy these with us as we re-experience God's loving guidance and healing in the lives of these people. We will highlight the Ministry Steps/Ingredients as we go along.

a. Joseph's Soul/Spirit Hurt

This portion of a Soul/Spirit Hurts session illustrates so well the perfect way that Jesus interacts with the ministry receiver to obtain maximum trust, obedience, and healing.

Ministry Receiver's Background

We were working with Joseph, an outstanding Christian leader who had come from a home where both of his parents were alcoholics. In Joseph's emotional abandonment, he had developed mistrust of both people and God. He acknowledged that he saw patterns in his own life of being aggressively controlling, self-sufficient, and independent.

Ministry Preparation

As we went through all the steps of preparation, Joseph became well-acquainted with the format we were about to use. We decided to start with the broad, general approach since he had hurts in many different areas. It seemed better initially not to restrict the healing to any specific focus.

Ministry

Instruction:

Listen, Report.

Minister (Listening Prayer): We are going to pray now and ask the Holy Spirit to bring into your awareness any key hurts and/or hurtful events that He wants to heal at this time. We want you to listen and then report to us any hurtful memory or impression, once it comes.

Wait upon the Lord. Pray, Listen.

(As we "Wait upon the Lord," we pray quietly in the Spirit, and listen for revelation about what God wants to do. We also try to discern any hindrances that may attempt to block the process. In this case, we don't discern any problems.)

Joseph (Receiving a memory): This memory is very clear. It was my wedding day, and I had forgotten something important I needed. I have to drive back to our house to get it before the wedding. My father begin to ridicule me about forgetting whatever it was.

Minister (Wanting to help specify feelings): What are you feeling as he is ridiculing you?

Joseph: I feel alone and angry. I am very angry. I immediately jump to the defensive mode. I guess I want to reject dad before he rejects me.

Minister (Feel the feelings): Let yourself feel your anger. Get more in touch with it.

Joseph: I am feeling my anger now. Actually, what I feel even more is hatred. I am feeling hatred toward my father. He ridiculed me so many times. He was never there for me when I needed him.

(Pause) I can also see Jesus over in the corner of the room. He is trying to get my attention, but I am ignoring Him. I am just too mad to listen.

(Notice, Joseph is aware that Jesus is already there. We don't need to have Joseph ask Him to come.)

Minister: Why don't you let Jesus talk to you?

Joseph: He already is. He is telling me that dad wanted to act right, but that he didn't know how. I am so mad that I am not interested in what He has to say.

(Long pause) I am driving away from the house now. Jesus is in the back seat of my car. He is telling me He has been waiting a long time for me to acknowledge Him. He is telling me to release my dad to Him; that He will change Dad, that I can't.

(Silence)

Minister (Checking the Results): What is happening to your anger?

Joseph: I am still feeling it. Jesus is asking me to let Him drive the car. He wants to take me to my dad. He is showing me that my dad has this covering over him. I have never realized that before. He is showing me what is underneath the covering, who my dad really is. I see my dad as a much younger person who is really scared and very ashamed.

(Long pause) I realize now that my dad needs my love and my support.

(Tearful) I never saw that before.

(Continues by describing his actions.) I am going over to my dad. I want to hug him but I am thinking of all the times he smelled like alcohol, all the times that he stunk. I'm going over anyway and putting my arms around him. I can't remember hugging him. I don't know what he will do. He is starting to hug me back. We are just holding each other. I am forgiving him for all the neglect, the times he wasn't there for me. I see that I have judged him and cut him out of my life. I am asking his forgiveness too. I thank him for being my dad.

Minister (Realizing that the Lord is healing years of Joseph's anger, stays quiet.)

Joseph: Now, I see myself back in the car. Jesus is in the front seat. He is telling me that He wants to make up for the things I have lost, but that He can't do it very well when He is in the back seat — when I am leaving Him out of my life. I am asking Him what I should do. He is telling me to trust Him, to let Him get in the driver's seat, to let him drive my car.

Minister (Wanting to follow the Lord's direction.): Just keep letting us know what you are doing.

Joseph: I'm telling the Lord that I have never been able to trust anybody. That is my problem. If I trust Him, I will have to get rid of all my crutches and strategies, all the things I have used to keep Him away and keep other people away.

(Pause)

Minister (Three-way conversation): Jesus, would You be willing to show Joseph how to let go of his mistrust?

Joseph: He's telling me He wants to do an exchange. He wants to take all of my strategies and give me what will be satisfying. We are making the exchange. Now I am transferring my trust to Him. I am going to trust Him.

(Pause) He says I am His son. He is telling me to focus on Him and that He won't walk away or leave me.

(Joseph's once tense and tearful face looks much more peaceful.)

Minister (Checking the Results): Would you look within yourself and see if you can find any anger or mistrust?

Joseph: There is no anger anywhere, or mistrust, but there is something left.

Minister: What is left?

Joseph: What is left is my concern about what others think. I have always been overly concerned. Jesus is asking me to write this fear on a card and give it to Him. He is saying that He will take care of what others think. He is taking away the card I have written on.

(Joseph looks up and begins to laugh in amazement at what the Lord has done.)

Minister (Checking the Results): Can you find any fear about what people think?

Joseph: No! No, Jesus has taken it all. I am at peace.

Minister: Where is Jesus now?

Joseph (With surprise in his voice, as if it should be obvious.): Oh, He's in the driver's seat, driving the car. I'm sitting next to him.

Minister: That's wonderful. Before we stop, we need to take care of just a few more things.

Discussion

Let's discuss this segment of Joseph's healing before going on to the Clean Up/Follow Up ingredient.

This healing was smooth and easy from the minister's point of view. We did not need to clarify the memory Joseph received. There were no blocks or hindrances. He was very able to identify his feelings and to feel them. He recognized anger, hate, and concern/fear. We did not need to have him ask for the Lord to come be with him since he was already aware of Jesus' presence. If Joseph had been unable to go on at this point of the healing, we would have suspected unforgiveness to be a hindrance. Clearly, however, he remained in good contact with Jesus. We just followed what he and the Lord were doing.

We skipped the step of "Pouring Out My Complaint" to the Lord. It wasn't needed to help him get in contact with a memory or in contact with the Lord. It wasn't needed to express and release the anger, hatred, and fear. Jesus took care of these directly.

Did you notice how He did it? Joseph's anger and hate left both when he forgave his dad and also when the Lord showed him his dad as he really was, ashamed and fearful. Jesus took his fear of "what others think" away on a card.

Out of Joseph's abandonment, he felt he couldn't trust God or anyone else to take care of him. As a result, he lived his life out of the Ungodly Belief, "I can't trust God to take care of me; I have to take care of myself." We identified several other related Ungodly Beliefs as well. He had to stay in control at all times. This problem of trust was directly dealt with as Jesus asked Joseph to trust Him and they made an exchange. The issues resulting from mistrust, control, and self-sufficiency were challenged as Jesus asked Joseph to let Him sit in the driver's seat, and Joseph yielded.

In this short healing session, Jesus also touched another related area: Joseph's deep sense of not belonging. Joseph's heart was touched as he was reconciled to his father and also as Jesus said, "You are My son."

Clean Up/Follow Up

The Clean Up/Follow Up ingredient was fairly simple. We ministered to the several Ungodly Beliefs, and helped Joseph formulate new Godly Beliefs for each one. The anger/hate/bitterness area needed to be broken as a Sin of the Fathers and as a Resulting Curse. Lastly, we added this grouping of demons, plus unforgiveness demons, to the list of demons to be cast out in the next session.

Because of Joseph's strong commitment to becoming all that God wants him to be, he has held on to his healing and seen outstanding changes in some major life-long patterns. It was a great privilege to be a part of God's healing of Joseph.

b. Cathy's Soul/Spirit Hurt

Let's look now at an excerpt from a Soul/Spirit Hurts session that includes some additional ingredients. In this session, we have to help our receiver stay focused on her memory, as well as stopping some demonic interference. Note also how we had the ministry receiver "Pouring Out My Complaint" to the Lord very early in the ministry.

Ministry Receiver's Background

Cathy, a strong, self-motivated leader and prayer warrior, is married to a Christian man who loves her. Over the twenty-plus years of their marriage, he has had several different periods of unfaithfulness that brought much pain to them both. Cathy and Dave have had ministry over the past year, but as they came to us, there appeared to be a subtle but real breach lingering between them, the kind that is hard to identify. We chose to go with a specific focus for the initial healing since their problem was both current and obvious.

Ministry

Minister (After Cathy has been prepared we direct Cathy to ask for a specific focus.): Would you just wait on the Lord now and ask Him to take you to a memory that has roots causing this current separation you are experiencing.

241

Cathy: I am seeing tons of different incidents.

Minister (Clarifying the memory): Ask the Holy Spirit to highlight one of them.

Cathy: I just feel so much anger at Dave.

Minister (Deciding to work with the feeling, thinking it can be used to help take Cathy to an important memory.): Let's start there. Just begin to pour out your complaint to the Lord. Tell Him all about your anger.

Cathy (Pouring Out My Complaint): Lord, I am so mad that this stuff keeps happening. It seems like Dave doesn't do what he needs to do to get over his problem. Lord, it creates a constant inner stress in me. I'm always wondering when the other shoe is going to drop. I hate living like this.

(Pauses) I am seeing a memory now of the early years of our marriage.

Minister (Clarifying the memory): Where are you and what is happening?

Cathy: We are in Kentucky. Dave has gotten into sexual trouble. I go to a pastor to get help. I come home and tell Dave what we need to do, but he won't listen. It's as if he doesn't hear me. He needs to get help. We both need help, fast, if we are going to save our marriage. I am so frustrated. Dave is looking at me and acting as if he is listening, but I know it's not penetrating.

Minister (Asking for the Lord's presence.): Would you ask the Lord to come be there with you.

Cathy: Jesus is already here. I can see Him. He is over in the corner of the room, listening.

Minister: Cathy, do you want to ask Him to help you with your frustration and anger?

Cathy (Starts to try to talk to Jesus but as soon as she starts, she comes out of the memory. She looks up and begins analyzing her past situation.)

Minister: Cathy, what just happened? You left your memory just as you were beginning to talk to Jesus. Would you see if you can go back to the memory and be there again.

Cathy (Takes a minute, closes her eyes.): Yes, I am here with Jesus.

Minister: Tell Him about your anger and frustration. Tell Him what that anger and frustration feel like to you. Tell Him what it made you want to do.

Cathy (Starts once again to talk to Jesus. She then looks up and goes into analytical mode for the second time.)

Minister (Briefly explains to Cathy that there is demonic blockage hindering her contact with Jesus.): We bind every antichrist demon and every demon of analysis. Cathy, now reenter the memory again, and see if you are able to talk to Jesus.

Cathy: Lord, I'm so angry with my husband. I am looking to him to be my covering. Lord, he is not even aware of my pain and how much he has hurt me. I want him to see and hear how bad he has hurt me. I want to make him repent.

(Continuing) Jesus is coming over to me. I can see this very large sword inside of myself. He is trying to pull it out of me.

(Pause. A minute or more go by before Cathy continues.) The sword is out now. Across it is written the words, "Man's Justice."

(Another pause) Lord, I repent of the lie that I have to be the one to bring Dave to a place of repentance, rather than You convicting him. Forgive me, Lord, for all of my anger and control.

Minister: What is happening to the sword? Are the words still there?

Cathy: I can't see the words any more. Jesus has put the sword into the fire. When it is tempered enough, He will give it back to me.

(The implication here is that when Cathy is healed, she will be able to (safely) use the sword, this time as a weapon of spiritual warfare.)

Minister (Checking the Results): Cathy, would you see if you can find any anger or frustration within yourself?

Cathy: There is none here, but I do see a very large void in me. That void held the anger and frustration and bitterness. It held my need to fix things myself and force my husband to repent. It is where the sword was.

Minister (Three-way conversation): Jesus, would You be willing to heal this void in Cathy?

Cathy: He is bathing me, washing me with His love. Jesus is just filling the void. It is going away. I also see His tears for Dave. He is hurting for my husband.

(As she sees this, Cathy's heart is softened toward her husband.)

Discussion

We made the decision to have Cathy begin the session by pouring out her complaint because often the feeling that is poured out will take the person directly back to a major memory. This happened in Cathy's case.

When Cathy tried to talk to Jesus, she came abruptly out of her memory instead. We suspected demonic blockage but we were not sure yet. When it happened a second time, we asked the Holy Spirit what demons were hindering and heard the words, "Antichrist" and "Analysis." These demons were trying to prevent Cathy from keeping contact with Jesus, her healer. (In another ministry time, it could be different demonic forces.) The demons responded to being bound in the name of Jesus. Otherwise, we would have stopped and done deliverance.

When Cathy saw the sword with "Man's Justice" written on it, she immediately saw the connection between "Man's Justice" and her own sin of trying to force her husband into repentance her way. She began to repent, without our having to intervene.

Lastly, note the significance of the final "Checking the Results." It was then that Cathy saw the void within herself, left by removing the sword. Filling the void was an important step. It needed to be done. It was also during the Checking the Results that Cathy saw Jesus' care for her husband and her heart toward him was softened.

Clean Up/Follow Up

The Clean Up/Follow Up part of the session included ministering to two Ungodly Beliefs: "I will be the one to cause Dave to see my pain and come to repentance," and, "My husband will never see the depth of my pain and repent from his heart." We also sensed that bitterness was a SOFCs, which we hadn't previously identified, so we ministered to it following the steps on the Ministry Card. Lastly, we did deliverance of the two demonic spirits identified, Antichrist and Analysis, as well as Bitterness and Control. We were out of time, but felt that in the next session, we would like to pursue Anger and Bitterness and make sure no more similar roots were hidden in other memories.

Rob's Soul/Spirit Hurt

Would you take a few minutes now to read Rob's healing testimony, "God's Healing Touch in One Man's Life" on page 245, so we can point out several areas that are different from the other two case histories.

Rob's Testimony: Discussion

Rob is an excellent example of a man who received life-changing healing through the pictures or images brought by the Holy Spirit. The pictures were of situations in his own life, i.e., teaching his child to swim and keeping a portfolio of his children's drawings and mementos. The point, however, is that these were not painful memories from which he needed healing. The Holy Spirit used these pictures as analogies. Just as Rob wanted his daughter to trust him and jump into the water, so God wanted Rob to trust Him. Rob immediately got the point. In the same way Rob, as a father, cherished his childrens' imperfect art work, God the Father loved and cherished the things that Rob gave Him, even when imperfect. These messages brought resounding truth. Rob was healed and basked in God's peace. Years later, the healing has not been lost. In Rob's session, the Clean Up/Follow Up included ministry to several Ungodly Beliefs.

4. Summary

Our job as ministers is to work with the Lord as He leads. If we need further clarification, we pray again for the interpretation until we know what needs to be done. We may need to lead our receiver in forgiving others, receiving more ministry concerning his ancestors' sins and curses, or reading certain scriptures, etc. The key is to listen to the Holy Spirit and to draw upon our knowledge of the ministry approach/process until we know how to pray for the situation and how to lead him.

So we pray and again wait upon the Holy Spirit to minister healing to the person. He never fails to do so! We then repeat the process for the next hurt that God wants to heal.

This is an amazing process, as we truly experience the unity of co-laboring[1] with God on our receiver's behalf. We pray to find out what God wants to heal, and God tells us. Then we pray for the healing, and God heals the Soul/Spirit Hurt. God effectively docs it all! What a privilege to serve a living God!

God always does it right.

We are continually awed by the "rightness" of what God shows and/or speaks as He brings complete healing and release. He knows the best way to present the information to our receiver. He may bring a vision. Jesus may be in the vision, either as an image or as a "felt" presence, but sometimes He is not. Sometimes, the remembrance is not a vision but an impression or a "knowing," etc. Sometimes, the receiver experiences a profound sense of peace and well-being, and he knows that Jesus is restoring that which was lost. It is always just right, perfect, and specifically for that special person. It is always far better than anything we could have thought of or prayed. It touches the heart where it is needed and accomplishes healing that can be obtained no other way.

L. Rob: God's Healing Touch in One Man's Life

Rob, a tall attractive man who had recently turned forty, approached ministry hoping against hope that somehow God was finally going to end the pain in his life. Although he had yearned for healing for a long time, his life had gone from bad to worse. It was with fear and trembling that he came. "What if this doesn't work? Where else can I turn? If this doesn't work, I am doomed to live with this pain the rest of my life!"

Background

His value came from "doing."

Rob grew up in a family where real communication was absent and high expectations of success through performance was demanded. To make matters worse, he had left a promising military career when God called him into the ministry — a decision his family of origin had never understood nor fully accepted. At the time he came for ministry, Rob was doing well in his ministerial position. Previously, however, he had experienced a heartbreaking season of "failure" in an earlier ministry setting. The life that he described to us was riddled with an intense fear of

He could never "do" enough.

failure that nagged at him no matter how much or how well he did. His performance never seemed to be good enough. Rob, like many of us, felt more like a "human doing" than a human being as he tried through achievements to prove that his life had value and worth. He was weary from his self-imposed treadmill.

His life was a mistake.

A second, related problem — and one that intensified Rob's performance orientation — was a deep sense that somehow his life was a mistake. Put another way, he felt that he didn't really have a "right" to exist. Although he had never verbalized this feeling before, it surfaced during ministry. At that point he related how he lived with a constant sense of having to justify his existence and prove that he was somehow worthy of being on this planet. He lived with the constant, heavy burden of having to prove his worth/value.

---

[1]   Please read I Cor 3:9.

Authorities can't be trusted.

Other hurts had led to his belief that authority figures could not be trusted and would humiliate and abuse him. The only way that he felt safe was to keep his heart closed, to keep his defenses up, and never to let himself be vulnerable.

Our Fourth Ministry Session

How to be a "success" with God.

Rob was quietly thoughtful as we met for our fourth ministry session one fall morning. We began dealing with his Ungodly Beliefs of "having to achieve" in order to be a "success" and have value. Chester posed the question, "What do you think being a success means to God?" As Rob was pondering this question, the Holy Spirit began to touch the deep hurt in his heart and to minister life-changing revelation to Rob. It came into his spirit as a beautiful, graphic picture, which he described as, "A weaned child on its mother's breast."[1]

Here is Rob's own interpretation. "This picture spoke of how I can be a 'success' with God regarding the 'being' side of who I am. I heard, 'Be still and know that I am God'[2] as I saw this picture in my mind's eye. The fact that the child was weaned is important in that the child was not desiring anything from his mother in the way of nourishment. He was simply enjoying being in the presence of his parent. There is a peace in knowing that one is loved and secure in the arms of his parent. Being able to rest in the love of God, secure in one's place as His child, constitutes 'success' in the eyes of God regarding the 'being' side of who we are."

Success is being secure in God's love and being at peace.

Then the Holy Spirit showed Rob that He wanted him to be that child — to be relaxed, at peace, and at rest. As we all continued praying, the Holy Spirit brought back a scene from a dream that Rob had shortly before beginning ministry. At the end of that dream, Rob remembered that God had leaned His head back on his chest. In the dream, there was such a sense of warmth and fellowship as they both enjoyed being in the other's presence. Rob had seen himself there, at ease and secure in being loved. God, through His Holy Spirit, was giving Rob a whole new definition of success — a definition radically different from the striving, proving mode that so encumbered his life. **Success is being secure in God's love and being at peace.**

Does excellence equal success?

God continued redefining "success" for Rob, who had forced himself to strive for "excellence" in order to be acceptable to God. Excellence was part of what it took to be a "success." The Holy Spirit next showed Rob a picture of an event that had happened many years earlier. In Rob's words, "God showed me as a father in a swimming pool with one of my little daughters standing at the edge. She was getting ready to jump in for the first time. When I told her to jump in, she trusted me. My daughter was a 'success' with me — not because she jumped in for the first time and began to do the butterfly stroke like an Olympian — but simply because she trusted me. It didn't matter that she went under the water and came up spluttering and coughing. It didn't matter that she couldn't even dog-paddle yet. I was tickled because she trusted me enough to try."

Does trusting God equal success?

---

[1] Please see Psa 131:2.
[2] Please see Psa 46:10.

Trusting God enough to try equals success.

"Suddenly, God flip-flopped the picture in my mind's eye. He became the one standing in the pool and I was the child at the edge. I immediately understood His message: He considers me a success in 'doing' when I simply trust God enough 'to try' when He asks me to do something. In that moment, I came to believe that **God the Father is just as pleased when we trust Him enough to try, regardless of how well we do or don't do.**"

Tears of freedom came as that truth resounded in Rob's spirit. He knew the truth that God had shown him would begin to free him from perfectionism, from never doing well enough, and from the tyranny of striving.

What it takes to be acceptable to God.

The Holy Spirit continued to elaborate on the theme of being acceptable to God as He showed Rob an image of himself getting out folders containing pictures his daughters had drawn over the years. These offerings were far from perfect, but they were sweetly representative of the ability and efforts of each girl at different times. There were colored pictures, little notes of affection, scribbles, and doodles; no masterpieces but still treasures to his father's heart. Then God began to speak to Rob that He had saved and treasured the things that Rob did in the same way. His Father's heart valued the offerings, the efforts, simply because He loved Rob so much. As Rob shared with us what God was revealing to him, we all basked in the deep peace of God's strong presence.

God always knows how to heal.

Because God knows us so intimately, He knew the amount of reassurance that our friend Rob needed that morning. He always knows what and how to heal.

His "Real" Fear

Rob begin to tentatively talk about his real fear: Could his hurt and damaged heart fully be healed after so many years of protecting it and not letting it be vulnerable. Could his heart somehow be connected to, or integrated with, his head. Could they work together after all this time?

"I was not sure of the condition of my soul when we started the ministry process. I had become aware that my 'head' (intellect) and my 'heart' (emotions) were not connected, not 'integrated.' I had prayed that God would help me get in touch and stay in touch with my feelings on an ongoing basis. I knew it was going to take some time, but I didn't know where I was in the process or whether it could even succeed after so long a time."

Rob described what happened next this way: "As I was praying, God brought back to me the memory of when I first saw my knee after an operation. I had torn a muscle off my knee, and the surgeon had reattached it. Since this was my first major operation, I was totally unprepared for the aftermath. The yellowish color of my skin — caused by the Betadine used during the operation — immediately caught my attention. Since I had no idea what it was, I immediately panicked. My badly swollen knee had what appeared to be yards of black, silk thread sticking out of it. When the doctor said, 'It looks great,' I remember staring at him in disbelief and yet hoping that what he said was true. Since I was unfamiliar with post-surgery after-effects, I had to trust the doctor. I clung to his assessment and fought back the fear that had gripped my heart."

"God then showed me that the condition of my 'head-to-heart' connection looked the same way. I remember I had cried out, fighting the fear that I was never going to be able to integrate my head with my heart. Now God seems to be looking at my heart and saying, 'It looks great!' That does not mean it is completely healed and fully functioning but that He has been able to attach the two together, and I am on the way to being healed."

With beauty, delicacy, and great tenderness, God the Holy Spirit healed the fear that had pervaded Rob's life — the fear that too much damage had already been done and that his heart and his head would never be able to function as integrated parts of his personality.

The Following Week

God was not finished with Rob's healing process. The following week as Rob returned to ministry, God dealt with two themes common to many of us: "victimization" and "feeling like an outsider."

As Rob offered his past hurtful experiences to the Lord and asked for His healing, Rob saw a picture of Jesus standing before the Sanhedrin. Rob reported to us, "This picture held special significance because I have felt victimized by authority figures. In this vision, I saw Jesus subject to the human authority of His time but not victimized by them. He 'bought into' the situation by subjecting Himself to their authority. He did not, however, compromise who He was or what He stood for. He did not give them the authority to determine His worth and status before God. His Father had already said, 'This is My beloved Son:' therefore, Jesus' identity was already settled. In like manner, I can be subject to human authorities, but I am not a 'victim' of them. I can choose to 'buy into' the situation and know that they cannot touch who I am and what I stand for as a person. God alone has that kind of authority, and He has already determined who I am. 'See how great a love the Father has bestowed upon us, that we should be called children of God; and such we are.'"[1]

Jesus says: I am the "Keeper of the House."

Finally that day, God touched Rob's feelings of continually being an outsider — the feeling of "not belonging." God brought to Rob a picture of himself **inside** the sheepfold with Jesus standing at the gate. Rob recounted this experience, "This vision followed an intense time of deliverance. I sensed that a wing of my house had been 'swept' in the process. I saw myself inside a large room and at the same time I felt this gnawing fear that I wasn't going to be able to keep it cleared. I sensed that God wanted me to rest in His ability to keep the enemy out of my life. As I began to think on this, I remembered the passage in John 10, 'Truly, truly, I say to you, I am the door of the sheep.'[2] I heard these words: 'Jesus is the Keeper of the house.' I also realized that, for the first time, I pictured myself inside the sheepfold and not on the outside looking in."

We rejoiced tremendously as we watched God change Rob's life. He changed how Rob viewed himself and his sense of belonging.

Let's look now at a fourth example of the Lord's powerful healing work as we return to Sandy's Story.

---

[1]   Please see 1 Jn 3:1.
[2]   Please see Jn 10:7.

M. Sandy's Story: Covered at Last

Sandy needed much Soul/Spirit Healing. Her wounding started while still in the womb. The abandonment, the occult terrorizing, the fears, the betrayal, the abuse, the occult control had all contributed to the tattered state of Sandy's heart. She was in so much pain herself that she could be a "tiger" in protecting those in her care. This may be one reason she became a counselor.

Much of the healing that the Holy Spirit brought to Sandy was done in combination with other ministry, but there was one very special healing encounter she had with the Lord that we would like to share.

Waiting Upon the Lord
We had done the preparation for the "Waiting Upon the Lord" Listening Prayer. Sandy was usually able to hear the Holy Spirit quite well, so this approach for praying for Soul/Spirit Hurts was working very effectively for her.

We had been praying for the wounds suffered while she was four to five years old and later at twelve to fourteen. She had felt particularly "exposed" during these periods. During early childhood she had been frequently left alone at home at night — an experience that caused much terror and feelings of being unprotected. The early teenage period brought the betrayal by her school girl "friends." We prayed for the healing of the sensitivity of being "uncovered" (unprotected), for the shame, and for the pain of betrayal. Then we became silent, quietly praying in the Spirit, "Waiting Upon the Lord."

Sandy began to cry with silent tears sliding down her face. We continued to wait, waiting until the Holy Spirit signaled to us He was finished.

"You know the story of Ruth and Boaz," Sandy said, still weeping. "I have always loved that story. Well, I saw Jesus come to me. He wrapped me in a cloak and took me away. He 'covered' me with His cloak."

The Holy Spirit also spoke the word "innocence" to Sandy.

"I lost my 'innocence' during that time. Jesus is healing the grief of my lost innocence and my lost childhood. He is covering me. I have never felt protected, and I still don't feel protected by the men in my life."

Sandy begin to sob as the fuller meaning of what Jesus had done for her began to sink into her spirit. No wonder the Book of Ruth had always been special to her. She had yearned for the "Kinsman Redeemer"[1] to come and provide the protection that she had never felt during her life. Now Jesus had done it, and He did it with the little four-year-old girl.

---

[1]   Please see Ruth 3:9.

Summary

Just as God healed Joseph, Cathy, Rob, and Sandy from heartaches and disappointments, our Heavenly Father wants to heal each of us. He wants us to have that life "more abundant" that is described in John 10 and cut the chains that hold us to our past. Jesus also wants to come back for a Bride without spot and without wrinkle.[1] We could add to that: without bruise, without hurt, without something blocking that maturing process in Him — and, most of all — without hindrances to hearing His voice and having a relationship with Him.

Will we let Him heal us? As long as we remain hurt, we put up walls that block unity in the church between us and other people. We draw back, we feel bad, we are consumed with self. To the degree that we are hurt, we stay focused on ourselves more than others.

As we let the Lord heal our Soul/Spirit Hurts and change our Ungodly Beliefs into Godly Beliefs, we become free to mature and be unified in His body. We can focus beyond ourselves and toward His plan and His purpose. How life changing to be convinced that God is truly able, willing, and eager to heal our hurts!

N. "Plan B" — Other Healing Prayer Approaches

*When the ministry receiver **cannot hear** the voice of the Lord.*

As we conclude this chapter, let us briefly present additional healing prayer approaches that are helpful when our ministry receiver is less able to hear the Lord, is totally unfamiliar with hearing the Lord, or has blockage that has not yet been removed. During these times, we pray prophetically, and/or chronologically. We use this approach as "Plan B."

Once again, the key question is, "Holy Spirit, how do You want us to pray? What areas do You want us to cover?" We may be led to pray over several hurts that we know are holding our receiver back, or we may pray chronologically through his life, praying for his hurts as the Spirit leads us.

1. Praying Prophetically

Pray as the Holy Spirit leads.

We start by instructing the ministry receiver to follow along with us and participate by fully setting his will in agreement with what we are praying.

We ask, "Holy Spirit, show us those hurts and situations that You want to heal."

We then pray prophetically as the Lord leads us. Sensing in our spirit what the Holy Spirit is saying, we pray it forth. We go to one hurt area at a time and focus on it. We may pray continually, speaking forgiveness, breaking curses and lies, praying for healing, etc., or we may interrupt our prayer and have our receiver participate more actively. Our prayer for David for a childhood hurt of rejection sounded like this:

---

[1] Please see Eph 5:27.

Lord, come and bring your comfort to this frightened, rejected little boy. David, we break the power of rejection that has affected you. We speak truth into your spirit and soul; truth that you are worthy of being loved and cared for. Lord, come now and touch those areas of his heart that look raw and painful. David, we want to break the power of that pattern within you where you always want to run away when you expect rejection. We speak to you that you are safe now. You no longer need to run away and isolate yourself.

David, will you forgive your father for leaving you? (He forgives.)

Now, will you repent of your pattern of isolation? (He does.)

Now would you break your agreement with the UGB that you have to run away and reject other people before they reject you? (He does, and we minister the steps for UGBs.)

(Now we are ready to do some deliverance.) David, would you renounce the demon of Rejection and tell it to leave, in Jesus' name? (He does.) (The demon manifests as it leaves.)

Next, the Holy Spirit shows us another painful incident in David's life. We see a picture of his being fired from a job. We ask him about it, and he validates that he was fired several years ago but had forgotten to mention it. We begin to pray for this hurt, and so it continues.

This kind of healing is usually not quite as powerful as when the receiver can hear the Lord for himself, and yet true healing does take place. Sometimes, as we pray prophetically, the Holy Spirit moves us from one episode in a person's life to another, with no apparent logic or order. Yet there are times when He wants us to pray in an orderly, chronological fashion.

2. Praying Chronologically

Sometimes it is appropriate to start at the beginning of our receiver's life and pray forward to the present. At the right time, we pray for healing for all of the major hurts that we have gleaned from him, as well as those the Holy Spirit reveals.

This approach is the favorite of many of the authors who write about inner healing. It is only hazardous if they also advocate "leading" the ministry receiver in "seeing" images of Jesus or control the process in other ways.

Pray along the person's lifeline. Generally, we start right at the beginning of life, while the infant was still being knit together in its mother's womb. We pray from the time of conception to birth, then through the traumatic birthing process on into the early parts of the person's life. We pray for the different parts of his life, until we arrive at the present.

*Be open for
prophetic prayer.*

It can be exhilarating to pray prophetically and chronologically, as the Holy Spirit shows us what to pray/declare at each stage of life. Even though we are moving along a timeline, we are also sensitive to what He is saying to our spirit. He will periodically show us brand new information as we are praying, or He may bring back into our remembrance previous knowledge that we add at the right point.

As in the illustration of ministry to David, we can ask our receiver to participate at important points. Sometimes the Holy Spirit brings back memories to him during this process even though, when we started the ministry, he thought he was "unable to hear the Lord."

Again we must state that this is not our preferred approach; however, because the Lord works through it, healing does take place.

We have included in the next several pages some information that has helped us to pray for people with greater effectiveness, particularly when led to pray chronologically. We want to be particularly sensitive to the following potential areas of hurt and to pray for them as impressed by the Holy Spirit.

a. Prenatal Issues

Some people are reluctant to pray for the ministry receiver before his birth, much less before he arrives at the age of accountability. We feel comfortable praying this way, particularly since David writes in Psalm 51:5:

> Psa 51:5
> Surely I was sinful at birth, sinful from the time my mother conceived me. (NIV)

We believe that this is a more accurate translation than the KJV and expresses David's understanding that we have iniquity in our hearts right from the beginning. He is not stating that he was conceived in sin, but that he already had a sinful nature.

*Rebellion may
begin in the
womb.*

We do find situations where people have apparently rebelled while they were still in the womb. You say, "Well, that seems very strange." And we agree, it is strange. But the rebellion is there, the Demonic Oppression is there, and the Soul/Spirit Hurts are there. Going through the forgiveness process and having the receiver pray for the hurts leads to healing and freedom.

Spiritual Environment in the Household

The rebellion, and other sins, can occur because of the spiritual environment in the house during the pregnancy. It is not unusual for the parents to experience fear, rejection, frustration, despair, depression, etc., during this time, particularly if the baby is unexpected and/or if money is tight. Also, if the parents are wanting a boy, and the baby is a girl, there seems to be a spiritual awareness in the baby of the anticipated disappointment. All of these possible influences can lead to various problems, such as rebellion, rejection, wrong sex identity, anger, etc., even before the baby is born.

Forgiveness

We have the receiver speak forgiveness to his parents for setting him up for hurt. We also have him ask forgiveness for his sins while in the womb.

b. Birth

There is usually trauma associated with the birthing process, as well as the initial few days in the hospital. If necessary, we pray for this part of a person's life.

Welcoming

Sometimes the Holy Spirit has us pray to welcome the person into the world in order to help bring the healing needed because of the parents' disappointment. God wasn't disappointed, surprised, unable to provide, etc., for the new baby. From God's point of view, this individual was right on time, of the right sex, in the right family. God has the perfect purpose, plan, and mission for him.

> Psa 139:13-16
> [13]For you created my inmost being; you knit me together in my mother's womb. [14]I praise you because I am fearfully and wonderfully made; your works are wonderful, I know that full well. [15]My frame was not hidden from you when I was made in the secret place. When I was woven together in the depths of the earth, [16]your eyes saw my unformed body. All the days ordained for me were written in your book before one of them came to be. (NIV)

Choosing Life

Sometimes the Holy Spirit will have us encourage the ministry receiver to make a decision to choose life. We have him cancel any rebellious decisions made within the womb, decide that he submits to God's will and accepts himself as God ordained him to be. We have him choose:

- sex/identity/appearance
- family
- God's plan and purpose for his life
- submission and obedience, rather than rebellion and self-will

This particular ministry can sometimes absolutely revolutionize a life that has been indecisive, wandering, "half here," etc. Rather than being here on the earth half-heartedly, living in spite of his rebellion in the womb, the person is able to fully embrace life and all that it and God have to offer.

Break Power of Received Lies; i.e., UGBs

As appropriate, we will use the power of the redemptive work of Christ on the cross to break the power of all lies involved in the above issues.

Time Factors

God is the same yesterday, today, and forever.

For those of you who are wondering about time: "Well, wait a minute, the person is forty years old, how can we pray for him as a baby?" Remember what God says, "I am the same yesterday, today, and forever."[1] God was there, and in one sense we could say, He is "there."[2] Whatever effect those hurts are having on us today, whether it's out of a painful memory or an ingrained habit pattern of response — or whatever — God can heal it so that tomorrow we are no longer affected by the old wound. We can respond to situations out of love rather than anticipated wounding and pain. It is a tremendous blessing.

c. Early Childhood

The growing up years provide many opportunities for deep emotional and psychological scarring. Interactions with parents, siblings, peers, school teachers (authority figures), etc., are issues for which we need to pray.

d. Young Adult

Puberty, attractions to the opposite sex, social blunders, sexual encounters, etc., cause the teenage years to be potentially very painful. In today's permissive and violent climate, many sins and resulting hurts are common. We pray with sensitivity through these years.

e. Marriage and Career

We pray for the major hurtful events of adulthood. We pray for former marriages with their times of hurt. We pray for any divorces that have occurred. We pray for the hurt with the person's spouse. (We do this even if it may not have been the intention of the spouse to hurt him. But we know that, in the normal course of living with another person, hurts occur.) We pray for the normal encounters with the world that provide ample opportunities for hurts.

Break soul ties.

Usually it is at this point that we also break ungodly Soul Ties with former relationships and parents. We do this not only with former lovers but also with inverted parental emotional connections and ungodly parental control that is still active. We discuss Soul Ties in Chapter XI.

---

[1] Please see Heb 13:8.
[2] Please see Jn 8:57.

O. Ministering to Soul/Spirit Hurts

Many of God's people merely plod through their Christian life. With hurts still needing the Master's touch, they lack both joy and growth. Does that describe you? If so, you may be wondering what is wrong and why you do not seem to care anymore. Do the same memories keep coming back even though you have spoken words of forgiveness over and over. Friend, you need God's healing! It is time for your Soul/Spirit Healing.

1. Final Thoughts before Ministry

Remember, that we, as ministers or as caring people praying for one another, cannot bring healing into anyone's life. Why, then, should we be anxious or concerned about what happens during ministry? If the Lord does not show up, there will be no revelations, no deliverance, no healing. It doesn't matter what *we* do, nothing of eternal value will happen unless the Lord accomplishes it. So, we might as well relax and enjoy the session.

Our responsibility is to pray and to be obedient. God's responsibility is to be faithful to His Word (which He is) and to fulfill it. He does watch over His Word to perform it.[1] So we can let go of any burden or false sense of responsibility for what happens to the person. We can't make anything happen on our own!

Also, remember that, as we are praying, the Lord may do a number of things for the ministry receiver as we have discussed throughout this chapter. Our job is just to bring the ministry receiver to Jesus, as Andrew did,[2] and let the Lord do what He wants to do.

> **Exercise:** We encourage you to use the "Wait Upon the Lord" Listening Prayer approach and move through the following Ministry Ingredients. The Holy Spirit will be faithful to bring to your awareness those hurts that he wants to heal and then, as you pray, He will heal them. You can do this in the privacy of your prayer closet. Give yourself permission to "feel" and to "be." This will free the Holy Spirit to minister to you at maximum effectiveness. May God bless you as you entrust yourself to Him!

2. Bind Demons

As we prepare to pray, it sometimes is helpful to again bind all demonic interference, even though we did this in the Opening Prayer. Otherwise, the demons may still try to block the receiving of the healing. They may also attempt to masquerade as angels of light, passing themselves off as angels or the voice of God. If we sense that there is a significant amount of Demonic Oppression within the person,

---

[1] Please see Jer 1:12.
[2] Please see Jn 1:40-42.

significant dissociation or a very confined range of emotions, we may "pray prophetically" or "pray chronologically," rather than relying on the person's ability to hear the Lord.

We may also go ahead and do some deliverance to clear out the blockages and then proceed with SSHs ministry.

3. Submission Prayer

We like to have the ministry receiver pray and submit to the healing process as we begin the actual "Waiting Upon the Lord" Listening Prayer. The following prayer is typical of what we ask him to pray.

SSHs Submission Prayer: Lord, I choose to be open and submitted to You today. Like David, I cry out to You and tell You my troubles. I ask You to bring my soul out of prison so I can praise Your name. I trust You not to give me more than I can handle. I can and do trust You to be my protector, my shield, and the revealer of my hurts.

Lord, only You know what lies in darkness, the deepest secrets inside me. I ask that You reveal the deep and hidden things to me and to my Ministers. Search me, and show us the hurts that You want to heal today. I trust You not to reveal more than I can bear.

I give You permission to dig deep for the roots of any hidden memories that are affecting my life. I ask You to take the keys to my heart now and unlock the doors. Bypass any denial or deception that may be blocking my memory. Bypass anything that has hindered me, or is hindering me, from receiving my healing.

Lord Jesus, I ask You to bring those things to the surface that You want to heal. I ask You to be with me as I re-experience any past hurt and pain. I want to be set free by the power of the Cross and Your Shed Blood.

In the Name of Jesus Christ I pray. Amen!

---

4. Ingredients/Steps for Ministering to Soul/Spirit Hurts

The ingredients/steps are helpful in preparing the way and then praying so the broken hearted ministry receiver can receive the healing of Jesus. This is a list of "ingredients" rather than the precise order of events. Use them as the Holy Spirit directs. Receiving healing for the hurts of the Soul/Spirit takes time as we wait upon the Lord, so don't feel in a rush. Relax and enjoy as the Lord of the universe operates on the ministry receiver as you watch from a ringside seat. Bless you as you take time to listen to the Lord with someone else or for yourself.

Ministry Steps/Ingredients[1]

1. **Prepare:** Explain the ministry approach. Let ministry receiver know that hindrances may be encountered but that they will be removed.

2. **Pray:** Have the ministry receiver pray the Submission Prayer on page 256.

3. **Determine Scope:** (You will have already determined the scope, either general or specific.)

4. **Wait on the Lord:** Ministry receiver "Waits on the Lord," listening to the Holy Spirit to bring the memory He wants to heal. (Throughout the ministry process, the minister listens as well, both for guidance and for revelation about hindrances.)

5. **Clarify Memory:** If needed, encourage the ministry receiver to work with the Holy Spirit for greater clarity of the memory/impression.

6. **Deal with Hindrances:** If needed, help the receiver work through any hindrances to receiving the memory, such as unforgiveness, anger with God, or demonic interference.

7. **Enter the Memory:** Help the ministry receiver enter the memory as he specifies the feelings and feel the feelings of the memory.

8. **"Pouring Out My Complaint":** Direct the ministry receiver to share his feelings honestly with the Lord.

9. **Invite Jesus In:** Have the ministry receiver invite Jesus into the memory. (Sometimes the receiver may not see Jesus in the memory, but he may have an awareness of God's presence.)

10. **Work Together:** Help the ministry receiver keep his focus on what Jesus is saying or doing. Have him report to you. Keep working with the receiver and the Holy Spirit until the hurt is healed.

11. **Address Hindrances:** If needed, help the ministry receiver remove any further blocks to healing. (At this point in the healing process, Demonic Oppression is the most common difficulty.)

12. **Take Notes:** Record what Jesus says and does as well as the Ungodly Beliefs revealed within each memory.

13. **Checking the Results:** Check with receiver to see if the negative emotion is truly gone/healed. If not, discern whether there is a further hindrance or whether the same negative emotion is stored in an additional memory or memories.

---

[1] A copy of a Ministry Card with a summary of these steps is in Appendix A.

14. **Clean Up/Follow Up:** Guide the ministry receiver in cleaning up any remaining healing issues from this memory or revelation. This may include:

- leading the ministry receiver through any remaining confession or forgiveness, including self-forgiveness.
- breaking Soul Ties.
- renouncing Sins of the Fathers and removing the Resulting Curses.
- breaking agreement with core Ungodly Beliefs (lies) embedded in the hurt and creating Godly Beliefs.
- removing demons associated with the memory and/or adding them to the deliverance list for the next session.

X

DEMONIC OPPRESSION

*I have given you authority to trample on snakes and scorpions
and to overcome all the power of the enemy; nothing will harm you.*
Luke 10:19

The Woman

The woman lived in a constant state of fear. She had never understood why she startled so easily, why she seemed to hear sounds that no one else heard, or why she would wake up at night drenched with the sweat of terror. Not even the reassurance of kindly parents, locked doors, and night lights quieted her quivering discomfort. Filled with shame, the woman hid her fear from everyone. A Christian from early childhood, she had experienced precious times of God's closeness and love. She had learned many scriptures and secretly memorized those that should directly counteract fear. Why did God's Word fail to bring peace and comfort as the evening shadows fell and night approached? She loathed her fear.

This woman's acute sense of failure resulted not from some besetting sin but rather from her inability to overcome her number one enemy: the paralyzing **fear**. She would ask herself, "How can I say that I trust God and still panic if the wind slams the door shut at night?" By age 40, she had become resigned to defeat and what she felt must be her "weak faith." Nothing had worked. Then something happened, something life-changing. She experienced the wonderful infilling of the Holy Spirit and soon afterward was prayed for in the area of deliverance. She had never contemplated the possibility that "demons" might be involved in her prevailing fear. The deliverance ministers, however, with their gifts of discernment and years of experience, easily saw the connection. They prepared the way early in the session and then went right for this enemy stronghold.

*Fear manifested and **lied** right to the very end!*

As the fear demons were forced out into the open and began to leave the woman, these evil beings made one last threat: "We are going to kill you. You will choke to death, and no one will help you. They will think that you are merely manifesting, but you are going to die before they realize what is happening." Sure enough, she began coughing and choking. Fear rushed through her whole being. Panic filled her as she realized the demons were right! She was going to die! There was nothing she could do about it! She couldn't yell out, **"Stop!"** with all of her coughing and choking. She was doomed!

259

Then it was over. "Out in the name of Jesus," the ministers commanded. "Out!" Quiet filled her. The fear was gone! She was still alive! She couldn't believe it! Was she really different? Was she really free?

Betsy was that woman. The answer was and has been a resounding, "**YES, YES, YES!**" The long-standing enemy of her soul had been defeated! She would never be the same again! The lengthening evening shadows had lost their threat. In a way she had never imagined, Betsy experienced the reality of:

> Prov 3:24
> When thou liest down, thou shalt not be afraid: yea, thou shalt lie down, and thy sleep shall be sweet. (KJV)

A. Christians and Demonic Oppression (DO)

Many fine Christians are like Betsy. They do not realize that they can be oppressed by demons. Consequently, they do nothing to stop this oppression, leaving themselves at the mercy of the Devil.

Yet he has no mercy. During the normal course of life, people are continually baffled by seemingly unexplained problems, calamities, failures, losses, interruptions, etc. It is only because of God's mercy and grace that Satan can not directly kill us during our time of immaturity.[1] In fact, none of us would probably survive childhood if not for God's grace. The longer we minister and learn more about the different ways Christians are hindered or defeated by demons, the more we are aware of the magnificence of God's grace.

God wants us to come into maturity regarding Satan and his demons. He wants us to enforce His victory over their kingdom of darkness. He wants us to "know the **Truth**, and the **Truth** shall make you (us) free."[2] He wants us to grow in maturity and faith and to appropriate His freedom by casting out demons.

Some Christians have concluded that the Holy Spirit will not co-habit with demons. They believe that, at the moment of salvation when we are born again, the Holy Spirit comes into us and all oppressing demons are forced to leave. Unfortunately, there is no scriptural basis for this teaching. In fact, the opposite is true. We can read in Ezekiel that the presence of God was in the temple with at least four groups of abominations. At some point, the cup of iniquity of the people became full. God withdrew from Israel, letting them go into exile.[3]

With Christians, the opposite process occurs. As the Holy Spirit comes and sets up house, He begins His work of sanctification. In the process, He brings us to an understanding of demons, increased faith, and eventual displacement and eviction of the demonic.

---

[1] Please see 1 Jn 2:12-14.
[2] Please see Jn 8:31-32.
[3] Please see Eze 8-10.

Derek Prince, the popular British speaker and Bible scholar was once asked publicly, "Can a Christian have a demon?" In his crisp British humor, he is said to have replied, "Yes, Christians can have anything they want to have."

Issue:

Can a Christian have a demon?

The deception inherent in the issue of whether Christians can have demons or not[1] can easily be exposed. How? By stopping to realize that we were all sinners before God mercifully gave us grace and faith to become saved.[2] Satan had plenty of time to infiltrate and oppress us before we changed kingdoms.[3] The ancestral sins, with the resulting curses, our Ungodly Beliefs and ungodly attitudes, and the hurts to our soul and spirit — all these have given Satan plenty of opportunity to ensnare us from the moment our earthly lives begin. Even though the Holy Spirit does inhabit us at the time of salvation — and even though some deliverance does frequently occur at that time — it is a mistake to conclude that we as Christians are totally free of Demonic Oppression.

Issue:

"Can a Christian have a demon?" is addressed in Appendix D.

We agree, however, with those who contend that Christians cannot be **"possessed"** by demons since possession involves **ownership.** On the other hand, we would *not* agree with those who say that Christians can't **"have"** a demon since this is an issue of harassment and oppression. For some people, the open door[4] for oppression is so large that the thief can easily do his stealing, killing, and destroying.[5] To stop Demonic Oppression, the "legal ground"[6] must be reclaimed. Then the trespassing demons can be easily evicted.

The ministry situation is an excellent place to accomplish this liberation. We can help fellow Christians mature in this area and move into their ordained place in the army of God so they can get involved in the spiritual warfare that is so prevalent.

Issues:

- *Do demons really exist?*
- *Can I cast them out?*

The two major blocks that keep Christians from dealing with the demonic world are both addressed during ministry. The first issue is, "Do demons really exist?" The second is, "Do I really have authority over demons, i.e., to cast them out?" These questions should and would not be issues if we literally believed the Word of God. But we don't, and they are. After demons have been cast out of a person, however, and he experiences them leaving when **"he"** gives the command, these two issues are usually settled forever.

Many excellent books have been written about demons, demonology, deliverance, and the subject of whether Christians can have demons, as well as the other issues touched on here. Several recommended authors are Basham,[7] Hammond,[8] and Philpott.[9]

---

[1] Please see Appendix D for a discussion on: "Can a Christian Have a Demon?"
[2] Please see Eph 2:8-10.
[3] Please see Col 1:12-13.
[4] Please see Gen 4:7.
[5] Please see Jn 10:10.
[6] Please see Eph 4:27.
[7] Basham, Don, *Deliver us from Evil,* New Wine Magazine, Mobile, AL, 1978.
[8] Hammond, Frank and Ida Mae, *Pigs in the Parlor*, Impact Books, Kirkwood, MO, 1973.
[9] Philpott, Kent, and Hymers, R. L., *The Deliverance Book,* Bible Voice, Inc., Van Nuys, CA, 1977.

Restoring the Foundations ministry is concerned with removing whatever basis (legal ground) has been allowing the Demonic Oppression and then casting out the demons. This is followed by teaching the ministry receiver how to stand against further attacks by the Devil. It is usually better, however, to delay the deliverance until the necessary forgiveness, repentance, renouncing, etc., has been done in the other three Problem/Ministry Areas. In this way, we can reclaim the "legal ground" for holiness. Otherwise we risk setting the stage for re-entry by other demons with similar natures.[1] Sometimes, though, it is necessary to do at least some deliverance before effective ministry can occur in one of the other Problem/Ministry Areas. In this case, we always come back and "check out" the same ground again during the deliverance time to cleanse it again if necessary.

The need for the Integrated Approach to Healing Ministry once again becomes relevant. Why? Because ministry to each of the four Problem/Ministry Areas works together. Let's look at the specific ways deliverance is related to the other Problem/Ministry Areas.

B. Understanding the Interrelationship of the Ministry Areas

Since deliverance normally comes after we have ministered to all of the other areas, it may appear to be the most important area. Nothing could be further from the truth. Each area is **equally important**. Each area needs to be ministered to so that ministry to the other areas is effective and remains completed. We don't want any openings left that would allow the healing and freedom to be undermined in the future.

1. How Deliverance is Related to Sins of the Fathers and Resulting Curses

When a particular type of generational sin occurs in two or more consecutive generations, we can expect to find demons of that same type in the family members of each generation, including the generation that has come for ministry.

Sometimes, a generational sin pattern may seem to skip a generation. This raises two questions: "Is this sin pattern really ancestral?" and, "Are demons actually involved with this sin?" Whatever the appearance may be, the answers are, "Yes!" The curse and the demons are present.

Generational sin and curses are passed down a family line, along with the demonic forces that help to carry them out. It does not mean, however, that every member of a particular generation will yield to any particular sin. Sometimes, godly teaching and guidance — and/or a quality decision on his part — will enable a person to resist. As a result, the curse does not manifest. The curse and the demons remain dormant, waiting for an opportunity in the next generation.

At other times, it seems that one person in a generation will receive **all** of the **evil.** His siblings may have some struggles but nothing compared to the extremes he

---

[1] Please see Lk 11:24-26.

experiences. He seems to be the **focus** of terrible Demonic Oppression. This seems very unfair, but perhaps we just don't understand the "setup" that has caused him to be a focus. The Good News, however, is that freedom is available, regardless of the intensity of the oppression or the demons "legal rights."

Neglecting to do Demonic Deliverance leaves a receiver at risk.

Even when the power of Sins of the Fathers and Curses is broken in a sin pattern area, it is rare that every demon will leave spontaneously. Normally, some do leave, but the majority will remain and pressure the person to continue in the same sin. He is extremely vulnerable to this demonic pressure, particularly if the core Ungodly Beliefs and/or Soul/Spirit Hurts have not also received ministry. To fail to do demonic deliverance would leave the ministry job unfinished. It would most likely bring confusion to the person who had anticipated freedom but instead still feels the same old pressure and temptation.

2. How Deliverance is Related to Ungodly Beliefs

Demons do not in themselves create a person's core Ungodly Beliefs. Their goal, however, is to help "engineer" circumstances that will cause the person to form the Ungodly Beliefs in the first place. They arrange for hurtful situations that cause the person to evaluate and make decisions about life which become beliefs. Then they further work to cement these untrue (based on God's Word) beliefs firmly into the core structure of the person. The demons continue to **reinforce the Ungodly Beliefs** by bringing them frequently to mind and by arranging experiences that verify the "truth" of the Ungodly Beliefs. They also try to **prevent** a person from hearing God's truth. They are ingenious and have numerous strategies. They will harass during church or Bible reading time and send all manner of distracting thoughts or even coughing spells or sleepiness. Demons will do anything to keep the Word of Truth from being planted and working in the person's life. In Mark we read:

> Mk 4:15b
> . . . And when they hear immediately Satan comes and takes away the word which has been sown in them. (NAS)

*The **Truth** of the Cross counters all lies.*

If a measure of truth is able to slip in, the demons will counter with thoughts such as, "That may work for some people, but it won't work for **me. I** am too bad. Look at all the sins **I've** committed." Unfortunately, the average Christian frequently buys into these lies and believe that he is the one thinking these thoughts. He passively sinks into defeated resignation, never countering with the Truth of the Cross. The Ungodly Beliefs continue to rule and reign.

Every area of Ungodly Belief is actually an area of **unbelief.** When a person has an **agreement** or covenant with unbelief in his life, the demon(s) has a legal right to stay. The person, his belief system, and the demon are all **in agreement.**

During one deliverance session, we actually had a demon say to a person, "I don't have to leave because you believe . . . ," and it went on to name the Ungodly Belief. Obviously, a person must break any and all agreements before the demon(s) can be evicted and before it will stay away. Also, the person must sincerely plant the new Godly Belief(s) in his heart if he is to stay free. We suspect that much deliverance, which is successful at the time, is short lived because the person's belief system has not been changed. This leaves the door open for other demons to reenter.

3. How Deliverance is Related to Soul/Spirit Hurts

The ministry area of deliverance relates to Soul/Spirit Hurts in several different ways.

Demons:

Remind,

Trap,

Amplify,

Agitate.

First, demons, which do their work primarily by putting thoughts into our minds, **remind** a person of his hurts. For example, a demon of rejection might say, "See there, **I** am left out again. **I** am always going to be a misfit."

Secondly, the demons will try to **reinforce the person's continuing in the same hurtful patterns.** They will put **explicit thoughts of temptation** into a person's mind. In addition, at a crucial time when the person's flesh is being tempted, the demon will **amplify** that thought. For example, the person may be feeling lonely and his flesh is tempted to have an alcoholic drink to block out these painful feelings. "Yes, yes, that is a great idea," the demon will say. "Why don't **I** cruise on down to the local bar right now?"

Lastly, demons seem to find ways to keep a Soul/Spirit Hurt **agitated to keep it from healing**. Just as germs must be cleansed from an infected wound, the Soul/Spirit Hurt must be "disinfected" before it can properly heal.

4. Summary

Dear reader, as we have elaborated on the intricate interconnectedness of these ministry areas, has it become clear to you why **the Integrated Approach to Healing Ministry** is both necessary and also powerful?

Let us turn our attention now to the scriptural basis for Demonic Oppression and deliverance.

C. Scriptural Basis for Deliverance

We want to look first at God's plan for deliverance from Demonic Oppression, as revealed in the second book of the Bible, Exodus. Then we will "consider"[1] examples of how Jesus dealt with demons. Next we will see His ministry multiplied as He sends out the twelve and then the seventy. Then, in the book of Mark, He commissions all believers to cast out demons. In other New Testament books, we will study scriptures about Satan, demons, and deliverance. The testimony of our early church fathers concerning demons and deliverance clearly indicates that the ministry of deliverance as Jesus did it was continued during the first several centuries of the Church. This section concludes with a challenge to us, the twenty-first century Church.

1. God's Strategy for Deliverance

God used the Israelites as examples for us.[2] The things He had them do in the natural are spiritual lessons for us. For example, He first gave them the promised land and then enabled them to fight and conquer it. In Exodus 23:20-33, He lays out His plan. This plan is repeated in Deuteronomy 7:1-26, where additional insights are provided. As we read these passages in the context of demonic deliverance, it is evident that God's heart and plan is to deliver His people and to bless them. In the Exodus passage, we read:

> Ex 23:29-31
> 29 **I will not drive them out from before thee in one year**; lest the land become desolate, and the beast of the field multiply against thee.
> 30 By **little and little I will drive them out** from before thee, **until thou be increased, and inherit the land**.
> 31 And I will set thy bounds from the Red sea even unto the sea of the Philistines, and from the desert unto the river: for **I will deliver** the inhabitants of the land into your hand; and **thou shalt drive them out** before thee. (KJV)

*God desires that we **increase** and **possess** our land.*

We see several principles in these three verses. First, God doesn't drive out the inhabitants of the land in one year (or one ministry session). He does it over time, using the criteria, "until thou be increased, and inherit the land." The NIV makes God's condition even clearer: "until you have **increased enough to take possession** of the land." As we grow in our Christian maturity, in our awareness of Satan, his schemes and his army, in our ability to wage the good warfare of faith, we are "increasing" and thus able to possess and manage more of the land. The land is "us." Each one of us is the "land." We are destined to become Holy land, dedicated and sanctified unto the Lord.[3] Part of this process is to remove the inhabitants of the land.

---

[1] Please see Heb 12:3.
[2] Please see 1 Cor 10:6, 11, and neighboring verses.
[3] Please see 1 Thes 4:3-4 and 2 Tim 2:20-21.

Thus, it is not uncommon to experience more than one deliverance over the course of several years, as we gain back "legal ground" deliverance after deliverance and then learn to live in that new freedom. We are continually going deeper — going for another cycle of regaining ground followed by consolidation.

The deliverance session Betsy described at the beginning of this chapter was actually her fourth experience that included casting out demons of fear. The earlier sessions were not failures on her part or on the part of the deliverance ministers. They were "gaining ground" sessions that enabled her to mature in her Christian walk. Eventually, she was ready for the final stronghold of the "fear of death" to be broken.

Today, she must merely resist periodic temptations to re-open the door to fear. If in a moment of weakness she does allow any fear to enter, it is a simple thing to repent and clean her "house" again.

*God **delivers** and we **drive** them out.*

Note in Exodus 23:31 that God **delivers** the inhabitants of the land into our hand, and we **drive** them out. This is another important principle shown in the above passage. It is our "partnership with God." We are to co-labor with Him. As we fulfill God's requirements concerning any **legal** rights the "inhabitants" suppose they have, their "status" changes from inhabitants to "trespassers," making it easy for us to "drive them out."

In Israel's case, the cup of iniquity of the inhabitants of the land became full[1] and God said, "That is enough. You have lost your rights to the land." In our case, we have God's provision (Jesus and the Cross) to remove the legal ground by forgiveness and dealing with the first three Problem/Ministry Areas. As we break any agreements that we have with the demonic and renounce them, God **delivers** them into our hands. Our part is to **drive** them out. This is the "casting out" process that Jesus did in His ministry and that He tells us to do in ours.

2. Jesus' Ministry Involved Demons

Two wonderful scriptures, First John 3:8 and Acts 10:38, provide summary statements about the purpose of Jesus' life and ministry. He came:

> 1 Jn 3:8
> . . . That He might destroy the works of the devil. (NAS)

And He fulfilled what He came to do:

> Acts 10:38
> You know of Jesus of Nazareth, how God anointed Him with the Holy Spirit and with power, and how He went about doing good, and healing all who were **oppressed** by the devil; for God was with Him. (NAS)

---

[1] Please see Gen 15:16.

We again see the Father's heart in the above passage. God equipped Jesus to accomplish His will, "doing good" and "healing all who were oppressed by the devil." Jesus was indeed "revealing" the Father to us.

Table R on page 269 lists a number of wonderful scriptures showing Jesus' authority over demons and His willingness to deal with them. Also included are scriptures about Believers casting out or being cautioned about demons and the Devil. Please refer to this table as we proceed through the following discussion.

The four Gospels offer numerous examples of Jesus casting out demons. One most noteworthy account involves the Gerasene demoniac.[1] Here, an insane, untamable man is restored to his right mind. The death demons, which had dominated him, are allowed/commanded by Jesus to go into the swine who rush rapidly to their death. The insane man becomes sane. He clothes himself and, as a result of his wonderful freedom, he wants to follow Jesus.

For 2000 years, the effects of deliverance have not changed. Deliverance brings freedom from torment and restoration to normalcy: normal mental states, normal physical states, and normal spiritual states. Deliverance creates a new desire in the Believer to want to stay close to Jesus.

When Jesus did demonic deliverance, it was never a strange or hidden part of His ministry. He never went to the "basement" of the synagogue and closed all of the doors. He did it in broad daylight and often with a crowd looking on in amazement. It was a normal part of His ministry as He showed us the Father's desire to bring healing and wholeness.

In Luke 4:18, Jesus proclaimed that part of His ministry was to "preach deliverance to the captives" and "set at liberty them that are bruised." Did Jesus accomplish His goal? Absolutely! Nearly one-fourth of the gospel accounts of Jesus ministry refer to His setting people free from Demonic Oppression.[2] In Matthew, Jesus says:

> Mat 12:28
> But if I cast out devils by the Spirit of God, then the kingdom of God is come unto you. (KJV)

Modern translations use the word "demons" rather than "devils." There is only one "Devil," but he has many "demons" in his fallen army.

The coming of God's kingdom includes freedom from Demonic Oppression. Jesus did not have merely a "deliverance ministry," but a "healing and wholeness" ministry that included: teaching, preaching, salvation, freedom, healing, and deliverance.[3]

---

[1] Please see Mat 8:28-34 and parallel passage Lk 8:26-39.
[2] Please note as examples Mat 4:24, 8:16, 8:31-32, 9:32-33, 12:22, 17:18, Mk 1:27, 3:10-11, 5:8-13, 7:26, Lk 6:18, 7:21, 11:14, 13:11-17, 13:32.
[3] Based on Lk 4:18.

3. Jesus' Ministry Extended

Jesus not only did deliverance Himself, but He extended His minist; first, by sending out the **twelve**[1] and then the **seventy**.[2] Finally, He commissioned all **"them that believe."**[3] In every case, besides the general command to extend the kingdom of God, He included the command to "cast out devils." In Mark He says:

Mk 16:17
And these signs will accompany **those who have believed: In My name they will cast out demons**; they will speak with new tongues; (NAS)

Basic criteria is that we "be a believer."

It is clear that Jesus expects us as believers to cast out demons, along with other forms of ministry that bring healing and freedom.

4. Believers Dealing with Demons

Scripture provides many examples of believers doing demonic deliverance.   In Acts 5:15-16, Peter is in Jerusalem, where the people were:

Acts 5:16
. . . bringing sick folks, and them which were vexed with unclean spirits: and they were healed every one. (KJV)

Notice the connection here between demons and being healed. Acts 8:7 records the work of Philip in Samaria:

Acts 8:7
For unclean spirits, crying with loud voice, came out of many that were possessed [with them]: . . . (KJV)

As we study the scriptures, the major requirement for doing demonic deliverance is being a Christian believer.[4] It definitely helps to be filled with the Holy Spirit and to have the various spiritual gifts in operation, but the basic criterion is to "be a believer."

A graphic, humorous account[5] of attempted deliverance is given of the seven sons of Sceva, who was a Jewish chief priest. These sons were not believers, but they had observed the power and effectiveness of Paul's deliverance ministry. They tried to duplicate it by saying:

Acts 19:13, 15-16
[13]. . . "In the name of Jesus, whom Paul preaches, I command you to come out."

---

[1] Please see Mat 10:1, 8, and parallel passages in Mk 3:15 and Lk 9:1-2.
[2] Please see Lk 10:1, 9, 17.
[3] Please see Mk 16:15-20.
[4] Please see Mk 16:17.
[5] Please see Acts 19:12-17.

Table R
Scriptures Concerning Deliverance

Jesus dealing with Demons

1 Jn 3:8	The purpose of Jesus' life is that he might destroy the works of the devil.
Acts 10:38	Jesus healing all who were oppressed by Satan, because God was with Him.
Mat 12:28, Lk 11:20	Jesus casting out by the finger of God. This brings the kingdom near.
Lk 8:31	Jesus has authority to cast demons into the abyss.
Lk 8:28	Jesus has authority and ability to torment them.
Mat 15:22, 28, Mk 7:26-30	Jesus casting out a spirit from a distance.
Mk 9:25	Jesus forbids any return of the demon.
Mat 4:24, Mat 8:16	Jesus heals all oppressed by demons.
Mat 9:32, Lk 9:42	Jesus casts out a dumb spirit.
Mat 12:22	Jesus casts out blind and dumb spirits.
Mat 17:18	Jesus casts out a mental illness demon.
Mk 1:39, Mk 5:2-13	Jesus casting out demons.
Mk 16:19	Jesus casts seven demons out of Mary Magdalene.
Lk 4:33-35	Jesus casting out demons.
Lk 4:40-41	Jesus heals all oppressed by demons.
Lk 13:12-16	Jesus frees woman from spirit of infirmity.
Jn 8:44	Satan's nature and character (murderer and liar).
Jn 10:10	Satan's nature and character (thief).

Believers dealing with Demons

Acts 5:16	Peter healing people afflicted with demons.
Acts 8:7	Philip casting out demons.
Acts 19:12	Paul casting out demons, even using cloth that had touched his body.
Mat 10:5-8	The twelve extending the kingdom of God.
Lk 10:17-19	Believers have power, authority, and protection.
Mk 16:17, 20	Believers shall cast out demons.
Jam 4:7	Believers resisting Satan.
Eph 4:27	Believers not giving place (legal ground) to Satan.
1 Pet 5:8	Believers are to be on guard.
2 Cor 2:11	Believers need to be aware of Satan's schemes, snares, devices.
	(Read 1 Tim and 2 Tim for many traps (particularly 2 Tim 2:26).

[15][One day] the evil spirit answered them, "Jesus I know, and I know about Paul, **but who are you?**" [16]Then the man who had the evil spirit jumped on them and overpowered them all. He gave them such a beating that they ran out of the house naked and bleeding. (NIV)

*In order for the demons to **know us**, we have to **know Jesus**.*

The sons got "cast out" instead of the demons! Why? Because they lacked the authority that true believers have. When the demons looked at them, they "did not know them." When demons look at us, we want them to see the Spirit of God with us, ready to drive them out.[1]

5. Additional Supporting Scripture

Additional key New Testament passages reveal the ways Satan and his legions try to oppress believers. These verses primarily give guidelines about how **not** to give him any place in one's life. Examples are the passages in James:

Jam 4:7
Submit yourselves therefore to God. Resist the devil, and he will flee from you. (KJV)

and in First Peter:

1 Peter 5:8
Be sober, be vigilant; because your adversary the devil, as a roaring lion, walketh about, seeking whom he may devour: (KJV)

These passages tell us to stand guard against our spiritual enemy. Although they refer to Satan and do not refer directly to demons, it would be presumptuous to think that Satan is personally, directly, attacking every single Christian. He delegates his authority down through the ranks of his multi-level organization until it gets to the demons that are assigned to us. Paul refers to this organizational hierarchy in Ephesians:

Eph 1:20-21
20 (God) . . . set [him] at his own right hand in the heavenly [places],
21 Far above all **principality, and power, and might and dominion, and every name that is named,** not only in this world, but also in that which is to come: (KJV)

Eph 6:11
For we wrestle not against flesh and blood, but against **principalities, against powers, against the rulers of the darkness of this world, against spiritual wickedness in high [places].** (KJV)

Somewhere below the top levels, we find the demons that oppress the average Christian. They are the ones who must flee when we resist the "lion" looking to chew on us[2] if we leave our "doors" open and let him into our house.

---

[1]   Please see Mat 12:28.
[2]   Please see 1 Pet 5:8.

Praise God that we know something about the organization and strategy of our enemy: that we are less and less "unaware" of his schemes: and that we are learning how to resist and defend ourselves. Praise God that He has given us authority and victory[1] over the Devil and that we don't have to be defeated Christians. We can go on the offensive and extend the kingdom within our lives and in others' lives. Praise God that in Revelation we know the end of the store: Satan's final defeat.[2]

While not much is written in other parts of the New Testament about demons and deliverance, there are some passing comments. These comments, along with the Gospels, indicate that the knowledge and understanding of demons, i.e., evil or unclean spirits, was common and widespread throughout all of the cultures of that region.[3] As we see in the next section, the concept of exorcism was well known.[4] As a result, the writers of the New Testament had no need to lay out the details concerning demonic deliverance for us in the twenty-first century. They did not know that modern Christians would "define" demons out of existence and ignore the reality of their presence.

6. Testimony of Early Church Fathers

It is a testimony to the powerful results of deliverance by Jesus and His followers that the ministry of deliverance was continued by the early church fathers, including Justin Martyr, Origen, Cyprian, Tertullian, and Hippolytus.[5] Justin Martyr, who was martyred in 165 AD, recorded these words:

> Many of our Christian men have exorcised in the name of Jesus . . . numberless demoniacs throughout the whole world and in your city. When all other exorcists and specialists in incantations and drugs failed, they have healed them and still do heal, rendering the demons impotent and driving them out.

The power and the practice was passed on in the first several centuries of the early Church.

7. Challenge for the Twenty-First Century

Ours is an age in which "seeing is believing." Truth has to be provable through visible, repeatable outcome to be accepted by many as truth. Anything invisible is discounted as **unreal**. Demons, of course, are delighted that the modern American ignores them, helping them remain hidden. For most Christians, accepting the reality of demons is a lot like accepting the reality of divine physical healing. It is hard to believe until experienced. Once it has been seen in a close friend or experienced personally, doubt vanishes. We know that it is true. Our eyes become open. "He who has ears to hear, let him hear."[6]

---

[1] Please see Col 2:15.
[2] Please see Rev 20:10.
[3] Please see as examples Mat 12:24-27, 14:26, Lk 24:37-39, Jn 7:20, 8:48-49, 52, 10:20-21, Acts 5:16, 8:7, 16:16-18, 19:12.
[4] Please see Mat 12:27, Mk 9:38, Lk 9:49, Acts 19:13-16.
[5] Cobb, Chris, *Deliverance: "the Children's Bread"*, a training manual, 1993, p.8, quoting from these early Christians and their writings.
[6] This admonishment is in Mat 11:15, 13:9, 13:16, Mk 4:9, 23, Lk 8:8, 14:35.

The deliverance ministry of Jesus is clear. Equally obvious is the fact that He delegated His authority and Name to believers to do deliverance. Why have we not gratefully embraced this ministry for the relief that it brings? Have we allowed ourselves the "privilege" of **selective reading**, somehow **discounting** or **retranslat- ing** any Bible passages that do not fit into our established theology or our religious tradition? Well, the days of selective belief of the Gospel are over. Jesus Christ is calling His Church to become fully healed, equipped, and committed to do battle at the end of the age.

> **Prayer:** Lord, give us ears to hear, eyes to see, and hearts to understand **all of Your Truth**. Lord, help us become Your faithful and trustworthy soldiers.

D. Demonic Oppression: Words and Definitions

When discussing the demonic kingdom, it is important that we to be clear about the meaning of several words that are used for Satan its leader, demons, and Demonic Oppression. Table S gives some definitions of these frequently used words.

The English words for Satan and Devil are transliterated Greek words meaning "adversary" and "accuser." Whenever we say "Satan" we are declaring his true nature of "adversary." Likewise, when we say "Devil," we are stating his true nature as "accuser."

For the word "demon," we have the excellent definition by Derek Prince, the British scholar who has studied and lectured widely about the demonic realm.

Definition of demons.

> **Definition:** Demons are invisible spiritual entities with minds, emotions and wills of their own, in league with, and under the control of Satan. They are out to do his bidding and to torment the people of God.

Now read this definition again and take a moment to think about it. What does it add to your current understanding of the demonic realm?

This definition is solidly biblical and has certainly been confirmed in our own experiences in dealing with demons.

The writers of the Bible did not deal directly with the issue of whether or not a believer can be "possessed" or "oppressed." In the Greek, they described people as "*daimonizomai*." This is best translated "**demon influenced,**" but "afflicted," "harassed" or "oppressed" are also correct. We could include other strong words such as "tormented," "tortured," "tried," "worried," "wronged." These words are defined in Table T. We understand that the literal meaning of "*daimonizomai*" is "to have a demon in one's possession" with the same connotation as "having a quarter in one's pocket."

We usually use the word "oppressed," as we have for the name of this fourth Problem/ Ministry area, because it avoids the issue of "ownership" and because Acts 10:38 uses this word to summarize the ministry of Jesus.

Table S
Kingdom of Darkness Definitions

Satan	Adversary. Adversary of God, Christ, and His people.
Devil **serpent** **evil one** **Beelzebub** **Abaddon** **Belial**	Accuser. Accuses saints before God. The Devil has many different names. These are only a few.
demon	Evil spirit, unclean spirit.
"de"	A prefix meaning: to distort, deceive, take away from, denude, or detract from. (This is just what demons do!)
"mon"	A suffix meaning: an entity, or "one".
"daimonizomai"	**Demon influenced**. (This word has been translated as "possessed" but "influenced" or "oppressed," or one of its synonyms as shown in Table T, is better.)
spirit (*"pneuma"* in the Greek)	Breath, air, or gas. This has connotations of the unseen, the invisible, the hidden.

Table T
Demonic Oppression Definitions

afflict	to inflict upon one something hard to endure.
harass	to make a raid on.
influence	to affect or alter by indirect or intangible means, to have an effect on the condition or development of.
oppress	to lower in spirit or mood.
torment	to cause severe suffering of body or mind.
torture	to punish or coerce by inflicting excruciating pain.
try	to subject to stress.
worry	to disturb one or destroy one's peace of mind by repeated or persistent torment.
wrong	to inflict injury on another without justification.

Acts 10:38

. . . Jesus . . . went about doing good, and healing all that were **oppressed** of the devil; for God was with him. (KJV)

> **"Demonic Oppression"** is the term used to represent the "pressure" exerted by demons to get us to sin, or to keep us bound in limitations. Usually they have an open door to gain access to us. Open doors come from SOFCs, UGBs, SSHs, and our own sin, as well as from witchcraft directed toward us.

Betsy, in her testimony at the beginning of this chapter, describes experiencing some, if not all, of these "influences." People suffering Demonic Oppression usually can relate to one or more of these synonyms in some areas of their lives.

We are not "possessed," but we can be "daimonizomai."

As we mentioned in the introduction to this chapter, we agree that Christians cannot be "possessed," or "owned," by demons since we are "owned" by Jesus Christ:[1]

1 Cor 6:20
You were bought at a price. Therefore honor God with your body. (NIV)

However, we hope that the above definitions clearly show that we can be "*daimonizomai*." We can be demon influenced, demon oppressed!

E. Operation of Demons

Let us now turn our attention to specific information about demons and how they operate. We can use the analogy of a high fidelity (hi-fi) amplifier. Just as the amplifier takes a weak signal and magnifies it, so the demons **sit** upon the places where we (or our ancestors) have given place to sin and they amplify/aggravate whatever weakness is there.

1. Important Facts about Demons

In Bible days, everyone knew about demons.

The Bible provides no description of demons. They are "just discussed," as if it is obvious to the reader what they are.

Are demons fallen angels?

In Ezekiel 28:12-19, there is a description of Satan's fall. His fall is also mentioned in Revelation 12:3-10, where one third of the angels fall with him. It seems likely that demons are fallen angels; but we do not know for sure.

It is clear, however, that they, like Satan, are created beings. As such, they ultimately are subject to the authority[2] of The Creator. Since God passed His authority

---

[1] Other scriptures of interest relating to this issue are: Mk 9:41, Rom 1:6, 7:4, 8:9, 14:8, 1 Cor 15:23, 2 Cor 10:7, and Gal 3:28-29, 5:24.

[2] Please see Job 1:12, 2:6, Lk 22:31, Eph 1:20-21.

on to the church, we, therefore, as believers do indeed have authority over the demons as well. We have authority to "cast them out."

Demons have personality: a will, mind, and emotions.

Demons are entities with a personality. They hear, speak, compete with each other, and have a will of their own. They are emotional, calculating, strategizing, sadistic, ruthless, and proud. They seem to come with different levels of ability and with different strengths and powers.

Demons have knowledge and may know our thoughts.

Demons have at least some knowledge. Revelation 9:4 shows that they know the difference between the saved and the unsaved since they can sting those without God's mark (of ownership) on their forehead. The question arises as to whether or not they know our thoughts. The answer seems to be a qualified "yes" for demons that are on the "inside" of a person, but "no" for those on the outside.

Satan's kingdom is highly organized, as the military.

We know from a number of scripture passages[1] that Satan's kingdom is highly organized. The demons we usually deal with are probably the low level peons in the hierarchy, but, nevertheless they are able to be effective in carrying out their master's purpose. The books by Frank Peretti, *This Present Darkness* and its sequel *Piercing the Darkness*,[2] have helped to bring much more awareness and understanding to the Body of Christ of the satanic kingdom.

Demons also seem to have a **region** or **home base** from which they have come and/or are assigned. In one incident, we felt the Holy Spirit impress us to cast out a witchcraft demon from Europe. So we said, "Get out, all you foul witchcraft demons from Europe." Then, speaking through the person, a demon said, "I'm not from Europe, I'm from Haiti." So we cast it out. Then the next one said, "I'm from Jakarta." So we cast it out as well. Finally, the next demon to manifest was the witchcraft demon from Europe. We had to laugh at how their arrogance and pride caused them to betray themselves as we cast out all of them.

The demon's purpose is to prevent or hinder salvation.

We do know that demons affect people today and that they affected people in Jesus' time. Their first goal is to **prevent someone from receiving salvation**. If that fails, they work at preventing **Christian maturity**. They try to shut us down and make us ineffective. Their chief strategy is **to try to get people to turn away from God**. They do this through many forms of **temptation,** many forms of **harassment**, and many forms of challenging our trust of God and His Word.

Demons take after their leader, Satan. John 10:10 states that Satan has come to "steal, kill, and destroy," and demons are the instruments through which he does much of his work. In John 8:44, Jesus states that Satan is a murderer, liar, and the father of liars. Listen to what He says in a heated conversation with the Jews.

> Jn 8:44
> Ye are of [your] father the devil, and the lusts of your father ye will do. He was a murderer from the beginning, and abode not in the truth, because there is no truth in him. When he speaketh a lie, he speaketh of his own: for he is a liar, and the father of it. (KJV)

Demons **lie to us** and work hard to have us **lie to ourselves** (i.e., self-deception).

---

[1] Please see Eph 1:21, 6:12, Col 1:16, 2:15, 1 Pet 3:22, and Dan 10:13.
[2] Peretti, Frank, *This Present Darkness* and *Piercing the Darkness*, Crossway Books, Westchester, IL, 1986 and 1989.

Another form of **harassment** is **accusation** and **criticism**. Demons, following their leader the Accuser, interject many condemning thoughts into the minds of believers. They particularly like to stir up the past with thoughts of "You really should have . . . ," or "If only you had done . . . differently." It is a comfort to know that the all-time great accuser is going to come to an end. In Revelation we read:

> Rev 12:10-11
> 10 And I heard a loud voice saying in heaven, Now is come salvation, and strength, and the kingdom of our God, and the power of his Christ: for the accuser of our brethren is cast down, which **accused them before our God day and night**.
> 11 And they overcame him by the blood of the Lamb, and by the word of their testimony; and they loved not their lives unto the death. (KJV)

The Bible tells us that we are at war with Satan. In fighting any war, one crucial ingredient is knowing all we can about the nature of our enemy!

2. Demons Affect All Parts of Man: Body, Soul, and Spirit

Demons don't "play fair."

Demons are on a "**seek and destroy**" mission. They work together. They strategize. They take advantage of weaknesses. They love times when people are either physically and/or emotionally weak and vulnerable. In short, demons don't play fair. They endeavor to affect all areas of a person, **body, soul and spirit**. Table U shows us some of the typical ways that they affect us.

Demons are out to do the same things that their leader does: that is, "to steal, kill, and destroy."[1] They do it at every level within the human personality that they can possibly access and through any open door that exists. Such was the case with our friend, Sandy.

3. Sandy's Story: Captured: Body, Soul, and Spirit

As Sandy's story continued to unfold during our ministry sessions, it showed the octopus-like grip of the enemy's tentacles woven around every area of her life: **body, soul and spirit.**

Sandy's pastor, himself also a childhood victim of sexual abuse, pleaded with her to fill needs that "only she could fill." Demons of deception obtained such a grip on her **mind** that she was convinced that his lies were truth. She believed that she was doing a "good thing" by helping him feel better about himself. Soon, she thought, he would reach a place of healing and confidence and all the church would benefit from what she had done in secret.

Sandy said that at times she would come to herself and vow never to sleep with him again, but a power seemed to draw her back. Her will was defeated. **Her mind and her will, such key parts of her soul, were no longer ruled by herself**, but by demons of deception, sexual perversion, and occult control.

---

[1] Please see Jn 10:10.

Table U
Typical Oppression by Demons

Body:	Appetites (lust, gluttony, sex, clothes, etc.), addictions (pornography, Internet, shopping, overeating, sports, gambling, TV, etc.), illness (cancer, arthritis, epilepsy, asthma, "incurable diseases," etc.), bodily states (sleeplessness, sleepiness, lethargy, pain, nervousness, etc.)
Soul/Mind:	Torment (thoughts of accusation, temptation, distraction, terror, insanity, death etc.), blocked memory, forgetfulness, lethargy, compulsive thoughts, blocked understanding of God's Word, etc.
Soul/Will:	Weak will. A will that has no follow through,
Soul/Emotions:	Exaggerated emotional states: fear, anxiety, anger, rage, shame, rejection, grief that is over-extended or out of proportion, etc.
Spirit:	Attempted prevention of salvation. Spiritual lethargy, doubt of salvation experience, unbelief. Can affect, harass, prevent maturing, but not take over (in a Christian).

She described her existence in this poem:

> I felt so lonely, Lord,
> And so empty.
> Finally, there was no laughter
> And happiness was a distant memory.
> Everything — even pleasant tasks —
> Became burdensome, loathsome.

Her life was tormented, devoid of joy. Since the enemy doesn't stop with one area, soon Sandy's **spirit** became clouded, like a thick cataract over an eye that longs to see. Though daily she would tell others of God's love for them, she couldn't experience it herself. She was serving water to others while she herself remained desperately thirsty.

Sandy's **body** was not immune to the demonic onslaught. In covering her secret life, she accepted the lie that if she worked harder and longer, she wouldn't feel so guilty. The demons drove her. She stayed at the church far too many hours. Exhaustion merged into numbness.

In addition, there was another strange kind of **physical** deception. For years, Sandy had endured multiple back surgeries, resulting from injuries in a car accident. She lived in constant pain. During the sexual encounters with her pastor, the demons would greatly reduce the pain. She felt enticed, and yet at the same time she felt trapped and defiled.

Sandy despaired of ever getting free, but finally her prayers were answered. Her freedom, however, came at great cost to herself, to the congregation, and to her pastor.

Those who have faced the depth of our great depravity may treasure beyond measure God's merciful forgiveness and deliverance. Here are the remaining stanzas of Sandy's poem which were written near the end of her ministry.

> Now, even the most difficult exercise
> Is touched with ease, with peace.
> Joy is more than just a word.
> Music dances through my heart,
> I have a new song—a song of hope.
> You exchange
> My death for Your life,
> My emptiness for Your fullness,
> My darkness for Your light.
>
> Rejoice, o my soul,
> And sing praises to the King;
> For He has set the captive free
> And brought home the destitute.
> His promises are true,
> His love is authentic,
> His mercy and loving kindness are
> From everlasting to everlasting.
>
> I will declare His faithfulness and goodness
> And follow after Him with my whole heart.
> He alone satisfies the soul!
>
> Sandy

God was setting Sandy free: **body, soul and spirit**. We will have more of Sandy's story later.

4. How Demons Enter: Open Doors

Since demons are such bullies, one might ask, "Do demons randomly pick on people, like the random checking done by the IRS on income tax returns?" While demons do target people (particularly those who are serious about serving God and who are advancing the kingdom of God), there are some very specific **"open doors"** by which demons frequently **gain entrance** into a person's life. Genesis 4:7b recounts what the Lord said to Cain after he expressed anger because his brother's offering was preferred:

> Gen 4:7
> . . . And if you do not do well, **sin is crouching at the door**; and **its desire is for you**, but **you must master it**. (NAS)

In general, it is our opening of the door that allows sin (and accompanying demons) to come in. The exception to this statement are the demons that come with our "inheritance" — those who have already entered while we were helpless in the womb. No one is immune unless our parents and/or other relatives knew to protect us with prayer and spiritual warfare.

Some of the "doors" through which demons come are shown in Figure 5 on the next page, as well as in the side margin. Lets look at these in some detail.

a. Inherited Curses and Accompanying Demons

Inherited Curses

Some demons apparently come down the family line. They often manifest soon after birth. We suspect that they are present even as the child is being formed. This seems particularly true of demons of fear, rejection, rebellion, anger, rage, shame, sexual perversion, control, and abandonment. They are able to enter at this early age because of the "legal ground" from Sins of the Fathers (and mothers). Because of the curses resulting from the generational sin, or because of others cursing the family line, the demons are able to pass from generation to generation to carry out the curses. The cycle continues as the demons put **pressure** on the person to **enter into** the same sins as his ancestors. As he yields to that pressure, the sin becomes his own, and he gives legal rights for the Demonic Oppression.

Another form of "inheritance" occurs when one or more of our ancestors have dedicated or committed their descendants to their particular god or occult guild, i.e., witchcraft or freemasonry. Here the demons claim "ownership" right from the womb and will do all within their power to prevent the person from hearing or understanding the Gospel.[1] This can be particularly severe if bloody oaths and/or sacrifices have been made. The good news is that the Blood of Jesus overrides and neutralizes any other blood that has ever been shed. As a result even people with major open doors of occult sin in their family line have the hope of freedom and healing.

---

[1] This is analogous to the seed sown on the path in Mat 13:4, 19.

In Second Samuel we have the example of David cursing Joab and his entire family line because Joab deceptively killed Abner after David had entered into an agreement with him. This was the **starting point**, or **entry point**, where demons were given legal right to enter a family and carry out the spoken curses. This curse, and its accompanying demons, will continue to move relentlessly down through the generations until it is finally broken and the demons are cast out.

> 2 Sam 3:27-29
> [27]Now when Abner returned to Hebron, Joab took him aside into the gateway, as though to speak with him privately. And there, to avenge the blood of his brother Asahel, Joab stabbed him in the stomach, and he died. [28]Later, when David heard about this, he said, "I and my kingdom are forever innocent before the LORD concerning the blood of Abner son of Ner. [29]**May his blood fall upon the head of Joab and upon all his father's house! May Joab's house never be without someone who has a running sore or leprosy or who leans on a crutch or who falls by the sword or who lacks food**." (NIV)

b. Sins of the Flesh

Sins of the Flesh o

By far, sins of the flesh are the **door that we most frequently open** to invite the enemy in to destroy us. This is especially true when the sin is repeated and becomes a pattern, leading to a lifestyle of indulging the flesh. Sin does not have to be "exotic" to provide an opening for demons. The "garden variety" sin will do the job just fine as far as the demons are concerned. Weakness of the flesh and demons **co-labor together** to keep a vicious cycle going. We sin, then the demons enter and help influence us to continue to sin in the same way. They usually work by putting persistent, deceptive thoughts into our minds. "The devil made me do it, **but** my flesh sure helped him out!"

The following list contains some very common areas in which we indulge our carnal appetites.

1. **Anger:** We give ourselves permission to vent our anger[1] on others. Anger can lead to violence, adding to the legal ground.
2. **Fear:** The Bible says "fear not."[2] Fear and worry often lead to sinful ways of coping. Since there are as many types of fear as there are possible ways to be injured or killed, there are many opportunities for demonic entry.
3. **Greed/Covetousness:** We are told not to covet, and we are warned about the severe consequences if we do.[3]
4. **Jealousy/Envy:** Envy is rottenness to the bones. It will make us sick.[4] James speaks of lusting to envy.[5] Lust and envy can work together.

---

[1] Please see Eph 4:26-32, Col 3:8, Jam 1:19-20,
[2] Please Lk 12:32, Jn 12:15, 2 Tim 1:7,
[3] Please see Ex 20:17, 1 Tim 6:9-10.
[4] Please see Prov 14:30 .
[5] Please see Jam 4:1-5.

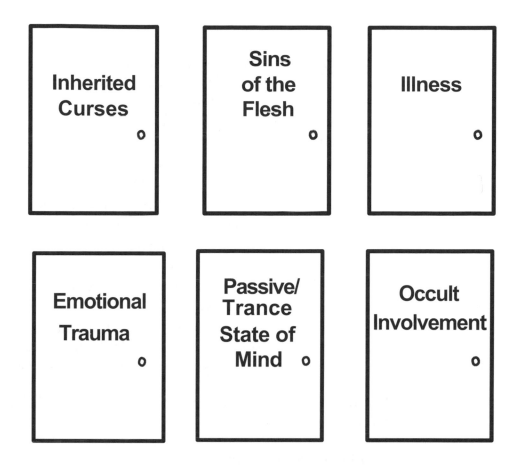

Figure 5: Open Doors for Demonic Entry

5. **Rebellion:** Ephesians speaks of walking in disobedience (rebellion).[1] First Samuel states that rebellion is "as the sin of witchcraft," abhorrent to God.[2]

6. **Pride:** This, the original sin of Satan, leads to many wrong actions. It is often the sin most hidden from us.

1 Jn 2:16	speaks of the lust of the flesh, lust of the eyes, and the pride of life. These incorporate all possible areas of pride.
I Tim 3:6-7	is a caution to protect novices (as well as the experienced) from being lifted up with pride.
Isa 14:12-17, Eze 28:12-19	demonstrate the "I" problem as well as the risk of putting value in achievements and possessions.

---

[1]   Please see Eph 2:2.
[2]   Please see 1 Sam 15:22-23.

7. **Lust:** Satan tries to arouse us to lust. His strategies are subtle. Samson provides us with a sad example, "Get her for me, for she pleaseth me well."[1]

8. **Gluttony:** *Aim* magazine reported that as much as 73 percent of the American population is overweight.[2] This is a serious national health problem. (Note: We must be careful, however, not to be judgmental in this area since there are **many reasons** for weight problems.)

9. **Gossip:** This sin gives Satan rich opportunity to work.[3]

10. **Strife:** James states that where envying and strife [is], there [is] confusion and every evil work.[4] God hates those who sow strife/discord.[5]

11. **Bitterness:** In Hebrews, God commands us to allow no root of bitterness.[6]

12. **Self-Righteousness:** "I am right and everyone else is wrong." This sin distances us from others in the church, as well as from God.

13. **Criticizing, Blaming, Judging:** In this sin, we often hold up our own life as the standard of rightness. Others are put down or seen as the cause/reason for everything being wrong.

14. **Unforgiveness:** God makes it very clear that forgiveness is an absolute requirement for freedom. The story of the unjust servant shows that if we do not forgive, God allows the tormentors (demons included) access to us.[7]

It's sobering to realize that any of these "ordinary" sins may provide an entrance for Satan's demons.

c. Illness and Accidents

Illness

○

Illness provides an opportunity for demons to enter. In these two forms of physical trauma — illness and accidents — defenses are lowered, the will is weakened, and the ability to pray for oneself is lessened. As previously pointed out, demons love to take advantage of our vulnerability and to kick us while we are down. With illness, we have the added liability of medical drug use. We have personally cast out many demons by the names of different drugs — even simple over-the-counter drugs such as **aspirin** — and seen amazing results. **Anything** that we are in bondage to is a potential open door for Demonic Oppression.

In accidents, during the time of shock and trauma, demons take advantage of our weakened defenses to "swarm" into our soul realm. Demons of "shock," "trauma," "depression," "accident," etc., will move right in, ignoring the fact that "it isn't fair." They sometimes are able to set up additional accidents, starting a cycle of "accident proneness."

---

[1] Please see Jud 14:3. Also 1 Jn 2:15-16.
[2] Aim magazine, January 1994, pg 9.
[3] Please see 1 Tim 5:13.
[4] Please see Jam 3:16.
[5] Please see Prov 6:19.
[6] Please see Heb 12:15.
[7] Please see Mat 18:21-35.

d. Emotional Trauma

> **Emotional Trauma** o

Emotional trauma is another common, yet unrealized, potential open door. A traumatic emotional or physical experience fractures the defenses that normally keep demons out. Many of us experience, at one time or another in our lives, the emotional trauma of loss. Common examples are the breakup of a relationship, divorce, unexpected death, job loss, and abuse. Other more severe forms of emotional and physical trauma include violence, rape, and ritual sexual abuse.

When any of these occur in our childhood, it can lead to fractured or multiple personalities as part of our "coping" mechanism for survival. Any or all of these personalities may also be oppressed by demons. This can complicate the job of ministering to these people considerably, as the minister needs the wisdom of the Holy Spirit to discern when he is dealing with a part of the personality and when it is a demonic entity.[1]

e. Passive or Trance State of Mind

> **Passive/ Trance State of Mind** o

Under normal circumstances, the mind has a protective wall around it, provided by the will — which is man's ability to say "No" to what is wrong, and "Yes" to what is right. When one gives up his will in a passive or trance state of mind, the door is opened for demons to invade. The person may become partially or even completely controlled by the demonic.[2]

There are three main ways that we allow our minds to enter the passive state that makes us so vulnerable to demons:

- **Trances:** When the mind is neutral, open, and unguarded (i.e., hypnosis).
- **Induced Mental States:** Voluntarily letting go, usually through drugs, chants, music (rock and roll), meditation [yoga or TM (mantra)], watching TV (yes, this can produce a trance).
- **Anesthesia:** When used during operations.

The experience of being anesthetized — though different from either self-induced passivity or a trance state — is similar in that it leaves the mind unguarded. In reality, it is a "drug induced" passivity or trance. We expect that much of the depression following surgery is caused by Demonic Oppression. Betsy experienced a severe depression following surgery in 1983. This ended dramatically as a result of deliverance. When our minds are passive because of anesthesia, a strong prayer covering can be very helpful, if not essential.

---

[1] The book by James G. Friesen, *Uncovering the Mystery of MPD*, Here's Life Publishers, Inc., San Bernardino, CA, 1991, presents an enlightened Christian approach to ministering to Multiple Personality Disorder.

[2] Philpott and Hymers, *The Deliverance Book,* op. cit.

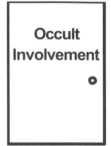

f.　Occult Involvement

The last open door through which demons enter that we want to discuss is the occult area. Occult involvement is the major form of idolatry.[1] The word "occult" means "hidden." Occult involvement means looking for knowledge and/or power in "hidden" sources, sources other than the true and living God. This eventually leads to allegiance or worship to those other sources.

Participation in occult activities amounts to rebellion against God. It is frequently driven by a **lust for power** through knowledge and control.

Occult involvement, like drug use or sexual sin, **is progressive**. It takes more and more to be satisfied. People start out with something mild, such as astrology, and progress to something more serious and eventually end up in witchcraft. This level of involvement puts a person into contact with demons.

Ignorance of the Law is no excuse.

Demons can enter even when we dabble in the occult areas in **ignorance**. Unfortunately, ignorance of the law is no excuse. Some of these activities are relatively minor and are done as "harmless fun." Yet, if an ancestral sin or curse is in operation, it takes very little "harmless fun," particularly in the occult area, to provide an opportunity for demon entry.

God hates the occult. This is clear through many scriptures, where God strictly forbids the following activities.

Deu 4:19	Astrology, and worshipping the stars.
Deu 18:10-12	Many things detestable (abomination) to the Lord are listed, such as sacrificing one's children, practicing divination, sorcery, interpreting omens, witchcraft, casting spells, mediumship, or consulting the dead.
Lev 20:2-5	Sacrificing children to false gods.
Lev 20:6	Consulting familiar spirits (mediums, witches, and wizards).
Lev 20:27	Being a medium, witch, or wizard.
Gal 5:20	Paul lists among the works of the flesh: idolatry, witchcraft.
Rev 21:8	Occult practitioners (sorcerers and idolaters) are headed for the lake of fire.

The demons of occult power are unusually strong when people have been involved in occult activities, or when the person is a generational "focus" for witchcraft or occult sin done in past generations. These demons can bring a wide variety of demonic gifts and oppressions. ESP gifts and psychic powers

---

[1]　Please see Ex 20:3-6.

provided by these demons are frequently seen in these people. It is important that the person renounce all desire for psychic (demonic) gifts and abilities and affirm that he wants only the giftings of the Holy Spirit to operate through him.

In addition to "special giftings" in a person, we can identify the presence of occult influence if the person has **several** of the following: **accident proneness** or **illness**, **sexual sins**, **strong fears**, and/or **strong control**.

> **Note:** Reading occult books does not automatically produce demonization, but unless the Holy Spirit directs you to absorb this kind of literature for the purpose of advancing the kingdom of God, you are taking a risk. Studying occult material does begin to produce a mind set (a set of Ungodly Beliefs) that makes one more and more prone to be drawn into the occult/demonic. Unless it is a part of the ministry that God has called you into, we suggest that you remain ignorant in this area.[1]

As we mentioned earlier in the Inherited Curses section, one frequently observed entry point for demons occurs when a person's **ancestors dedicate their descendants** to their particular god. We have seen this repeatedly with occult and/or secret organizations, such as the Mason's bloody oaths, Indian ancestor dedications, and witchcraft.

The Generational Patterns Form is helpful.

The Generational Patterns Form, included in Appendix A, is helpful because it provides the ministry receiver an opportunity to list all occult activities in which he or his ancestors have participated. Often, a prospective ministry receiver will begin to do some family research as he prepares for ministry, and in the process he will find some very significant information. During the ministry session, the Holy Spirit also will show occult activities and other open doors, of which the ministry receiver and RTF ministers have no previous knowledge.

g. Summary

While the six doors of demonic entry we have just discussed are not the only ways that demons infiltrate our personhood, they do appear to be the major ways. It is important to be aware of them as we each become better equipped to minister to the Body of Christ.

> **Exercise:** Think about the six doors of entry we have just discussed and whether one or more may be in operation in your life. Also, pray and ask the Holy Spirit to reveal to you any open doors that you are not aware of, either in your own life or in your ancestors. We suggest that you jot down some notes so that when we come to the Ministry Steps section, you can either do some self-deliverance and/or enlist the help of a mature Christian.

---

[1] Please see 1 Cor 14:20.

5. Testing Your Knowledge

As ministers, when we hear descriptions of these "open doors" in a ministry receiver's life, we want to check out whether the doors have been used for **demonic entry** and **influence**. So, to help you practice your increased knowledge and understanding of this important subject, you can consider the following situations to determine whether or not demonic activity may be involved.

a. Situation 1

A young woman attending Bible College had a severe problem with masturbation. As a small child she had been molested by a neighbor and began masturbating soon after this incident. She contacted us for ministry after she had spent a month of frequent fasting and much prayer, only to have her problem get worse.

- Is demonic activity indicated? No: _____   Yes: _____
- If yes, what is the probable door of entrance? _____
- Is it primarily a problem of undisciplined flesh? No: _____   Yes: _____
- Is it a case where both flesh and demons may be involved? _____
- Is there insufficient information to determine clearly?: _____

b. Situation 2

David, a man in his early thirties, moved away from his lover, whose life was becoming more erratic and more eccentric. He found out later that she had gotten a scary message from her Ouija board about their future together, and she had basically given up on him. The following year, David was led to salvation by a street evangelist and shortly thereafter married a Christian girl. Over the next five-year period, David, whose job involved much travel, was in three rear-end collisions. One required extensive hospitalization and follow-up chiropractic treatment. He came to us, trying to decide whether or not to take a job with less travel. "My life just seems to be jinxed," he said.

- Is demonic activity indicated? No: _____   Yes: _____
- If yes, what is the probable door of entrance? _____
- Is it primarily a problem of undisciplined flesh? No: _____   Yes: _____
- Is it a case where both flesh and demons may be involved? _____
- Is there insufficient information to determine clearly?: _____

c. Situation 3

Sam and Jenny were having marriage difficulties. Both had grown up in single parent families and had been given much responsibility early in life. They both liked things to be neat and orderly. The trouble was that each had his own definition of "neat and orderly," and each wanted things his way. Each felt more in control when he was "running the show." Sometimes what started as a simple conversation erupted into violence when they disagreed and ended with Jenny throwing kitchen utensils and Sam pushing her against the wall. A friend jokingly said he was going to report them to the police if they didn't learn to calm down.

- Is demonic activity indicated? No: _____ Yes: _____
- If yes, what is the probable door of entrance? _____
- Is it primarily a problem of undisciplined flesh? No: _____ Yes: _____
- Is it a case where both flesh and demons may be involved? _____
- Is there insufficient information to determine clearly?: _____

d. Situation 4

The Browns lived with Mr. Brown's father, a melancholy man who had lost everything in the Depression. Though he had been able to start a business again and make a go of it, somehow he had never been able to relax or enjoy his work. The Browns also had been through years of tumult, with their little upholstery busi-ness humming along some years, and then barely making it others. "I guess we are just doomed not to get ahead," Mr. Brown said after looking at their accounts. They didn't really mind not having a lot, but what really puzzled them was that their son, who had been valedictorian of his high school class, was having one business failure after another.

- Is demonic activity indicated? No: _____ Yes: _____
- If yes, what is the probable door of entrance? _____
- Is it primarily a problem of undisciplined flesh? No: _____ Yes: _____
- Is it a case where both flesh and demons may be involved? _____
- Is there insufficient information to determine clearly?: _____

As we listen to our ministry receiver's life story, we, as ministers, want to begin to learn to "tune in" to possible Demonic Oppression open doors. As we practice listening to them and to the Holy Spirit, our spiritual discernment will increase.[1]

---

[1] Please see Heb 5:14.

6. Behavioral Indicators of Demonic Oppression

Learn to recognize the clues.

As a child, did you ever go on a treasure hunt in which you had **clues** to follow in order to find the treasure? Well, many demons leave "clues" in the form of behavioral manifestations, which are an easy give-away if you know how to recognize them. This section should help you become a "demon detector," as well as helping you learn to use the wonderful gift of discernment.

This list of Behavioral Indicators was originally developed by Ernest Rockstad.[1] We have confirmed and expanded it. Table V shows the listing (a "Who's Who" in the demonic-manifestation world). Following is a discussion of each item.

a. Incapacity for Normal Living

This symptom manifests in a variety of ways. Some examples are:

- The **inability to feel joy** or satisfaction in life. A person experiences ongoing feelings of confusion, heaviness or depression, similar to dragging an anchor. This occurs at times when there is no particular external situation causing stress.

- **Agitation at gospel meetings** that keep one from truly entering in or from receiving the message. Demonic strategy can often be seen in causing restlessness, irritation, sleepiness, or even physical attacks or coughing, especially as the main truths of the gospel are being read or preached.

- In the **yo-yo effect,** a person goes from **one extreme to another.** For example, he is not happy in a crowd and not happy alone. He may yo-yo between exuberance and depression, between being very disciplined and undisciplined, between having much sexual passion and being frigid.

b. Extreme Bondage to Sin

The person is **unable to stop the sin** even when trying very hard. He becomes hopeless and defeated. This is the case in some besetting sin.[2]

Examples might include a person who can't stop abusing his own children, can't stop temper tantrums, can't stop shoplifting, can't stop involvement with pornography, etc.

c. Deception about Normal Personality

Demons masquerade as part of our personality. They hide within our personhood. The person thinks, "This is just the way I am. This is part of my personality, or, a **normal** part of my family characteristics." (The Smiths have always been hot-tempered; the women in this family have always been bossy, controlling, etc.)

---

[1] Rockstad, Ernest B., *Enlightening Studies in Spiritual Warfare*, Faith and Life Publications, Andover, Kansas 67002, 1985. Also an earlier tape series on *The Christian Life and Studies in Demonic Deliverance.*

[2] Please see Heb 12:1.

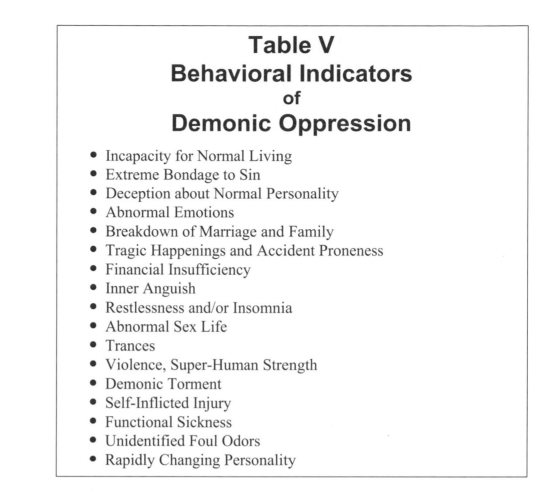

Table V
Behavioral Indicators
of
Demonic Oppression

- Incapacity for Normal Living
- Extreme Bondage to Sin
- Deception about Normal Personality
- Abnormal Emotions
- Breakdown of Marriage and Family
- Tragic Happenings and Accident Proneness
- Financial Insufficiency
- Inner Anguish
- Restlessness and/or Insomnia
- Abnormal Sex Life
- Trances
- Violence, Super-Human Strength
- Demonic Torment
- Self-Inflicted Injury
- Functional Sickness
- Unidentified Foul Odors
- Rapidly Changing Personality

This deception about a person's true identity is frequently seen in connection with the Shame-Fear-Control Stronghold. With this stronghold, the person has accepted the lie that he is shameful and must control to avoid any exposure and further shaming. Please see Chapter XIV for an explanation of this stronghold and how to remove it from your life.

When the demons are cast out, the person frequently experiences a transitional time of loss and instability as he becomes familiar with his real personality.

d. Abnormal Emotions

Demons can cause a person's emotions to become exaggerated, intense, out of control, or all consuming. This is particularly true with fear, anger, jealousy, grief, shame, resentment, and unforgiveness. Betsy's past fear of death is an example.

e. Breakdown of Marriage and Family

We believe demons are at work in the break-down of family life and in many cases of divorce. We know some people whose Control demons continually battle each other. Think about the families that you know. There are families where divorces are rampant, others where there are none at all.

f. Tragic Happenings and Accident Proneness

A woman who has been a special friend to us endured more heartbreak in one year than we have had in a lifetime. She herself struggles with her sexual identity and fights wrong sexual relationships. Her brother died of AIDS. Her sister was in a terrible wreck the month before the brother died. The sister's husband is a drug user. This woman's younger brother, who has border-line retardation, has been reported for exposing himself. This young woman's mother has begun radiation treatments for a breast malignancy. Her father, who is often in and out of work, spends much time depressed. Our friend prays to be a light for God in the midst of her circumstances!

g. Financial Insufficiency

Demonic infestation is particularly indicated in situations where there is an adequate supply of income and there "should be enough," but there isn't.

h. Inner Anguish

This anguish takes many forms, such as pressure on the inside, turmoil, depression, despair, mental lapses, and the inability to concentrate. The anguish exists even when there are no obvious pressures from the external environment.

i. Restlessness and/or Insomnia

The demon's strategy: "Let's wear him out." Demons may be present when a person can't slow down, when he is impelled to be busy. He will over exert, then go to bed and not be able to sleep. Note: There are other causes for this behavior, so one must be careful not to judge or label too quickly.

j. Abnormal Sex Life

Demons may cause a person to have abnormal sexual patterns, demanding too much or too little. They can also cause spouses to have the opposite desires, i.e., one will have excessive need while the other is frigid. Demons can cause the same adverse effect in families over the generations. We know of one family line where for three generations one woman in each generation was frigid.

k. Trances

A person is demonized if he goes into a trance-like state, even in an uncontrolled way. We are not saying that all trances are demonic, but it is likely that many trances are. If anyone "falls" into a trance from time to time, and perhaps a physician has been consulted and no explanation found, then the condition is likely to be demonic in nature.

The mediumistic trance is the ultimate form of demonization — a state where the demon is in complete control, and the person has "willed" to yield totally to their "spirit guide."

l. Violence, Super-Human Strength

Demons can cause people to have super-human strength. We have the scriptural example of the Gerasene demoniac[1] who could not be bound. We suspect that many violent people in mental institutions, who have to be drugged to be controlled, are actually manifesting demons of violence. In our experience, these violent manifestations can be partially, though not necessarily completely, controlled through binding the demons in the Name and Authority of Jesus Christ. The degree of success in binding depends on the degree of submission of the person to the demonic.

m. Reporting of Demonic Torment

One year, our daughter brought two friends home during her spring break from college. We were trying to be on our best behavior and not mention demons at the dinner table or do anything to embarrass her. After dinner, she said to one of her friends, "Why don't you tell them what has been going on. They are used to this stuff. Nothing shocks them." We were pleased by her vote of confidence, but a little surprised as her friend begin to describe two occasions where she woke up to find her bed several feet off of the floor. Needless to say, we stopped trying not to talk about demons and launched ahead. She had a glorious deliverance!

We have ministered to more than twenty people who have experienced such strange phenomena as having doors slam when there is no wind, having their bed a foot or more off of the floor, hearing voices when there is no one present, having the light go on or off by itself. These are all forms of demonic torment. Other people, usually those who themselves or their ancestors have a background of occult practices, have experienced sexual intercourse with an Incubus (male) or Succubus (female) spirit. These demonic torments are very real.

n. Self-Inflicted Injury

Demons, like their leader, are working to kill us. If they can cause a person to harm himself, they are accomplishing their mission. Scratching one's arms, cutting, other forms of mutilation, are signs of demonic mental anguish and pain. Both suicidal fantasies and suicidal attempts can be caused by demons.

o. Functional Sickness

Functional sickness includes pain or sickness at inopportune times (such as at church or in ministry sessions) and undefined pains that move around the body.

It seems very likely that demons are involved with many, if not all, of the "incurable" illnesses, such as MS, cancer, AIDS, arthritis, ringing in the ears, etc. They may not always be the root cause, but they certainly make the illness worse.

---

[1]   Please see Mat 8:28-34, Lk 8:26-39.

p. Unidentified Foul Odors

On rare occasions people will emit a strong unpleasant odor which has no physical cause. One possibility is that the source of the odor is a demon. Occasionally, we have experienced a brief, intense stench during deliverance. Was this the odor of a leaving demon? When Betsy was working at a Mental Health center, she saw a young woman in her twenties whose life was miserable because she couldn't get rid of a reeking odor. It accompanied her every where, and no doctor had been able to discover a cause. It truly smelled like a dead animal. However, one possibility had not been considered. Could demons have caused her odor?

q. Rapidly Changing Personality

Sometimes, very rapid changes of personality occur for no external reason. Demonic Oppression is one possible cause. (Chemical and hormonal imbalances and multiple personalities are other possible causes.)

This is a long but important list of behavioral indicators which we may observe as we grow in our ability to recognize demonic influence and the resulting manifestations. You can use this list to alert you to possible Demonic Oppression.

7. Demonic Oppression Groupings

Like many other people involved in deliverance, we have benefited from the early work of Frank and Ida Mae Hammond.[1] Over the years, we have adapted their "groupings" list to match what we were finding with the people coming to us for ministry. Since the major Demonic Oppression groupings will be different in each group of people — i.e., different in different churches because of the principalities that have "place" over each church — this list may need to be adapted for each deliverance minister. If you haven't yet formulated a list, however, the lists on pages 294 and 295 can provide a starting point.

In the Generational Patterns portion of the Application Form in Appendix A we have a modified set of these lists. They have been incorporated into the Application Form to serve as interview sheets, to be used for the SOFCs ministry, and to be used for the deliverance session.

8. Demonic Interconnectedness

We can take the demonic grouping concept a step further and construct a simplified diagram showing the interconnectedness, mutual support, and protection that the various demonic groupings provide for each other. While it is true that demons are very competitive, cut-throat, and ruthless, they will work together in their mission to destroy the person they inhabit.

---

[1]   Hammond, Frank and Ida Mae, *Pigs in the Parlor*, op. cit.

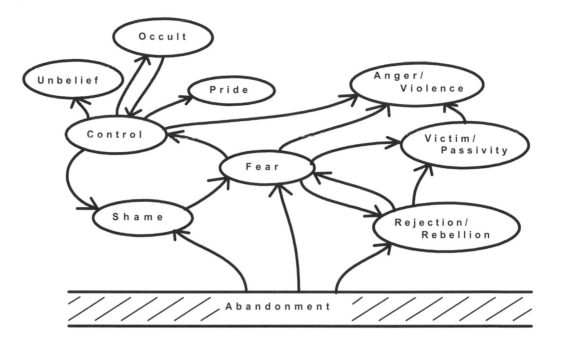

Figure 6: Demonic Grouping Interconnectedness
and Support Diagram

The above example diagram applys to a particular individual, with Abandonment as the root/foundational problem in his life. (Remember, we are trying to show the main functions and not all of the detail that is actually present.) We saw that Abandonment interconnected to and supported Shame, Fear, and Rejection/ Rebellion. Shame also fed into Fear, which gave place to Control and the Victim groupings. (Note the presence of the Shame-Fear-Control Stronghold. This is the topic of Chapter XIV.)

Anger and Violence came out of the Victim, Fear, and Control groupings. The Occult both drew from the rest of the demonic groupings and fed power and support into every other grouping through the Control grouping. In actuality, the Occult probably interconnected into every other grouping directly, but the Control group was its main partner in oppressing the person. With this diagram, we had a better grasp of how to do the deliverance for this person, i.e., in what order we should attack and disassemble out the demonic groupings.

Sometimes the Holy Spirit directs us to start at the outer fringes of the Demonic Oppression groupings. Then we work through the "weak" groupings first and move toward the root grouping(s) last. In this approach, we are "undercutting" the support from the "mutual aid society" that the demonic groupings provide for each other. As we approach the final groupings, even though they are strong in themselves, they have lost the support of the other groupings and are more easily removed.

Figure 7: DEMONIC OPPRESSION GROUPINGS*

Name: _____   Page 1

Abandonment
Isolation
Loneliness
Not Acceptable
Not Belonging
Rejection
Self-Pity
Not Wanted
Victim

Addictions/
Dependencies/
Escape
Alcohol
Caffeine
Cocaine
Computers
Downers/Uppers
Food
Gambling
Marijuana
Nicotine
Non-prescription
 Drugs
Pornography
Prescription Drugs
Sports
Street Drugs
Television
Tranquilizers
Video Games

Anger
Abandonment
Feuding
Frustration
Hatred
Murder
Punishment
Rage
Resentment
Spoiled Little
 Boy/Girl
Temper Tantrums

Anxiety
Burden
False Responsibility
Fatigue
Heaviness
Nervousness
Restlessness
Weariness
Worry

Bitterness
Accusation
Blaming
Complaining
Criticalness
Fault Finding
Gossip
Judging
Murmuring
Ridicule
Unforgiveness

Competition
Driving
Jealousy
Possessiveness
Striving

Control
Appeasement
Denial
Domineering
Double Binding
False Responsibility
Manipulation
Male Control
Occult
Passive Aggression
Possessiveness
Pride (I know best)
Selfishness
Witchcraft
Female Control

Deception
Confusion
Lying
Self-Deception

Depression
Despair
Despondency
Discouragement
Hopelessness
Insomnia
Oversleeping
Self-Pity
Suicide fantasies
Suicide attempt
Withdrawal

Emotions, Bound
Hindered

Escape
Fantasy
Forgetfulness
Lazy
Lethargy
Passivity
Procrastination
Sleep/Slumber
Withdrawal
_____
_____
_____

Failure
Performance
Pressure to Succeed
Striving

Fears
Anxiety
Bewilderment
Burden
Dread
Harassment
Heaviness
Horror Movies
Intimidation

Mental Torment
Over-Sensitivity
Paranoia
Phobia
Superstition
Worry
Fear of Authorities
Fear of being
 Attacked
Fear of being a
 Victim
Fear of Cancer
Fear of Death
Fear of Diabetes
Fear of Demons
Fear of Failure
Fear of Infirmities
Fear of Man
Fear of Performing
Fear of Punishment
Fear of Rejection
Fear of Sexual
 Inadequacy
Fear of Sexual
 Perversion
Fear of Singing
Fear of Violence
_____
_____
_____

Financial Bondage
Greed
Irresponsible
 Spending
Job Failures
Job Losses
Poverty
Stinginess

Greed
Cheating
Covetousness
Idolatry
Stealing
_____

Grief
Crying/Weeping
Heartbreak
Loss
Sadness
Sorrow
Trauma

Idolatry
Appearance/Beauty
Clothes
Food
Money
Position
Possessions

Infirmities/
Diseases
Accidents (falls,
 cars)
Anorexia/Bulimia
Asthma
Barrenness/Mis-
 carriage
Cancer
Congestion (lungs)
Diabetes
Fatigue
Female Problems
Heart/Circulatory
 Problems
Mental Illness
MS
Migraines-Mind
 Binding
Physical
 Abnormalities
Premature Death

Judgment
Blaming
Criticalness
Fault Finding
_____
_____
_____
_____
_____
_____
_____
_____
_____

* Use check mark if applicable, use cross mark when accomplished.
  Some groups from "Pigs in the Parlor" by Frank and Ida Mae Hammond.

DEMONIC OPPRESSION GROUPINGS*

Name: _____   Page 2

Mental Illness
Craziness
Compulsions
Confusion
Hallucinations
Hysteria
Insanity
Mind Binding
Paranoia
Schizophrenia
Senility

Mind Influence
Double Minded
Binding
Blocking
Racing

Mocking
Laughing
Ridiculing

Music
Heavy Metal
Rock and Roll

Not Belonging
Abandonment
Isolation
Loneliness
Not Acceptable
Not Wanted
Rejection
Self-Pity

Occult
Accident Proneness
Antichrist
Astral Projection
Astrology
Automatic Writing
Black Magic
Books,
   Occult/Witchcraft
Clairvoyance
Crystal Ball
Death, Suicide
Dispatching Demons
Eight Ball
ESP
False Gifts
Fortune Telling
Gypsy
Handwriting Analysis
Horoscopes
Hypnosis
I Ching
Idolatry (of
)
Indian Burial Ground
Indian Occult Rituals
Jewelry, Occult
KKK
Levitation
Mental Telepathy
Movies, Science
   Fantasy
Movies, Horror
Music, Heavy Metal

Necromancy
Non-Christian
   Exorcism
Ouija Board
Pagan Temples
Palm Reading
Past Life Readings
Pendulum
Psychic Healing
Science Fantasy
Seances
Sorcery
Spell or Hex, Casting
Spirit Guide(s)
Spiritism
TM
Tarot Cards
Tea Leaves
Victim
Voodoo
Water Witching
White Magic
Witchcraft
Yoga Meditation

Pride
Arrogance
Self-Importance
Vanity

Rebellion
Disobedience
Independence
Insubordination
Lying
Self-Will/Sufficiency
Stubbornness
Undermining

Rejection
Mistrust (of others)
Mistrust (by others)
Not Wanted
Perceived Rejection
Perfectionism
Prejudice/Slavery
Self-Rejection

Religious Spirits
Antichrist
Catholicism/Other
Legalism/Rules
Liberalism
New Age
Traditionalism

Self-Accusation
Anger
Condemnation
Guilt
Inferiority
Self-Hate
Self-Punishment

Sexually Confusion
Deception
Homosexuality
Lesbianism
Pornography
Trauma
Unprotected

Sexual Sins
Adultery
Bestiality
Demonic Sex
Defilement/Unclean
Exposure
Fantasy Lust
Fornication
Frigidity
Homosexuality
Incest
Incubus
Lesbianism
Lust
Masturbation
Pornography
Premarital Sex
Prostitution/Harlotry
Rape
Seduction/Alluring
Sexual Abuse
Succubus

Shame
Anger
Bad Boy/Girl
Condemnation
Embarrassment
Guilt
Hatred
Inferiority
Overweight/
   Underweight
Self-Hate

Strife
Arguing
Bickering
Contention
Cursing
Fighting
Mocking
Quarreling

Trauma
Accident
Emotional Abuse
Little Boy/Girl
Loss
Physical Abuse
Sexual Abuse
Shock
Verbal Abuse
Violence

Unbelief
Doubt
Rationalism
Skepticism

Unforgiveness
Bitterness
Religious
Pride

Unwanted
Abandonment
Not Belonging
Victim

Unworthiness
Inadequacy
Inferiority
Insecurity
Self-Accusation
Self-Condemnation
Self-Hate

Victim
Appeasement
Helplessness
Hopelessness
Mistrust
Self-Pity
Suspicion
Trauma

Violence
Cruelty
Destruction
Feuding
Hate
Murder
Retaliation
Torture/Mutilation

Withdrawal
Isolation
Blocked Intimacy
Loneliness

* Use check mark if applicable, use cross mark when accomplished.
   Some groups from "Pigs in the Parlor" by Frank and Ida Mae Hammond

Other times the Holy Spirit directs us to "go for the jugular," and we penetrate into the center of the enemy's camp and cast out the foundational demonic grouping(s) first. We usually have to command a separation of the groupings in this case by isolating the main ones from each other. Then we pick off these "strong men," casting them and their associated demons out. This is followed by moving out to the weaker and weaker groups. The diagram helps us understand how to separate groupings and move from one group to the next as we demolish the Demonic Strongholds within the person.

Some of you may be asking, "Where do these diagrams come from?" Well, they come partly from experience, but mostly from praying through the notes taken throughout the ministry sessions. We ask the Holy Spirit to show us the structure of the enemies' camp, i.e., how all of the different parts are connected. The components of the structure have been assembled from the Sins of the Fathers and the Resulting Curses, and from the place(s) given by the Ungodly Beliefs and Soul/Spirit Hurts. Then, as the Holy Spirit shows us, we sketch the diagram. We try not to have too much detail but just the right amount. Then we can see how the major demon groupings are cooperating so as not to lose their "house," keep the person captive, and carry out their work of "stealing, killing, and destroying."[1]

F. Preparation for Deliverance

Let's look at some significant preparation information we need to understand before we can safely ministry deliverance.

1. Deliverance in the RTF Ministry Context

God's heart has always been to see His people set free. He has sovereignly delivered His people from many demonic forces, particularly at the important times of their salvation, water baptism, and the baptism of the Holy Spirit. He has supernaturally delivered His people from Demonic Oppression in response to prayer, repentance, and fasting. Great deliverance has taken place during times of revival. God loves to see His sons and daughters shake loose from the enemy's clutches. He is present, through the power of His Holy Spirit, for us to co-labor with Him to bring about deliverance.

We want the best possible situation for effective and lasting deliverance.

In the RTF ministry situation, we have the most advantageous setting for effective and lasting deliverance to take place. First, the minister can assure the salvation and seriousness of the ministry receiver. Both factors are very important for a successful outcome. Then there is time for proper preparation. Also, in this context, the person is able to:

- Build trust and thus more easily . . .
- Share intimate areas where repentance and forgiveness are needed.

---

[1] Please see Jn 10:10.

This context also has the advantage of the integrated nature of this ministry, where the minister has opportunity to:

- Break Sins of the Fathers and Resulting Curses
- See that major Ungodly Beliefs are dealt with
- Minister to Soul/Spirit Hurts that have given legal ground to demons

In other words, in the context of RTF ministry, the legalities and ground work can be done which allow the best possible situation for casting out demons and ensuring that new demons won't come in at a later time.

We have seen the greatest fruit when both the minister and the ministry receiver are rightly **prepared** for the deliverance. Let's turn our attention to what that preparation involves.

2. Preparation of the Minister

The RTF minister needs to be thoroughly convinced of two things: that demons really exist and the Jesus has given us authority over them. This conviction will occur as he experiences deliverance himself and as he works with an experienced deliverance minister. Once these issues are settled, then it is a simple matter of listening to the Holy Spirit to obtain God's order and strategy for doing the deliverance.

a. Remembering Who He is In Christ

The minister must be confident in Christ's position of rule and authority over Satan and all his legions, and then in his own position in Christ. He needs to have it settled in his own heart that he is truly seated with Christ in the heavenly places and ruling with Him in authority[1] and that **everything** is under his feet as well as the feet of Christ.[2] The minister must **know that he knows** that Christ has given him authority and that he can stand in that authority.

*We need to **Know** our authority.*

He needs to know that his authority is based on God's Word. He must believe the truth spoken by Jesus:

> Mk 16:17
> And these signs will accompany those who have believed: in My name they will cast out demons, . . . (NAS)

In Luke 10:19, Jesus speaks to the seventy excited deliverance ministers. He addresses the issues of authority and safety:

> Lk 10:19
> Behold! I have given you **authority** and **power** to trample upon serpents and scorpions, and (physical and mental strength and ability) over all the power that the enemy [possesses], and **nothing shall in any way harm you**. (AMP)

---

[1] Please see Col 1:15-17 and Eph 2:6.
[2] Please see Eph 1:20-23.

John, in First John, also reassures the minister that God's power and authority operating in his life is greater than any power of Satan and his demons. Furthermore, as he comes against the powers of darkness, he is doing what Jesus has told him to do and he is safe doing it.

> 1 Jn 4:4
> . . . because greater is he that is in you, than he that is in the world. (KJV)

> 1 Jn 5:18
> . . . but he that is begotten of God keepeth himself, and that wicked one toucheth him not. (KJV)

b. Remembering Who the Deliverer Is

The minister, to be rightly prepared, needs to remember that "Jesus is the Deliverer." Deliverance is something we do, yet it is something Jesus does, and in another sense, it has already been done. You might reread the section "God's Strategy for Deliverance" on page 265 again to refresh your memory of how God has delivered the enemy into our hands. We are to drive them out, as we co-labor with Christ. Paul speaks of this human-divine interaction in First Corinthians:

> 1 Cor 3:9
> For we are labourers together with God. . . . (KJV)

God hasn't changed this fact in 2000 years. Again Paul expresses it:

> Col 1:29
> To this end I labor, struggling with all his energy, which so powerfully works in me. (NIV)

Jesus is the Deliverer.

We are pursuing the ministry and issuing the commands, but Jesus is the actual/ true Deliverer. The demons leave as they are escorted away by the finger of God,[1] which is the Holy Spirit.[2]

Retaining this **truth** prevents anxiety and fear from hindering the deliverance ministry. It also gives the person ministered to a sense of security and confidence.[3]

c. Depending on the Holy Spirit

The last part of the minister's preparation is to develop a list of the specific demons (demonic groupings) and Demonic Strongholds to be cast out. We start by looking back over the Generational Patterns sheets in the Application Form (see Appendix A), and noting the SOFCs groupings we ministered to earlier. We also prayerfully go back over notes of the previous sessions, noting the person's main problem areas. Many times, God will show which category/ group of demons or which Demonic Stronghold[4] to deal with first. At times, He has given a strategy

---

[1] Please see Lk 11:20.
[2] Please see Mat 12:28.
[3] Philpott and Hymers, *The Deliverance Book,* op. cit., page 83.
[4] Some schools of deliverance ministry have developed lists of "The Proper Names of Demons." These have been gleaned from what the (continued)

that appears to be analogous to the disarming and disassembly of an armed fortress.[1] He will reveal a plan of attack if it is needed.

Always cover the areas of: Occult, Control, Sexual Sin, Fears, and Physical Ailments.

It is wise to **always cover** the areas of: the occult, control, sexual sin, fears, and physical ailments. Even though the ministry receiver may have never sinned in any of these areas, it is almost a certainty that some of his ancestors have, resulting in curses of defeat, failure, and entrapment in these areas.

In summary, the minister needs to approach the time of deliverance spiritually prepared and mentally set in his knowledge and focus.

3. Preparation of the Ministry Receiver

How can the ministry receiver be best prepared for deliverance? We like to cover the following items.

a.   Requirement: Salvation, Seriousness

First, it is highly preferable — shall we say "essential" — that the ministry receiver be saved. We verify his salvation condition in the first ministry session as part of reviewing his Application Form.[2] We proceed with introducing him to Jesus if he isn't saved. Of course, in a church setting, it is unlikely that anyone will come for Christian ministry unless he is saved, but it doesn't hurt to check.

The ministry receiver should be serious, yet we must be prepared to "stand in the gap."

In addition to being saved, it is important for the ministry receiver to be serious in wanting deliverance. After all, it is his house that needs the cleansing. He should want to cooperate with the process and actively engage in setting his will and joining in with the deliverance process. Also, since he is the one who must "walk it out," he needs to be serious about appropriating God's provision so he can be successful in maintaining lasting victory.

The balancing word for the previous paragraph is that someone severely oppressed by curses and demons may need help before he can come into a condition of seriousness. There are times when it is the minister's faith and determination, his "standing in the gap,"[3] that brings that measure of freedom and healing that enables the person's own will and faith to begin to operate. Once again we are "forced" to rely on the Holy Spirit in these situations to see what we need to do. Do we confront the ministry receiver's passivity and encourage him to "get determined?" Do we press ahead and confront the demons on his behalf? Or do we do both things?

---

minister has heard in the spirit realm and what he has experienced in the response of demons. This knowledge may prove helpful in some instances but generally is not essential for deliverance once the legal ground of the first three Problem/Ministry Areas has been recovered. Please see books by Win Worley for further information in this area.

[1]   This is discussed in detail in Chapter XII, "Demonic Strongholds."
[2]   Sample Application Form is in Appendix A.
[3]   Please see Eze 22:30 and Mk 2:3-5.

© 1994, 1996, 2001 Proclaiming His Word, Inc.

We follow the Holy Spirit's leading on fasting and praying?

One additional measure of a ministry receiver's seriousness is his willingness to enter into praying and fasting before he comes for deliverance. We do not make a rule about the fasting part of this, but usually leave it to the ministry receiver to do as he desires and God directs. We personally do not generally fast before a deliverance session because we would not eat very often if we did. When, however, we are coming against major occult strongholds, we are very likely to fast beforehand. We also enlist intercessory support, which has proven to be vital at times.

Intercessors can be vital.

b. Specific Information for the Ministry Receiver

As it seems relevant for a particular ministry receiver, we may cover some or all of the following points with him. In addition, we review the "Ministry Steps" at the end of this chapter so that he will be familiar with the process. Obviously what we discuss depends on his maturity level, his understanding of the demonic kingdom, and his previous experiences with demonic deliverance.

Some ministry receivers may be fearful and anxious before the first deliverance session. Fear of the unknown, particularly of the spiritual realm, can be extremely unnerving. Some of the ministry receiver's anxiety may be alleviated by instruction on what to expect and how to constructively participate.

Unconfessed Sin/Need for Forgiveness

Demons will cling to any hidden or **unconfessed sin** so it is very important to make sure that repentance and the forgiveness of others is as complete as possible. This is especially true in the occult area, so double check! It is better to be too thorough than not thorough enough. What's not already covered will become apparent during the "casting out" phase if and when strong resistance is encountered.

Occult Objects

If the ministry receiver still possesses **occult books** on magic, fortune telling, astrology, sexual perversion, witchcraft, psychic gifts, etc., he needs to agree to get rid of them. This is also true of trinkets or jewelry with magical and/or idolatrous significance. Use of the Occult section on the Generational Patterns form in Appendix A can be helpful in bringing items to the person's remembrance.

It's the Truth that sets us Free, not Force

It's our Authority, not our loudness, that drives them out.

By the time we start deliverance, the ministry receiver's UGBs should be "on the way out" and being replaced with God's truth as expressed in his GBs. In addition, it may be helpful to ensure that the receive **knows** the truths that Jesus has defeated, disarmed, and triumphed over all the power of the enemy.[1] Demons have to leave because He has given us authority over them and we are releasing the Word of truth. It is the Truth that sets people free and not the volume of our voices nor the force of our will. The lies contained in the UGBs gave demons "place" and these have been exposed and dealt with. We can proclaim the Truth by using Scripture and praise as part of the deliverance, if necessary.

---

[1] Please see Col 2:13-15.

Have Him Set His Will

Once the legal ground has been recovered by ministering to the first three Problem/Ministry Areas, the determination and setting of the ministry receiver's will becomes the critical factor regarding long term freedom. In fact, the degree of his desire and persistence to be free is the deciding factor between an easy versus a difficult deliverance. When he has purposed in his heart that the demons have to leave and he stands on the truth and authority that Jesus has given him, there is no contest. The demons are in his house, and he needs to insist that they go. The last thing we want is a passive ministry receiver. If necessary, we help him be active and involved.

Speak in English and Keep Eyes Open

Normally, we ask the ministry receiver to speak in English and not in tongues during the "casting out" process. There is some indication that "tongues" hinders the demons departure through the mouth. We don't make a "federal case" of this, however. If the person repeatedly switches back to tongues without realizing what he is doing, we drop the matter. Of course, the tongues stir them up and encourage the demons to leave, but then, so does English.

It also helps us (and him) if he keeps his eyes open. This helps him stay in control and not go into a trance-like or passive state. In addition, the minister will sometimes see a demonic presence through the eyes of the person. Occasionally his eyes change as a demon manifests, so it is another indicator of how the deliverance is going.

Laying on Hands

Often our discernment is increased if we lay hands on the ministry receiver during the deliverance. Before touching him, we are careful to ask for his permission. We, of course, use discretion about where we place our hands, particularly for members of the opposite sex. We recommend touching the person's shoulders only, which is generally safe.[1]

The presence of hands with the anointing of the Holy Spirit often further agitates the demons, which can make the receiver upset. When that is the case, we need Holy Spirit wisdom to determine whether the stirring of the demons is more beneficial than any confusion to the person.

Joint Effort

Instruct the receiver that we will all be commanding and putting pressure on the demon(s) at the same time. This is no time for polite conversation, not even in the South!

---

[1] Please see our cautions regarding "laying on of hands" in Chapter XVI, "Final Thoughts for RTF Ministers."

Reporting

Let the ministry receiver know that he can help by reporting any negative experiences such as thoughts tempting him to withdraw from the deliverance process, strong negative feelings, and/or any physical symptoms (i.e., moving pains, dizziness, confusion, etc.).

Expect Hindrances

Demons will try to block the deliverance. That is just part of the warfare. We explain to the ministry receiver the "log jam" concept used by "blocking demons" to hinder us. We also inform him of strategies we will use if we run into hindrances. (See the following section on "What to do with Obstinate Demons.")

Use of Scripture, Praise

Demons hate any talk or songs about the Name of Jesus, the Blood, the Cross, certificates of debt,[1] the resurrection, Satan's defeat, their defeat, the lake of fire, etc. They get stirred up, agitated in different ways, and have a hard time remaining hidden. They particularly hate scripture, especially verses about the fall or the defeat of Satan. The ministry receiver should be ready to say or read scripture and to join the ministers in praise. (See the following section on "What Demons Hate.")

Possible Manifestations

Let the ministry receiver know that there may be manifestations, both of resistance and as the demons leave. The most common signs of resistance are thoughts such as, "This won't work," or "Demons aren't real." The receiver may experience sharp pains that move about his body, sleepiness, changing body temperature, and/or tightness somewhere in his body. Sometimes demons mock the process. At these times, the receiver may appear to be sarcastic, sneering and/or uncooperative. Demons generally manifest according to their type or function. For example, a demon of anger will cause a person to feel angry, a demon of shame, shameful, etc. Occasionally, the demon will manifest in a physical struggle. Also, occasionally the demons may speak through the person. Be prepared for whatever form the manifestations may take. Assure the ministry receiver that you will limit the extent of the manifestations if they become distracting or potentially harmful to him.

Explain how Demons Leave

Demons usually leave with the breath, through a yawn, cough, sigh, burp, hiccup, deep exhalation, laughter, crying, or a scream. Sometimes, as an act of the will, it is helpful to have the person breathe deeply and then to forcibly breath out, even to cough. This seems to help encourage the demons to leave, especially if they are already close to leaving. While the breath or cough does not cause the demons to leave, it provides the receiver an opportunity to exercise faith that the demons are leaving. Screams may occur, but this happens infrequently and usually when related to occult, witchcraft, or death demons. Demons may also leave through gas expulsion, but we usually don't mention this manifestation until it occurs!

---

[1]   Please see Col 2:14, NAS.

Sometimes There Are No Manifestations

Sometimes we see no manifestation when the demons are leaving, but the ministry receiver experiences a release of tension and/or a greater degree of peace and/or clear-headedness. It is helpful for the receiver to know how he manifests, even if only internally. Of course, we are doing our best to exercise the gift of the discernment of spirits so we know where we are in the "casting out" process. We want to be able to verify when a particular demon (or grouping) is gone.

c. Summary

As we go through this information with the receiver, we leave time for questions and then pray and have the person pray. Frequently, we find ourselves praying spontaneously. We ask the ministry receiver to do likewise as led by the Holy Spirit. Other times we ask the ministry receiver to read/pray a written prayer as part of starting the deliverance ministry. We particularly like a prayer originally shared with us by friends and fellow ministers, Mike and Michelle Green. We have it at the end of this chapter to use as we prepare to go through the Ministry Steps for deliverance.

G. Doing the Actual Deliverance

While there are potentially many different ways to do deliverance, we use the following procedure. We prefer to use this procedure because it helps the ministry receiver to learn how to do self-deliverance. We want him to be able to continue the spiritual warfare to clean his "house," as the Holy Spirit brings into his awareness other areas of Demonic Oppression as he is ready to deal with them.

1. Commanding

The minister's attitude is one of commanding. He needs to be firm and prepared to press in. He does not need to be loud. (Demons are not deaf.) The ministers' commanding attitude resembles that of a person speaking to a little "yappy" dog commanding him to go home and stop barking. We also want the ministry receiver to set his will to resist and then command the particular demon or grouping of demons to leave him, in Jesus' name. This is repeated until the demons are gone.

We also want the ministry receiver to set his will to resist and then command the particular demon or grouping of demons to leave him, in Jesus' name. This is repeated until the demons are gone.

2. Affirming

It is usually good to have the ministry receiver affirm that he is serving God, that all of him belongs to Jesus Christ, and that he is a child of the living God. He is no longer in the kingdom of darkness but in the kingdom of light.[1] The Submission Prayer at the end of this chapter contains these elements.

---

[1] Please see Col 1:13.

3. Equipping

During the initial phase of the deliverance, we take the lead and guide the ministry receiver through the Ministry Steps. This way, he learns what to do while we are dealing with the stronger demonic groupings. Then we gradually shift the lead over to the person as we move more into a supporting role. This helps him learn to do self-deliverance, an "equipping" that he will use for the rest of his life.

4. Dealing with Manifestations

We have full authority to allow or not allow the demons to manifest as they are leaving.[1] We usually allow manifestations because they help the ministry receiver accept the reality of demons and their oppression. Manifestations also clearly show Christ's victory over the forces of darkness and the authority that Jesus has given to us, His Church. On the other hand, we command the demons to stop the manifestations if they become excessive, harmful, or distracting to the person.

5. Identifying additional Demons

Besides the preparation before the ministry session as discussed above, it is normal to identify additional demons during the actual session. This occurs through the discerning of spirits either by the ministers or the ministry receiver. Sometimes, the person's behavior reveals the presence of a demon. During the ministry session, the demon may speak through the person in a recognizable way or try to put the person to sleep, etc. Sometimes, as the demon is stirred up, the type of manifestation exhibited by the person reveals the demon's identity. Be alert to changes in the receiver's emotions, physical actions, appearance, and voice pitch or level.

For example, on one occasion as we were ministering deliverance to a young woman, she raised her arms and began "pumping iron" as her voice dropped to a much deeper pitch. We immediately asked, "Who are you?" The demon replied, "Workout." Needless to say, "Workout" was directed to another place where he could work on building up his muscles!

> **Note:** Sometimes, it is helpful to ask the demon's name, but normally we do no more than this. They sometimes talk; they may even threaten the person or you. They have been known to say, "I am going to kill you," and other unsavory phrases. Command them to be quiet in the Name of Jesus.
>
> It is important to be alert. You may think that the ministry receiver is speaking when it is actually a demon. Demons sometimes tell the truth, but mostly they don't, so it is risky to put much stock in what they say. They are so arrogant, however, that they frequently reveal significant information that allows you to get a firmer "grip" on them. As they reveal more of their legal ground, you can do what is necessary to reclaim the ground, making it easier for you to cast them out.

---

[1]   Please see Mat 16:19 and 18:18.

6. Sending Demons to Jesus

We are frequently asked what to do with the demons after we cast them out. Scripture is not specific about this issue, however we have a hint in Luke.

> Lk 8:31
> And they besought him that he would not command them to go out into the deep (abyss). (KJV)

Our suggestion is simply to say, "I command you to go where Jesus sends you." This is scripturally safe. However, as we sought the Lord about this issue, we felt He was saying He does indeed, "send them to the abyss," which is the same as the "outer darkness" and "dry places."

7. Preventing Demons Returning

Jesus our model told the epileptic demon never to come back:

> Mark 9:25
> . . . Jesus . . . rebuked the evil spirit. "You deaf and mute spirit," he said,
> "I command you, come out of him and never enter him again." (NIV)

By forbidding the demons to return and turning them over to Jesus to go wherever He sends them, the demons being cast out of the person are essentially removed from our planet. Thus, their ability to oppress the ministry receiver, or anyone else for that matter, comes to an end.

However, plenty of other demons of "like nature" (i.e., having the same function, such as anger) are waiting in the wings ready to tempt the delivered person as they strive to find a home. If the recently delivered ministry receiver yields to the temptation, the door may be reopened. The "replacement" demons can then set up housekeeping, drawing the person back into bondage.[1] So while we need not fear the "previous" demons re-entering, we do want to warn our ministry receiver to be on the alert against counterattacks from **replacement** demons trying to infiltrate.

---

[1]   Please see Mat 12:43-45.

8. Continuing The Deliverance

We continue the "casting out" process until one of the following occurs:

- All identified demons and all those revealed by the Holy Spirit are removed from the person.
- We have done enough for a particular session.
- The Holy Spirit indicates that we are to stop. Usually, this means that we need to allow the person to "increase and possess the reclaimed land"[1] before moving on to the next round of warfare.

As we "wrap up" the deliverance session, we:

- bind the remaining demons.
- command the demons to stay separated and isolated, and forbid any manifestations, particularly the interjecting of thoughts into the person's mind.
- cancel the assignments of all demons assigned to replace the evicted demons.
- pray for the Holy Spirit to fill all of the vacated areas.
- pray for restoration of the areasaffected by the demons, including physical healing.

H. What to do With Obstinate Demons

Demons don't like ***Eviction Day****.*

When Eviction Day arrives, the demons are not excited. Their bags are not packed and they have not bought their airline tickets in advance. Rather, they will do everything within their power to hinder and block their departure. They will continue to resist right up to the very last moment.[2]

They may claim "squatter's rights," saying "I have been here a long time, and I don't have to leave." They may say, "He (the ministry receiver) doesn't want us to leave." They may even have a group meeting and strategize how to interfere, confuse, sidetrack, and even prevent the deliverance. Sometimes the "strongman" will force the weaker demons to be "sacrificed," hoping that the ministers will think that they have evicted the "big guy" who will attempt to remain in hiding and not be cast out. This is why we need the Gifts of the Holy Spirit in operation so we are not deceived.

It is better to take care of the legalities.

This section centers around what to do when you meet the enemy face to face and he says, "I'm not leaving." In principle we could "force" him to leave because of the authority given to us by God. In practice, however, the ministry receiver is usually (unknowingly) giving "legal ground" to the demon(s). Thus, rather than fighting against the demon (and the receiver), it is much better to take care of the "legalities." Then we can easily cast the demon out and a new demon of "like nature" won't be able to find an open door for re-entry.

---

[1] Please see Ex 23:29-31.

[2] This occurred in Betsy's deliverance described at the beginning of this chapter.

1. Blocking Demons

Deliverance can be like a log jam.

Sometimes deliverance resembles an old West **log jam**. As the logs came down the river, maybe first one and then another would get stuck and cause other logs to begin to pile up around them. These might block other logs, until the entire flow of logs was brought to a stop. The loggers, using long poles, would poke and prod and pry to find the "**key**" log. When the key log was loosed and set free, the entire jam would release and move on down the river.

Getting demons out can be very similar to breaking up a **log jam**, particularly when we are dealing with a Demonic Stronghold.[1] Like the loggers, we poke around, prying a little here, pushing a little there, following the leading of the Holy Spirit as we recover legal ground. When we get things loosened up, and we find and remove the "key" log (strongman demon), the remaining demons generally leave quite easily.

At other times, the enemy may have a definite plan to stop the deliverance process. His tactics, however, are all doomed to failure since the victory has already been won. All we have to do is to follow the Holy Spirit's leading to remove the various obstacles that the demons erect until all blocks are gone.

a. Mental-Blocking Demons

Mental-Blocking demons strategize to prevent deliverance of other demons. They whisper messages to the person's mind such as: "Demons are not real. This is an outdated concept. My problems are really psychological." They may say, "This is not going to work. It works for other people, but it is not going to work for me." They have even been known to say, "I'm not here," as the deliverance minister called their names.

Common Blocking Demons: Doubt, Unbelief Skepticism, Rationalism, Pride.

These demons work to affect the person's belief system and, thus, his will. The most common blocking demons are **doubt**, **unbelief**, **skepticism**, **rationalism**, and **pride**. Pride, of course, attempts to keep the person from admitting that he could "have" such a thing as a demon.

This demonic strategy needs to be met with a strong biblical offensive. Share scriptures about demons, illustrations of Jesus doing deliverance, and stories of deliverance in your experience. Also specifically bind the blocking demons, or proceed with their deliverance. Go through the usual forgiveness, renouncing, and casting out process. Forgiveness, in this case, includes having the ministry receiver ask forgiveness for giving place to the blocking demons and agreeing with their lies.

---

[1] Please see Chapter XII.

b. Other Commonly Occurring Blocking Demons

Many other types of blocking demons exist, but these are the more common ones:

Fear demons may try to block through threats. They may say, "I'll kill you," or "I'll kill your family," or "You can't make it without me."

Control demons try all sorts of tactics and will do anything to stay in control and not have to come out. They may have the ministry receiver talk incessantly and/or change the subject away from deliverance. The minister must stay alert and retain "legitimate" control.

Passivity demons try to keep the ministry receiver from exerting his will and choosing to get rid of his (passivity) demons.

Pain and Distraction demons cause various kinds of pains and distractions. These pains can move rapidly from one part of the body to another.

We bind all these blocking, hindering, and distracting demons. The ministry receiver is often not even aware that he is being demonically influenced. We tell him to stay in control and explain that Jesus gives him power to resist. If necessary, we have him begin to quote scripture verses about the defeat of Satan and his demons.

c. Remaining Legalities

Sometimes certain legalities have not yet come to our attention. Demons may claim these as justification for remaining. Thus they are effectively "blocking demons." These legalities usually fall into the following categories.

Unconfessed "Secret" Sin and/or Vow: In the ministry receiver's mind, shame magnifies the past sin into the "untellable," unpardonable deed. Sexual sins particularly fall into this category. Sometimes a long forgotten vow, brought to light by the Holy Spirit, will need to be nullified.

Open Doors from Generational Sin: It is common for the ministry receiver to have a specific ancestral sin that a demon is using for legal ground. Here we need the Holy Spirit's revelation gifts to show us what the legal ground is and how to minister so that the demon(s) loses all "rights."

Occult/Witchcraft: Open doors from past, generational sins frequently reside in the occult/witchcraft areas. Sin in these areas seems to particularly empower curses to propagate down the family line as well as strengthening other demons and strongholds. These curses, however, are broken by confession and the power of the Cross as readily as curses from any other source.

The identity agreement is the most difficult for the Receiver to see.

Agreement: Every Ungodly Belief is a potential agreement with the forces of darkness that provides legal ground for Demonic Oppression. The most severe agreement is the Identity UGB. That is, a belief about who "I am" as a person. Examples might be "I am an angry person," "I am ashamed," or "I am depressed." Notice the "I am" identity phrase. This type of identity agreement is generally hidden from us because it is buried so deeply within our personhood. While it is expected that we will have normal human emotions of anger, shame, or depression, an identity UGB may give place to demons that magnify and manifest anger, shame, or depression. When we provide this legal ground to demons, they won't leave until we exert our free will and cancel (renounce) the agreement on the basis of the Cross and the Lordship of Jesus Christ. Of course, any needed forgiveness should also be accomplished.

Since God doesn't violate our free will, we, likewise, cannot override the free will of our ministry receiver. However, our job is to help him become aware of the lies (UGBs) he has believed about who he is. The demons, of course, don't want to lose their place and so they try to prevent the person from becoming aware of his Identity UGB. If he does become aware, the demons try to fool him into believing that he and the Demonic Stronghold are the same. They deny that a "false" identity is at work as well as the real one. It often takes time for the person to become increasingly aware of the deception and to become hopeful of being freed from the old, destructive patterns. He must become determined to be free from the false demonic identity.

God honors our agreements with the enemy.

In the Old Testament, God expressly forbids agreements (covenants) with the Canaanite inhabitants of the land. Joshua and the Israelites, however, formed a covenant with the Gibeonites.[1] Although it was done through deception and without the Israelites "asking counsel at the mouth of the Lord," God expected the Israelites to honor their commitment. In fact, it was Saul's breaking of this covenant that provided the final straw and lost him the kingship.[2] We are truly blessed that our covenant with Jesus Christ can be used to override and cancel all agreements with the demonic "inhabitants" of our land. We need to apply this covenant and remove all false identity demons.

2. What Demons Hate

Demons hate many things. At the top of their list are God, His Word, and humans. We can make use of this when we are casting them out. We can "stir them up" with things they hate, forcing them out of hiding and maybe even pressuring them to leave.

Demons really hate Bible scriptures like the ones on the next page. Read these out loud to magnify God and minimize Satan. Taunt the demons with scriptures about the fall and the defeat of Satan. They will reveal themselves as they cry out in defense of Satan and their position in his kingdom. Reading these scriptures to the demons (and the ministry receiver and ministers) during deliverance is guaranteed to bring **good** results.

---

[1] Please see Josh 9:3-27.
[2] Please see 2 Sam 21:1-2.

We encourage you to read through these scriptures for yourself. Let the **truth** of God expressed in these verses penetrate your heart. These are **Godly Beliefs** that will set you free from fear and concern about the Devil and enable you to minister freedom to others.

Please particularly note the last phrase of Isaiah 14:17 (in the table). The scripture contends that Lucifer (the Devil) "would open not the house of his prisoners." When we cast out demons, we are **forcefully** going into the prisons of the kingdom of darkness and **forcefully** opening the house of Satan's prisoners and setting them free. It is good work. It is what Jesus said would be happening.

> Mat 11:12
> From the days of John the Baptist until now, the kingdom of heaven has been forcefully advancing, and forceful men lay hold of it. (NIV)

Demons also hate praise and worship of God. The importance and power of adoration of God the Father and the Lord Jesus Christ during the deliverance session cannot be underestimated, particularly if any resistance arises.

Demons hate any talk about the Name of Jesus, the blood, the Cross, the resurrection, Satan's defeat, and the lake of fire. Songs about the blood of Jesus will definitely "stir" them up and force them to reveal themselves. Speaking in tongues will also aggravate them nicely. Use the weapons God has provided us to maximum advantage when dealing with obstinate demons.

3. Additional Considerations in Removing a Resistive Demon

If you still have an obstinate demon (or stronghold) after employment of the previously discussed items, completing the removal of legal ground may require one or more of the following tactical maneuvers. We use these when the Holy Spirit indicates in order to complete the deliverance.

Sever ancestral ties. Affirm and declare that all ties are broken — from the time of conception in the womb right up to the present.

Speak forgiveness to any ground that the demon(s) may be standing on (using), and/or to any agreements that the ministry receiver may have with the demon(s). Lastly, speak forgiveness[1] to the person for his putting up with, entertaining, catering to, and/or giving place, to the demon(s).

Break any agreements/lies/contracts/covenants still remaining between the ministry receiver and demon (s).

Appropriate the Blood of Jesus over any legal ground the demons think they have and nullify all agreements. Declare that every part of the ministry receiver's life, all of his "land," is holy ground, dedicated and consecrated unto the Lord.

---

[1] Please see Jn 20:23.

Table W
Scriptures that Demons Hate

1 Jn 3:8 . . . For this **purpose** the Son of God was manifested, that he **might destroy** the works of the devil. (KJV)

Acts 10:38 How **God anointed** Jesus of Nazareth with the Holy Ghost and with power: who went about **doing good**, and **healing all** that were **oppressed** of the devil; for God was with him. (KJV)

Col 2:15 . . . God made you **alive** with Christ. He forgave us all our sins, (NIV) having **canceled out the certificate of debt** consisting of decrees against us and **which was hostile to us**; and He has taken it out of the way, having **nailed it to the cross**. When He had **disarmed the rulers and authorities**, He made a public display of them, having **triumphed over them** through Him (by the Cross). (NAS)

Heb 2:14-15 . . . he also himself likewise took part of the same (flesh); that **through death he might destroy him that had the power of death**, that is, **the devil**; And **deliver them** who through f**ear of death** were all their lifetime **subject to bondage**. (KJV)

Lk 10:18-19 . . . I beheld **Satan as lightning fall from heaven**. Behold, I give unto you **power to tread on serpents and scorpions**, and **over all the power of the enemy**: and **nothing shall by any means hurt you**. (KJV)

Lk 11:20 But if I with the **finger of God cast out devils**, no doubt the **kingdom of God is come upon you**. (KJV)

Mk 16:17 And these signs shall **follow them that believe**; **In my name** shall they **cast out devils**; (KJV)

Isa 14:12-17 How art **thou fallen from heaven**, O **Lucifer**, son of the morning! [how] art **thou cut down to the ground**, ... For **thou hast said in thine heart, I will ascend** into heaven, **I will exalt** my throne above the stars of God: **I will sit** also upon the mount of the congregation, in the sides of the north: **I will ascend** above the heights of the clouds; **I will be like the most High**. **Yet thou shalt be brought down to hell**, to the sides of the pit. They that see thee shall narrowly look upon thee, [and] consider thee, [saying, **Is**] **this the man that made the earth to tremble, that did shake kingdoms**; **[That] made the world as a wilderness**, and **destroyed the cities thereof**; [that] **opened not the house of his prisoners**? (KJV)

Eze 28:17-19 **Your heart became proud** on account of your beauty, and **you corrupted your wisdom** because of your splendor. So I **threw you to the earth**; **I made a spectacle** of you before kings. By your many sins and dishonest trade you have desecrated your sanctuaries. So I made a fire come out from you, and it consumed you, and I reduced you to ashes on the ground in the sight of all who were watching. All the nations who knew you are appalled at you; **you have come to a horrible end and will be no more**.

Rev 12:11 . . . Now is come salvation, and strength, and the kingdom of our God, and the power of his Christ: for the **accuser of our brethren is cast down**, which accused them before our God day and night. And **they overcame him by the blood of the Lamb**, and **by the word of their testimony**; and **they loved not their lives unto the death**.

Rev 20:10 and fire came down from God out of heaven, and devoured them. And **the devil** that deceived them **was cast into the lake of fire and brimstone**, (KJV)

Taunt the Demons, continuing to stir them up as discussed earlier. Remind them that they are losers who are working for, and in league with, a loser.[1] Tell them that Satan and all his demons were defeated at Calvary. Remind them that Jesus went into hell and defeated them all and made an "open show" of Satan as Jesus disarmed and triumphed over him.[2] Remind the demons that all certificates of debt[3] have been nailed to the Cross. Tell them that they do not have any legal ground remaining. **So leave!**

4. How to Know when the Demon is Gone

The minister usually has a sense or a "witness" in his spirit when the demon(s) is gone. His spirit is at peace again. Also, the gift of the discernment of spirits is most helpful. While this gift may manifest in any of the ways that we can hear God's voice, frequently the Holy Spirit will give us visual, symbolic images showing what is going on in the spirit realm as the demons are leaving.

In addition, the ministry receiver may report a change, a release, a sense of peace, and/or an end to whatever manifestations he was experiencing. However, the most reliable guide is the "fruit." Does the ministry receiver report a changed life in the days and weeks following the deliverance. For example, he may report that his temper is now under his, and not the demon's, control. He may indicate that he no longer has lustful thoughts or that he is no longer riddled with insecurity.

Having removed the demons, the next step is to keep the "house" in such condition that other demons of like nature have no opportunity to come in.

I. Post Deliverance: Keeping the House Cleansed

No one wants to go through deliverance only to have seven more demons worse than the original ones come take their place.[4] As the Demonic Oppression session comes to an end, we pray for the Holy Spirit to fill all of the places that have been vacated by demons. Yes, the battle was won, and the demons are out, but the war is not over.! We can be assured that Satan and his army will do their best to launch a counterattack. So the smart thing to do is to anticipate the counterattack and attack first. As they say in the military, "The best defense is an offense." If we have the ministry receiver immediately begin the following activities, there will be no opportunity for Satan's counterattack. The person, whose "house" the demons were in, **must go on the offensive** and take a number of assertive steps to guard his victory. He is to live in a way that is actually a counterattack against the demonic. This lifestyle should be the "normal Christian" life.

The best defense is an offense: against evil and toward good.

> Rom 12:21
> Be not overcome of evil, but overcome evil with good. (KJV)

---

[1] Please see Eze 28:19.
[2] Please see Col 2:15.
[3] Please see Col 2:14, NAS.
[4] Please see Mat 12:43-45.

What is involved in keeping one's deliverance? The following suggestions are a combination of our own insights, plus those of Frank and Ida Mae Hammond[1] and Chris Cobb.[2]

1. Put on the Whole Armor of God

Ephesians 6:10-18 commands us to be properly **clothed** in the whole armor of God as we walk through this life. This is even more critical as the ministry receiver begins to walk in the newfound freedom and healing from several ministry sessions. Please refer back to Chapter V, "God's Weapons for Spiritual Warfare," for an in-depth discussion of the armor of God and its importance.

2. Guard Our Mind

You know the saying that we have no control over whether a bird flies over our head, but we do have control over whether he builds a nest in our hair! Replacement demons most often try to reenter the same way they got in originally: through our thoughts. God's Word tells us to take control of our thoughts.

> 2 Cor 10:5
> . . . bringing into captivity every thought to the obedience of Christ;
> (KJV)

Think about what you are thinking. You do not have to be a victim of your own thoughts. Chester says there is an area of weakness in his life where a demon tries to gain entry occasionally. The demon usually suggests something like, "I am really too tired to deal with this. I think I will just give in." Then Chester realizes what is happening and he counters with, "No, I'm not too tired. Get away from me and stop your harassing."

If you start hearing critical, condemning thoughts such as, "I am no good," you should be able to recognize the source. (Hint: It isn't you or the Holy Spirit!) Determine to put ungodly thoughts out of your mind. Stop what you are doing and read, pray, or sing the Word. Replace the wrong thoughts (UGBs) with pure ones (GBs). Change what you allow to be "centerstage" in your mind. If needed, change activities or locations.

Most of us have at least one or two important weak areas where the flesh has habitually ruled and/or been pampered. Be on guard in these areas. Attacks on the flesh always start in the mind, so stay on **double guard** in those vulnerable areas. Don't give in an inch. Each victory we win in the thought realm strengthens us for the next victory. It is an upward trend. We must be walking in James 4:7 on a continual basis.

> Jam 4:7
> Submit therefore to God. Resist the devil and he will flee from you.
> (KJV)

---

[1]   Hammond, Frank and Ida Mae, *Pigs in the Parlor*, op. cit.
[2]   Cobb, Chris, *Deliverance: "The Children's Bread"*, op. cit.

3. Guard Our Mouth

In the Psalms we read:

> Psa 141:3
> Set a guard over my mouth, O LORD; keep watch over the door of my lips. (NIV)

Life and death are in our tongues.[1] We can speak life or death over ourselves. We need to make a decision **not** to confess doubt, unbelief, or whatever is negative (ungodly) about ourselves or anyone else.   Rather, we should seriously follow Paul's admonishment to:

> Phil 4:8-9
> [8]Finally, brothers, whatever is true, whatever is noble, whatever is right, whatever is pure, whatever is lovely, whatever is admirable—if anything is excellent or praiseworthy—think about such things. [9]Whatever you have learned or received or heard from me, or seen in me—put it into practice. And the God of peace will be with you. (NIV)

4. Crucify/Control the Flesh

Don't give in to the lusts of the flesh. Crucify/control the flesh. It will always try to act as if it is ruling and reigning instead of our spirit man. Submit the flesh to the Lordship of Jesus Christ and the discipline of the Holy Spirit.[2]

5. Overcome by the Word of Our Testimony

Our testimony about the victories God has accomplished in our lives and the stability He has brought brings a strengthening to our spirit.[3] It builds up our faith. It provides a strong force against the enemy.

6. Resist the Devil

A basic scripture that applies here is:

> Jam 4:7
> Submit therefore to God. Resist the devil and he will flee from you. (KJV)

This resistance involves the strategies listed above, as well as doing further self-deliverance if needed. Also, it is important to cover (pray for and bind Satan out of) our households, which includes all that God has given us and all for which we are responsible.

---

[1] Please see Prov 18:21 and Jam 3:2-12.
[2] Please see Rom 6:6-7, Gal 2:20, and Gal 5:24.
[3] Please see Rev 12:11-12.

7. Move Into and Stay in Fellowship and Be Accountable.

We are instructed not to forsake gathering together[1] because we are built up and strengthened, as well as confronted, by God's people and hearing His Word.

8. Be Totally Committed to Christ

This can only happen when we have an active prayer life, study the Word, continually submit our plans to Him, and listen for Him to guide our steps. As we yield ourselves to Christ, He will speak to us about all areas of our lives: relationships, places to go, things to do, what to let ourselves see and experience, etc.

9. Praise God in the Middle of the Battle

God is ever present with us and, therefore, our strength and protection as we praise Him.[2] Demons flee as we celebrate God's victory over our enemies.[3]

J. Ministering Deliverance from Demonic Oppression

In the usual flow of the ministry process, deliverance comes after the other three Problem/Ministry Areas. At times, however, it is necessary to accomplish some deliverance before effective ministry is possible in the first three Problem/Ministry Areas.

Sometimes the ministry receiver's ability to forgive is hindered, or he is not able to pray to receive a Godly Belief after renouncing the Ungodly one. Perhaps he is unable to receive God's healing in the area of Soul/Spirit Hurts. Demons can block any of these ministry areas. Remember, there is no rigid structure to the ministry process. There is only a guiding framework. We want the Holy Spirit to be in charge of the ministry session. Whenever the Holy Spirit impresses upon us that we need to alter the "normal" process in order to continue effective ministry, we do so, including the casting out of demons.

1. Final Thoughts before Ministry

Remember, it is not by our might or our power that we cast out demons to help people be set free. It is also not by our knowledge or position in the church. It is by knowing the **Truth** about Christ's victory and the transference of His authority to us, His Church, that we are able to deliver people from the bonds of darkness. Our job is to impart the **Truth** into the people, so that they walk in freedom the rest of their lives in fellowship with God the Father and with Jesus and with the Holy Spirit.

---

[1]   Please Heb 10:25.
[2]   Please see Psa 22: 3 and Psa 5:11-12.
[3]   Please see Psa 27:6 and Psa 149:6-9.

> **Caution:** If this is your first experience with deliverance, we highly recommend that you enlist the help of an experienced deliverance minister. It is not that you can't do self-deliverance yourself. Rather, it is that you don't know what type of manifestations, degree of resistance, or demons/strongholds you might encounter. When you are both the "ministry receiver" and the "minister," it is harder to deal with these potential problems. This is a time for godly wisdom. Have someone help you the first time. Later, you will know what to expect and so can judge when self-deliverance is appropriate.

> **Exercise:** If you have worked through the ministry of the other three Problem/Ministry areas, then you are ready for the final cleansing. Collect your Generational Patterns, Ungodly Beliefs, Soul/Spirit Hurts, and Demonic Groupings worksheets and review them. Then ask the Holy Spirit to give you a strategy for the order of deliverance, i.e., which demonic grouping to cast out first, second, etc. Use the following Submission Prayer to position yourself properly, and then proceed through the Ministry Steps to evict the trespassers from your land! God Bless you as you receive more fully the freedom for which Christ paid so dearly.

2. Submission Prayer

We are ready to help our ministry receiver pray and submit to God's deliverance process. This is very important. It is good for the demons to clearly hear the receiver's determination and commitment to freedom.

> **DO Submission Prayer:** Lord Jesus Christ, I believe that You died on the cross for my sins and rose again from the dead. You redeemed me by Your blood, and I belong to You. I thank You, Lord Jesus, for Your shed blood, which cleanses me from all sin. I want to live for You. I come to You as my Deliverer.
>
> I now confess all of my sins, known and unknown. I repent of them and ask you to forgive me. I renounce them all. I forgive others as I want You to forgive me. Forgive me now and cleanse me with Your blood. I repent of any way I have given place to the enemy.
>
> You know my special need: to obtain freedom from things that bind me, torment me, and defile me. I need freedom from every evil and unclean spirit. I claim the promise of Your Word, "Whoever calls upon the Name of the Lord Jesus Christ shall be delivered."
>
> I call upon You now, Lord Jesus. Deliver me and set me free. I renounce Satan, all his works, and all of his workers. I loose myself from Satan in the name of Jesus Christ. I command you, Satan, you and your demons, to leave me now. All this I do in the Name, and on the authority, of Jesus Christ of Nazareth. Thank You Lord Jesus. Amen!

3. Steps in Ministering to Demonic Oppression

The steps for ministering are listed below. As with Ungodly Beliefs, the post ministry follow-up is very important for maintaining one's deliverance.

Ministry Steps[1]

1. **Listen:** Identify the groupings of demons and any sins that provide open doors for Demonic Oppression. [Generally, you will have these well in hand before the time of the deliverance session.]

2. **Forgive:** Have ministry receiver forgive any people, events, or situations that have not already been forgiven while ministering to the other three ministry areas. [It is not uncommon during a deliverance session for additional areas to come up that require forgiveness. Have the receiver forgive as needed. This is **the** major step in removing any excuse (legal ground) that a demon may use to avoid being cast out.]

3. **Repent:** Have receiver ask God's forgiveness for "putting up with," for "entertaining," and for "agreeing with" demons by catering to their demands and desires. [If there is any sin in the receiver's life that has not already been confessed, repented of, and forgiven, have him do so at this time.]

4. **Forgive:** Have receiver forgive himself.

5. **Renounce:** Have receiver renounce any more involvement in the sins associated with a demonic grouping. [He renounces all agreements that he has made with demons and renounces giving power or control to the demons or Satan.]

6. **Command:** Have receiver set his will to "cast out" the demon(s) and then command the particular grouping of demons to leave him. Then proceed to cas out one demon at a time to avoid confusion as to which demons have left and which ones are still present. [If necessary, the commanding should be repeated until the demon(s) are gone. The minister adds his faith and authority in Jesus Christ in agreement with the receiver.]

Repeat the above steps until all demon groupings have been cast out.

7. **Restore:** Pray for a new infilling of the Holy Spirit into all of the newly cleared out regions of the receiver. Pray for physical, soul, and/or spirit healing of any damage done by the presence of demons. Pray that the Holy Spirit would make the receiver very sensitive to falling back into old thought patterns or sinful habits that would begin to reopen any doors.[2]

---

[1] A copy of a Ministry Card with a summary of these steps is in Appendix A.
[2] Please see Jn 5:14, 8:11.

Post-Ministry

Once some deliverance has taken place, the minister should discuss the following areas with the ministry receiver to prepare him for the "walking it out" phase of deliverance. This begins immediately after the first demon has been cast out! These items are based on the earlier section "Post Deliverance: Keeping the House Cleansed" on page 312.

1. Assure him that the **power** of the demons **is broken** but that the Devil will present new opportunities to sin, especially in the areas where he has had strongholds and in the past given in to his flesh. Temptations frequently occur right after the victory of deliverance. Temptation, however, will now come from the "outside" rather than the "inside." This form of temptation really has much less power and he will be able to resist if he **wills to resist**. He will have to keep the doors shut to the old fleshly ways. The Holy Spirit will provide all of the grace and power necessary if he wills to call on the Lord.

2. Inform him that **active warfare** will likely continue until the demons assigned by Satan become convinced that he is indeed firm in his resolve. The stronger he sets his will (the will of his spirit as well as the will of his soul), the sooner the battle will be over.

3. Instruct him **to take the offense and bind** daily any and all demons that are still "on the inside" and those "on the outside" assigned to tempt him back into the old ways. Render them inactive.

4. Encourage him to move into **active mode and give no place to the enemy** by guarding his mind, his mouth, and his activities. Discuss possible changes that may need to be made in his lifestyle and/or friends, in order for him to keep his deliverance.

5. Instruct him to **quickly repent** if he sins. Remind him how to do **self-deliverance** so he can cast out demons in the future as needed.

6. Encourage him to be **daily in the Word**, to pray, to commune with God. Remind him that it is only those who do the will of God and whom Jesus "knows" that will enter the kingdom of God.[1]

7. Remind him to **praise God** for his victory. Also in times of temptation, praise God as a way of defeating the enemy.

8. Charge him to **be in a place where he is accountable, where he can receive prayer support and encouragement.** It may also be helpful for him to have a one-on-one relationship for accountability with someone other than yourself.

---

[1] Please see Mat 7:21-23.

Part 3

Foundational Applications

With the Foundational Understandings and the four Foundational Problem/Ministry Areas clearly in our minds and hearts, we are equipped to minister to each of the areas. Now it is time to learn how to apply what we have learned.

We will start by looking at Soul Ties. This is a simple, yet very significant, ministry application of the Integrated Approach to Healing Ministry. Many people are bound by ungodly Soul Ties to another person without any awareness of the significance of the bondage.

Next we will "dig" into a profoundly important topic, Demonic Strongholds. This is a particularly "strong" or "vicious" structure of SOFCs, UGBs, SSHs, and DO all associated with a main theme. It is one level higher in complexity and strength compared to a demonic grouping.

We then move up another level of complexity and strength into the subject of "super" strongholds. We discuss two super strongholds to illustrate this concept. The Control-Rebellion-Rejection Stronghold has three individual strongholds working together, as does the Shame-Fear-Control Stronghold. Using traditional ministry approaches, these super strongholds are nearly impossible to penetrate and destroy. Once we understand how Demonic Strongholds work, however, we can be led by the Holy Spirit to destroy, totally and permanently, these evil structures!

XI

SOUL TIES, THE TIES THAT BIND

Know ye not that your bodies are the members of Christ?
shall I then take the members of Christ,
and make [them] the members of a harlot? God forbid.
What? know ye not that he which is joined to a harlot is one body?
for two, saith he, shall be one flesh.
But he that is joined unto the Lord is one spirit.
1 Corinthians 6:15-17

Soul Ties are invisible ties that bind to another person, organization, or thing. Our focus will be on ungodly Soul Ties that create emotional and spiritual connections with another person that are perverted, dysfunctional, and/or sexual.

Let's "paint" a word picture to illustrate Soul Ties.

Imagine that you have a number of rubber bands attached to your head.[1] Imagine that the rubber bands are connected to each person with whom you have had an unhealthy, emotional relationship. Now imagine more rubber bands connecting you with each person with whom you have had a sexual relationship. Those rubber bands exert a subtle pressure that pulls you toward each of these people. Can you imagine what this picture of you looks like?

The rubber band, representing a long-term, intense emotional involvement, may be very thick. Then next to it might be a very skinny rubber band, representing a "one-night stand." Perhaps next to that would be another thick band, representing your relationship with your mother, who has never released you to grow up and have your own life. As you try to move forward in life, you feel pulled in many directions. You try to make love to your spouse, but you have memories of other lovers at the same time. You don't feel free, and you are not free. These Soul Ties need to be broken.

As we minister to a person using the Restoring the Foundations Integrated Approach to Healing Ministry, the need to break/cut ungodly Soul Ties may arise at any point in the ministry process.

---

[1] Burkett, Sandy and Greg. Illustration from "Healing the Broken Hearted," Marion Christian Center, Marion, OH 43302, March 2000.

If parents or distant ancestors are involved, Soul Ties may be a part of the Sins of the Fathers and Resulting Curses ministry. Ungodly Beliefs are always a part of the Soul Tie relationship. For example, a person may be involved with perversion because he "believes" that unhealthy co-dependency is "normal." Soul/Spirit Hurts frequently occur as a part of the functioning of Soul Ties. The dysfunction leads to many inner wounds and tears. As usual, demons take advantage of these vulnerable areas, and keep us "wrapped up" with the other person in our emotional life as well as our thought life. "Familiar" spirits, along with other demons attached to the Soul Ties, need to be cast out.

A. Definition: Soul Ties

> Soul Ties are an ungodly covenant with another person, organization, or thing based on an unhealthy emotional and/or sexual relationship/attachment. This covenant binds the two people together or it binds a person to an organization or thing. God "honors," or recognizes, these covenants. He leaves each one of us free to decide when and if we will appropriate His provisions to break/cut the ties and release ourself from the attachment or the other person. The other person is also set free in the process.

We define "Soul Ties" as an ungodly covenant between two people. This is a serious situation because God is serious about covenants. As a covenant-making and covenant-keeping God, He is very interested in covenants — even when they are with our enemies and/or are ungodly.

We see this principle at work in the story about the Israelites and the Gibeonites.[1] First Joshua makes a covenant with the Gibeonites, a Canaan tribe, against God's direct commandment to kill all of the people of the nations of Canaan.[2] Then, many years later, King Saul attempts to kill the remaining Gibeonites, even though the covenant is an eternal one. This results in a curse of three years of drought during the reign of King David because the covenant was violated. Breaking the covenant released a curse even though it appears that Saul is carrying out God's earlier commandment. God honors, i.e., recognizes and upholds the covenant even when it is with His enemy.

The same principle operates today. God "honors" covenants, even ungodly ones that we have made. This is exactly the same concept expressed in the Ungodly Belief Chapter, where we illustrated that God "honors" UGBs as covenants with our enemy, Satan. To break them, we must "appropriate" His provision and renounce any ungodly covenants, i.e., ungodly Soul Ties, that have been established.

---

[1]   Please see Josh 9:3-27 and 2 Sam 21:1-3.
[2]   Please see Ex 23:24, 32-33, Deu 7:2-3, 16, 24, as two examples.

B. Godly Soul Ties

Before we go further, let us assert that "godly" Soul Ties also exist. We find these in healthy parent-child relationships, in balanced, close friendships, and in intimate, healthy marriages. These ties are a blessing from God. In First Samuel 18:1, we see an example of a godly soul/spirit covenant (Soul Ties). Jonathan became one in spirit with David, and "He loved him as he loved himself." This describes the type of covenant that God wants in marriage. Naturally, we do not want to interfere with godly Soul Ties. This nation needs more of them!

C. Sexual Ungodly Soul Ties

Soul Ties formed with others, both before and during marriage, interfere with our lives and, particularly, with our marriage. The following example from our ministry experience demonstrates the emotional damage caused by Ungodly Soul Ties.

We were asked to minister to an attractive missionary couple who had been sent home from the mission field because of severe marital problems. They arrived emotionally and physically exhausted. Upon interviewing them, we found that both had been involved with street drugs and many sexual relationships before marriage. Soon after marriage they were radically saved and made an equally radical change in lifestyle. They were instantly delivered from all former addictions and their permissive lifestyles. They went to Bible college and then headed for the mission field.

When asked about their marriage, they described it as "It has just been Hell!" Both wept openly as they described the misery of their sex life, which had been "incredible" before they married. "We just don't understand it," they confided.

"Tell us what it is that makes your love life so miserable," we inquired, already suspecting that we knew the answer. They went on to report feeling as if they had all of their old "lovers" in bed with them. That was quite a picture to imagine: more than 40 people with them in the bed! They had memories of these old lovers that they just could not get away from. They felt defiled and as if they were being intentionally unfaithful. All the "rubber bands" of the old lovers were pulling on them, pulling them away from each other and from God.

We dealt with each spouse in individual sessions and began by breaking generational sexual sin and the accompanying curses. Then we moved to the area of their own sin and read with them:

> 1 Cor 6:15-16
> 15 Do you not see and know that your bodies are members (bodily parts) of Christ, the Messiah? Am I therefore to take the parts of Christ and make [them] parts of a prostitute? Never! Never!
> 16 Or do you not know and realize that when a man joins himself to a prostitute he becomes one body with her? The two, it is written, shall become one flesh. [Gen 2:24] AMP

Each spouse confessed and repented of sexual sin with each of his/her former lovers. Each one that he/she had been joined with needed to be confessed/named individually. Why was this necessary? Because each one was a separate covenant, a separate "joining."

Next, we helped them break the Soul Ties with each past "lover," using the prayer in this chapter. We also cast out the demons using the Soul Ties as "legal ground" to torment.

(Note: When the ministry receiver can't remember the name of the person but can remember the face, the former lover can still be presented before the Lord the same way as a name. In most cases, he or she describe the place or the circumstances and usually something about the person. Any of these characteristics will serve to identify the person and the time of "covenant making" in order to break the Soul Ties and annul the covenant.)

During the next session with our couple, we brought them back together and suggested they ask forgiveness from each other for the way they had defrauded the other by:

1. Having sex with others:
2. Having sex with each other before they were married:
3. Defiling each other within the marriage with the "old" sexual covenants.

In short, they had entered into their marriage relationship on a faulty foundation. Once the forgiveness was completed, we prayed with them to establish a new covenant before God that based their marriage on a "restored foundation."

That week they began to taste the sweetness of God's freedom. The torment, the shame, the feelings of dirtiness were gone. As this couple shared physical intimacy, they felt as if they were coming together for the first time. Each gave full attention to the other in a true giving and receiving of love. They continued the intimacy through closer communication. Although other areas still needed ministry, the turnaround had begun!

Although not always this dramatic, this same scenario has been repeated numerous times. As old Soul Ties were removed/annulled, new freedom came into the marriage.

D. Unhealthy Emotional Soul Ties

Ungodly Soul Ties also exist within any relationships with strong, unhealthy emotional bonds. Girl/boy friends, parents, and/or children can all be trapped in codependent relationships and have Soul Ties that need to be broken. Sometimes a child has becomes a surrogate mate for his own parent. Sometimes children are "not allowed" to leave home.

Several relevant questions need to be asked about any relationship: Is each person free to be himself and to move toward his purpose in life? Or, is the relationship inhibiting to him in some way? Is it negative? Is it built on unhealthy love?

Let's look at several ministry situations that illustrate this problem.

One spouse is still playing the "What if . . .?" fantasy game. That is, Bob wonders frequently, "What if I had married Doris rather than Beverly (his wife)?" Bob is trapped in a Soul Tie. This can happen even if a serious relationship with "Doris" had never existed, but Bob had "hoped" for a relationship with her. Even without sexual involvement, a past "almost" relationship can continue its tantalizing appeal, particularly during times of stress in the current marriage. This can be just as detrimental to a marriage as a previous sexual relationship.

Note that Soul Ties between a ministry receiver and his/her "first love" are often particularly strong and need to be broken. Breaking Soul Ties sets both parties free.

In another instance, we were ministering to a man we will call "Don." During the Soul/Spirit Hurts session, it became obvious that his mother was very involved in his household. In fact, Don and his wife, Sue, lived just 1/2 block away from his parents' house. Further, the mother was either on the phone or in her son's house an hour or more every day. Don's wife, of course, felt like an "outsider" and complained that Don spent more time with his mother than with her. Sue was heartbroken because Don seemed to have a more intimate relationship with his mom than with her. In effect, the mother was taking the place of the wife, who felt she was not "number one" in Don's heart.

Do you think that this is co-dependency? Do you think ungodly Soul Ties are present?

Well, Don could not see it. He contended that he was, "Just honoring my parents." In reality, he was afraid to get too far away from his mother.

We presented God's "oneness" scripture, Genesis 2:24, and explained to Don how he had effectively "never left home," particularly his mother, and had certainly not "cleaved" to his wife.

> Gen 2:24
> Therefore shall **a man leave his father and his mother**, and shall **cleave unto his wife**: and **they shall be <u>one</u> flesh**. (KJV)

As Don began to understand, he opened up to receive ministry. We broke the strong Soul Ties with his mother and also dealt with other issues. Then, when Don and his wife both had received significant ministry, they renewed their marriage vows. For the first time, they established a covenant based on the Word of God, particularly Genesis 2:24 and Ephesians 5:22-33.

Everyone was much happier after this, except for the mother. Following the shock of losing her place as the surrogate wife, she began to put more time and energy into her own marriage. In the end, however, even *she* decided that "things" were better.

Another young man handled the "mother issue" in a completely different way. While ministering to Jack during the Sins of the Fathers and Resulting Curses session, we were surprised when he stated, "That's right, I hate my mother. I never call or talk to her anymore. Its been many years since I last talked to her." Of course, we did not show our surprise. We acted as if this was just another day in the life of an RTF minister. As we probed deeper, we found that she had controlled all of Jack's decisions while he was growing up.

Finally, he left home just to get away from "Mom." While not a conscience decision, Jack punished his mother by letting his anger keep him from communicating with her.

We all rejoiced as he was freed of these "long-held" bindings.[1] You can imagine his mother's shock and joy when Jack called her the next week.

E. Ministry to Ungodly Soul Ties

Here is a sample prayer that you can use to break Soul Ties and help yourself, as well as others, to be free. We suggest you repeat the third paragraph for each relationship/attachment in which you have an ungodly Soul Tie.

Prayer: Father, in the Name of Jesus, I submit myself completely to You. I confess all of my emotional and sexual sins, as well as my ungodly Soul Ties. [(*If your Soul Tie is with an ancestor, or if you see this sin and curse in your family line, also include:*) I confess my ancestor's sin of maintaining ungodly Soul Ties.] I choose to forgive my ancestors and each person with whom I have an ungodly Soul Tie. I ask You, Lord, to forgive me for my sin that resulted in ungodly Soul Ties. Lord, I receive Your forgiveness. Thank You for forgiving me and for cleansing me.

I choose to forgive myself for this involvement. I will no longer be angry at myself, hate myself, or punish myself.

Lord, I break my ungodly Soul Ties with _____. I release myself from him/her/it and I release him/her from me. As I do this, Lord, I pray that You would cause him/her to be all that You want him/her to be and that You would cause me to be all that You want me to be.

Lord, please cleanse my mind from all memories of ungodly unions so I am totally free to give myself to You and to my spouse.

I renounce and cancel the assignments of all evil spirits attempting to maintain these ungodly Soul Ties.

Lord, thank you for restoring my soul to wholeness. I choose to walk in holiness by Your grace. In the Name of Jesus Christ I pray. Amen.

---

[1] Please see Jn 11:44, about removing the "binding" grave clothes from Lazarus.

XII

DEMONIC STRONGHOLDS

A wise man attacks the city of the mighty (demonic)
and pulls down the stronghold in which they trust.
Proverbs 21:22

He (God) flashes destruction on the stronghold
and brings the fortified city to ruin.
Amos 5:9

We want to present an extension to the normal understandings of Demonic Oppression, demonic groupings, and demonic interconnectedness, that we call "Demonic Strongholds."

We first recognized the presence of Demonic Strongholds in 1991. Now that we are aware of them, we can look back and see that the evidence of their existence was there all along. In fact, they are quite common. Most of us have at least one or two Demonic Strongholds, at least until we receive deliverance. They usually can be demolished using the normal deliverance approaches since they are generally relatively weak. Thus we don't realize that we are dealing with strongholds. This is particularly true when the Integrated Approach to Healing Ministry is used since the effectiveness of removing legal ground undermines the strength of the stronghold(s) regardless of the efforts of the inhabitants of each stronghold.

The usual "sign" of the presence of a significant Demonic Stronghold occurs when we meet an area of resistance during deliverance that forces us to seek God for the remaining legalities and the appropriate order of ministry, i.e., strategy. It is as if we "run into a brick wall," whether large or small. The most severe strongholds deceive us into believing that they are a part of our personality. They are well camouflaged. It requires the discernment of the Holy Spirit to separate the true personality from the demonic. It requires the word of God that can divide between soul and spirit, between the real person and the counterfeit person with its evil characteristics.[1] Intercession, fasting, getting a number of people involved, is sometimes necessary to bring real freedom from a Demonic Stronghold.

Our experience in ministering freedom from the "Evil Core" Stronghold with Sandy is a good example of this deep, deceptive, masquerading type of Demonic Stronghold, and how the Holy Spirit led us step by step as we disassembled and demolished the stronghold. You can review her story on page 169.

---

[1]   Please see Heb 4:12.

A. Understanding Demonic Strongholds

First, we need to be able to recognize their presence. Then we can "go after" the significant Demonic Strongholds that are "entrenched and fortified." Such demonic structures require a determined and "God-revealed" strategic approach in order to successfully attack and destroy them. In order to do this, we must apply an important military principle: "Know your enemy."

1. Evidence of the Presence of a Demonic Stronghold

Evidence that we are dealing with a significant Demonic Stronghold may include any or all of the following (not necessarily an exhaustive list):

- A person with a besetting sin.[1]
- A person living below his potential and destiny, not to mention his inheritance as a child of God.
- A person who has already received much counseling and ministry yet is still in bondage.

- Strong resistance during deliverance. This usually comes from fortified occult demons that exhibit extreme manifestations.
- Failure to effect significant freedom and healing using the traditional deliverance approaches. Little, if any, progress takes place, and the person receiving ministry does not report any significant change.
- Failure of the ministry receiver to retain his deliverance and healing in the days following ministry, even when he is really trying.

2. A Physical Analogy of a Demonic Stronghold

We sometimes visualize a stronghold by imagining a large grassy plain with a castle sitting on it. The Sins of the Fathers and resulting Curses provide the foundation, representing the starting point or "set up" into which each of us is born. In more severe cases, some of the superstructure (i.e., towers, walls, etc.) may also already be in place at our birth. These would represent dedications and/or

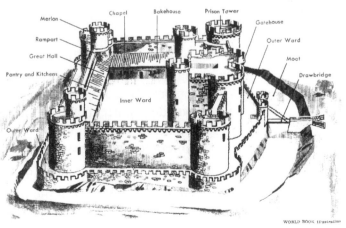

A Mature Stronghold.

---

[1] Please see Heb 12:1.

ancestors had made. If they worshipped and/or served other gods, and/or engaged in blood covenants (i.e., the occult), considerable structure and interconnectedness could exist between the various parts of the castle. All of this could be in place at the time of our birth.

Then, as we commit our own sins and others sin against us, curses result. The structure then grows and becomes more mutually reinforcing as the different parts (sins) of the stronghold intertwine. The mortar between the bricks or stones may represent our Ungodly Beliefs and Soul/Spirit Hurts. The bricks or stones may represent the demons. As a result, our UGBs and SSHs hold the structure of demons together while the Sins of the Fathers and Resulting Curses provide a "place" or foundation. The extent of the initial set up by our ancestors — plus what is added with our own sins and others' sin against us — determine how big a castle we build and the number of adjoining towers, rooms, dungeons, etc.

3. Definition of a Demonic Stronghold

The above considerations lead to the definition of a Demonic Stronghold.

> **Definition:** A Demonic Stronghold is a structure composed of a foundation provided by SOFCs and walls/towers/rooms/ etc. made from Self-Sins, UGBs, SSHs, and DO. The complexity of this structure can range from relatively simple to quite complex, with many different parts and interconnections.
>
> This structure must be identified, disassembled, and demolished one part at a time, following a **strategy** given by the Holy Spirit. This **strategy** involves repetitive application of the Ministry Steps for the four Problem/Ministry Areas to each part of the structure, until complete removal of the stronghold is accomplished.

B. Holy Spirit Led Strategy

The word "strategy" is used in the above definition of "Demonic Stronghold." Why do we use this word? Strategy has to do with planning, following a procedure, and knowing the right timing. We will need all of these as we come against a Demonic Stronghold.

We depend on the Holy Spirit to reveal the strategy necessary to systematically clear the legalities, break the bondages, and evict the demons. We need this strategy because the "standard" flow of the RTF ministry process does not lead to full freedom. In other words, moving directly through the four Problem/Ministry Areas in sequence is not adequate. The key phrase distinguishing a Demonic Stronghold from other Demonic Oppression and groupings is: **the need for a Holy Spirit led strategy**.

1. Why There is a Need for a Strategy

In a significant stronghold, a great multiplicity of reinforcing and intertwining of the various problems make up the stronghold. The "normal" ministry procedure/approach of dealing with, first, Sins of the Fathers and Resulting Curses and Self-Sins, and then Ungodly Beliefs, next Soul/Spirit Hurts, and finally Demonic Oppression may not be adequate to demolish the stronghold. The normal process only lets us deal with the "surface" of the stronghold. We are not able to penetrate into the depths of it. We are blocked by "what hasn't already been dealt with."

For example, we may deal with forgiveness at the outer layer, but more forgiveness is needed deeper within. We may break all of the ancestral curses at the boundary, but more curses may exist further inside. In fact, ancestral dedications and commitments may need to be broken. After we expose and deal with Ungodly Beliefs at the surface, more will be deep within. We have to repeatedly break ungodly agreements between the ministry receiver and the demonic, regardless of how deep and how many layers we must remove.

We pray for God to touch the hurts accessible near the outer wall. Other hurts, however, are covered by demons, lies, curses, and layers of negative emotions such as anger and rage. We may cast out the demons clinging to the castle wall, but the powerful "strong men" are barricaded behind layers of other demons, curses, lies, and sins.

Following the normal procedure for deliverance may not be adequate to do severe damage to a major stronghold. We may not be able to to demolish and remove it completely.

In order to work our way into and throughout the stronghold, we need a strategy — a definite sequence of Holy Spirit led steps, involving repeated ministry in each of the four Problem/Ministry Areas. Our goal is to recover the "legal ground" given away by our ancestors (SOFCs). This happens by repeatedly removing the mortar (UGBs and SSHs) from between the bricks and then dismantling the bricks (DO) until nothing remains. We want to disassemble the structures, groupings, and the interconnectedness until the stronghold is gone. Our final objective is to remove all of the resulting debris and dispose of it, leaving an empty, green, grassy, peaceful plain. We want **all** of the land reclaimed for the Kingdom of God.

This is not to say that only one strategy will work. Many different procedures could result in the demolishing of a Demonic Stronghold. We need at least one strategy that will work.

2. How We Learn God's Strategy and Apply It

How do we obtain a truly effective strategy? From only one source: the Holy Spirit. While this statement is generally true in deliverance it is particularly true when dealing with a significant Demonic Stronghold. We are alerted to the need for a Holy Spirit strategy in Second Corinthians. Let's look at this passage from the Amplified version of the Bible:

> 2 Cor 10:3-5
> [3]For though we walk [live] in the flesh, we are not carrying on our warfare according to the flesh and using mere human weapons.
> [4]For the **weapons of our warfare** are not physical (weapons of flesh and blood), but they **are mighty** before God **for the overthrow and destruction of <u>strongholds</u>**,
> [5][inasmuch as **we] refute arguments and theories and reasonings and every proud and lofty thing that sets itself up against the (true) knowledge of God**; and **we lead every thought and purpose away captive into the obedience of Christ**, the Messiah, the Anointed One, (AMP)

We used this scripture in Chapter V, "God's Weapons for Spiritual Warfare," when we discussed our (spiritual) weapons. We must use these weapons to defeat and overthrow Demonic Strongholds.

Notice that the battleground is the mind, the location of our Ungodly Beliefs. The war is over arguments, theories, and reasonings, and every proud and lofty thing that sets itself up against the true knowledge of God. The war is over who we are in agreement with, have a contract with, are in covenant with. Is it Christ or the enemy? The enemy is trying to prevent a true knowledge of God, leading to Godly Beliefs. Satan will do everything possible to keep us from thinking or living in obedience to Christ.

We must use spiritual weapons and Holy Spirit led strategies to overthrow and destroy the strongholds. As we repeatedly apply the Ministry Steps associated with the four Problem/Ministry Areas to the specific sins, curses, UGBs, SSHs, and demons making up the stronghold, the entire structure finally collapses.

3. Biblical Examples of God Providing the Strategy

We appreciate that God has given us a number of examples in the Bible where He provided the strategy for the victory. In fact, in a few cases, God provides the strategy and also conducts the warfare, winning without any help from the Israelites!

- At the stronghold of Jericho, God gives the strategy to Joshua, and the people of God carry out the battle plan.[1]
- At the stronghold of Ai, we see the same process repeated.[2]

---

[1] Please see Josh 6:2-24.
[2] Please see Josh 8:1-26.

- With Gideon, God not only gives the strategy, but He goes to great effort to raise up Gideon to lead the people to defeat the Midianites, Amalekites, and the "sons of the east." While Israel kills the main kings, Judges 7:22 states, "the LORD set the sword of one against another even throughout the whole army" (NAS). So besides the strategy, God also caused the army to largely destroy itself.[1]

- When the Moabites, Ammonites, and Meunites come against Jehoshaphat, God gives the strategy and He also wages the warfare. The people simply have to be obedient and march before the enemy praising and singing.[2]

- When David attacks the stronghold of Jerusalem, he and his army do the fighting. They surprise the Jebusites, however, by a sneak approach into the center of their stronghold by entering through one of the water passages. The scripture does not explicitly state that God gave the strategy to David, but it was David's practice to "inquire" of the Lord[3] before undertaking any major campaign. The fact that the strategy was an unusual one makes it likely that it was God's strategy.[4]

When we analyze the situations in which God gives the strategy, we see that:

- God gives the strategy and battle instructions.
- God generally has men carry out the plan.
- It is not the same strategy every time.
- The strategy is usually not logical nor satisfying to the rational mind.
- The strategy may involve confusion and/or surprise for the enemy.
- Strongholds are generally defeated one at a time.
- It takes time to completely clear the land.
- Occasionally God does everything by Himself without man's help.

As we come against the more complex strongholds in people's lives, we find that the above principles are still valid. Sometimes we start at the outside and work our way in. Other times, God will have us "jump" into the middle of the stronghold and we work our way out. In other situations, He does the majority of the "clearing out" and we mostly observe the destruction of the stronghold. On other occasions, He leads us step by stp, as if we are recapturing a city, room by room, house by house, block by block.

Working with the Holy Spirit at this level of warfare is very exciting. It takes a close "co-laboring" with Him and a consistent flowing in all of the gifts to bring this degree of freedom into a person's life. We feel as if we are an extension of the kingdom of God here on the earth. Needless to say, it is very satisfying work.

As you might suspect, we were first introduced to Demonic Strongholds while ministering to Sandy, as the Holy Spirit had us remove both the "Evil Core" Stronghold and the "Five Tower" Stronghold. This led us to "super" Strongholds.

---

[1] Please see Judg 6:33-35, 7:1-8:12.

[2] Please see 2 Chr 20:15-17, 20-27.

[3] Please see examples of times when David did inquire of the Lord: 1 Sam 22:10, 23:2, 4, 30:8, 2 Sam 2:1, 5:19, 23, 21:1, 1 Chr 14:10, and 14.

[4] Please see 2 Sam 5:6-9 and 1 Chr 11:4-7.

C. "Super" Strongholds

After we have "mastered" ministry to "ordinary" Demonic Strongholds, the next level of complexity of demonic structures is the "super" Stronghold.

> A "super" Stronghold is a combination of two or more strongholds, joined together and working together toward the destruction of their host. Each stronghold provides support and defense for the other. It appears as a city, as if there are "castles" located next to each other.

The Five Tower Stronghold described in the next installment of Sandy's story provides an example of a "super" Stronghold. In the following chapters, we discuss other powerful and vicious strongholds: the Control-Rebellion-Rejection Stronghold and the Shame-Fear-Control Stronghold.

Other combinations are certainly possible — and common. "Super" Strongholds frequently contain Demonic Strongholds such as Abandonment, Pride, Fear, Failure, Sexual Sins, Religiosity, Bitterness, Anger, Violence, Victim, Unworthiness, Addictions, Occult, etc. The list goes on and on. Be on the lookout for "super" Strongholds as you minister. Take them apart one stronghold at a time.

D. Sandy's Story: Five Tower Stronghold

As we continued to minister to Sandy,[1] we came across demonic groupings so extremely intertwined and resistive that they were nearly impossible to evict. To our surprise, we discovered the existence of Demonic Strongholds and even a "super" Stronghold.

One day, as we were studying and praying our way through the notes from our sessions with Sandy, Chester felt impressed by the Holy Spirit to get a pencil and paper and draw some circles. His drawing is shown in the next figure.

First he wrote "Abandonment" and drew a circle around that word. Then he moved to the upper right and wrote "Occult." As the Holy Spirit led him, he wrote and drew the remaining three strongholds. Then he listed the demonic groupings within each stronghold. When he finished, we realized that we had discovered a more complex interrelationship among the demonic groupings that would allow us to penetrate further into the enemy camp that had oppressed Sandy for so long. We named this structure the "Five Tower Stronghold."

The Holy Spirit showed us that each of the five major strongholds was an "entrenched and fortified" stronghold with a "Wall of Deception" surrounding the entire structure. Throughout Sandy's life, the "Wall of Deception" had successfully hidden these strongholds from her awareness.

---

[1] Please note other parts of Sandy's testimony throughout this book.

Wall of Deception

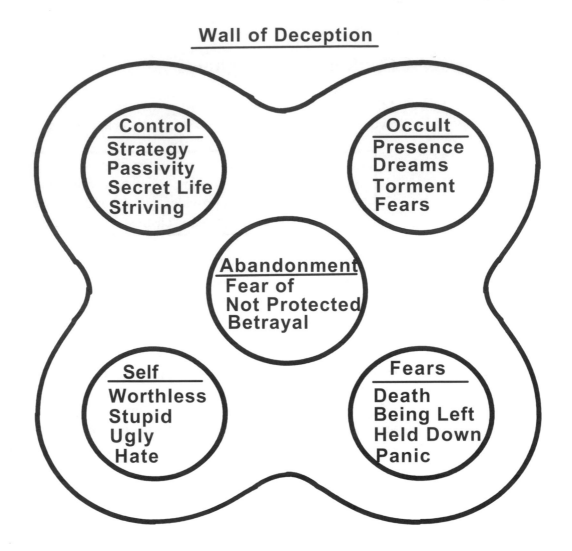

Figure 8: Five Tower Stronghold

Wall of Deception

In earlier ministry sessions, God had shown us a number of ways that deception was a major factor in Sandy's family line. She was set up for deception by the Sins of the Fathers and the Resulting Curses. During one of our sessions, we suggested to Sandy that, "Deception could be a major part of what is going on." Sandy was shocked at the possibility and convinced that deception had never been an issue. (This was deception about deception.) During the next session, however, she came back to this topic and admitted that God had been speaking to her. "Maybe deception does have a small role in the total scheme of things," she told us. By the following session, she was sure that deception had thrown a large veil over her mind and life. "All my life," she said, "I have been leading a 'double-life,' a life of deception."

By age six, Sandy was already living a secret life. Various demonic visitations of a "presence" (evidence of the occult in her family line) caused her to be terrified on the inside. On the outside, however, she gave the appearance she was fine.

Table X
Five Tower Stronghold Demonic Groupings

Abandonment	Control By Others	Occult Oppression	Fears	Self
Fear of Abandonment	(Allowed so others	Presence	of death, murder,	Worthless
Not Protected	wouldn't abandon her.)	("No move, no sound,	"killer"	Stupid (to be afraid)
Vulnerable	Strategizing,	or I'll kill you")	of Bodily Harm	Ugly, Awkward
Betrayed	Planning, etc.	Dreams	of Being Left	Deceived
Isolation	Performance	("sly, leering things")	of Being Abandoned	Hate
Alone	Passivity	Being Controlled by	(Don't get too close	Ego, Pride
Displaced	(Do whatever you	Others	to me!)	Righteous
Rejected	want to me.)	Mental Torment	of Not Being Taken	Comparison
(By Girlfriends)	Double/Secret Life	- Blocking	Care of	Passive
	Striving for Acceptance	- Mind Clamp	of Forgetting	Lack of Discipline
	Man-Pleasing	- Veil	of Freezing	Ashamed, Shame
		- Confused	of Being Left Alone	Guilt
		Fears	of Being Held Down	Bad/Evil Core
			of Being Crippled	Arrogant, Prideful
			Non-Trusting	Spiritual, Religious
			Panic, Terror, Cold	Indignant
			Terror	Obnoxious
				Helpless, Hopeless,
				Depression, Despair
				Criticalness

Sandy would be or do anything anybody wanted her to be or do. When she was being controlled by others or in need of being accepted, Sandy became completely passive. When *she* was in control, however, her strong-willed and assertive personality flared. She smoked and had other self-destructive habits but, interestingly, was not sexually promiscuous. Sexual sin was not the main stronghold that pressured Sandy to enter into adultery.

In high school and college, others saw Sandy as popular, fun, outgoing, and a good friend. She saw herself, however, as not close to anyone since she felt compelled to hide her "true" self from them and "wear the mask."

During the eight years of adultery with her Pastor, she led a double life. His "hypnotic" (occult) eyes, she said, left her powerless to resist. During these years of adultery, she believed that, by her submission, God would bring this man to a healed state and use him to accomplish greater things. This is the kind of blatant deception that obviously had a tremendous hold on Sandy's life. Yes, deception was an issue for Sandy.

Tower Inhabitants

In each tower, many more inhabitants reside than are shown in the figure. As the Holy Spirit showed us the names of the inhabitants, we listed them as shown in table X. All of these demonic groupings were oppressing Sandy one way or another and at one time or another. By joining together in strongholds, they had more power over her and were better protected. Their legal ground "glued" them together.

Interestingly, some duplication of demonic groupings exist within the various towers. For example, "Fear" groupings are listed in three other towers besides the "Fear" tower. A demonic group "Deception" occurs within the "Self" tower in addition to the demons making up the Wall of Deception. Note the "Rejection" grouping within the "Abandonment" stronghold. This "duplication" is not uncommon since different "legal" ground can be found within each stronghold. This explains why, on some occasions, deliverance ministers find themselves casting out a demon having the same name/function as an earlier one. This causes questioning, such as, "Did that one just get back in?" or, "Were we just fooled, thinking that demon had left? Yet, it still seems to be here!" The answer to both questions is most likely, "No." The deliverance ministers are merely working within another Demonic Stronghold or grouping.

Holy Spirit Strategy

At the time of drawing the Five Tower Stronghold, the Holy Spirit had revealed the problem but He had not shown the strategy. We were forced to constrain our enthusiasm until the next ministry session when the Holy Spirit revealed the strategy for disassembling the stronghold step by step. We also realized the Holy Spirit had a reason for waiting to show us.

We explained to Sandy what God had revealed to us. She was surprised but, by this time, ready to try whatever God was telling us to do. Joining us in agreement, she whole-heartedly submitted and said: "I'm ready to be rid of whatever is there."

As we laid our hands on Sandy and began to pray in the Spirit, the Holy Spirit said to Chester, "Open up a hole in the 'Wall of Deception,' and go into the center tower. Remove it first." So, by faith, Chester commanded that a hole open. Then he declared that we were through it and positioned at the Abandonment tower.

The Holy Spirit's gift of discernment was operating in Sandy, and she said, "Oh, they are surprised. They didn't expect you to do that. They had all of their forces marshaled to protect the wall."

We continued to follow the leading of the Holy Spirit, disassembling the Abandonment tower first.

336

Then the Holy Spirit moved us to the "Control by Others" stronghold. The Holy Spirit begin to give all of us a symbolic, pictorial view (gift of discernment) of what was taking place. As we approached the second tower, we saw nervous, anxious figures looking down from the top of the Control tower, fearing that their end was near. First, we worked through the legal ground given to the kingdom of darkness by Sandy's ancestors and her own sin. Then, we dealt with her Ungodly Beliefs associated with allowing others to control her and prayed for healing of the Soul/Spirit Hurts received as others had controlled her. At that point, we realized that the mortar between the stones was crumbling. Next, the stones — sometimes one at a time and sometimes an entire wall or part of a room — were removed until whole sections of the tower were dismantled as we commanded the demons to leave. Eventually, the entire demonic structure collapsed like a pile of rubble on the ground. We continued to command and cast out until nothing was left except a level, green, grassy, peaceful plain. It was glorious!

We continued on to the other three towers, going next to the "Occult" tower. Although much stronger than the "Control by Others," it, too, was disassembled until nothing was left. It was a pleasure removing this tower, knowing how destructive the "Occult" combined with "Control by Others" had been in Sandy's life. These main forces had "set her up" to be **used** by spiritual leaders who themselves were oppressed by the occult.

The Holy Spirit, then, directed us to the "Fears" tower with the same procedure and result. Lastly, He had us demolish the "Self" tower, which held all of Sandy's accusations and fears about herself as well as various coping/defense mechanisms (sin) that had given place to the demonic, such as "Self-Righteous." It was **good riddance** for all of it.

At this point, only the "Wall of Deception" remained. As we addressed the demons of deception making up this wall, the Holy Spirit opened Sandy's eyes and allowed her **literally to see** it. She gasped, "There are thousands of them, all flowing together, intermeshed, holding on to each other. I have never seen so many demons in my life!"

Finally convinced that deception was indeed or, rather, **had** indeed been an issue in her life, Sandy received massive freedom. We rejoiced at seeing her possess her land more than ever before. We also rejoiced at receiving a Holy Spirit education in demonology and demonic strongholds that money could not buy.

XIII

CONTROL-REBELLION-REJECTION STRONGHOLD

Even if Babylon (witchcraft) reaches the sky and fortifies her lofty stronghold,
I will send destroyers against her, declares the LORD.

Jeremiah 51:53

One particular stronghold surfaces in almost everyone to whom we minister. In fact, we had to deal with this stronghold in our own lives. (By now, we trust that you are no longer surprised by the number of different hurts and wounds we had.) We call it the "Control-Rebellion-Rejection Stronghold." These three "strongholds in one" form a "super" Stronghold. From an academic point of view, this dynamic pattern is fascinating. In "real" life, however, this very destructive stronghold can devastate relationships, individuals, and families.

We suspect that all dysfunctional families exhibit this pattern. Its main consequence creates a feeling of being trapped within the family. All members within the family believe they cannot leave and live their own lives. The children usually respond either by staying in the family long after the normal time for doing so, or by breaking away (rebelling) at their first chance. It is not a healthy pattern.

Girls get married just to escape the family. Such marriages, however, usually end in divorce. Why? Because the same SOFCs are perpetuated in their new family, and the girl feels just as trapped, or more so, as in her original family. Boys, on the other hand, have fights with their dads and run away from home. They start their own families and become massive Controllers, trying to force peace where there is no peace.

This stronghold has two basic cycles. As one person Controls another, the second person reacts with Rebellion and also with feelings of Rejection. The second person, out of both the Rebellion and Rejection, also becomes a Controller, as they resist the Control of the first person. The cycles are also active in all their other relationships. As a result, two cycles operate within the same person. We frequently see these cycles continuing down through the generations as the parent's excessive Control[1] provokes Rebellion and Rejection in their children, and then the children become Controlling parents with their children.

---

[1] Please read Eph 6:4.

A. Legitimate Control

Legitimate control should lead to willing submission and cooperation.

Before we start into the details of this chapter, we need to make it clear that not all Control is "bad." There **is** "legitimate Control." When someone has received — or been delegated — legitimate responsibility and authority over something or someone, there is a basis for legitimate Control. For example, the boss at the work place has legitimate responsibility and authority. He is therefore expected to exert, within the boundaries of the job, legitimate Control over his employees. Parents have a God-ordained responsibility and authority with their children. Therefore, they are expected to use legitimate Control to raise their children in a way that will prepare them to live godly lives.[1] Of course, as the children grow up, the time comes when a gradual releasing of the legitimate Control is necessary. As that happens, the children learn to be responsible and exercise legitimate authority and Control over their own lives and come into their rightful places as mature people responsible before God.

Christ has transferred legitimate control to His Church.

Jesus Christ legitimately received "all authority on heaven and earth," from the One who had the authority to declare His victory in His triumph over Satan.[2] Christ then gave this authority to us, the Church. Thus, the Church has legitimate responsibility, authority, and Control over the forces of darkness and over the affairs of the earth — but not over the free will of individual people.

Legitimate Control does exist. Not all Control is bad. When, however, undelegated, unauthorized Control occurs, the Control-Rebellion-Rejection Stronghold is given "place," along with its destructive consequences for everyone involved.

We want to look at why people Control, how people Control, the dynamics of Control, and the consequences of Control. We will see how Rebellion and Rejection complete these destructive cycles.

B. Why People Control

While there may seem to be many reasons why people Control, when we dig down to the bottom, only two root causes exist.

1. People Control for Power

It may surprise you to learn that the most obvious reason for controlling — controlling for power, particularly power over other people — is actually somewhat rare. Perhaps Hitler and other dictators Control for this reason. In reality, however, we believe that only a small percentage of the world's population enjoys controlling for power.

---

[1] Please read Prov 22:6.
[2] Please read Col 2:14.

Exercise: To help you become attuned to the Control portion of the Control-Rebellion-Rejection Stronghold, please take a moment and think about the questions in this exercise.

Think of the person who has controlled you more than any other during your lifetime.

Questions

1. How did he (or she) do it? What was his method of controlling?
2. Why did he do it? What was his motive?
3. How did you respond? Did you have any coping mechanism or defense?
4. If you had a defense mechanism, how successful were you in coping with his Control of you (i.e., avoiding being controlled)?
5. Did being controlled cause you to have any feelings? What did the Control cause you to want to do? Did it stir up godly or ungodly responses?
6. How has being controlled caused you to become a Controller yourself?

It is unlikely that we will find one of these Control-type people in the ministry room. First of all, they are unlikely to come to church. If they do come, they probably would not submit to anyone, much less ask for help from RTF ministers. We probably will not find these people among those to whom we minister.

Victims become Victimizers

One group of people may seem to be controlling for power: those who victimize others, such as perpetrators of sexual abuse. While an element of raw power is definitely involved, these people usually use Control to avoid pain and to express their anger from the abuse they have suffered.

2. People Control to Avoid Pain

We believe that the main reason that most people Control is to cover over their existing pain and to avoid further hurt and pain at all cost. We estimate that 90 to 95 percent of the controlling people to whom we have ministered Control for this reason. These people will do almost anything to hide from pain, prevent potential pain, or divert pain. They will Control, strategize, manipulate, reason, argue, etc. Logical people will behave illogically. Weak people will become strong. Gracious people will become rude. They will do anything in order to get their way so that **maybe** they can cover over the existing pain and feel secure and protected. Since lasting security or protection is not available through Control, they always need to do more even though they know deep inside that they cannot do enough. As a result, they experience no rest, no peace, but only a constant, relentless drive that consumes them their entire life — unless they receive freedom from this insidious pattern.

Control leads to hurt, which leads to Control.

What types of hurts lead to this controlling-type behavior in order to avoid further pain? Hurts such as being abandoned, suffering abuse of any kind, being controlled, and being devalued. Along with these painful experiences come all the hurts resulting from the Control itself, including the withholding of approval. Such devastating, major experiences usually result in much internal pain. This pain, in turn, frequently leads to a victim mentality, in which the victim becomes a Controller to avoid any set up for future pain.

Mistrust of God is also usually present.

The key underlying issue with people who control to avoid further hurt is mistrust of others. This usually also includes mistrusting God. Since they don't trust anyone, they must do everything themselves, and they must Control everyone else to prevent additional hurt. Out of this deep need to Control comes many different manifestations of Control. Let's look at a few of them.

"Protecting" Others

It is not uncommon for people to put a lot of effort into "protecting" others. They say that they are protecting you, but they are really protecting themselves. These are the ones who "know what's best for you." How many of you have had mothers or fathers who knew what was best for you, and they controlled you excessively? Their hidden motive was to Control you so they would not experience further hurt or pain from what you might do if you were not controlled. Ungodly, illegitimate Control occurred when they imposed their will over your will in an excessive manner — when they went beyond legitimate authority, regardless of how noble the reason.

Examples of "protection Control" might be, "I'll pick out the college for you to attend;" "I'll help you find the best wife for you;" "I'll decide what you should name your children." Getting "A's" on your report card was very important. Doing well in sports, music, or other extracurricular activities. Such attempts to control usually involves a large element of false responsibility and an even larger element of pride.

Filling the Vacuum

People Control for another reason: What we call "filling the vacuum." Filling the vacuum occurs when no one else is in charge. The underlying motivation is, "I have to control in order to avoid disaster." This is so understandable since the one stepping into the vacuum fears he or she will otherwise be hurt.

A wife fills the vacuum left by the husband.

This motive for Control most often occurs in a husband-wife situation. The couple usually has the "classic" complementary UGBs that were discussed in Chapter VIII, "Ungodly Beliefs." For example, the husband might believe, "Wives are controlling." The wife believes, "Husbands are passive." Such thinking keeps each spouse trapped into this complementary, re-enforcing, Ungodly Belief cycle. The force of the wife's Ungodly Beliefs plus the husband's own beliefs and personality pressure him to succumb to passivity and to give up his God-given authority as head of the house. As a result, a vacuum is created. The wife, because she doesn't expect her husband to function as leader and is suffering the consequences, "naturally" fills the vacuum. She takes over, usually a little at first but gradually more and more. It is almost impossible for the wife **not** to take control. Unfortunately, in the process she "enables" the husband to become more and more trapped in his passivity.

Since God did not ordain the wife to function in the headship position, her "filling the vacuum," even to avoid the immediate disaster, will lead to a larger disaster in the long term. The vicious cycles of the Control-Rebellion-Rejection Stronghold continue to escalate until something "explodes." The only way for them to get free is for one or the other of them to realize what is going on, to understand the destructive consequences, and decide to get free. It will take both of them desiring freedom in order for it to occur without destroying the marriage.

Preventing Chaos and Uncertainty

When we are surrounded by unpredictability, violence, yelling, chaos, and shame-producing experiences, we want to "take over" so we can bring order into the situation and have peace and quiet. In later life, we will Control to ensure that chaos doesn't have an opportunity even to arise.

C. Effort Required to Control

Controlling the Universe can be exhausting.

People who control (and we all do to some degree) exert a lot of energy. They can become exhausted, physically, mentally, and spiritually. We like to joke with them that they are "controlling the universe." Most of the time, however, they don't laugh. After all, it takes an awful lot of energy to Control the universe! Making sure every person is in the right place at the right time and ensuring that nobody is going to cause conflict with anyone else can lead to exhaustion. Controllers are almost always tired.

Have you had people over for dinner?

A common situation occurs when a number of people are invited for dinner. The hostess carefully plans where each guest will sit in order to avoid any potential controversies or unpleasant encounters. Such intricate planning involves filling out the name tags and putting them in the right places: strategizing, thinking, worrying, fretting, and never-ending activity. "I can't put Aunt Susie across from Uncle Bill because they have a five-year feud going, and . . . When I talk to cousin Nancy, I must make sure my husband isn't around because he hates Nancy. I have to make everything perfect so nobody will have a reason to be mad at me!" Whew, it's exhausting just to think about it.

We have all experienced situations that we thought required our intervention in order to maintain "the peace" or keep our reputation in tact. In the back of our minds, we think, "Maybe I can avoid being embarrassed, or shamed, or yelled at, or this or that, if I Control one way or another."

D. Enabling Others in Their Sin

God wants us free of "enabling," as well as freeing the other person.

The previous sections presented some of the major motives that people have for controlling. Some of these motives involve **enabling.** That is, in order to avoid pain, people enable somebody else to stay in his sin. This might be the controlling wife helping her passive husband continue to be passive. If she takes over the checkbook to keep him from spending all the money, then she is enabling him to remain immature and not grow in that area. If no one confronts the alcoholic in the family, he or she may be enabling him to continue his irresponsible addiction. God doesn't want us to be enablers of sin, nor does He want the ones being "enabled" to stay in their sin. Godly counsel will likely be necessary to help the person learn how to become free of Control and also how to intervene so that the "enablee" can get free of his sin.

E. How People Control

How direct is the control?

There are many methods of controlling. In fact, there are probably as many different ways and methods of controlling as there are people. Table Y on the next page is divided into four categories based on the "directness" of the Control. Please note that the placing of a particular method of Control into any one category is subjective, and that some forms of Control could be in more than one category.

1. Direct Control

In many ways, Direct Control is the most honest. At least it is out in the open, and everybody knows that it is happening. If, however, it is illegitimate Control, it is still sin. Table Y lists four common, direct methods of Control.

2. Overt Control

Our use of the term Overt Control means direct, but not necessarily obvious, Control. This may result in situations where one person is in Control, but the motive for Control may be unclear. It may be causal, as in the turning of a conversation, or "sugar coated," as in "helping out."

Chester used to frustrate Betsy when she was telling a story. Chester likes clarity (all of the detail necessary for sufficient understanding should be included in the story). Betsy, on the other hand, likes to hit the high points (without necessarily telling the whole story or not telling it in chronological order or properly "setting the stage"). Chester liked to "help" Betsy by interjecting the missing parts. He thought that it was nice of him. Betsy thought that it was rude and uncalled for. She felt Chester was taking over the story and trying to Control her. The message she received was, "You are not doing it right, therefore, you are not adequate." We, of course, no longer (well, hardly ever) do this anymore.

The person in the family who manages the checkbook or Controls the car and/or other equipment may be a Controller.

The one who decides how and where the family time will be used may be a Controller.

Some people Control by their "superior" knowledge. This is akin to, "I know what is best for you," but it takes a different slant when they dominate conversations, decision making, and elevate themselves over others.

Table Y
Some Methods of Control

Direct Control (out in the open)

Giving commands	Being bossy, even if it is sugar coated
Telling somebody "how to do something"	Using force, physical violence

Overt Control (not necessarily obvious)

Steering conversations	Controlling the finances, i.e., the checkbook
Insisting on perfection	Controlling the car, i.e., other peoples' freedom
Providing money for support	Deciding where to go on vacations
Refusing to listen to or acknowledge loving feedback	Deciding how family time is used, i.e., social life

Indirect Control (manipulation)

Deliberately pleasing someone	Using sex, i.e., as a reward or payoff
Promoting loyalty	Having a "headache"
Withdrawing, pouting, "pity party"	Shedding tears
Being angry and/or moody, even violent	Accusing, criticizing
Withholding approval	Needing to work
Promoting shame, i.e., guilt and/or embarrassment, humiliation. "Jewish" mother	Using fear, i.e., threats
Getting terribly wounded and hurt.	Blaming
"How could you do this to me?"	"Look how much you've hurt me."
Making excuses	"You have no appreciation for all that I've done for you."

Hidden Control (occult)

Being incapacitated. Everyone must consider "me" before themselves	Withholding information, lies, deception
Invalid	Having family idols to measure up to
Alcoholic	Unintentional Witchcraft (#1 problem in Church according to Derek Prince)
Paranoid	Casting spells, hexes, etc., i.e., witchcraft

345

3. Indirect Control

Indirect Control is more hidden than Overt Control, but it can still be easily discerned once you become aware that it exists and become attuned to it.

Withdrawing from, or rejecting, is a indirect way of controlling another person.

Some people Control through anger and moodiness. They can keep the whole household wrapped up around them. Everything can be nice and peaceful, and in they walk. In three minutes everybody is attending to them in an attempt to regain the peace. They "enable" the Controller by catering to the Controller's needs and emotions at the expense of their own.

What is the traditional way that women Control? That's right, they cry. Or they "have a headache." Maybe it's the "wrong time of the month."

But what about men, how do they Control? The most common way is probably withdrawal. They punish their wives by not being available. He will give her "the silent treatment." Or he may say, "Have to work late tonight. Sorry honey. Of course, I am doing this for you, so you can live in the lap of 'luxury'." In reality, he is escaping from the chaos in the household and possibly the controlling wife. At work he can be in Control and maintain the peace.

We control by withholding approval and being critical.

Withholding approval and being critical can be Control. Messages that communicate, "You don't dress right," "You don't talk right," "You don't walk right," "You don't do it the way I want you to do it," are messages of disapproval. Unfortunately, parents often use this method to Control their children.

4. Hidden Control

Hidden control is an opening for occult power.

Hidden Control is the hardest to discern when it is happening. It either looks like something else, or we are not even aware that anything is going on, i.e., witchcraft. Whether deliberate witchcraft or not, it almost always provides an opening for occult power to become involved. This tends further to entrap both the person doing the controlling and the person being controlled. Why? Because deception and demonic powers bind the minds and actions of the people.

We may control through sickness.

One of the most insidious forms of hidden Control is displayed through being incapacitated. Now, not everyone who is incapacitated is necessarily a Controller, but it is a possibility to consider. If the person enjoys being sick, or if he does not seem to want to get well — regardless of how much you pray for him — and he never prays for himself to be healed, then you have reason to suspect hidden Control. If he seems to *enjoy* controlling, be even more concerned. He may like the attention of having the entire life of the family revolving around him. "Let's see, is it time for another pill. Thank you for getting it for me." Or, for three days before the big event, everybody is kept informed, "Oh, I have a doctor's appointment. Sorry you have to miss your basketball practice, but you need to take me to the doctor." It just goes on and on. All of the different facets of illness provide means of entrapping the family into taking care of the invalid.

We control through family idols.

Some families Control through family idols. They elevate some virtue or characteristic onto a pedestal and then insist that each family member adhere to it. Some families insist on "correct" feelings. Everyone must always be happy or be at peace or at least be quiet. If you try to express any negative emotions, you are punished and shamed into line. From the outside, the family may seem like a nice family but, inside, everyone is seething from stored up frustration, anger, rage, hurt, etc., because it is not possible to work out conflict. The family is dysfunctional. Because everyone is always "good," the family maintains the idol of being a wonderful, happy family.

One family that we know has made an idol out of beauty. All of the girls in the family are compared with each other and with their mother in terms of appearance and looks. These are the standards by which everything they do is judged and controlled.

Another idol that families frequently have is self-sufficiency. Everyone in the family is judged and controlled relative to his being able to take care of himself. This starts in the early years in sibling fights (not being allowed to cry) right on into the middle-aged years, where the size of the saving accounts, the importance and security of the job, etc., are used as measures of value and worth.

Control invites deliberate witchcraft.

Witchcraft is imposing one's will onto another.

Of course, deliberate witchcraft (using occult means to direct curses and/or demons to other people) is the worst form of hidden Control. It is done in secret, using deception and unseen spiritual powers, with purposed intent to impose one's will onto another person. Consider this interesting fact: Although the target of the Control does not know that the Control is being directed toward him, he responds according to the Control-Rebellion-Rejection Stronghold dynamic cycles.

F. Control-Rebellion-Rejection Stronghold Dynamics

Understanding the dynamic cycles of the Control-Rebellion-Rejection Stronghold can be a big help in the ministry situation, not to mention the benefit of avoiding this trap in our own lives. Figure 9 on the next page contains a sketch of the dynamic cycles.

1. Controller

Control begets Rebellion and Rebellion begets Control.

As the Controller controls (on the left), he "projects" his Control toward the recipient. Since the recipient normally reacts out of the old nature (walking in the flesh), he allows both Rebellion and Rejection to be triggered within himself. We like to say that "Control begets Rebellion and Rejection." Then the rebel "enters" into Control, hoping to Control the situation so as to avoid further hurt. Thus "Rebellion begets Control," "Rejection begets Control," and the cycles continue.

Remember that people become Controllers because they are wounded. They are involved in controlling in order to avoid further hurt and pain. In their constant scheming and strategizing, they expend tremendous amounts of intellectual and emotional energy. They are persistently involved with "what ifs." What if this happens? What if that happens? They are always planning ahead, trying to cover every possible contingency. They are very, very busy, very, very worried about all kinds of things. In order to enforce their way, they often use illogical reasoning and arguing, even though they pride themselves on their logical ability and calmness of personality.

By imposing their will onto other people, they manifest illegitimate Control, unauthorized authority, and false responsibility. All of their energy is focused like a projectile toward others.

The people being controlled react with both Rebellion and Rejection. Let's talk about the Rebellion cycle first.

2. Rebel

Rebellion may be Active or Passive.

The Rebellion may be either active or passive. Some people react against the Control with arguments, shouting, violence, etc. They want to punish and strike back. Others are passive rebels. They say "yes" but do whatever they wanted to do in the first place. They are resistive and uncooperative.

We choose Eruption or Stuffing.

One good thing can be said for active rebels: They usually outwardly vent most, if not all, of their negative emotions. The bad thing is, in the process, they cause much hurt and destruction to others. Passive rebels, on the other hand, generally have stuffed all of their feelings inside — maybe for years. This can create a volcano, waiting for a small trigger shock to erupt all over somebody. Active rebels often wonder why they get so angry over what appear to be insignificant issues. These outbursts occur because of the "pile" of past hurts and wounds — along with all of the negative emotions — they have stored.

Which is the worst sin?

We might ask, "What is the worst sin, Rebellion or Control?" To get the answer to this question, we can read First Samuel, where God has some strong words concerning harmful behaviors and attitudes of the heart.

> 1 Sam 15:22-23
> 22 And Samuel said, Hath the LORD [as great] delight in burnt offerings and sacrifices, as in obeying the voice of the LORD? Behold, to obey [is] better than sacrifice, [and] to hearken than the fat of rams.
> 23 For **rebellion [is as] the sin of witchcraft**, and **stubbornness [is as] iniquity and idolatry**. Because thou hast rejected the word of the LORD, he hath also rejected thee from [being] king. (KJV)

God is looking for hearing ears and obedience.

Rebellion is as the sin of witchcraft; stubbornness (or arrogance) is the same as iniquity and idolatry. It is common in Hebrew poetry to have a repeating line with the second line amplifying and adding to the first line. In this verse, God is equating Rebellion and witchcraft, i.e., Control. Then He uses stubbornness as a synonym for Rebellion, and iniquity and idolatry as synonyms for witchcraft. The answer to the question seems to be that God hates both Rebellion and Control and related manifestations of them. He is looking for people with hearing ears and a willingness to obey His voice.

The rebel then moves into Control to try to avoid further Control and the pain, hurt, and separation that comes with it. The cycles continue.

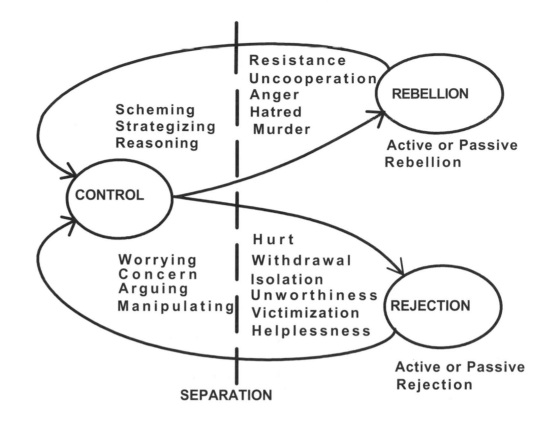

Figure 9: Control-Rebellion-Rejection Stronghold
Dynamic Cycle.

3. Rejectee

Is it possible to both rebel and feel rejected at the same time?

Looking at the Rejection cycle, we find that the very same person who is rebelling is also experiencing Rejection. The force of the Control causes him to draw back from the Controller and feel separated, put down, shut down. The message from the Controller is, "You are not adequate, so I've got to take charge. You need **me** to tell you what to do."

Rejected people, of course, feel hurt and are hurt. Their personhood has probably been violated. They may feel unappreciated and devalued. Their wounds tend to lead to a low self-esteem. They may conclude that they are bad and inherently defective. They may decide that they are "just" victims with no power over their own lives. They can't even make their own decisions.

Active or Passive Rejection results.

They may react **actively** by withdrawing and isolating themselves physically at the same time they are violently striking back at the controller (rebelling).

They may react **passively** by withdrawing within. Feelings of isolation and not belonging may overwhelm them. Continued over time, these tend to break down the bonding between the people involved, i.e., the family members.

349

As the hurts accumulate, the person may become very sensitive to any degree of Control, even perceiving Control when there is none. They may become uncorrectible, unteachable, opinionated. Carried to an extreme, they may become potentially useless in the Kingdom of God, not to mention the world, as they wall themselves off from all potential hurts.

Then, because of all these wounds and hurts, the person moves into the position of being a Controller, and the Rejection cycle continues.

G. Control-Rebellion-Rejection Stronghold Consequences

Throughout this chapter, we have alluded to many consequences of the Control-Rebellion-Rejection Stronghold. Now we want explicitly to list a number of consequences that may be less obvious and yet of major importance.

The Control-Rebellion-Rejection Stronghold:

- Produces new crops of controllers, rebels, and rejected people generation after generation.
- Isolates parents from children, children from each other, and promotes wars.
- Isolates husband and wife and promotes wars.
- Brings division and strife as each one attempts to protect himself.
- Distorts our view of God as we project our experience with our father onto Him.
- Produces people that rebel against authority, both secular and spiritual, and God.
- Allows Satan to do his work of stealing, killing, and destroying.[1]
- Causes people to give up, to become victims: "I can never please," "I am always rejected," "I have no power," etc.
- Causes stifled emotional development. A portion of the person's emotional personality may be stifled or shut down because of trauma.

Two Controllers!

The above consequences occur with even greater intensity in situations where there are two Controllers. For example, when two Controllers marry, there is seldom peace in the household. They are both trying to avoid pain. In the process, they defend themselves and wound, reject, and punish the other. When two

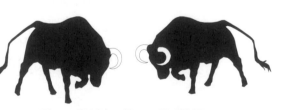

Two Controllers Colliding

Controllers are both trying to be in charge of a meeting, an organization, etc., it usually leads to "fireworks." It would be funny if it were not so destructive. Helping these people become free of the tyranny of the Control-Rebellion-Rejection Stronghold is very satisfying work. It "looses" two strong survivors into their productive place in the Body of Christ.

---

[1]　Please read Jn 10:10.

H. RTF Ministry Considerations

If one component is present, then all three components are usually present.

The Control-Rebellion-Rejection Stronghold Dynamic Cycle is a common pattern. As ministers, we need to be aware of it and the many forms in which it comes. Having this sensitivity to the pattern will enable us to better serve those coming to us for help. For example, if a person comes to us for ministry, and we see at least one of the three components of the stronghold, we are alerted to look for signs of the other two components. If we have a Rejected person, we look for the Control and Rebellion. If Control is obvious, we look for the Rebellion and the Rejection. Generally, all three components are there, even if hidden or subtle. One component may dominate, but the other two will generally be evident. All three need to be removed.

Care is needed in order to not "lose" the person.

*Ladies (and men) are **not** Jezebels. Demons are Jezebels.*

Our job is gently to help the person become aware of his Control — and the accompanying Rebellion and Rejection — and to see it all as sin. This usually needs to be done gently so we don't lose the person before we have an opportunity to help him become healed. Since Controllers usually seek to Control the ministry situation, they can become quite offended if we seem to be accusing them. Ladies are particularly sensitive to being labeled as "controlling" because they are so often accused of being a "Jezebel." Rather than confronting the person directly, we normally assume a permissive attitude and lead him along with questions. This allows him to discover for himself that he is a Controller.

Revelation brings freedom.

Asking questions to expose the extent of his Control and then helping him to receive revelation as to why he is controlling usually paves the way for freedom. He needs to realize that he is not on a power trip, nor is he a "naturally born" defective (his unspoken fear), but he is trying to survive and avoid further hurt.

Control is frequently hidden. It is a blind spot.

Some individuals have a hard time recognizing their Control. When we first bring it up as a possibility, they will be quite surprised and even hurt (see the Control?). "Oh no, not me. I'm a victim. There is no way that I could be a Controller." As we continue through the ministry procedure, as trust builds between us, as he sees that we have his best interest at heart, soon he will say, "Well, I see that it is a possibility, but probably not." Eventually, God's grace opens up his eyes, and he sees the extent of his Control.

Explaining the Control-Rebellion-Rejection Stronghold, its dynamics and the reasons why he has controlled usually helps him accept the reality of his Control. He can face the fact that he has controlled, and that it is not the "unpardonable sin."

Then we can help him decide to become healed and free from this sin. If he will acknowledge the sin and confess it, he can get free of it. That's the requirement that God puts on us all, regardless of the kind or type of sin.[1]

---

[1] Please read 1 Jn 1:9.

He must make
a quality decision.

The Controller must choose to remove himself (with God's Grace) from **all** Control, Rebellion, and Rejection in which he is involved. He **must** refuse to participate.

You can help him learn how to "stand aside" when Control comes at him and to let it "pass on by." Basically, this requires walking in the Spirit rather than in the flesh.[1]

Clarify boundaries
between legitimate
and
illegitimate control.

Sometimes he will need help in clarifying the boundaries of legitimate and illegitimate Control. He needs to learn God's framework of authority, responsibility, and Control.

It may require careful, delicate work to help a strong Controller become free. Yet the rewards for him, his family, and the Kingdom of God make it well worth the effort.

---

[1]   Please read Gal 5:16.

XIV

SHAME-FEAR-CONTROL STRONGHOLD

*Rather, **we have renounced secret and shameful ways;***
*we do not use **deception**, nor do we **distort the word of God**.*
On the contrary, by setting forth the truth plainly
we commend ourselves to every man's conscience in the sight of God.
2 Corinthians 4:2 (NIV)

*Instead of **their shame** my people will **receive a double portion**,*
*and instead of **disgrace** they will rejoice in **their inheritance**;*
and so they will inherit a double portion in their land,
and everlasting joy will be theirs.
Isaiah 61:7 (NIV)

In our years of ministering freedom and healing to the Body of Christ, one revelation stands out above the others. It is the way the strongholds of Shame, Fear, and Control work together as one "super" Stronghold. In order to quickly spread this revelation to others, we released the basic teaching as a two-tape resource, plus some handouts.[1] This chapter on the Shame-Fear-Control Stronghold (SFC) will further help others learn about and get free of this stronghold. In order to get help to the largest number of people, we will release a book about this stronghold in the future. Another resource, *Double Honor: Uprooting Shame in Your Life* by Melodye Hilton,[2] describes the author's journey out of the Shame-Fear-Control Stronghold after she and her husband received ministry in the Healing House.

A. What is Shame?

Sandra Wilson, in her book, *Released From Shame*, defined shame as that awful sense of "being uniquely and hopelessly flawed."[3] Like rejection, it is a common malady for many of us who accepted the lie, "This is who I am," and believed that our core personhood is one of Shame. **This is the worst kind of Ungodly Belief — a false belief about our identity**.

---

[1] Please see the resource page 436 for information on the Shame-Fear-Control Stronghold resource.

[2] Hilton, Melodye, *Double Honor, Uprooting Shame in Your Life,* Double Honor Ministries, Elizabethville, PA 17023, 1999.

[3] Sandra D. Wilson, *Released From Shame*, Intervarsity Press, Downers Grove, IL 60515, 1990.

> Shame is that awful sense of "being uniquely and hopelessly flawed."

B. How does Shame "Give Place" to Fear and Control?

Those of us living with Shame must constantly attempt to cope with the painful thought that "I am uniquely and hopelessly flawed." At the same time, we also struggle to survive in a world where other people might "reject us." As a result, we unintentionally give place to Fear and allow it to intertwine with Shame. In reality, this merely amplifies our human fear: "What if they find out?! Then I will really be in trouble!" This frightful thought opens the door for Control — and its deceptive promise of protection and cover-up — which gives it a place with Shame and Fear. "If I maintain Control over others, no one will ever find out how different (bad) I really am." Figure 10 on the next page depicts this cycle of deception and entanglement. Notice the basic lies involved with each stronghold making up this "super" Stronghold.

Too shamed to admit it?

Control, however, is unable to deliver on its promise of protection. Life's shaming events continue to torment us. Over the years we continually yield to and cooperate with these three demonic strongholds since we know no other alternative. We think that these manifestations are simply a part of our personality. Talk about the perfect trap!

Consider this final "catch 22": Since we would be "shamed" if we admitted to being "uniquely and hopelessly flawed," we draw back from God's requirement to "confess our sin." The very thing (the exposure of our shame) that we are working (i.e., controlling) day and night to prevent, we have to do in order to get free!

> Rom 7:24
> O wretched man that I am! who shall deliver me from the body of this death? (KJV)

Praise the Lord, Paul gives us the answer in the next verse:

> Rom 7:25
> Thanks be to God—through Jesus Christ our Lord!" (NIV)

C. Source of Shame-Fear-Control

Original Source

Where did Shame originate? Yes, you guessed it! From our dear father and mother Adam and Eve. We were excited to discover in the first book of the Bible:

> Gen 3:10
> And he (Adam) said, I heard thy voice in the garden, and **I was afraid**, because **I [was] naked**; and **I hid myself.** (KJV)

After Adam and Eve rebelled against God and His commandment, the **Shame** of their nakedness caused them to be **Fearful,** to take **Control** of the situation, and to hide themselves — first with fig leaves and then within the garden. They had not known that they were naked before the fall. Now they did. They tried to cover their Shame themselves.

354

Figure 10: Basic Lies that Enable the SFC Stronghold.

Control, in an effort to cover the Shame and keep it from being exposed, seems to use separation, withdrawal, and abandonment.

In this case, Adam and Eve abandoned God, forcing Him to abandon them.

> **The root of Shame is Abandonment.**

Current Source

For most people — and maybe all of us — the SFC stronghold is inherited. It comes down the family line as one of the Sins of the Fathers and Resulting Curses. The Demonic Strongholds are passed down the family line, generation after generation, producing a line of isolated and hiding people.

The demons look for an opportunity to cause that first shaming experience. Their goal is to "set up" the person to enter into the sins surrounding Shame. Then they will have established "legal ground" within the person just as an army establishes a beachhead. After that, it is merely a matter of continuing to take ground.

Abandonment, rejection, isolation, and various forms of abuse are the most common initial shaming events. These forms of shaming are used in the deliberate traumatizing of babies by those practicing SRA and psychological programming. Extreme shaming can lead to dissociation as the person struggles to separate from the pain.

A person need not be in a SRA family, however, to experience shaming events. For example, just going to school has done it for many of us. Being laughed at by one's classmates or receiving the teacher's scorn can be the beginning of a life of shame. Failing to meet our parents' expectations in such areas as beauty, intellect, athletics, family pride areas, etc., will also do it quite well, thank you. All of these events cause us to feel separated (rejected), isolated, and abandoned.

The demons do not care what gives them legal ground. They will continue to engineer shaming experiences so that their deceptive lies can be put forth and accepted (agreed to) by their host. Fear grows, getting a firmer grip on the "life" within the person. At the same time, Control builds the wall higher and thicker. As time goes by we learn ever more effective weapons to use to keep everyone away from our fortress. We will NOT be exposed.

Each stronghold of Shame, Fear, and Control interacts with, supports, and cooperates with the other demonic groupings and strongholds to bring about Satan's "stealing, killing, and destroying." Please refer back to the Demonic Interconnectedness and Support Diagram on page 293 for an example of a complex demonic structure containing the SFC stronghold as a part.

D. Symptoms and Sources of Shame-Fear-Control

It would make life easier if we would all wear signs advertising what type of Ungodly Beliefs we have about our Identity. That is, if we would inform others just which, if any, counterfeit identity Demonic Strongholds we have. Then we could do a better job relating to each other. We could deal straight with each other rather than getting caught up in "games" and other camouflage strategies.

Do you have the counterfeit identity of Shame-Fear-Control? Table Z on the next page shows some of the many sources, manifestations, and symptoms of the SFC counterfeit identity stronghold. While we hope that you do not find yourself on this list, more than likely you will. ☺

However, we can not go entirely by the symptoms or sources to determine the presence of the SFC stronghold as an identity. Rather, we need to know what the person believes about who he is. Does he believe "I have **done** sometime shameful," or, "**I am** something shameful."

Table Z
Symptoms and Sources of the
Shame-Fear-Control Stronghold

Shame	Fear	Control
Abandonment	of Exposure	Prideful
Abuse	of Rejection/	Unteachable
- Emotional	Abandonment	Easily Offended
- Physical	of being Vulnerable	Defensive/
- Sexual	of receiving Ministry	Justifying
- Spiritual	of Failure	Denying
- Verbal	of Success	Lying
Adoption	of being Wrong	Blame Shifting
Alcoholism	of making a Mistake	Criticalness
Abortion	of loss of Reputation	Judging
Barrenness		Bitterness
Burden		Passivity
Poverty	(And many other fears	Under-Achiever
Failure	too numerous to list.)	Withdrawn
Illegitimacy		False Humility
Unworthiness		Co-dependency
Confusion		Need to be Right
Deficiency		Over-Achiever
Unwanted		Perfectionism
Not Belonging		Clowning
Neglected		Talkative
Shame Bearer		Aggressive
(Scapegoat)		
Victimized		

E. Demons Present

The above table, besides containing symptoms and sources, also indicates the types of demons that are usually part of each of the Shame-Fear-Control Strongholds as well as the Shame, Fear, and Control demons themselves.

Almost any type (function) of demon may be found in any of the strongholds. The particular demons that oppress a particular person are strongly effected by the heritage and the choices one makes as he goes through life. For example, since all of us chose different methods of control, the intensity of the Control stronghold can vary considerably. It may contain demons that are "laid back" and use passivity as their main method of Control. Or it may have demons that are more assertive and forceful, giving place to the more vicious type of controlling demons such as Religious and Jezebel demons.

F. RTF Ministry Considerations

Ministering to those afflicted by the SFC stronghold is an interesting and exciting challenge. When the Control portion of the stronghold is very strong — perhaps at a "Jezebel" level — even more finesse is required. Helping a person gain enough trust to let down his walls requires the utmost care. It takes much grace for him to begin to hope that you are presenting him with the truth. It takes faith for him to believe that a counterfeit identity — and not "himself" — has created all the turmoil in his life. The hope that he might be able to get free of this life-long entrapment frequently takes every ounce of courage he can muster.

None of us will open up and confess our innermost weaknesses to another person until we feel safe. The SFC stronghold is very deceptive and the hiddenness of the false identity is extremely deep. Establishing trust, therefore, is essential. Only then can we expect our ministry receiver to begin to "entertain" the possibility that the beliefs he has accepted all of these years are lies. He must make the paradigm shift that his own shameful personality is not really himself but rather a separate entity — a group of demons, a stronghold masquerading as his true self. This is heavy-duty stuff!

We recommend that you start early in the ministry process — as soon as you sense the likelihood of the presence of the SFC stronghold — to begin to bring up the possibility that "Shame may be a factor in your life." Normally this will be a complete surprise, resulting in his immediate rejection of the idea. Don't let this bother you. Just begin to point out to him the "clues" that he is giving you.

As you begin to share with your ministry receiver the symptoms you are seeing, it is essential to insure that he understands that you are describing a Demonic Stronghold and not him. Your job is to enlist the receiver on your side and get him to stop cooperating with the stronghold. This is not easy for him. You are asking him to change a lifelong pattern. How well you succeed will be greatly influenced by his personality and his acceptance of your caring concern.

Throughout the ministry time continue to build on the Shame, Fear, Control theme and minister to it within each of the four Problem/Ministry Areas. Remove the effect of the ancestral sins and curses. Start working on the core SFC Ungodly Beliefs. Notice that many of the theme headings in the Ungodly Beliefs About Ourselves and Others tables (Tables H and I) have to do with this stronghold. Observe which UGBs your ministry receiver relates to — if he has the courage to admit it. Deal with the SSHs that were part of the shaming events. Then cast out the demons using your knowledge of how to disassemble and destroy Demonic Strongholds, even "super" Demonic Strongholds.[1]

You will be thrilled as you watch from your "close-up" vantage point God free people from this stronghold!

---

[1] If you are going to minister to people and help them gain freedom from the SFC stronghold, we strongly encourage you to obtain the SFC tape and handouts resource. Please check the resource page 436.

Part 4

Foundational Implementations

In presenting a broad view of the four different RTF Ministry Formats — Altar ministry, Issue-Focused ministry, Thorough ministry, and Extended ministry — our goal is to answer the question, "What do we do when?"

In the final chapter, we would also like to leave some final thoughts for ministers, particularly RTF ministers. Please take these to heart. We don't want you to be one of the causalities in this war.

XV

RTF MINISTRY FORMAT[1]

Therefore confess your sins to each other and
pray for each other so that you may be healed.
The prayer of a righteous man is powerful and effective.
James 5:16-18 (NIV)

Now that we understand the Integrated Approach to Healing Ministry, the four Problem/Ministry Areas and the importance of ministering to all four of these areas simultaneously, Soul Ties, Demonic Strongholds, and "Super" Strongholds, these questions remain when ministering to a person:

- How do we put these understandings into practice?
- How much time to we take?
- What format do we follow?
- How prepared, or qualified, do we have to be?

The answer to all these questions is: "It depends!"

We have found the Restoring the Foundations (RTF) ministry can be used in many different situations. There is no limit to the number, type, or variety of applications where one can pray more effectively using this approach and expect to see greater results. As we have stated throughout this book, the Lord Jesus Christ is so interested in seeing His Body healed and set free that He will work with us in every possible way to accomplish this goal. The structured approach of RTF ministry insures that we meet the conditions expressed within God's conditional promises. It qualifies the RTF minister to consider how the four Problem/Ministry Areas have affected the ministry receiver's life. If we do our part, God will do His. The situation in which we find ourselves is not the determining factor.

To illustrate the flexibility of the RTF ministry, several "formats," or "types," of ministry are presented. These formats can range from a few minutes at the church altar on Sunday morning (or on the phone) to a church leader ministering in his office. The format might be a team ministering for several sessions to a church member, or a team involved in in-depth, long-term ministry.

*Categorize Format by **ministry time** and **preparation/ training** requirements.*

When we categorize the different formats/types of ministry, two parameters help us differentiate them from one another: (1) the total **ministry time**; (2) the amount of **preparation or training** required of the RTF minister.

---

[1]   Please see a condensed description of the training process for RTF lay ministers on page 433.

In this chapter, we present four RTF ministry formats and their differences related to the required ministry time. We start with the briefest, which is the Altar Ministry and move through to "Extended" RTF ministry, which takes an undefined amount of time.

A. Formats

Four ministry formats are discussed in this chapter. Their main distinguishing characteristics are based on **duration** of the ministry, **where** the ministry normally occurs, **for whom** the ministry is appropriate, the minimum **preparation/ training** requirement, and the level of **qualification** for the RTF ministers performing the ministry.

- **Altar Ministry**

Duration: Three to ten minutes.
Location: Church.
For Whom: Appropriate for any church member.
Training: Issue-Focused RTF Ministry.
Minister(s): Local church Altar ministry individuals and teams, plus those more prepared/trained.

- **Issue-Focused RTF Ministry**

Duration: Three to six hours. (One to two sessions)
Location: Church office, or cell/small group leader's living room.
For Whom: Appropriate for any church member.
Training: Issue-Focused RTF Ministry.
Minister(s): Local church cell/small group leaders and assistants, plus those more prepared/trained.

- **Thorough RTF Ministry**

Duration: Fifteen hours. (Five, three hour sessions)
Location: Church, RTF minister's home, or Healing House.
For Whom: Appropriate for church leaders and any church members needing or wanting more than Issue-Focused Ministry.
Training: Issue-Focused RTF Ministry, plus two weeks of apprenticeship with supervision, plus personal Thorough RTF ministry.
Minister(s): RTF lay ministry teams (two people per team), plus those more prepared/trained.

- **Extended RTF Ministry**

Duration: Undefined amount of time.
Location: Healing House and/or residential program.
For Whom: Appropriate for very wounded Christians.
Training: Same as for Thorough RTF Ministry, plus RTF ministry experience. May involve specialty training.
Minister(s): Healing House Network ministry teams (two people per team), plus those specially prepared/trained for the severely wounded.

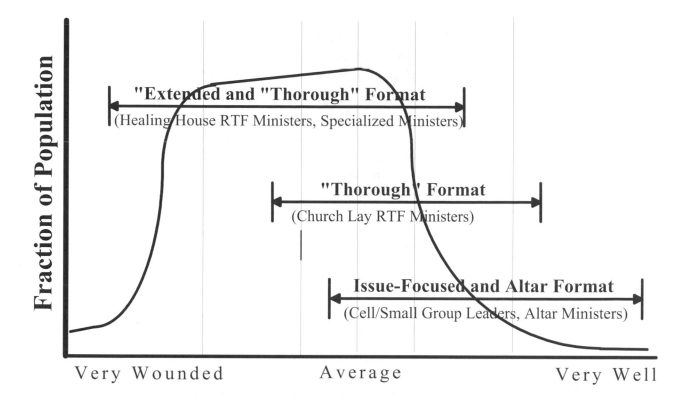

Figure 11: Christian Population Degree of Wellness

Who Ministers to Whom?

When considering the people for whom these different formats are appropriate and why we have four different formats and levels of preparation, the charts on this page help answer this question.

The first chart depicts the degree of wellness (or woundedness) on the horizontal axis. On the vertical axis, we have sketched a curve to represent the number of people at each degree of wellness. This shape is not based on actual research but is an adequate approximation for the sake of this discussion.

The middle of the chart shows the people who have an average, or normal, amount of wounding. This is where most of us are. The right side of the chart indicates a much smaller number of people who grew up and lived their lives

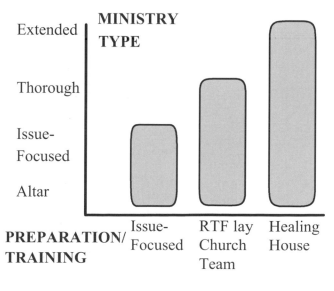

Figure 12: Qualification Levels of RTF ministers

experiencing a relatively small number of wounds. (We haven't met many of these people yet, but we like to think that they are "out there.") The left side of the chart represents the significant number of people who are more severely wounded. These people need major ministry to receive God's full restoration.

This chart highlights two important points. First, it takes more preparation and training to be able to minister to the more deeply wounded people. That is why we require additional preparation/training for RTF ministers who participate in the more advanced ministry. This is the principle. We don't want a hospital orderly doing heart surgery, and we don't want the heart surgeon changing the bed pans. The ministers' level of call/preparation/training/anointing/qualifying determines the appropriate groups of people to whom they can minister.

Secondly, overlapping is inevitable when it comes to "who can minister to whom." Looking at the center of the chart, it appears the "average" person could receive ministry either from his cell group leader, and/or from the church RTF lay ministers, and/or from a Healing House team. Likewise, this "average" person can choose his "doctor" from those trained as a general practitioner, an internist, a clinician, or many other levels of preparation/qualification.

While all of these trained ministers are equipped and able to help our "average" person, it only makes sense to start with the least trained and move up the hierarchy as needed. Just as we would prefer to keep the heart surgeon in the operating room, where his highly trained specialty skills can be put to best use, we probably would not want our highly trained and qualified Healing House teams ministering to a mostly "well" person.

The second chart further amplifies these points. It shows that the more prepared/trained/qualified RTF ministers are equipped to function in a variety of formats. Those trained as Issue-Focused ministers can minister at the Altar, as cell/small group leaders, or as church leadership. Those prepared as church lay RTF ministers can function in the Thorough format, as well as the Issue-Focused and Altar ministry. Healing House Network teams can minister using all of the formats.

B. Altar Ministry

This ministry is characterized by the very short amount of time available. It is usually conducted by trained altar ministers, which may include healing teams, deliverance teams, prophetic teams, and small group leaders, as well as other church leadership, i.e., elders and pastors. Altar ministers may minister individually or in pairs (married couples, men's and women's teams).

Besides the usual preparation and training for altar ministers, we recommend that they also be equipped, at least, to the level of Issue-Focused RTF Ministers. This enables them to bring the entire revelation of *Restoring the Foundations* into their ministry at the altar.

How do we "apply" the RTF ministry at the altar? Let's "walk" through a typical example to see how the process might occur. We are going to put you in the lead.

At the Altar

Imagine that you are a part of an altar ministry team. Your job is to effect significant change while functioning within the constraints of the situation. A member of your congregation is in front of you, seeking immediate help but not extensive ministry. Your "interview" consists of one or two questions for clarification.

Once the church member states his issue, you first ask yourself, "What does God say about this situation?" It doesn't matter what you already know, think, or want to do. Religious prayers, regardless of how well intended, will not accomplish God's will. No, in this brief period of time, you want to determine: "What areas of ministry are the most essential in order to bring God's healing to this person?" You pray briefly, in the Spirit, seeking God's Rhema Word.[1]

At this point, you can bring your understanding of the Integrated Approach to Healing Ministry before the Lord as a canvas upon which the Holy Spirit, through the Rhema Word, will "paint" the picture of what you are to do.

As you pray, you are asking the Holy Spirit a number of questions. "Is forgiveness needed?" Perhaps you need to ask the member, "Is there anyone toward whom you are holding unforgiveness?" Or, your question may be even more direct: "Have you forgiven your wife for doing that?"

While listening to your ministry receiver's answers, you check with the Holy Spirit to see if one or two key ancestral sins/curses underlie the problem. Are these giving place to demons that are really stirring up the issue? What are his Ungodly Beliefs in this area? Do you need to help him see his agreement with the enemy or his cooperation in keeping the problem going? What old hurts are getting triggered? Is the real problem a childhood issue that has never been healed?

The church member's simple request for prayer falls like a seed into a fertile garden. You are the "garden," which includes your understanding of the four Problem/Ministry Areas and the Integrated Approach to Healing Ministry. The rich, organic, black earth is waiting for the Rhema seed. Into your "garden" comes the voice of the Lord: "Do these things!" As you do them, the harvest of healing and freedom quickly springs to life.

Focusing on the key areas revealed by the Lord, you pray, bind, release, break, declare, command, etc., as needed. You may stop, ask questions, and/or give instructions, as appropriate. You may lead the person in speaking forgiveness, asking forgiveness, repenting of his UGBs, etc., as the Holy Spirit continues to lead.

At this point, you are ready to pray for healing and restoration and/or for deliverance and freedom. As you continue following the Rhema Word, you bring God's intervention into the member's situation. You do your best to be Christ's Body and do as He did. Jesus spoke and "did" as He had heard and seen the Father doing.[2] Now you are speaking and doing as His Holy Spirit is leading you.

The short amount of time available at the altar requires a slightly different approach to ministry. It is preferable, of course, to have the ministry receiver involved in the work of bringing God's authority and solution into the situation. This requires him to use his will and helps him learn how to receive for himself.

---

[1]   We defined God's "*rhema*" word in a footnote on page 2.
[2]   Please see, for example, Jn 5:19, 30; 8:38.

At the altar, however, there is time only for rapid **and** effective ministry. You must take the initiative to bring God's authority and solution into the situation.

Tears, laughter, smiles of gratitude, a quick "Thank you, God bless you," and the ministry is completed. As the minister, you also thank the Lord and rejoice in the opportunity to be an instrument in the Master's hand.[1] Then the next person appears, ready to share his heart.

More Ministry Needed?

It should be obvious that our goal as ministers is to leave the person better off at the end of the ministry than at the beginning. Sometimes, it is apparent that the person requires more ministry than can be accomplished in the few minutes available at the altar. In these cases, we do what we can (i.e., what the Holy Spirit shows us to do), and then we "tie up" the rest for another day, rather than opening "things" up without being able to come to a satisfactory resolution. It is important to be sensitive to the Holy Spirit as to the best approach for each individual.

We recommend to the member that he pursue more ministry, either with his cell/small group leader or with one of the church's RTF lay ministry teams.

C. Issue-Focused Ministry

Several years ago, the Lord said to us, "I want this ministry taken to the 'grass roots' of My Church." We knew what He meant. He wants the RTF ministry "taken to **every member** of the Body of Christ" so everyone has the opportunity to receive a significant touch from Him. The Lord desires to restore one or more of the areas of the believer's life where significant hindrances remain. Our heavenly Father longs to see **every one of His children** "going on" in a satisfying Christian walk, enabled to fulfill his call, purpose, and destiny in this life.

The Lord had us start with the original Thorough RTF ministry format and apply the same ministry principles to one significant problem, or issue, in a person's life. The Issue-Focused Ministry format is the result of this effort. Compared to the 15 or more hours needed for the "Thorough" RTF ministry, the time required for the Issue-Focused Ministry normally involves one session, lasting two to three hours. We knew this was the best way to reach as many people as possible.

The Lord also had us develop a training procedure that was straightforward, that would allow many leaders and potential leaders in the church to be quickly equipped and released to conduct the Issue-Focused Ministry.

Availability

Rapid availability is a great advantage of this abbreviated format. The time required is short enough that every church member can receive some ministry help. Every need may not be met, but, in this case, some significant help is better than no help.

---

[1] Please see 2 Tim 2:21 (NIV).

Where Used?

This shorter format works well for a cell or small group leader who notices one of his members struggling with an issue. He can invite the member to his home for an evening of ministry. This format can also be used as a basis for group ministry, in which everyone is ministered to at the same time. Church educational classes or a *Restoring the Foundations* seminar provide an appropriate setting. Lastly, this abbreviated format proves helpful during a scheduled one-hour appointment in which a church member comes to the pastor (or elder) with a problem.

The usual setting for this ministry is the living room of a cell or small group leader. It is evening time, and the leader and his assistant (spouse) have two to three hours to minister. In preparation, the leader has studied in detail the completed Questionnaire section of the Member's Guide, which he had previously provided to his cell member. The leader and his assistant are prayerfully prepared and expecting God to touch the member's life and entirely free him from the problem/issue.

Issue-Focused Ministers

Issue-Focused ministry can be conducted by cell/small group leaders and their assistants, by RTF lay ministers, and by other trained church leadership. For cell/small group leaders, or RTF lay ministers, this could be a husband/wife team, or two men or two women. We would strongly recommend that two people of the opposite sex **do not** minister together if they are not married (to each other). Also, we would strongly recommend against one cell leader meeting with one member of the opposite sex. Please see the cautions in the next chapter on this subject on page 375.

Preparation/Training/Qualification[1]

The Issue-Focused ministry training consists of two seminars, the RTF Healing/Deliverance Seminar, and the RTF Issue-Focused Activation Seminar. (These seminars are also part of the preparation for more advanced RTF ministers.) For cell/small group leaders, Issue-Focused Ministry training is in addition to their preparation as leaders for the cell/small group model being used by their church.

Publications

Two publications work together to help accomplish the Issue-Focused Ministry. The first is the Member's Guide. In 16 pages, this Guide presents to the cell/small group member (ministry receiver), the essence of the Integrated Approach to Healing Ministry. It prepares the cell member to receive RTF ministry that applies to one problem area/issue in his life. It also contains a questionnaire to fill out, which is returned to the person doing the ministry (Leader). This allows the Leader to fully prepare and maximize benefit of the ministry time.

---

[1]   The ***Issue-Focused Ministry*** training seminars and publications are discussed on page 433. You may call **877-214-8076** for more information, and/or go to our web site at **www.issuefocused.org**.

The second publication, the Leader's Guide, is a 30 page booklet, showing in step-by-step detail, how to bring the Integrated Approach to Healing Ministry to bear on one issue. It "leads" the Leader through the interview and then through the Sins of the Fathers and Resulting Curses, Ungodly Beliefs, Soul/Spirit Hurts, and Demonic Oppression as he ministers to the receiver's major issue. This Issue-Focused Ministry can all be accomplished in one session.

Staying Focused

For the Issue-Focused Ministry, we basically put a "fence" around the problem and the direct influences on it, allowing us to concentrate on what is "inside the fence." We stay very focused. In a relatively short time, we want to effectively remove **all** of the legal ground, hurts, and oppression associated with the one issue/problem. Our goal: a problem attacked, a stronghold demolished. We want it **entirely gone** so that no open doors remain for future "reinfestation."

Number of Meetings

After one or two different ministry sessions, the Member should have his major one or two key problem/issue areas taken care of.

For some of the people in the church, except for the very wounded, Issue-Focused Ministry will "jump start" them and release them to move ahead in their sanctification walk. This may be all that they need. They may be able to work directly with the Holy Spirit to continue receiving healing, deliverance, and freedom in other areas of their life.

For others, however, these one or two sessions will bring relief and hope but will not be enough to take care of the degree of significant issues in their lives. In fact, they may become aware of just how much healing they need. This is not necessarily bad. Once we know we are unhealed, and we learn what God has for us, most of us get more serious about seeking God for the healing. Going through the Issue-Focused ministry, however, will often stabilize people until they have an opportunity to continue with the Thorough RTF format.

Five-Fold Ministers

We always recommend that those who are called as five-fold ministers complete the Thorough RTF ministry format. Why? Because their healing, or lack of it, significantly impacts many lives. Their ability to fully accomplish God's call on their lives may be critically dependent on their degree of wellness.

D. Thorough RTF Ministry

We are ready now to look at the "Thorough" ministry format. This is the original format in which we applied the Integrated Approach to Healing Ministry. It is a "very" Thorough approach, generally providing the Lord ample opportunity to bring major healing and freedom to the person receiving ministry.

In this format, we use a ministry structure with five individual sessions, each with a designated purpose. We consider this basic structure as a framework within which the Holy Spirit fills in the pieces for each individual, showing us step-by-step the details of what needs to be done.

RTF Ministry Team

This ministry is conducted by an appropriately trained RTF ministry team. A team is defined as two people, patterned after Jesus sending his disciples out "two by two."[1] A team is usually made up of a husband/wife (see page 375 in the next chapter for reasons why), but it can also be two men or two women. As we stated earlier, we strongly recommend that two people of the opposite sex **not** minister together if they are not married to each other.

Preparation/Training/Qualification[2]

As we move to the more advanced ministry, we require more preparation for the RTF ministers. Besides the two seminars used to train Issue-Focused Ministers, those preparing to use the "Thorough" format go into the ministry room for the final two steps of their training. This is apprenticeship or "hands-on" training. In the first step, they observe at least one person (it is better to observe a couple) receiving Thorough ministry (at least 15 hours). The apprentices are actively involved, taking notes, and planning the ministry as if they were the lead ministers, but they are not.

In the last step, they become the lead RTF ministry team. They minister to two people (a couple), taking them completely through the Thorough RTF ministry. Of course, a RTF trainer is with them the entire time, including the extensive pre- and post-session training, as well as during the actual ministry.

Additional Training Publication[3]

In addition to the general information and the Ministry Steps provided in each of the core chapters of this book, we have developed an even more specific training resource for the Thorough RTF ministry format: *Ministry Tools for Restoring the Foundations*. This manual is used for training church RTF lay ministry teams. This detailed, step-by-step manual, guides the ministry team through each of the needed ministry sessions. Many of the teams minister with *the Ministry Tools* manual lying open on their laps since it is such a helpful reference book.

Session Frequency

A typical church RTF lay ministry team will minister once a week using a three-hour block of time. Some ministry teams may have more time, such as retired people, and are able to minister twice a week. This frequency works well when ministering to a married couple since each spouse can come for ministry once a week. Having the couple simultaneously going through the ministry process enables them to move into open and honest sharing, which adds greatly to the healing process.

---

[1] Please see Mk 6:7 as one example.

[2] The RTF Thorough ministry training information is presented on page 433. You may call **877-214-8076** for more information, and/or go to our web site at **www.phw.org**.

[3] Information about the ***Ministry Tools*** manual is included in the resource section on page 435.

In the Healing House, where the RTF teams are involved full-time, the frequency of ministry is once, and sometimes twice a day, to one person. If a couple is receiving ministry, one spouse is seen in the morning and the other in the afternoon.

Session Length

The normal session length is three hours. Compared to a one- or two-hour time block, this length of time is actually more efficient. It avoids additional starting and stopping and the time needed to report on activities between sessions.

On the other hand, going more than three hours begins to put a strain on the person receiving ministry, not to mention the RTF ministers. An occasional session might last four to five hours because of a difficult deliverance or intense Soul/Spirit Hurts session when issues of safety and peace are at stake.

Number Of Sessions

Five sessions for each person normally yields effective results. This number can be extended by one or two sessions if more ministry is needed in any one Problem/ Ministry Area. We do not, however, recommend going more than seven sessions. It is important to have a definite "stopping" time so the person can "walk it out" for a season, consolidating his newfound healing and freedom.

Content

Normally, we move through the interview and the four Problem/Ministry Areas using the standard five session format.

The first session includes "getting started" activities plus an Interview to supplement the information in their Application Forms.

During the next four sessions, we move through each of the four Problem/Ministry Areas in the normal order of progression. At least, it sometimes works out this way. More commonly, as we have mentioned more than once, the contents of the five sessions are "blended," as the Holy Spirit orchestrates the details of the ministry.

- Joint Session: • Initial Joint Session for a Married Couple
- Session One: • Individual Interview Session
- Session Two: • Ministry to Sins of the Fathers and Resulting Curses
- Session Three: • Ministry to Ungodly Beliefs
- Session Four: • Ministry to Soul/Spirit Hurts
- Session Five: • Ministry to Demonic Oppression
- Session Six: • Optional (if needed to complete any Ministry Area)
- Joint Session: • Final Joint Session for a Married Couple

Ministering to Married Couples

When ministering to a married couple, we have two additional "joint" sessions: one at the beginning, before starting the individual sessions; and one at the end, after the individual sessions have been completed. As a result, couples have a total of 12 sessions.

The first joint session is designed to determine how the couple relates to one another in their marriage and the main issues facing them as a couple. We make sure to address these issues during their individual sessions.

The final joint session provides an opportunity for the couple to share the results of their RTF ministry, to ask each other's forgiveness as appropriate, and to agree on some guidelines for the future to help each one move ahead in their healing. In this session, we show the couple their mutually reinforcing negative (UGBs) patterns and help them plan strategies for a new approach. Although RTF ministry is **not** marriage counseling/ministry per se, the marriage relationship and its dynamics are greatly affected as each spouse receives his/her individual ministry.

E. Extended RTF Ministry

For some people the above ministry formats are not enough. Their degree of wounding requires more time, more specialized ministry, and more accountability than the five-session Thorough RTF ministry is designed to accomplish. This is where the Extended ministry format comes into play.

Who For?

As mentioned throughout this book, these people are characterized as:

- Bound by addictions.
- Crushed by sexual or physical abuse.
- Tormented by gender, or other, identity confusion.
- Traumatized so deeply as to fragment and isolate portions of their personality, causing dissociation. This trauma may be deliberately imposed, such as in SRA, DID, political programming, etc.

Others have been extensively wounded as they were raised up and dedicated by their ancestors:

- Into one of the various witchcraft guilds.
- To the god of a secret society, a false religion, or a cult.

The use of blood and bloody oaths is common in these organizations. Always, it seems, the attempt is made to counterfeit, or replace, the blood of the Lamb, the Lord Jesus Christ. The use of blood, sexual torment or encounters, terror, and extreme victimization are all designed to increase the degree of submission (i.e., slavery) and to gain power through demonization and dissociation.

Who Can, and Cannot, Minister?

People with any of these very wounding backgrounds should not be ministered to by church volunteers. The usual RTF lay ministry team conducts one three-hour session once a week. They have jobs, families, and are involved in church and other activities. They do not have the time, training, or anointing to deal with the more wounded people. The cell/small group leader, trained in Issue-Focused ministry, already has an entire group of people under his care and cannot provide an appropriate solution.

God has been, and is, raising up an army of five-fold ministers to help these people gain their freedom. Full-time, experienced RTF ministers are one branch of this army. These people have answered God's call to serve the entire Body of Christ. A number of them are already working in the Healing House setting. They have gone beyond the training and preparation required to serve their local church and have become prepared to bring RTF ministry to everyone — from Christian leaders to some of the severely wounded people discussed above. They have become extremely proficient in working with the Holy Spirit to tear down strongholds and to bring in God's grace and mercy.

Specialists/Residential Programs

Some in this five-fold ministry army are called by God to become specialists further trained in the "Extended" format. They have a heart and a call to minister to those people with a particular type of wounding.

Residential programs are, and will be, more and more available as the Body of Christ mobilizes to provide resources, i.e., ministers (RTF and others), facilities, and jobs, to help the severely wounded become free.

Content

In the simplest terms, the Extended format is the same as the Thorough format, but it is repeatedly applied to deeper and deeper layers of a person's life or personality. In many ways, the process is the same as ministry to a Demonic Stronghold, as we discussed in Chapter XII. The understanding of the Integrated Approach to Healing Ministry, Demonic Strongholds, and the Shame-Fear-Control "Super" Stronghold are essential to effective Extended ministry.

Are You Called to this Arena?

To discuss this ministry format further is beyond the scope of this book. If, however, you feel God is calling you to this level of ministry — and you would like more information about how to become qualified as a Healing House RTF ministry team member — please call either the Proclaiming His Word Ministries office at **877-214-8076**, or the Healing House Network office at **800-291-4706.** You may also EMail us at **office@phw.org** or **office@healinghouse.org**.

If you have an interest in establishing a RTF ministry program in your church and possibly a regional Healing House for your community, please call and ask for the booklet, *Establishing a RTF Ministry Program*.

XVI

FINAL THOUGHTS FOR RTF MINISTERS

Behold, I send you forth as sheep in the midst of wolves:
*be ye therefore **wise as serpents**, and **harmless as doves**.*
Matthew 10:16

... you will be called priests of the LORD, you will be named ministers of our God.
All who see them will acknowledge that they are a people the LORD has blessed.
Isaiah 61:6, 9

As we near the end of this journey through *Restoring the Foundations*, we hope it has been a profitable trip for you and that the keys referred to in the Introduction Chapter are now firmly in your grasp. Many of you are now serious about the prospect of having your foundation restored and also have a strong desire to help others as well. As we finish, we want to leave you with some final thoughts.

A. Straight Talk

Now, dear fellow minister, allow us to pass on some hard-won wisdom for your consideration. This wisdom can be expressed as several levels, or intensities, of cautions. Our presentation would not be complete if we failed to share some important lessons learned over the years through our own experience and growth (you may read this as "mistakes and foolishness," if you like). By heeding these warnings your ministry will be much safer and more effective for you and your ministry receiver.

In fact, we can express this thought even more strongly. Heeding these guidelines, cautions, safeguards, and "No, No's" will greatly reduce the likelihood of opening a door for Satan's demons. Their mission is to bring you down. Don't cooperate. Make it hard for them. In today's world, one must be careful without becoming fearful. As expressed in the above scripture (Mat 10:16), Jesus instructed His disciples long ago, "be wise as serpents, and harmless as doves."

Another relevant scripture is:

> Proverbs 22:3
> A prudent (wise) [man] **foreseeth the evil**, and **hideth himself**: but the simple (foolish) pass on, and are punished. (KJV)

The *New International Version Bible* helps us further understand the caution:

> Proverbs 22:3
> A prudent (wise) man **sees danger** and **takes refuge**, but the simple (foolish) keep going and suffer for it. (NIV)

We would prefer not to be counted among the foolish. Let's do what we can do to avoid the evil danger.

1. General Guidelines

Spiritual Oversight

When you are ministering, stay under authority and accountability. Please don't become an independent, "loose gun" prophetic counselor or RTF minister. Ensure that your spiritual oversight knows you and your ministry receiver. He must be in agreement with the theological understandings presented in *Restoring the Foundations*. Be convinced that he will pray for you, support you, and stand with you when the attacks come.

Ensure Clearance

Engage in RTF ministry only when the Lord says, "Yes." When you are asked by your Oversight Pastor and/or the Church Placement Committee (or whoever is responsible for placing ministry receivers with ministers), be sure the Lord has spoken to you. Continue to pray until you are sure, and the word from the Lord is "Yes," loud and clear. You are not supposed to be able to minister to everybody. If the Lord says, "No," refuse the request for ministry.

No "Parking Lot" RTF Ministry

Don't let people try to manipulate you into serious RTF ministry to them "on the side." Tell anyone who asks, "All requests for RTF ministry have to go through the placement office/committee. You can fill out an application and turn it in to them. They determine which teams see which people. If you want to request that we minister you, that will be fine." Of course, only make this last statement if it is true.

If the word gets out that you will "pray" for people "on the side" and significant fruit is coming from your ministry, you will be inundated with requests for "just a little prayer." Having a screening and placement office/committee is designed to protect you, the people receiving ministry, and the church.

Limitations

Know your skill level, training level, experience, and anointing. Know your limitations. Know the arena to which the Lord has called you. If you get in over your head, let your Oversight Pastor know immediately. Call for reinforcements. Ask for more intercessors. Bring in the "big guns" by having a supervisory team "sit in" to add their discernment and greater experience.

As a last resort (don't wait too long), inform the ministry receiver that you are not able to help him and that you need to refer him back to the Oversight Pastor/placement officecommittee. This should be done only after much prayer and after agreeing with the Oversight Pastor/ placement office/ committee that you should discontinue. If at all possible, have your Oversight Pastor with you when you inform the person about the referral. Be ready with another possible referral. Be careful not to blame the person. Lead up to this referral in an appropriate manner. You don't want the person to suffer more rejection wounds in your very own ministry room!

2. Stay Focused

Discipline

Try to stay "focused." The time allotted for the RTF ministry is limited. This is not a time for discipleship nor for prolonged Bible study, teaching, or preaching. Do what is needed to prepare the receiver effectively and then proceed directly into ministry. Don't consume your time talking needlessly. Be on guard, because most people have a tendency to "do" their "gifting" during RTF ministry. Stay focused.

Stay in Charge

Ensure that you have enough time available to do the ministry fully. If the person receiving ministry is late to the sessions, address this issue. If you have a person who talks too much or gets off on rabbit trails, take charge. These actions can be the enemy's decoy! He doesn't want your ministry receiver healed nor free.

3. Cautions in the Sexual Arena

Today's sexual climate in the USA has been fully exploited by Satan and his hordes to bring down Christian leaders. Most likely you can immediately think of more than one high-profile leader who has allowed himself to be deceived in this area and given Satan the opportunity to "take him out." None of us want to be among this group. We don't want to put ourselves or any RTF teams at unnecessary or foolish risk. There is no justification to do this. To put it very plainly: No crisis is so great, nor any emergency so immediate, that we should put ourselves or any ministry team into this kind of risk.

Full-time pastors and other ministers may have to violate the "rules" we are about to give you. But even in their case, they can and should take "extreme" precautions to minimize the risk.

Protection

We are totally convinced that team ministry is the most effective ministry approach for many reasons. Near the top of the list is the protection provided for the members of the team, particularly for husband-wife teams.

Healing/Deliverance ministry is an intimate activity. Emotions and feelings are expressed and often intense. Also, the person receiving ministry experiences listening and loving care for an extended period of time. In fact, it may be the most care and concern he/she has ever experienced. This combined with the presence of the Lord can cause a strong association of God's love with the RTF minister. It is not uncommon for the person to think that he/she has fallen in love with the minister, particularly if part of his wounding is lack of love and acceptance.

Because of this intensely intimate nature of the ministry relationship, we desire to provide safety for both the ministry team and the person receiving ministry. Our goal is to insure that everyone is protected. We want singles to be healed and strengthened, not led astray or leading a minister astray. We want married couples growing closer to **each other** as they minister in this intimate atmosphere. It is inappropriate, therefore, for a man and a woman not married to each other to minister together as a team. Likewise, it is inappropriate for one or two men to minister to a single lady, or vice versa. It is too emotional, too intense, too intimate. It is too risky. Don't do it!

Father/Mother Figures

One final consideration before we give you our rules. When there is a large difference in age between the ministry team and the person receiving ministry, this does provide a place for some grace. If you and your spouse are father/mother figures in the Body of Christ, and your ministry receiver needs spiritual fathering and mothering, then with caution provide this nurturing. This may be part of God's healing that you are to bring to that person. The key is to use wisdom. Don't open the door to any expectations on the person's part that you are not able nor called to fulfill.

With this background, dear fellow RTF minister, we give you the following rules. (This is the only place in our ministry where we are legalistic, but legalistic we are. We do not apologize for this.)

Rules

1. Never minister **with** a member of the opposite sex as your ministry team mate unless he/she is your spouse.
2. Never minister **to** a member of the opposite sex unless your spouse is with you as your team mate.
3. A male team or a female team may only minister to others of the same sex.
4. Never lay hands on the person receiving ministry without asking his/her permission first. Then, place your hands **only** where appropriate.
   - *Men:* Don't mess up a lady's hair. Place your hands on her shoulders. This is always safe. Also be careful about where you put your hands on another man. Be sensitive to the possibility of a feminine spirit issue. You don't want to "stir up" any spirits before it is the right time to deal with them. Again, shoulders are almost always safe for both sexes.

376

- *Women:* maintain some reserve with a man. Likewise, placing your hand on his shoulder is usually appropriate. As with the instructions for a man, be careful about putting your hands on another woman. We recommend you **not** place your hand(s) on another women's knee. Be sensitive to the possibility of the masculine spirit issue. Again, you don't want to "stir up" any spirits before it is the right time to deal with them. You do not want the person blocked from receiving ministry from you because she feels attracted to you.

4. High Risk Ministry

Friends and Family

In most situations, it is very unwise to minister to your relatives or your close friends. It is difficult, after one has been in a RTF ministry relationship (where there is an authority/ submission relationship), to change back to a normal peer, give-and-take relationship that friends and family should have. It can be done, but it takes a clear understanding on both sides of what is involved **before** beginning the ministry.

After completing the ministry, it takes a conscious agreement to re-establish the friendship and move out of the RTF ministry relationship. The hazard is that one couple remains the "authority" with the answers to the other's problems and the other couple/person continues to look to them for help. This could possibly create a co-dependent relationship with both sides losing good friends and/or relatives.

Cell/Care/Home Groups

It is also unwise to do in-depth RTF ministry in a cell or care group setting. It is one thing to pray for each other, but it is another to start digging into and exposing roots and hidden sin. Even if the person(s) gives his permission or asks for deeper ministry, it can go further than planned and bring up areas in his life that he does not want publicly exposed. RTF ministry should never be done in such a way that others can hear private, personal information. This principle applies even to a care group where everyone is close. In some cases, the other people in the group may draw back or even leave the group, if they feel they, too, may have to expose their "dirty laundry" someday. Intensive, public ministry in a cell or small group has been known to destroy the group.

5. The Real "No No's"

You probably think that we have already covered the most important issues. Maybe so, but here are some more very important considerations. (If you get mad at us for including any of these topics, we encourage you to take a serious look at what might be behind the anger. It is possible that there is more healing for you.)

a. Offenses

Don't take on the offenses of your ministry receiver. Remember, you are hearing just one side of the story! This is especially true when he is telling you everything that is wrong with his pastor, or he/she is telling you about his/her spouse!

Pastors

Almost everyone, even a loyal church member, has some offense with his pastor. This can be a trap that you definitely need to avoid. Keep in mind that God is probably using the pastor to bring to the surface areas that need to be dealt with in the person. Your job is to take advantage of what is stirred up and bring God's redemptive healing into it through forgiveness and release, "Waiting upon the Lord" Listening Prayer, and removing aggravating demons. Also explore what UGBs are being activated.

Even if the pastor has clearly been in the wrong, guard against becoming offended, being judgmental, or taking sides. It is okay to join with the person in praying for God's healing and freedom for the pastor, as long as it is a heartfelt desire for restoration on all sides and not a "Get him, God," type of prayer. If it is appropriate, help him decide whether he needs to go to his pastor with his offense. If he and the Holy Spirit are in agreement with this, then help him prepare for the meeting.

Spouses

Concerning the story you are hearing about the person's spouse, this is one case where there really are "two sides to the story." More than once, after interviewing a husband and wife, we have been convinced that they were married to someone else and not the other person we had interviewed. Their stories were completely different. Each spouse complained of being victimized or not being appreciated, or . . . , and it was all the other person's fault!

The extreme cases are almost always associated with strong occult forces accompanied by much deception, shame, control, and bitterness. It really does take the grace and discernment of the Holy Spirit to work through the maze of protective devices erected by the receiver and help him/her get free from the "snare of the fowler."[1]

b. Decisions

Don't make decisions for your ministry receiver. It's okay to help him explore his alternatives and insure that he being realistic regarding the possible outcome. Bring out what the Bible has to say on the subject, and help the person realize the possible consequences of his decision. But **never, never** take away from him **his** responsibility to live accountable before God and his fellow man. Help him pray and make his decision with the Holy Spirit's guidance. Help him ensure that God's peace is in the decision.

> Isa 55:12
> For ye shall go out with joy, and **be led forth with peace**: (KJV)

> Col 3:15
> **Let the peace of Christ rule in your hearts**, since as members of one body you were called to peace. And be thankful. (NIV)

---

[1] Please see Psa 91:3.

c. Money

In some situations, one of the problems facing the person may be lack of money. If you desire to help him and the Holy Spirit prompts you to do so, fine, but please, heed this caution.

First of all, don't "loan" him any money. Don't put him in the position of being obligated to you.[1] This will "muddy" your relationship with him. Either give him the money with no strings attached, or don't get involved with money at all.

Secondly, do your best to give the money in such a way that he doesn't know that you have done it. For example, give the money to the church's benevolence fund and have them pass it on to the person. If this won't work, get it to him in some other round-about way, such as leaving an envelope in his mailbox. Do your best not to foster any co-dependence or expectations of "more" in the future around the issue of money.

Thirdly, help him pray for Holy Spirit favor with employers, etc., and for creative ideas to turn his situation around. Your RTF ministry to him should begin to help him become more and more free from the financial curses, bondages, Ungodly Beliefs, and demons that have been holding him in lack. You should begin to hear some praise reports from him as God intervenes in his situation. You might refer him to Tim's testimony at the beginning of the Ungodly Belief Chapter for some inspiring reading.

d. Self-Disclosure

Be careful with self-disclosure, i.e., what you share out of the details of your life. Share only what would be edifying or pertinent to the person's greater understanding of his own problem. If God has brought you out of a similar problem, your testimony may provide hope to the person. The main guideline for self-disclosure is **not to glorify Satan** or the darkness of his kingdom but **to glorify God** and what He has done in your life. Don't disclose details of your life that might diminish the person's ability to receive God's freedom and healing through you.

e. Co-Dependence

Be careful not to develop a co-dependent relationship with your ministry receiver. It is fine to care about him, but it is unacceptable to need him to satisfy something in your own life or to somehow make him part of "your family." If you keep this up with person after person, you will soon have a very large and co-dependent family.

Co-dependence will cause you, at some point, to avoid RTF ministry because it has become "so hard and exhausting." With so many people to take care of, you will have to "drop out" as a RTF ministry team because your new "family" is taking all of your time.

---

[1] Please see Prov 22:7.

At the same time, the people you have "adopted" are not maturing in their Christian walk nor in their ability to wage their own spiritual warfare. They need you to "help" them. You have gotten in the way of the Holy Spirit's continuing sanctification and are interfering with God's process. Only negative consequences can come out of a co-dependent relationship with your ministry receiver. (Please check your "mad" scale to see if this is a sensitive area for you.)

f. Releasing the Person

We do have the responsibility to "carry" the person while we are ministering to him. We "stand in the gap" through intercession and by seeking the Lord for revelation that will help the person receive God's freedom and healing. We do this during the time he is under our covering receiving RTF ministry.

As we cautioned earlier, however, don't make decisions for the person nor try to live his life for him. You can't carry his pain nor shield him from dealing with the consequences of past failures, mistakes, and sin — nor, for that matter, future failures, mistakes, and sin.

When the ministry is completed, we strongly encourage you to "turn him over" to the Lord. That is, release him completely!

Sometimes it is even necessary to consciously do this after a RTF ministry session if it has been especially intense. Pray and cleanse the house or meeting room, and ask the Lord to be with the person, comforting and protecting as necessary.

Finally, please don't "carry" the person as a prayer "burden" once you have finished the ministry to him. Release him "completely" to the Lord. If possible, transfer him back to his cell/care group leader, or other spiritual oversight, for ongoing discipleship and prayer coverage.

It will be time for you to turn your intercessory anointing and heart toward the new person, bringing your specialized RTF training and equipping to bear on his issues. What special miracles and life transformations will God do this time?

B. Blessings

Talking to you about the blessings of RTF ministry falls into the same category as, "Let me tell you about my grandchildren." Innumerable blessings could be recited, but we will include the most frequent and permanent.

The blessing we experience repeatedly is the great joy of seeing "up close" God's gracious love and His deliverance. Those who minister healing and freedom are an extension of Christ's nature used in sanctifying His people. Sometimes we witness outstanding miracles (we see "normal" miracles as lives are transformed). Often, we stand in awe as it becomes obvious that He does know and does care about the intimate details of our lives! He knows what we need. We love seeing changed lives as the captives are set free. We delight in watching couples grow in intimacy, unity, and emotional closeness in their lives.

Another great blessing is the deep and abiding sense of fulfillment that comes from knowing that we, personally, are right where God wants us — in the center of His will. We are fulfilling His purpose for our lives. We also benefit personally as God continues to bring us healing at the same time we are His instruments to bring healing to others. In the RTF ministry, as in all other places, the Law of Sowing and Reaping is at work. We have reaped much healing. You, dear fellow RTF minister, will also reap much healing!

C. A Final Word

Thanks be to God for His indescribable gift,[1] the gift of His Son, and His eternal plan of restoration and healing. Thanks be to Him for the wonderful gifts of the Holy Spirit and the presence of the Spirit in the ministry sessions. Thanks be to Him for the great changes we have experienced and seen in the lives of others.

May God bless all who labor to bring freedom, healing, and deliverance to the members of the Body of Christ, establishing many overcoming Christians who are strong, effective warriors in the army of God and part of a bride that "hath made herself ready."

> Rev 19:7-9
> 7 Let us be glad and rejoice, and give honour to him: for the marriage of the Lamb is come, and **his wife hath made herself ready**.
> 8 And to her was granted that she should be arrayed in fine linen, clean and white: **for the fine linen is the righteousness of the saints**.
> 9 And he saith unto me, Write, Blessed (are) they which are called unto the marriage supper of the Lamb. And he saith unto me, These are the true sayings of God. (KJV)

---

[1] From 2 Cor 9:15, KJV.

Epilogue
Sandy's Story

"How is Sandy today?" you must be asking.

As we were finishing this book (first edition, 1996),[1] we contacted Sandy to ask if she would be willing to share with us (and you) how she is doing five years after going through Restoring the Foundations ministry. These are some excerpts from her letter.

> It would be untrue and even unkind to suggest that I am living a "Tinkerbelle existence," flying gaily through each day in a sort-of Christian fantasy land. No, Christ has called me to reality, and reality is not always easy. I have found that becoming who I am, and relating to God and others in a healthy way, is totally foreign to me. Every day I am learning how to do it "right." It isn't comfortable to go around without any makeup when I have worn a mask all my life. It isn't easy to simply let Christ clothe me when I have spent a lifetime sewing fig leaves to cover myself. And it doesn't always feel safe to walk around in the harsh world with no protection except that which the Lord has promised to provide as we need it.

Sandy is living in a world of God-centered reality rather than her old world of pretense and fantasy. She is quick to say that complete and lasting change is a slow process.

> Sometimes I feel as if the person I was is completely gone — not even any fingerprints left for identification. The challenge is to discover who I am in Christ. Each new step, each new challenge, is painfully difficult, like a child learning to walk. But it is also lovely to begin to discover who I really am.

Sandy talks about how difficult it has been to get totally rid of the old lies and enter into Christ's truth.

> In a recent, particularly hurtful situation, I found myself slipping back into the lie that controlled me for so long, that "I am so flawed that I am without hope." It's such an absurd lie for anyone to believe (even for a moment), especially for anyone who walks with such a continual realization of God's love and acceptance as I do now. I'm amazed at the powerful effect it had on me. On the other hand, having embraced this lie as "truth" for 50 years, isn't it incredible that I was able to see the deception so quickly and walk away from it? (I can almost hear a chorus singing in the background, "Oh Love, that will not let me go . . .")

---

[1] As we finish this second edition at the end of 2000, we are happy to report that Sandy continues to gain in peace and rest in the Lord. All of the past striving for recognition and control is gone. While she is grateful to do and to share as the Lord provides opportunities, she doesn't "need" to do anything but fellowship with Jesus. Many people envy (in a godly way, of course) her peace.

Throughout her ministry, Sandy was ardent about getting rid of all demonic influence, including those in the "Evil Core" and "Five Tower Stronghold."[1] At the same time, she shares the reality that deliverance has a challenging, "walking-it-out" aspect.

> While the demons have been forced to release their grip on my life, I was left to deal with a lifetime of patterns of behavior which **were** my life for so long. One cannot release such patterns instantly, nor without struggle. The old **is** passed away, but the new **must be entered into**. The old was deadly, but familiar; the new is life-giving, but unfamiliar. Daily I have been confronted with choices . . .

Sandy goes on to describe the tremendous extent to which her guilt and shame have been healed. She says that before her ministry,

> I never could go fast enough to outrun my shame, nor could I perform well enough to overcome my guilt.

Then she adds,

> While I do retain a sense of shame about what I became and for what I have done, I am no longer haunted by the **shame** that defined my life prior to my healing. I wanted to move to a new place and start a new life; instead, I have stayed in the same place and have a redeemed life.

> I have done all that I know to do based on the scripture to be reconciled to those I hurt. I can never forget the pain that my sin brought to them. I know the cost to my family and to the Body of Christ that my actions incurred, and I am forever available to be part of their restoration, whenever they desire my help. I know the boundless grace that is mine through Christ and I am confident that the One Who heals me is able to heal those I've offended. I trust Him with my life and with theirs.

Sandy writes that while she once struggled to "perform" in order to achieve perfection for approval (especially in ministry), God has released her from that struggle and even redefined the meaning of ministry. Although she now teaches weekly at the county jail, it is no longer a performance for her but rather a ministry from her heart. She writes,

> God has shown me that "Ministry" is running errands for my mother, seeing a movie with my granddaughter, or reading and eating popcorn with my husband in the evening, just as much as it is teaching Bible in the jail.

For the first time in her life, Sandy is free from the fear of not-being-accepted, i.e., **abandonment**. She has taken painting classes and is becoming a gifted painter.

> It's the first time I have wanted to do well but been unafraid for others to see my imperfection. It's a delight for me to paint, and my performance is irrelevant.

---

[1] Sandy's testimony about getting free from these strongholds is in the Uugodly Beliefs and Demonic Strongholds Chapters.

Sandy is a gracious person and very easy to love. Her deep appreciation for us and all that God did through us was tenderly expressed in her letter.

> The writers of this book, Chester and Betsy Kylstra, were sent to me in a most miraculous way. They were God's choice to be trustworthy instruments in His hands. Less tender hearts or loving spirits would have destroyed me. Conversely, their determined commitment to nothing less than complete deliverance for me was equally essential. God alone knows the depth of my gratitude to these beloved ones.

We want to close by sharing a few more powerful paragraphs from Sandy's letter.

> Out of the ashes beauty has emerged. Because my husband's love for God and commitment to His will was greater than his own pain, I have not had to walk alone. His love and forgiveness have enabled the Lord to use our marriage as the primary (ongoing) forum for my healing. Together, we are learning to lay down our lives for one another, thus enabling God to give us His life. Our children, my mother, and other family members have been selfless in their love and support of me. They suffered deeply because of my sin and have had to endure the pain of my disclosure. But, they have also been beneficiaries of the healing touch of Christ as He has extended it into their lives as well. Our family is restored and blessed, precious friends have remained in our lives, new ones have been added, and we are seeing foundations restored in other lives as God's healing touch continues to be extended.

> Since I was a child, the Word of God has been the one source of truth to which I have returned. Its power has been, and continues to be, a source of sustenance throughout the healing process. Through it, God gives direction, imparts hope, builds faith, and reveals the truth that sets me free. We can discover a lot about ourselves by the scriptures He sets before us. For as long as I can remember, He has brought Isaiah 30:15 to me. It says this:

> > In returning and rest is your salvation;
> > In quietness and trust is your strength.

> How hard it has been for me to walk in those words until now; they seemed difficult for me to even comprehend. Every time I read "rest" and "quietness" and "trust," my heart yearned to experience them. Such beautiful, wonderful words, but for me they were as unknowable as the stars. Today, they are a part of my life, and the reality with which I live. God has fulfilled His word to me.

> > > > Sandy
> > > > 1996

APPENDICES

A

RTF MINISTRY FORMS

The following ministry forms are presented here as examples that you may use in your Restoring the Foundations ministry. You may copy them "as is" or adjust them to suit your purposes. You are granted permission to use them for your own use but not to sell or incorporate them into another publication. We hope that these forms will be a blessing for you.

Forms in this Appendix

1. Application Form for RTF Ministry
2. Ministry Notes Form
3. Ministry Card
4. Lead Team Summary Report

Application for Restoring the Foundations Ministry

_____ Church

DESCRIPTION OF RESTORING THE FOUNDATIONS MINISTRY

The _____ Church Restoring the Foundations (RTF) ministry is for people needing short term help, generally five to six ministry sessions. Ministry sessions are normally scheduled once a week, and are approximately three hours duration. The RTF ministry team may at times be assisted by an intercessory prayer team or by a supervisory team.

The RTF ministry teams are an extension of the pastoral ministry, and as such, are submitted to the pastoral authority of the church. In order to better serve you, it is possible that the ministry team may consult with the Church Pastor(s) and/or their designated representative(s) (i.e., the oversight minister and/or supervisory ministers) concerning their ministry to you.

Please read the following statements, and sign that you acknowledge and understand your commitment and your ministry team's commitment. Please complete these forms and return them to the Church office as soon as possible.

PERSONAL INFORMATION

Name: _____ Address: _____

City/State/Zip: _____ Home Phone: _____

Date of Birth: _____ Age: _____ Male: ___ Female: ___ SS#: _____

Marital Status: Single ___ Married ___ Separated ___ Divorced ___ Widowed ___ Remarried ___

Presently living with: Parents ___ Spouse ___ Alone ___ Other _____

Occupation: _____ Hours worked/week: _____ EMail Address: _____

Employed by: _____ Work Phone: _____

Your Personal Purpose in Life: _____

_____

PURPOSE FOR SEEKING RESTORING THE FOUNDATIONS MINISTRY

_____

_____

EXPECTATIONS OF YOUR COMMITMENT

Your RTF ministry team will be making a major commitment to you; first as they schedule their time to be available to you, and also as they pray, prepare, and then minister to you. Likewise, it is expected that you will be committed to obtaining the maximum benefit possible from your ministry time. You can facilitate this by being on time to ministry sessions and by completing "homework" assignments given to you. Most of all, it is expected that you will have a sincere desire to overcome whatever problems are hindering you, and that you will cooperate fully with your RTF ministry team and with the Holy Spirit in order to maximize your receiving God's help.

We ask you, by your signature, to commit to one month of serious prayer and Bible time following the completion of your ministry. This would include one hour per day (at least five days per week) devoted to prayer and Bible reading. This hour should include at least fifteen minutes of prayer and meditation on your new Godly Beliefs (GBs).

We also ask you to call your ministry team two and four weeks after your ministry, to report your progress, to be accountable as you meditate on your GBs, and to obtain any needed prayer and support.

REFERRAL

Either before you come for ministry, or after the completion of your ministry, your RTF ministry team, in conjunction with the Pastor(s) and/or their designated representative(s), will assist you in planning for on-going support and accountability in situations where it could be beneficial to you.

Also, if your RTF ministry team is not equipped or able to minister to your particular need, or if you need longer term ministry, they, in conjunction with the Pastor(s) and/or their designated representative(s), will help you find appropriate referral resources.

WAIVER OF LIABILITY

I understand that I will be seeing RTF ministers who will be able to listen, support, encourage, pray with, and minister to me to help me overcome my problem(s) and to grow in my Christian life. I accept that they are not licensed counselors, that they minister by the Christian Bible, and that they may or may not be ordained and/or full-time ministers, pastors or counselors. **I acknowledge that all ministry is under the direction and control of the Holy Spirit, and that no guarantees are made, nor can be made, by anyone or any organization that I will or will not receive any particular healing.** Thus I waive all rights to claims of liability. I accept that they may recommend further ministry for me by a pastor, counselor, home ministry group, support group, and/or other agency in my community.

WAIVER OF CONFIDENTIALITY

I am aware that all statements that I shall make to my RTF ministers are of a confidential nature, including all written information, and that legally and ethically these may not be disclosed without my written consent. **However, I waive my right to "complete" confidentiality in the following situations:**

1. I accept that my ministry team will give a brief summary report of the results of the ministry to the Church Pastor(s), and/or the oversight team.
2. I accept that my ministry team may consult with the Church Pastor(s), oversight ministry team, and/or their designated representatives, concerning their ministry to me.
3. I accept that my home/cell ministry leaders may be informed of some aspects of the ministry to me, to better equip them to help me after the prayer ministry.
4. I accept that the Church Pastor(s), and/or their designed representative(s), will be informed of any ongoing, willful sin in which I am involved.
5. I accept and acknowledge that pastors, counselors, Restoring the Foundations Ministers, or any other persons involved in working with adults and children in a helping setting, are either encouraged or required by law to disclose to the appropriate person, agency, or civil authority, any harm or potential harm that a person may attempt or desire to do to himself or to others.
6. I accept and acknowledge that they are also required to report any reasonable suspicion of physical or sexual abuse that has been done, or that is being done to a minor child.
7. I accept that all pastors, counselors, and RTF ministers at _____ Church , reserve the right to make such reports as mandated by law, whether or not they confer with me first.

By my signature I acknowledge that I have read and understand all of the above provisions, including the Waiver of Liability and Waiver of Confidentiality, and that I accept the stated conditions and limits of liability and confidentiality. Further, I agree to the "Expectations of Your Commitment," including the post-ministry prayer, Bible reading, meditation for at least 30 days on my Godly Beliefs, and the two and four week progress report.

Signature: _____ Date: _____

Printed Name: _____

Name: _____

Background Information

_____ Church

The following information, which will become a part of your confidential file, will help your RTF ministry team focus more clearly on the areas in which you need and/or desire ministry. Please fill these forms out as honestly and as completely as you can, and return them to the Church office.

FAMILY BACKGROUND

Natural Parents: Married ___ Separated ___ Divorced ___

Rate your parent's marriage: Unhappy ___ Average ___ Happy ___ Very Happy ___

If separated or divorced, how old were you at the time of the divorce? _____

Father remarried when you were age _____. Mother remarried when you were age _____.

You lived with: Mother ___ Father ___ Foster ___ Other Family Member ___

Step-Parents (if applicable): Married ___ Separated ___ Divorced ___

What kind of relationship did/do you have with your parents and/or step-parent(s)?

_____

Father deceased? Yes ___ No ___ How old were you at the time? _____

Mother deceased? Yes ___ No ___ How old were you at the time? _____

EDUCATIONAL BACKGROUND

Circle last year of school completed:

Grade school 1 2 3 4 5 6 7 8   High school 9 10 11 12   College 1 2 3 4 5 6 +

Degrees in? _____

MARITAL BACKGROUND

Name of spouse: _____ Occupation: _____

Is your spouse willing to participate in ministry? Yes ___ No ___ Uncertain ___

Have you ever been separated? Yes ___ No ___ When? _____

Marriage(s): Please give the following information for your marriage(s).

Date Married	Your Age	Their Age	Name of Spouse	Duration	Reason that it Ended

Children: Please give the following information about each of your children.

Name	Age	Sex	From Which Marriage?	Self-Supporting?	Married?	Still Alive?	Age at and Cause of Death

MEDICAL/MINISTRY/COUNSELING BACKGROUND

Describe any physical problems or handicaps that require medication or physical care:

Are you currently receiving medical treatment? Yes ___ No ___ For what purpose?

_____

_____

Have you used drugs for other than medical purposes? Yes ___ No ___

What drugs? _____ When? _____

Have you ever been in counseling/therapy/mental health care? Yes ___ No ___

When? _____ With whom? _____

For what reason? _____

Have you ever taken medication prescribed for emotional reasons? Yes ___ No ___

When? _____ For what reason? _____

Are you currently taking medication prescribed for emotional reasons? Yes ___ No ___

What medication? _____

If the ministry team feels that it would be best for you to have a physical before ministry, would you be willing to do so? Yes ___ No ___

SPIRITUAL/RELIGIOUS BACKGROUND

Have you made a commitment to Jesus Christ as Lord and Savior? Yes ___ No ___ When? _____

Please tell what happened: _____

_____

_____

_____

Have you received the Baptism of the Holy Spirit? Yes ___ No ___ When? _____

Has that experience been accompanied by the evidence of speaking in tongues? Yes ___ No ___

Describe your present relationship with the Lord: _____

_____

_____

Please list all church affiliations: _____

_____

_____

WHAT HAS PROMPTED YOU TO SEEK MINISTRY AT THIS TIME?

	Started?		Started?		Started?
Abuse		Fear/Phobia		Self-Esteem/Perfectionism	
Addiction/Compulsion		Financial/Legal		Sexual issues/Incest	
Anger/Aggression		Grief/Loss		Spiritual concerns/Values	
Church Split		Parental/Family/Child		Stress/Anxiety	
Depression/Suicide		Premarital/Marital		Trauma	
Divorce/Separation		Relationship/Loneliness		Vocational/Educational	

Please comment: _____

_____

_____

Name: _____

Generational Patterns Questionnaire
_____ Church

PURPOSE

The purpose of this questionnaire is to help you and your RTF ministry team identify Sins of the Fathers and Resulting Curses and negative patterns that may be hindering you, as well as identify those areas in your heritage or in your life that lead to Ungodly Beliefs and/or Soul/Spirit Hurts, and/or that may be openings for Demonic Oppression. Please fill these forms out as honestly and as completely as you can, and return them to the Church office.

GENERAL QUESTIONS

From what country or countries did your ancestors originally come? _____

What are the prominent ethnic backgrounds of your ancestors? _____

What are the church backgrounds of your ancestors? _____

In what geographic areas within America have they primarily lived their lives? _____

Is it possible that they were connected with slavery, i.e., either owners, traders, or slaves? _____

Is it possible that they were involved in unfair business practices? _____

Is it possible that they were involved in the occult? _____

On a scale of 1 to 10, indicate how much each parent loved you. Give examples of how they showed their love.

_____

_____

_____

_____

_____

_____

Who in your life has caused you the most pain or disappointment? Give an example of how it happened.

_____

_____

_____

_____

_____

List the main issues in your life that you and God are working on at this time.

_____

_____

_____

_____

_____

FAMILY TREE FACTS

To help us with your ancestors, please fill in the requested information for each of your two parents (F/M), your four grandparents (GF/GM), and your eight great grandparents (GGF/GGM), to the best of your knowledge.

FATHER'S FAMILY

Example:
Name _____
DOB   DOD   Age
# of Children _____
Occupation _____
Cause of Death _____

GGF _____
_____
_____

GF _____
_____
_____
_____

GGM _____
_____
_____

F _____
_____
_____
_____
_____

GGF _____
_____
_____

GM _____
_____
_____
_____

GGM _____
_____
_____

Names of Siblings/Age
_____
_____
_____
_____
_____
_____

MOTHER'S FAMILY

GGF _____
_____
_____

GF _____
_____
_____
_____

GGM _____
_____
_____

M _____
_____
_____
_____

GGF _____
_____
_____

GM _____
_____
_____
_____

GGM _____
_____
_____

FAMILY PATTERNS (Please check if common in your immediate or extended family.)

(**Note:** Your extended family includes aunts, uncles, and cousins.)

___ Lack of communication between spouses
___ Lack of intimacy (in marriage, other)
___ Men dominant over women
___ Women dominant over men
___ Men/women workaholics
___ Success/failure cycles
___ Deceptive business practices
___ Family secrets
___ Business, financial, or other losses
___ Broken promises (in relationships/finances)
___ Unfilled lives and/or destinies
___ Abuse: _____
___ Addiction: _____
___ Co-dependency
___ _____
___ _____

___ Lack of communication between parents/children
___ Children favored, idolized
___ Children not valued, neglected
___ Children taking care of parents
___ Children dishonoring parents
___ Sibling rivalry, fights, feuds
___ Broken marriages/divorce
___ Pride and arrogance
___ Idolatry of _____
___ Chronic illness/sickness
___ Premature deaths
___ Most received salvation
___ Most were not saved
___ _____
___ _____

OPEN DOORS (Gen 4:7)

Please put a check under the **A** (Ancestors) category if you know about, or have observed, any of these characteristics, events, or involvement, in your immediate or extended family. If any of these is (or was) also true for you, put a "**C**" for current or a "**P**" for past in the **S** (Self) category.

A S

ABANDONMENT
Abdication
Blocked Intimacy
Desertion
Divorce
Isolation
Loneliness
Neglect
Rejection
Separation
Self-Pity
Victimization

REJECTION
Expected Rejection
Perceived Rejection
Self-Rejection
FINANCES
Bankruptcy
Cheating
Covetousness
Debt
Deception
Delinquency
Dishonesty
Failure
Greed
Idolatry of Possessions
Irresponsible Spending
Job Failures
Job Losses
Lack
Neglect
Poverty
Robbery
Robbing God (not Tithing)
Stealing
Stinginess

A S

RELIGION
Antichrist
Betrayal
Denominationalism
Division
Hypocrisy
Injustice
Legalism
Liberalism
New Age Practices
Religiosity
Rules, Excessive
Spiritual Pride
Traditionalism
Unforgiveness

PERFORMANCE
Competition
Driving
Envy
Jealousy
People Pleasing
Perfectionism
Possessiveness
Rivalry
Striving
Workaholism

ANXIETY
Burden
False Responsibility
Fatigue
Heaviness
Nervousness
Restlessness
Weariness
Worry

A S

DECEPTION
Blindness
Cheating/Stealing
Confusion
Denial
Fraudulence
Infidelity
Lying
Secretiveness
Self-Deception
Treachery
Treason
Trickery
Untrustworthiness

MENTAL PROBLEMS
Craziness
Compulsions
Confusion
Distraction
Forgetfulness
Hallucinations
Hysteria
Insanity
Mind Binding
Mind Blocking
Paranoia
Mind Racing
Schizophrenia
Senility

OPEN DOORS (Gen 4:7) *(Continued)*

UNBELIEF
- Apprehension
- Double-Mindedness
- Doubt
- Fear of being Wrong
- Mind Blocking
- Mistrust
- Rationalism
- Skepticism
- Suspicion
- Uncertainty

MOCKING
- Blaspheming
- Cursing
- Laughing
- Profanity
- Ridicule
- Sarcasm
- Scorn

ADDICTIONS/ DEPENDENCIES/ ESCAPE
- Cocaine
- Downers/Uppers
- Marijuana
- Non-Prescription Drugs
- Prescription Drugs
- Street Drugs
- Tranquilizers

- Alcohol
- Caffeine
- Cigarettes
- Computers
- Food
- Gambling
- Internet
- Pornography
- Overspending
- Sex
- Sports
- Television
- Video Games

ESCAPE
- Daydreaming
- Fantasy
- Forgetfulness
- Hopelessness
- Isolation
- Laziness
- Passivity
- Procrastination
- Sleep/Slumber/Oversleeping
- Trance
- Withdrawal

UNMOTIVATED
- Irresponsibility
- Laziness
- Procrastination
- Undisciplined

PRIDE
- Arrogance
- Conceit
- Controlling
- Egotistical
- Haughtiness
- Leviathan
- Prejudice
- Self-Centeredness
- Self-Importance
- Vanity

REBELLION
- Contempt
- Deception
- Defiance
- Disobedience
- Independence
- Insubordination
- Resistance
- Self-Sufficiency
- Self-Will
- Stubbornness
- Undermining

ANGER
- Abandonment
- Feuding
- Frustration
- Hatred
- Hostility
- Murder
- Punishment
- Rage
- Resentment
- Retaliation
- Revenge
- Spoiled Little Boy/Girl
- Temper Tantrums
- Violence

BITTERNESS
- Accusation
- Blaming
- Complaining
- Condemnation
- Criticalness
- Gossip
- Judging
- Murmuring
- Ridicule
- Slander
- Unforgiveness

VIOLENCE
- Abuse
- Arguing
- Bickering
- Cruelty
- Cursing
- Death
- Destruction
- Feuding
- Hate
- Mocking
- Murder/Abortion
- Retaliation
- Strife
- Torture/Mutilation

DEPRESSION
- Dejection
- Discouragement
- Despair
- Despondency
- Gloominess
- Hopelessness
- Insomnia
- Misery
- Oversleeping
- Sadness
- Self-Pity
- Suicide Attempt
- Suicide Fantasies
- Withdrawal

TRAUMA
- Abuse, Emotional
- Abuse, Physical
- Abuse, Mental
- Abuse, Sexual
- Abuse, Spiritual
- Abuse, Verbal
- Accident
- Loss
- Imprisoned
- Rape
- Torture
- Violence

GRIEF
- Agony
- Anguish
- Crying
- Despair
- Heartbreak
- Loss
- Pain
- Sadness
- Sorrow
- Torment
- Weeping

SHAME
- Abandonment
- Anger
- Bad Boy/Girl
- Condemnation
- Defilement
- Different
- Disgrace
- Embarrassment
- Guilt
- Hatred
- Inferiority
- Illegitimacy
- Occult Involvment
- Self-Accusation
- Self-Hate
- Self-Pity

UNWORTHINESS
- Inadequacy
- Inferiority
- Insecurity
- Self-Accusation
- Self-Condemnation
- Self-Hate
- Self-Punishment

VICTIM
- Appeasement
- Betrayal
- Deportation
- Entrapped
- Helplessness
- Hopelessness
- Mistrust
- Passivity
- Self-Pity
- Suspicion
- Trauma
- Unfaithfulness

FAILURE
- Boom/Bust Cycle
- Defeat
- Loss
- Performance
- Pressure to Succeed
- Striving

OCCULT INDICATORS/OCCULT OPEN DOORS (Gen 4:7) *(Continued)*

A S　　　　　　　　　　　　**A S**　　　　　　　　　　　　**A S**

INFIRMITIES/DISEASE
- Accidents (falls, cars, etc.)
- Anorexia/Bulimia
- Arthritis
- Asthma
- Barrenness/Miscarriage
- Bone/Joint Problems
- Cancer
- Congestion/in lungs
- Diabetes
- Fatigue
- Female Problems
- Heart/Circulatory Problems
- Lung Problems
- Mental Illness
- MS
- Migraines/Mind Binding
- Physical Abnormalities
- Premature Death
- _____
- _____

CONTROL
- Appeasement
- Denial
- Domineering
- Double Binding
- Enabling
- False Responsibility
- Female Control
- Jealousy
- Manipulation
- Male Control
- Occult Control/Jezebel
- Passive Aggression
- Passivity/Ahab
- Possessiveness
- Pride (I know best)
- Witchcraft
- _____
- _____
- _____

FEARS
- Anxiety
- Bewilderment
- Burden
- Dread
- Harassment
- Heaviness
- Horror Movies
- Intimidation
- Mental Torment
- Over-Sensitivity
- Paranoia
- Phobia
- Superstition
- Worry
- Fear of Authorities
- Fear of being Abused
- Fear of being Attacked
- Fear of being Wrong
- Fear of being a Victim
- Fear of Cancer
- Fear of Death
- Fear of Diabetes
- Fear of Demons
- Fear of Exposure
- Fear of Failure
- Fear of Heart Attack
- Fear of Inadequacy
- Fear of Infirmities
- Fear of Loss
- Fear of Man
- Fear of Performing
- Fear of Poverty
- Fear of Public Singing
- Fear of Punishment
- Fear of Rejection
- Fear of Sexual Inadequacy
- Fear of Sexual Perversion
- Fear of Success
- Fear of Violence
- _____
- _____
- _____

SEXUAL SINS
- Abortion
- Adultery
- Bestiality
- Demonic Sex
- Defilement/Uncleanness
- Exposure
- Fantasy Lust
- Fornication
- Frigidity
- Homosexuality
- Illegitimacy
- Incest
- Incubus
- Lesbianism
- Lust/Fantasy Lust
- Masturbation
- Pornography
- Premarital Sex
- Prostitution/Harlotry
- Rape
- Seduction/Alluring
- Sexual Abuse
- Succubus
- _____
- _____
- _____
- _____
- _____
- _____
- _____
- _____
- _____
- _____
- _____
- _____
- _____
- _____

OCCULT
- Abortion (Molech)
- Accident Proneness
- Ahab
- Animal Spirits
- Antichrist
- Astral Projection
- Astrology
- Automatic Writing
- Behemoth
- Black Magic
- Books, Occult/Witchcraft
- Clairvoyance
- Conjuration
- Control, Occult/Witchcraft
- Crystal Ball
- Death, Suicide
- Demons, Dispatching
- Demon Worship
- Divination
- Eight Ball
- Evil Eye
- ESP
- False Gifts (Occult)
- Fortune Telling

- Handwriting Analysis
- Hexing
- Horoscopes
- Hypnosis
- I Ching
- Idolatry (of _____)
- Incantations
- Jezebel
- Levitation
- Leviathan
- Mediumship
- Mental Telepathy
- Necromancy
- Non-Christian Exorcism
- Ouija Board
- Palm Reading
- Past Life Readings
- Pendulum Readings
- Psychic Readings
- Psychic Healing
- Python
- Reincarnation

- Satanic Worship
- Seances
- Slavery, Occult
- Sorcery
- Spells
- Spirit Guide(s)
- Spiritism
- Superstition
- Table Tipping
- Tarot Cards
- Tea Leaves, Reading
- Third Eye, Using
- Trance
- TM
- Vampire
- Victim, Occult
- Voodoo
- Water Witching
- Werewolf
- White Magic
- Wicca
- Witchcraft
- Meditation, Eastern

ACTIVITIES/INVOLVEMENT OPEN DOORS (Gen 4:7) *(Continued)*

HAVE YOU EVER:	ANCESTORS INCLUDE:	HAVE IDOLATRY OF:
Cast a Spell/Hex	Africans	Appearance
Drunk Blood or Urine	American Indians	Beauty
Had Hard Rock Music	Asians	Children
Had Heavy Metal Music	Europeans	Clothes
Had Masonic Jewelry	Germans	Food
Had Occult Jewelry	Gypsies	Ministry
Had Occult/Witchcraft Books	Latin America	Occupation
Had Pagan Fetishes	South Pacific	Position
Had Punk Rock Music		Possessions
Had Violent Rap Music		Power
Heard Voices on the "Inside"		Social Status
Heard a Voice, "Kill Yourself!"		Sports
Joined a Coven		Spouse
Played Dungeons & Dragons		Wealth
Made a Blood Pact		
Made a Bloody Oath or Vow		
Participated in Martial Arts		
Seen a Sacrifice		
Seen Demons		
Seen Horror Movies		
Seen Science Fantasy Movies		
Selected a Guru		
Used Mantras		
Visited Pagan Temples		
Visited Indian Burial Grounds		

FAMILY INVOLVEMENT IN:
SECRET SOCIETIES, CULTS, FALSE RELIGIONS, OCCULT AND MIND CONTROL ORGANIZATIONS

(The following are examples of groups which omit the foundations of the Christian Faith, such as the Trinity, the Atonement, the Blood of Jesus, or the Divinity of Jesus.)

Armstrong/Radio Church of God	Inner Peace Movement	Scientology
Bahai	Islam	Shamanism
Buddhism	Jehovah's Witnesses	Shintoism
Buffaloes	Job's Daughters Lodge	Shriners
Christadelphians	Kabbala	Silva Mind Control
Christian Science	KKK	Spiritualism
College Fraternities	Knights of Columbus Lodge	Swedenborgianism
College Sororities	Masonic	Knights Templars
Daughter's of the Nile	Moonies	The Way International
De Molay Lodge	Moose Lodge	(Renamed the Christian
Druids Lodge	Mormonism	Educational Society)
Eastern Religions	New Age Movement	Theosophy
Eastern Star Lodge	Odd Fellows Lodge	Unitarian Church
Edgar Cayce	Orange Lodge	Voodoo
Elks Lodge	Rainbow Girls Lodge	Wicca
Freemasonry	Rebekahs Lodge	White Shrine
Hare Krishna	Religious Science	Witchcraft
Hinduism	Rosacrucianism	
Indian Occult Rituals	Santeria	
	Satanism	

Ungodly Beliefs About Myself

Read the following UGBs, check the ones that you relate to, or agree with. Ask the Holy Spirit to show you other UGBs that you may have. (By the way, all of us have Ungodly Beliefs! ☺)

Theme: Rejection, Not Belonging

____ 1. I don't belong. I will always be on the outside (left out).
____ 2. My feelings don't count. No one cares what I feel.
____ 3. No one will love me or care about me just for myself.
____ 4. I will always be lonely. The special man (woman) in my life will not be there for me.
____ 5. The best way to avoid more hurt, rejection, etc., is to isolate myself.
____ 6. _____

Theme: Unworthiness, Guilt, Shame

____ 1. I am not worthy to receive anything from God.
____ 2. I am the problem. When something is wrong, it is my fault.
____ 3. I am a bad person. If you knew the real me, you would reject me.
____ 4. I must wear a mask so that people won't find out how horrible I am and reject me.
____ 5. I have messed up so badly that I have missed God's best for me.
____ 6. _____

Theme: Doing to achieve Self-Worth, Value, Recognition

____ 1. I will never get credit for what I do.
____ 2. My value is in what I do. I am valuable because I do good to others, because I am "successful".
____ 3. Even when I do/give my best, it is not good enough. I can never meet the standard.
____ 4. I can avoid conflict that would risk losing others' approval by being passive.
____ 5. God doesn't care if I have a "secret life," as long as I appear to be good.
____ 6. _____

Theme: Control (to avoid hurt)

____ 1. I have to plan every day of my life. I have to continually plan/strategize. I can't relax.
____ 2. The perfect life is one in which no conflict is allowed, and so there is peace.
____ 3. _____

Theme: Physical

____ 1. I am unattractive. God shortchanged me.
____ 2. I am doomed to have certain physical disabilities. They are just part of what I have inherited.
____ 3. It is impossible to lose weight (or gain weight). I am just stuck.
____ 4. I am not competent/complete as a man (woman).
____ 5. _____

Theme: Personality Traits

____ 1. I will always be _____ (angry, shy, jealous, insecure, fearful, etc.).
____ 2. _____

Theme: Identity

____ 1. I should have been a boy (girl). Then my parents would have valued/loved me more, . . . etc.
____ 2. Men (women) have it better.
____ 3. I will never be known or appreciated for my real self.
____ 4. I will never really change and be as God wants me to be.
____ 5. _____

Theme: Miscellaneous

____ 1. I have wasted a lot of time and energy, some of my best years.
____ 2. Turmoil is normal for me.

Ungodly Beliefs About Others

Theme: Safety/Protection

____ 1. I must be very guarded about what I say, since anything I say may be used against me.

____ 2. I have to guard and hide my emotions and feelings. I cannot give anyone the satisfaction of knowing that they have wounded or hurt me. I'll not be vulnerable, humiliated, or shamed.

____ 3. _____

____ 4. _____

Theme: Retaliation

____ 1. The correct way to respond if someone offends me is to punish them by withdrawing and/or cutting them off.

____ 2. I will make sure that _____ hurts as much as I hurt!

____ 3. _____

Theme: Victim

____ 1. Authority figures will humiliate me and violate me.

____ 2. Authority figures will just use and abuse me.

____ 3. My value is based totally on others' judgment/perception about me.

____ 4. I am completely under other people's authority. I have no will or choice of my own.

____ 5. I will not be known, understood, loved, or appreciated for who I am by those close to me.

____ 6. _____

____ 7. _____

Theme: Hopelessness/Helplessness

____ 1. I am out there all alone. If I get into trouble or need help, there is no one to rescue me.

____ 2. _____

____ 3. _____

Theme: Defective in Relationships

____ 1. I will never be able to fully give or receive love. I don't know what it is.

____ 2. If I let anyone get close to me, I may get my heart broken again. I can't let myself risk it.

____ 3. If I fail to please you, I won't receive your pleasure and acceptance of me. Therefore, I must strive even more (perfectionism). I must do whatever is necessary to try to please you.

____ 4. _____

____ 5. _____

Theme: God

____ 1. God loves other people more than He loves me.

____ 2. God only values me for what I do. My life is just a means to an end.

____ 3. No matter how much I try, I'll never be able to do enough or do it well enough to please God.

____ 4. God is judging me when I relax. I have to stay busy about His work or He will punish me.

____ 5. God has let me down before. He may do it again. I can't trust Him, or feel secure with Him.

____ 6. _____

____ 7. _____

PRAYER MINISTRY NOTES

Page ___ of ___

Name: _____   Location: _____

Date: _____   Session #: _____

Forgiveness(**O, G, S**)
|Sins of the Fathers
__|**Self**-Sins
___|Curses (**G, O, S**)
____|Ungodly Beliefs
_____|Affirmation/Declaration/Renounce
_____|Pouring Out Complaint
_____|Soul/Spirit Hurt
_____|Deliverance
_____|**O**ther

F	S	S	C	U	A	P	S	D	O	
F	S	S	C	U	A	P	S	D	O	
F	S	S	C	U	A	P	S	D	O	
F	S	S	C	U	A	P	S	D	O	
F	S	S	C	U	A	P	S	D	O	

Ministry Card

The detailed Ministry Steps for each of the four Problem/Ministry Areas are presented at the end of each Problem/Ministry Area chapter. Please refer to these chapters for an "in-depth" study of how to minister to each of these areas. The Ministry Card contains a summary of the most important steps.

This page contains a copy of the "inside" of the Ministry Card.[1] We give this Card to the person receiving ministry, to help him know what we (and God) are expecting of him. We encourage him to keep, and to continue to use the card.

<u>Sins of the Fathers & Resulting Curses</u>	<u>Soul/Spirit Hurts</u>
1. I *confess* the sin of my ancestors, my parents, and my own sin, of _____. 2. I choose to *forgive* and *release* them; for the sin, the curses, and the consequences in my life. (Be specific.) 3. I ask You to *forgive* me, Lord, for this sin; for yielding to it, and to the resulting curses. I *receive* Your forgiveness. 4. On the basis of Your forgiveness, Lord, I choose to *forgive* myself for involvement in this sin. 5. I *renounce* the sin and curses of _____. I *break* this power from my life, and from the lives of my descendants, through the redemptive work of Christ on the Cross. 6. I *receive* God's freedom from this sin and from the resulting curses. I *receive* _____.	1. I *Ask* You Holy Spirit to reveal the hurt You want to heal. (*Listen/watch* as He tells/shows it to you.) 2. I choose to *pour out* my heart, to *express* my hurt and frustration, my pain, fear, or anger. (Be honest with God about how you feel.) 3. (Take care of any hindrances. I.e., unforgiveness, repentance, demonic interference, etc.) 4. (Listen to the Holy Spirit and/or interact with Jesus about your hurt.) 5. I *receive* Your healing touch. (*Listen/watch* as He brings His healing. Allow the Holy Spirit and/or Jesus ample time to minister to you.) 6. I **break** my agreement with any and all of the UGBs (lies) found in this hurt.
<u>Ungodly Beliefs</u>	<u>Demonic Oppression</u>
1. I *confess* my sin ((if appropriate) and my ancestor's sin) of believing the lie that _____. 2. I *forgive* those who contributed to my forming this UGB. (Be specific.) 3. I ask You, Lord, to *forgive* me for receiving this UGB, for living my life based on it, and for any way I have judged others because of it. I *receive* Your forgiveness. 4. On the basis of Your forgiveness, Lord, I choose to *forgive* myself for believing this lie. 5. I *renounce* and **break** my agreement with this UGB. I **break** my agreement with the power of darkness. I *cancel* all agreements with demons. 6. I choose to *accept*, *believe*, and *receive* the GB that _____.	1. (Include the following steps if not yet accomplished:) • I *confess* my sin of _____ and *forgive* all who may have influenced me to sin. • I *repent* for giving place to demons of _____. • I *forgive* myself for the pain and limitations I have allowed the demons to inflict upon me. 2. In the Name of Jesus, I *renounce* and **break** all agreements with the demons (stronghold) of _____, including all associated demons of ____, _____, etc. 3. I take *authority* over the demons (stronghold) of _____ and *command* you to leave me now based on the finished work of Christ on the Cross.

[1] If you are interested in obtaining copies of this Ministry Card, you may call **Proclaiming His Word Ministries (877-214-8076)** for additional information. They are printed on beautiful, heavy card stock, for long duration use.

LEAD TEAM SUMMARY REPORT
RESTORING THE FOUNDATIONS MINISTRY
_____ CHURCH

RTF Ministers: _____ Date: _____

Intercessors: _____

Dates seen: _____ Total hours: _____

Person receiving ministry: _____

Reasons for seeking ministry: _____

_____

_____

_____

RTF Minister's Report:

Major problems: _____

_____

_____

_____

Areas receiving ministry: _____

_____

_____

_____

_____

_____

_____

_____

Comments/Referral/Consultation? _____

_____

_____

_____

B

WHY NAMED "SOUL/SPIRIT" HURTS

Introduction

Why use the phrase "Soul/Spirit" Hurts for the Problem/Ministry Area having to do with wounds to our "inner" man (or woman)? Why not use one of the more well-known phrases, such as inner healing, healing of memories, soul healing, emotional healing, healing damaged emotions, etc.?

We have two reasons for the use of the term "Soul/Spirit." One reason is more for "fun," the other one is more serious.

The first reason comes out of the wounds in our own backgrounds. We both grew up wanting to "keep the peace" and not get involved in conflict and controversies. So one day we said (to each other), "If we use a phrase that no one knows, maybe we can avoid controversy about whether what we are doing is valid or needed and whether we are 'doing it right.' Maybe we can pray for someone, and he'll be healed before he gets a chance to think about arguing with us!" We are happy to report that this tactic has worked well for us.

The second reason comes out of the general lack of knowledge about the "non-physical" part of man and about what "part" of man actually does need healing.

The Inner Makeup of Man

The real reason for using the phrase "Soul/Spirit" comes from the fact that we don't know that much about the "inner" invisible part(s) of the human being — what we refer to as the soul and spirit of man.

Do we "really" know the inner makeup of man?

We can read how God created man in Genesis 1 and 2. From this we know that we are made in the image of God, that He fashioned our bodies from the dust of the earth, that He breathed His Breath into our father Adam, and that he and we become a "living soul."[1] Beyond this, most of us have not done much study on the inner (i.e., non-physical) makeup of man.

---

[1] Please see Gen 2:7.

407

Some years ago, there was a period of time during which Dennis and Rita Bennett, along with other teachers, were teaching the Body of Christ about the three-part makeup of mankind — the triune nature of man: body, soul, and spirit.[1] We enjoyed and benefited from their teaching. As we began to study the scriptures in this area, however, we found that the concept was not well supported. We want to share with you some of the things we learned.

The most familiar definition of mankind, based on the three-fold description of man, is that the soul contains the will, the emotions, the intellect, memory, etc. The spirit part is not as clearly nor cleanly defined. Usually it is described as the "essence" of each person; that is, the central part, perhaps the "heart" of man — the core of his being.

Problems with definition: which attributes are within the soul, spirit, and/or body.

There are problems with this definition.

First of all, we can't find scripture that backs up this definition. A big problem arises when **we remove from the spirit realm** such characteristics as the emotions, will, intellect, memory, etc.

One Example

One simple example will demonstrate the problem.

> Jn 4:24
> God [is] a **Spirit**: and they that worship him must worship [him] in spirit and in truth. (KJV)

God is a Spirit.

God has emotions, intellect, memory, etc.

We are made in His image.

Therefore, our spirit has . . .

Probably all of us agree that God does not have a body (except for Jesus the Christ, who currently has a human spiritual body with no blood). Also, God does not have a soul. The scripture says that God is spirit and **only spirit**. God has no body or soul, yet He has a will. He also has emotions, intellect, memory, etc.

Since we are made in His image,[2] *ergo,* we must have a will, emotions, intellect, memory, etc., **of the spirit** as well as of the soul. The scripture says that we **must** worship Him from our spirit. This is a very strong indication that we have the ability to make a **decision** (i.e., set our will) within our spirit to worship God.

If we try to use the "triune nature of man" definition of the soul, attributing the usual characteristics only to the soul realm, the above scripture doesn't make sense. We must realize that we have a will of the spirit and a will of the soul. We have emotions of the spirit and emotions of the soul. We have a memory of the spirit as well as a memory of the soul. And we have hurts in the spirit as well as hurts in the soul.

Let's dig a little deeper.

---

[1] Dennis and Rita Bennet, *Trinity of Man*, Plainfield, IL, Logos International, 1979.
[2] Please see Gen 1:26-27.

Table 1
Definitions of "Soul, Mind," and "Spirit, Heart"

Word	Old Testament	New Testament
Soul	**5315 nephesh {neh'-fesh}** 1) soul, self, life, creature, person, appetite, mind, living being, desire, emotion, passion 1a) that which breathes, the **inner being** of man 1f) seat of **emotions** and **passions** 1g) activity of **mind** 1h) activity of the **will**	**5590 psuche {psoo-khay'}** 1) breath 2) the soul 2a) the seat of the feelings, desires, affections, aversions (our **heart**, soul etc.) 2b) the (human) soul . . . regarded as a **moral being** designed for everlasting life
Mind	**5315 nephesh {neh'-fesh}** **Same as for Soul**	**1271 dianoia {dee-an'-oy-ah}** 1) the mind as a faculty of understanding, **feeling**, desiring 2) understanding 3) mind, i.e. **spirit**, way of thinking and **feeling** 4) thoughts, either good or bad
Spirit	**7307 ruwach {roo'-akh}** 1) wind, breath, **mind**, **spirit** 1e) spirit (as **seat of emotion**) 1f) spirit 1f1) as **seat** or organ of **mental acts** 1f2) rarely of the **will** 1f3) as seat especially of **moral character**	**4151 pneuma {pnyoo'-mah}** 1) a movement of air (a gentle blast 2a) the **rational spirit**, the power by which the human being **feels, thinks, decides** 2b) the **soul** 5) the disposition or influence which fills and governs the **soul** of any one
Heart	**3824 lebab {lay-bawb'}** 1) inner man, **mind**, **will**, **heart**, **soul**, **understanding** 1a) **inner part**, midst 1a3) **soul**, heart (of man) 1a4) **mind**, knowledge, thinking, reflection, memory 1a5) inclination, resolution, determination (of **will**) 1a6) **conscience** 1a7) heart (of **moral character**) 1a9) as seat of **emotions and passions**	**2588 kardia {kar-dee'-ah}** 1b) denotes the **centre** of all **physical** and **spiritual** life 2b) the **centre** and **seat** of **spiritual life** 2b1) the **soul** or **mind**, as it is the fountain and seat of the **thoughts, passions, desires, appetites, affections, purposes, endeavours** 2b2) of the **understanding**, the faculty and seat of the **intelligence** 2b3) of the **will** and **character** 2b4) of the **soul** as the seat of the sensibilities, affections, **emotions,**

Definitions

Using *Strong's Concordance,* we looked up the Strong's numbers and worked with the original Hebrew and Greek words that have been translated into the English words **"soul"** and **"mind**," and **"spirit"** and **"heart**." We assumed that "mind" is an approximate synonym for "soul" and that "heart" is an approximate synonym for "spirit." Table 1 on the previous page gives the Biblical definitions of these Hebrew and Greek words. Note that we have included only the definitions associated with each of these four words. We eliminated the ones not directly relevant to the discussion at hand in order to keep the table size to one page.

There is much overlap in the definitions of soul, spirit, mind, and heart.

You can see the overlap among the definitions. For example, all four words have definitions including both spiritual characteristics and soulish characteristics. The meanings for the word "heart" seems to overlap completely the meanings of "soul" and "spirit."[1]

Searching the Bible

What characteristics and attributes are found in both soul and spirit?

We then used the English words and the Strong's number for the Hebrew and Greek to search the Bible for references to the "soul" and "spirit," as well as the words "heart" and "mind." We wanted to know the characteristics and attributes that the writers of the Bible assigned to the soul and spirit. Did they overlap? Was there a "blur" among the functions of the "soul," "mind," "heart," and "spirit?"

We eventually had over four pages of characteristics and attributes that were "attached" to both the "soul" and "spirit." We have narrowed the list down to one page, which is shown in Table 2 on the next page.

Characteristics and Soul/Spirit in Same Verse

The first group of six characteristics, found in 14 verses, are particularly interesting because they contain our key words (soul/mind and spirit/heart) in the same verse, with the same characteristic. So we have a direct linking of the soul and spirit. These characteristics of loving, obeying, turning, observing, memory, and serving include characteristics normally associated with either the soul or the spirit but not both.

Characteristics in Different Verses

The rest of the characteristics in Table 2 are also attributed to both the soul and the spirit but are from different verses found throughout the Bible.

Specific Characteristics

Where is our "Lover?"

The first characteristic is **"loving."** We are to **love** God with all our spirit, soul, mind, strength. Six different verses declare this fact. Jesus proclaims this as the greatest commandment. As a result, every part of our being is capable of loving. God wants our entire being to love Him.

---

[1] No wonder that translators have such a hard time selecting an English word for each Hebrew or Greek word. They have to take into account the context within which the word is found. The word they select, of course, is strongly influenced by their theology, including their understanding of the "soul" and "spirit" of man.

Table 2
Comparison of Soul and Spirit Characteristics

Characteristic Attribute	Soul (5315 OT *nephesh*) (5590 NT *psuche*) Mind (5315 OT *nephesh*)		Spirit (7307 OT *ruwach*) (4151 NT *pneuma*) Heart (3824 OT *lebab*)	
Loving	Deu 6:5	Deu 13:3	Deu 6:5	Deu 13:3
	Josh 22:5	Lk 10:27	Josh 22:5	Lk 10:27
	Mat 22:37	Mk 12:30	Mat 22:37	Mk 12:30
Will (obedient)	Deu 30:2, 6		Deu 30:2, 6	
Turned	Deu 30:10		Deu 30:10	
Observe	Deu 26:16		Deu 26:16	
Memory (lay up)	Deu 11:18		Deu 11:18	
Serve	Deu 10:12		Deu 10:12	
	Josh 22:5		Josh 22:5	
	1 Chr 28:9		1 Chr 28:9	
Willing	2 Cor 8:12		Ex 35:5, 21, 22	Mat 26:41
Ready	2 Cor 8:19	1 Pet 5:2	Hos 7:6	Mk 14:38
Purposed			2 Cor 9:7	Acts 19:21
Decreed			1 Cor 7:37	
Trusted	Psa 57:1		Psa 28:7	Psa 112:7
	Isa 26:3		Prov 3:5	Prov 31:11
Humbled	Psa 35:13		Psa 51:17	
Troubled	Jn 12:27		Jn 13:21	Jn 14:1, 27
	2 Thes 2:2		Gen 41:8	
Discouraged	Psa 57:6		Psa 42:6, 11	Psa 43:5
Distressed	1 King 1:29		Acts 5:33	Acts 7:54
Grieved	Jud 10:16		Gen 6:6	
	Psa 31:9		1 Sam 1:8	1 Sam 2:33
Anguished			2 Cor 2:4	
Fearful	Acts 2:43		Psa 27:3	
Trembling			Deu 28:65	
Sorrowful	Mk 14:34		Jn 16:6	
Hateful	Isa 1:14		Lev 19:17	

411

Where is our "Will?"

Let's look at the characteristic of being **"willing."** This requires the presence of a "will," the ability to make a "decision." Based on scripture, both the soul (or mind) and spirit (or the heart) can be "willing." Both the soul and the spirit are able to make decisions, able to exert a will, able to have purpose.

Where do we decide to be "Obedient?"

The characteristic of **"obedience"** appears both in Deuteronomy 30:2 and 6. God wants us to be obedient at every level of our personality, within both the soul and spirit. We can't be obedient at any level unless we have a will at each level with which to "decide" to be obedient.

Where is our "Memory?"

The characteristic of **"memory"** appears in Deuteronomy 11:18, for both the mind and the heart. God says basically to make up your mind, to set your mind, and to set your heart. In the KJV, NIV, NAS, and AMP versions of the Bible, the translation is essentially the same.

> Deu 11:18
> You shall therefore **impress** these words of mine on your **heart** and on your **soul**; and you shall bind them as a sign on your hand, . . . (NAS)

God is commanding the people to get His word on the inside — into their heart and their soul and store it there. In other words, He is telling them to **memorize** His word. Therefore, both the spirit (heart) and the soul must have a memory.

Emotional Characteristics

Where are our emotional characteristics?

The next major group are those characteristics that have to do with the emotions. Either the soul or spirit can be: humbled, troubled, discouraged, distressed, grieved, fearful, sorrowful, even hateful.

This information encourages us to be not too dogmatic about how God made man, how we are constructed on the inside in the inward, invisible parts.

Let's look at some other scriptures that touch on different aspects of this issue of soul and spirit.

God has both a Heart and a Mind?

We quoted John 4:24 earlier, which states that God is (a) Spirit. But does He have a heart and mind as well? First Samuel seems to indicate that He does.

> 1 Sam 2:35
> And I will raise me up a faithful priest, [that] shall do according to [that] which [is] in mine **heart** and in my **mind**: . . . (KJV)

Where is God's heart and mind? It must be in Him, and He is Spirit!

Spirit of your Mind?

Paul uses an interesting phrase in Ephesians.

> Eph 4:23
> And be renewed in the **spirit of your mind**; (KJV)

Does our mind have spiritual characteristics? What are they? This verse is very similar to Romans 12:2, where Paul admonishes us to "be transformed by the renewing of our mind." Our belief system needs to be renewed, wherever it is located.

Paul and the Triune Nature versus the Dual Nature

In First Thessalonians, Paul does refer to the triune nature of man.

> 1 Thes 5:23
> . . . and [I pray God] your whole spirit and soul and body be preserved blameless . . . (KJV)

This is the only reference in the Bible to the triune nature of man. This is interesting because, in Paul's other writings, he refers to the dual nature of man. He uses the phrases "old man" and "new man," or he talks about the "flesh" and the "spirit."[1]

Jesus and Dual Nature

Even Jesus referred to the "flesh" and the "spirit."

> Mat 26:41
> . . . the **spirit** indeed [is] willing, but the **flesh** [is] weak. (KJV)

Conclusion

After studying the above, we find it hard to be dogmatic about "what is where" on the inside of man. Rather than spending our time dividing ourselves up into parts and trying to figure out what needs healing, it seems a better use of our time to simply pray for God's healing to come, wherever a person may need it, whether in the soul/mind and/or the spirit/heart and/or the body.

We will let God figure out exactly where the healing is needed. The Bible states that only the Word of God can discern this anyway.

> Heb 4:12
> For the word of God [is] quick, and powerful, and sharper than any two-edged sword, piercing even to the **dividing asunder of soul and spirit**, and of the joints and marrow, and **[is] a discerner of the thoughts and intents of the heart**. (KJV)

We don't think that mankind has the ability to separate between the bone and the marrow, so likewise, we also can't discern between soul and spirit. Only the Word of God can do this.

Let's decide to do what He has called us to do — which is to pray for the sick to be healed[2] — and let God do what He does best, which is to bring the healing wherever it is needed.

---

[1] The majority of Paul's writings treat man as having two parts: the "flesh" or "old man", and the "spirit" or "new man". Examples are: Rom 2:28-29, 7:5-6, 7:25-8:16, 1 Cor 5:3, 6:20, 2 Cor 7:1, Gal 3:3, 5:13-6:8, Eph 4:22-24, Phil 3:3, Col 2:5, 3:9-10.

[2] Please see James 5:14.

C

CONTROVERSIES CONCERNING INNER HEALING

The topic of healing of the inner person has generated much controversy. We would like to illuminate the issues, at least to some degree, so you can add our thoughts to your own. This appendix may also help you be prepared to discuss the concerns that the person to whom you are ministering might have.

Before we discuss the controversy, let's us list a few of the books that have been written on both sides of the issue.

Concerned Authors

- Dave Hunt and T.A. McMahon, *The Seduction of Christianity: Spiritual Discernment in the Last Days* (Eugene: Harvest House Publishers, 1985).

- Martin and Deidre Bobgan, *Psycho Heresy: The Psychological Seduction of Christianity* (Santa Barbara: Eastgate Publishers, 1987).

- Don Matzat, *Inner Healing: Deliverance or Deception?* (Eugene: Harvest House Publishers, 1987).

Advocating Authors:

- Rita Bennett, *How to Pray for Inner Healing for Yourself and Others* (Old Tappan: Fleming H. Revell Comp., 1984).

- Pat Brooks, *Healing of the Mind* (Fletcher: New Puritan Library, 1978).

- John and Paula Sandford, *Healing the Wounded Spirit*, (South Plainfield: Bridge Publishing, Inc., 1985).

- David A. Seamands, *Healing for Damaged Emotions* (Wheaton: Victor Books, 1981).

- David A. Seamands, *Healing of Memories* (Wheaton: Victor Books, 1985).

- Ruth Carter Stapleton, *The Experience of Inner Healing* (Waco: Word Books, Publisher, 1977).

Major Problems

As we read through these books and other similar ones, two basic controversies surface: Whether or not there is a need for inner healing, and whether or not the terminology/method(s) used for inner healing are scriptural.

Is there a Need for Inner Healing?

Three basic questions about inner healing.

Since we have written an entire chapter on how to pray for Soul/Spirit Hurts, we obviously believe that there is a need for ministry to the inner person — whatever name is used to label the ministry. We will not address this issue further.

Non-Scriptural Terms and Concepts

One objection people have is that practitioners of inner healing use terminology that is clearly not in the Bible. Rather, they make extensive use of secular psychological terms and concepts. Does the use of these non-biblical terms invalidate the ministry?

Use of Visualization or "Guided" Prayer

A second objection is the use of visualization, imagination, and suggestions made by the minister to the ministry receiver. Suggestions might be about "seeing" Jesus in the situation, and/or "imagining" that Jesus is "doing something." These suggestions are similar to (or exactly like) hypnosis. This rightly concerns all Christians.

Let's look at these objections in more detail.

Secular Psychological Terms and Ministry

Is non-scriptural language "bad?"

Simply because a term or concept is used by secular psychology does not in itself make it "bad." After all, we all use a lot of words that are not in the Bible. To us, the real issue is not whether the terms or concepts are in the text of Scripture, but whether the practice or ministry is based upon the truth of God. It is "how" the practice or ministry is being done that is important. We want everything we do to be based on the Bible; that is, based on the principles and precepts of the Word of Truth.

It seems that the main thrust of the secular approach to counseling is to help people understand themselves. The goal seems to be to understand their hurts and learn to accept themselves as they are. In other words, to learn to "cope" with their problem(s).

God doesn't want to leave us where we are. He wants to change us!

As Christians, it is clear that God doesn't want us merely to accept how we are or settle for "coping." He wants to change us. He wants to improve us; He wants to turn each of us into an image of Jesus.

The real test of a ministry.

So the real test of any ministry — whether it goes under the name of secular psychology or Christian psychology or something else — is whether it "leaves people where they are" or helps them appropriate God's provision for freedom and healing. Does it leave them in their sin, with their wounds, and with the guilt they feel? Or does it present the good news of God's forgiveness of sin, His resurrection power, and His plan for restoration?

Those who minister by helping the person accept himself as he is and teach him how to cope with his "problem" may be, in reality, aiding and abetting sin.

Use of Visualization or "Guided" Prayer

When we come to the "methods" of inner healing, we encounter much diversity in the concepts and methods used. There are almost as many approaches as there are authors of books and practitioners of inner healing. This makes it difficult to define what exactly is meant by the various terms.

A valid concern regarding visualization and imagery.

We agree, however, that valid concerns should be voiced when we come to the use of visualization and imagery under the control of the minister. This involves the use of "active" suggestions by the minister, directing his ministry receiver what to see and perceive. Minister controlled and directed imagery creates a potential hazard for the person. It actually "sets up" the person for:

- Possible control (fostering co-dependence) by the counselor/minister.
- Possible infiltration by demons (spirit guides).
- Possibility of opening up areas that neither the person nor the minister are equipped or ready to handle.

God is "for" Visualization (Visions)

The key to the solution concerning visualization is to realize that God "is for" visualization. In the Bible this is called a "vision." (See our section on how to hear God in Chapter IV, "Hearing God's Voice.")

There are many visions in the Bible.

Jesus had many visions.

In the Bible, we read about the prophets who saw visions. John in his revelation saw several visions. We have accounts of Jesus seeing visions. In fact, based on Jesus' statements, He was in continual communication with God the Father via visions. In John, He frequently states words to the effect, "I only do what I **see** the Father doing and I only say what I **hear** the Father saying."[1]

The difference between a Bible "vision" and Active or Guided Visualization is in **who initiates the vision**. In the Bible, God takes the initiative and presents a vision to a man. The man is passive and simply "receives" the vision. In what we are calling "active visualization," a man is taking the initiative and presenting the vision (imagination) to God. In effect, the man is saying, "God, fit into this vision, and do as I direct." We are more than uncomfortable with this approach.

---

[1] Example passages are: Jn 5:19-20, 8:26, 38, 55, 12:49-50, 14:10, 16:13-14 (the Holy Spirit), 17:8, 14.

"Waiting Upon the Lord" Listening Prayer

As God was drawing us more and more into Restoring the Foundations ministry, we were very concerned about the inner healing aspect. We prayed for some time about the above issues. We wanted to minister in a way that was safe for everyone concerned: the ministry receiver, the ministers, and the Holy Spirit. At the same time, we wanted to provide God the maximum opportunity to bring His healing to the person. The approach we present in the chapter on Soul/Spirit Hurts of "Waiting Upon the Lord" Listening Prayer is what He gave to us. It meets all of our criteria and more!

*God always
does it best!*

We find that when we "Wait Upon the Lord," He frequently selects wounds to heal that are not on our list of Soul/Spirit Hurts for the person. Of greater importance is the revelation that He brings to the person during the healing time. It is always much more profound and significant to the person than anything we could have thought up. Our heavenly Father always knows exactly the very thing that the person needs in order to have a major healing. There is no need for us to try to guide the ministry direction. We could not do it as well as the Holy Spirit!

D

CAN A CHRISTIAN HAVE A DEMON?

Derek Prince, the popular British speaker and Bible scholar, was once asked publicly if a Christian can have a demon. In his crisp British humor, he is said to have replied, "Yes, Christians can have anything they want to have."

Assuming that we can not be oppressed by demons leaves us defenseless.

The following discussion is a serious one, however, because this question is an important one to many Christians. We encourage you to look again at Scripture to see the validity of deliverance for Christians. This is an area where assuming that demons aren't a problem for Christians causes us to give up our God-given rights and adopt a passive stance. This leads to total helplessness at the hands of the enemy since we allow him to do as he wishes.

What about before we were saved?

All we really have to do in order to realize the likelihood, and reality, of oppression by the demonic is to remember that there was a period in our lives when we were not Christians. During this time, we were totally unprotected (unless we were in a godly family that knew how to protect us, at least to some degree). In most cases, we were wide open to all of the demonic oppression coming down the family line, as well as whatever wanted to come through the doors we opened ourselves. We have had a lifetime of accumulating demonic oppression. Unfortunately, these demons don't automatically leave when we are "born again."

God's grace can cause deliverance during special encounters with Him.

Some deliverance can, and frequently does, take place at the moment of Salvation. Deliverance can also take place at other moments when we have a special encounter with God, such as receiving the Baptism in the Holy Spirit. Anytime the demons lose their "legal" right to occupy an area of sin, there is the potential for some deliverance taking place spontaneously. It seems, however, that there is always **more** that can be, and that needs to be, accomplished.

God's Strategy for Deliverance

As we read in Exodus,

> Ex 23:30
> Little by little I will drive them out before you, until you have increased enough to take possession of the land. (NIV)

God used the nation of Israel to teach us many spiritual truths. In giving the Israelites His plan for removing the inhabitants from the promised land, He was (and is) teaching us His plan for removal of the "inhabitants" from **our** "promised land." In other words, He is showing us what to expect as we receive freedom from demonic oppression. He is showing that it doesn't happen all at once, but that it is "little by little" — that there is always **more** we can look forward to.

God's "rate" for setting us free from Demonic Oppression.

When we ask how fast "little by little" is, or "How fast am I going to be set free from demonic oppression?" the answer is given in the later portion of the verse. It is based on how rapidly we are able to "increase and possess the land." It is based on the rate that we mature in our spiritual walk, which is the rate that we work with the Holy Spirit to "sanctify" us.

Our freedom also depends on our ability to maintain our possession once we have obtained it. God doesn't want us to fall back and reopen the door(s) to the demonic. Losing one's deliverance can be hazardous, and God doesn't want us to end up even more oppressed. This is why — once we have stabilized in possessing the ground that has already been cleared during previous deliverance — God always **has more** deliverance for us.

Scriptures relating to Christians and demons

No verse in the Bible says, "Christians can be oppressed by demons." It would be nice if it were that plainly stated, but God did not see fit to include this statement. For that reason, we have to see what is inferred and allow the scriptures to help us make sense of our experiences.

On the next two pages, we have collected a number of scriptures that relate to the issue at hand. We encourage you to study carefully what is being implied, check the reality of your experiences and those of others you trust, and then ask the Holy Spirit to clarify this most important issue for you.

May God Bless you as you study His Logos Word. May you be led by the Living Word.

Table 3
Scriptures Concerning Christians and Demons

Peter and Judas

Mat 16:23, Mk 8:33	Jesus says to Peter: "Get thee behind me Satan." The implications are that Satan himself or his representatives are speaking through Peter.
Lk 22:3, Jn 13:27	We read: "and Satan entered into Judas . . ." We could question whether or not Judas was saved, but regardless, out of his sin, he opened himself to being controlled by either a high level demon or Satan himself, to accomplish Satan's will.

Spirit-filled Christians dealing with the Demonic

Mk 16:17	Believers are to cast out demons. From whom are we to cast them out? Unbelievers? This is not wise. They have no protection or defense to prevent re-entry.
Acts 5:3	Peter says to Ananias, "Why has Satan filled your heart to lie to the Holy Spirit?" This (Spirit-filled) couple had opened a door to Satan, and he had come through it.
1 Cor 10:18-22	Paul doesn't want us to be in agreement (partners) with demons.
1 Cor 12:2-3	Paul, writing to Spirit-filled believers, states that no one, if speaking by the Spirit of God, can curse Jesus. He leaves open a question about believers speaking by other spirits than the Spirit of God.
2 Cor 2:10-11	This scripture shows that there is a potential for Satan to outwit us. We must be aware of his schemes (devices, snares, hooks, intentions). In this context, it is the possibility of the sin of unforgiveness opening the door for demonic oppression.
2 Cor 11:4	Here we see the potential for deception by the serpent's cunning. There is a possibility to receive a different spirit than the spirit received previously.
2 Cor 12:7	This scripture points out the potential for a messenger of Satan to torment (buffet) us, particularly when pride is an issue. (Remember Satan's persecution of Christians via the pride of the Pharisees, with Paul being one of the most zealous ones.) Paul was not exempt from having the curse of sowing and reaping work in his life.
2 Tim 2:25	Paul writes: ". . . if God peradventure will give them repentance to the acknowledging of the truth." They have lost the truth due to being taken captive.
2 Tim 2:26	"And [that] they may recover themselves out of the snare of the devil, who are taken captive by him at his will." There is a potential for being taken captive by the devil, at his will, to do his will. Remember, Paul is writing to Timothy, and he is talking about Spirit-filled Christians.
James 4:7	The devil will be near anytime he thinks that we are vulnerable. Anytime there is a possibility that we will let him reclaim ground that he has previously lost, he will come around. Or if he thinks that we will give up and let him have new ground, he will be there to tempt us. He will have plenty of his demons available to come in and occupy whatever he can get.
	Even in a time of weakness or overwhelm, we must exercise our authority that we obtain when we submit to God. We must resist him. When he sees that we are determined, that we are not going to give place to his temptations, but that we are using the Word of God against him, he will flee.

Table 3 (continued)
Scriptures Concerning Christians and Demons

Spirit-filled Christians dealing with the Demonic (continued)

1 Pet 5:8	"Be self-controlled and alert. Your enemy the devil prowls around like a roaring lion looking for someone to devour. Resist him, standing firm in the faith, . . ." We have here a clear implication that Spirit-filled Christians can be devoured, if we don't resist.
1 Jn 4:1-3	John instructs us to test the spirit(s). In who? In Spirit-filled Christians?
1 Jn 5:18-19	These verses show potential for harm from the evil one. It is necessary that we "keep" ourselves protected. The whole world is under the control of the evil one.

Can the Holy Spirit of God co-habit with demons?

Eze 8-11	The Glory of the Lord finally leaves the temple, as the abominations increase beyond God's limit of tolerance. In this case, the Spirit of God is co-existing with the demonic, until God eventually leaves.
	In the case of a Christian, God goes through the opposite process. The Holy Spirit comes into the new temple (us), and proceeds to clean it out over a period of time.

Four Levels of Abominations: Things that drive God far from His Sanctuary

Eze 8:5-6	Idol named "Jealousy" at North gate. It provokes (God) to "Jealousy."
Eze 8:7-13	70 elders worshipping idols (demons) inside of the temple, in the dark, (where God can't see!).
Eze 8:14-15	Group of women weeping for Tammuz (a Babylonian god, who was supposed to die annually and subsequently be resurrected!).
Eze 8:16-18	25 priests with backs toward the temple and faces toward the east, bowing down to the sun (god).

Four Steps taken as the Glory of the LORD leaves the Temple

Eze 9:3, 10:4	From throne above the cherubim to the threshold of the temple.
Eze 10:18-19	From threshold of the temple to the entrance to the east gate of the Lord's house.
Eze 11:22-23	From within the city to the mountain (Zion) east of it.
	Finally, God completely leaves.
	When the Holy Spirit comes and sets up His habitation within us, the new believer, the reverse process occurs. He progressively "cleans" the house as we allow and work with Him (II Cor 7:1, Phil 2:12-13) until it is completely Holy. This is the Sanctification process.

About the Authors
(updated for fifth printing)

God called Chester and Betsy in mid-life from careers in aerospace software engineering and mental health counseling to new careers as teachers and ministers in the Body of Christ. During their preparation time at Liberty Bible College,[1] God began both to heal them and to reveal the elements of Restoring the Foundations ministry. They started to minister, teach, and train other couples to function as Restoring the Foundations (RTF) Ministry Teams to help bring freedom and healing to church members.

Since 1990, when they begin to minister full-time, God has continued to expand their vision. While still active in personal ministry, they have now established healing ministry programs within churches in many locations. They conduct Healing/Deliverance, Activation, and Training Seminars throughtout the USA and internationally. They continue to train healing ministry teams and trainers of RTF Ministry Teams throughout the USA and in other nations.

"Proclaiming His Word Ministries" was founded in 1992 in response to God saying that others would be joining them and to prepare a covering organization to take care of them. This did occur, as over the years a number of top-quality RTF ministry teams joined PHW and ministered within the CI/PHW Healing House and throughout the nation. By the year 2000, over sixteen trained ministers and trainers, as well as office staff, worked with Proclaiming His Word. Chester and Betsy were traveling extensively by this time, bringing the good news of how to receive God's Healing throughout the world.

In the meanwhile, in 1993 they were called by Dr. Bill Hamon to Christian International in Flordia to minister to the CI Leadership. This lead to the first "Prophetic Counseling" conference in March of 1994, which included the launch of the "Christian International/Proclaiming His Word Healing House." The relationship with CI and Dr. Bill Hamon continucs as Chester and Betsy are ordained by CI and serve on the CI Board of Governors.

In 2001 they launched the Healing House Network as a covering membership organization for the many qualified RTF Ministry Teams ministering at the Healing House level of professionalism. This network is providing quality training and oversight, as well as functioning as a nationwide and international referral center.

In 2004, the prophecies concerning an eventual training center came to fulfillment. Echo Mountain Inn in Hendersonville, NC, was purchased as the home of the "Restoring the Foundations International Training Center" and became the new ministry base, as the entire ministry moved from near Christian International in Florida to North Carolina. This training center has allowed a great accceleration in the preparation and release of RTF ministers into the Body of Christ.

---

[1] Betsy has degrees in Counselor Education (MA, EdS). Chester has degrees in Mechanical (BS) and Nuclear Engineering (MS, PhD). They both earned their Masters Degrees in Theology at Liberty Bible College, Pensacola, Florida.

They have developed a number of resources to help train RTF ministers. *Restoring the Foundations* was their first book. A smaller version of the RTF, entitled *An Integrated Approach to Biblical Healing Ministry*, was created in 2003 and published by Sovereign World Publishers, UK, for sale in bookstores and for easier translation into other languages. This book was then released in the USA by Chosen Books, under the title *Biblical Healing and Deliverance*. Along with Dorathy Railey, a reference manual was written for RTF ministers to take into the ministry room. It is entitled *Ministry Tools for Restoring the Foundations*. This book is what it's title indicates, a manual with "tools" to increase the effectiveness of the ministering process.

In 2006 another expansion of the Restoring the Foundations revelation came to fruition as the book *Transforming Your Business* was released. It applies the principles of the Integrated Approach to Ministry to organizations, particularly businesses. (Please learn more at: www.TransformingYourBusiness.org.)

Because of the widespread use of the Restoring the Foundations book, in 2006 the leaders of the ministries agreed to consolidate all of the ministries under the banner of "Restoring the Foundations Ministries."

A number of the resources available from Restoring the Foundations are described on the last pages of this book. You may also visit the web site to learn about all of the available resources. (www.RestoringTheFoundations.org)

Chester and Betsy have four adult children; James, Lewis, Eric, and Pam.

You may contact Chester and Betsy through:

> Restoring the Foundations Ministries
> 2849 Laurel Park Highway
> Hendersonville, NC 28739
> **828-696-9075**
>
> office@RestoringTheFoundations.org
> www.RestoringTheFoundations.org

You may learn more about the several ministries they have founded by clicking on the differnt links at the (above) main web site.

Healing House Network

RTF International Training Center

Transforming Your Business: www.TransformingYourBusiness.org

Issue-Focused Ministry

The Restoring the Foundations International Training Center is located at Echo Mountain Inn in Hendersonville, NC. This facility is operated year-round as a Bed and Breakfast Inn. You may learn more about the Inn and its features at:

Echo Mountain Inn: www.EchoInn.com

INDEX

G

Garden of Eden, 108
Gibeonites, 309, 322
Gideon, 133, 332
gifts of the Holy Spirit
   see 'Holy Spirit, gifts of'
gluttony, 282, 398
God, 104, 309
   and covenant, 322
   and the occult, 284
   anger/disappointment with, 94, 215, 220
   hated, 113
   jealous, 113
   nature and character of, 105, 107
   of justice, 105, 107, 117, 119
   of mercy, 105, 107, 117, 123
   relationship with, 215, 226
   separation from, 40
   submit to, 253
   the Father, 235
   trust, not, 110, 215, 220, 342
   trust Him, 228, 239, 247, 259
God's
   armor, see 'armor'
   army, 261, 381
   blessings, 24, 150
   care, 215
   conditions, see 'God's, requirements'
   covenant, 24
   economy, 81
   family, 106, 153
   favor, 379
   forgiveness, see 'forgiveness'
   healing, 199, 206, 216, 217
   heart, 95, 267
   kingdom, 352
   Law, 29, 38, 107
   love, 22, 259
   measuring stick, 69
   mercy and grace, 260
   peace, 259, 378
   point of view, 104, 122
   promises, 5, 27, 32, 41, 45, 51, 56, 63, 64, 68, 76, 80, 91, 93, 107, 136, 142, 144, 148, 164, 169, 176, 179, 184, 199
   provision, 19, 21, 68, 106, 107, 169, 299, 322
   purpose, 204, 223, 250, 253, 381
   requirements, 20, 27, 32, 35, 37, 39, 41, 64, 68, 84, 87, 91, 93, 105, 106, 114, 132, 139, 169, 266, 268
   responsibility, 255
   strategy for deliverance, 265, 331, 419
   voice, 2, 49, 59, 150, 215
   will, 235, 381
   Word, 259, 261
Godly Beliefs, 25, 45
   also see 'Ungodly Beliefs'
   definition of, 157
gossip, 170, 179, 282, 398
grace, 20, 29, 36, 83, 85, 88, 92, 133, 188, 192, 213, 260, 261, 318, 351, 358, 376, 378
   abuses of, 32
greed, 280, 397
groups, 366, 367, 377
   leader, xviii, 364, 367, 372, 380
guard, 313, 314
guidelines, 374
guilt, 8, 39, 398

H

Hammond, Frank and Ida Mae, 261, 292, 294, 313
handicapped, 130, 210
harassment, 263, 275
hatred, 83, 90, 113, 180, 239, 241, 398
healing, 27, 107, 199, 306, 380
   hindrances to, see 'hindrances'
Healing House, xii, xvi, 62, 353, 370, 372, 423, 424, 434
   Network, 423
   team, 364
helplessness, 62, 398, 419
   also see 'victim'
Hilton, Melodye, 353
hindrances
   analytical thinking, 220, 242, 243
   anger/disappointment with God, 220
   blocked emotions, 223
   dealing with, 232, 234, 235
   demonic, 227, 241, 243
   major fears, 219
   medications, 220
   removing, 231
   to healing, 217
   unconfessed sin, 218
   unfamiliarity, 217
   unforgiveness, 218
   Ungodly Beliefs, 229
holy, 5, 24
Holy Spirit, xvii, 5, 6, 12, 24, 38, 41, 56, 60, 68, 79, 90, 151, 171, 172, 200, 246, 255, 260, 306, 308
   and dreams, 55
   baptism of, 259
   directed by, 64, 79, 221, 227, 233, 235, 293, 307, 310, 315, 329, 331, 336, 378
   gifts of, 2, 57, 62, 107, 283, 285, 306, 312, 329, 336, 378
   listening to, 63, 86, 97, 98, 235
   sanctification, see 'sanctification'
   temple of, xvii, 5
home groups, see 'groups'
hopelessness, 62, 93, 169, 170, 171, 174, 288, 398
hypnosis, xxii, 172, 399

I

Identification Repentance, 106, 144
identity, false, 168, 213, 214, 289, 309, 327, 353, 356, 358, 436
idolatry, 112, 114, 143, 284, 348
infirmities, see 'disease'
inheritance, 7, 23, 69, 76, 105, 114, 123, 148, 162, 165, 262, 265, 279, 284, 285
   Christ's, 116
   from father Adam, 140
   greatest, 108
   of iniquity, 105
   of shame, 355
iniquity, 105, 114, 120
   definition of, 115
   inherited, 105, 108, 124, 252
inner healing, see 'Soul/Spirit Hurts'
Integrated Approach to Healing
   Ministry, xvii, xxiv, 2, 64, 133, 365
     Demonic Oppression, 110, 159, 203, 262
     Sins of the Fathers, 109, 158, 203, 262
     Soul/Spirit Hurts, 110, 159, 203, 264
     Soul Ties, 322
     Ungodly Beliefs, 110, 158, 203, 263
intercession, 74, 90, 130, 149, 221, 235, 300, 327, 375, 380, 391
interconnectedness, 264, 292, 293, 330, 356
interview, xx, 111, 292, 365, 368, 370, 378, 436
intimacy, 214, 324, 380, 397
isolation, 397
   also see 'withdrawing'
Issue-Focused Ministry, 359, 364, 366, 424

J

jealousy, 280, 397
Jeremiah, 22, 51, 120, 122, 205
Jesus Christ, see 'Christ Jesus'
Jezebel, 115, 116, 351, 357, 358, 399
Joshua, 309, 322, 331
judging, 282, 398
justice, 105

K

key to freedom, 1, 47, 81, 98, 117, 188, 373
kingdom
    of darkness, see 'Satan, and his kingdom'
    of God, see 'God's, kingdom'
Kylstra, Chester and Betsy
    see 'Authors'

L

lake of fire, 302, 310
Lamb
    blood of, 129
    provision, 21
    sacrifice, 35, 76
    slain, 19, 68, 95
land, 265, 337
    holy, 310
Law, 29, 33, 36, 68, 106, 148
    and Jesus, 34
    and RTF ministry, 42
    and Ungodly Beliefs, 44
    of believing in your heart, 45
    of judgment, 36, 41, 117, 124, 132, 135, 136
    of multiplication, 36, 44
    of sowing and reaping, 30, 36, 42, 117, 124, 135, 136
    of time to harvest, 44
    relating to, 35, 37
    types of, 30
    understanding, 36
    violation of, 30, 33, 39, 41, 46, 148
laying on of hands, 77, 301
    appropriately, 376
Lazarus, 237
Lead Team Summary Report
    see 'Forms'
legal ground, xix, 7, 9, 40, 57, 101, 110, 127, 159, 170, 204, 217, 218, 237, 261, 262, 263, 266, 279, 280, 296, 297, 306, 308, 310, 312, 324, 330, 336, 337, 356, 368
    establishing, 356
legalism, 223, 397
    avoid, 218
licensed counselor, 3
life
    also see 'Christ Jesus, and life'
    mistake, 245
    secret, 334
lifestyle, 323
    futile, 23, 148
log jam, 307
loss, 174, 283, 289, 398
love, 22, 25, 107

Lucado, Max, 208
lust, 139, 280, 282, 284, 314, 399
lying, 132, 142, 143, 173, 397

M

man
    dual nature, 413
    nature of, 252
    triune nature, 200, 408, 413
marriage, 323, 397
    and hurts, 254
    covenant, 325
    defrauded, 324
    foundation of, 324
    oneness, 325
    spouses, 377
    unfaithfulness, 241
Mary, 116
masks, see 'identity, false'
Masons, see 'Freemasons'
medications, 220, 398
memory, 200
    blocking ministry, 227
    clarifying, 234
    contents, 228
    entering, 232, 234
    inviting Jesus, 234
    listening for, 233
    not entering, 220
    work within, 234
mental problems, 290, 397
mercy, 105, 260
mind, 186, 200, 220, 313
ministers, five-fold, xviii, 368, 372
ministers, RTF
    cautions, 375
    father/mother figures, 376
    function of, 3, 55, 62, 79, 86, 88, 89, 94
    guidelines, 374
    high risk, 377
    limitations, 375
    No, No's, 377
    preparation of, 151, 194, 217, 228, 255, 296, 297, 315, 362, 365, 367
    protection, 376
    qualifications of, 7, 216
    releasing, 380
    rules, 376
    scriptures for, 87, 96, 121, 137, 145, 177, 181, 185, 187, 207, 221, 224, 269, 311, 411, 421
    staying focused, 375
    staying in charge, 375
    straight talk, 373
    training, 423
    wisdom, 373

ministry
    effective, xv, xvii, 2, 7, 17, 73, 77, 97, 130, 150, 158, 159, 190, 199, 201, 215, 218, 249, 252, 262, 268, 296, 315, 327, 331, 361, 366, 370, 372, 373, 376, 423
ministry, RTF, 6
    also see 'ministry sessions, RTF'
    Altar, 364
    blessing of, 380
    cautions, 375, 377
    considerations, 215, 221, 226, 296, 310, 351, 358
    Cross basis for, 17
    deliverance, 296
    Extended, 371
    formats, 361
    guidelines, 374
    high risk, 377
    Issue-Focused, 366
    No, No's, 377
    overview, 362
    post-ministry, see 'post-ministry, RTF'
    preparing for, 111, 150, 151, 194, 228, 230, 255, 315, 367, 435
    Problem Areas, see 'Problem Areas'
    process, 27, 64, 81, 82, 98, 101, 160, 221, 224, 229, 234, 237, 296, 302, 312, 315, 321, 323, 324, 329, 364
    program, see 'church RTF program'
    purpose, 4, 63, 261
    sessions, 368, 369
    specialists, 227, 372
    steps, 151, 196, 256, 317
    strategy, 150
    Thorough, 368
    to anger, 225
    to blocked emotions, 223
    to children, 149
    to DO, 315
    to family & friends, 377
    to SOFCs, 150
    to Soul Ties, 322, 326
    to SSHs, 255
    to UGBs, 194
    training, 2, 7, 14, 79, 168, 199, 362, 364, 366, 367, 369, 372, 375, 433, 435
Ministry Areas, see 'Problem Areas'
Ministry Card, 190, 229, 231, 404
    also see 'Forms'
Ministry Notes Form, see 'Forms'
ministry receiver
    ask him questions, 234
    blocked emotions, 223
    cautions, 230
    co-dependency, 379

Soul Ties, 172, 199, 321
   and first love, 325
   breaking, 237, 254, 321, 324, 325
   definition of, 322
   emotional, 324
   godly, 323
   illustration, 321
   ministering to, 326
sowing and reaping, see 'Law'
specialists, 372
spirit
   of man, 200, 407
spirit guides, see 'demons'
spiritual warfare, 6, 11, 67, 69, 70, 261,
   272, 331
   how to fight, 79, 80, 265, 270
   spheres of, 78
spouses, see 'marriage, spouses'
SRA, see 'dissociation'
stealing, xxiv, 40, 132, 261, 296, 397
steps, see 'ministry, RTF, steps'
strategy, 150, 329, 371, 419
   also see 'deliverance, strategy'
   also see 'God's strategy for
      deliverance'
   military, 312
strife, 282, 398
strongholds
   see 'Control-Rebellion-Rejection
      Stronghold'
   see 'Demonic Strongholds'
   see 'Shame-Fear-Control
      Stronghold'
success, 246
surrogate
   mate, 324
   wife, 325
survival, 213, 227, 239
symptoms, 63

T

teams, 199
   benefits of, 376
   definition of, 369
Ten Commandments, 106
terror, 259, 277, 334, 399
testimonies, xviii, 82, 91, 238, 245, 259,
   271, 314
thoughts, 220, 230, 307, 313
time to harvest, see 'Law'
tongues, 310
torment, 32, 39, 50, 86, 87, 172, 173,
   259, 267, 272, 277, 282, 290, 291,
   399
training, xviii
trapped, 213, 214, 398
   also see 'Satan, schemes'
trauma, 216, 217, 227, 253, 282, 283,
   398

trust, 65, 113, 239, 246, 250, 358
   God, 220, 247
   lack of, 215
truth, 25, 247, 260
   knowledge of, 94
   prevent hearing, 263

U

unbelief, 125, 158, 164, 184, 185, 189,
   194, 227, 263, 277, 295, 307, 314,
   398
unfairness, 105, 108
unfaithfulness, 323, 399
unforgiveness, 89, 218, 282, 398
   also see 'forgiveness'
   consequences, 86
   Satan's trap, 91
Ungodly Beliefs, 7, 45, 46, 313, 330
   also see 'Integrated Approach to
      Ministry'
   and forgiveness, 86
   and Law, 44
   and Soul/Spirit Healing, 229
   and the Cross, 25
   Belief-Expectation cycle, 162
   blocking, 229
   core lies, 229
   definition of, 157
   ministering to, 194, 229
   post-ministry, 198
   replacing, 188
   scriptural basis for, 176
Ungodly Beliefs Worksheets
   see 'Forms'
unity, 250, 380
unsaved, 18, 33, 46, 69, 70, 149, 179,
   275
unworthiness, 25, 46, 60, 62, 93, 96,
   125, 184, 295, 398

V

victim, 62, 69, 83, 89, 158, 170, 174,
   248, 276, 293, 313, 333, 349, 378,
   398
victory, 314
Virkler, Mark and Patti, 59
visions, 172, 244, 246, 248
visualization, 201, 416, 417
voice of the Lord, 2
   learning to recognize, 49, 50, 51, 52,
      59
   listening to, 63, 150, 217, 220, 230,
      232, 235
   not hearing, 215, 250
   recording, 61
   ways God speaks, 52
vows, 308

W

Waiting Upon the Lord Prayer, 56, 59,
   199, 201, 232, 233, 249, 256, 378,
   418
   case histories, 238, 241, 245, 249
   ministry ingredients, 228, 232, 233
   preparation for, 228, 230, 233
walking it out
   see 'post-ministry, for DO'
warning, 316
warriors, 381
weapons, 331
   defensive, 73
   offensive, 74
What if ...?, 325
will, 200
Wilson, Sandra, 90, 212, 353
wisdom, 373
witchcraft, 113, 132, 170, 208, 275,
   279, 281, 284, 300, 302, 308, 346,
   347, 348, 399
withdrawal, 214, 346, 349, 356, 398
worship, see 'praise'
woundedness, degree of, 363

Restoring the Foundations Ministries
Training Steps

Prerequisites

These items must be completed before a team embarks on the process of becoming equipped as either an Issue-Focused Minister or as a Thorough Format Minister.

Commitment
It is expected that a team will make a personal commitment to submit to their recognized church oversight (or appropriate spiritual oversight) and to the church RTF ministry policies.

Reference
A team (two people)[1] needs a personal reference from their pastor validating their commitment, call, level of maturity, and character.

Supervision
A commitment is needed from the team's pastor (or oversight) to provide supervision, prayer covering, and a place to exercise their ministry once the training is completed.

Initial Equipping (by attending the Healing/Deliverance Seminar)
Some initial equipping is required. This may be accomplished by attending a RTF Healing/Deliverance Seminar, and/or by watching the DVDs of this seminar, and/or by reading and understanding the healing and deliverance concepts and principles as expressed in the book *Restoring the Foundations*.

Receiving RTF Thorough Format (15 hours) Ministry
Every RTF team is encouraged to receive healing. Issue-Focused Ministers receive IFM ministry. They may elect to receive the Thorough Format ministry. Teams desiring to be trained to do the Thorough Format Ministry must receive the Thorough Format ministry from a recognized RTF ministry team, preferably before starting the training process, however, it must be completed before the Third (and final) Training Step.

Training Process

(Step 1) Attend and Complete a RTF Activation Seminar
Attending a RTF Activation Seminar provides a safe place to practice the RTF Issue-Focused Ministry (IFM) format. In this seminar, a team receives teaching, demonstration, activation (practice), and impartation covering the key aspects of the IFM process. Teams are released to minister the IFM after successfully completing this seminar. (At least 18 hours of training.)

---

[1] Please read the definition of a team on page 369.

(Step 2) Observing Step

For those teams desiring to be trained for the Thorough Format Ministry, they are to proceed through the second and third Training Steps. In Step 2, a trainee team (actively) observes an experienced team conduct the entire RTF ministry process "live" with two ministry receivers. Observing ministry to a couple is preferred for "couple" teams, a womens team may observe ministry to two women. This helps the team gain an understanding of how the different parts of the integrated ministry fit and flow together. The observing trainee team is fully involved with every aspect of the ministry, except the "doing," i.e., having the responsibility of conducting the ministry. (Approximately 40 hours of training, including the preparation and evaluation time.)

(Step 3) Ministering Step

In the Third Step, the trainee team receives supervised training as they minister to two receivers (normally a couple). The trainee team demonstrates all of their knowledge and anointing as they apply the RTF Integrated Approach to Healing Ministry. (Generally 50 hours, including the preparation and evaluation times.)

Other Training

Annual Advanced Conferences (regional and international)

These conferences help RTF ministry teams to continue to advance in skill, understanding, and anointing, as well as an opportunity to fellowship with others of like heart and calling. The conferences are different each year as the Lord releases new revelation and anointings. You can check on when and where the upcoming Advances will be by going to www.RestoringTheFoundations.org and clicking on the Healing House Schedule link.

Specialized Seminars

These seminars provide advanced and ongoing training in specialized areas of RTF ministry.

Trainer Training

For those called to train/teach RTF ministry teams, there are several approaches. One approach is to come a Healing House Network member team and be trained as part of the ongoing ministry activity. Another approach is to be trained within a local church that a recognized Restoring the Foundations Ministry program.[1] A third approach is to come to the Restoring the Foundations International Training Center in Hendersonville, NC, and attend one or more of the Training Modules and ongoing mentoring opportunities. (Visit www.RestoringTheFoundations.org and click on "Training Center Schedule" for more details.)

Other training of trainers includes the Seminar Leader seminar to prepare a team to teach the RTF Healing/Deliverance Seminar and the RTF Activation Seminar within the local church. All of the training is designed to promote the multiplication of available RTF Ministers within the Body of Christ while preserving the integrity of the God-given revelation.

---

[1]   If you are interested in the details of establishing a RTF ministry within your church, please call the office at 828-696-9075 for the booklet: *Establishing a RTF Ministry Program.*

Healing God's world, one life at a time

Restoring The Foundatons Ministries

2849 Laurel Park Highway
Hendersonville, NC 28739
828-696-9075
resources@RestoringTheFoundatons.org
www.RestoringTheFoundatons.org

Resources: Books, Training Manuals, DVDs, CDs and MP3 CDs

Authors and Teachers: Chester and Betsy Kylstra, unless otherwise noted.

Book/Training Manual: *Restoring the Foundations,* Second Edition

This is the book that you are holding. It contains sixteen chapters and four appendices covering foundational topics and all ministry topics for Restoring the Foundations ministry. Hard cover, 460 pages, 8 1/2 by 11 inches.

Price: $36. S&H: **$10**. If sold within Florida or North Carolina, please add sales tax: **$2.52.**
Totals: $46 with S&H, or **$48.52** with Florida/North Carolina sales tax.

Training Manual: *Ministry Tools for Restoring the Foundations,* Second Edition
with Dorathy Ferguson Railey

A workbook containing all of the essential ministry aids, ministry steps, example prayers, and other teaching/explanation information that a Restoring the Foundations ministry team needs as they prepare for ministry or while they are in the ministry room. It leads them step-by-step through everything that needs to be done. 110 pages, 8 1/2 by 11 inches, three-ring binder. Included are 45 plastic page protectors so that you can get "hard use" from this workbook. Packs of Ministry Cards also available.

Price: $24. S&H: **$8**. If sold within Florida or North Carolina, please add sales tax: **$1.68**.
Totals: $32 with S&H, or **$33.68** with Florida/North Carolina sales tax.

Book: Twice Chosen. *One Woman's Story of Healing* by Betsy Schenck Kylstra

"I loved being twice adopted, twice chosen." Betsy shares how God set her free from her "dark side," and brought her out of "no right to exist" into the fullness of His destiny. A paperback book, 208 pages.

"You will be blessed and enlightened as you read this book. It will cause you to laugh and to cry. It will cause you to contemplate and meditate on God's goodness and faithfulness.

Twice Chosen gives a vivid portrayal of God's providential purpose being worked out in an individual's life. Betsy's life reveals that God chooses us before we know we have been chosen. It demonstrates God's timing and seasons that cause things to happen in a chain of events to bring one forth to divine destiny." Bishop Bill Hamon

"Twice Chosen is a book about adoption by God, as well as by human parents. Through it, I came to better understand myself as well as my adopted friends. Thank you, Betsy, for writing this book." A Friend

Price: $10. S&H: **$5**. If sold within Florida or North Carolina, please add sales tax: **$0.70**
Totals: $15 with S&H, or **$15.70** with Florida/North Carolina sales tax.

Book: Transforming Your Business

The revelaiton in TYB builds upon the Restoring the Foundations ministry, taking it into the organizational world of business, churches, civic clubs, etc. The book explains the spiritual dynamics of organizations including the five negative spiritual roots underlying all organizational problems, how to remove the root's effects, and how the business can become all that God has destined for it. The book is available as a hardback, 6x9 inches, 368 pages.

Price: **$50**. S&H: **$10**. If sold within Florida or North Carolina please add sales tax: **$3.50**.
Totals: **$60** with S&H, or **$63.50** with Florida/North Carolina Sales tax.

Book: Effective Listening, *Interview Skills for the Christian Counselor,* Second Edition
by Mike Green

Sit down with Mike for a "fireside chat" on how to "listen." He wants you to be the best possible Holy Spirit led counselor/minister you can be. He will share with you the various ways that we communicate, and how you can use your understanding to help your counselee/ministry receiver obtain his healing. A paperback book with 72 pages.

Price: **$8**. S&H: **$5**. If sold within Florida or North Carolina, please add sales tax: **$0.57**
Totals: **$13** with S&H, or **$13.57** with Florida/North Carolina sales tax.

CDs, or MP3 CD: Shame-Fear-Control Stronghold Teaching/Ministry

Explains the strongholds of Shame, Fear, and Control, and how they work together (support each other) to deceive us into accepting a counterfeit/false identity that is extremely hindering to our Christian walk and destiny. Includes identifying characteristics and an actual one hour ministry session demonstrating the strategy for disassembling and demolishing the strongholds.

Price: **$18**. S&H: **$5**. If sold within Florida or North Carolina, please add sales tax: **$1.28**
Totals: **$23** with S&H, or **$24.28** with Florida/North Carolina sales tax.

DVDs: 15-hour RTF Healing and Deliverance Course

Enjoy fifteen 50 minute life-changing classes revealing the transforming power of the Integrated Approach to Ministry as presented in the book, *Restoring the Foundations*. Experience the transforming power of the integrated approach with teaching, demonstration, and group ministry. Eight DVDs.

Price: **$160**. S&H: **$10**. If sold within Florida or North Carolina, please add sales tax: **$11.20**.
Totals: **$170** with S&H, or **$181.20** with Florida/North Carolina sales tax.

Music CD or Tape: *Jesus My Healer*

Original healing songs and music to relax and meditate on God's goodness and virtue, to receive His healing power into your body, soul and spirit.

Price: **CD/Tape $15/10**. S&H: **$5**. If sold within FL or NC, please add sales tax: **$1.05**.
Totals: **$20/15** with S&H, or **$21.05/16.05** with Florida/North Carolina sales tax.

RESOURCES

Shame-Fear-Control Stronghold

This "super" stronghold afflicts over half of the Body of Christ with a counterfeit identity. Is this stronghold lying to you about who you really are? You can learn how to identify, disassemble, and demolish it. You can participate in the ministry session at the end and start on the road to freedom from Shame, from Fear, and from Control. (CDs and MP3)

See Resources page for more information.

Transforming Your Business

The revelation in TYB builds upon the Restoring the Foundations ministry, taking it into the organizational world of business, churches, etc. The book explains the spiritual dynamics of organizations including the five negative spiritual roots underlying all organizational problems, how to remove the root's effects, and how the business can become all that God has destined for it.

RESOURCES

Twice Chosen

Twice Chosen gives a vivid portrayal of God's providential purpose being worked out in Betsy's life. She is adopted and raised in a godly home, yet tormented by deep rejection and demonic fears. Laugh, cry, and be profoundly encouraged as you learn how God restores her and brings her into her destiny.

Effective Listening

Restoring the Foundations ministry involves listening. Lots of listening. Let Mike share with you important principles of how to listen not only to the content of what a person says, but also how he says it. What is his body language saying? Furthermore, what can you do to help him tell you his story? Do you help him "open up" to share deeply, or do you "shut" him down? You will be challenged to become a more Effective Listener.

Healing God's world, one life at a time

Restoring the Foundations Ministries

2849 Laurel Park Highway
Hendersonville, NC 28739
828-696-9075
resources@RestoringTheFoundations.org
www.RestoringTheFoundations.org

RESOURCE ORDER FORM

Date: Date Shipped:	Method of Payment:
Name:	Check #:
Church/Organization:	Credit Card # :
Address:	Expiration Date:
City/State/Zip	Telephone:

Quantity:		Price:	S/H:	Total:
	B: *Restoring the Foundations*, Second Edition	$35	$10	
	B: *An Integrated Approach to Healing Ministry*	15	5	
	B: *Transforming Your Business*	50	10	
	B: *Twice Chosen* (*Autobiography by Betsy Kylstra*)	10	5	
	B: *Effective Listening*, Second Ed. *(by Mike Green)*	10	5	
	B: *Prodigal Daughter* (by Kathy Tolleson)	18	5	
	DVDs: **Healing/Deliverance Course** (15 classes)	160	10	
	Manual: *Ministry Tools for RTF*, Second Edition	25	10	
	A: **Essential Teachings (over 12 hrs in-depth Teachings)**	55	5	
	A: **Shame-Fear-Control Stronghold**	20	5	
	A: **Lifestyle of Deliverance**	10	5	
	A: **Sexual Imprinting/Soul Battles/Post-Abortion**	20	5	
	A: **Advanced RTF Teaching #1**	30	5	
	A: **Principles of Deliverance**	20	5	
	A: **Knowing and Releasing Your Authority**	20	5	
	A: **Orphan Lifestyle/Father's Heart**	15	5	
	A: **Dethroning Jezebel /Removing Fiery Darts**	15	5	
	A: **Original RTF Course, 27 Hour**	55	10	
	CD/Tape: **Jesus My Healer**	15/10	5	
	Cards: **Ministry Prayer Cards:** Packs of 10/25/50/100	5/10/15/25	1/3/4/5	
	B: These Resources are Books.			
	A: These Resources are Audio CDs			
	and/or MP3 CDs.			

Sub Total			
Sales Tax (Florida or North Carolina 7%)			
Canadian & Foreign S&H			
Total			

Thank you for purchasing Proclaiming His Word's resources and helping to spread the Good News!